NINTH EDITION

Rockin' in Time

A Social History of Rock and Roll

David P. Szatmary

Former Vice Provost, University of Washington, Seattle

Pearson

330 Hudson Street, NY NY 10013

Portfolio Manager: *Bimbabati Sen*
Content Producer: *Kani Kapoor*
Portfolio Manager Assistant: *Anna Austin*
Product Marketer: *Jessica Quazza*
Art/Designer: *Integra Software Services Pvt. Ltd.*
Full-Service Project Manager: *Integra Software Services Pvt. Ltd.*

Compositor: *Integra Software Services Pvt. Ltd.*
Printer/Binder: *LSC Communications, Inc.*
Cover Printer: *Phoenix Color*
Cover Design: *Lumina Datamatics, Inc.*
Cover Art: *Shutterstock*

Acknowledgments of third party content appear on pages within the text.

Library of Congress Cataloging-in-Publication Data

Name: Szatmary, David P., author.
Title: Rockin' in time/David P. Szatmary.
Description: Ninth edition. | Boston: Pearson, 2018. | Includes bibliographical references and index.
Identifiers: LCCN 2018020057 | ISBN 9780134791357
Subjects: LCSH: Rock music—United States—History and criticism. | Rock music—Social aspects—United States.
Classification: LCC ML3534 .S94 2018 | DDC 781.660973—dc23
    LC record available at https://lccn.loc.gov/2018020057

1 18

Books a la Carte:
ISBN-10:   0-13-479135-5
ISBN-13: 978-0-13-479135-7

Instructor Review Copy:
ISBN-10:   0-13-479280-7
ISBN-13: 978-0-13-479280-4

To My Wife, Mary

Contents

Preface

New to this Edition

I have used many new photos and images to make the text more relevant and to better show the connection of rock and roll to social history. I have added new material, including the following:

- New chapter on Delta blues
- New section on fusion jazz
- New chapter on the electronic dance movement
- Additional new material incorporated into each chapter

I have also corrected any errors in the text. I hope that you find this revision useful and would appreciate any comments as you read it.

This text is available in a variety of formats—digital and print. To learn more about our programs, pricing options, and customization, visit www.pearsonhighered.com.

Music for this title is available through Spotify. The link to the title-specific Spotify playlist can be found on this title's page at www.pearson.com.

Acknowledgments

Thanks to several people who helped me with this book: Bill Flanagan, Timothy Leary, Michael Batt, Jamie Steiwer, Peter Blecha, Chris Waterman, Charles Cross, Gene Stout, John Shannon, Richard Carlin, Gary June, Joe Moore, Dave Rispoli, Jerry Schilling, Keith John, Joel Druckman, W. Michael Weis, and Sonny Masso offered perceptive comments and constant help on various drafts of the text. I also thank Robert Palmer, Bob Guiccione, Jr., Alan Douglas, Mike Farrace, Gregg Vershay, and Bob Jeniker for their encouragement. I especially want to thank Stewart Stern, Richard Hell, Sebastian, Frank Kozik, Mark Arminski, Alex Conry, Emek, and rapper Ed "Sugar Bear" Wells for their insights. Obviously, none of those who provided assistance can be held responsible for the contents of this book.

I have others to thank as well. Jerry Kwiatkowski (Kaye) introduced me to the world of rock and prodded me to listen to everyone from Captain Beefheart to Eric Clapton. Mike Miller helped me explore the summer concert scene in Milwaukee. Neil Fligstein, Eileen Mortenson, Gail Fligstein, Tom Speer, and Pete Acevez did the same for me in Tucson and Seattle. On the East Coast, Dave Sharp fearlessly accompanied me on journeys to see Sid Vicious and explore the meanings of Root Boy Slim.

I want to acknowledge my former coworkers at Second Time Around Records in Seattle—owners Wes and Barbara Geesman, Dan Johnson, Mike Schwartz, Dave Wolter, Howie Wahlen, Jeff Taylor, Rob Innes, Michael Wellman, and Jim Rifleman—for adding to my understanding of rock music and the rock business. At the University of Arizona, Donald Weinstein graciously allowed me to teach a class on the social history of rock and roll, which served as the beginning of this book; Rick Venneri did the same at the University of Washington. Students in those classes added to my knowledge of rock music. Thanks to Dudley Johnson at the University of Washington for initially putting me in contact with Prentice Hall.

I owe a special debt to the late Bob "Wildman" Campbell, the king of psychedelia who spent many hours with me analyzing the lyrics of Larry Fischer, the nuances of Tibetan Buddhists chants, Bonzo Dog Band album covers, and the hidden meaning behind the grunts of Furious Pig. He shared with me his definitive psychedelic record collection, mentored me about the beats, and suggested that we venture into CBGBs to see the Voidoids. Besides reading and commenting on this manuscript, he expanded my musical horizons with a series of demented tapes and letters, which twisted this book into shape. Such a debt can never be repaid, and he will be sorely missed.

Thanks to my late parents, Peter and Eunice, for instilling in me a love of music and the written word. A special appreciation goes to my mother who commented on the manuscript and gave me suggestions for a title.

A special thanks to my grandson, Alexander Fantl who constantly expands my musical boundaries.

My daughter Sara constantly brought me back to reality, when I became overly absorbed in the manuscript, and showed me that energy can be boundless. She provided needed guidance about music in the twenty-first century and gave me hope that rock and roll will never die. In the last several editions, she offered insightful editorial comments about the newest music on the charts and provided invaluable research.

Most of all, I want to thank my wonderful wife Mary for her love and companionship, her openness to all types of music, her editorial comments, her willingness to attend concerts when we were both too old for the venue, and her indulgence of my vinyl and rock-poster addictions. For this edition, she continually provided me rock-and-roll material for sources, which I would otherwise have not seen. I could never have completed nine editions of this book without her understanding, interest, encouragement, and love. I dedicate this book to her with all my heart.

Introduction

"Rock and roll will be around for a long, long time. Rock and roll is like hot molten lava that erupts when an angry volcano explodes. It's scorching hot, burns fast and completely, leaving an eternal scar. Even when the echoes of the explosion subside, the ecstatic flames burn with vehement continuity."

—Don Robey, owner of Peacock and
Duke Records, in *Billboard*, March 1957

This book is a social history of rock and roll. It places an ever-changing rock music in the context of American and, to some extent, British history from the early blues to the present. *Rockin' in Time* explains how rock and roll both reflected and influenced major social changes during the last eight decades. As Ice-T explained in 1997, "albums are meant to be put in a time capsule, sealed up, and sent into space so that when you look back you can say that's the total reflection of that time."

Rockin' in Time deals with rock music within broad social and cultural settings. Rather than present an encyclopedic compilation of the thousands of well-known and obscure bands that have played throughout the years, it examines rock and rollers who have reflected and sometimes changed the social fabric at a certain point in history. It concentrates on rock musicians who most fully mirrored the world around them and helped define an era.

Rockin' in Time emphasizes several main themes, including the importance of African-American culture in the origins and development of rock music. The blues, emanating from American slaves, provided the foundation for rock and roll. During the early Fifties, African-Americans who migrated from the South to Chicago created an urbanized, electric rhythm and blues that preceded rock and roll and served as the breeding ground for pioneer rock and rollers such as Little Richard and Chuck Berry. African Americans continued to develop new styles such as the Motown sound, the soul explosion of the Sixties, fusion jazz, the disco beat, house music, techno, and hip-hop.

Many types of rock coincided with and reflected the African-American struggle for equality. The electric blues of Muddy Waters became popular amid the stirrings of the civil-rights movement. During the early Sixties, as the movement for civil rights gained momentum, folk protesters such as Bob Dylan and Joan Baez sang paeans about the cause. In 1964 and 1965, as Congress passed the most sweeping civil rights legislation since the Civil War, Motown artists topped the charts. When disgruntled, frustrated African Americans took to the streets later in the decade, soul artists such as Aretha Franklin gained respect. During the late Eighties and throughout the Nineties, hip-hoppers such as Public Enemy rapped about inequality and renewed an interest in an African-American identity.

White teenagers embraced rock and roll, when the civil-rights struggle cultivated an awareness of African-American culture. Youths such as Elvis Presley listened to late-night, rhythm-and-blues radio shows that challenged and broke down racial barriers. During the Sixties, white teens readily accepted African-American performers such as the Ronettes, the Temptations, and the Supremes who had been carefully groomed for success in a mainstream market. At the same time in Britain, teenagers such as the Rolling Stones became obsessed with Chicago blues and brought their version of the blues back to adoring fans in America. Later in the decade, white youth bought soul records and revered Jimi Hendrix as the ultimate guitar hero. By the Eighties, young white suburbanites wore baggy pants and chanted the lyrics of inner-city rappers. In the new century, American teens danced at massive festivals to the African-American sounds of house music and techno. During the last eight decades, black and white Americans have been integrated through rock and roll.

Population shifts and generational changes, the second theme of this book, provided an audience for African-American-inspired rock and roll. During World War II, African Americans from the South streamed into large Northern cities such as Chicago in a Great Migration. Blues musicians such as Muddy Waters came north along with thousands of African-American migrants who provided a ready audience for the electrified blues.

When the war ended, soldiers came home to their wives and had children who as a group became the baby boom and represented one of the most populous generations of all time. By the mid-Fifties, an army of youngsters demanded their own music. Along with their older brothers and sisters who had been born during the war, they latched onto a young, virile Elvis Presley who attracted hordes of postwar youth.

Until the early Eighties, rock music reflected the interests of the baby-boom generation. The music of the Dick Clark era, Brill Building songwriters, the Beach Boys, Motown artists, and the early Beatles focused on dating, cars, high school, and teen love for young boomers. Catering to post-teen baby boomers during the Sixties, rock morphed into the serious protest music of Bob Dylan and psychedelic bands that questioned basic tenets of American society. When college-age boomers were threatened by the Vietnam War military draft and the prospect of fighting in an unpopular war, the music turned harsh and violent with heavy metal and then escapist after the student killings at Kent State. During the Seventies, after the war ended and when many college rebels landed lucrative jobs, glitter rock and disco exemplified the excessive, self-centered behavior of the boomers. During the Eighties, artists such as Bruce Springsteen reflected the baby-boom yearning for the Sixties spirit of social change.

The sons and daughters of the baby boom, born between 1965 and 1981 and called Generation X, carried forward the rock-and-roll banner. Disaffected youths born on the cusp of the new generation delivered a stinging British punk rock and an American hardcore to vent their anger. Other youth from Gen X watched and listened to British dance music, Michael Jackson and a pop-oriented version of heavy metal on the MTV television network. As they grew older, Generation X confronted sobering social conditions with thrash, grunge, death metal, and rap.

By the late Nineties, a third generation of youth, born between 1982 and 2001 and referred to as the Baby Boom Echo, Generation Y, or the Millenials, developed their own rock. Confronted by a plethora of economic, environmental and political problems, they flocked to socially conscious singer-songwriters and rappers. During the past decade, amid a conservative upheaval in the United States, many Millenials listened to the traditional message of a country rock and escaped their troubles by dancing to electronic beats.

The roller-coaster economic times of the post–World War II era serve as a third focus of this book. A favorable economic climate initially allowed rock to flourish by permitting baby boomers in the United States to live in relative affluence. During the Fifties and early Sixties, sizeable allowances enabled teens to purchase the latest rock records and buy tickets to see their favorite heartthrobs. During the next fifteen years, unparalleled prosperity allowed youth to consider the hippie counterculture and led to cultural excesses and booming record sales.

When the economic scene worsened during the mid-to-late Seventies in Britain, youth spat out the sneering protest of punk that reflected the harsh economic realities of the dole. Throughout the most of the Eighties and early Nineties, American youth coped with few career prospects and little family stability through shattering hardcore punk, pounding industrial music, a bleak grunge, growling death metal, and a confrontational rap. During the mid-Nineties, when the economy brightened for several years on both sides of the Atlantic, teens turned to a bouncy, danceable Britpop and

Sixties-style, eclectic jam bands. From 2007 to the present, as the worldwide economy settled into one of the worst recessions in one hundred years, youth listened to a conservative country rock and escaped reality through massive electronic-dance-music festivals, which featured fantastic Disneyland-like settings.

Advances in technology shaped the sound of rock and roll and provide another framework for *Rockin' in Time*. The solid-body electric guitar, invented and popularized during the Fifties by Les Paul and Leo Fender, gave rock its distinctive sound. Mass-produced electric guitars such as the Fender Telecaster, appearing in 1951, and the Stratocaster, first marketed three years later, enabled blues musicians and later white teens to capture the electric sound of the city and the passion of youth. During the late Sixties and early Seventies, guitar gods plugged into a wide array of electronic devices such as the distortion box and the wah-wah pedal to deliver slashing, menacing heavy metal. Later technologies such as the synthesizer, the sequencer, and the sampler allowed musicians to embellish and reshape rock and roll into different genres.

Several technological breakthroughs helped popularize rock and roll by making records easily and inexpensively accessible. The reasonably priced 45-rpm record, introduced in 1949 by RCA, prodded youths to purchase the latest hits and replaced the more brittle shellac 78-rpm record. Starting in the mid-Sixties, the extended format of the long-play, 12-inch, 33-1/3-rpm record, which Columbia had commercialized in 1948, perfectly fit such rock music as the experimental psychedelia. The LP remained the dominant medium for rock until the laser-powered compact disc became widely available in 1982. Advances in the quality of sound such as high fidelity, stereo, component stereo systems, and digital sound transferred the immediacy of the live performance to the home and enhanced the rock experience.

Television popularized rock by broadcasting it to teens in their homes. Elvis Presley and the Beatles leapt into American homes on *The Ed Sullivan Show*. Dick Clark's offered the popular *American Bandstand*, and during the Sixties programs such as *Shindig* aired regularly. In Britain, television shows such as *Thank Your Lucky Stars*, *Ready Steady Go!*, and *Juke Box Jury* lured teens to rock and roll. In the early Eighties, MTV changed the way youth thought about music by making it visual as well as aural.

Several technological devices fundamentally transformed rock and roll. The portable cassette tape player-recorder, the portable CD player, and, most recently, the iPod gave teens an opportunity to listen to their favorite songs in the privacy of their rooms, at school, or on the streets. By the Nineties, the Internet enabled youths to listen, trade, download, and burn their favorite music and learn about new bands. It greatly enhanced the scope of music available to the rock fan.

Political events, another theme of this book, directly impacted rock and roll. During the late Sixties, the Vietnam War drew the ire of rock musicians from Jimi Hendrix to Black Sabbath. In 1994, the British Criminal Justice and Public Order Act specifically targeted the rave culture and evoked opposition from bands such as Prodigy and Orbital. The 2004 Presidential election united rockers from all genres in opposition to George W. Bush and his foreign policies and his stance on environmentalism.

Gender serves as another focus of this book. Initially, hormonally motivated girls served as screaming fans for male rock stars such as Elvis, Fabian and the Beatles. During the early Sixties, women emerged as performers in singing groups such as Ronettes and the Supremes. Women similarly contributed to rock as Seventies singer-songwriters such as Carole King and country–rock singers such as Linda Ronstadt. In a largely male-dominated rock field, females first strapped on guitars and sat behind drum sets in great numbers during the punk era with Siouxsie and the Banshees, the Slits and Chrissie Hynde. Riot grrrls bands such as Bikini Kill continued the role of women as performing musicians. In hip hop, several women such as Queen Latifah joined male rappers, and the Spice Girls swept the international charts with their slogan of "girl power." The changing role of women in rock reflected the increasing acceptance of females in the workplace and as equals in American society.

Rock music has been entwined with the development of the music industry, another feature of this book. Rock and roll has always been a business. It started with small, independent companies such as Chess, Sun, Modern, and King, which delivered a new sound to the public. As it became more popular among teens, rock and roll sparked the interest of major record labels such as RCA, Decca, and Capitol, which in the Sixties dominated the field. By the Seventies, major companies aggressively marketed their product and consolidated ranks to increase profits and successfully build an industry more profitable than network television and professional sports. In 1978, as the majors experienced a decline in sales, independent labels again arose to release new rock styles such as punk, rap, grunge, and techno. Within a decade, the majors reasserted their dominance of the record industry, by the signing new acts that had been nurtured by the independents and by introducing the compact disc that enticed many record buyers to purchase their favorite music in a different, more expensive format. As the new century unfolded, major record labels confronted and protested against the Internet, which created a fundamentally new business model for the music industry by allowing musicians to release and distribute their music inexpensively to a worldwide audience without an intermediary.

Though a business, rock music has engendered and has been defined by rebellion, which manifested itself through a series of overlapping subcultures. Youths used rock and roll as a way to band together and feel part of a shared experience. As Bruce Springsteen mentioned about his own background, rock music "provided me with a community, filled with people, and brothers and sisters who I didn't know, but who I knew were out there. We had this enormous thing in common, this 'thing' that initially felt like a secret. Music always provided that home for me." "Rock provides a family life that is missing in America and England," agreed David Bowie. "It provides a sense of community."

During the last eight decades, identifiable rock-and-roll communities assumed specific characteristics, fashion, and styles. Fueled by uncontrolled hormones during the Fifties and early Sixties, rockabilly greasers challenged their parents by wearing sideburns and long greased-back hair and driving fast hot rods. Their girlfriends sported tight sweaters, ratted hair, pedal-pusher slacks. During the 1960s, serious clean-cut, smartly dressed, college-aged folkniks directed their frustration and anger at racial and social injustice by taking freedom rides to the South and protesting against nuclear arms. A few years later, hippies flaunted wild, vibrant clothing, the mind-expanding possibilities of LSD, sexual freedom, and a disdain for a warmongering capitalism that they expressed in their swirling psychedelic poster art. In the next decade, baby boomers attended stadium concerts to collectively celebrate sexually ambiguous, theatrical, and extravagant superstars. A few years later, women wore flowing, revealing dresses and men favored gold medallions and unbuttoned silk shirts as they discoed to the steady beats of deejays.

During the late 1970s, angry rock subcultures emerged. Sneering British punks grew spiked hair, wore ripped, safety-pinned T-shirts, and pogoed straight up and down to lash out against economic, gender, and racial inequities. In America, Mohawked youths congregated in small clubs and slam danced to hardcore punk. Around the same time, a hip-hop subculture of rap music, graffiti and break dancing unabashedly assaulted racial prejudice and its effects on African Americans in the inner cities to highlight the racial injustice that the civil-rights movement of the Sixties had not erased. Within a decade and into the new century, the inner-city b-boy subculture spread to white suburbs, where gun-toting teens looked for ho's and wore Adidas, sagging pants, baseball caps (preferably New York Yankees) turned backward, loose T-shirts, and, depending upon the year, gold chains.

In the Eighties and Nineties, Generation X youth voiced frustration and despair through a series of subcultures that included a gothic-looking industrial style; a long-haired, leather-jacketed thrash and death metal; and the self-described "loser" community of grunge, which adopted the idealized look of the working class: longish, uncombed hair, faded blue jeans, Doc Marten boots, and T-shirts. Until subverted and incorporated into the mainstream by fashion designers, Hollywood, and big business, these subcultures knit together distinct groups of youth with common ways of looking at the world.

By the start of the new century, rock and roll splintered into a variety of subcultures. Black metal adherents wore corpse paint on their faces, studded black leather outfits, and long hair to demonstrate their disgust with current society. Young suburban country fans sported cowboy hats and cowboy boots and swing danced to a largely conservative version of country rock. During the past several years, youth danced all night in furry boots, underwear as outerwear and tutus to party with thousands of others at electronic-dance-music festivals such as the Electric Daisy Carnival.

History seldom can be separated into neat packages. Many of the different rock genres and their accompanying subcultures overlapped with one another. From 1961 to the advent of the British invasion in 1964, Brill Building songwriters, surf music, and Bob Dylan coexisted on the charts. Motown, the Beatles, the Rolling Stones, and soul music occurred approximately at the same time. Most recently, rap, country rock and electronic dance music coincided with one another. Though sometimes intersecting with one another, the different subcultures of rock and roll have been divided into distinct chapters in this book to clearly distinguish the motivating factors behind each one.

Rockin' in Time attempts to be as impartial as possible. Even though a book cannot be wrenched from the biases of its cultural setting, I have tried to present the music in a historical rather than a personal context and to avoid effusive praise or disparaging remarks about any type of rock. To paraphrase Sting, lead singer of the Police, there is no bad music, only bad musicians.

These pages explore the social history of rock and roll. During the last eight decades that it has been an important part of American and British culture, rock and roll has reflected and sometimes changed the lives of several generations. It has morphed into a plethora of creative forms and will continue to amaze, shock, entertain, and inform fans in the future.

Chapter 1
The Birth of the Blues

"The blues can't die because spirituals won't die. Blues—a steal from spirituals."

—Big Bill Broonzy

In 1912, Blind Lemon Jefferson and his companion, Leadbelly, rode the T & NV railroad line through Texas. They needed no fare because they carried guitars with them. "We didn't have to pay no money in them times. We get on the train, the driver takes us anywhere we want to go," Leadbelly recalled. "The conductor says, 'Boys, sit down. You going to play music?' We tell him, 'Yes.' We just out collecting money."

When stopping at a small town, the two guitar players left the train and entertained people at the station. Blind Lemon picked out tunes and Leadbelly accompanied him with rhythm to marvel listeners. They smiled when someone threw a nickel on the ground near their feet.

Sometimes, the two men stayed in town to continue their makeshift concert and then traveled dusty roads toward adjoining towns. Every Saturday, Jefferson played in Wortham, Texas, in front of Jake Lee's barbershop, where residents gathered to hear him. "Lemon started out playing his guitar on these streets," reminisced Quince Cox, a resident of Wortham. "I pitched quarters and nickels to him, and he'd play his guitar." When evening came, Jefferson and his sidekick walked seven or eight miles to Kirvin, Texas. The next night, they headed toward Streetman and Groesbeck to other appreciative audiences. The wandering Blind Lemon and Leadbelly played a new style, which applied secular themes to African-American spirituals. They called it the blues.

The blues formed the foundation of rock and roll. It provided the necessary elements and inspiration for rock and rollers from Elvis to Nirvana. Born in slavery, the music combined African and European elements in a unique way. It first surfaced in African-American church music and gradually transitioned to a secular context, when inexpensive acoustic guitars became readily available at the end of the nineteenth century. By the mid-1920s, rural country blues appeared on record to set the stage for the development of rock and roll.

Born in Slavery

American slaves guarded and repurposed musical traits from Africa to create work songs, field hollers, and spirituals that predated and shaped the blues. Wrenched from their kin, enduring an inhuman journey from their homes in West Africa to the American South on slave ships, and forced into slavery, Africans retained continuity with their past in a variety of ways, including music. They sang between the lines of the more rigid diatonic European music scale by using a pentatonic scale and flattening or bending 3rd, 7th, and sometimes 5th notes, which became known as "blue notes." To plantation owners and overseers, the slave songs of seemingly sliding notes or glissando appeared to make the music rise and fall and sound off-key. One observer found the music of slaves "to strike sounds that cannot be precisely represented by the gamut, and abound in 'slides' from one note to another."

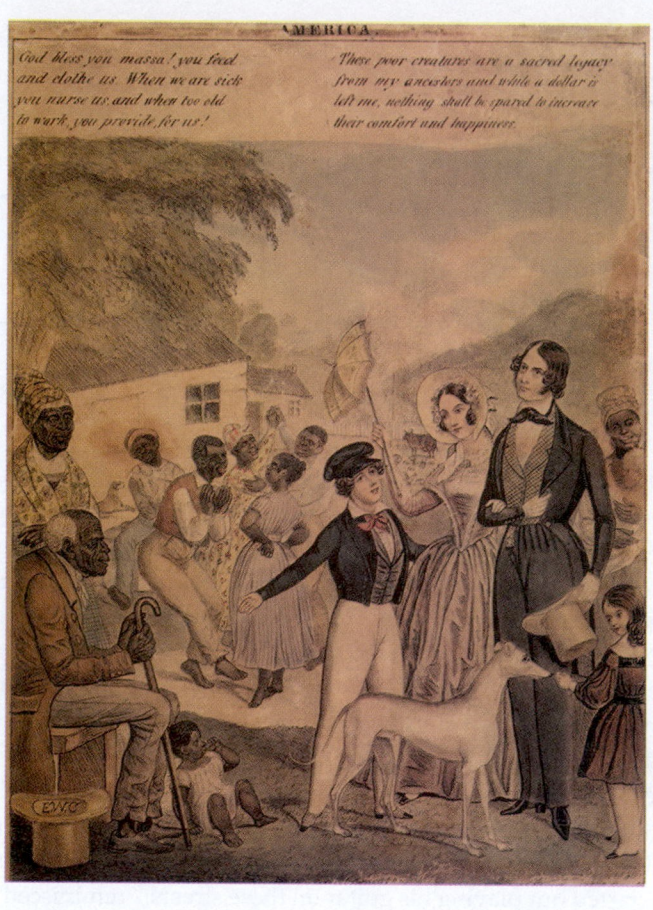

Slaves patting juba, 1841.

Library of Congress Prints and Photographs Division [LC-USZC4-5950].

Slave songs involved calculated repetitions in a call-and-response pattern. Often used to decrease the monotony of work in the fields, one slave called or played a lead part, and another slave followed with the same phrase or a variant of it until another took the lead. As Sir Charles Lyell, a British geologist traveling in America, wrote of his African-American oarsmen in 1845, "One of them, taking the lead, first improvised a verse, paying compliments to his master's family, and to a celebrated black beauty." "The other five then joined in the chorus, always repeating the same words," he explained. In 1853, Frederick Law Olmstead, a journalist, conservationist, and a pioneer in landscape architecture traveled through South Carolina, when "suddenly one slave raised such a sound as I have never heard before, a long, loud musical shout, rising and falling, and breaking into falsetto." "As he finished," continued Olmstead, "the melody was caught up by another, and then, another, and then, by several in chorus." Some slaves, especially those originally from the Bantu tribe, whooped or jumped octaves during the call-and-response, which served as a basis for field hollers.

Slaves concentrated on rhythm. They had been accustomed to dancing and singing to the beat of drums in Africa but had been barred from using percussion instruments in the American South by plantation owners who feared that drums would be used to coordinate slave insurrections. To offset anti-drum laws, slaves focused on rhythm in other ways. In a single song, they clapped, danced, and slapped their bodies in several different rhythms to compensate for the absence of drums. Solomon Northup, an ex-slave writing in 1853, called the practice "patting juba." Slaves performed it by "striking the right shoulder with one hand, the left with the other—all the while keeping time with the feet and singing." In contrast, noted President John Adams, whites "droned out [Protestant hymns] ... like the braying of asses in one steady beat."

Many times, slaves laced rhythm on top of rhythm to create a polyrhythmic music. The editors of *Slave Songs* noticed the "effect of a marvelous complication and variety [of rhythm], and yet with the most perfect time, and rarely with any discord."

They heard "the curious rhythmic effect produced by single voices chiming in at ir-regular intervals."

Slaves accented different beats of the melody to create syncopation. The editors of *Slave Songs* noticed the "apparent irregularities in the time" of the songs that they collected. A few years later, Georgia-born poet Sidney Lanier insisted that syncopations "are characteristic of Negro music. I have heard Negroes change a well-known melody by adroitly syncopating it."

The African-American Church

African Americans used their African musical traits in religious ceremonies. One writer in the *New York Nation* described a "praise-meeting" held in May 1867: "At regular intervals one hears the elder 'deaconing' a hymn-book hymn which is sung two lines at a time, and whose wailing cadences, borne on the night air, are indescribably melancholy." The response from the congregation to the bluesy call of the minister resulted in a call-and-response, a rhythmic complexity, and the minor-key sound common in African music.

The religious ceremonies featured the ring shout. According to the *Nation*, this rite took place on Sundays or at a special praise day in a room in which the benches had been pushed against the wall to allow maximum floor space for the congregation. The participants first walked and then began "shuffling round, one after the other, in a ring. The foot is hardly taken from the floor, and the progression is mainly due to a jerking, hitching motion." As the ring shout progressed over four or five hours, some of the congregation fell from the ring and lined the walls of the building. They shouted praise and slapped their knees and sides to create multiple rhythms.

African-American religious ceremonies combined European elements with African musical traits. The parishioners sang songs from *A Collection of Spiritual Songs and Hymns* (1801), which ex-slave Reverend Richard Allen, founder of the African Methodist Episcopal Church (AME), had assiduously compiled from the official Methodist songbook. The songs generally used a centuries-old, twelve-bar, European harmonic progression in a standard 4/4 time. Grafting African elements onto the white Protestant hymns, the congregation created a call-and-response effect by reiterating a line three times before embellishing it with a third line in a pattern called AAAB. They employed flatted notes in the songs and focused on a three-note, bass riff for a dominant rhythm sometimes called a "groove" or a "shuffle." The resulting music, commented the compilers of *Slave Songs*, became "imbued with the mode and spirit of European music—often, nevertheless, retaining a distinct tinge of their native Africa."

The Birth of the Blues

African-inspired, Protestant-based church music, known as spirituals by the 1860s, served as a basis for blues, when singers applied the religious music to secular themes. Blues players adopted the twelve-bar format, blue notes, syncopated polyrhythms, and call-and-response to chronicle their personal situations or recent natural disasters such as a flood. Following the example of African griots who relayed oral traditions by telling stories to the beat of music, bluesmen chronicled everyday events by adapting spirituals, work songs, and field hollers.

Many bluesmen equated the blues with spirituals. "Some of the church songs, you can't hardly tell them from the blues," insisted Jack Owens (b. 1904), a farmer from Bentonia, Mississippi, who played guitar and operated a juke joint on the weekends. "Some of us sang the church songs, some of us sang the blues, some of us sang both." Charlie Patton, a Delta blues guitar innovator who launched his career around

1906, sandwiched church songs in his performances. "Right in the middle of a dance, it didn't make him no difference," his protégé Booker Miller recalled. "If it hit him he'd just go to playing church songs right there." "He could have preached if he a-wanted to," added Eddie "Son" House about Patton. Bluesman Big Bill Broonzy, who recorded nearly 200 songs from 1925 to 1952, maintained that "the blues can't die because spirituals won't die. Blues—a steal from spirituals."

The Baptist church assumed an especially prominent role in the lives of some bluesmen who both played guitar and served as itinerant ministers. Skip James both ministered and played the blues. "I didn't like the way he was doing it, preaching a while, then playing the blues a while," groused his friend Jack Owens. "I'd play the blues with him Saturday night, and the next morning he'd be preaching church." Big Bill Broonzy began playing music, then "started to preaching and I preached for four years, and then I went back to playing again," when he realized that music could be more lucrative. Son House embarked a similar split career by serving as a minister in Northern Mississippi. "If Son House couldn't make enough playing the guitar, he gonna pick up a [church] collection," sniffed blues guitar player Willie Brown. "He'd preach a year, somethin' like that six months again. He could *preach*, you know." "I was trying to hold the blues in one hand and God in the other," admitted House.

Blues musicians generally performed on the acoustic guitar. Many poor aspirants started with a one-string instrument called a diddley bow, which they built by unraveling the wire that had been wrapped around the straw of a broom and then attaching one end of the wire to a stationary object like a barn. They placed a bottle underneath it as a bridge. To get a sound, they plucked the instrument or ran a knife or bottleneck across the wire. Throughout most of the nineteenth century, few slaves and sharecroppers owned a manufactured guitar. In a survey of ex-slaves, 205 mentioned fiddles, another hundred spoke about banjos on the plantation, and only fifteen referred to guitars.

During the 1890s, inexpensive guitars could more easily be bought. Manufactured by the Oscar Schmidt Company starting in 1899, Stella guitars could be purchased. Itinerant bluesman Ishmon Bracey bought one for eleven dollars in Memphis, and Huddie Ledbetter, popularly known as Leadbelly, who started performing on guitar before 1900, played a Stella. Charlie Patton favored a Stella as his "favorite box" as did Blind Lemon Jefferson (b. 1893), a guitarist from Coutchman, Texas.

The prices of the guitars dropped even further, when retailers Montgomery Ward and Sears, Roebuck & Company mass marketed them through mail-order catalogs. First selling mail-order goods in 1875 to farmers in rural areas, in 1894 Montgomery Ward introduced American-made guitars in their catalogs. In 1899, when Sears overtook Montgomery Ward in total mail-order sales, it offered relatively inexpensive Harmony and Stella guitars to its national customer base. Sears sold the Troubadour for $2.95; the Encore for $3.60; the Oakwood for $4.95; the Columbian, designed to honor the Columbian Exposition, for $7.95; and the Magnolia, "the handsomest guitar made," for $8.95. High-end consumers could buy the more expensive Washburn models, which were crafted by the Lyon & Healy Company in Chicago from rosewood with a cedar neck and an ebony finger board for more than $20. By the turn of the century, companies sold 78,500 guitars annually.

With instruments available at somewhat affordable prices, blues guitarists appeared in rural areas of the South. Booker Miller (b. 1910) asserted that his grandfather, Jim Brown, "was a guitar player." Charleston resident Stanford Bennett entertained at local joints before the dawn of the twentieth century. By 1905, Mississippian Rich Dickson had been regarded an accomplished guitar player, when he taught Henry Stuckey the instrument. Henry Thomas (b. 1874) played the blues before 1900. Leadbelly (b. 1888) remembered his uncles Bob and Terrell playing guitar to him as a young child. Uncle Bob sang "The Cleveland Campaign Song" about the election

African-American man playing guitar, 1909.

Library of Congress Prints and Photographs Division [LC-USZC4-5950].

of Grover Cleveland as president in the 1884 election, perhaps indicating that he played his guitar by then. Before 1900, Leadbelly himself played guitar at local dances. Together with his cousin Edmond Ledbetter, they "used to make music. Sometimes I played a mandolin and I'd second him [by chording] with a guitar and sometimes we played the guitar together."

Guitarists who performed publicly played a variety of music for their audiences. Initially, they favored versions of sixteen-bar rags, popular songs such as "My Bucket's Got a Hole in It" and four-bar, up-tempo breakdowns that consisted of chord changes at the beginning of each measure. "We'd play whatever the people request," informed Booker Miller, a protégé of Charlie Patton, who performed with his mentor in the Mississippi Delta. "Lemon could play anything he had to play," recalled a Wortham, Texas, resident about Blind Lemon Jefferson. Texas bluesman Mance Lipscomb likewise performed a variety of material for his listeners and called himself a "songster."

Around 1900, a few musicians transformed a sixteen-bar rag into a twelve-bar blues by repeating the four-bar phrases of spirituals three times and substituting secular themes for religious topics. Big Bill first heard the blues "Cryin' Joe Turner'" about the disastrous flood of 1893. Booker Miller dated the first blues to "a little before 1900." Sam Chatmon (b. 1899), speaking about his early boyhood, indicated: "Never heard nobody pick no blues till my brother Bud and Charlie Patton, they're about the first." Nehemiah "Skip" James (b. 1902), raised in Bentonia, Mississippi, "hadn't heard of blues" as a child, "but after a little period of time, I heard my mother and them speak about 'singin' the blues." The "Reverend" Robert Wilkins, born six years before James, heard the twelve-bar blues version of such rags as "Spoonful" in his hometown about the same time. "They started in Hernando, [Mississippi], about 1904, something like that," he recalled. Whatever the exact date of the birth of the secular blues, by 1910 Charlie Patton had written a series of now classic blues such as "Pony Blues," "Banty Rooster Blues," and "Mississippi Bo Weevil Blues" to add to his repertoire.

Most of the budding bluesmen toiled in the fields during part of the year and rambled with their guitar for the remainder of it. Charlie Patton who "dressed like a plough-hand" "picked cotton in the fall, but long in the former part of the year he'd be here and yonder," remembered Tom Cannon, Patton's nephew. "He never did settle down for no farmin'." Bluesman Ishmon Bracey worked in the fields during the spring and summer and then traveled throughout the South during the fall to earn money with his guitar.

Given their wandering ways, the bluesmen earned poor reputations. Charlie Patton "didn't want to do nothin' but run all over the country and play guitars and pick up every woman he sees," sniffed fellow Mississippi guitarist Eddie "Son" House. "A man that was singin' the blues," observed Henry C. Speir, the white music-store owner who discovered and helped many of the bluesmen land record contracts, "couldn't intermix with the people too much. He didn't have too much education, he was what we call a 'meat barrel type.' Smell a little bit, you see." "These people," added Speir, "they're not stable."

Train Stations, Frolics, and Juke Joints

Itinerant blues guitarists entertained black and sometimes white Southerners in a variety of places. Some traveled by rail to play their songs. W.C. Handy regularly observed "blind singers and footloose bards that were forever coming and going." "Some came sauntering down the railroad tracks, others dropped from freight cars, while still others caught rides on the big road and entered town on top of cotton bales." Using railroad stations as their concert halls, they performed to "crowds of country folk" who ate fish, bread, and other staples while they waited for their trains.

In small Southern towns, some bluesmen played on the street corners for spare change. In 1903, a young Leadbelly performed on the streets for storeowners to attract business. By 1910, a thirteen-year-old Memphis Minnie (b. Lizzie Douglas) had run away from home and supported herself by roaming from town to town between her home in Walls, Mississippi, and Jackson to entertain passersby on the streets.

Blues performers many times appeared at country frolics. Bluesmen ventured to a country plantation on Saturday nights to play a frolic in someone's house. Sometimes, the guitarist appeared as a solo act. Other times, two guitar players accompanied one another: one picking on single strings and the other chording behind him. During the day before the frolic, they played in the town center to advertise the upcoming event. By evening, the musicians made their way toward a two-room house with a bonfire in front to denote to nearby sharecroppers that a frolic would be held that evening. The guitarists played for a crowd assembled in the ramshackle house, where the furniture had been pushed aside so two or three dozen tightly packed neighbors could dance to the music and purchase peanuts, candy, apples, fish as well as chicken and ham.

A few of the guitar players entertained their clientele with a wild stage act. Charlie Patton "loved to 'clown' with his guitar, just puttin' it all under his legs and back behind him, takin' a hand and puttin' it all back his head," remembered Sam Chatmon. Patton's neighbor Frank Howard saw him put his guitar "'round his head, than change hands with it, play off with his feet and all that kinda stuff."

At times, the frenzied atmosphere at the plantation frolics turned violent. As early as 1881 on a visit to an Alabama plantation during Christmas week, Booker T. Washington attended a frolic. "This meant a kind of rough dance, where there was likely to be a good deal of whiskey used, and where there might be some shooting or cutting up with razors," he remembered. When Willie Morris and Charlie Patton played for revelers at a frolic on the Red Gun Plantation near Leland, Mississippi, "this guy starts shooting, and they all runned out and got in them cotton fields and corn fields, man," Mance Lipscomb described typical violence at frolics. When Mance played at the frolic in Brazos, "long about twelve or one o'clock, you'd hear a gun somewhere, in the house or the outhouse. 'Boom,' Somebody died."

Some of the violence did not escape punishment. Son House shot a man at a frolic in Lyon, Mississippi, and for the next two years labored at the notorious

Dancers at a juke joint, 1930s.

Library of Congress Prints and Photographs Division [LC-USZC4-5950].

maximum-security Mississippi State Penitentiary, also known as Parchman Farm, which was memorialized by the song, "Parchman Farm," by bluesman Bukka White, who also served time there for killing two men. Leadbelly shot and killed a man and ended in the Shaw State Prison Farm and then the Central State Prison Farm, referred to as "Sugarland." After seven years of incarceration, Leadbelly received a pardon from Texas Governor Pat Neff after the governor heard him sing on a visit to Sugarland.

Juke joints or barrelhouses, where proprietors generally required clientele to check their weapons before entering, offered a somewhat safer venue for the blues guitarists. Located near a train station in the town center or a saw mill, turpentine camp or another type of work camp, the juke joints usually included rooms for gambling, drinking, prostitution, and dancing, and sometimes served as a makeshift boarding house. They opened on Friday night to provide a recreational outlet to their sharecropping and laboring customers until Sunday. Usually, fifty to seventy-five people crammed the barrelhouses at one time. "They'd stay alla night long," recalled Elizabeth Moore, who operated a Mississippi juke with her husband. A barrelhouse generated as much as $1,500 a weekend.

The jukes attracted an unsavory crowd. "They called 'em 'juke house people,' or otherwise they just didn't like em'," contended barrelhouse proprietor Elizabeth Moore. "Them there Saturday night folks, good people don't be out with 'em, that's a bad class of people, bad *type* of people, bad *character*." Son House referred to Saturday night at the barrelhouse as "the devil's night," establishing the connection between the blues and the devil's music.

Blues guitarists competed with pianists for audiences at the dangerous saw mills and turpentine camps, located near juke joints, which invested in cheap upright pianos. Charles "Cow Cow" Davenport, the son of a Baptist minister born in Anniston, Alabama, incorporated blues songs into his act, including his signature tune, "Cow Cow Blues," and moved from camp to camp with his music. Clarence "Pine Top"

Listening to the blues, 1930s.

Library of Congress Prints and Photographs Division [LC-USF34-031941-D].

Smith, heralding from Alabama, played "Pine Top's Boogie Woogie" for camp laborers. Tennessean "Cripple" Clarence Lofton (b. 1887) did the same throughout the South.

More commonly, pianists with blues material performed in the cities, especially in Louisiana. "You couldn't fool with no piano too much, not for the country gang or goin' to have a ball here, yonder, and like that," explained Son House. "They couldn't fool with the piano much, you know, 'cause they'd be too much to move all the time." In contrast, many barrooms in Southern cities such as New Orleans owned pianos and regularly hired pianists to entertain customers.

The Rural Blues Explosion

By the mid-1920s, records offered rural Southerners a way to hear rural bluesmen without braving the sometimes dangerous frolics and juke joints. During and after World War I, the fledgling record and phonograph industries expanded dramatically. From 1914 to 1919, phonograph sales exploded from $27.1 million to $158.7 million. In 1917, record companies sold 25 million discs and just four years later increased sales to 100 million, more than half of them sold by record giant, the Victor Company.

A proliferation of record companies, including labels that focused on the blues, accompanied the dizzying growth. Paramount, a subsidiary of the Wisconsin Chair Company located in Grafton, Wisconsin, played a pivotal role in the dissemination of the blues. Started in December 1915 as part of a couch subsidiary, the recording arm of the diversified company burgeoned after the parent group experimented with the manufacture of phonographs and decided to stock records for their phonograph cabinets. Initially, the company pressed German, Scandinavian, and Mexican music; popular dance bands; and vaudeville comedians. In 1922 amid fiscal troubles, general manager Maurice Supper and chief executive Otto Moeser decided to offer "race" selections. "We could not compete for high-class talent with Edison, Columbia and Victor, and we had inferior records: so we went with race records," explained Moeser.

In early 1926, Paramount ignited an interest in rural, male blues guitarists, when it recorded Blind Lemon Jefferson. The label received a tip from Dallas record retailer

Juke joint, 1930s.

Library of Congress Prints and Photographs Division [LC-USZC4-5950].

R.T. Ashford about Texas guitarist/singer Jefferson, who he had played near Ashford's shop on Elm Street and Central Avenue. Beginning in March 1926, Paramount achieved commercial success with Jefferson, who recorded a series of now classic guitar blues, including the 1926 hit "Long Lonesome Blues." "Blind Lemon sent out a record about 'Catch my pony, saddle up my black mare,'" recalled Booker Miller about Jefferson's "Black Horse Blues" (1926). "Man, you oughta been there! That thing went like *wildfire* all over the country."

Paramount, emboldened by their success with Jefferson, signed other male bluesmen. The company hired talent scouts such as Henry Speir who auditioned countless blues guitarists at his music store on Farish Street in the black section of Jackson, Mississippi. Through Speir's tips, Paramount snagged Charlie Patton who recorded his bevy of blues for the label. The company recorded such Son House titles as "Preachin' the Blues" and "Mississippi County Farm Blues." By the end of the 1920s, Paramount had become one of the preeminent blues labels in the country with a recording studio, fifty-two record presses that could produce 35,000 records a day and subsidiary labels.

Vocalion Records helped popularize the blues. Launched in 1915 and acquired by Brunswick records ten years later, in 1926 the company developed a "race" series that included blues. Most notably, the label signed Robert Johnson who generated only moderate interest at the time but became the model for many rock-and-roll guitarists with his "Cross Roads Blues," "Love in Vain," and "Come On in My Kitchen." Johnson released the timely "Sweet Home Chicago," which detailed a mass migration of Southern Blacks to the North.

The Great Migration

Many African Americans, disgusted with discrimination and sharecropping, migrated to Northern cities for better lives. As World War I progressed in Europe after 1914, the demand for industrial workers grew acute in the United States, which supplied manufactured goods for the conflict. Steel mills and other manufacturing companies desperately needed laborers to fulfill orders that poured in from across the Atlantic as well as at home after 1917, when the United States entered the war and severely restricted immigration into the country.

African Americans from the American South provided an alternative workforce to Northern manufacturers who no longer could rely on inexpensive labor from Eastern Europe. They had been anxious to leave the harsh conditions of a Jim Crow South, which implicitly condoned regular lynching and overt discrimination of African Americans during the post-Civil War era. One woman in New Orleans dreamed about the "great chance that a colored person has in Chicago of making a living with all the privilege that whites have, and it makes me the most anxious to go." "They said it was a place of freedom," echoed "Georgia" Tom Dorsey, a bluesman and later the father of gospel music. "I was looking for that." "Take some of the sections from which the Negro is departing and he can hardly be blamed when the facts are known," reported the Houston *Observer* on October 21, 1916. "He is kicked around, cuffed, lynched, burned, homes destroyed, daughters insulted and oft times raped, has no vote nor voice, is underpaid, and in some instances when he asks for pay received a 2 × 4 [board] over his head."

As well as constant fear of death and racial discrimination, natural disasters plagued African-American sharecroppers. First hitting the cotton fields of Mississippi in 1907, by 1914 boll weevils caused general devastation in the state. Two years later, the insects ruined fields in Alabama. Creating uncertainty in the cotton market by 1916–1917, the pests created a credit crisis throughout the South by making it more difficult for poor farmers to get money in advance to plant their crops. To add to the troubles of sharecroppers, in 1912 and 1913 crippling floods of the Mississippi River wiped out entire crops. In 1915, drought followed the floods.

Pushed from their land by racism and natural disasters, African Americans flooded into Chicago and other Northern cities. Thousands saved cash for the trip to the Windy City that cost two cents a mile for fare. Some rode for free with tickets from agents employed by major Northern manufacturing companies, which sent representatives to the South to recruit cheap labor. In Decatur, Alabama, during 1917, a

African-American sharecroppers working the field in Georgia, 1937.

Library of Congress Prints and Photographs Division [LC-DIG-fsa-8b32081].

remaining resident saw the result of the mass African-American exodus to the North: "You could see hundreds of houses where mattresses, beds, wash bowls and pans were thrown around the back yard after the people got through picking out what they wanted to take along" on their trips.

Chicago, the terminus of the Illinois Central Railroad line, attracted the greatest influx of African Americans. In 1900, 3,000 African Americans called Chicago their home. Ten years later, Chicago had 44,103 African-American residents out of a total population of nearly 2.2 million. By 1920, the African-American population in the city skyrocketed to 109,458 and congregated mostly in the southern and west sides of the city.

The same population explosion occurred in other large Northern cities. From 1910 to 1920, the New York African-American population increased from 91,709 to 152,467; Detroit's once-miniscule African-American community mushroomed from only 5,741 to 40,838; Philadelphia added nearly 50,000 African Americans; Cleveland saw an increase in the African-American population from 8,500 to 34,500; and the St. Louis African-American population grew by nearly 25,000 for a 58 percent increase.

Most African-American newcomers found employment. In Chicago, the male migrants worked in meat-packing plants and steel mills, which had mechanized and required primarily unskilled laborers. "A Negro could always get a job in the stockyards," asserted a black porter. Other African-American males readily found work in the steel mills. "They were hiring day and night," recalled one migrant. "All they wanted to know was if you wanted to work and if you had a strong back." During the great migration, workers in the meat-packing houses and steel mills earned an average of $5.00 a day or 50 cents an hour compared to 65 cents a day in the Southern cotton fields. Approximately 15 percent of female migrants worked with men in the factories, and the majority toiled as domestic servants.

Though the migrants did not escape racism in Chicago and other Northern cities, they still believed that they lived better than in the rural South. One migrant to the Windy City just began "to feel like a man." "My children are going to the same school with the whites, and I don't have to humble to no one. I have registered—will vote the next election, and there isn't any 'yes sir'." Delta-born pianist Eddie Boyd "thought of coming to Chicago where I could get away from some of that racism and where I would have an opportunity to, well, do something with my talent... . It wasn't peaches and cream [in Chicago], man, but it was a hell of a lot better than down there where I was born."

The migrants, flooding into the Northern cities and making more money than they had ever earned in the South, created a market for records by African-American performers. During World War I, W.C. Handy "was convinced that our people were lovers of music and they were great buyers." "The market was definitely there, waiting to be tapped," he continued. "In Chicago, I had seen cooks and Pullman porters buying a dozen or two dozen records at one time. Not sophisticated music, of course, but oddities that appealed to them, and blues—always blues." George Leaner who distributed blues discs in Chicago during the 1930s recalled that "the Illinois Central Railroad brought the blues to Chicago. With the thousands of laborers who came to work in the meat-packing plants and the steel mills came the blues." Upon their arrival in the North, many of these workers bought records by blues shouters.

The Blues Singers

Female blues singers recorded African-American blues for the masses of urban African Americans. Combining the spirituals with their minstrel show and vaudeville backgrounds, they delivered a citified blues for the recently arrived African Americans in the North. Rather than a single singer with a guitar, the blues shouters blasted their blues over trombones, clarinets, trumpets, and violins.

The female blues mania began on a hot, sweltering day in New York City in August 1920, when African-American singer and Broadway performer Mamie Smith recorded a James P. Johnson composition, "Mama's and Papa's Blues," which she and her manager, Percy Bradford, renamed "Crazy Blues." Smith cut the song for Okeh Records, a fledgling company established by Otto K. E. Heinemann. As musicians for the date, the label's talent scout and director of record production Ralph Peer enlisted the help of pianist Willie "The Lion" Smith as well as a trombonist, a violinist, a cornet player, and a clarinetist. He did not bother with either drums or bass because those instruments could not be heard distinctly on early studio recordings. "The tune," insisted The Lion, "was just an ordinary blues strain."

Released in November, the record met an enthusiastic response. "In no time at all it was selling like hot cakes in Harlem," observed Willie Smith. In one week, Harlemites bought 75,000 copies of the record. Within a few months, the disc sold by the thousands throughout the rest of the country. In less than a year, "Crazy Blues" racked up sales of more than a million copies, most bought by urban African Americans.

Mamie Smith paved the way for other female blues singers. Smith, remarked fellow blues belter Alberta Hunter, "made it possible for all of us, with her recording of 'Crazy Blues,' the *first* blues record." "After 'Crazy Blues' became a bit hit," explained Willie "The Lion" Smith, "every record company and every colored singer got on the old bandwagon. They began to turn out blues records by the ton." The African-American female blues artists included Gertrude "Ma" Rainey; the Georgia-born Lucille Hegamin; Katie Crippen who performed with a young William "Count" Basie; and the tough-talking Smiths—Trixie, Clara, and Laura.

Bessie Smith took her blues to the top. In February 1923, she recorded her debut "Down Hearted Blues," a song written by fellow blues siren Alberta Hunter and pianist and band leader Lovie Austin. Bessie sold 780,000 copies of the disc during its first six months and eventually registered sales of more than 2 million discs. Smith scored with two more hits the same year—"Baby Won't You Please Come Home" and "Tain't Nobody's Biz-Ness If I Do." During the next four years, Bessie delivered six more top blues selections, including a version of W.C. Handy's "St. Louis Blues" and "Careless Love Blues," to become the most commercially successful female blues singer. In all, she recorded more than 160 songs, mostly for Columbia Records, and became independently wealthy at a time, when women lobbied for suffrage and adapted a flapper look and demeanor.

Like the music of the rural blues guitarists, the blues of Bessie Smith had musical elements of the African-American church. New Orleans guitarist Danny Barker felt that "she had a church deal mixed up in it." "The South had fabulous preachers and evangelists. Some would stand on corners and move the crowds from there. Bessie did the same thing on stage." Ethel Waters, the sweet-voiced blues singer who scored with a series of hits starting in 1921 with "Down Home Blues" and "They'll Be Some Changes Made," believed that "Bessie's shouting brought worship wherever she worked." During many of Bessie's performance, wrote one contemporary, "Amens rent the air."

Unlike the rural bluesmen, the blues shouters combined the influence of the African-American church with their experiences in minstrel and vaudeville shows and sometimes Broadway plays. Before recording "Crazy Love," Mamie Smith sang in the chorus of the Broadway play *The Smart Set*. Ma Rainey performed in the Rabbit's Foot Minstrel Show and later established her own vaudeville show with her husband—Rainey and Rainey, Assassinators of the Blues. After busking with her brother in front of saloons in her hometown of Chattanooga, Tennessee, in 1912 Bessie Smith joined the traveling troupe of Moses Stokes as a dancer and shared the stage with singer Ma Rainey. She later followed Rainey into the Rabbit's Foot Company. By 1918, the 24-year-old Smith headed her own review. At age 14, blues singer Ida Cox, who recorded seventy-eight blues and earned the nickname, "Uncrowned Queen of the

Bessie Smith in action during her prime.

Library of Congress Prints and Photographs Division [LC-USZ62-100863].

Blues," left home to tour with White and Clark's Black & Tan Minstrels. She graduated to other minstrel shows such the Florida Orange Blossom Minstrels, the Silas Green Show, and the Rabbit's Foot Minstrels. Other blues shouters followed the same pattern early in their careers. Louisville-born Sara Martin sang in vaudeville starting in 1915; Esther Bigeou began in vaudeville two years earlier; and Chippie Hill worked with Ma Rainey in the Rabbit's Foot Company.

The vaudeville and minstrel show experience of the female blues shouters, combined with their church backgrounds, gave African-American migrants to the North a new style of the blues, which matched their new surroundings. Steeped in the church but honed on the stage, the music of the blues shouters provided transplants with a familiar but slicker version of the blues. It offered a citified blues for new urban dwellers who wanted to forget their sharecropping past.

By the late 1920s when the female blues mania subsided, bluesmen who joined the great migration to Chicago offered another option. Migrants to the Windy City included Big Bill Broonzy, an ex-slave's son who worked as a plow hand in Mississippi and laid railroad track in Arkansas. He reached Chicago in 1920. Five years later, guitarist Tampa Red (b. Hudson Woodbridge) headed from Florida to the same destination, where he scored with the double entendre "Tight Like That" in 1928. Pianist Eurreal "Little Brother" Montgomery, born in 1906 on the grounds of a Louisiana lumber company, performed at logging camps until he ended up in Chicago in 1928. In 1934, harmonica wizard John Lee "Sonny Boy" Williamson, the first Sonny Boy, migrated from Jackson, Tennessee, to the Windy City, where three years later he cut "Good Morning Little School Girl." "The reason why Chicago was different than all the other places, 'cause all the singers migrated to Chicago, because all the people came to Chicago," explained bluesman Billy Boy Arnold. "All the jobs—the people came here for the jobs."

Lester Melrose, a white talent-scout, produced many of the early Chicago bluesmen and promoted a new acoustic blues style. He became a fixture at Tampa Red's house, where many of the blues transplants met and wrote songs. "That was his kind of headquarters," recalled bass player Willie Dixon who came to Chicago to pursue a boxing career but became a preeminent blues songwriter. "If it sounded like it was alright, then Melrose would say, 'Well, looky here, we'll try it out and see what happens.'" From the mid-thirties, Melrose boasted that "I recorded at least 90 percent of all rhythm-and-blues talent for RCA and Columbia Records," including Big Bill Broonzy, Tampa Red, Sonny Boy Williamson, and many others. By using several of his artists in one session, Melrose featured vocals, a guitar, and a piano to create an acoustic Chicago blues sound more enlivened and sophisticated than the more subdued country blues that some called the "Bluebird beat" after RCA's Bluebird label. The guitar-based blues had arrived in the city.

Chapter 2
The Advent of Rock and Roll

"Blues had a baby and they called it rock and roll."

—Muddy Waters

Late on a Saturday night in 1950, Muddy Waters entered a smoke-filled Macomba Lounge on the South Side of Chicago. He wore an electric green suit, baggy pants, a white shirt, and a wide, striped tie. He sported a 3-inch pompadour with his hair slicked back on the sides.

Waters walked onto a small, dimly lit stage behind the bar in the long, narrow club and joined his band. With half-closed eyes, the guitarist peered through the smoke and saw a bar jammed with African-American patrons, many of whom had just made the journey from the South to the Windy City to find jobs. Waters gripped an oversized electric guitar—an instrument born in the postwar urban environment—and caressed, pulled, pushed, and bent the strings until he produced a sorrowful, razor-sharp cry that cut into his listeners who responded with loud shrieks. As he growled out the lyrics of "Rollin' Stone," Waters' face contorted in a painful expression that told of cotton fields in Mississippi and the experience of being black in Middle America at midcentury. Muddy Waters delivered a new, electrified music called "Chicago blues," which encapsulated his urban environment and reflected a new mood among African Americans. Some called it rhythm and blues to fit neatly into the prevailing categories of the record charts, which had replaced the "race" category with "rhythm and blues" in 1949.

The music of Muddy Waters and other Chicago bluesmen served as a direct precursor to the birth of rock with the success of Chuck Berry and Little Richard. Despite their innovative roles, African-American artists seldom received the recognition or the money that they deserved. Established crooners, disc jockeys, and record company executives, watching their share of the market dwindle with the increasing popularity of electric blues and its rock-and-roll offspring, tried to torpedo the new music by offering toned-down, white copies of black originals that left many African-American trailblazers bitter and sometimes broken.

Muddy Waters and the Postwar Electric Blues

Muddy Waters (b. McKinley Morganfield), who grew up in Clarksdale, Mississippi, and traveled to Chicago, adapted his Delta influences to his new environment. He had his first introduction to music in church. "I used to belong to church. I was a good Baptist, singing in church," he recollected. "So I got all of my good moaning and trembling going on for me right out of church." Muddy started with harmonica and at seventeen bought his first guitar. "The first one I got," he recalled, "I sold the last horse we had. Made about fifteen dollars for him, gave my grandmother seven dollars and fifty cents, I kept seven-fifty and paid about two-fifty for that guitar. It was a Stella. The peoples ordered them from Sears-Roebuck in Chicago." A young Muddy, influenced by Son House and Robert Johnson, played locally around his home base, a plantation owned by Colonel William Howard Stovall. In 1941, Muddy, then a tenant farmer, recorded for musicologists Alan Lomax and John Work who were on a trip to the Mississippi Delta in search of Robert Johnson, for the Library of Congress. "You just make up things when you're working out on the plantation," Waters explained. "You just get lonesome and tired and hot, and you start to sing."

In 1943, Muddy moved to Chicago "with a suitcase, a suit of clothes, and a guitar," to "get into the big record field." "I wanted to get out of Mississippi in the worst way," remembered Waters who joined thousands of other African Americans that make the wartime trek to the Windy City. "They had such as my mother and the older people brainwashed that people can't make it too good in the city. But I figured if anyone else was living in the city, I could make it there, too." By day, Muddy worked in a paper-container factory and then as a truck driver. At night, he performed his blues at parties and backed several established bluesmen such as Sunnyland Slim. Muddy electrified his sound. In 1944, he outfitted his hollow-body acoustic guitar with a De Armond pickup to electrify it and bought a small amplifier, and two years later, he formed his first electric combo.

The archetype of Chicago blues artists, Muddy Waters felt compelled to electrify his sound in Chicago. "When I went into the clubs, the first thing I wanted was an amplifier. Couldn't nobody hear you with an acoustic." At least partly out of necessity, Muddy combined his Delta blues with an electric guitar and amplifier, which blasted forth the tension, volume, and confusion of the big-city streets. By combining the sounds of the country and city to achieve a loud, pounding music that forced club customers to listen, Muddy Waters reflected the proud attitude of postwar African Americans, who questioned the discrimination around them.

The urban music contrasted sharply with the more sullen country blues, born in slavery. Willie Dixon, a bassist from Vicksburg, Mississippi, and composer of blues-rock classics such as "(I'm Your) Hoochie Coochie Man," "I'm a Man," and "I Just Want to Make Love to You," recalled that "there was quite a few people around singin' the blues but most of 'em was singing all sad blues. Muddy was giving his blues a little pep." "We kept that Mississippi sound," explained Muddy. "We didn't do it exactly like the older fellows—with no beat to it. We put the beat with it. You know, put a little drive to it." The peppy, hard-driving blues of artists like Muddy Waters became known as Chicago blues or rhythm and blues to reflect the record charts.

After three years of perfecting his electric sound in Chicago clubs, Muddy signed with Aristocrat Records, owned by local entrepreneur Evelyn Aron in partnership with Jewish immigrant brothers Leonard (b. Lejzor Shmuel Czyż) and Phil Chess (b. Fiszel Czyz), who had immigrated from Poland as youths and operated several South Side bars, including the Macomba Lounge. At first, reminisced, Leonard Chess found it difficult to understand Waters and wanted to reject him but Evelyn Aron suggested that they record him. When he released his first hit on a Friday in September 1948, "I Can't Be Satisfied," backed with "(I Feel Like) Going Home," reminisced Waters, "you couldn't buy one Saturday evening, you couldn't get one in Chicago nowhere. They sold 'em out." "I had a hot blues out, man. I'd be driving my truck and whenever I'd see a neon beer sign, I'd stop, go in, look at the jukebox, and see my record on there," Waters related. "Pretty soon I'd hear it walking along the street. I'd hear it driving along the street."

Encouraged by success and the abandonment of the blues market by RCA and Columbia, in December 1949 the Chess brothers bought out their partner Evelyn Aron, changed the name of the company to Chess, and released a series of Muddy Waters sides that became hits on the "race" charts. They first cut "Rollin' Stone" backed by the Robert Johnson tune "Walkin' Blues." In 1951, the Chess bothers followed with the Waters hits "Long Distance Call" and "Honey Bee."

Muddy Waters, 1950s.

Everett Collection Inc./Alamy Stock Photo.

By the mid-1950s, Leonard and Phil Chess rode Muddy Waters to success with a raucous, urbanized, electric Delta blues, which sold largely to an African-American audience. They scored with such Waters hits as "Mad Love," "I'm Your Hoochie Cooche Man," "Mannish Boy," "Just Make Love to Me," and "I'm Ready," among others. They repeatedly recorded Muddy Waters and his band, which included Otis Spann on piano, Little Walter on harmonica, Jimmy Rogers on guitar, and Leroy "Baby-Face" Foster on drums, and represented one of the most explosive Chicago blues units ever assembled.

The Wolf

Chester "Howlin' Wolf" Burnett, another Chess discovery, rivaled Muddy Waters with a raw, electrified Delta blues. In 1926, a teenage Burnett, living on the Young and Morrow plantation near Ruleville, Mississippi, met Charley Patton who lived nearby on Will Dockery's plantation. "Charley Patton started me off playing," he insisted. "He took a liking to me, and I asked him would he learn me, and at night, after I'd get off work, I'd go and hang around." A few years later, he heard the country yodeling of another Mississippian, Jimmie Rodgers, and tried to emulate the white country singer. Never mastering the yodeling technique because of his harsh, raspy voice, the blues singer earned a series of nicknames for his distinctive style, which included "Bull Cow," "Foot," and "The Wolf." "I just stuck to Wolf. I could do no yodelin' so I turned to howlin'," remembered Burnett. To perfect his raspy blues, Howlin' Wolf traveled across the Delta during the next two decades and played with prominent blues artists of the area, including Robert Johnson and Sonny Boy Williamson II (b. Rice Miller).

In 1948, at age 38, the Wolf plugged his Delta blues into an electric amplifier. In West Memphis, he formed an electric band, the House Rockers, which at times included harmonica players James Cotton and Little Junior Parker. The Wolf and his band landed a regular spot on radio station KWEM that gave them national exposure. Four years later, the Wolf joined the exodus to Chicago. He stayed at Muddy Waters' house for about two months, and Muddy introduced him to various club owners. "When Muddy went on the road, Wolf just stepped in his shoes," recalled Wolf's guitarist Hubert Sumlin.

A competition developed between Waters and the Wolf, who quickly established himself among the Chicago blues crowd. "Ever since the Wolf came to Chicago and started taking over, Muddy didn't like him too well," pointed out Sumlin who played for Wolf and Muddy. "A kind of rivalry started up between them about who was the boss of the blues." Willie Dixon, hired by the Chess brothers in 1950 as a songwriter and talent scout, recalled that every once in a while [the Wolf] would mention the fact, "Hey man, you wrote that [song] for Muddy. How come you won't write me one like that?" Dixon finally resorted to reverse psychology by telling the Wolf " 'Now here's one I wrote for Muddy, man.' 'Yeah, man, let me hear it,' an enthusiastic Wolf replied. 'Yeah, that's the one for me.' "

The Wolf scored a series of hits with Dixon's songs and traditional blues standards that influenced the course of rock and roll. He recorded his calling card, "Moanin' at Midnight"; "Killing Floor," later recorded by Jimi Hendrix; "How Many More Years," which became Led Zeppelin's "How Many More Times"; and "Smokestack Lightning," later popularized by the Yardbirds.

Wolf's stage demeanor presaged later rock-and-roll antics. At the end of one performance, the 300-pound, six-foot-three singer/guitarist raced toward a wing of the stage, took a flying leap, and grabbed onto the stage curtain, while still singing into his microphone. As the song built to a climax, the Wolf scaled the curtain. As the song drew to a close, he slid down the drapery and hit the floor just as the song ended to the screams of the audience. "God, what it would be worth on film to see the fervor in that man's face when he sang," recalled Sam Phillips, the genius behind Sun Records who recorded a few Howlin' Wolf songs and sold them to Chess. "His eyes would light up, you'd see the veins come out on his neck and, buddy, there was nothing on his mind but that song. He sang with his damn soul."

Bo Diddley and Other Chess Discoveries

The Chess brothers recorded other hard-driving electric blues performers from the Delta. Born Ellas Otha Bates McDaniel in McComb, Mississippi, Bo Diddley moved to the Windy City with his family, when he was six years old. He first played violin and then turned to the electric guitar by fashioning pick-ups from old radio components. He perfected an insistent, thumping beat, which he learned from "sanctified churches, Holy Rollers." "Oh, I played the street corners [on Maxwell Street] until I was nineteen or twenty, from about fifteen on," he told an interviewer. "Then I walked the streets around Chicago for about twelve years, before I got somebody to listen to me." Eventually, he landed a job at the 708 Club.

Diddley joined Chess Records almost by accident. In 1955, the guitarist walked down an alley three blocks from his house, when he saw a man dumping broken records into a trash bin. Bo asked the man about the building. After the man replied that Chess Records rented the building, Diddley mentioned that he "had a little band." The man suggested that Bo come to the front and talk to the Chess brothers. "I went there and made an audition with 'em," Diddley laughed, "so here I am." In June, signed with Chess Records, where reputedly he took the name Bo Diddley from a local comedian. That year, after a television appearance on the "Ed Sullivan Show," Diddley topped the R&B chart with "Bo Diddley" backed by "I'm a Man." He subsequently charted with "You Can't Judge a Book by Its Cover," and "Say Man." Though appealing to rock-and-roll fans, Diddley stood firmly rooted in the electrified Delta sound. The striking similarity between his "I'm a Man" and Muddy Waters' "Mannish Boy," both recorded in 1955, attests to Bo Diddley's Delta underpinnings.

Chess signed two pioneers of the amplified harmonica: Sonny Boy Williamson II (b. Aleck 'Rice' Miller) and Marion Walter Jacobs, otherwise known as Little Walter. Miller, the undisputed king of the blues harmonica, gained popularity through his long-running *King Biscuit Time*, a daily fifteen-minute radio show on station KFFA, broadcast from Helena, Arkansas. Although already a popular artist, when he signed with Chess in 1955, Sonny Boy cut a number charting singles for the Chicago label, including "Don't Start Me Talking."

Little Walter grew up in the cotton fields of Louisiana. He learned to play harmonica or the harp during his teens by patterning himself after Sonny Boy. In 1946, Walter left home for Chicago, where he joined the Muddy Waters band. In 1952, backed by the Muddy Waters group, he topped the chart with "Juke," which remained in the Top Ten R&B chart for fourteen weeks. Little Walter quickly formed his own band, the Night Cats, and followed with more than a dozen hits, including his signature, "My Babe" (1955), a Willie Dixon composition based on the gospel song "This Train."

By the mid-1950s, the Chess brothers had offered a new blues sound to record buyers. As Billy Boy Arnold, the harp player who backed Bo Diddley on his first Chess recording, explained, blues "changed drastically from 1940 to 1950. ... The saxophone players couldn't hardly get jobs. And piano was just about obsolete," with the notable exception of Otis Spann in the Muddy Waters' band. In their place, continued Arnold, Fifties Chicago blues featured "that harmonica blastin' on the amplifiers. Two guitars strumming behind 'em. ... Electric blues and harmonica and Muddy's type of country singing and low-down blues was at its pinnacle at that time." In the Windy City, the entrepreneurial Chess brothers had captured the new sound on vinyl to popularize the guitar-driven, amplified blues, which reflected postwar America, which became the bedrock of rock and roll.

Modern Records: B. B. King, Elmore James, and John Lee Hooker

Modern Records and its various subsidiaries, owned by the Jewish Bihari brothers of Los Angeles, gave Chess Records its stiffest competition in the search for blues talent. Launching their label in 1945, Jules recorded the artists, Saul pressed the records, and Joe promoted and sold the discs. The brothers focused on the blues. As Jules explained, "I was an operator of pinball machines and jukeboxes. I operated mostly in Negro areas, as far as jukeboxes were concerned. So naturally I took a liking to blues records." "So one day Jules said, 'If we can't buy them, let's start making [blues records],' " continued Joe Bihari. "Saul got out of the army and he had the money; he saved eight hundred dollars." With Saul's capital, the brothers started a record label.

During the early 1950s, Joe and Saul took numerous scouting trips to the Mississippi Delta and Arkansas. As Joe Bihari told it, "I traveled looking for those country blues singers and musicians. Some were from the cotton fields and plantations, some walking down the highway with an old guitar slung across their backs, others playing in juke joints, nightclubs and the backwoods gambling joints." To help with their search, the brothers hired talent scout and pianist Ike Turner who then was the leader of the Rhythm Kings and later gained fame as half of the Ike and Tina Turner duo.

The Biharis signed one of the most successful blues artists, Riley "Blues Boy" King. Born on a cotton plantation near Itta Bena, Mississippi, the heart of the Delta, King worked the fields by age 9 and earned $1.75 a day for picking 480 pounds of Delta Pinelent cotton. "I guess the earliest sound of blues that I can remember was in the fields while people would be pickin' cotton or choppin'," King recalled. One lead picker would sing, "just what he felt at the time. When I sing and play now I can hear those same sounds that I used to hear as a kid," he said.

As with many blues performers, King began his musical career in the church. He and his cousin sang in the church choir. "Singing was the thing I enjoyed doing, and when I started in school, I sang with a group: a quartet singing spirituals," King remembered. In 1940, a 15-year-old King bought a red Stella guitar for a month's wages that quickly became the boy's constant companion. He continued to "sing gospel music, using the guitar to tune up the group I played with," he related. When inducted into the army at age 18, King "started playing around little towns, just standing on the corner. People asked me to play gospel tunes and complimented me real nicely: 'Son, if you keep it up, you're going to be real good someday.' But the people who asked me to play the blues tunes normally tipped me, many times getting me beer. So that motivated me to play the blues." "The only difference is that 'my Lord' has turned into 'my baby,'" he added.

After being discharged from the army, King moved back and forth from Indianola, Mississippi, to Memphis, Tennessee. In 1946, the guitarist hitchhiked to Memphis where he moved in with a cousin, Booker T. "Bukka" White, a renowned Delta blues figure, and found a job at the Newberry Equipment Company. Two years later intent on a career in music, he permanently relocated to the city, where he performed on radio station WDIA in a program sponsored by the blood-building, alcohol-based tonic Peptikon. King initially had a ten-minute slot during the mid-afternoon by himself, then added drummer Earl Forrest and Johnny Ace [b. John Alexander] on piano, and eventually served as a disc jockey with two hour-long shows and a fifteen-minute program.

After nearly a year on WDIA, King, now called "Blues Boy," or "B. B." for short, signed a contract with Modern Records and its subsidiaries RPM, Kent, and Crown. He fused his Delta influences with a piercing falsetto vocal style and a jazzy, swinging, single-note electric guitar attack borrowed from Texas bluesman Aaron "T-Bone" Walker, who had adapted the country blues of Blind Lemon Jefferson to an electric guitar. "When I heard Aaron 'T-Bone Walker," King admitted, "I flat-out lost my mind. Thought Jesus Himself had returned to earth playing electric guitar." King learned from Walker about a style, in which "blues were as blue as the bluest country blues with attitude as slick as those big cities." Within a few years, King produced dozens of urban blues hits, which rock guitarists either copied or stolen, including "Whole Lotta' Love," "Woke Up This Morning (My Baby She Was Gone)," and "You Upset Me Baby" as well as his first chart topper "3 O' Clock Blues."

Elmore James joined B. B. King at Modern Records. Born on a farm near Richland, Mississippi, James taught himself guitar by stringing a broom wire to a wall of his cabin and plunking on it. He traveled with Delta giants such as Robert Johnson and Sonny Boy Williamson II and by the late 1940s had become a master slide guitarist. James first recorded with Trumpet Records, which Lillian McMurry started in Jackson, Mississippi. In 1952, James released a gut-wrenching, slashing, electric version of Robert Johnson's "Dust My Broom," which hit the Top Ten on the R&B chart. The next year, Elmore journeyed to Chicago, where he recorded for the Meteor and Flair labels, subsidiaries of Modern Records. As with his fellow Delta performers, Elmore James captured the pain and anguish of three centuries of slavery and tenant farming. Bobby Robinson, the African-American owner of Fire Records who recorded James, urged record buyers to listen to the "raw-nerved, spine-tingling picking of the guitar and the agonized screams and the soul-stirring of Elmore James. Close your eyes, you'll see the slave ships, the auction blocks, the cotton fields, the bare backs straining, totin' that barge and liftin' that bale. You will smell the sweat, feel the lash, taste the tears and see the blood."

The Biharis discovered John Lee Hooker, the Delta-born guitarist who traveled north to Detroit during World War II. Hooker learned guitar from his stepfather Will Moore who had performed with Charley Patton on Dockery's plantation. He sang with various gospel groups in the Delta, left home by age 14, and in 1943 moved to Detroit. "Detroit was *the city* then," enthused Hooker. "Work, work, work, work. Plenty work, good wages, good money at that time."

In the Motor City, Hooker worked by day as an orderly, a janitor at the Dodge automobile factory, and Comco Steel. At night, he played in various Detroit nightclubs. After a few years, he boasted, "I became the talk of the town around at the house parties. Finally I met this very, very great musician, who I loved so much, I treasured him like I would a piece of gold, the great T-Bone Walker. He was the first person to get me my electric guitar." Like Muddy Waters and other urban bluesmen, Hooker embraced the electric guitar because it allowed him to play over the din at dances and in bars.

Hooker joined the Modern Records roster. In 1948, he met record distributor Bernie Besman who recorded Hooker and then leased the acetate to Modern. With the single, "Boogie Chillin'," Hooker conjured an electric, chantlike, dark, superstitious-sounding stomp that vividly described black Detroit's main thoroughfare, Hastings Street. According to the guitarist, the single "caught fire. It was ringin' all around the country. When it come out, every juke box you went to, every place you went to, every drug store you went, everywhere you went, department stores, they were playin' it in there." Hooker followed with a series of discs such as "Crawlin' King Snake," "Hobo Blues," and the chart topper "I'm in the Mood" for a variety of companies, including Modern, Chess, and Besman's Sensation label.

Other Discoveries

Jimmy Reed entered the Chicago blues fray with Vee-Jay Records. Born on a plantation near Dunleith, Mississippi, Reed discovered the guitar with friend and later backup musician Eddie Taylor, whose style derived from Charley Patton and Robert Johnson. He learned harmonica by "listening to Sonny Boy Williamson [Rice Miller]. … I'd slip out of the fields and go up to the house to listen to them do the fifteen minutes he had to do over the radio show. He was broadcastin' for King Biscuit flour out of Helena, Arkansas." In 1943, Reed joined the rush to Chicago, where he worked at various steel mills and foundries. During his breaks and lunch hours, he practiced one-chord, Delta guitar shuffles and a laid-back vocal style that masked the biting lyrics of songs such as "Big Boss Man." In 1953, after moving to Gary Indiana, and being rejected by Leonard Chess, Reed signed with the newly organized, Chicago-based Vee-Jay Records, which was established by African-American disc jockey Vivian Carter and her husband James Bracken. In 1955, he first reached the Top Ten of the R&B chart with "You Don't Have to Go" and followed with a series of hits that included "Ain't That Lovin' You Baby" and "Honest I Do."

Small, independent record companies in Los Angeles, the new home of thousands of African Americans who migrated to the city during World War II to secure jobs, specialized in different styles of the electrified blues. Aladdin Records, begun by brothers Leo and Edward Mesner, recorded postwar sounds that spanned the relaxed vocal stylings of Charles Brown to the more jumpy blues of Amos Milburn who hit the chart in the late forties and early fifties with such chart toppers as "Bad, Bad Whiskey" and "Roomin' House Boogie." In late 1956, the company released Shirley and Lee's number one "Let the Good Times Roll," which became a rallying cry for rock-and-rollers.

Antoine "Fats" Domino signed to the Los-Angeles-based Imperial Records, which Lew Chudd established in 1945. Born in New Orleans, Domino learned to play the barrelhouse piano at age 9 and as a teenager worked in a bedspring factory by day and in local bars at night. In 1949, signed with Imperial. He debuted with the single "Fat Man," which sold 1 million copies. Domino followed with a string of number-one hits, including "Ain't That a Shame," "Blueberry Hill," "I'm in Love Again," "Blue Monday," and "I'm Walkin'." From 1949 to 1962, Fats delivered forty-three records that made the *Billboard* charts, twenty-three gold records, and record sales of 65 million units.

By the mid-1950s, Jewish entrepreneurs operated dozens of urban-based independent companies to record the African-American blues. The Jewish business included the Chess Brothers, Syd Nathan (b. Sydney Kriviansky), who established the King label; radio pioneer Herman Lubinsky who started Savoy Records; and Hy Weiss, a onetime distributor of Chess Records, who opened Old Town Records in New York City with his brother Sam. "We were people who had an understanding" with the African-American musicians, asserted Dave Usher, a Jewish music entrepreneur who worked as a talent scout for the Chess brothers. "You've got to understand, you're talking about Eastern European Jews that were persecuted," reasoned fifties' disc jockey Harold "Mr. Blues" Ladell. "So they're not ones to look down upon the blacks; they'd just come out of persecution."

The Jewish-owned companies cornered the blues market. In 1953, independents accounted for more than 80 percent of the burgeoning blues product. In just two more years, the labels produced 92 percent of all blues releases and dominated an emerging market.

The Blues Audience

The market for the new sound expanded with the number of African Americans who flooded into northern and western cities during and after World War II.

A second massive migration of African Americans from the rural South to Chicago and other Northern cities provided the context and a market for the music of Muddy Waters and other electric bluesmen.

The mechanical cotton picker pushed many Southern African-American sharecroppers to the North. In 1931 after several years of design work, two brothers, John and Mack Rust, developed a prototype for a mechanical cotton picker. By 1936, they demonstrated the new machine to bankers, scientists, plantation owners, and the press at the Delta Experimental Station in Stoneville, Mississippi. In one hour, the machine picked 400 pounds, which equaled four days of work for a cotton picker.

The invention of the Rust brothers struck fear among poor Southerners who relied on picking the puffy, white staple fiber for their livelihoods. The *Memphis Commercial-Appeal* printed a cartoon of an African-American cotton picker on an empty cotton sack, complaining that "if'n it do my work, whose work I gonna do?"

At the same time, the North beckoned rural African Americans. As the threat of war materialized, Northern industrial companies needed African-American workers and offered them more money than they had ever earned. In 1941, the year that the United States entered the war, prospects for work in Northern factories seemed even more encouraging, when President Franklin Roosevelt issued Executive Order 8802 that forbade "discrimination in the employment of workers in defense industries or Government because of race, creed, color or national origin."

African Americans flocked to Northern cities such as Chicago. During the forties, 214,000 Southern African Americans migrated to the Windy City to grow the African-American population by 77 percent in just one decade. Half the migrants came from the Mississippi Delta, a 200 mile region from Memphis to Vicksburg. Many saved $15 over several years for the day-long trip on the Illinois Central Railroad to the Windy City.

Other Northern cities experienced a similar influx of Southern African Americans. During the forties, the African-American population in New York skyrocketed from 458,444 to 748,000, a 63 percent increase. The African-American community in Cleveland jumped from 84,504 to 148,000; and in Philadelphia the African-American population climbed from 250,888 to 376,000. "Detroit became a haven for a lot of the immigrants from the South, like people from Alabama, Georgia, parts of Florida, Mississippi," recalled African-American songwriter Billy Davis who lived in the Motor City. "You found a lot of black families come up to

Black and white shipyard workers Oscar Sean and Jerry Evans at the site of building the SS Frederick Douglas, May 1943. Six thousand blacks had been recently hired at the shipyard.

Library of Congress Prints and Photographs Division [LC-USW3-024175-D].

Detroit because there was work available in the automobile plants." On the West Coast, the African-American population of the Los Angeles area mushroomed from 75,496 in 1940 to 134,519 just four years later. In April 1945, a writer for *The Chicago Defender* described "the great Negro march on freedom northward of the present war period" as "a chapter as significant in the life of mankind as the ancient Hebrew migration out of Egypt."

Most African-American migrants found jobs. Within a year of Roosevelt's executive order, shipbuilding plants hired thousands of the transplants. The U.S. Navy likewise employed African Americans in 37 different crafts, including first-class machinists. By 1945, approximately 1 million African Americans had been added to the national workforce.

Like the African Americans who traveled North during and after World War I, African-American migrants during World War II landed jobs in defense factories and earned higher salaries than their paltry wages as sharecroppers and cotton pickers. "The war inevitably improved the financial lot of the Negro," observed sociologists Alfred Lee and Norman Humphrey in 1943. "His labor became an essential part of the manpower pool, and he is being rewarded more adequately than ever before in his experience."

The migrants, most of them having extra cash for the first time, looked for entertainment, but faced discrimination. "Harlem folks couldn't go downtown to the Broadway theaters and movie houses," recalled Ahmet Ertegun, cofounder of Atlantic Records. "Downtown clubs had their ropes up when they came to the door. … Even radio was white-oriented. You couldn't find a black performer on network radio. And when it came to disc jockeys on the big wattage stations, they wouldn't play a black record."

For their leisure, some African Americans in urban areas frequented segregated clubs such as the Roosevelt in Pittsburgh, the Lincoln in Los Angeles, the Royal in Baltimore, Chicago's Regal, the Howard in Washington, and the now-famous Apollo Theater in New York City. The owners of Town Hall, the only large dance hall in Philadelphia that admitted African Americans, claimed that "swollen Negro paychecks at local war plants and shipyards" helped increase their profits. Other African Americans went to segregated taverns and demanded music by African-American artists on the jukeboxes, which numbered 400,000 by 1950.

The majority of migrants, bound closer to home by their families, found entertainment through recorded music. As Ahmet Ertegun suggested, most "black people had to find entertainment in their homes—and the record was it." They bought 78-rpm discs by their favorite artists in furniture stores, pharmacies, barber shops, shoeshine stands, and other local businesses. Most favored the electrified blues. "The black people, particularly the black people I knew," Art Rupe (b. Art Goldberg), the owner of Specialty Records, recalled of the late forties, "looked down on country music." In Rupe's experience, black people wanted to distance themselves from rural stereotypes, and this desire extended to music.

At first, the sales of blues discs depended on African Americans. Johnny Otis (b. Ioannis Veliotes), a white bandleader who grew up in a black section of Berkeley, California, and later helped many African-American artists rise to stardom, noticed the trend. "As far as black music was concerned we had what was known as race music. Race music was Big Bill Broonzy, he observed. The blues were "very much part of the black community but they didn't occur anywhere else and these cats could hardly make a living plying their trade." An extremely successful blues recording sold a maximum of 400,000 copies and, according to Jerry Wexler of Atlantic Records, "sales were localized in ghetto markets. There was no white sale, and no white radio play."

During the early 1950s, more and more white teenagers became aware of the blues and purchased the music. Initially, young Southern whites bought records by African-American artists. As Jerry Wexler observed about his experience during the early 1950s, "We became aware that Southern whites were buying our records, white kids in high school and college." In California, at the same time, Johnny Otis saw the changing demographics of the blues audience, which was becoming dotted with white faces. In 1952, the Dolphin Record store in Los Angeles, which specialized in blues and jazz records, reflected the trend by reporting that 40 percent of its sales were to whites. Eventually, white teens in all parts of the country turned to blues. In April 1955, Mitch Miller, then head of Columbia Records and later famous for the sing-along craze he masterminded, complained that "rhythm-and-blues songs are riding high." This " 'rock-and-roll' began among Negro people, was first recorded by Negro performers and had its following among Negroes in the South and also Negro urban areas in the North." Miller noticed that "suddenly millions of white teenagers who buy most of the 'pop' records in America have latched onto rhythm and blues."

Rock and Roll Emerges: Little Richard and Chuck Berry

The white teenage blues record buyers favored a few showmen who delivered a frenetic, hard-driving version of an already spirited electric blues that became known as rock and roll. They especially idolized young blues performers with whom they could identify. By 1955, Muddy Waters had turned 40, Howlin' Wolf was 46, Sonny Boy Williamson was 56, John Lee Hooker was 35, B. B. King was 30, and Elmore James was 37.

Little Richard and Chuck Berry, significantly younger and wilder than most electric blues performers, became heroes to white teens. Little Richard, born Richard Penniman in Macon, Georgia, on December 5, 1932, sang in a Baptist church choir as a youth and traveled with his family gospel troupe, the Penniman Family. He joined various circuses and traveling shows, and in the Broadway Follies met gospel/blues shouter Billy Wright, who secured a recording contract from RCA Records for the 18-year-old Little Richard. In late 1951 and 1952, Richard cut eight sides for RCA, which failed to chart.

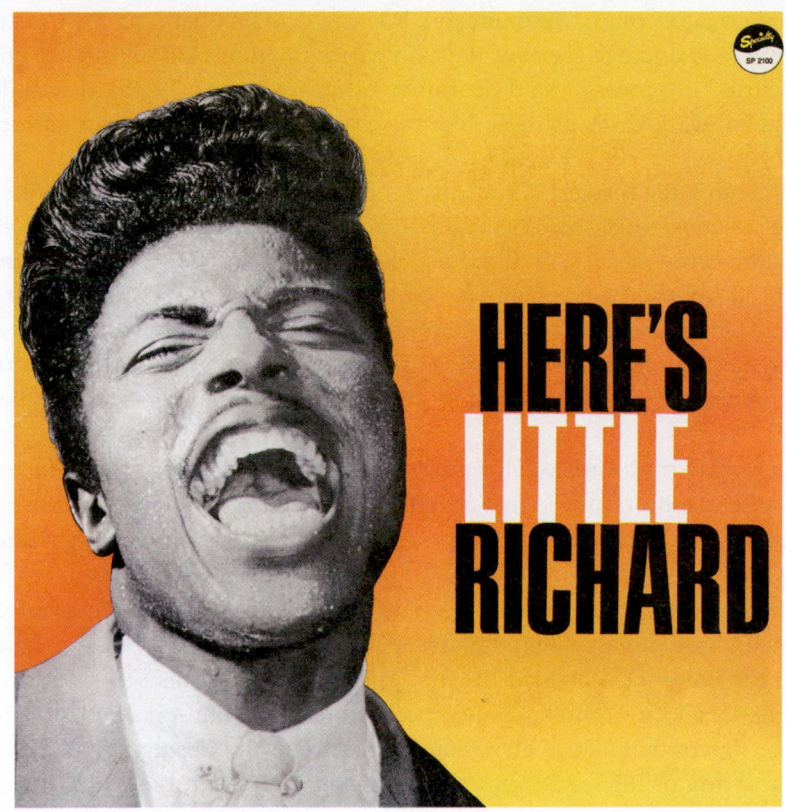

The fabulous Little Richard.

Courtesy of Concord Music Group.

Little Richard returned home, when a local tough shot and killed his father, the owner of the Tip In Inn. To support the family, Richard washed dishes in the Macon Greyhound Bus station by day and at night sang with his group, the Upsetters, at local theaters for $15 a show. "We were playing some of Roy Brown's tunes, a lot of Fats Domino tunes, some B. B. King tunes and I believe a couple of Little Walter's and a few things by Billy Wright," remembered Little Richard.

After a few years of one-night stands in Southern nightclubs, Penniman changed his style. He transformed himself from a traditional blues singer into a wild-eyed, pompadoured madman who crashed the piano keys and screamed nonsensical lyrics at breakneck speed. Not content to deliver Chicago blues, he pounded the piano with a boogie-woogie bass line, played right-hand notes at double speed, and howled high-pitched screams. On the advice of blues singer Lloyd Price of "Lawdy Miss Clawdy" fame, Richard contacted Specialty Records in Los Angeles. He sent a demo tape of two rather subdued blues tunes to label owner Art Rupe, who had recorded Price as well as blues artists such as Roy Milton. According to Specialty's musical director Bumps Blackwell, Richard wrapped the tape "in a piece of paper looking as though someone had eaten off it." Blackwell opened the wrapper, played the tape, and recommended that Rupe sign Little Richard.

On September 14, 1955, Richard arrived in New Orleans for his first Specialty recording session. He started with a few blues songs. During a break in the session, someone heard him playing "Tutti Frutti" on the piano and asked about the song. Little Richard edited the obscene lyrics from the tune, recorded it, and within a week sold 200,000 copies. During the next three years, Richard cut a wealth of rock-and-roll standards, which defined the new music: "Long Tall Sally," "Slippin' and Slidin'," "Rip It Up," "Ready Teddy," "The Girl Can't Help It," "Good Golly Miss Molly," "Jenny, Jenny," "Keep a Knockin'," and "Lucille."

Little Richard, dressed in flamboyant clothing with a pompadour hairstyle and makeup, developed a wild stage show. His band "the Upsetters wasn't just a name;

when we'd go into a place, we'd upset it! We were the first band on the road to wear pancake makeup and eye shadow, have an earring hanging out of our ear and have our hair curled in process," said drummer Charles Conner. "Richard was the only guy in the band that was actually like that, but he wanted us to be different and exciting."

Along with Little Richard, Chuck Berry created rock and roll. Berry, unlike almost all other blues musicians, spent his youth in a sturdy brick house on a tree-lined street in the middle-class outskirts of St. Louis. He first sang gospel at home with his family and at the Antioch Baptist Church. "Our family lived a block and a half from our church, and singing became a major tradition in the Berry family. As far back as I can remember, mother's household chanting of those gospel tunes rang through my childhood," he explained. "Looking back I'm sure that my musical roots were planted, then and there."

The young Berry heard country music and the blues on the radio. "The beautiful harmony of the country music that KMOK radio station played was almost irresistible," recalled Berry. By his teens, Berry also had become a fan of several bluesmen, especially Muddy Waters.

After a three-year stay in reform school and several jobs, which included work as a cosmetologist and an assembler at the General Motors Fisher Body plant, Berry turned to the blues. He obtained his first guitar from St. Louis blues performer Joe Sherman and, in 1953, formed a blues trio with Johnnie Johnson on piano and Ebby Harding on drums that played at St. Louis bars such as the Cosmopolitan Club.

In the spring of 1955, a 28-year-old Berry and a friend traveled to Chicago, the mecca of urban blues. He watched the shows of Howlin' Wolf, Elmore James, and Muddy Waters who to Berry "was the godfather of the blues. He was perhaps the greatest inspiration in the launching of my career." After a late-night set, Berry approached Waters for his autograph and got "the feeling I suppose one would get from having a word with the president or the pope." When Berry asked Muddy about his chances of making a record, Waters replied, "Yeah, [go] see Leonard Chess, yeah. Chess Records over on Forty-Seventh and Cottage." Chuck Berry took Muddy Waters' advice. The next day, he rushed to the Chess offices and talked with Leonard Chess who asked for a demo tape of original songs within a week. Berry returned with a tape that included a traditional song, "Ida Red," which had been popularized in 1938 by Bob Wills and his Texas Playboys. Chess, recalled Berry, "couldn't believe that a country tune (he called it a 'hillbilly song') could be written by a black guy. He wanted us to record that particular song." In the studio, on the advice of Willie Dixon who played bass on the session, Berry added a heavy back beat and a bluesy element to the tune, renamed it "Maybelline," after the trade name on a mascara box in the corner of the studio, and backed it with a slow blues, "Wee Wee Hours."

Berry convinced Chess to release "Maybelline," a traditional song adapted to an upbeat, rolling boogie-woogie beat on the guitar, which hinted at the marriage between country and blues that reached full fruition with the rockabillies. Within weeks, Berry's song received national airplay and by the end of August hit *Billboard's* Top-Five pop chart.

Berry's debut attracted a teen market. "The kids wanted the big beat, cars, and young love," recalled Leonard Chess about the market for the song. "It was a trend and we jumped on it." The guitarist-songwriter followed with such teen-oriented pop hits as "School Day," "Rock and Roll Music," "Sweet Little Sixteen," "Johnny B. Goode," and dozens of other songs. He embarked on a whirlwind tour of the country by playing 101 engagements in 101 nights, during which he perfected his trademark duck walk.

By 1956, Chuck Berry and Little Richard had bridged the short gap between the electric Chicago blues and what became known as rock and roll, originally an

African-American euphemism for sexual intercourse. They delivered a frantic, blues-based music to teens who claimed it as their own. "It used to be called boogie-woogie, it used to be called blues, used to be called rhythm and blues," explained Chuck Berry, "but it's called rock now."

Rock and Roll and the Changing American Culture

A rapidly changing American culture during the fifties, distinguished by television, civil rights and a baby boom, nurtured and made possible the popularity of a wild, teen-oriented rock and roll. Television made radio space available to more recording artists. Before the 1950s, network radio shows, many of them broadcast live, dominated the airwaves and, as Johnny Otis argued, "in the thirties and forties, black music was summarily cut off the radio." After World War II, television became more popular and affordable. By 1953, more than 300 television stations in the United States broadcast to more than 28 million television sets. By absorbing the network radio shows to fill a programming void, television created airtime for a greater variety of records, including discs by African-American artists.

Many of the disc jockeys who spun rock-and-roll records became die-hard advocates of the music. During the fifties, B. Mitchell Reed, who jockeyed on a leading Los Angeles station KFWB-AM, became "enthralled with rock" and convinced management to switch from a jazz format to rock and roll when he "realized that the roots of the stuff that I was playing—the rock—had come from the jazz and blues I'd been playing before." Even earlier than Reed's conversion to rock, the Los Angeles "dean of the DJs," Al Jarvis, introduced African-American artists on his show.

Alan Freed became rock and roll's superpromoter. Freed, launched his broadcasting career in New Castle, Pennsylvania, on the classical station WKST. After a stint on a station in Akron, Ohio, in 1951, he landed a job in Cleveland on the independent station WJW. Prodded by record-store owner Leo Mintz, Freed began to play rock-and-roll records on his program. He picked the jumping "Blues for the Red Boy," a release by boogie-woogie pianist Todd Rhodes, for his theme song and named his show *The Moondog Rock 'n' Roll House Party*.

Freed ceaselessly marketed the new music. In 1952 and 1953, the disc jockey organized racially integrated rock-and-roll concerts in the Cleveland area that met with enthusiastic responses. For the first, the "Moondog Coronation Ball," he attracted 18,000 teens to an auditorium that seated 9,000 and was forced to cancel the show. By late 1954, the successful Freed landed a key nighttime spot on New York station WINS. While there, he introduced thousands of young whites on the East Coast to African-American music by consistently befriending African-American artists who recorded on small, independent labels. Freed also managed several rock-and-roll acts and in 1956 appeared in movies such as *Don't Knock the Rock* with Little Richard *Rock, Rock, Rock!* with Chuck Berry and *Rock Around the Clock*, which caused riots in the United States and Europe and further familiarized white youths with R&B, now being called rock and roll by Freed.

Young teens listened to disc jockeys such as Freed on a new gadget, the portable transistor radio, which by 1954 became available to the general public. Within a decade, more than 12 million consumers, many of them teens, bought the handheld radios each year. Teens on the move bought the increasingly inexpensive radios to experience the exciting new music called rock and roll.

The car radio served the same purpose as the portable transistor model. Standard equipment by the late thirties by 1946 more than 9 million car radios blasted forth from dashboards of automobiles, which sped down the highways and back roads of

America. During the fifties, car radios introduced rock and roll to many teens who used the automobile in such rites of passage as the school prom and the first date. In 1956, a car radio allowed Chuck Berry to detail his exploits in a Ford with a V8 engine to a cocky boy behind the wheel of his own car who raced his friend on a deserted road. The car radio helped deliver rock and roll to a mobile, young, car-crazy generation.

The less expensive, more durable 45-rpm record helped disseminate rock and roll to a teen market. On March 31, 1949, it had been introduced by RCA amid a high-profile marketing campaign. By 1956, the new 7-inch record accounted for $70 million in sales, mostly for jukeboxes and to teenagers who preferred the less breakable and more affordable record. Two years later, the 45-rpm disc accounted for nearly 66 percent of all vinyl sales compared to the classical-music friendly 33 1/3, which grabbed 24 percent and the heavy, breakable 78 rpm that had fallen to less than 3 percent. For nearly a decade, the 7-inch format became synonymous with rock and roll.

The civil-rights movement helped white teens accept American–inspired rock and roll. In 1954, with the advent of rock and roll, the Supreme Court handed down *Brown v. Board of Education of Topeka*. Convinced by the arguments of Thurgood Marshall, counsel for the NAACP and later a Supreme Court justice himself, the Court unanimously banned segregation in public schools and ordered school districts to desegregate. "In the field of public education," Chief Justice Earl Warren contended, "the doctrine of 'separate but equal' has no place. Separate educational facilities are inherently unequal." By overturning the "separate but equal" doctrine of the 1896 *Plessy* v. *Ferguson* case, the Court strongly endorsed African-American rights and furthered a civil-rights movement that fostered an awareness and acceptance of African-American culture, including the African-American–based rock and roll.

The number of youths who felt the impact of the *Brown* decision was growing rapidly. In 1953, approximately 13.6 million teenagers lived in the United States. Six years later, the number climbed to 15.4 million; and in 1960, the number of teens increased to 18.4 million. Observers called it the "wartime baby boom."

Many of these teens enjoyed prosperous times and had money in their pockets to spend on records. In general, Americans had more leisure time than during the war and benefited from financial credit, which had been extended to them for the first time since before the Great Depression. Most Americans spent much of this extra money on consumer items such as paperback novels, television sets, cameras, and electrical appliances. Teenagers received sizable allowances. In 1956, America's 13 million teenagers earned a total of $7 billion with a weekly income of $10.55. A year later, they

School integration, Tennessee, 1956.

Library of Congress Prints and Photographs Division [LC-U9-657B-14].

had more than $9 billion to spend much of which was expended on records. Along with other factors, an increasingly affluent and consumer-based society paved the way for the mass consumption of rock and roll.

By 1954, rock and roll achieved widespread popularity among white youths. Teens bought discs by Chuck Berry and Little Richard and soon danced to the music. While touring with Fats Domino, Chuck Berry saw audiences beginning to integrate racially: "Salt and pepper all mixed together, and we'd say, 'Well, look what's happening.' " "'Tutti Frutti' really started to bring the races being together," boasted Little Richard. "The white kids would jump over the balcony and come down where I was and dance with the blacks. We started that merging all across the country."

Ralph Bass, a producer for King and then Chess Records, found the same phenomenon, when he went on the road with African-American acts. By the early fifties, he observed, "They'd have white nights, or they'd put a rope in the middle of the floor. The blacks on one side, whites on the other, digging how the blacks were dancing and copying them. Then, hell, the rope would come down, and they'd all be dancing together." "It was a revolution," Bass proclaimed. "Music did it. We did as much with our music as the civil rights acts and all of the marches, for breaking the race thing down."

Chicago blues and early rock and roll helped racially integrate America, when white teens began to accept aspects of African-American culture. "By their new-found attachment to rhythm and blues," suggested Mitch Miller in April 1955, "young people might be protesting the Southern tradition of not having anything to do with colored people." Rock-and-roll music, *Cashbox* editorialized a few months earlier, "has broken down barriers which in the ordinary course of events might have taken untold amounts of time to do." Rock and roll "is doing a job in the Deep South that even the U.S. Supreme Court hasn't been able to accomplish," the jazz magazine *Downbeat* contended the same year. "In some areas, areas where segregation is the most controversial, audiences will often be half colored and half white, not in separate accommodations."

Racist Backlash

The integration of white and black youths elicited a racist response from many white adults. In 1956, as white Southerners lashed out against desegregation and attacked civil rights workers, Asa "Ace" Carter of the White Citizens Council of Birmingham, Alabama, charged that rock and roll—"the basic, heavy-beat music of the Negroes"—appealed to "the base in man, brings out animalism and vulgarity" and, most important, represented a "plot to mongrelize America." One Southerner equated rock and roll with "the death song of America and the white race."

Other whites expressed their fear of race mixing by complaining about the sexual overtones of the new music. Testifying before a Senate subcommittee in 1958, Vance Packard—the author of *Hidden Persuaders*—cautioned that rock and roll stirred "the animal instinct in modern teenagers" by its "raw savage tone." "What are we talking about?" Packard concluded, quoting an article from a 1955 issue of *Variety*. "We are talking about rock 'n' roll, about 'hug' and 'squeeze' and kindred euphemisms which are attempting a total breakdown of all reticences about sex." *Cashbox* similarly warned that "really dirty records" had been "getting airtime" and suggested that companies "stop making dirty R&B records." Russ Sanjek, later vice president of Broadcast Music, Inc. (BMI), which initially licensed most rock-and-roll songs, explained the white fear of possible white and African-American sexual relations: "It was a time when many a mother ripped pictures of Fats Domino off her daughter's bedroom wall. She remembered what she felt toward her Bing Crosby pinup, and she didn't want her daughter creaming for Fats."

A few adults defended the teen music. In 1958, one mother from Fort Edward, New York, found that rock and roll eased the boredom of her housework: "After all, how much pep can you put into mopping the floor to 'Some Enchanted Evening,' but try it to 'Sweet Little Sixteen' by Chuck Berry and see how fast the work gets done." She added that "rock and roll has a good beat and a jolly approach that keeps you on your toes."

To jazz innovator William "Count" Basie, the uproar over rock and roll reminded him of the racist slurs hurled at his music two decades earlier. After living through the "swing era of the late 1930s, when there was a lot of screaming, pretty much like the furor being stirred up today," he remembered "one comment in the 1930s, which said 'jam sessions, jitterbugs, and cannibalistic rhythm orgies are wooing our youth along the primrose path to hell.' The funny thing is, a lot of the kids who used to crowd around the bandstand while we played in the 1930s are still coming around today to catch us. A lot of them are parents in the PTA, and leading citizens."

Many whites, rejecting the Count's logic, tried to waylay expected integration by outlawing rock and roll. In 1955, the Houston Juvenile Delinquency and Crime Commission sent local disc jockeys a list of nearly 100 songs that it considered objectionable, all of them by African-American artists. Blues singer Jimmy Witherspoon, living in Houston at the time, felt that "blacks were starting a thing in America for equality. The radio stations and the people in the South were fighting us. … They banned Little Richard's tune ('Long Tall Sally') in Houston."

The same year, anti-rock-and-roll crusaders in other cities followed the Houston example. In Memphis, station WDIA, the station that B. B. King helped popularize, banned the recordings of thirty African-American rock-and-roll singers. Radio program managers in Mobile, Alabama, similarly pledged that "the offensive will be discarded." In Long Beach, California, the sheriff banned "offending" records from the town's jukeboxes. In nearby Los Angeles, twenty-five disc jockeys agreed to "do everything possible to avoid public airing of records which [were] believed to be objectionable."

In some cases, racist violence erupted over the new music. Bo Diddley reminded an interviewer that "we used to have funny things like bomb scares and stuff like that because we were in South Carolina where the Ku Klux Klan didn't want us performing."

The Music Industry versus Rock and Roll

The music industry, stunned by the popularity of the new music, organized against rock and roll. Crooners whose careers tumbled because of the new music bitterly condemned it. Testifying before Congress in 1958, Frank Sinatra called rock "the most brutal, ugly, desperate, vicious form of expression it has been my misfortune to hear." Though he had been a teen idol only a decade before, Sinatra labeled rock and rollers "cretinous goons" who lured teenagers by "almost imbecilic reiterations and sly—lewd—in plain fact *dirty*—lyrics." By such devious means, he concluded, rock managed "to be the martial music of every sideburned delinquent on the face of the earth." A year earlier, Sammy Davis, Jr., an African American who had achieved success with a smooth crooning style, threatened that "if rock-'n'-roll is here to stay I might commit suicide." Crooner Dean Martin cryptically ascribed the rise of rock and roll to "unnatural forces."

Disc jockeys who lost listeners from their pop and classical programs to rock-and-roll stations spoke out against their competition. In 1955, Bob Tilton of WMFM in Madison, Wisconsin, called for "some records for adults that don't rock, roll, wham, bam, or fade to flat tones." To Chuck Blower of KTKT in Tucson, the year 1955, "with the tremendous upsurge of R&B into the pop crop—the almost complete absence of good taste, to say nothing of good grammar—this has been the worst and certainly the most frustrating pop year I have ever known." In the same year, a *Billboard* survey indicated that "many jockeys believe the quality of the pop platter has seriously deteriorated in the past year. … Several jockeys are strongly opposed to the rhythm-and-blues influence in pop music."

Songwriters in the American Society of Composers, Authors, and Publishers (ASCAP) exhibited an equal disdain for rock and roll. Because the new music usually was written by the performers, professional songwriters who had been dominant in the music industry since the days of Tin Pan Alley scrambled for work and soon complained. Lyricist Billy Rose, then a board member of ASCAP, labeled rock-and-roll songs "junk," and "in many cases they are obscene junk, pretty much on a level with dirty comic magazines." Meredith Wilson, the playwright of the Broadway smash *The Music Man* and a classical composer, charged that "rock-and-roll is dull, ugly, amateurish, immature, trite, banal and stale. It glorifies the mediocre, the nasty, the bawdy, the cheap, the tasteless."

ASCAP took action against their competitors. To reassert their control, in November 1953, ASCAP songwriters initiated a $150 million antitrust lawsuit against the three major broadcasting networks, Columbia Records, RCA, and Broadcast Music, Inc. (BMI), a song performance/licensing competitor that had been formed in 1939 by 250 broadcasters and catered to blues, country music, and the rock and roll. ASCAP songwriters eventually took their battle to a congressional subcommittee, but failed to squelch the popularity of rock and roll.

The Blanching of Rock

Many record executives complained about and successfully undermined African-American rockers and their music. Some leaders of the music industry personally disliked rock and roll. RCA vice president George Marek did not "happen to like [rock] particularly, but then I like Verdi and I like Brahms and I like Beethoven." Explained Ahmet Ertegun, who had recorded blues artists on his Atlantic Records: "You couldn't expect a man who loved 'April in Paris' or who had recorded Hudson DeLange in the '30s when he was beginning in the business, to like lyrics like 'I Wanna Boogie Your Woogie,' and 'Louie, Louie.' He had always thought race music and hillbilly were corny, and so he thought rock-'n'-roll was for morons."

More important than their personal tastes, established record executives feared the economic consequences of a new popular music that they did not control. Outdistanced by independent labels that had a virtual monopoly on rock-and-roll acts, they worried about their share of the market, especially when white teens started to buy rock-and-roll records en masse.

To reverse this trend, larger, entrenched companies signed white artists to copy, or "cover," the songs of African-American artists, and sometimes sanitize the lyrics. Charles "Pat" Boone, a descendent of pioneer Daniel Boone, epitomized the successful cover artist of the era. He wore a white sweater and white buck shoes, had attended college, and idolized Bing Crosby. After hosting the "Youth on Parade" radio program on Nashville station WSIX, in early 1955 Boone signed with Dot Records. The singer, though speaking out against racism, refused "to do anything that will offend anybody. If I have to do that to be popular, I would rather not be an entertainer. I would rather not have a voice."

Boone topped the chart with his cover renditions of popular blues and rock-and-roll songs. In September 1955, Boone topped the chart with a cover of Fats Domino's "Ain't That a Shame." During the next two years, he scored hits with other covers such as "At My Front Door" by the El Dorados, Big Joe Turner's "Chains of Love," and "Tutti Frutti" and "Long Tall Sally" by Little Richard. All told, Boone recorded twenty-nine Top-Twenty-Five hit singles, six of them reaching the-number-one spot. He appeared in more than a dozen films and wrote several teen books, including *The Care and Feeding of Parents*.

Boone many times toned down the originals. He reworked T-Bone Walker's "Stormy Monday" by substituting the phrase "drinkin' Coca-Cola" for "drinkin' wine." When covering "Tutti Frutti," Boone explained, "I had to change some words, because they seemed too raw for me. I wrote, 'Pretty little Susie is the girl for me,' instead of 'Boys you don't know what she do to me.' I had to be selective and change some lyrics, but nobody seemed to care," the singer recalled. "It made it more vanilla."

Boone, as well as some other cover artists, believed that his versions furthered the development of rock and roll. "R&B is a distinctive kind of music; it doesn't appeal to everybody. So if it hadn't been for the vanilla versions of the R&B songs in the 1950s, you could certainly imagine that rock-'n'-roll, as we think of it, would never have happened," argued Pat Boone. "Imitation may be the sincerest form of flattery, but that kind of flattery I can do without," countered LaVern Baker, who hit the pop chart with "Tweedle Dee" (1955) and "Jim Dandy" (1956) and saw her songs covered by white singers.

To sell these imitations and their pop records, Columbia, Capitol, Decca, and RCA employed new marketing techniques. The companies placed product on racks in suburban supermarkets, which by 1956 sold $14 million worth of discs and within a year sold $40 million of records, which accounted for nearly 20 percent of all sales. In addition, Columbia and then RCA and Capitol introduced mail-order record clubs to further build market share.

Many disc jockeys aided major companies rather than the independent labels. Although a few broadcasters such as Alan Freed refused to spin covers, most DJs gladly played "white" music. "It was a picnic for the majors," Ahmet Ertegun of Atlantic Records huffed. "They'd copy our records, except that they'd use a white artist. And the white stations would play them while we couldn't get our records on. 'Sorry,' they'd say. 'It's too rough for us.' Or: 'Sorry, we don't program that kind of music.' " Danny Kessler of Okeh Records found that "the odds for a black record to crack through were slim. If the black record began to happen, the chances were that a white artist would cover—and the big stations would play the white records. ... There was a color line, and it wasn't easy to cross."

Industry leaders even succeeded in banning some African-American artists from the airwaves. In one instance, CBS television executives discontinued the popular *Rock 'n' Roll Dance Party* of Alan Freed, when cameras strayed to a shot of African-American singer Frankie Lymon of the Teenagers dancing with a white girl. African-American artists developed the music and got "ripped off and the glory and the money goes to the white artists," grumbled Johnny Otis.

The Story of Arthur "Big Boy" Crudup

The saga of Arthur "Big Boy" Crudup bears testimony to Otis' charge. Crudup, born in Forest, Mississippi, worked as a manual laborer in the fields, logging camps, sawmills, and construction projects until his thirties. In 1940, he headed to Chicago with other African-American hopefuls and signed a contract with RCA. Between 1941 and 1956, Crudup released more than eighty sides, which included "Rock Me Mama," "So Glad You're Mine," "Who's Been Foolin' You," and "That's All Right Mamma," which have been subsequently reworked by Elton John, Rod Stewart, Canned Heat, Johnny Winter, and many others. By the late 1950s, Crudup quit playing. "I realized I was making everybody rich, and here I was poor."

Arthur "Big Boy" Crudup.
Courtesy of Delmark Records.

In 1968, Dick Waterman, an agent and a manager for many blues artists, began the fight for Crudup's royalties through the American Guild of Authors and Composers. After four years, he reached an agreement for $60,000 in back royalties with Hill and Range Songs, which claimed ownership of Big Boy's compositions. Crudup and his four children traveled from their home in Virginia to New York City and signed the necessary legal papers in the Hill and Range office, a converted four-story mansion. John Clark, the Hill and Range attorney, took the papers to Julian Aberbach, head of Hill and Range, for his signature, while Waterman, Crudup, and his children "all patted each other on the back and congratulated Arthur that justice had finally been done." But, according to Waterman, "the next thing, John Clark comes back in the room, looking stunned and pale, and says that Aberbach refused to sign because he felt that the settlement gave away more than he would lose in legal action. We all waited for the punch line, for him to break out laughing and whip the check out of the folder. But it wasn't a joke." Crudup who once said, "I was born poor, I live poor, and I'm going to die poor," passed away three years later, with little money.

Though Crudup did not reap the benefits of his innovations, he did not go unheard. Years later, one rock-and-roll star acknowledged his debt to Crudup. "If I had any ambition, it was to be as good as Arthur Crudup." The admission came from Elvis Presley.

Chapter 3
Elvis and Rockabilly

"[Rock and roll is] a combination of country music, gospel, and rhythm and blues. As a child, I was influenced by all of that."

—Elvis Presley

Rockabilly Roots

Elvis Presley, a kinetic image in white suede shoes, an oversized, white-checkered jacket over a jet-black shirt with an upturned collar and *no tie*. He violently shook his black loose-fitting pants as he gyrated his hips and legs. A sneering, rebellious expression covered Presley's face, and his greased hair fell over his sweat-drenched forehead. The singer grabbed a microphone as though he was going to wrench it from its metal base, and he barked, whimpered, and shouted into it. Elvis warded off screaming fans who pulled at his trousers, his suit, and his shirt, lusting to tear off a piece of the raw energy that burst forth. Swaggering across the stage, he sang a sexually charged music that fused a white country past with African-American sounds. Elvis Presley, singing to hordes of adoring, frantic teens, delivered a sound called "rockabilly" that changed the direction of popular music.

White teenagers from poor southern backgrounds, growing up in the border states where black-and-white cultures stood face-to-face over a seemingly impassable chasm, concocted the pulsating mixture of African-American-inspired rhythm and blues and country and western known as rockabilly, a term coined by *Cash Box* editor Ira Howard. The young rockabilly pioneers included Jerry Lee Lewis, who leapt on his piano, banged the keys with his feet, and heaved his jacket, and sometimes his shredded shirt, to the audience; the more subdued Carl Perkins, writer of "Blue Suede Shoes," "Boppin' the Blues," and many other classics; Johnny Cash, who launched his career with several rockabilly gems; Johnny Burnette, the cofounder of the crazed Rock-and-Roll Trio with his brother Dorsey and Paul Burlison; the quiet, bespectacled Texan, Charles "Buddy" Holly; and, of course, Elvis Presley, the pacesetter of the new music, whose raw edge drove crowds to a frenzy. Despite the warnings of many horrified adults, these poor southern whites spread the message of rock and roll to millions of clamoring teenage fans and vaulted to the top of the national charts.

Most rockabillies never dreamed of such success. Presley, the king of swagger and the musical embodiment of James Dean's celluloid image, grew up in a 30-foot-long, two-room house in the poorest section of Tupelo, Mississippi. His father Vernon sharecropped and worked odd jobs, while his mother Gladys did piecework as a sewing machine operator. For several months, Vernon served time at the notorious Parchman prison for forging a check to make ends meet. On January 8, 1935, when Elvis was born, his parents "didn't have insurance," one neighbor remembered, "so Gladys stayed at home." During Elvis's childhood in Tupelo, the Presleys defaulted on the payment of their mortgage and drifted from house to house. In September 1948, the Presley family moved from Mississippi to Memphis, Tennessee. Vernon Presley packed the family's belongings in cardboard boxes and roped them on top of their

Elvis in Concert, 1956.

Pictorial Press Ltd./Alamy Stock Photo.

run-down 1939 Plymouth and set out on the road. "We were broke, man, real broke, and we left Tupelo overnight," Elvis recalled, "Things had to be better."

In Memphis, the standing of the Presleys did not improve initially. Vernon worked for a tool company, as a truck driver, and finally, in 1949, landed a job as a laborer at the United Paint Company. Earning less than $40 a week, he paid the rent on an apartment in Lauderdale Courts, a federally funded housing project. Elvis attended the nearby L. C. Humes High School, "a lower poverty-type school, one of the lowest in Memphis," according to one of Presley's classmates. After graduating from Humes High in 1953, he did factory work at M. B. Parker's Machinists' Shop, then worked at the Precision Tool Company, and finally worked as an apprentice electrician, delivering electrical parts throughout town in a small black Chevrolet truck for the Crown Electric Company, until he turned to music. Jane Richardson, one of two home-service advisors working for the Memphis Housing Authority, summed up the condition of the Presleys during their first years in Memphis: "They were just poor people."

Other rockabilly stars came from similarly impoverished backgrounds. Jerry Lee Lewis, who scored hits with "Great Balls of Fire" and "Whole Lotta Shakin' Goin' On," was born on September 29, 1935, on a farm outside Ferriday, Louisiana. His father Elmo eked out a living by doing carpentry work and growing surplus produce on the farm. Johnny Cash was born on February 26, 1932, into a poor country family in Kingsland, Arkansas. When Franklin D. Roosevelt's New Deal came to the South, the Cash family moved to Dyess, Arkansas, as part of a resettlement program for submarginal farmers. Johnny later enlisted in the U.S. Air Force and after his discharge sold refrigerators in Memphis. The boredom of the sales job prompted him to write the classic "I Walk the Line." Carl Perkins grew up only a few miles from Johnny Cash on the Tennessee side of the Mississippi on a cotton plantation. At age 6, Perkins began picking cotton and worked in the fields for years until he could fill five 65-pound bags in one day. When writing "Blue Suede Shoes," Perkins lived in a government housing project with his wife Valda. He had the idea for the song after "seeing kids on the bandstand so proud of their new city shoes—you gotta be real poor to care about new shoes like I did—and that morning I went downstairs and wrote out the words on a potato sack—we didn't have reason to have writing paper around."

The Rockabilly Sound

These poor youths combined two indigenous musical forms of the rural American South: the blues and country music. Like the Delmore Brothers who in the 1930s combined blues and folk into an emerging country music, Elvis Presley looked to both African-American and white music for inspiration.

Elvis listened to Mississippi Delta bluesmen such as B. B. King, John Lee Hooker, and Chester "Howlin' Wolf" Burnett on late-night radio and in the clubs along Beale Street in Memphis, a four-block thoroughfare of African-American music and culture in the South. Blues great B. B. King met Elvis in a pawn shop on Beale Street, where they hung out and insisted that Beale Street was one of the "only places where the races really got along."

Beale Street in Memphis, Tennessee, a hub of the postwar Southern blues scene and a favorite hangout of many rockabilly artists.

"The colored folks been singing it and playing it just like I'm doin' now, man, for more years than I know," Elvis contended in 1956. "I dug the real low-down Mississippi singers," recalled Presley in early 1957, "although they would scold me at home for listening to them. 'Sinful music,' the townsfolk in Memphis said." The Presley sound also derived from the country-and-western tradition of the South. In late 1954, Elvis, then called the King of the Western Bop, played at the Bel Air Club in Memphis with bassist Bill Black and guitarist Scotty Moore in Doug Poindexter's Starlite Wranglers. At that time, recalled Poindexter, "We were strictly a country band." Presley's first recordings revealed his dual influences: a "race" number written by bluesman Arthur "Big Boy" Crudup, "That's All Right, Mama," and a Bill Monroe country tune, "Blue Moon of Kentucky." As Presley insisted at the time, "I love the rhythm and beat of good rock-and-roll music and I think most people like it too. After all, it's a combination of folk or hillbilly music and gospel singing." A 1954 *Louisiana Hayride* program, noticing the singer's musical hybrid, referred to Presley as "the youngster with the hillbilly blues beat." *Billboard* first characterized Presley's style as "a white voice with a Negro rhythm which borrows in mood and emphasis from a country style."

Ironically, at least to self-righteous Northerners, southern whites first incorporated African-American sounds into their music and challenged the prevailing racism of the day. Change did not originate in the North observed Atlantic Records cofounder Ahmet Ertegun. "No, it was 'prejudiced' white Southerners who began programming R&B." "Young white teenagers heard them on those top-of-the-dial stations and began requesting them," he continued. "What the hell was Elvis listening to when he was growing up?" Sam Phillips, founder of the Memphis-based Sun Records likewise identified "a tradition in the South, between the blacks and the whites, where they have much more in common, than is generally known."

As with most blues artists, Elvis and other rockabilly musicians first found music in the southern churches. Presley attended the evangelical First Assembly of God Church. "There were these singers, perfectly fine singers, but nobody responded to them," recalled Elvis. On the other hand, the preachers "cut up all over the place, jumpin' on the piano, movin' ever' which way. The audience liked 'em. I guess I learned from them." At church, he listened to spirited white gospel singers, especially the Blackwood Brothers Quartet who performed and were members of the First Assembly of God Church in South Memphis.

For a few wild rockabilly musicians such as Jerry Lee Lewis, the close connection to the church not only provided musical bedrock but also engendered a sense of guilt when they turned to rock and roll. As a youth, Lewis attended the Pentecostal Holiness Assembly of God, where he heard fire-and-brimstone sermons. At 17 after witnessing a revivalist preacher, he enrolled in the Southwestern Bible Institute in Waxahachie, Texas. Though expelled from the Institute for unleashing a boogie-woogie version of "My God Is Real" in a school assembly, Lewis never lost the urge to become a preacher. "Jerry, he thought he was going to hell for not preaching," mused Johnny Cash years later. One night Lewis told Cash that "we all were going to hell for singing the kind of music we were singing." Cash responded that "maybe you're right, Killer, maybe you're right."

Sun Records and Elvis

Many southern rockabillies recorded their brand of raucous black-and-white blues at the Sun Record Company in Memphis, which was owned by Sam Phillips. Phillips, growing up near Florence, Alabama, and working in the cotton fields as a boy, seldom noticed "white people singing a lot when they were chopping cotton," but "never heard a black man who couldn't sing good. Even off-key, it had a spontaneity about it that would grab my ear." He immediately became entranced with rhythm and blues.

During the early 1940s, a young Phillips landed a job as a disc jockey at WLAY in Muscle Shoals, Alabama, moved to WLAC in Nashville, and ended up at WREC in Memphis.

In January 1950, Phillips, earning his certification as a radio engineer through a correspondence program, built a recording studio in a converted radiator shop at 706 Union Avenue in Memphis to record R&B artists, since, in his words, "there was nobody on the [Memphis] scene recording black music." He cut sides and sold them to such independent companies as Chess and Modern with such performers as Howlin' Wolf, Big Walter Horton, Joe Louis Hill, Rosco Gordon (who began to combine R&B and country), B. B. King, and Jackie Brenston, who with the Ike Turner band cut "Rocket 88." In January 1953, Phillips established his own record company, Sun Records, to record these blues and R&B artists.

The R&B orientation of Sun Records changed during the early 1950s. Many of the best African-American performers in Memphis, such as Howlin' Wolf, moved to Chicago, the rhythm-and-blues capital of the world, and the artists remaining at Sun sold only a few discs. Phillips, still in his twenties, also wanted his records to appeal "most especially to young whites, young blacks, and then thirdly to the older blacks.... There was just no music for young people then except for a few little kiddy records put out by the major labels." Faced with a declining business in R&B, Phillips confided to his office manager, "If I could find a white man who had the Negro sound and the Negro feel, I could make a billion dollars."

Elvis Presley walked into the Sun Records studio and gave Sam Phillips the sound he sought. On July 18, 1953, 18-year-old Presley recorded "My Happiness," a 1948 pop hit for Jon and Sandra Steele, and the Ink Spots' "That's When Your Heartaches Begins" as a present for his mother at the Memphis Recording Service, a branch of the Sun studio at which anyone could record a 10-inch acetate for $4. On Friday, January 4, 1954, he returned and cut his second disc—a ballad, "I'll Never Stand in Your Way," and a Jimmy Wakely country song, "It Wouldn't Be the Same without You." Marion Keisker, a Memphis radio personality and a front office staff person at the studio, taped the takes and rushed them to her boss.

After some initial reluctance, by April 1954 Phillips brought Presley into the studio. He first held an unsuccessful session on the ballad, "Without You." In late June, the Sun owner teamed Presley with guitarist Scotty Moore and bass player Bill Black and on July 5 recorded the trio. The combo struggled without results until finally a disgusted Phillips went back to the booth and left the microphones on. "I think that Elvis felt like, 'What the hell do I have to lose? I'm really gonna blow his head off, man.' And they cut down on 'That's All Right, Mama,' and, hell, man, they were just as instinctive as they could be," related Phillips. Uninhibited, Presley hiccupped the words in an animated fashion. "My legs were shaking all over," Elvis intimated, "mostly because I was so nervous and excited, but also I can feel the music more when I just let myself react." Moore banged out the melody on his amplified guitar, and Black slapped the bass like the forties hillbilly boogie of the Maddox Brothers and their sister Rose, creating a steady, repetitive boogie-woogie bass line to help define the rockabilly sound. The next day, Presley and his group cut a rockin' version of the country song "Blue Moon of Kentucky."

"Daddy-O" Dewey Phillips, the WHBQ Memphis disc jockey who hosted the R&B radio show *Red Hot & Blue*, received an advance acetate of the record from the Sun owner four days later. On the evening of July 10, 1954, recalled Sam Phillips, Dewey "played that thing, and the phones started ringing. Honey, I'll tell you, all hell broke loose." Locating Elvis in a local Memphis movie house after a frantic search, the disc jockey rushed the new sensation into the radio studio. In Dewey's words, "I asked him where he went to high school and he said Humes. I wanted to get that out, because a lot of people listening thought he was colored." In the nine days before the release of the Presley record on July 19, more than 5,000 orders streamed into the Sun offices for the disc that hit the top position on the Memphis chart by the end of the month.

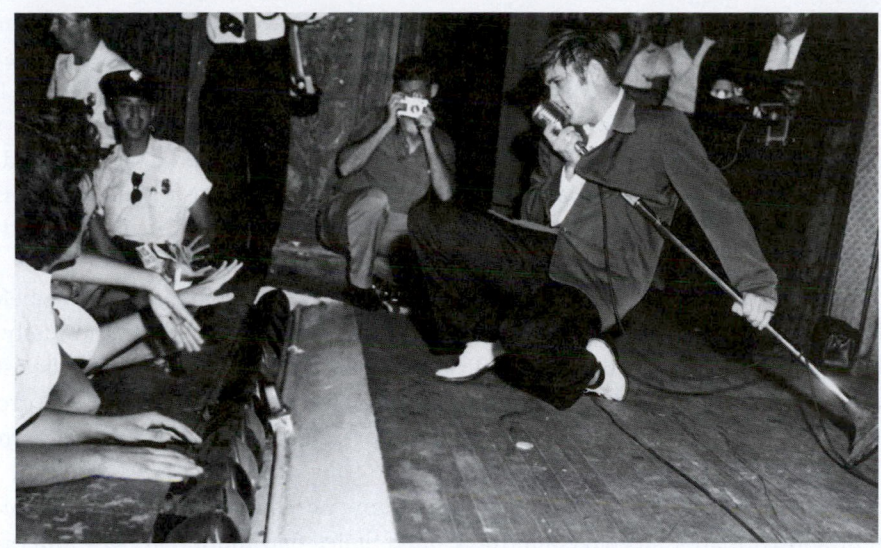

Elvis in Concert, 1956.

Pictorial Press Ltd./Alamy Stock Photo.

Elvis's live performances contributed to the hysteria. For Presley's first public show, Sun Records scheduled a performance at a small Memphis joint out on the highway at Summer and Medenhall, and Sam Phillips introduced him. "He ain't necessarily playing rhythm and blues, and he didn't look conventional like they did. He looked a little *greasy*," recalled Phillips. "And the reaction was just *incredible*."

During the summer of 1955, the wild reaction over Presley intensified during Elvis's tour of the South. In Jacksonville, Florida, at the Gator Bowl on May 13, rabid fans chased Elvis backstage and cornered him. According to Mae Axton, a concert promoter, an English teacher in Jacksonville, Florida, and cowriter of "Heartbreak Hotel," fifty girls "were tearing at Elvis. They'd pulled off his coat and shirt and ripped them to shreds." Elvis started running and climbed on top of a shower stall. The girls pulled his shoes and socks off and tried to pull his pants down when Axton arrived with a security guard to rescue the singer. Afterward, Presley told country singer Faron Young, who also appeared on the bill at the concert, that "them little girls are strong." "Yeah," agreed Young, "fifty of 'em get a hold of your ass, and it's just like a vacuum cleaner sucking on you. You can't get away." From then on, Young remembered, Presley's female fans tried "to get him, tear his clothes off, pull out his hair."

As Faron Young noticed, the Presley mania continued unabated. On July 4, 1955, in DeLeon, Texas, fans shredded Presley's pink shirt—a trademark by then—and tore the shoes from his feet. One female admirer from Amarillo, Texas, suffered a gash in her leg at the concert. "But who cares if it left a scar," she told a *Coronet* reporter. "I got it trying to see Elvis and I'm proud of it."

Country singer Bob Luman recalled a similar scene at Kilgore, Texas. A 19-year-old Elvis emerged from backstage in red pants, a green coat, and a pink shirt and socks. He defiantly sneered at the audience and stood behind the microphone for five minutes, before moving. Then Elvis played one chord on his guitar and broke two strings. Though their idol "hadn't done anything yet," related Luman, "these high school girls were screaming and fainting and running up to the stage." Finally, Presley "started to move his hips real slow like he had a thing for his guitar" and the entire crowd erupted. Presley also appealed to African-American teens. In 1956, the new sensation agreed to appear at Ellis Auditorium at the WDIA Goodwill Revue in Memphis to benefit needy African-American children. "For a young white boy to show up at an all-black function took guts," asserted B. B. King, who also played at the event. When Presley took the stage, remembered emcee Rufus Thomas, "people just leapt out of their seats and started screaming. They came running down the aisles trying to get Elvis. There was complete pandemonium."

The extreme reaction to Presley came from teens, especially teenaged girls, born during and immediately after World War II, who had just reached adolescence. In 1932, one of the worst years of the economic depression in the United States, less than 1 million Americans repeated their marriage vows. As the depression lifted and America entered World War II, more and more Americans decided to get married. In 1937, nearly 1.5 million Americans registered for marriage licenses, and by the first two years of the war, more than 1.7 million citizens annually recited their mutual pledges at the altar.

These couples decided to have children in record numbers. In the ten years before 1941, no more than 2.5 million children were born in the United States annually. In 1941 as young soldiers left their wives to fight in Europe and Asia, the number skyrocketed to 2.7 million and two years later hit 3.1 million newborns. By 1956, the growing legion of teens numbered 15.4 million and represented a 16 percent increase from just the beginning of the decade.

The teens had money to spend on entertainment. At a time of low unemployment and low inflation, teenagers in the United States had more than $8.4 million in discretionary income. Nearly 80 percent of them owned radios and 60 percent owned their own phonographs. Of the teens, many bought at least two records a month. A 1956 survey by the Bureau of Advertising called the teen market "big and lively and responsive."

Teenage girls offered Elvis a perfect demographic for his stage act, perceiving Elvis's stage act as a sexual call to arms. "The girls went crazy!" remembered guitarist Scotty Moore. "When we came off the stage, somebody told Elvis it was because he was shaking his leg. That was the natural thing for him. It wasn't planned." "I was scared stiff," Elvis admitted. "With those old britches that we wore," laughed Scotty, "it made it look like all hell was going on under there." Once Presley heard the reaction, Moore recalled, "He started embellishing on that real quick." To the adolescent girls in the audience such as one screaming, teary-eyed Florida fan, Elvis became "just a great big, beautiful hunk of forbidden fruit."

The teenage boys flocked to Elvis for his perceived rebellion against the adult world. Presley's pompadoured, slicked-back hair that he combed into a "ducktail" style, his sideburns, loose-fitting, zoot-suit pants, wildly colored shirts and jackets that he found on Beale Street, and his ever-present sneer seemed to embody a rejection of mainstream values and a sense of danger. At a time when his fellow high school students wore T-shirts, jeans, and loafers, Presley's appearance seemed to herald a new and defiant era and during the fifties defined the height of "cool" for young men.

A radio show helped spread the sexually charged, cool image of Elvis. On October 16, 1954, he started a thirteen-month-long stint on the influential *Louisiana Hayride* radio show, which had brought initial popularity to country stars Hank Williams, Webb Pierce, Faron Young, and others. Broadcast on KWKH in Shreveport, Louisiana, to listeners as far away as California and televised locally on the weekends, by the end of 1955 the *Hayride* helped propel Presley's "Baby, Let's Play House" to number ten and "I Forgot to Remember to Forget" to the top slot on the national country-and-western chart. In 1955, observed the *Memphis Press-Scimitar*, "A white man's voice singing Negro rhythms with a rural flavor has changed life overnight for Elvis Presley."

"The Killer"

Sam Phillips, buoyed by his success with Presley, recorded other young Southerners who possessed the same gritty, jumpy, seemingly rebellious sound. In 1956, a persistent Jerry Lee Lewis, nicknamed "The Killer" in high school, joined Sun. First playing piano publicly at age 14 with a local country band in a Ford dealership parking lot, Lewis found his musical roots in the blues and country music. As a young boy, he snuck into Haney's Big House in Ferriday, Louisiana, "a knock-down-drag-out colored joint," according to Jerry Lee, where blues artists such as B. B. King performed. He also listened to such country stars as Jimmie Rodgers. "He'd play a lot of boogie woogie and blues, and some country" in the house, his sister Linda Gail remembered of her brother in his early years. Mickey Gilley, Lewis's cousin and later a country musician, pinpointed the same influences for Jerry Lee. "With his left hand, he'd play what the black rhythm 'n' blues players used to do, with the boogie beat," he explained. "On the right hand, you'd hear the old [country] Moon Mullican style. He put those things together."

At 19, a determined Jerry Lee sold thirty-nine dozen eggs to pay for the gas for a trip from Ferriday to Memphis to meet Jack Clement, the producer at the Sun studio. According to Lewis, Clement initially brushed off the aspirant until Jerry Lee "told him he was going to do it or I'd whip him." Clement replied, "Well, if you feel that strongly about it, you must be good." When Sam Phillips returned from a long-deserved vacation at Daytona Beach, Clement put Lewis's "Crazy Arms" on the sound system, and the Sun owner screamed, "Where the *hell* did that man come from? He played that piano with abandon," Phillips later remembered. On December 1, 1956, Sun released Lewis's "Crazy Arms," which failed to compete with the number-one country version by Ray Price.

For the next year, Jerry Lee kept trying to breakthrough into the high reaches of the chart. He backed a few lesser-known Sun acts and added drummer James Van Eaton and guitarist Roland Janes to his band. On February 5, 1957, Lewis and his new band ripped through an earth-shattering version of a Johnny Littlejohn blues gem "Whole Lotta Shakin' Goin' On" for his second Sun disc and sold 60,000 copies regionally soon after its release. "It was never done like that before," explained Lewis. A trade magazine characterized the disc as a "driving blues shouter in the Sun tradition."

Phillips, in dire financial straits, decided to put Sun's efforts behind the single. "I knew the only hope to make Sun a successful and a big company was that we take Jerry Lee Lewis and put everything behind him and use his talent to create all the other Sun personalities," remarked Judd Phillips, Sam's brother and a Sun executive. The promotion package included a spot on the popular *The Steve Allen Show*—a close rival of *The Ed Sullivan Show*—which on July 28, 1957, showcased Lewis frantically banging the keys, kicking the piano stool into the audience, and shaking his mop of curly blonde locks until he looked like Lucifer's incarnation. The teens in the audience erupted, while the stage crew peered in disbelief. After the performance, the switchboard lit up. Scandalized adults screamed their dissatisfaction but shaky-voiced teenagers called to find out more about their new idol. In an uncharacteristic understatement, Lewis related: "Then I got on *The Steve Allen Show* and it busted wide open." By June, "Whole Lotta Shakin' Goin' On" reached number three on the *Billboard* singles chart and hit the number-one slot on both country-and-western and R&B charts. By November, Lewis neared the top of the singles chart with "Great Balls of Fire," which borrowed its bass line from Little Richard and also nearly topped both country and R&B charts.

"Blue Suede Shoes"

Lewis's success was matched by a steady stream of Sun rockabilly talents, among them guitarist-songwriter Carl Lee Perkins. Born near Tiptonville, Tennessee, on April 9, 1932, like many poor black Southerners Perkins constructed his first guitar from a cigar box and a broomstick and began to perfect a unique style. Since he seldom had cash for new strings, he once told a reporter, "I'd slide along to where I'd had to tie a knot and push up on a string 'cause I couldn't jump over the knot. Maybe if I'd been wealthy and could have bought new strings, I'd have slid down it and not developed the pushing up on the strings."

By the age of seven, Perkins learned guitar from his black neighbors. Chopping cotton in the fields for fifty cents a day, Perkins worked alongside black sharecroppers and "used to sing in the cotton fields." After work, he headed to the home of local bluesman John Westbrook, where he sat on the porch and learned blues licks. Carl produced a sound that resembled the music of other rockabillies, a merger of blues and country-and-western, and the slapped-bass boogie woogie beat. He "liked [country guitarist] Bill Monroe's fast stuff and also the colored guys, John Lee Hooker, Muddy Waters, their electric stuff. Even back then, I liked to do Hooker's things Monroe style, blues with a country beat and my own lyrics." He soon played music that sounded very much like Presley's. Bob Neal, then a disc jockey at Memphis radio station WMPS and later Presley's manager, recalled that he and Elvis saw Perkins perform in the fall of 1954 and "we were both struck by the sound Perkins was getting. It was very similar to Elvis' own." After hearing Presley's first Sun recording, Perkins himself felt that "it was identical to what our band was doing, and I just knew that we could make it in the record business after that."

Perkins and his band, which included his brothers Clayton on stand-up acoustic bass and Jay on rhythm guitar as well as drummer W. S. "Fluke" Holland, signed with Sun in October 1954. The band began touring from the back of a truck, charging $1 to watch the show. In 1955, the Perkins band released "Movie Magg," backed by "Turn Around," on the Sam Phillips' subsidiary label Flip and "Let the Jukebox Keep Playing" with the hard-bopping "Gone, Gone, Gone" on the Sun label. On December 19, 1955, Perkins cut the smash "Blue Suede Shoes," which within four months topped country-and-western chart, nearly did the same on R&B and reached the number-three slot on the pop chart.

As he vied for the rockabilly crown, on March 22, 1956, Perkins faced tragedy. Just before sunrise on the way to New York City for an appearance on the television blockbuster *The Perry Como Show*, outside of Dover, Delaware, he was involved in a car crash with a pickup truck that nearly killed his brother Jay and hospitalized him with a broken collarbone, three fractured vertebrae in his neck, and a severe concussion. "I was a poor farm boy, and with 'Shoes' I felt I had a chance but suddenly there I was in the hospital," Carl recalled bitterly.

Perkins never attained the stardom of Presley, who, according to Perkins, "had everything. He had the looks, the moves, the manager, and the talent. And he didn't look like Mr. Ed, like a lot of us did. Elvis was hitting them with sideburns, flashy clothes, and no ring on the finger. I had three kids," added Carl. After Presley hit the chart with his version of "Blue Suede Shoes" in April 1956, Perkins became known more for his songwriting than for his performing and worked in the shadow of the King.

Johnny Cash

Johnny Cash became the other stellar Sun rockabilly beside Elvis, Jerry Lee Lewis, and Carl Perkins. The son of a sharecropper, Cash joined the U.S. Air Force where he started writing songs, including "Folsom Prison Blues." By 1953, he joined a small group in his barracks, singing country songs by such stars as Hank Williams and Hank Snow.

The blues also attracted Cash. "My favorite music," he recalled, "is people like [country bluesman] Pink Anderson, Robert Johnson, the king of the Delta blues singers, Howlin' Wolf, Muddy Waters.… Those are my influences in music, those are the ones I really loved."

The songwriter signed with Sun Records in early 1955 with his brand of rockabilly. He first hit the Top-Twenty country-and-western chart with "Cry! Cry! Cry!" Convincing Sam Phillips that he should record his next composition rather than baritone singer Tennessee Ernie Ford, Cash followed with "Folsom Prison Blues," which reached number four on the country chart. In May 1956, Cash released his signature "I Walk the Line." Initially, Cash wrote the song for Elvis "but it came time for my next single release and Sam said, 'Elvis can't have that!' … So Sam released it with 'Ballad of a Teenage Queen,' which got the most play for a long time." By September, the tune hit the Top Twenty and peaked at the top of the country singles.

The Sun Rockabilly Stable

The Big Four of Sun—Presley, Lewis, Perkins, and Cash—supported a battalion of lesser-known but nonetheless hell-bent rockabillies. Billy Lee Riley exemplified the group. The wild Riley, part Native American who played guitar, harmonica, drums, and bass, formed the Little Green Men in 1955. By 1957, he signed with Sun and released the seminal "Flying Saucer Rock-and-Roll" and "Red Hot" and drove crowds to a frenzied pitch with his onstage antics. During one memorable performance, he hung from the water pipes near the stage with one hand and clutched the microphone with the other, screaming the lyrics of a song until his face turned bright pink. He delivered a music that "was still country, but it had the black feel, which I was brought up on."

Sonny Burgess, another slightly crazed rockabilly in the Sun fold, produced raw rock that attracted a local audience. A farm boy from Newport, Arkansas, Burgess traveled to Memphis in 1955. His music, best exemplified by his 1956 minor hit "Red Headed Woman," which sold 90,000 copies, combined a country Arkansas heritage and African-American rhythm and blues. "We were doing rhythm and blues and fast country," he explained. Ray Harris, who cut "Come On Little Mama" for Sun in 1956, exhibited an intensity similar to other rockabillies. Bill Cantrell, then a Sun employee, felt that "Ray wanted to be another Elvis. He couldn't sing and he wasn't good to look at but he didn't care. Man, he was crazy. You would go to visit him and hear him practicing there on Ogden [Street] from two blocks away." In an understatement, *Billboard* referred to his hit "Little Mama" as "excitable."

Some Sun rockabillies took a more subdued approach to their music. Roy Orbison, raised in Wink, Texas, formed the Wink Westerners, later renamed the Teen Kings, while in high school. After a year of college, the singer remembered, "I met a couple of guys who had written 'Ooby Dooby' and what convinced me I was in the wrong place at the wrong time was I heard a record by a young fellow on the jukebox called 'That's All Right.'"

Orbison headed for Memphis and on March 27, 1956 recorded the Sun-issued "Ooby Dooby." It sold nearly a half million copies and reached number fifty-nine on the *Billboard* singles chart, which was the best chart position of a Sun disc other than hits by the Big Four of Sun.

The singer, identifiable by his sunglasses, black clothes, and a near-operatic, high-pitched, ethereal voice, followed with "Rockhouse," but only reluctantly. Said producer and songwriter Jack Clement: "I recorded 'Rockhouse' with Roy and it was good but Roy was not into what the Sun studio was capable of back then." Roy confirmed, "I was writing more ballads then [1957], but I didn't bother to ask Sam to release them." Sun "didn't have the ways to get into the audience I wanted to go for." Orbison eventually signed with Monument Records, and during the early 1960s achieved popularity with a series of songs that built to powerful, dramatic, emotional crescendos: "Only the Lonely," "Crying" and the number-one hits "Running Scared," and "Oh, Pretty Woman."

The Decca Challenge

The major record companies competed with Sun for the rockabilly market. Decca Records took the lead, signing Bill Haley and the Comets. Born in Detroit, Michigan, Haley in 1948 formed a band, the Four Aces of Western Swing, who played on a radio show that he hosted on station WPWA in Chester, Pennsylvania. As the Ramblin' Yodeler, he recorded country music with the Four Aces and subsequently with the

Saddlemen. "My dad, who was from Kentucky, played mandolin. And I suppose that was where the country influence came from," he revealed.

In June 1951, Haley and the Saddlemen covered Jackie Brenston's "Rocket 88," which convinced him to combine country swing music with the boogie-woogie "jump beat" of Louis Jordan. "We'd begin with Jordan's shuffle rhythm," said Milt Gabler, the Comets' producer at Decca, "I'd sing Jordan riffs to the group that would be picked up by the electric guitar and tenor sax, Rudy Pompilli. They had a song that had the drive of [Jordan's] Tympany Five and the color of country and western. Rockabilly was what it was called back then."

Haley used a different term for his music. "We started out as a country western group, then we added a touch of rhythm and blues," Haley recalled. "It wasn't something we planned, it just evolved." "We were something new." He continued: "We didn't call it that at that time, but we were playing rock-and-roll."

Haley took his rock and roll to Decca. In 1953, after reaching the number-twelve slot with "Crazy, Man, Crazy" on the small Essex label, Haley and his Comets signed with Decca Records. On June 7, 1954, the Comets released a slightly countrified version of the Joe Turner R&B classic, "Shake, Rattle and Roll," which hit the Top Ten for Haley. Though recording it on April 12, 1954, the Comets followed the next year with "(We're Gonna) Rock Around the Clock," after the director of the film *Blackboard Jungle* featured it throughout the film.

Blackboard Jungle gave a voice to Haley and the growing legion of teens. It recounted the challenges of a fictional inner-city teacher played by Glen Ford harassed by several disruptive students, including a young Sidney Poitier. Featuring "(We're Gonna) Rock Around the Clock" at the opening credits and during the first scene, the middle of the movie and at the end, the film became a battle cry for the swelling number of youths, some of whom rioted during and after the film. In the process, by early 1955 "(We're Gonna) Rock Around the Clock" shot to number one on *Billboard*. Haley continued to churn out hits. During 1955 and 1956, he scored with twelve other Top-Forty records, including "See You Later, Alligator," "Burn That Candle," "Dim, Dim the Lights," and "Razzle-Dazzle." On August 7, 1955, Haley and his Comets appeared on the popular *Ed Sullivan Show*. The next year, he appeared in two movies, *Rock Around the Clock* and *Don't Knock the Rock*, which featured his music.

Though predating Elvis and laying claim to the first rockabilly success, Haley never wrenched the rock crown from Presley. He delivered a smoother sound than the jagged-edged music of Presley. The singer and his Comets also offered a tamer stage show. In 1956, Haley warned that "a lot depends on the entertainer and how he controls the crowd. The music is stimulating enough without creating additional excitement," an apparent jab at Elvis. Just as important, Haley's age and appearance—pudgy, balding, and 31 years old in 1956—compared unfavorably to the image of the young, virile, swivel-hipped Elvis in the eyes of teenaged rock-and-rollers driven by raging hormones.

Decca, hoping for a larger share of the teen market, signed brothers Johnny and Dorsey Burnette along with their friend Paul Burlison who called themselves the Rock 'n' Roll Trio. Growing up in Memphis, bassist Dorsey and lead guitarist Burlison worked together at the Crown Electric factory, the same company that employed Presley, and in 1953 joined with rhythm guitarist and vocalist Johnny Burnette as a trio. Initially, they played in a Hank-Williams country style.

The group, exemplified by Burlison who backed Howlin' Wolf on a radio broadcast in West Memphis, became intrigued by black culture and started to blend country music with electric blues. Beale Street in Memphis "was really happening in those days, and my dad and his friends would go down there a lot and listen to the blues guys," remembered Billy Burnette, the son of Dorsey, who continued the rockabilly tradition of his father. "They'd buy their clothes on Beale Street, at Lansky Brothers, where all the black people shopped."

The Trio, which delivered a white-and-black musical hybrid, caused disturbances throughout the South with songs such as "The Train Kept a Rollin'," "Rock Billy Boogie," "Tear It Up," and "Rock Therapy." During one performance of the Trio, reported the Evansville, Indiana, *Courier* on October 20, 1956, "the crowd of about 2,000 people kept up a continuous howl that all but drowned out the singer's voice." When Johnny Burnette tried to leave the stage, hundreds of wild-eyed girls attacked him and "tore his shirt to bits for souvenirs." According to the *Courier*, "the singer, who had all but exhausted himself in the performance, was in sad shape when he reached the car. 'I should'a laid off that last 'Hound Dog,'" he panted.

In early 1956, when the Trio lost their day jobs in Memphis, they moved to New York City with hopes of national success. After winning first prize on Ted Mack's *Amateur Hour* twice, the group signed to Coral, an offshoot of Decca and recorded one seminal album before disbanding.

That same year, Decca discovered Buddy Holly (b. Charles Hardin Holley), a skinny teenager from Lubbock, Texas, who wore thick-rimmed glasses and a shy grin. Holly had heard R&B through records and on radio programs, such as *Stan's Record Rack*, broadcast from Shreveport, Louisiana by Stan Lewis from his record shop. As Holly's friend Bob Montgomery explained, "Blues to us was Muddy Waters, Little Walter, and Lightnin' Hopkins."

As with other rockabillies, Holly also gravitated toward white country music, especially bluegrass and western swing. He listened to stars such as Hank Snow and Hank Williams and, in 1953, with friends Bob Montgomery and Larry Welborn, formed a country music trio that performed on the *Big D Jamboree* radio show broadcast from Dallas and regularly played on station KDAV as *The Buddy and Bob Show*. By his sixteenth birthday, Buddy already had "thought about making a career out of western music if I am good enough but I will just have to wait and see how that turns out."

Elvis Presley changed Buddy's plans. In October 1955, when Elvis arrived in Lubbock for an engagement at the Cotton Club, Holly and Bob Montgomery drove the new sensation around town. The next day, Holly and his group backed Elvis at the grand opening of a local Pontiac car dealership. "And when the next KDVA Sunday Party rolled around, Buddy was singing Elvis songs," recalled a Lubbock local. Added Larry Holly, Buddy's brother, "He was on an Elvis Presley kick—he just idolized the guy. And, I mean, he sounded exactly like him. He did Elvis Presley things on the Jamboree." Holly, interested in leatherwork at the time, even crafted a wallet with "ELVIS" emblazoned in pink letters on it, and in early 1956 he left the wallet at Sun Studios as a present for Presley.

Holly incorporated Presley's style in a unique sound. By early 1957, when he formed the Crickets with Joe B. Mauldin on stand-up bass and Jerry Allison on drums, he had perfected a light, bouncy, bright rockabilly that bore only traces of the unique Presley sound.

Holly searched for the producer who could capture his sound. He first inked a deal with Decca Records but had little success with the pop-orientation of "Love Me" and "Modern Don Juan." He then took his music to the small studio of producer Norman Petty, who had already recorded hits for the Rhythm Orchids—"Party Doll" and "Stickin' with You," released under the names of singer Buddy Knox and bassist Jimmy Bowen. In 1957, with Petty's help, the Crickets crafted "That'll Be the Day," which showcased Holly's sound. The group signed to Brunswick and Coral Records, both subsidiaries of Decca, and hit the top of the singles pop chart with the tune. Throughout 1957 and 1958, they followed with a series of fresh rockabilly tunes that became rock-and-roll classics, including the number two "Peggy Sue," the Top Ten "Oh Boy!" and the Top Twenty "Maybe Baby."

Rockabilly Sweeps the Nation

Other record companies searched for their own acts to enter the rockabilly market. Capitol Records, a major label, nabbed Gene Vincent (b. Eugene Vincent Craddock), a Korean War veteran who was born in the southern Navy town of Norfolk, Virginia. In 1956, with his band the Bluecaps, Vincent released the unforgettable "Be-Bop-a-Lula" after reading a Little Lulu comic book. By June, the song hit the Top Ten. In 1956 to 1957, Vincent cut such boppers as the Top Twenty-Five "Dance to the Bop," "Bluejean Bop," and "Race with the Devil."

Cadence Records, a small, New York–based independent company owned by Archie Bleyer, scored with the Everly Brothers. Sons of country stars Ike and Margaret Everly, the two Kentucky-born brothers, Don and Phil, toured with their parents and performed on a family radio show on KMA in Shenandoah, Iowa. For a while, they lived in Chicago, where their father took them to Maxwell Street, which was filled with "blues players from Mississippi and Alabama" on every street corner. There, the brothers listened to "the blues, and black music was really important."

In 1955, the duo headed for Nashville in search of stardom. They first sold a few songs to a country music publishing firm owned by country guitarist extraordinaire Chet Atkins. Less than two years later, the Everly Brothers signed with Cadence Records after being promoted by music publisher Wesley Rose. By May 1957, the duo neared the top of the chart with "Bye Bye Love."

The song, dominated by bright, warm, country-style harmonies that they had learned from their father, had an R&B beat. As Don pointed out, "I loved Bo Diddley; I told Chet Atkins, 'That's what I want my guitar to sound like.... The intro to 'Bye Bye Love' was inspired by Bo Diddley." Don called the music "the white blues."

In 1957 after appearances on *The Ed Sullivan Show* as well as on other television variety programs, the Everlys became national rockabilly mainstays. They followed their first hit with the number-one singles, "Wake Up Little Susie," "All I Have to Do Is Dream," and "Bird Dog," racking up sales of $35 million by 1962.

Imperial, the label that featured Fats Domino as its star, snagged Ricky Nelson (b. Eric Nelson) in the rockabilly sweepstakes. The son of jazz bandleader Ozzie Nelson and singer Harriet Hilliard, the young Nelson idolized Carl Perkins. "I used to go and buy every Sun record that I could get my hands on back in the Fifties 'cause they were such a really good sound."

Nelson entered the music business through the new medium of television. With his mother, father and brother David, Ricky portrayed himself on the syndicated radio show, *The Adventures of Ozzie and Harriet*. Beginning on October 3, 1952, the show aired on television under the same name. On April 10, 1957, to impress a girlfriend Ricky covered Fats Domino's "I'm Walkin'" on the show and, after a wild teenage response to the program, Verve Records released his version of the song. Attesting to the importance of television, the song sold 60,000 copies in three days. Ricky continued to sing one of his songs on many of the subsequent episodes of the show, ending the segments by belting out a song at the sock hop of his television high school.

In September 1957 when Verve Records withheld royalties, Nelson signed with Imperial. His first Imperial single, "Be-Bop Baby," sold a million copies and hit number three on the chart. From 1957 to 1959, he followed with the Top Ten "Stood Up," "Poor Little Fool," "Lonesome Town," and "It's Late." He also scored with songs written by Johnny and Dorsey Burnette such as "Believe What You Say" and "A Little Too Much."

Liberty Records jumped onto the rockabilly wagon with Eddie Cochran. The son of two Oklahoma City country-western fans, Eddie moved with his family to Bell Gardens, California. As a teen, he appeared with several country-and-western bands and in 1954 formed the Cochran Brothers who delivered mostly country music with a dash of rhythm and blues. While thumbing through the racks of a local record store in

October 1955, Cochran met Jerry Capehart, who became his songwriter-collaborator throughout his career. In 1956, Capehart wrote and Cochran performed "Skinny Jim," which flopped. Several months later, a movie producer in Los Angeles spotted Cochran and offered him a small part in the film *The Girl Can't Help It*, in which he sang "Twenty Flight Rock."

Trying to secure better distribution for their discs, Capehart convinced Si Waronker, president of Liberty Records, to invest in the rockabilly talent of his partner. After releasing a few unsuccessful singles, in late 1958, Cochran alternated between an Elvis-like whimper and a gravel-voiced growl in an anthem of teenage frustration, "Summertime Blues." Cochran's bopping call to arms, striking a chord among teenagers who were gaining increasing power through their numbers, hit the Top Ten.

The Selling of Elvis Presley

RCA Victor lured to its label the performer who became known as the king of rock and roll. In 1955, amid a competitive bidding war for Presley, Steve Sholes, who produced country and western acts for RCA, convinced his company to offer Sun Records $35,000 plus $5,000 in back royalties owed by Sun to Elvis for the rights to Presley's recorded material. Sam Phillips accepted the money and surrendered all of the Presley tapes that Sun had produced. Phillips hoped to "get myself out of a real bind," explained Phillips. "I mean I wasn't broke, but man, it was hand-to-mouth."

Elvis had been sold to RCA by a new manager, Colonel Tom Parker. Born in 1909 in the Netherlands, Parker (b. Andreas Cornelis van Kuijk) started his career in carnivals. Since the circus life, according to the Colonel, "was a day-to-day living," he used his ingenuity to make money. For one of his ploys, he rented a cow pasture adjacent to the circus grounds and during the night herded the cows on the only road through the field, which served as the sole exit from the carnival. When unsuspecting circus goers reached the exit the next day, they could either walk through ankle-deep manure or pay the Colonel a nickel for a pony ride through it.

By the 1950s, Parker abandoned the circus and applied his ingenious techniques to the music business. By the mid-1940s, he marketed the careers of such country singers as Eddy Arnold. On November 21, 1955, Parker signed the new sensation to an exclusive contract. As one of Elvis's neighbors remembered, the Colonel, "in the most polished Machiavellian way," convinced Vernon to sign his son to the Colonel's management company. "Colonel Tom was a salesman, I'll give him that. He sure knew how to sell."

Almost immediately, the Colonel began to market Elvis Presley to the media. "The Colonel doesn't sell Elvis to the public, dig?" Jon Hartmann, one of Parker's employees, rhetorically asked. "He sells Elvis to the people who sell to the public, and those are the media people—the television and motion picture personalities, the executives and businessmen who control the networks, the important radio people." The Colonel considered "Elvis, as a product, always in the state of being sold."

As part of his media strategy, Parker tried to sell Presley on the powerful new medium of national television. Developed during the 1920s, televised images had first been witnessed by the public during the 1930s as a novelty. In 1948, the Columbia Broadcasting System (CBS) and the National Broadcasting Company (NBC) offered regular television programming, soon followed by the American Broadcasting Company (ABC). By 1950, more than 7.3 million Americans had bought television sets, prodded by the lure of short-term consumer credit, which increased from $8.4 billion in 1946 to more than $45 billion twelve years later. By the time Colonel Parker began to manage Presley, there were 37 million TV sets in American homes with nearly 628 stations televising many programs that previously aired on radio. Americans watched television while feasting on prepackaged TV dinners, introduced by C.A. Swanson and Sons in 1953, and read about their favorite programs in the *TV Guide* magazine, first published in April the same year

Parker immediately attempted to slot the photogenic Elvis on television. After being rejected by every other variety show on national television, Presley landed a spot on the January 28, 1956, airing of *Stage Show*, a half-hour variety program hosted by jazz band leaders Tommy and Jimmy Dorsey and produced by Jackie Gleason as a lead-in to his popular *The Honeymooners* comedy show. Though some organizers of the show objected to the rock-and-roller, Jackie Gleason backed Elvis. Supported by Gleason, Presley appeared five more times on *Stage Show*, last appearing on March 24, 1956. On April 3, as a favor to Colonel Parker, comedian Milton Berle scheduled the singer for his program in the first of two appearances. On July 1, impressed by the reaction to Presley on *The Milton Berle Show*, Steve Allen featured Presley on his prime-time program.

Ed Sullivan, who earlier had condemned Presley as unfit for "his family-type show at any price" noticed the reaction to Presley on *The Steve Allen Show*, his prime-time competitor, and signed the rising rockabilly star. He agreed to pay the new rock star $50,000 for three appearances on his show, one of the two most popular television programs in America at the time. Sullivan booked Presley for a first appearance on September 9, 1956. Fearing a backlash from his usual viewers and prodded by the publicity-hungry Colonel Parker, the television host ordered that Elvis be filmed from the waist up, allowing the teenaged television audience to only imagine the pelvic gyrations that took place off screen. Creating one of the most legendary moments in television history, Sullivan attracted nearly 54 million viewers, or almost 83 percent of the television audience, to his show and helped lift Presley into national prominence.

Presley's televised appearances exemplified the power of national television. By the time he finished his six appearances on *Stage Show* in March 1956, Presley had sold nearly 1 million copies of "Heartbreak Hotel" and generated more than 300,000 advance orders of his first, self-named album. On May 5, less than a month after appearing on the influential *The Milton Berle Show*, which attracted 25 percent of the viewing public, "Heartbreak Hotel" became Presley's first number-one single. A few weeks after singing "Hound Dog" and "I Want You, I Need You, I Love You" on *The Milton Berle Show* and *The Steve Allen Show*, Presley again hit the top of the singles chart with both songs. After Elvis debuted "Love Me Tender" on his first *Ed Sullivan Show* segment, RCA was forced to advance ship the single to demanding fans who made the record another number-one smash.

During the next few months, Presley continued his domination of the singles chart with a number of songs, many of which he had sung during his television appearances: "Too Much," "Don't Be Cruel," and "All Shook Up," the last two written by African-American songwriter Otis Blackwell, who had penned "Great Balls of Fire" for Jerry Lee Lewis. "It was television that made Elvis' success possible," related Steve Allen who favored jazz. "What his millions of young fans responded to was obviously not his voice but Elvis himself. His face, his body, his hair, his gyrations, his cute, country-boy persona."

Film served as another medium to plug Presley, as it had for other male singers, from Rudy Valle to Frank Sinatra. "I knew there was an acting possibility from the beginning," explained RCA publicist Anne Fulchino. "He understood all this. He wanted it, and he had the talent." Elvis hoped to emulate his film heroes, James Dean and Marlon Brando. At first enthusiastic about his acting career, in August 1956 Presley started on the production of his first feature-length film, *Love Me Tender*. Director and cowriter Hal Kanter expanded a role to fit Presley and included songs to help sell the picture. On November 15, 1956, the film opened in 550 theaters across the country to enthusiastic crowds, despite poor reviews of Elvis's performance.

A new Top-Forty format on radio also helped promote Presley. It was pioneered in 1954 by radio-chain owners Todd Storz and Gordon McLendon to rescue radio from a five-year decline caused by the popularity of television. Top-Forty radio involved an instant news concept, disc jockey gags and patter, and a limited play list of roughly forty hits that disc jockeys spun in constant rotation.

Top-Forty radio, promoting the songs of only a few artists, fueled the meteoric rise of Elvis. "There was a huge change overnight," recalled Russ Solomon, founder of the Tower Records chain. "Everybody was interested [in Presley]. At the same moment, Top-Forty radio came into play. As a result there was a very dramatic change in the way you perceived selling records. Your hit titles became more and more important."

In mid-1956, Hank Saperstein joined Colonel Parker in the Presley media blitz. Saperstein had become successful in the advertising industry through his marketing efforts for television creations such as *Lassie, Wyatt Earp*, and *The Lone Ranger*. Not to be outdone by his competitors, he had even stuffed plastic blowguns in cereal boxes to increase the sales of Kellogg's Cornflakes. Saperstein recognized the "universality" of the Presley appeal and began to plaster Elvis's name and picture on all types of products. "We wanted to manufacture a phenomenon," reasoned Saperstein. "My mission was to create someone whose name and image flashes in your mind without having to think. If you have to ask, 'Who?' then we did *not* do our job." By 1957, Saperstein and Parker had saturated the American market.

If a loyal fan so desired, she could immerse herself in Elvis. She could put on some Elvis Presley bobby socks, Elvis Presley shoes, skirt, blouse, and sweater, hang an Elvis Presley charm bracelet on one wrist, and with the other hand smear on some Elvis Presley lipstick—either Hound Dog Orange, Heartbreak Hotel Pink, or Tutti Frutti Red. She might fold an Elvis Presley handkerchief in her Elvis Presley purse and head for school. Once in the classroom, she could write with her green Elvis Presley pencil, inscribed "Sincerely Yours," and sip an Elvis Presley soft drink between class periods. After school, she could change into Elvis Presley Bermuda shorts, blue jeans, or toreador pants, write to an Elvis Presley pen pal, or play an Elvis Presley game, and fall asleep in her Elvis Presley pajamas on her Elvis Presley pillow. Her last waking memory of the day could be the Elvis Presley fluorescent portrait that hung on her wall. All told, a diehard fan could buy seventy-eight different Elvis Presley products that grossed about $55 million by December 1957. In addition to 25 percent of Elvis's performance royalties, Colonel Parker received a percentage of the manufacturer's wholesale price on each item.

By early 1958, Elvis Presley had created a seismic shift in the music industry by bringing rock-and-roll to the mainstream. "If you look at the album charts in '55, what are you going to see?" asked Irv Lichtman, a former editor of the industry standards *Cash Box* and *Billboard*. "Soundtracks, Broadway, Perry Como and Frank Sinatra, they were the great guns." During the next two years with the success of Presley, asserted Lichtman, "it just broke apart. Yes, revolution is a good word; it was a revolution."

Reactions Against the Presley Mania

The press and national leaders disparaged the revolutionary change in the music industry by criticizing Presley for a variety of reasons. Many targeted his sexual innuendo. In one review, Jack Gould, television critic for *The New York Times*, wrote that "Mr. Presley has no discernible singing ability." He especially blasted his "accented movement of the body that heretofore has been primarily identified with the repertoire of the blonde bombshells of the burlesque runway. The gyration never had anything to do with the world of popular music and still doesn't." A scandalized Jack O'Brien of the *New York Journal-American* agreed that "Elvis Presley wiggled and wiggled with such abdominal gyrations that burlesque bombshell Georgia Southern really deserves equal time" and described his act as "the weirdest and plainly planned, suggestive animation short of an aborigine's mating dance." *Time* magazine called Presley a "sexibitionist," who lived "off what most parents would agree is the fat of teenagers' heads," and *Look* accused him of dragging "'big beat' music to new lows in taste."

Religious leaders, guarding the moral fabric of America, especially felt compelled to speak out against the gyrating Presley. Reverend Charles Howard Graff of St. John's Episcopal Church in Greenwich Village called Elvis a "whirling dervish of sex," and evangelist Billy Graham did not "want my children to see" Elvis. Reverend Robert Gray of the Trinity Baptist Church in Jacksonville, Florida, believed Presley "achieved a new low in spiritual degeneracy" with his stage performance. In his sermon "Hot Rods, Reefers, and Rock-and-Roll," Gray warned the youth in his congregation not to attend an upcoming Presley show, which featured the singer's sexual moves.

The concern over Elvis's risqué stage act engendered fears over changing racial mores. Though Elvis was white, he clearly integrated black rhythm-and-blues music in his style and borrowed many of the ribald stage routines from his African-American influences. Bill Haley explicitly linked his music to an assault on racial intolerance. "Rock and roll does help combat racial discrimination," he asserted. "We have performed to mixed groups all over the country and have watched the kids sit side by side." In August 1956, during one Carl Perkins performance, black and white teens started to dance together. "For the first time in history, Negro and white couples danced on the same floor," read the *Pittsburgh Courier*.

As teens began to listen to a music at least partly based on African-American culture, parents worried about the social implications of race mixing. When one southern teen in 1957 declared that "I'm not afraid of Negroes, I'm afraid of parents," the fabric of society seemed to be unraveling for many adults, who lived in a more stratified, racist society. They referred to rock and roll as a "jungle strain" and "vulgar", "animalistic", etc. On April 23, 1956, the White Citizens Council contended that "rock 'n' roll is the basic heavy beat of the Negroes" and a subversive "plot to mongrelize America." One Southerner bitterly characterized rockabilly as the "death song of America and the white race."

Fears over increasing juvenile delinquency also underlaid much of the backlash against Presley. The dark image of the alienated, shiftless, and violent street tough in a black leather jacket who dangled a cigarette from his lips had been popularized in books and films. The preoccupation with the teenage delinquent was reflected in paperbacks such as *Blackboard Jungle, Gang Rumble, The Hoods Ride In*, and countless others. It also appeared in movies such as *The Wild One* (1954), which showcased Marlon Brando as the leader of a heartless motorcycle gang, and *Rebel Without a Cause*, released the next year, which starred James Dean, who with Brando symbolized teenage rebellion.

Released in 1955 and starring actor James Dean, *Rebel Without a Cause* epitomized the rebellious youth of the 1950s. The film, explained Stewart Stern, who wrote the screenplay, dealt with "the phenomenon of what was called in those days juvenile delinquency, happening not in families that were economically deprived but in middle-class families that were emotionally deprived. Partly, people felt it had to do with the war, the fact that so many women were working for the first time away from the home, that older brothers and fathers who would have been role models for the young weren't there, and the tremendous drive for material 'things.' When the kids saw that the material goods that were supposed to make their parents happy really didn't, they began to doubt their parents' authority," said Stern. "The lesson of *Rebel*," concluded the screenwriter, "was that if the kids could not be acknowledged or understood by their parents, at least they could be acknowledged by each other."

Many concerned middle-class adults directly linked the poor southern style of Presley, including his wild clothes, swagger, slicked-back hair, and sideburns, to the violence of juvenile delinquency. On April 11, 1956, *Variety* connected a Presley-driven rock to a "staggering wave of juvenile violence and mayhem.... On the police blotters, rock-'n'-roll has been writing an unprecedented record. In one locale after another, rock-'n'-roll shows, or disc hops where such tunes have been played, have touched off every type of juvenile delinquency." The Pennsylvania Chief of Police Association contended that rock music provided "an incentive to teenage unrest," and Pittsburgh Police Inspector Fred Good felt "wherever there's been teenage trouble lately, rock-and-roll has almost always been in the background."

Teen riots at concerts fueled the fear of rock-and-roll delinquents and prompted officials to bar promoters from holding rock concerts in civic buildings. In San Jose, rock fanatics routed seventy-three policemen and caused $3,000 in damage, convincing the mayor of nearby Santa Cruz to ban rock concerts. On May 3, 1958, violence erupted after an Alan Freed–hosted rock revue that headlined Jerry Lee Lewis. When police turned on the house lights before the show ended, Freed huffed, "I guess the police here in Boston don't want you kids to have a good time," and teens streamed into the street. As *Time* reported, "All around the arena common citizens were set upon, robbed and sometimes beaten," and nine men and women required hospitalization. Though the arena had been the site of previous muggings and teens likely did not participate in the violence, in 1956, Boston mayor John Hynes barred rock-and-roll shows from the city. Officials in New Haven and Newark followed the Boston example, canceling scheduled Freed-sponsored shows. After a melee among 2,700 fans at a rock show, Mayor Roland Hines of Asbury Park, New Jersey, banned all rock concerts from city dance halls. Mayor Bernard Berry of nearby Jersey City did the same a few days later.

Disc jockeys who broadcast classical and pop music took action to protect their jobs. In Halifax, Nova Scotia, station CJCH rigidly forbade the airplay of any Elvis discs. Nashville jockey "Great Scott" burned 600 Presley records in a public park, and a Chicago station manager smashed Elvis 45s during a broadcast. In Wildwood, New Jersey, a local disc jockey started an organization to "eliminate certain wreck and ruin artists" such as Elvis. For many, the rock and roll embodied in Elvis Presley had become a menace to society that needed to be eradicated.

Elvis Becomes a Respectable Icon

RCA Victor and Colonel Parker responded to the reaction against Presley by modifying the singer's wild act. Presley's appearance on *The Steve Allen Show* provided an early example. "We'd recognized the controversy that was building around Elvis and so we took advantage of it," confessed Allen. The host dressed Presley in a tuxedo and forbade him to hold his guitar. He then forced him "to stand perfectly still, and we positioned a real hound dog on a stool next to him—a dog that had been trained to do nothing but sit and look droopy." Elvis's respectable behavior on the show stood in marked contrast to his earlier hip-shaking performances and foreshadowed a change in image.

Throughout the late 1950s and into the 1960s, Presley became more subdued and enlarged his audience with a new style. In September 1957, the rising star split with two members of his original band, Scotty Moore and Bill Black, who had helped pioneer the distinctive Presley sound. Elvis recorded with them only sporadically during the next decade. After his return from the Army in 1960, Presley recorded an operatic ballad "It's Now or Never," based on the Italian standard "O Sole Mio," which separated the singer even further from his rockabilly roots. "After the Army you had a totally polished performer," explained RCA executive Joan Deary. "These records ['It's Now or Never' and the 1961 number-one hit 'Are You Lonesome Tonight,' a hit for Vaughn Deleath in 1927] were not at all based on the same appeal as 'That's Alright (Mama)' and 'Hound Dog' and 'Don't Be Cruel.' Suddenly Elvis was just not for kids."

With an expanded audience, Presley began to sell more records. He sold more than 20 million copies of "It's Now or Never," his best-selling single. Though briefly revisiting his rock roots in his 1968 television comeback, in the 1960s and 1970s Elvis followed with thirty gold records, which were mostly pop ballads. Appealing to a wide range of record buyers, Presley sold a total of more than 250 million records by the end of his career. In the history of recorded music, only Bing Crosby neared Elvis's mark with about 200 million records sold. Frank Sinatra, the bobby-socks sensation of the 1940s, sold only about 40 million discs.

Presley also broadened his fan base by opting for a safe, clean-cut image in the movies. He starred in thirty-one feature films such as *G.I. Blues, Flaming Star, Wild Star, Blue Hawaii, Follow That Dream, Kid Galahad*, and *Girls! Girls! Girls!* Though offered dramatic roles in films such as *Thunder Road, Midnight Cowboy*, and *West Side Story*, Elvis obeyed Colonel Parker and settled for parts in movies written around songs, which for the most part abandoned gut-bucket rockabilly for a soothing ballad style that reinforced his new image. "Elvis would go ahead with the program and get the picture done," remembered D. J. Fontana, the drummer who played with Elvis from 1954 to 1968. "You see, the Colonel's thought was *don't make any waves*; don't let me have to make a deal with these people." Gene Nelson, director of two Elvis movies, recalled, "The Colonel's stock answer was just 'You come up with the money; we'll do the picture.' He wasn't interested in Elvis' latent dramatic abilities." In many of his films, Presley reluctantly but obediently finished his work. "Come on, guys," recalled Scotty Moore, "let do this piece of shit and get it over with."

Presley, appealing to a wider audience, received awards of all types. In 1959, the Mississippi legislature passed a resolution that lauded Elvis as a "legend and inspiration to tens of millions of Americans," who "reaffirms a historic American idea that success in our nation can still be attained through individual initiative, hard work, and abiding faith in one's self and his creator." A few months later, a joint session of the Tennessee legislature honored Presley.

The young, working-class Presley, ceaselessly marketed by RCA and Colonel Parker, was swept away by stardom. "My daddy and I were laughing about it the other day," he told a reporter in late 1956. He "said, 'What happened, El? The last thing I remember is I was working in a can factory and you were still driving a truck.'" "It just caught us up," Elvis shrugged.

The famous star enjoyed a newfound wealth. Elvis bought a fleet of Cadillacs, including one in his favorite color—pink; a $40,000, one-story ranch house in Memphis; and then a $100,000 mansion, Graceland, for himself and his parents. He purchased an airplane, a truckload of television sets, a horse ranch, dozens of motorcycles and cars, and hundreds of gadgets, which he freely gave as gifts to his friends and employees.

The rock-and-roll star paid dearly for his fame. As his popularity mounted, Elvis found it difficult to protect his privacy. "Even today [late sixties] I'd be willing to bet a thousand dollars he could draw a hundred people in five minutes anywhere he went," mused Neal Matthews, one of the Jordanaires, Elvis's backup singing group. "And he knows this. It's bound to make him unhappy. He'd like to be able to walk down the street like a normal human being." Presley could only venture out late at night, when he rented an entire skating rink or movie house and invited a few close confidants to be with him. On his 1969 tour of Hawaii with Minnie Pearl, Minnie remembered 500 women who swarmed the taxi when they tried to get to the hotel. Elvis grabbed her arm, and the women mobbed them. "I felt my feet going out from under me," she related. As Minnie Pearl and her husband enjoyed the Hawaiian sun, Elvis never left his room, except for an occasional midnight swim. "We'd get out and act crazy, having the best time in the world, and we'd look up there and Elvis would be standing at the window, looking down at us," Minnie recalled.

Eventually the isolation began to affect Presley. As early as 1957, he told the pastor of the Assembly of God Church that "I am the most miserable young man you have ever met. I have more money than I can ever spend. I have thousands of fans out there, and I have a lot of people who call themselves my friends, but I am miserable." Trapped in a creative wasteland by Colonel Parker who forced him to keep churning out B-grade movies, Elvis progressively became more despondent. "You know, you

Elvis in his comeback concert, 1968.

Pictorial Press Ltd./Alamy Stock Photo.

all are lucky," Presley told D. J. Fontana and his wife in 1968. "I'm so tired of being Elvis—I don't know what to do. I just wish I could do something else."

A depressed Elvis resorted to drugs. Even early in his career, Presley like many other performers at the time turned to amphetamines to deal with the hectic touring and movie schedule that he had been asked to meet. As the years progressed and his fame overwhelmed him, he turned to a smorgasbord of pills. "The drugs were a band-aid for a lack of a creative outlet," explained Elvis's friend Jerry Schilling.

Elvis's drug habit and the constant pressure of his fame sometimes led to violence. He destroyed television sets, pool cues, jukeboxes, and cars. "The temper was the hardest thing to take," one friend recalled. "One day he'd be the sweetest person in the world, the next day he'd burn holes in you with his eyes."

In the end, Elvis Presley became a larger-than-life icon to the world, which looked at him in superhuman terms. Elvis the man, a small-town Southerner with a cornball sense of humor and a sense of evangelical religion, became superseded by media expectations, which his handlers had created and which could never be fulfilled by any human being. He became the premier American legend, known in nearly every part of the globe, who could find little human interaction or peace and who needed to piece together a lonely, isolated life to exist. As singer Johnny Rivers (b. John Ramistella), who during the 1960s scored with a string of hits including "Secret Agent Man," concluded, Elvis "had created his own world. He had to. There was nothing else for him to do." His retreat into himself ended with an untimely death on August 16, 1977, at the age of 42.

Elvis Presley had been trapped by success. The gyrating, sneering Elvis, who taunted his audiences and worked them to a fevered pitch, gave way to a more haggard, bloated performer adorned by extravagant, sequined costumes, singing ballads to the well-dressed clientele of Las Vegas nightclubs. Sometimes the old magic sneaked through the weary flesh, but most of the original vibrancy and vitality had disappeared. Elvis was transformed from an innocent country boy who belted out a hybrid of black rhythm-and-blues and country music with animalistic intensity to a well-groomed, multimillion-dollar product. The change, starting when Presley signed with RCA and becoming more pronounced during the 1960s after Presley returned from the Army, signaled the end of rockabilly dominance.

Though becoming more sedate, Elvis had established a mass market for rock and roll and in the process assaulted racial barriers in the United States. "Not only did Elvis entertain the world, he socially changed the way we thought," reminisced Elvis's friend Jerry Shilling. "A pivotal part was that he helped bring the races together." Soon teenaged crooners schooled by Dick Clark would vie for the mantle of the King.

Chapter 4
The Teen Market: From *Bandstand* to Girl Groups

"I hope someday that somebody will say that in the beginning stages of the birth of the music of the Fifties, though I didn't contribute in terms of creativity, I helped keep it alive."

—Dick Clark

"Elvis in the army, Buddy dead, Little Richard in the ministry, Berry nabbed by the Feds" became the chant of a bewildered rock-and-roll generation. An important part of American culture just three years earlier, by 1959 rock and roll had lost many of its heroes. Elvis Presley had been inducted into the army, Buddy Holly had been tragically killed, Little Richard had suddenly joined a fundamentalist religious sect, and Chuck Berry had been arrested and stood trial.

Two young entrepreneurs—Dick Clark and Don Kirshner—produced a new crop of idols and a fresh batch of songs for rock-starved teens. Beginning in 1957, Clark found photogenic, well-groomed Italian teens, promoted them on his television show, and almost single-handedly created the Philadelphia sound. Only the payola scandal slowed Clark's success. A music publisher in the Tin Pan Alley tradition, Kirshner assembled teams of young, talented songwriters in the Brill Building in New York City and from 1960 to 1963 churned out hundreds of tunes that he placed with scores of budding girl groups. For nearly three years, he helped set the direction of rock and roll. From 1958 to 1963, in the absence of Presley and other rock pioneers, two businessmen reshaped rock and roll and made it respectable.

Lost Idols

During the late 1950s, rock-and-roll fans either lost or rejected their heroes. On October 12, 1957, the flamboyant Little Richard renounced his jeweled bracelets and wild parties for the ministry of the Seventh Day Adventist Church. He had frequently threatened to quit rock. Chuck Conners, the drummer in Little Richard's band, remembered that Richard "had been talking about giving up rock-'n'-roll and devoting his life to God for a long time." Then, on his way to Australia, as Little Richard looked out the window of the plane, the engines seemed to burst into flames, doused only by the saving efforts of yellow angels. A few days later in Sydney, on the fifth day of a two-week tour, Richard walked away from rock and roll in the middle of a show and in front of 40,000 fans. As he looked into the sky, he saw overhead the first *Sputnik*, the Soviet Union's first satellite in outer space. To Richard, it looked like a "big ball of fire. It really shook my mind. I got up from the piano and said, 'This is it. I am through. I am leaving show business to go back to God.'" True to his word, Richard deserted his fans for Jehovah. Said the singer: "If you want to live for the Lord, you can't rock-and-roll, too. God doesn't like it." Not until 1964 during a tour of England did Little Richard again raise the standard of rock.

Two months later, twenty-two-year-old Jerry Lee Lewis married his thirteen-year-old third cousin, Myra Gale Brown, who was the daughter of Lewis's bass player. It was Lewis's third marriage. During his first performance on a 1958 tour of England, the crowd greeted the rockabilly star with silence and then sporadic heckling. Some of the audience yelled "baby snatcher" at the rockabilly star. The reaction to Lewis's marriage caused promoters to cancel thirty-four of the thirty-seven scheduled shows. For more than a decade, the public censured the "Killer," who gravitated more and more toward country music. "When I married my cousin, I paid," moaned Lewis. "I didn't know the hole could be that deep."

On March 24, 1958, the king of rock and roll, Elvis Presley, entered the army for a two-year stint and became U.S. Private 53310761. On orders from his manager, Colonel Tom Parker, he refused to sing for the army and spent much of his time in West Germany, where he met his future wife, Priscilla Beaulieu. When discharged on March 5, 1960, as a sergeant, Presley concentrated his efforts on motion pictures and only in 1968 returned to the stage.

In 1959, two of rock's pioneers left the stage. On February 3, tragedy struck. Rockabilly singer and songwriter Buddy Holly, the shy, bespectacled youth from Texas, died when his four-seat Beechcraft Bonanza plane crashed in a cornfield near Mason City, Iowa, after a show during a midwestern tour. J. P. Richardson, the disc jockey known as the Big Bopper, who in 1958 hit the chart with "Chantilly Lace," and the seventeen-year-old sensation Richie Valens (a.k.a. Richard Valenzuela), who had just scored hits with "La Bamba" and "Donna," were killed in the same crash.

Chuck Berry was forced from the music scene by a federal court. On December 23, 1959, Berry faced charges when a 14-year-old girl who the rocker had transported from El Paso, Texas, to St. Louis, Missouri, to work in his club as a hatcheck girl accused him of immoral behavior after he fired her. Testimony at the two-week trial revealed that the girl had been a prostitute when Berry first met her and that she had come willingly to St. Louis. In March 1960, the court initially found Berry guilty, but a retrial was scheduled because of racist remarks by the judge. After an appeal, in June 1961 the jury in a second trial convicted Berry of a violation of the anti-prostitution Mann Act and sentenced him to three years in the federal penitentiary at Terre Haute, Indiana. After an unsuccessful appeal, Berry served prison time from February 1962 to October 1963.

An automobile accident robbed rock and roll of two other hit makers. On Saturday, April 16, 1960, after a successful tour of England, Eddie Cochran, Gene Vincent, and Sharon Sheely, Cochran's girlfriend, who subsequently wrote many of Ricky Nelson's hits, rode to the airport in a Ford Consul taxi. En route near Chippenham, Wiltshire, a tire blew out, the driver lost control, and the car smashed into a lamppost. Within hours, Cochran died from multiple head injuries the next day at Bath Hospital. Sheely and Vincent survived, but the accident derailed Vincent's career.

The Booming Teen Market

Rock-and-roll tragedy occurred amid booming economic conditions. During the 1950s, the gross national product (GNP), the indicator of U.S. economic growth, rose from $213 billion to $503 billion. The personal per capita income in the country increased from $1,526 in 1950 to $2,788 ten years later, an increase of 82 percent. Throughout the decade, unemployment remained low, fluctuating between 4 percent and 5.5 percent.

The recording industry, reinvigorated by rock and roll, shared in the general prosperity. Record sales in the United States skyrocketed from $189 million in 1950 to nearly $600 million by the end of the decade. In 1959, the industry chalked up almost

$200 million in sales of 45-rpm records, which usually were manufactured for teens, who could afford the comparatively inexpensive discs. Though more than 5,000 record labels competed for a share of the market, four major companies—RCA Victor, Columbia, Decca, and Capitol—racked up nearly 75 percent of total sales.

The major labels increased their sales through innovative marketing techniques. In 1955, Columbia launched the Columbia Record Club, which by the end of the year sold 700,000 records worth $1.174 million to more than 125 thousand members. By the next year, the mail-order business boasted 687,000 members who bought nearly $15 million worth of records. Capitol and RCA Victor quickly followed with their own disc clubs. In addition, the record giants started to sell their product in supermarkets, which by the end of the 1950s had nearly replaced neighborhood grocery stores.

The burgeoning pocketbooks of teens fueled this growth. In 1957, teens possessed nearly $9 billion in disposable income. Six years later, adolescents spent more than $20 billion, much of it on entertainment. At the time, the sum represented twice the gross national product of Austria.

Reflecting a postwar trend in U.S. business, the record industry expanded into the international market with rock and roll. RCA vice president George Marek observed in 1959 that "rock-and-roll is popular not only in this country but it has swept the world, the world where there are no broadcasting stations even: It is relatively popular in conservative England, in Australia, India, Germany, wherever you go." An early Decca press release of the 1960s described the state of the music business: "The recording industry, a fledgling during the heyday of vaudeville, has shown a steady, remarkable growth until today it stands as a major factor in the world's economy."

Dick Clark and *American Bandstand*

Dick Clark, a marketing genius from upstate New York, delivered new stars to the increasing rock-and-roll audience. Born in 1929, Clark attended Syracuse University and studied advertising and radio. In 1951, he landed a part-time job as an announcer for station WOLF while attending college and then worked for his father, who managed WRUN in Utica, New York. In 1952, Clark accepted a job at WFIL in Philadelphia, at first announcing a radio show of popular and classical music. "I was a great pitchman" he related. "I sold pots and pans, vacuum cleaners, diamond rings, Mrs. Smith pies, the works."

In July 1956, Clark moved to WFIL's television station and hosted the Philadelphia show *Bandstand*, which showcased local high school students dancing to popular hit records. He replaced disc jockey Bob Horn, who, in October 1952, had launched the program, but four years later resigned due to adverse publicity surrounding a drunken driving citation and a statutory rape charge.

Dick Clark initially knew little about the rock-and-roll music that the program highlighted. During his first *Bandstand* appearance as the regular host on July 9, Clark said he arrived on the set "with only a foggy notion of what the kids, music, and show were really about. I don't understand this music."

The new host of *Bandstand* quickly became familiar with the commercial potential of the new music. "The more I heard the music," Clark later related, "I knew that if I could tune into them and keep myself on the show, I could make a great deal of money." Clark—voted by his high school classmates as the "Man Most Likely to Sell the Brooklyn Bridge"—felt that behind his "bland twenty-nine-year-old face lay the heart of a cunning capitalist" who wanted to "defend my right and your right to go to a church of our choice, or to buy the record of our choice."

Clark's business savvy transformed a local telecast into a national phenomenon. To get sponsors for the show, he traveled to New York, visited advertising agencies on Madison Avenue, and eventually snagged the lucrative Beechnut Spearmint Gum account.

Bandstand, built upon a solid advertising base by Clark, broadcast nationally on television as *American Bandstand*, premiering on August 5, 1957, on sixty-seven stations coast to coast to more than 8 million viewers. It aired from Philadelphia for ninety minutes every weekday afternoon and on Mondays from 7:30 to 8:00 P.M. The show featured 150 teenagers in the audience, many of whom danced to the popular hits and listened to the smooth patter of Dick Clark. "It's been a long, long time since a major network has aimed at the most entertainment-starved group in the country," Clark told *Time* magazine. "And why not? After all, teenagers have $9 billion a year to spend."

Droves of teenage girls responded to Clark's brand of rock and roll. After school hours, hordes of pubescent girls rushed home and feverishly tuned into *American Bandstand*. Usually with their best girlfriend or sister, they danced to the music on their living-room floors, identified with the regular dancers, and fantasized about stardom on the dance floor of *American Bandstand*. The girls flooded the show with up to 45,000 letters a week and helped the program gross $500,000 a year and net ratings that equaled the combined ratings of the shows telecast by two rival networks. "We love it," gushed one girl from Charleston, West Virginia. "When I hear a Beethoven symphony I don't feel anything. When I hear our kind of music, I feel something way down deep." In the absence of major rock stars and working on the new medium of television, the farsighted Clark created a rock and roll that emphasized the audience as much as the music. By the end of 1959, Clark attracted more than 50 million teens to his show.

Clark and *American Bandstand* brought respectability to rock and roll that had not existed with the suggestive, greasy rockabillies. Clark himself portrayed a prim, clean-cut image. *Newsweek* referred to him as "genial and soft spoken," and *Time* characterized the announcer as "personable and polite, he manages to sound as if he really means such glib disc jockey."

The dancers and performers featured on *American Bandstand* mirrored the clean-cut demeanor of the host. Clark insisted on a dress code, forcing boys to wear a jacket

Dick Clark with the hit records.

or sweater and tie. "Nobody dressed that way in real life," beamed Clark, "but it made the show acceptable to adults who were frightened by the teenage world and their music. Girls couldn't wear slacks, tight sweaters, shorts, or low-necked gowns—they had to wear the kind of dresses or sweaters and skirts they wore in school." To further purge sexuality from the airwaves, the announcer refused to say "going steady" and banned the Alligator and Dog dances as "too sexy." "We just didn't deal with sex," Clark later wrote. *Newsweek* approvingly reported that "Clark enforces strict rules: No smoking, no tight sweaters or dresses, no slacks, no hats or overcoats, no gum chewing." "We've never had an incident," Clark boasted to *Time* in 1958.

One of Clark's books about teenage etiquette, *To Goof or Not to Goof*, exemplified his dampening of teenage rebellion. The dust jacket read: "How to have morals and manners and still have fun." The contents dealt with such burning questions "to successful teenaging" as "Where do your elbows go when you're not eating?" "How long should it take to say good night to a girl? To her father?" "Do nice girls call up boys?" and "How far is friendly?"

Clark's Creations

Dick Clark, though showcasing a variety of rock-and-roll acts on *American Bandstand*, created a stable of mostly poor, Italian, Philadelphia-bred youths whom he groomed, promoted, and cast as the stars of his show. Fabian became one such idol. One day in 1957, a South Philadelphia policeman, Dominick Forte, suffered a heart attack on the street. Bob Marcucci, co-owner of Chancellor Records, offered help and noticed Forte's 14-year-old son Fabian. Impressed with Fabian's resemblance to Elvis Presley, the manager asked the teen if he had an interest in music. When Fabian's father could no longer work steadily, Marcucci signed the youth and gave him voice and etiquette lessons for two years and then tried to market the teen by buying full-page ads in the music industry trade papers. "I was molded, manufactured to fit a certain ideal, and I'll probably wind up with a plastic tombstone," complained Fabian years later.

In 1959, Dick Clark agreed to promote Fabian, who lip-synced "Turn Me Loose," "Tiger," and the Elvis Presley imitation, "Hound Dog Man" on *American Bandstand*. Though believing that the singer "got screams though he couldn't sing a note," Clark transformed Fabian from a $6-a-week drugstore clerk into an overnight sensation. Within a year, Clark helped the Philadelphia teen to sell almost 1 million copies of his signature song "Tiger," appear on *The Ed Sullivan Show*, and receive coverage in *Time* magazine. "Dick Clark was the only way to get your artist to be seen throughout the entire country in the matter of one day," commented Bob Marcucci about the importance of *American Bandstand*.

Dick Clark also launched the career of Frankie Avalon, another regular on *American Bandstand*, who was managed by Bob Marcucci. Born Francis Avallone, Avalon played trumpet for the Philadelphia group Rocco and the Saints, and in 1958 debuted his solo single "DeDe Dinah," which reached the number-seven slot on the chart. Through repeated appearances on *American Bandstand*, the teen scored number-one hits with songs such as "Venus" and "Why." Remarked Frankie about "Venus": "Dick got behind it and it sold a million and a half copies. He's the greatest."

Bobby Rydell, born Robert Ridarelli in Philadelphia, followed his friend Frankie Avalon on the path to stardom. Also a member of Rocco and the Saints, Rydell started a solo career in 1958 that was unsuccessful until he joined *American Bandstand* a year later. In 1959 and 1960, he scored hits with "Kissin' Time," "Volare," and "Swingin' School," and within four years, he chalked up eighteen Top-Thirty chartbusters. Rydell's music consisted of a teenage version of the smooth ballads delivered by Italian crooners of the 1940s and early 1950s such as Frank Sinatra, Perry Como, and Dean Martin.

Clark also brought fame to Ernest Evans, another Philadelphian who became known as Chubby Checker and popularized an international dance craze. In the summer of 1960, Clark noticed an African-American couple on *American Bandstand* "doing a dance that consisted of revolving their hips in quick, half-circle jerks, so their pelvic regions were heaving in time to the music." Clark screamed to his producer, Tony Mammarella, "For God's sake, keep the cameras off that couple. ... It looked like something a belly dancer did to climax her performance."

The announcer soon realized the commercial potential of the dance and suggested that Cameo Records—a company that he owned partially—cover Hank Ballard's 1959 "The Twist." For a singer the company turned to one of the very few African Americans on its roster, Chubby Checker, who had attended high school with Fabian and Frankie Avalon and already had cut a novelty disc for Cameo. At the time, he was working at Fresh Farm Poultry in the Italian market of Philadelphia cleaning chickens. In 1960, *American Bandstand* played Checker's "The Twist" until it hit the top of the chart. By 1963, Checker had sold 70 million singles, 30 million albums, and had starred in two movies, *Twist Around the Clock* (1961) and *Don't Knock the Twist* (1962).

A new dance craze, started on the program, accompanied the song. To do the dance, teens placed one foot in front of them and pretended to extinguish a cigarette butt with their big toes. At the same time, they moved their arms and bodies as if they were frantically drying their backs with towels. The twist craze reached international proportions and spawned a series of records: "Twist with B. B. King," the Isley Brothers's "Twist and Shout," "Twist with Bobby Darin," Sam Cooke's "Twistin' the Night Away," "Twistin' with Duane Eddy," and many others. Both in 1960 and 1961, Checker's version of the song hit the number-one spot.

Dick Clark marketed other dances and their theme songs on his television show. "Many of these dances," admitted the announcer, "came out of Philadelphia and were associated with songs done by artists on Cameo Records." Chubby Checker instructed fans to dance to the R&B gem the Hucklebuck as well as the Pony, the Limbo, and the Fly. Bobby Rydell popularized the Fish. The white Philadelphia doo-wop group the Dovells introduced the Bristol Stomp and the Continental, and singer Dee Dee Sharp exhorted television viewers to jump to the Mashed Potato.

Though creating teen idols and dance steps for his television viewers, Clark remained center stage. He received the attention of the trade publications and the popular press. *Time* labeled him "the Pied Piper of the teenagers." Even the teens themselves swooned over Clark. During the first year of *American Bandstand*, more than 300,000 fans requested Clark's photo, and in 1958, *Life* printed a revealing shot of an awestruck 16-year-old, June Carter, during "her great moment" when Dick Clark kissed her cheek.

For Clark, popularity led to wealth. The announcer collected a sizable salary each year for work on television programs such as *American Bandstand* and *The Dick Clark Show*, a Saturday-night variety show started in February 1958, and the road show *Dick Clark's Caravan of Stars* begun in 1959. In addition to the income from his appearances on television and at concerts, he earned $50,000 a year spinning discs at record hops, which led to the formation of his first corporation, Click. Clark slowly gained a financial interest in local record companies. By 1959, Clark had accumulated a part of Chancellor Records, which featured Fabian and Frankie Avalon; Cameo-Parkway, which recorded Bobby Rydell, Chubby Checker, and the Dovells; one-half ownership of Swan Records in Philadelphia; and 25 percent of Jamie Records. During the 1950s, Dick Clark held at least some share in thirty-three corporations. He also owned the copyrights to over 160 songs, including the top-selling "At the Hop" by Danny and the Juniors and "Sixteen Candles" by the Crests "I was making a killing, racing around trying to make all the money I could," confessed Clark. "My tentacles went in every direction." By April 8, 1958, *Time* reported that "television's newest rage consists of a jukebox full of rock-'n'-roll records, a studio full of dancing teenagers, and Dick Clark, a suave young (twenty-eight) disc jockey full of money."

The Payola Investigation

Clark's interlocking interests became painfully public during the payola investigations of 1959 and 1960. Payola, or "play for pay," had been an accepted practice in the music industry, dating back to the vaudeville era. "Historically, payola is an outgrowth of a music business tradition—song promotion," noted Paul Ackerman, music editor of *Billboard*.

The payola investigations of 1959–1960 began with fraud on television. In November 1959, Charles Lincoln Van Doren admitted before the House Special Committee on Legislative Oversight that two years previously he had been given answers in advance as a contestant on NBC's *Twenty-One* quiz show. Reeling from the revelation of cheating, the networks discontinued many game programs. NBC canceled *Tic Tac Dough* and *The Price Is Right*; CBS eliminated all quiz shows from its schedule and fired the president of the network, who had been closely associated with *Quiz Kids, Stop the Music*, and *The $64,000 Question*, the most popular show in America.

The scandal spread to the music industry with the prodding of the American Society of Composers, Authors, and Publishers (ASCAP), a song/performance-licensing concern that, through the 1950s, had attacked the interlocking interests of radio, network television, and the record companies represented by the rival licensing agent, Broadcast Music, Inc. (BMI). Concerned about rock performers such as Little Richard and Chuck Berry, who wrote their own material, the professional songwriters of ASCAP used the payola investigation to lash out bitterly against BMI and the rock and roll it licensed. The songwriters hired Vance Packard, author of *Hidden Persuaders*, who tried to demonstrate that rock and roll was "largely engineered, manipulated for the interests of BMI, and that would be the point, that the public was manipulated into liking rock-and-roll." ASCAP member and well-known Broadway songwriter Oscar Hammerstein asked, "What do you think is going to happen to rock-and-roll songs? . . . They die as soon as the plug stops."

Congressmen in charge of the investigation, hoping to impress their conservative constituencies during an election year, joined in the attack on rock and roll. "Suppose John Smith owns a record company and then buys a broadcast station," postulated the counsel for the committee. "Suppose he dumps its personnel and its good music format to put on his own label, generally only rock-and-roll. . . . Now, that's not in the public interest." Without payola, "a lot of this so-called junk music, rock-'n'-roll stuff, which appeals to the teenagers would not be played," stressed Congressman John Bennett of Michigan. Such "trash" as rock music had been "pushed" on unsuspecting teens, agreed Representative John Moss of California.

The committee focused on disc jockeys who played rock and roll. Boston jockey Norm Prescott told the House committee that "bribery, payola, has become the prime function of this business to get the record on the air at any cost" and that he had taken almost $10,000 from various record distributors. Another Boston announcer, WBZ's Dave Maynard, admitted that a record distributor had helped finance his purchase of two cars and had given him $6,817 in cash. Alan Dary, also of WBZ, received cash, a hi-fi, liquor, and carpeting for his master bedroom. By 1960, investigators announced that 207 rock-and-roll disc jockeys in forty-two states had accepted more than $263,000 in payola. President Dwight Eisenhower instructed the committee, headed by Oren Harris of Arkansas, "to clean up this whole mess."

Some rock DJs immediately felt repercussions from the payola investigation. In Detroit, WJBK's Tom Clay was fired after he admitted to taking $6,000 in a year and a half. In Boston, three top disc jockeys on the rock station WILD—Stan Richards, Bill Marlowe, and Mike Eliot—found themselves unemployed. And in New York, premier rock announcer Alan Freed was dismissed by WABC when he admitted that he had taken $30,650 from six record companies. Complained a bitter Freed, "What they call payola in the disc jockey business they call lobbying in Washington."

Dick Clark came under especially close scrutiny. As Representative John Bennett of Michigan put it: "I think it is pretty convincing that Clark was involved with payola as all other disc jockeys, but on a much larger scale." Illinois Congressman Peter Mack called him "the top dog in the payola field," and Representative John Moss of California began to refer to the investigations as "Clarkola."

However, Clark escaped the payola investigation with his job and reputation intact. Wearing a blue suit, a button-down shirt, and black loafers, the announcer uncategorically informed the House committee in April 1960 that "I have never agreed to play a record in return for payment in cash or any other consideration." When grilled about promoting artists who recorded for companies in which he owned an interest, a cool Clark replied softly that "I did not consciously favor such records. Maybe I did so without realizing it." The host of *American Bandstand*, projecting an air of respectability to the congressional investigators, slipped through the committee unscathed. At the end of his testimony, he was told by Chairman Oren Harris: "You're not the inventor of the system or even its architect. You're a product of it. Obviously, you're a fine young man."

Alan Freed, a tireless champion of black performers who wrote their own songs and had created rock and roll, did not fare as well. As the payola investigation ended in 1960, an unemployed Freed was charged with commercial bribery in connection with payola by an eight-member grand jury in New York. Blackballed by the music industry after the payola scare, the former disc jockey, penniless, stood trial in December 1962 and pleaded guilty to two counts of commercial bribery. He was fined $300 and given a six-month suspended sentence. Less than two years later, on March 16, 1964, Freed was charged with income tax by another grand jury, which ordered him to pay the Internal Revenue Service almost $38,000 in back taxes. Later in the year, a broken, unemployed, despondent Alan Freed entered a California hospital, suffering from the effects of alcoholism. On January 20, 1965, he died at age 43.

Don Kirshner Takes Charge

The payola investigation had an immediate impact on rock and roll. As the established tunesmiths in ASCAP had hoped, songwriters became a dominant force in the new music. Ironically, from 1960 to 1963, a new breed of songsmiths nurtured by New York music publisher Don Kirshner outdistanced recognized Tin Pan Alley songwriters to corner the teen market. They produced romantic lyrics and upbeat melodies for and about teenagers and placed the songs with gospel-influenced, African-American girl groups, who gradually became more popular than the white, male, Italian teen idols of the Dick Clark era.

Don Kirshner masterminded the takeover of rock by the songwriters. The son of a Bronx tailor, Kirshner began to write songs professionally in 1958 and hoped to reshape Tin Pan Alley for the expanding teen market. He idolized songwriters Max and Louis Dreyfus who had built the music publishing firm, Chappell Music, and had mentored such notable songwriters as George Gershwin, Richard Rodgers and Cole Porter. "My philosophy—my dream—was that we were approaching a new era in the music business with room for new people to accomplish what the Dreyfuses had," Kirshner related. "And I believed that if I got the chance to sit behind a desk in the music business, I'd be the guy to accomplish that."

Chasing his dream, a 21-year-old Kirshner, along with Al Nevins, guitarist for the pop group The Three Suns, established Aldon Music in 1958 in search of new, young writers. The business partners rented office space across the street from the famed Brill Building at 1619 Broadway, which housed the well-known publishing firms so important to Tin Pan Alley pop music. "The Brill Building," reminisced songwriter Mike Stoller, who collaborated with Jerry Leiber on a number of songs recorded by

Elvis Presley, the Coasters, and many others, "had music publishers on every floor. Frequently ... writers would go [there] to peddle their songs, and they'd go from door to door trying to sell them."

Kirshner quickly discovered teams of young songwriters who challenged the established firms across the street. One afternoon, just two days after Aldon Music opened its doors for business, two aspiring Brooklyn writers who had been neighborhood chums, Neil Sedaka and Howie Greenfield, walked into the office. Sedaka and Greenfield had just been rejected by Hill and Range publishers and approached Kirshner. Kirshner, looking for talent, bubbled, "I'm the guy!" to the incredulous duo. Kirshner rushed the team to the home of a friend, pop singer Connie Francis (b. Concetta Franconero), who heard and then recorded the Sedaka/Greenfield song, "Stupid Cupid," which in 1958 hit the Top Twenty. Neil Sedaka, unlike almost all of the other songwriters at Aldon, recorded his own material. After the Connie Francis hit, Sedaka, who was a classically trained pianist, believed that the singers who recorded his songs "couldn't feel it the way I could. I used to play songs for people and then play the record, and they would say, 'We like the way you do it better.'" In 1958, Al Nevins took Sedaka to RCA, which signed Sedaka. The label recorded "The Diary," a Sedaka/Greenfield collaboration, which, after a $100,000 promotional campaign, became Sedaka's first hit as a singer. During the next four years, Sedaka followed with the Top-Ten chartbusters "Breaking Up Is Hard to Do," "Calendar Girl," "Happy Birthday, Sweet Sixteen," and "Oh! Carol," all Sedaka/Greenfield originals.

The Sounds on the Streets

Don Kirshner found some successful songwriters who helped extend the boundaries of doo-wop. Doo-wop originated on the streets of New York City, where groups of young African-American males, too poor to afford instruments, sang in harmony. Many groups fashioned themselves after the Ravens. Formed in early 1946, the four-man group featured the deep bass tone of leader Jimmy Ricks and released singles for several independent labels before signing with Columbia in 1950. They hit the R&B Top Ten with "Write Me a Letter" and on January 2, 1949, appeared on Ed Sullivan's *Toast of the Town* television program. During the 1950s, the Ravens inspired dozens of groups named after birds, including the Larks ("Heaven and Paradise"), the Swallows ("Itchy Twitchy Feeling"), the Cardinals, the Robins ("Smokey Joe's Cafe"), the Jayhawks ("Stranded in the Jungle"), and the Penguins, who in 1954 perhaps achieved the greatest commercial success with "Earth Angel."

Doo-wop groups also looked to Clyde McPhatter and the Drifters for inspiration. As with most doo-wop harmonizers, McPhatter first joined a gospel group, the Dominoes, which was managed by Billy Ward. Soon after their television debut on *The Arthur Godfrey Show*, the Dominoes recorded R&B numbers, and in May 1951, released the classic "Sixty Minute Man." Within two years, McPhatter bolted from the Dominoes to form the Drifters, settling on the name because the members "drifted" from one group to another. The quartet signed with Atlantic Records and in September 1953 scaled the chart with the million-selling "Money Honey." In 1954, they followed with such hits as "Such a Night," "Honey Love," and "Bip Bam," which all hit the R&B Top Ten.

Influenced by the success of the Ravens and Drifters, several new doo-wop groups formed around New York music entrepreneur George Goldner. Originally in the garment business, Goldner recorded Latin acts during the late 1940s, and then, in March 1954, he took a chance on the doo-wop group the Crows, which unexpectedly attracted an R&B and pop following with "Gee."

Encouraged by his success with the Crows, Goldner signed several harmonizers, including Frankie Lymon and the Teenagers. The Teenagers, fronted by 12-year-old

Lymon, practiced on street corners, in a junk-filled backyard, and on the top of a Harlem tenement house. One day, Richard Barrett, the lead singer of another Goldner act, the Valentines, overheard the Teenagers as he passed by a street corner. Excitedly, he brought the boys, all in their teens except Lymon, to Goldner's office, where they sang "Why Do Fools Fall in Love." The next day, the Teenagers recorded the song. Released in January 1956, the song became a Top-Ten pop hit within a month. Goldner followed with many other doo-wop groups such as the Wrens, the Flamingos, and the Channels. "His gift was that he could recognize and manipulate talent with an uncanny ear for commercial potential," remarked Herb Cox, lead singer of the Cleftones, who hit with "Little Girl of Mine."

By the mid-1950s, hundreds of young African-American males, most of whom had just graduated from high school, harmonized on the streets of urban America. Most of them came from New York City, including the Paragons ("Florence"), the Jive Five ("My True Story"), the Jesters ("The Plea"), the Chords ("Sh-Boom"), and the Charts ("Desirie"). Other cities contributed to the movement as well. From Los Angeles came the Penguins, the Olympics ("Western Movies"), the Hollywood Flames ("Buzz-Buzz-Buzz"), and the Jacks ("Why Don't You Write Me"). The Five Satins, who hit with "In the Still of the Night," came from New Haven, Connecticut; the Charms ("Hearts of Stone") sang on the streets of Cincinnati; the Monotones ("Book of Love") grew up in Newark, New Jersey; and the Dells ("Oh, What a Night") came from Chicago.

Many of the doo-wop groups named themselves after hallmarks of the urban streets. Some borrowed their names from the automobiles that glided past the streets on which they sang: the El Dorados, the Cadillacs, the Edsels, the Fiestas, the Impalas, the Imperials, and the Belvederes. Dion and the Belmonts ("I Wonder Why" and "Teenager in Love"), one of the few white doo-wop groups, named themselves after Belmont Avenue in the Bronx near their neighborhood. Reflecting life in urban America of the 1950s, these teens created a sound that would reverberate throughout the history of rock and roll.

The Girl Groups

Don Kirshner hired teams of young New York City songwriters who built upon the doo-wop tradition by writing teen-oriented songs for a bevy of African-American female vocal groups. Carole Klein, the subject of a Neil Sedaka song ("Oh! Carol"), who later became known as singer/songwriter Carole King, helped write Aldon Music's first smash hit, which set the direction of the company for the next three years.

King churned out chartbusters with collaborator and then husband Gerry Goffin. King learned piano at age 4 and in high school formed her first band, the Co-sines. While attending Queens College in New York in 1958, she met lyricist Gerry Goffin, who started to write songs with her in the evenings. The King–Goffin team joined Aldon Music and began to compose Tin Pan Alley songs designed especially for teens. Goffin told *Time*, "Lyrics will hurt a song if they're too adult, too artistic, too correct. You should shy away from anything too deep."

In 1960, the King–Goffin duo composed the teen ballad "Will You Love Me Tomorrow." Initially, Kirshner brought the song to Mitch Miller, then the head of Artists and Repertoire (A&R) at Columbia Records, but the conservative Miller rejected the song. Turning away from the musical establishment, Kirshner took the song to a New Jersey–based independent company, Scepter Records. He approached its owners and recommended the song for the Shirelles, an African-American, all-girl act on the label. Kirshner convinced them to record "Will You Love Me Tomorrow," which in October 1960 became a number-one hit, a first for an all-girl group.

Kirshner hired other teams of songwriters who worked side by side to compose teenage-oriented tunes for other doo-wop-influenced, African-American girl groups who became some of the first female rock-and-roll performers. Paying his composers about $150 a week, he snagged the songwriting teams of Barry Mann–Cynthia Weil and Ellie Greenwich–Jeff Barry, who joined about thirty other young tunesmiths at Aldon Music during the early 1960s. "It was insane," recalled Barry Mann. "Cynthia and I would be in this tiny cubicle, about the size of a closet, with just a piano and chair; no window or anything." Every morning, the duo would write songs all day, next to other closet-sized rooms occupied by Carole King–Jerry Goffin and Neil Sedaka–Howie Greenfield who all feverishly banged on their pianos and composed teenage anthems. "All of us," added Barry, "were so insecure that we'd never write a hit again that we constantly wrote in order to prove we could."

The two teams of Mann–Weil and Greenwich–Barry crafted a number of songs during 1962–1963 for two of the premier African-American girl groups, the Ronettes and the Crystals. Mann and Weil wrote the Top-Twenty hits "Uptown" and "He's Sure the Boy I Love" for the Crystals and "Walking in the Rain" for the Ronettes. The more prolific Greenwich–Barry team authored "Be My Baby" for the Ronettes and "Da Doo Ron Ron" and "Then He Kissed Me" for the Crystals. They also composed "Today I Met the Boy I'm Gonna Marry" for Darlene Love, who sang lead vocal on many of the Crystals' hits.

Darlene Love (born Darlene Wright) infused the girl-group sound with a gospel flavor. "My father was a minister, and I used to sing all the time in the church choir," remembered Love. At age 16, she joined the Blossoms, a female vocal group in Los Angeles. In 1962, Darlene Love sang lead vocal on the Crystals' number-one hit "He's a Rebel," instilling her gospel influences in the song. With the Blossoms, the singer cut many other gospel-influenced records officially released under the Crystals' name. Ellie Greenwich described Love as "a typical sixties soulful street gospel singer."

Despite her success singing Aldon's material, Darlene Love complained that "many of the singers [in the girl groups] that sung those songs didn't really want to sing them. We called them bubblegum songs. The lyrics were really not even teenage. I say kid, you know ten to twelve, the market was geared for them."

Phil Spector, owner of Philles Records, which recorded the Crystals and the Ronettes, surrounded the teen-oriented, gospel-flavored tearjerkers of Aldon Music with a "wall of sound" to create distinctive, girl group music. Spector, born in the Bronx, moved to Los Angeles with his mother when his father died. After a short-lived success with the rock combo the Teddy Bears, he found employment with independent producers Lester Sill and Lee Hazelwood, who in 1960 sent Spector to New York to serve an apprenticeship with songwriters Jerry Leiber and Mike Stoller. In 1961, the 21-year-old Spector and Lester Sill, a former promotion man for Modern Records, formed the New York–based Philles Records, which Spector owned solely by 1962.

While recording the Crystals and the Ronettes for Philles, the producer perfected his now-famous wall of sound, which involved overlays of the same instruments as well as multiple instruments in a song to create a dense, full-blown, orchestral sound. Ronnie Bennett, the lead singer of the Ronettes, who later married and then divorced the producer, remembered that "everything was done double. I mean where most people have one guitar or one drummer we had two of everything, so that's what made that wall of sound." Spector took this lush instrumentation and doubled it through an elaborate echo system. "You had live sound going to the [echo] chamber and you had a delayed sound going to the chamber at the same time, and the result was that it repeated in the chamber, so when it came back it was just a big blur," explained music engineer Bones Howe who worked with Spector on several songs.

The resulting music sounded heroic and monumental. "Well, I know that Phil's favorite composer was Wagner, no question, power, bigness," commented Ellie Greenwich. "Wagner was his idol and Wagner was power and bigness and heavy and all that and I think he was going after that in his records." Spector himself called the new sound "a Wagnerian approach to rock-and-roll; little symphonies for the kids." The power of Spector's production that surrounded gospel-flavored songs of teenage romance resulted in the bright, upbeat, almost ethereal girl group sound.

The Dream

The rags-to-riches success stories of the girl groups added to the romantic appeal of the music for thousands of school-age girls. The Crystals, a group of Brooklyn teens, had been discovered by Phil Spector while auditioning in New York City. The Shirelles had begun singing at school shows and at parties, and in 1958 had been signed to Scepter Records by Florence Greenberg, the mother of one of their high school classmates. The Chantels, five New York teens who sang in the youth choir of a local Catholic grade school, were signed to a contract when a talent scout inadvertently heard them harmonizing at a Frankie Lymon concert. In 1958, they hit the Top Twenty with "Maybe."

Other girl groups had similar stories. The Chiffons, high school friends who sang during lunch breaks and in the neighborhood after school, were discovered by songwriter Ronnie Mack, who groomed the girls until they made their chart-topping "He's So Fine" in early 1963. The Dixie Cups, singing together since grade school, were spotted at a local New Orleans talent contest by singer/pianist Joe Jones, who became their manager and in 1964 helped them top the chart with the Greenwich–Barry song "Chapel of Love." The Shangri-Las, one of the few white girl groups of the era, grew up in a tough section of Queens, New York, and sang together as young teenagers. One day, producer Shadow Morton, a friend of Ellie Greenwich, happened to hear the four girls—Mary Weiss and her sister Betty and the Ganser twins, Marge and Mary Ann—and signed them to the new Red Bird label, which had been started by doo-wop impresario George Goldner and R&B songwriters Jerry Leiber and Mike Stoller. In late 1964, when Mary was only fifteen, the group hit the Top Ten with "Remember (Walking in the Sand)" and later the same year topped the singles chart with "Leader of the Pack."

The discovery of the Ronettes—sisters Veronica and Estelle Bennett and their cousin Nedra Talley—probably offered teenage girls the most encouraging story. In 1961, the three girls became resident dancers at the Peppermint Lounge, a focus of the twist craze in New York City. In August, the group signed with Colpix Records and released four unsuccessful songs. After a show at the Peppermint Lounge in June 1963, Ronnie Bennett casually walked into a bar and saw Phil Spector sitting at the piano. Their eyes fastened on one another, and Spector softly asked Ronnie to sing. After a few bars, the producer exclaimed, "That's the voice, that's the voice I've been looking for."

Such tales of instant stardom, coupled with the dramatic, romanticized music of the girl groups, created the fantasy among many young girls that they too could become famous. "You see them coming from the cities, mostly groups, off the streets, hanging around Tin Pan Alley on Broadway near the Brill Building," noticed Phil Spector at the time. "They're usually between sixteen and nineteen, anxious to record, anxious to be a singer." Although few traveled to New York in search of their dreams, millions of girls lay on their beds, listened to their transistor radios, and fantasized about impending stardom. Songwriter Jerry Leiber characterized the era as "very naive, very innocent, full of hope, full of fantasy, full of promise." *Life* magazine referred to the new sound as "a fairy tale called the pop-record business" and identified Don Kirshner as "the grand wizard of the fairy tale."

The fantasies of teenage girls helped Don Kirshner establish a music publishing empire. "The fastest rising phenomenon in the business is a Tin Pan Alley octopus called Aldon Music Inc., which has thirty-five boys and girls busy night and day composing songs," reported *Time* in March 1963. A few months later, *The Saturday Evening Post* renamed Tin Pan Alley, "Teen Pan Alley," and told its readers that "Broadway's

Brill Building, once the home of jelly-jowled, gray-headed music publishers, is now being refurbished with youthful executives who have grown up to no other kind of music than the beat of today. ... One of the typical—and prime—figures in youth's takeover of the pop-record business is a onetime unsuccessful songwriter named Don Kirshner." By the end of the year, Kirshner had sold hundreds of songs that dominated the music charts and grossed millions of dollars.

In 1963, Don Kirshner and his partner Al Nevins sold Aldon Music. "The money just kept rolling in, and the hits kept rolling in," shrugged Kirshner, "and you walk away at twenty-eight years of age with a $2 million check with your partner, it's difficult to turn down." Kirshner left for a lucrative job in the Columbia Screen Gems Television Music Division, where he supervised the record and music publishing interests of the company. He had left Aldon just when the surf had begun to rise.

Chapter 5
Surfboards and Hot Rods: California, Here We Come

"We sang about California and being young."

—Dean Torrence

Eureka, a Greek word meaning "I have found it," was selected by state legislators as a motto in 1850, at the end of the great Gold Rush, when California became the thirty-first state. Especially during the late 1950s and early 1960s, it aptly characterized the sentiments of the droves of migrants from the Midwest and the East Coast who traveled to California with hopes of sun, fun, and jobs. A new indigenous music, a bright, bouncy sound that glorified beaches, bikinis, and hot rods, embodied and promoted the California myth.

Postwar California had advantages over most other states. It enjoyed an abundance of natural resources, including lumber, oil, and many minerals. In 1961, the state produced more fruit, vegetables, and nuts than any other state and topped the number-two farm state, Iowa, by more than $700 million in total produce. Ushering in the computer age, in 1961 the state procured almost half of the $6 billion in Defense Department research-and-development contracts, and during the 1950s, it attracted 200 electronic firms such as Western Electric, Raytheon, Remington Rand, Zenith, and Motorola, to the aptly named Silicon Valley, which contained deposits of silica used in manufacturing transistors and computer chips. Probably most important, third only to Alaska and Texas in size, California boasted a wide range of terrains and climates from the desert of Death Valley to the damp, forested mountains in the north and from the central farm valley to the beaches of Malibu.

The resources of California, especially a healthy economy and the sunny, balmy climate of the southern part of the state, drew throngs of migrants after World War II. In 1940, the population of the state stood at almost 7 million. Within ten years, it increased to 10.6 million, bolstered by many Texans and Oklahomans who journeyed there during the war for employment in government factories. People continued to stream into California during the next decade, until, by late 1962, with its population expanding by 1,700 daily, California had more than 17 million inhabitants and became the most populous state in the country. About 60 percent of the people lived in the ten southernmost counties of the state.

Many of the migrants looked for the mythical California of fun and prosperity that had been promulgated by the press. In a late 1962 article, "What to Know About and Look For," *Life* focused on California's "bigness, bustle, and boom." The reporter described a state with a per capita income 25 percent above the national average, a wide-open job market, "plenty" of houses equipped with swimming pools, 160 state parks (a third of which were beaches), and the best college system in the country and supermarkets and roadside stands that would "stagger most Easterners." At the same time, *Newsweek* emphasized the "happy hedonism" of the California transplants.

"Californians take their relaxation seriously," it asserted. "Unassuming and carefree, they break with the staid ways of their former communities, dip freely into credit for financing luxury items, and start experimenting in weird and wonderful ways." California, concluded a writer in a September 1962 issue of *Look*, "presents the promise and the challenge contained at the very heart of the original American dream."

Several homegrown California attractions and consumer items symbolized the fairyland aura of fun, sun, and whimsical hope of the nation's most populous state. Disneyland, a 160-acre theme park, opened to the public on July 18, 1955. The brainchild of animation king Walt Disney, it featured fantasy neighborhoods such as Frontierland, Adventureland, Fantasyland, and Tomorrowland, the last of which Disney described as "designed to give you an opportunity to participate in adventures that are a living blueprint of our future." Each section of the $17 million, brightly-colored extravaganza included theme-inspired rides on rivers, waterfalls, mountains, spaceships, and spinning teacups with employees dressed in larger-than-life cartoon costumes greeting the visitors. By 1965, more than 50 million children and their parents had entered the gates of the magic kingdom to enjoy an otherworldly and unforgettable experience. A television show, *The Mickey Mouse Club* series, which premiered on October 3, 1955, and featured Mouseketeers such as Annette Funicello, added to the California-centered Disney craze.

Toy manufacturer Mattel, producing Disney-licensed merchandise, created another product that pandered to the idealized image that California backers promulgated. In 1958, Ruth Handler, the wife of one of Mattel's cofounders, unveiled an 11.5-inch fashion doll, which she dubbed "Barbie" after her daughter. Unlike stuffed animals or traditional porcelain dolls, Barbie sported the anatomically unrealistic measurements of 39-21-33, if magnified to human proportions. Debuting at the 1959 New York World's Fair, the Mattel doll gave young girls an impossible goal and provided boys with a buxom, blonde, ever-smiling, and totally passive ideal. "That's a doll for little girls?" blurted future Beach Boy Dennis Wilson, then a young boy in Hawthorne, California, where Mattel had its headquarters. "Whoa! I'd rather have this in my room than a stag magazine!" In 1961, Ruth Handler developed a trim, muscular male counterpart to Barbie, which she named "Ken" after her son.

Surfing U.S.A.

A buoyant surf music, born amid the California boom, reflected and promoted the myth of the California wonderland. It glorified one of the most attractive elements of the California myth: the sun-drenched Southern California beaches dotted with tanned, blonde, bikini-clad, Barbie-like beauties.

Surfing, the sacred sport of Hawaiian kings that began in the fifteenth century, was introduced to California at the turn of the twentieth century. In 1959, the sport received a boost from the movie *Gidget*, a tale about a young girl who spent a summer on the beach and fell in love with two surfers.

The same year, the innovations of two surfboard companies, Hobie Surfboards in Dana Point and Sweet's Surfboards in Santa Monica, further popularized the sport. Hobie Alter and Dave and Roger Sweet replaced the heavy wooden board with a lightweight polyurethane foam strip coated with fiberglass and glossed with a polyester resin that could be handled more easily, an important consideration for the teen market.

Almost immediately, young people in Southern California started to buy the new plastic boards and took to the waves. In late September 1961, *Life* commented that "now the surf that sweeps in on the beaches bears flotillas of enthusiasts standing on long buoyant boards. ... Surfing has become an established craze in California." "If you're not a surfer," explained one high school boy, "you're not 'in.' If you're a good surfer, you're always in. All you've got to do is walk up and down the beach with a board and you've got girls."

By August 1963, reported *Time*, "every weekend an estimated 100,000 surfers paddle into the briny on 7 ft. to 12 ft. balsa or polyurethane boards, struggle upright into a precarious balance with nature, and try to catch the high breakers coming in." Bill Cooper, executive secretary of the U.S. Surfing Association, calculated that "ninety percent are beginners. Half of them give it up in a year or two, but then there are more."

The new legion of predominantly male, white teenage surfers began to develop its own culture, dressing, and speaking in a distinctive way. At high school, the bleached-blonde surfers wore Pendleton shirts, sandals, white, tight, and somewhat short Levis, and baggies—very large, loose boxer-style shorts. After school, they jumped into an oversized station wagons with wooden sides (a "woodie"), which transported their "polys" (surfboards), drove to the beach, and dashed toward the ocean. They ran with their "sticks" (surfboards) into the "soup" (the foaming water near the beach) and tried to catch a wave. Some would only "fun surf" on 3- to 6-foot waves. Other more daring surfers would carry their "big guns" (surfboards designed for riding tall waves) into the water, pick up a "hairy" wave (a fast wave that is difficult to surf), and "shoot" (ride) it, sometimes "hot dogging" (performing tricks) to impress the "bunnies" (girls) on shore. All surfers showed disdain for the poorly skilled or fraudulent, to whom they referred to as "gremlins" or "kooks." After packing their gear, jumping in their woodies, and reaching their homes they devoured magazines such as *Surfer* and *Surfer Illustrated* and watched surfing films by director Bruce Brown such as *Slippery When Wet* (1960) and *Barefoot Adventure* (1961), or the more commercial *Beach Party* (1963), *Muscle Beach Party* (1964), and *Bikini Beach* (1964), which starred two Dick Clark regulars, Frankie Avalon and former Mouseketeer Annette Funicello.

The Sound of the Surf

Surfers listened to their own style of music, which originated with Dick Dale and his Del-Tones. Born in Boston, a teenage Dale (b. Richard Monsour) moved with his family to El Segundo on the Southern California coast and joined the hordes of young surfers. "I found myself out on a surfboard being taught how to surf at the Santa Ana River Jetty," he fondly remembered. "Soon I was surfing all over the place."

A guitar enthusiast who had released a few unremarkable singles on his own label in 1959 and 1960, Dale experimented with electronics. He worked closely with Leo Fender, the manufacturer of the first mass-produced, solid-body electric guitar, to improve the Showman amplifier and develop a reverberation unit that gave his guitar a distinctively fuzzy sound. He and Fender also perfected a speaker that could withstand the Dale's loud, distorted music.

Dick Dale fused his two passions—surfing and the guitar—to create a new music for surf fanatics. "There was a tremendous amount of power I felt while surfing and that feeling of power was simply transferred into my guitar when I was playing surf music," he recalled. Dale created a style of instrumental music, which provided him with "that good rambling feeling I got when I was locked in a tube with the white water caving in over my head. I was trying to project the power of the ocean to the people," added the guitarist.

During the summer of 1961, Dale and his band unveiled the new surf sound during weekend dances at the Rendezvous Ballroom in Balboa, California. Dale owned a small record/phonograph repair shop across the street from the Ballroom and convinced the owner, Thelma Neufeld, to allow his band to play there. On July 1, the Deltones started a long engagement at the club that attracted wildly enthusiastic fans. The Rendezvous, remembered Paul Johnson, later a member of the surf group the Bel-Airs, had a capacity of one thousand spectators. Dale's "music was huge and throbbing, especially when combined with all those sandals stomping on the wooden floor." By late 1961, when he first arrived on the West Coast, disc jockey and producer Jim Pewter found that "the word was 'Let's go to a Dick Dale dance,' so my girl and I motivated to the Rendezvous and checked it out, only to return again and again."

Dick Dale and the Del-Tones released records for the surf crowd. In late 1961, "Let's Go Trippin'" topped the California charts and a few months later edged toward the national Top Fifty. Dale followed with "Surfbeat," and in May 1962 produced the classic surf instrumental "Miserlou." In March 1963, Capitol Records recorded Dale and pegged him as the "King of the Surf Guitar." The same year, the guitarist landed a spot in the William Asher–directed movie *Beach Party*, and by the end of 1963, he had become a California celebrity.

The Beach Boys

The Beach Boys brought surf music to national prominence. Raised in the suburb of Hawthorne, California, the boys—leader Brian Wilson, his brothers Carl and Dennis, cousin Mike Love, and Al Jardine, a classmate of Brian's at El Camino Junior College—began to play in 1961. After trying out several names, they settled on the Pendletones, a play on the Pendleton shirts that were favored by California teens.

The band smoothed the rough edges of the fuzzy, twanging surf instrumental. As with Dick Dale, the boys favored a swinging electric-guitar sound of the 1950s. "'Rock Around the Clock' shocked me," Brian Wilson told a reporter. "I mean, I was so electrified by the experience—that song was really it." The group combined the rawness of the 1950s rock with glossy harmonies gleaned from white vocal groups such as the Four Freshmen, a jazz-based quartet formed in 1948 and reaching mass popularity during the mid-1950s. The blend resulted in a bright, airy, snappy sound that embodied the California myth and reflected the general optimism of the Kennedy presidency, which promised a Camelot of full employment, civil liberties, and victory in the space race.

These California teens recorded their new sound with the help of their domineering, sometimes abusive, father, Murry Wilson, who managed a heavy machinery import business and in his spare time composed songs. Murry introduced the boys to music publisher Hite Morgan who was looking for new material. In October 1961, the band auditioned for Morgan. "We've written a song about the surfing sport and we'd like to sing it for you," pestered the Wilson brothers. Morgan quietly listened to the tune and exclaimed, "Drop everything; we're going to record your song." Within two hours, the group recorded "Surfin'." Morgan took the demo to the local Candix label, which released the record in December 1961 and changed the group's name to the Beach Boys. Commented Mike Love about the name change: "We didn't even know we were the Beach Boys until the song came out." Within weeks, "Surfin'" topped the California charts and reached number seventy-five on the national Top One Hundred.

Good luck temporarily deserted the Beach Boys. Two months after the success of "Surfin'," the Beach Boys recorded four more songs, but before they could be released, Candix Records, plagued by financial difficulties, ceased operations. Murry Wilson, by this time the manager of the group, played the demos to a variety of labels, all of which rejected the songs because, in the estimation of an executive at Dot, "surfing music was a flash in the pan." Al Jardine, disgusted with the failures, quit the band to begin dental school but would rejoin the group nearly a year later.

Murry Wilson finally brought the demos to Nick Venet of Capitol Records. After listening to the songs, the producer rushed into the office of his supervisor and boasted, "Boss, I've got a double-sided smash for Capitol." The label signed the Beach Boys and in June 1962 released "Surfin' Safari," which reached number fourteen on the

The Beach Boys.

Pictorial Press Ltd./Alamy Stock Photo.

national singles chart. Later in the year, Capitol followed with an album of the same name, which cracked the Top Thirty-Five.

In May 1963, Capitol released the breakthrough Beach Boys album *Surfin' U.S.A.* The cover featured an action photo of a surfer cutting a path across a 30-foot wave and included a headline that hailed the Beach Boys as "the number-one surfing group in the country."

The Beach Boys applied their trademark harmonies to the title track on the album. "*Surfin' U.S.A.*," a note-for-note reworking of Chuck Berry's "Sweet Little Sixteen," hit the number-three slot on the national singles chart. The other selections on the album included covers of Dick Dale's "Miserlou" and "Let's Go Tripping" and other odes to surfdom such as "Lonely Sea," "Surf Jam," and "Noble Surfer." The album established the Beach Boys as the kings of surf, and *Surfin' U.S.A.* helped spread the surfing craze across the nation.

During the next few months, the Beach Boys fortified their reputation. In late 1963, they scored with "Surfer Girl," and in 1964, they topped the singles chart with "I Get Around." The group reflected and enforced the California myth with their chart-busters "Fun, Fun, Fun" (1964) and "California Girls" (1965). By the mid-1960s, the Beach Boys had brought a bright, bouncy surf music that extolled sun and fun to teens throughout the country.

Jan and Dean

Jan and Dean delivered the same message of the California surf to American teenagers. Becoming friends at Emerson Junior High School in West Los Angeles, Jan Berry and Dean Torrence began their partnership by recording teen ballads. In October 1959, they reached the Top Ten with "Baby Talk" and appeared on the nationally televised *American Bandstand.* Further paeans to teenage love followed, until the duo joined the ranks of surfdom with the help of the Beach Boys. "When 'Surfin' came out," recalled Dean, "we heard it and liked it. I think we sensed that it was going to be good for business." Because "Jan and I were physically involved with surfing, it was just natural that we became involved with the music."

In late 1962, Jan and Dean became converts to surf music after performing with the Beach Boys. At one show, the Beach Boys first played a few songs, including "Surfin'" and "Surfin' Safari," and Jan and Dean followed with three or four songs. After receiving an enthusiastic reaction from the crowd, Jan and Dean asked the Beach Boys, "Hey, do you want to do your set again, and we'll sing with you guys?" "Gee, you'll sing our songs," responded an awestruck Brian Wilson. "Sure," replied Dean, "I think your songs are really fun to sing." Jan and Dean backed the Beach Boys on two numbers, and the crowd went wild.

The collaboration convinced Jan and Dean to include a surf song on their upcoming album, which featured the song "Linda." As Dean told it, their record producer and manager Lou Adler suggested, "Why don't you take Linda surfing … That gets it all in there." Dean agreed but "didn't know any surfing songs except the two that the Beach Boys had done." He called Brian Wilson and asked if the group would play the instrumental parts and perform back-up vocals on "Surfin'" and "Surfin' Safari" on the album. Dean recalled that Brian "was just totally knocked out that we were going to record his songs! He said, 'Sure, I'll get the guys,' " who dashed to the studio. While at the session, Brian also sang the opening line of a new song, which he offered to Jan and Dean. The duo added lyrics and recorded it as "Surf City," a tune that in 1963 went to the top of the charts. As part of the California myth of abundance, the tune promised "two girls for every boy." The next year, they followed with "Ride the Wild Surf" and "Sidewalk Surfin'."

By the end of 1963, surf music had become a national craze. The Surfaris recorded "Wipe Out," which reached number two on the national chart. Modeling their sound after Dick Dale by using his reverberation unit, the Chantays hit the Top Five with "Pipeline," which in surf parlance referred to the curl of a wave before it broke. Duane Eddy, the king of twang, recorded "Your Baby's Gone Surfin'," the Trashmen from the Midwest cut "Surfin' Bird," and the Astronauts from Colorado released "Surfin' with the Astronauts." A spate of other surf-inspired albums emerged: *Surfin' with the Challengers, Surfin' Bongos, Surfin' with the Shadows*, the Marketts' *Surfers Stomp, Surfbeat* by the Surfriders, and *Surf Mania* by the Surf Teens. Chess Records even released the album *Surfin' with Bo Diddley*, without informing the guitarist who did not play on the LP. By the mid-1960s, the California surf had risen.

Drag City

Many of the surfer groups glorified another aspect of the sprawling Southern California landscape: the automobile. By the early 1960s, a maze of highways connected the inhabitants of Southern California. "California," *Life* informed its readers in October 1962, "has 1,000 miles of freeways and blueprints for many more." The magazine described more than 850 miles of California expressways and 2,400 miles of multilane highways.

The tangle of roads forced most Californians to own at least one automobile. "In California, a car is like an extra, highly essential part of the human anatomy," explained *Life*, which estimated that the 8.5 million cars in the state, positioned bumper-to-bumper, would extend more than 27,000 miles. The magazine equated life in California without an automobile to "a fate roughly equal to decapitation."

The importance of cars in California led to a subculture that, as with the surf ethos, involved distinctive dress and language. Teenagers, mostly males, lusted for their first automobile. Rather than a staid family car, they cast their eyes upon "asphalt eaters" (dragsters) such as Cudas (Plymouth Barracudas) or GTOs (Grand Turismos), propelled by huge engines such as the "rat motor" (a 427-cubic-inch Chevy engine) or the Chrysler Hemi (a 426-cubic-inch engine equipped with hemispherical combustion chambers). Like cowboys on their horses, teens with greased hair and tight black pants drove their machines to seldom used roads and waited for a competitor to drag (race). They anticipated the flash of a light, "dropped the hammer" (released the clutch quickly), and sped away, "shutting down" (defeating) an opponent. By the end of the 1950s, the dragsters raced legally on such strips as the one at the Orange County Airport near Santa Ana. "Kids love dragging a car," gushed auto customizer Ed Roth.

The hot rod subculture was promoted through the press and on film. *Hot Rod* magazine, which became standard reading for car-crazed California youth, first rolled off the presses in 1947. Casting hot-rodders as juvenile delinquents on wheels, movies such as *Hot Rod Girl* (1956), *Dragstrip Riot* (1958), and *Teenage Thunder* (1959) further popularized drag racing among an element less clean-cut than the surfer crowd.

Roger Christian, a Los Angeles disc jockey who was tagged "Poet of the Strip," helped surfer bands such as the Beach Boys write songs about dragsters, even though die-hard surfers considered hot-rodders, or "ho-dads," as they called them, rivals. "Roger was a guiding light for me," revealed Brian Wilson of the Beach Boys. After Christian's late-night radio show, Brian and the disc jockey would "go over to Otto's, order a hot fudge sundae, and just … whew! talk and talk." He told *Life* in 1964 that "Roger is a real car nut. His normal speech is only 40 percent comprehensible. And he has a tremendous knack for rhyming things with *carburetor*." In early 1963, Christian and Brian Wilson first collaborated on "Shut Down," which backed "Surfin' U.S.A." and became nearly a Top Twenty hit. They continued their partnership with "Little Deuce Coupe," "Don't Worry Baby," and "Spirit of America," the last of which celebrated Craig Breedlove's three-wheeled, 7,800-pound jet car that broke land-speed records.

Roger Christian also composed songs for Jan and Dean. In 1963, at Jan's request, Christian and Brian Wilson wrote "Drag City" for the duo, which reached the Top Ten. The disc jockey penned most of the other songs on the album of the same name, including "Hot Stocker," "I Gotta Drive," "Schlock Rod," and "Dead Man's Curve."

The Christian-created "Dead Man's Curve" became eerily prophetic. On April 2, 1966 on his way to a meeting to establish his own record company, Jan Berry smashed his Corvette Stingray into a parked truck at 65 mph in Beverly Hills at a treacherous place in the road called Dead Man's Curve. He sustained major head injuries and took years to recover, derailing the careers of Jan and Dean and dealing a blow to the car-inspired song craze.

But in 1964 before the accident, several other bands had jumped on the car-craze bandwagon. The Rip Chords, a studio band formed by Bruce Johnston, a neighbor of Jan Berry and later a Beach Boy, scored with "Hey, Little Cobra." Gary Usher, who had helped pen some of the Beach Boys' early songs, formed the Hondells who covered the Beach Boys "Little Honda" to extol the virtues of Honda motor bikes, which during the early 1960s became popular in Southern California. The Nashville-based Ronny and the Daytonas hit with "G.T.O." Dick Dale and the Del-Tones checked in with the album *Mr. Eliminator*; Jerry Kole and the Stokers released the album *Hot Rod Alley*; the Hot Rodders cut "Big Hot Rod"; and the T-Bones released *Boss Drag at Hot Rod Beach*. Even artist Ed "Big Daddy" Roth who provided the car culture with such graphic art images as Rat Fink, recorded an LP, *Rods and Ratfinks*, under the name Mr. Gasser and the Weirdos. In November 1964, *Life* noted the proliferation of "love songs to the carburetor."

By 1964, jangling harmonies celebrated and enhanced the California myth. "I think we had a lot to do with the population rush to California," asserted Beach Boy Al Jardine. "People hearing the Beach Boys' songs envisioned California as sort of a golden paradise where all you did was surf and sun yourself while gorgeous blondes rubbed coconut oil on your back." Dean Torrence also tied his music to the California dream. "We sang about California and being young," he explained. However, as the Beach Boys and Jan and Dean promoted surf boards and hot rods, folk singers in New York City such as Bob Dylan sang about another America, where African Americans protested and died for their civil rights.

Chapter 6
The New Frontier of Folk

"There's other things in this world besides love and sex that're important."

—Bob Dylan

Early on a Saturday night in April 1961, a 20-year-old singer carrying an oversized guitar case walked into a dimly lit folk club, Gerde's Folk City, in Greenwich Village, New York City. He was dressed casually: worn brown shoes, blue jeans, and a black wool jacket covering a plain yellow turtleneck sweater. A jumble of rumpled hair crowned his head, which was topped by a black corduroy Huck Finn cap. He pressed his lips together tightly and glanced at the tables of patrons, who sipped espresso and seemed to be arguing feverishly about current events. The singer looked serious and exhibited a nervousness that a friend had earlier tried to calm with four jiggers of Jim Beam bourbon. He slowly mounted the stage, opened his guitar case, and carefully took out an old, nicked, six-string acoustic guitar, which he treated like an old friend. He fixed a wire harmonica holder around his neck and pushed a harmonica into place. As the singer stood alone on stage, motionless, a hush descended upon the coffeehouse.

The audience, mostly white middle-class college students, many of them attending nearby New York University, politely applauded the singer. For a moment, the scene appeared to epitomize Eisenhower gentility and McCarthy repression: boys with closely cropped hair, button-down shirts, corduroy slacks, Hush Puppy shoes, and cardigans; and rosy-cheeked girls dressed in long skirts, bulky knit sweaters, and low-heeled shoes, who favored long, straight, well-groomed hair.

The singer shattered the genteel atmosphere when he began to strum a chord and sing. He was young Bob Dylan, who had just recently arrived in New York City to sing songs of social protest. As civil rights marchers protested in Birmingham and as President John F. Kennedy announced plans for a new frontier, many college-age youths heard the stirring message of Bob Dylan, who leveled his guitar at racism and the hypocrisy of corporate America. Growing older, the first baby boomers were starting to become aware of the world around them.

Songs of Protest

The foundation for the 1960s' protest music was laid at the turn of the century by the International Workers of the World (IWW). Members of the group, known as Wobblies, first penned protest songs in the United States as part of their drive to achieve equality for American workers. While marching in demonstrations, the radical unionists sang from the *Little Red Songbook*, first published in 1909 and compiled by organizers Ralph Chaplin and Joe Hill (b. Joel Emmanuel Hägglund), the last a Swedish immigrant who six years later was executed in Utah for his political beliefs. The Wobblies adopted as their anthem Chaplin's "Solidarity Forever," a protest song set to the music of the

"Battle Hymn of the Republic." During the Red Scare that followed World War I when federal and state authorities raided and closed IWW offices, the union and its protest songs declined and by the mid-1920s faded from the limelight.

Woody Guthrie continued the IWW's legacy of the protest song. Born on July 14, 1912, to a poor family in Okemah, Oklahoma, Woodrow Wilson Guthrie left home at age 16 and drifted through the Southwest during his teens, working as a newsboy, sign painter, and farm laborer. While visiting his uncle, Jeff Guthrie, in Pampa, Texas, in 1929, the young Woody learned to play guitar. The youth performed on street corners and continued to work odd jobs until 1937, when he became a performer and the host for a program on Los Angeles radio station KFVD, on which he read radical newspapers over the air. Within two more years, he moved to New York City and began writing a daily column for the Communist party's newspapers *People's Daily World* and the *Daily Worker*. In 1940, Guthrie recorded for folklorist Alan Lomax, who taped the singer for the Library of Congress.

After a two-year stint in the merchant marine and the army during World War II, Guthrie returned to New York City, where he penned many of his 1000 songs, including "This Land Is Your Land," "Tom Joad," "Billy the Kid," and "Pastures of Plenty." "I don't sing any songs about the nine divorces of some millionaire play gal or the ten wives of some screwball," he later explained. "I sing the songs of the people that do all of the little jobs and the mean and dirty hard work in the world and of their wants and their hopes and their plans for a decent life." The motto emblazoned on his guitar summed up his message: "This Machine Kills Fascists."

Pete Seeger joined Woody Guthrie, roaming the countryside to sing songs to and about the American worker. Born on May 3, 1919, in New York City to a musical family, Seeger quit Harvard University during the late 1930s and worked with folklorist Alan Lomax at the Library of Congress. In late 1940, he founded the Almanac Singers with Guthrie, Lee Hays, and Millard Lampell who vowed to promote peace through their songs. Two years later after the Federal Bureau of Investigation hounded them, the group disbanded and Seeger entered the military to serve in World War II. On December 31, 1945 upon the end of the war, Seeger co-established People's Songs, a quarterly song-publishing newsletter, and booking agency, which attracted 3000 left-leaning members. In November 1948 the politically energized singer/songwriter formed the Weavers with Lee Hays, Ronnie Gilbert, and Fred Hellerman, who found work at the Village Vanguard and popularized folk songs such as "On Top of Old Smokey,"

Pete Seeger at a union event, 1944.

Library of Congress Prints and Photographs Division [LC-USW3-040956-D].

Leadbelly's "Good Night Irene," Guthrie's "So Long, It's Been Good to Know You," and "The Hammer Song" written by Seeger and Hays. "Like the Almanac Singers," recalled Seeger, "the Weavers also hoped to sing for peace and civil rights." Gilbert added about the Weavers, "We were four very politically motivated people interested in doing what we could for the music we loved and for social action."

The McCarthyite witch hunt derailed protest singers such as Seeger and the Weavers. In early 1950, pro-business Republican Senator Joe McCarthy from Wisconsin fanned the flames of anti-Communist paranoia by claiming without evidence that he possessed a list of 205 current members of the State Department who had membership in the Communist Party. *Washington Post* cartoonist Herbert Block coined the term McCarthyism for the Senator's bombastic, baseless insinuations and allegations.

Though rebuked by a special Congressional committee that dismissed McCarthy's charges, the Wisconsin Senator continued his scare tactics, which manufactured fear and foreboding in America. Later in 1950, McCarthy attacked a mysterious "Mr. X" with no evidence. The next year, he assailed George Marshall, the Army Chief of Staff during World War II and then Secretary of Defense and Dean Acheson, Secretary of State, describing a "conspiracy so immense, an infamy so black, as to dwarf any in the previous history of man." Five months later, he memorialized his vitriolic outburst in book form, *America's Retreat from Victory*. In January 1952, he blasted *Time* magazine for an article that it had printed about him and threatened to induce advertisers to pull their marketing dollars from the publication.

The Wisconsin senator and his adherents criticized liberal entertainers such as Woody Guthrie and Pete Seeger, who were blackballed by television and radio networks and the recording industry. By 1952, the Weavers had scaled the chart with several hits and had been offered a national half-hour television program, sponsored by Van Camp's Pork and Beans. Amid the McCarthy fever and an article from the right-wing press about the Communist tendencies of the Weavers, Van Camp pulled its sponsorship. "The jobs started vanishing, and pretty soon we were down to singing at Daffy's Bar and Grill on the outskirts of Cleveland," explained a bitter Pete Seeger. Though the destructive effects of McCarthyism abated for the Weavers by December 1955, when they triumphantly performed at Carnegie Hall, the group never regained its pre-McCarthyite popularity until the early 1960s' folk revival.

The Folk Revival

Folk music reappeared, when the number of college students increased. In 1954, 2.4 million students attended college across the country. In 1961, more than 4 million studied within the ivy halls, an increase of nearly 70 percent.

These college-age youths searched for an alternative to the popular, romanticized hit singles of Don Kirshner's songwriters who composed for the young teen market. "Today," observed *Look* in early 1961, "the fifteen- to twenty-year-olds, especially those in college, are showing their musical curiosity in ways that don't appear on single-record popularity charts." Two years later, the magazine reported that college students were "weary of the more and more juvenile level of 'pop' music, frustrated by the dearth of good Broadway show tunes, and slightly befuddled by the growing complexity of jazz, [and were] ready to turn solidly folknik."

The Kingston Trio started the folk revival. Formed in 1957 by three college students—Bob Shane, Nick Reynolds, and Dave Guard—the Trio scored a number-one hit in 1958 with "Tom Dooley," based on a version of the song by North Carolina banjo player Frank Proffitt. The threesome followed with a series of successful albums for Capitol Records, which in four years grossed $40 million, and they surpassed Frank Sinatra as Capitol's number-one moneymaker. By June 1960, *Time* called the "rockless, roll less and rich" trio the "hottest group in U.S. popular music."

The Kingston Trio projected a safe, corporate image. "They are 'sincere' without being 'serious,'" reported singer Will Holt about the Trio in 1961. "They are the kids who sing Saturday nights at fraternity house parties, and the audience gets the comfortable feeling that anyone can do it." Pictures in national magazines featuring the well-groomed, well-dressed Trio at poolside with their wives further promoted the image of stability.

The wholesome Trio profited from their success. In 1962, the threesome averaged $10,000 per concert in a large hall, earned nearly $300,000 in record sales, and grossed $1.7 million in total earnings. The group established Kingston Trio Inc., a ten-company investment firm that owned an office building in San Francisco, a land-development concern, a restaurant, a concert-promotion agency, and a group of music publishing companies. "When we fight nowadays," one of the Kingston Trio told *Time* in 1960, "it's mostly about business—what to invest in."

The commercial success of the Kingston Trio encouraged other apolitical, clean-cut folkies to form singing groups. In July 1959, 36-year-old Lou Gottlieb, an arranger for the Kingston Trio who had earned a Ph.D. in musicology from the University of California, Berkeley, Alex Hassilev, an actor and a University of Chicago graduate, and 39-year-old Glenn Yarbrough began to sing as the Limeliters. Within a year, the group commanded $4,000 a week for their performances and recorded their debut. In 1961, they hit the Top Five with their *Tonight: In Person*. "If the button-down, scrubbed-looking, youthful Kingston Trio are the undergraduates of big-time U.S. folksinging," *Time* reported in June 1961, "the Limeliters are the faculty."

As the Limeliters scaled the chart with their debut, ten folksters banded together into the blatantly commercial New Christy Minstrels, named after the mid-nineteenth-century, blackface minstrel troupe. "When I chose our people," explained founder Randy Sparks, "I made it a point to shy away from questionable people. I looked for the all-American boy or girl who had no political complaints and no sexual problems anyone would be interested in." The "sporty, clean New Christy Minstrels," reported *Time*, offered "a bland mix of broad harmonies, familiar tunes, corny humor and just enough of the folk music spirit to cash in on the most avid adult record buyer." The group sold over 100,000 copies of its first album, the 1962 Top-Ten *Presenting The New Christy Minstrels* (aka *Exciting New Folk Chorus*), and the next year hit with two more Top-Ten albums. In 1964, Sparks sold his interest in the group for $2.5 million.

By the early 1960s, folk music had become a craze. Coffeehouses were opened in most major cities. Boston folkies frequented Club 47; in Chicago folk played at the Gate of Horn owned by Albert Grossman; in Los Angeles folk dominated the Unicorn and McCabe's. In New York, the epicenter of the folk revival, such coffeehouses as the Bitter End, the Café Wha? and Gerde's Folk City entertained folksters, and Izzy Young opened the Folklore Center in Greenwich Village to provide records, books, music and a gathering place to the folk crowd.

Becoming more visible, folk music developed into a commercial enterprise. College-age folk fans, having more money than young teens, abandoned 45-rpm hit singles for long-playing albums (LPs) of their favorite groups that helped double sales of LPs from 1956 to 1961. Beginning in early April 1963, 11 million folk fans watched *Hootenanny*, an ABC nationally broadcast, Saturday-night television show that each week took viewers to a folk concert on a different campus. They bought hootenanny sweat shirts, played hootenanny pinball games, read hootenanny magazines, and even watched the feature film *Hootenanny Hoot*. "Yesterday, it was the esoteric kick of history buffs and music scholars. Today, it's show biz," *Look* told its readers in 1963. "With a hoot and a holler, folk music has taken over from coffeehouse to campus to prime-time television."

The commercial folk boom ironically led to the rediscovery of traditional folk. "Commercialization has actually helped folk music," claimed Pete Seeger in 1963. "It revived interest in it in the cities, where it had almost died. Country interest never really stopped. Now, there are kids all over the nation plinking their banjos, and folk music is a living, vibrant thing again." College-age youths began to listen to Seeger, the re-formed Weavers, the spiritual, operatic singing of Odetta, and Jean Ritchie, who sang Appalachian folk ballads to her own accompaniment on the dulcimer. In search of folk authenticity, some record collectors searched for and rediscovered pre-World War II acoustic blues players such as Mississippi John Hurt who had disappeared into obscurity. Blues fanatic Tom Hoskins found Mississippi John Hurt by tracking him down in Avalon, Mississippi, from the title of Hurt's "Avalon Blues." "Before 1963, the idea that bluesmen we listened to on old records might still be alive somewhere really hadn't occurred to us," recalled record collector Phil Spiro. "That all changed when Tom Hoskins rediscovered Mississippi John Hurt." Once resurrected, Hurt released a series of albums on the folk-based Vanguard label, re-recording some of his originals from 1928.

Once Hurt re-emerged, blues fans frantically unearthed other vintage acoustic blues men. Blues aficionados Ed Denson and John Fahey found Booker "Bukka" White, prominent in the 1930s, by offering him a recording contract on Fahey's Takoma Records. Folk singer/songwriter Eric Von Schmidt and collectors Nick Perls, Phil Spiro, and Dick Waterman located Eddie "Son" House who in 1964 again started to record his hard-edged brand of Mississippi Delta blues. Fahey, Bill Barth, and Henry Vestine, later a member of Canned Heat, uncovered Nehemiah "Skip" James who in 1931 had delivered for Paramount Records a unique and eerie blues style from the Delta. Blues enthusiasts Dick and Louisa Spottswood found the Reverend Robert Wilkins who had recorded during the twenties and thirties before turning to the ministry. By 1964, Delta blues musicians had been lionized as the originators of the blues and mainstays authentic American folk music. Even electric bluesmen such as Muddy Waters and Howling Wolf each released albums called *The Real Folk Blues* and *More Real Folk Blues* to keep pace with the folk-blues frenzy.

Sit-Ins, Freedom Rides, and Marches

The growing clamor of African Americans for civil rights coincided with and shaped the burgeoning folk music scene. On February 1, 1960, four African-American freshmen from the Agricultural and Technical College in Greensboro, North Carolina, entered a Woolworth's variety store, made several purchases, and ordered coffee at the lunch counter reserved for whites. Although refused service and told to leave, the students remained at the counter until the store closed. The next day, the four freshmen were joined by twenty other students. By the end of the week, nearly a thousand students, both African American and white, crowded around the lunch counter until Woolworth's closed its doors to business until further notice. This tactic of passive resistance, the sit-in, attracted national attention to the civil rights movement, which challenged segregation in privately owned facilities.

Protests soon ignited in other Southern cities. Within a week, students in neighboring Durham and Winston-Salem, North Carolina, "sat in" at lunch counters to demonstrate the need for equal treatment of blacks, a method employed as early as May 1942 by the Fellowship of Reconciliation (FOR) and the Congress of Racial Equality (CORE). Within another week, college students demanded equal treatment at lunch counters in more than fifteen cities in South Carolina, Virginia, and Florida.

Sit-ins occurred in Nashville, Tennessee, where activists had trained for the nonviolent strategy. In early February, 500 students marched into the local branches of three nationally based five-and-ten-cent stores, occupied the lunch counters, and returned each day. On February 27, violence erupted. While blacks occupied seats at the lunch counter in a Woolworth store, several young white toughs charged the counter and "started pulling and beating primarily the young women," recalled John Lewis, then a student at the American Baptist Theological Seminary in the city. "They put lighted cigarettes down their backs, in their hair, and they were really beating people." In a few minutes, the police arrived but arrested all the black protestors instead of the whites who had been the instigators. Not deterred, the college students returned to the lunch counter after authorities released them. Within a few weeks, downtown Nashville looked deserted. Fearing violence, whites refused to travel to the downtown area. Blacks supported the college students by boycotting businesses. On May 10, 1960, after nearly three months of sit-ins, six Nashville lunch counters began to serve black patrons.

By May 1960, sit-ins had become a national phenomenon. In seventy-eight cities throughout the South, the tactic disrupted the business of downtown stores. More than fifty thousand demonstrators, mostly black, entered stores and remained in their seats to demand equality. Of the nonviolent protesters, two thousand had been dragged to jail by authorities.

In 1961, civil rights demonstrators employed another tactic, the freedom ride. In 1946, the Supreme Court banned segregation on buses and trains engaged in interstate travel, and fourteen years later applied its ruling to bus and train terminals. Caught during a snow storm on their way to New York City, Gordon Carey and Tom Gaither, two field secretaries for CORE, decided to test the law banning segregation in terminals. They devised a bus trip to New Orleans with stops in Southern bus terminals to challenge Southern racism in those facilities.

The two friends pitched their idea to CORE director James Farmer, who supported the notion of a nonviolent "interracial group ride throughout the South." "The whites in the group would sit in the back of the bus, and the blacks would sit in the front of the bus, and would refuse to move when ordered," explained Farmer. At every rest stop, the whites would enter the waiting room for blacks, and the blacks would occupy the waiting room for whites, refusing to leave. CORE hoped to antagonize Southern racists and thereby "create a crisis" to compel the federal government to enforce the law, which Southern bigots violated on a daily basis. "We figured that the government would have to respond if we created a situation that was headline news all over the world," disclosed Farmer.

On May 4, 1961, seven black and six white freedom riders of various ages boarded buses in Washington, D.C. They intended to ride through Atlanta, then Alabama, and Mississippi and on May 17 arrive in New Orleans.

The white segregationists created the crisis that Farmer had envisioned. White racists brutally attacked the riders in Anniston, and Montgomery, Alabama. "I was hit with a sort of crate thing that holds soda bottles—and left lying unconscious there, in the streets of Montgomery," recalled rider John Lewis. When arriving in the segregated bus terminal in Jackson, Mississippi, more than 300 freedom riders, mostly college students, ministers, and professors, were arrested and jailed. Though the freedom riders never reached their New Orleans destination, they attracted the attention of the nation and forced the intervention of federal troops two weeks before a Kennedy–Krushchev summit in Vienna.

In 1963, the demand for civil rights among African Americans escalated in Birmingham, Alabama. On April 3, protesters, marched in the downtown area to desegregate stores and end discriminatory hiring, led by Martin Luther King, Jr. and Reverend Fred Shuttlesworth, the head of the Birmingham chapter of the Southern Christian Leadership Conference (SCLC). The demonstrators slowly increased in numbers, reaching more than 3000 in a month. On May 2, Theophilus "Bull" Conner, the head of the fire department as well as the police, arrested 500 marchers, most of them school children. The next afternoon, another 900 students, chanting "Freedom! Freedom! Freedom!" and singing "We Shall Overcome," were assaulted by Connor's men, who unleashed dogs, wielded electric cattle prods, and used fire hoses to disperse them. "They're rolling that little girl there, right in the middle of the street," screamed David Vann, a white attorney who sympathized with the protesters. On May 4, another one thousand marchers appeared, and Connor continued to pummel them with fire hoses. Within two more days, Bull had jailed two thousand high-school marchers. The appalled editors of the *New York Times* editorialized that "no American schooled in respect for human dignity can read without shame the barbarities committed by Alabama police authorities against Negro and white demonstrators for civil rights."

A week later, when racists bombed the house of a demonstrator and an African-American–owned motel, 2500 African Americans spilled out into the streets and overturned automobiles, and burned six small stores and an apartment building. They confronted police and pelted them with bricks and bottles. By May 12, when the violence ended, Birmingham officials had agreed to desegregate many of the downtown public facilities, to hire and promote African Americans in local businesses, and to establish a permanent biracial committee to deal with future problems. The riot in Birmingham quickly spread to other cities such as Tallahassee, Nashville, New York, and Cambridge, Maryland.

More racist-inspired violence erupted in June. That month, racists in Jackson, Mississippi, ambushed and killed Medgar Evers, the Mississippi field secretary of the National Association for the Advancement of Colored People (NAACP), near his home. Police in Danville, Virginia, arrested 347 protesters and injured forty others, when they turned fire hoses on the crowd. Racists shot and killed white civil rights crusader William Moore, who was walking near Attalla, Alabama, with a sign demanding equal rights. White supremacists pelted 10 "freedom walkers" with rocks and eggs as they attempted to continue Moore's march. By early July 1963, authorities had arrested almost 15,000 civil rights advocates, who participated in 758 demonstrations in 186 cities.

On August 28, 1963, 250,000 white and African-American civil rights partisans converged on Washington, D.C., a march conceived by A. Philip Randolph, who had envisioned the event as early as 1941. "Black people voted with their feet," civil rights leader Bayard Rustin recollected. "They came from every state, they came in jalopies, on trains, buses, anything they could get—some walked." They proceeded to the steps of the Lincoln Memorial and listened to ten civil rights leaders, including the rousing "I Have a Dream Speech" by Martin Luther King, Jr. Both the NBC and ABC television networks paused their normal programming to broadcast King's moving speech.

Civil rights march on Washington, D.C., August 1963. Photo by Rowland Scherman.

Library of Congress Prints and Photographs Division.

Kennedy and the New Frontier of Racial Equality

President John F. Kennedy, elected in 1960 and a passive supporter of the March on Washington, offered civil rights crusaders hope that King's dream could become reality. The young, energetic Kennedy assured the nation that the United States was approaching a "new frontier." In his inaugural speech, the president specifically focused on "human rights to which this nation has always been committed."

Kennedy acted on his promise to provide equal rights to blacks. On September 20, 1962, as part of an ongoing effort to desegregate public schools, Kennedy sent federal troops to the University of Mississippi in Oxford, at which James Meredith, an African-American Air Force veteran, attempted to enroll. When resisted by state troops mobilized by the governor to bar Meredith from the university, Kennedy federalized the Mississippi National Guard and on national television appealed to the students at the university to accept desegregation. After a racist-inspired riot left two dead, the president ordered a guard of U.S. marshals to protect Meredith, who began to attend classes.

In June 1963, the president sent federal troops to the University of Alabama to safeguard two new African-American enrollees, Vivian Malone and James Hood. He ordered federal marshals to dislodge Alabama Governor George Wallace, who physically positioned himself in the front doorway of a university building and denounced "this illegal and unwarranted action of the Central Government." In a televised broadcast after the Wallace incident, Kennedy told the nation that the civil rights question was "a moral issue ... as old as the Scriptures and ... as clear as the American Constitution." He committed his administration to the proposition "that race has no place in American life or law."

Kennedy took further action the same year. The protests for civil rights, he declared, "have so increased the cries for equality that no city or state or legislative body can prudently choose to ignore them." The president proposed wide-reaching civil rights legislation to guarantee equal access to all public facilities, to attack employment discrimination based on race, and to empower the attorney general to file suit on behalf of individuals whose civil rights had been violated.

Many college students pledged their energies to the new frontier of racial equality. They perceived Kennedy, the youngest elected president in U.S. history, as an energetic visionary who stood in sharp contrast to the grandfatherly Dwight Eisenhower. College-age youth felt an affinity to the Harvard-educated president, who surrounded himself with academics such as Harvard professor Arthur Schlesinger, Jr., and in his inaugural address, told a national audience that "the torch has been passed to a new generation of Americans."

College students devoted themselves to Kennedy's program for civil rights. "This generation of college students has begun to react against being treated like adolescents," reasoned a writer in a 1961 issue of *The New Republic*. "They have been willing to associate themselves with nonconformist movements, despite warnings by parents and teachers that such activities will endanger their personal as well as their job security." Driven by a Kennedy-inspired idealism, college students became freedom riders, marched for desegregation, and gathered in Washington, D.C., to demand equality.

Student civil rights activism led to one of the first major campus protests, the free speech movement. As they returned to school on October 1, 1964, students at the University of California at Berkeley discovered that tables, which previously had been reserved for the distribution of political leaflets, had been banned on the Bancroft Strip at the Telegraph Avenue entrance to the campus. "We knew at the time that it was aimed at the civil rights movement and at progressive organizations and at those of us interested in the peace movement and civil rights," recalled Jackie Goldberg, who

Attorney General Robert Kennedy at a civil rights rally, June 1963.

The Daily of the University of Washington.

participated in the subsequent protests. When authorities arrested CORE activist Jack Weinberg, who ignored the new policy and coined the phrase "Don't trust anyone over thirty," the Berkeley students began a three-month protest. Sparked by Mario Savio, who had participated in civil rights activities in Mississippi and headed the Campus Friends of SNCC, the students occupied campus buildings and eventually found faculty support for their free speech demands. "Last summer I went to Mississippi to join the struggle there for civil rights," Savio shouted to his fellow students during one demonstration. "This fall I am engaged in another phase of the same struggle, this time in Berkeley. The two battlefields seem quite different to some observers, but this is not the case." Students at Berkeley identified their protest with the struggle for African-American civil rights.

College students fueled the growing market for folk music dealing with social issues. "Students that support 'causes' support folk music," *Newsweek* reported as early as 1961. "Find a campus that breeds Freedom Riders, anti-Birth demonstrators and anti-[nuclear] bomb societies, and you'll find a folk group." "The connection," the magazine instructed, "is not fortuitous."

Bob Dylan: The Music of Protest

The demand for civil rights on college campuses and the folk music revival led to the mercurial rise of Bob Dylan and his brand of protest folk music. Born on May 24, 1941, to the owner of a hardware store in Hibbing, Minnesota, Robert Allen Zimmerman grew up near the Mesabi copper range. Being Jewish in an area with few Jews, Dylan felt isolated. As Dylan's high school girlfriend later confided: "The other kids, they wanted to throw stones at anybody different. And Bob was different. He felt he didn't fit in, not in Hibbing." Dylan told a reporter from *The Saturday Evening Post*, "I see things that other people don't see. I feel things that other people don't feel. It's terrible. They laugh. I felt like that my whole life. … I don't even know if I'm normal."

To cope with the isolation, Dylan turned to music. He first listened to country star Hank Williams. As with thousands of other youths at the time, Dylan sat transfixed near his radio and tuned into late night programs, which featured Muddy Waters, John Lee Hooker, Jimmy Reed, and Howlin' Wolf. "I used to stay up until two, three o'clock in the morning," he confided.

A fan of both country and the electric blues, Dylan almost naturally embraced the new music of rock and roll. When the film *Rock Around the Clock* showed in Hibbing, Dylan shouted to a friend outside of the theater, "Hey, that's our music! That's written for us." He began to idolize Little Richard and then Elvis Presley and Buddy By his freshman year in high school, Dylan formed several bands including the Golden Chords, which played rock and roll at local functions.

Dylan turned to folk music when it reached the Midwest. "I heard a record—the Kingston Trio or Odetta or someone like that," he remembered, "and I sort of got into folk music. … I traded my stuff for a Martin [acoustic guitar]." In 1959, he began to perform traditional folk and bluegrass in coffeehouses around the University of Minnesota under the name Dillon and then Dylan.

Bob Dylan encountered his most important early influence while in Minneapolis. As he told it, "I heard Woody Guthrie. And when I heard Woody Guthrie, that was it, it was all over." Dylan searched for and bought any Guthrie album he could find. "Woody was my god," he revealed. In December 1960, Dylan traveled from Minnesota to New York City to visit the dying Guthrie at a state hospital in nearby New Jersey. Dylan's first album, recorded in October 1961 for $402, included a song dedicated to Woody.

In Greenwich Village, at clubs such as Gerde's Folk City, the Gaslight Coffeehouse, and the Village Gate, Dylan sang his own songs of social protest. Remembered Terri Thal, Dylan's first manager and married at the time to folk-blues guitarist Dave Van Ronk: "He was beginning to think about and talk about people who were being trod upon [by 1961]. Not in any class way, but he hated people who were taking people." Some observers suggested that Dylan's girlfriend influenced him. Suze Rotolo, Dylan's then-girlfriend who was pictured on a windswept New York street with Dylan on the *Freewheelin'* cover, worked as a secretary for the civil rights group CORE. She likely caused Dylan to write 'The Ballad of Emmett Till,' a song about the brutal murder of a 14-year-old African American from Chicago, who in August 1955 traveled to Money, Mississippi, to visit relatives. As one observer in the Village mentioned, "Suze came along and she wanted him to go Pete Seeger's way. She wanted Bobby to be involved in civil rights and all the radical causes Seeger was involved in." By 1962, Dylan had become friends with civil rights activists such as James Forman, Bernice Johnson, and Cordell Reagon of the Student Non-Violent Coordinating Committee and began publishing his songs in *Broadside*, a mimeographed newsletter printed by folksters Agnes Cunningham and Gordon Friesen, to encourage young folk singers to compose topical songs.

Composing songs about current social issues, rather than singing traditional or commercialized folk, Dylan politicized the 1960s' folk music scene with his second album, *The Freewheelin' Bob Dylan*. The album, released in May 1963, featured "Blowin' in the Wind," a song based on the melody of an old spiritual that became an anthem for the civil rights movement. "The idea came to me," Dylan said, "that all of us in America who didn't speak out were betrayed by our silence." Dylan told of the ordeal of James Meredith at the University of Mississippi in "Oxford Town" and composed "Hard Rain's A-Gonna Fall" about the Cuban missile crisis, which occurred in

October 1962, when the United States threatened nuclear warfare if Russia did not remove its missiles from Cuba. He penned "Talkin' World War Three Blues," a humorous but somber picture of life after a nuclear holocaust and blasted government leaders in the vitriolic "Masters of War." At the time, the singer felt that "there's other things in this world besides love and sex that're important, too. People shouldn't turn their backs on them just because they ain't pretty to look at."

Dylan continued to pen protest songs for his next album, *The Times They Are A-Changin'*, released in January 1964 and hitting the Top Twenty. The title song became a battle cry of the emerging social revolution. He wrote about the murder of civil rights leader Medgar Evers in "Only a Pawn in Their Game." Dylan chronicled the sobering realities of African Americans in "The Lonesome Death of Hattie Carroll," based on the 1963 killing of a middle-aged African-American barmaid by a white Maryland tobacco farmer who received a sentence of only six months in prison and a $500 fine for the murder.

Dylan reinforced his politicized music through a number of public actions. On May 12, 1963, he refused to perform on *The Ed Sullivan Show* when CBS censors banned him from singing "Talkin' John Birch Society Blues." On July 6, he gave a concert outside Greenwood, Mississippi, with Pete Seeger to promote African-American voter registration initiated by the Student Non-Violent Coordinating Committee. Later in the month, he appeared on a local New York television program dealing with "freedom singers." On August 28, Dylan performed at the March on Washington, D.C.

Bob Dylan began to serve as the focal point for the community of protest singers. On September 29, 1961, Robert Shelton of the *New York Times* covered a Dylan concert at Gerde's and characterized him as "a bright new face in folk music" who seemed to be going "straight up." In 1962, *Newsweek* tagged him "the newest rage" in folk music, and *Time* sarcastically mentioned that Bob Dylan delivered "his songs in a studied nasal that has just the right clothespin-on-the-nose honesty to appeal to those who most deeply care." The next year, the sales wing of Columbia Records promoted Dylan as a "rebel with a cause."

In 1963, Bob Dylan attracted a national audience with the assistance of two music entrepreneurs, Albert Grossman and John Hammond. In 1957, Grossman opened one of the first folk clubs, the Gate of Horn, in Chicago; two years later, he collaborated with George Wein to launch the first Newport Folk Festival. In 1960, Grossman met politically minded folk singer Peter Yarrow, whom he signed to a management contract. Grossman introduced Yarrow to one-time Broadway singer Mary Travers and

Bob Dylan and Joan Baez at the March on Washington, August 1963.

Library of Congress Prints and Photographs Division.

stand-up comic Noel Paul Stookey, who began to perform as Peter, Paul, and Mary. "It was Albert's idea to make a group, and it was Albert's suggestion that it contain a comedian, a very strong energetic woman's voice—ballsy is I guess the term that you might use—and that I would be the serious presenter onstage and the sensitive male lead singer," explained Yarrow. "Albert Grossman," added Stookey, "had a vision of a more accessible form of folk entertainment."

The folk trio, propelled by Grossman's vision, hit the charts. In April 1962, they scored with "Lemon Tree" and six months later cracked the Top Ten with Pete Seeger's and Lee Hays's "If I Had a Hammer (1949)," an anti-right-wing song, which brought folk protest to a national audience. The group's debut album, which included both hits, topped the album chart in late October and would eventually sell 2 million copies. The next year, the trio reached number two on the singles chart with Dylan's "Blowin' in the Wind," which had been given to them by their manager, who had signed Dylan in June 1962. They quickly followed with "Don't Think Twice, It's Alright," another Dylan composition. "It was Bobby Dylan's writing that put us on another level," confessed Peter Yarrow.

Dylan soon captured the national spotlight. In addition to Peter, Paul and Mary's successful renditions of his songs, in October 1961 Dylan snagged a deal with Columbia Records, masterminded by John Hammond who had discovered Count Basie. "I was just waiting for somebody with a message for kids when I met Bob," the politically minded record producer explained. In March 1962, he released his first album with little fanfare. On May 27 the next year, he offered the politically potent *The Freewheelin' Bob Dylan*, which neared the Top Twenty and started to gain a following outside the small circle of folk enthusiasts.

The singer/songwriter solidified his national reputation with his appearance at the Newport Folk Festival. The festival had been engineered by Albert Grossman, jazz entrepreneur/pianist George Wein and jazz promoter Eddie Sarkesian. On July 26, 1963, in front of 47,000 eager folkies, Dylan sang his protest anthems such as the antiwar "With God on Our Side" and "A Hard Rain's Gonna Fall." He capped an evening performance with "Blowin' in the Wind" and the civil-rights paean "We Shall Overcome" to a roused, standing audience. By the end of the year, Bob Dylan symbolized protest music and the yearning for change. To Joan Baez, herself active in the protest movement, "Bobby Dylan says what a lot of people my age feel but cannot say."

Joan Baez

Joan Baez was Bob Dylan's female counterpart in folk protest. The daughter of a Mexican-born physicist and a Scotch-Irish mother who taught English drama, the dark-skinned Baez faced racial discrimination at an early age. As a girl in Clarence Center, New York, a town of 800 people, she felt that "as far as the [townspeople] knew we were niggers" [Quotation reproduced exactly from the original source].

Baez moved with her family to Boston, where, during the late 1950s, she began to perform traditional folk songs in coffeehouses around Harvard, such as Club 47, the Ballard Room, and Tulla's Coffee Grinder. In 1959, Baez debuted to 13,000 people at the first Newport Folk Festival. "A star was born," wrote Robert Shelton in *The New York Times* after the performance, "a young soprano with a thrilling lush vibrato and fervid and well-controlled projection." Baez continued to attract a following, selling out a Carnegie Hall performance two months in advance. From 1960 to 1963, she recorded four albums, all of which either neared or hit the Top Ten. By 1962, *Time* referred to Joan "as the most gifted of the newcomers to the folk scene" and featured her on the cover of its November 23 issue.

The singer, though composing few of her own songs, took a decidedly political stance. She sang topical songs such as the antiwar "Last Night I Had the Strangest

Joan Baez at the March on Washington, August 1963.

Library of Congress Prints and Photographs Division.

Dream" and a parody of the House Un-American Activities Committee, which ceaselessly tracked supposed Communist sympathizers. The singer refused to appear on ABC's *Hootenanny* when the show blacklisted Pete Seeger, and rejected more than $100,000 in concert dates during a single year because, as she told *Time*, "folk music depends on intent. If someone desires to make money, I don't call it folk music." In 1963, Baez demonstrated in Birmingham for desegregation and in August marched on Washington, D.C. "I feel very strongly about things," Joan told *Look* in 1963. "Like murdering babies with fallout and murdering spirits with segregation."

The Singer-Activists

Other folk singers followed the path of protest. Texas-born Phil Ochs, the son of a Jewish army physician, studied journalism at Ohio State University, where he won his first guitar by betting on John Kennedy in the hotly contested 1960 presidential election. A year later, he composed his first song, "The Ballad of the Cuban Invasion," about the American invasion of Cuba at the Bay of Pigs, and joined a radical singing group called the Sundowners or, sometimes, the Singing Socialists, with roommate Jim Glover, who later became half of the pop duo Jim and Jean. In 1962, Ochs dropped out of Ohio State and journeyed to New York City to start his folk-protest career in earnest, describing himself as a singing journalist. He performed at the 1963 Newport Folk Festival with the Freedom Singers, Dylan, Baez, and helped at Newport's songwriters' workshop. Ochs hoped to crystallize the thoughts of young people who "have stopped accepting things are they are."

Ochs, looking for a forum to propagate his radical ideals, churned out protest songs dealing with the issues of the day. His first album, *All the News That's Fit to Sing*, released by Elektra in April 1964, included "Too Many Martyrs," "Talkin' Cuban Crisis," and "Talkin' Vietnam." Subsequent albums delivered other protest hymns such as "Ballad of Oxford, Mississippi," "Draft Dodger Rag," and "I Ain't Marching Anymore."

Phil Ochs backed his words with action. In 1964, when he heard that the bodies of three murdered civil rights workers had been found buried under an earthen dam, he headed for Mississippi. Ochs later traveled to Hazard, Kentucky, to help striking miners, who were engaged in a bloody struggle with mine owners who were trying to bypass provisions of the Mine Safety Act. Phil's song "No Christmas in Kentucky" became a battle cry among the workers. When Phil and folk singer Tom Paxton played a benefit for the miners, members of the John Birch Society and the Fighting American Nationalists picketed the concert with placards that read "Agrarian Reformers Go Home."

Tom Paxton raised his voice in protest for other causes. Born in Chicago, a young Paxton traveled to Oklahoma with his family. At the University of Oklahoma, Paxton discovered the music of Woody Guthrie and, like Dylan, became radicalized. "Woody was fearless; he'd take on any issue that got him stirred up … and he became one of my greatest influences," explained the folk singer. After a stint in the army, in the early 1960s Paxton moved to New York City, where he started to write songs and perform at the Gaslight Café in Greenwich Village. In 1963, he appeared at the Newport Folk Festival, and Pete Seeger recorded a few of his songs, including "What Did You Learn in School Today." By 1964, Paxton landed a recording contract with the then folk label, Elektra Records, and offered a series of protest songs in *Ramblin' Boy*. The next year, he recorded one of his most political albums, *Ain't That News!*, which included "Lyndon Johnson Told the Nation," "Buy a Gun for Your Son," and the title song. Paxton explained about "Ain't That News": "When Negroes, disenfranchised for years, are lining up by the thousands to register to vote; when mass demonstrations and teach-ins protest this government's foreign policy," he wrote in the liner notes of the album, "that's news."

By 1964, the protest songs of Bob Dylan and others such as Tom Paxton climbed the charts, telling of racial injustice and the need for change. Their songs reverberated throughout the campus halls of the country, reaching college students who intently listened to their words and sometimes took action.

Dylan's Disenchantment

During late 1963, folk music started to change. On November 22, in Dallas, rifleman Lee Harvey Oswald shot and killed President John Kennedy, who was riding in a motorcade with his wife Jackie and Texas Governor John Connally and his wife. The assassination shocked and horrified the nation, which mourned a president who symbolized energy, action, and optimism.

Folk musicians felt especially disillusioned by the assassination. Phil Ochs sensed "a definite flowering-out of positive feelings when John Kennedy became president. The civil rights movement was giving off positive vibrations. There was a great feeling of reform, that things could be changed." When Kennedy died, Ochs felt that "it ruined the dream. November 22, 1963, was a mortal wound the country has not yet been able to recover from."

Bob Dylan experienced the same pain and confusion over Kennedy's death. As folk singer/songwriter Eric Andersen told it, "you can't separate Dylan from history in the sense of what was going down, the way he reacted to a chain of events. The first being Kennedy's death; I think that got him out of politics." The "force had lost out. And people were depressed," added Andersen.

In the wake of the Kennedy assassination, Dylan became somewhat disillusioned with political activism. "I agree with everything that's happening," he told writer Nat Hentoff over dinner in October 1964, "but I'm not part of no Movement." "Those [protest] records I already made," said Dylan, referring to his first three albums, "I'll stand behind them, but some of that was jumping on the scene to be heard and a lot of it was because I didn't see anybody else doing that kind of thing. … You know—be a spokesman." Dylan criticized Joan Baez for her involvement with the Institute for the Study of Nonviolence at Carmel, California, established to "root out violence in ourselves and in the world." By 1965, Dylan abruptly informed a *Time* reporter that "there's no message [in my songs]." "I've never written a political song," he continued. "Songs can't save the world. I've gone through all that. When you don't like something, you gotta learn to just not need that something."

In place of social protest, Dylan crafted complex, personal, and sometimes cryptic songs. "I have to make a new song out of what *I* know and out of what *I'm* feeling," he asserted. "I once wrote about Emmett Till in the first person, pretending that I was him. From now on, I want to write what's inside *me*." The aptly titled *Another Side of Bob Dylan*, recorded on June 9, 1964, featured such nonpolitical poetry as "Chimes of Freedom" and more pop-oriented tunes such as "All I Really Want to Do" and "It Ain't Me Babe." It explicitly repudiated the composer's folk protest in "My Back Pages." "I think it is very, very destructive music," complained Joan Baez about Dylan's new orientation. "I think he doesn't want to be responsible for anybody, including himself."

Dylan's next album, *Bringing It All Back Home*, released in early 1965, edged toward an electrified rock. On one side backed by the Chicago-based electric blues of the Paul Butterfield Blues Band, it highlighted bitter, dark songs such as "Subterranean Homesick Blues," "She Belongs to Me," and "Maggie's Farm." The acoustic flip side included "Mr. Tambourine Man," "Gates of Eden," and "It's All Right, Ma (I'm Only Bleeding)."

On July 25, 1965, at the Newport Folk Festival, Dylan unveiled his new electric sound and brand of songwriting to the folk community. Behind the stage, some of the folk performers tried to prevent Dylan from playing his electric music with the Paul Butterfield Blues Band. "On one side you had Pete Seeger, [concert organizer] George Wein, the old guard," remembered Paul Rothchild, who mixed the Dylan set and had recently recorded the Butterfield band. "Pete is backstage, pacifist Pete, with an ax saying, 'I'm going to cut the fucking cables if that act goes onstage.'" Eventually, Seeger dashed to his "car and rolled up the windows, his hands over his ears." When Dylan unleashed the electrified "Maggie's Farm," recalled Elektra Records owner Jac Holzman, "suddenly we heard booing, like pockets of wartime flak." Irwin Silber, editor of the radical folk magazine *Sing Out!*, lamented "I wouldn't mind so much if he sang just one song about the war." Peter Yarrow later related, "People were just horrified. It was as if it was a capitulation to the enemy—as if all of a sudden you saw Martin Luther King, Jr. doing a cigarette ad."

Dylan, angry and shaken, stormed off the stage. Encouraged backstage by Johnny Cash and prodded from onstage by Peter Yarrow, he returned a few minutes later, alone. Dylan asked for a D harmonica from the crowd, which soon carpeted the stage with the instrument and hoped that the request signaled a victory for acoustic music. He sang "Mr. Tambourine Man" and "It's All Over Now, Baby Blue" and walked off the Newport stage for the last time. "To me, that night at Newport was as clear as crystal," explained Paul Rothchild. "It's the end of one era and the beginning of another." On August 30, Dylan released *Highway 61 Revisited*, which featured an all-out rock sound with the impressionistic, beat-inspired poetry of "Desolation Row," "Ballad of a Thin Man," and "Like a Rolling Stone."

Though ridiculed by folk purists, Dylan secured a national audience with the electric sound. He snagged the number-two spot with "Like a Rolling Stone," his first hit single. He also first hit the Top Ten with *Bringing It All Back Home* and neared the top of the chart with *Highway 61 Revisited*. In 1966, the singer again cracked the Top Ten with *Blonde on Blonde*, which made the transition complete from folk protest to an electrified poetry inspired by the Beatniks, and raised the bar for anyone who hoped to write rock lyrics. Dylan had become a commercial success with a sound that inspired a folk-rock boom.

Folk Rock

Folk music fundamentally changed into folk-rock for the masses. By 1965, bands took the introspective songs of an electrified Bob Dylan and combined them with the jangly sound of the British Invasion to create a new music. Following Dylan in his abandonment of the protest song for Beat-inspired, personal lyrics and influenced by the dizzying success of four lads from Liverpool, these groups combined two of the dominant trends of the early 1960s for an escapist music that the nation embraced following the assassination of President John F. Kennedy.

The Byrds led the folk-rock boom. In early 1964, Gene Clark sat in a bar in Norfolk, Virginia, and looked at the selections on the jukebox. In August of the previous year, he had been recruited by the folk group, the New Christy Minstrels, and was touring with them. Unsuspectingly, he chose the song "She Loves You" by a new group from Liverpool called the Beatles. "I might have played it 40 times in the two days the New Christy Minstrels were playing that town," he later enthused. "I knew, I *knew* that this was the future." After hearing the Fab Four, Clark quit the New Christy Minstrels and moved to Los Angeles where he went to the Troubadour folk club and met Roger McGuinn, another folkie who had been converted by the Beatles. Within months, the duo joined with bluegrass bassist Chris Hillman of the Hillmen, drummer Michael Clarke, and Troubadour regular and guitarist David Crosby in a band that they called the Byrds, intentionally misspelled to emulate the spelling error of the Beatles' moniker.

The Byrds combined their folk backgrounds, which had been rooted in Dylan, with the music of the Beatles. "I did feel that the real folk scene was in the Village," remembered Roger McGuinn. "But the Beatles came out and changed the whole game for me. I saw a definite niche, a place where the two of them blended together. If you took Lennon and Dylan and mixed them together, that was something that hadn't been done." McGuinn and his band grafted the bouncy, jangling harmonies of the mop-tops from Liverpool onto Dylanesque folk.

In 1965, the Byrds scaled the charts with their new sound. After obtaining a test pressing of Dylan's "Mr. Tambourine Man" from Dylan's producer Tom Wilson, the Byrds meteorically rose to the top of the chart with a version of the song that featured bouncy vocal harmonies and a ringing twelve-string Rickenbacker guitar. The group followed with electrified, harmony-rich versions of Dylan's "All I Really Want to Do," "Spanish Harlem Incident," "The Times They Are A-Changin'," and "Chimes of Freedom," as well as the chart-topper "Turn, Turn, Turn," a song adapted by Pete Seeger from the biblical Book of Ecclesiastes. "I changed the chord structure to be more like, kind of Beatley, and we changed the beat," intimated Roger McGuinn about "Turn, Turn, Turn." "We put a kick, that Phil Spector beat, to it."

Other groups adopted the folk rock formula of electrified renditions of Dylan songs sung in harmony with a Beatles beat. In 1965, the ebullient Turtles, a band that had switched from surf music to folk the year before, hit the Top Ten with "It Ain't Me Babe." The same year, a husband-wife team, Sonny and Cher, released the million-selling, Dylan-sounding "I Got You Babe." Cher (b. Cherilyn Sarkisian), a former backup singer for the Ronettes, scored a Top-Twenty solo hit with Dylan's "All I Really Want to Do." "What do we sing? We call it folk and roll—a sort of folk music with a rocking beat. But with a smile," gushed Sonny Bono to *Melody Maker*. "Ours is happy music—we haven't any message to impart."

Paul Simon and Art Garfunkel joined the folk-rock crowd. Two high school friends in Queens, New York, in 1957 the duo attracted notice as Tom and Jerry with "Hey! Schoolgirl" and appeared on *American Bandstand*. In 1964, after being influenced by the folk boom, they reemerged with a collegiate image and an album of soft harmonies, *Wednesday Morning, 3 a.m.* The album showcased Dylan's "The Times They Are A-Changin'" and Simon's composition, "The Sound of Silence," which in late 1965 became a number-one hit when Tom Wilson, Dylan's producer at the time, remixed the track by adding drums, percussion, and electric guitar.

Mimicking Dylan by wearing a denim cap and using a racked harmonica, Donovan Leitch of Scotland became the British answer to Dylan. In 1964, Donovan began performing folk music in clubs throughout the United Kingdom. The next year, he landed a spot on the British television show *Ready, Steady, Go!*, on which he appeared with a guitar that had the Woody Guthrie–inspired message: "This guitar kills." "I knew immediately that I would be to the European youth what Bob Dylan was to America, the European Bob Dylan," recalled Donovan. After appearing on the television show, Donovan hit the British singles chart with the acoustic "Catch the Wind," which bore an obvious resemblance to the Dylan title, "Blowin' in the Wind." Later in 1965, Donovan penned the antiwar "Universal Soldier," written by Native American Buffy Saint-Marie. After appearing at the 1965 Newport Folk Festival, Donovan turned to folk rock. He heard the Beatles sing "Love Me Do" and "knew in an instant that this is what I would do—merge the acoustic guitars with the pop music form." In 1966, amid the folk-rock craze, Donovan scored his first American success with the chart-topping "Sunshine Superman," which featured cryptic lyrics and a rock band. In three months, Donovan snagged the number-two slot with the equally impressionistic "Mellow Yellow," which featured vocal assistance from Beatle Paul McCartney.

The Lovin' Spoonful joined the folk rock legion. Formed in 1965 by John Sebastian, who had backed several folk groups in Greenwich Village including Dylan before forming the Spoonful, the band admitted its debt to Dylan. Sebastian insisted that Bob Dylan acted as "a force on our music, just like the 'Star Spangled Banner.' We all heard it." The group also attributed its music to the Beatles, delivering an upbeat electric sound similar to British invasion bands. They called their sound "good-time music." In August 1965, the Lovin' Spoonful hit the Top Ten with "Do You Believe in Magic?" The next year, they followed with several Top Ten tunes and their blockbuster "Summer in the City."

By the mid-1960s, the escapist Dylan-Beatles amalgam of folk rock had permeated popular music. In September 1965 alone, reported *Billboard*, various folk rockers had recorded snappy versions of forty-eight different Dylan songs, most of them concerned with topics other than protest. According to *Newsweek*, "healthy, cheap, moral or venal, folk rock is what's happening at this moment in the dissonant echo chamber of pop culture." As well as Dylan, the new sound owed its existence to four mop-topped lads from Liverpool who had just invaded America.

Chapter 7
The British Invasion of America: The Beatles

"We were just the spokesmen for a generation."

—Paul McCartney

On Friday, February 7, 1964, at Kennedy International Airport in New York City, a mass of screaming teenagers covered the rooftop on one of the airport wings. The crowd, mostly pubescent girls, had been waiting for more than eight hours in the cool and windy winter air. They considered themselves lucky: Only those with special passes had been permitted on the roof, patrolled by dozens of uniformed security police.

Inside the terminal, huddled around the gate that admitted incoming passengers from London, more than 9,000 teenage girls, adorned with bouffant hairdos, oversized jewelry, and their mothers' makeup, shoved, clawed, and pushed each other in a mad attempt to get to the arrival entrance. They were separated from their goal only by a thin white nylon rope and a few airport guards. As the minutes passed slowly and the intensity mounted, a WINS radio broadcast comforted the girls that the plane had left London at 6:30 A.M. Beatle time. Four of the passengers on Pan American flight 101 felt uneasy. "We did all feel a bit sick," remembered one. "Going to the States was a big step. People said just because we were popular in Britain, why should we be there?" asked another. A third worried about his hair. The fourth, the oldest and the leader of the group, sat silent and motionless in his seat.

As the plane neared its destination, a few wild screams from the airport crowd broke the tense silence. Then an entire chorus of cries from girls on the rooftop alerted the crowd inside of the group's arrival. In a few moments, the frenzied wails of pent-up teenage passion sent tremors throughout Kennedy International Airport, increasing at a deafening rate. The girls started to half chant, half sing, "We love you Beatles, oh yes we do."

The plane landed safely and reached the hangar. Scurrying attendants pushed a platform toward the jet, the door swung open, and passengers descended the steps. Employees of Capitol Records shoved Beatle kits complete with wigs, autographed photos, and a button with the message "I Like the Beatles" at them. At last, four young Englishmen, who sported button-down, Edwardian suits from French designer Pierre Cardin and mushroom-shaped haircuts, walked out. After almost 150 years, the British had again invaded the United States. This time, they would emerge as the victors. The Beatles had arrived in America. The four lads from Liverpool—John, Paul, George, and Ringo—dashed toward a chauffeured airport limousine. They leapt into the car, locked the doors, and rode toward the terminal, assaulted by hundreds of girls who hurled themselves at the slow-moving automobile, clinging to the hood, the roof, and the sides. As they inched away, the foursome saw, pressed against the windows, the contorted faces of teenage fans who tried to catch a glimpse of their heroes before a fellow Beatle maniac pulled them away.

The foursome broke loose from the crowd and headed toward the airport complex. After a short press conference, the Beatles jumped back into the limousine and sped down the Van Wyck Expressway, reaching Manhattan about an hour and a half later. Though swarmed by hundreds of fans when the car stopped at New York's plush Plaza Hotel, the Beatles managed to pry the doors open and somehow make it into the hotel lobby, where they were escorted to a twelfth-floor room. There they discovered three screaming girls in the bathtub and called the service desk for help. Throughout the night and for the next few days, the Beatles were protected by armed guards from ingenious girls, who climbed the fire escapes, and from conspiring groups of teens, who checked in at the hotel, using the names of their well-to-do parents to penetrate the twelfth floor. Outside, the Liverpool lads heard fans keep a twenty-four-hour vigil by chanting, "We want the Beatles, we want the Beatles." Beatlemania had overtaken America.

The Mods, the Rockers, and the Skiffle Craze

Beatlemania had its genesis in a wartime and postwar baby boom and in an economic depression that spawned gangs of British working-class youths. As with the United States, England experienced a baby boom after World War II. "That was the Bulge, that was England's Bulge," Pete Townshend, lead guitarist for the Who, told a reporter. "All the war babies, all the old soldiers coming back from the war and screwing until they were blue in the face—this was the result. Thousands and thousands of kids, too many kids, not enough teachers, not enough parents." By the late 1950s and early 1960s, many English baby boomers had become teenagers, who were ready for rock and roll.

At the same time, England faced economic hardships. Crippled by the war, it continued to enforce wartime rationing until 1954 and tried to rebuild with little help from wartime allies. "World War II went on there for another nine years after it finished everywhere else," recalled Keith Richards of the Rolling Stones. "I remember London, huge areas of rubble and grass growing."

During the mid- to late 1950s, many British teens, unlike their American counterparts, faced hard times upon finishing school at age 15 or 16. By March 1964, Harold Wilson, a Labour Party leader from Liverpool and later prime minister, regarded "as deserving of the utmost censure and condemnation a system of society which, year in, year out … cannot provide employment for its school-leavers." British youths felt especially directionless due to the change in English conscription laws. The draft ended in 1960, remembered Ringo Starr, "and so at eighteen you weren't regimented. Everyone was wondering what to do."

Idle working-class teens formed rival gangs: the Rockers and the Mods. The Rockers, modeling themselves after the tough Teddy Boys of the 1950s, wore black leather jackets, tight-fitting pants, and pointed boots or suede shoes. They greased back their hair in a pompadour style and sometimes donned sunglasses in beatnik fashion, roaring down the streets on motorcycles.

The Modernists, shortened to Mods, favored "teenage Italian-style clothes," according to Townshend, himself a Mod. They had "short hair, money enough to buy a real smart suit, good shoes, good shirts; you had to be able to dance like a madman. You had to be in possession of plenty of pills all the time and always be pilled up [especially with Drynamil, an amphetamine commonly known as a 'purple heart']. You had to have a scooter covered in lamps." The Mods sometimes adopted different fashions weekly. "One outfit might be twelve quid, a week's wages, and the next week you'd have to change the whole lot," recalled Townshend. Reacting against the generic simplicity necessitated by the impoverished conditions following World War II, they especially favored brightly colored, eye-catching styles. "I remember growing up as a kid in black and white," explained Kenny Jones, a Mod who played in the band the Small Faces. "We were the people to wear color, and it was amazing. We started to wear all these bright things, and it was alright to dye your hair then. A lot of Mods actually dyed their hair blonde." The fashion-conscious Mods fueled the rise of the now-famous alternative clothing district at and near Carnaby Street in London, where music blared from shops packed with teens searching for the newest trend.

As with the Rockers, the Mods "were nothing. They were the lowest," recalled Pete Townshend. "Most Mods were lower-class garbage men, you know, with enough money to buy himself Sunday's best."

The lower-class Mods, buying snappy, preppy clothes, for the first time took away the fashion mantle from the British upper crust. "Once only the rich, the Establishment, set the fashion. Now it is the inexpensive little dress seen on the girls in the High Street," asserted 1960s fashion queen Mary Quant. "The voices, rules, and culture of this generation are as different from those of the past as tea and wine," she continued. "They represent the whole new spirit that is present-day Britain, a classless spirit that has grown out of the Second World War." Quant created "an innocent child look" as her statement and sold the clothes to both men and women in her shop, Bazaar.

The Mods, blurring the class lines in British society, fostered a sense of belonging among some lower-class British youths. Pete Townshend knew "the feeling of what it's like to be a Mod among two million Mods and it's … that incredible feeling of being part of something. … Any kid, however ugly or however fucked up, if he had the right haircut and the right clothes and the right motorbike, he was a Mod. He was a Mod!" exclaimed Townshend.

The Mods and the Rockers, each group bound by a common appearance, fought one another for dominance. During the Easter weekend of 1964 at Clacton-on-Sea, Essex, a few hundred young scooter riders from the eastern and northeastern parts of London attacked motorcycle gangs of Rockers. According to D. H. Moody, chairman of the Urban District Council, "they insulted passersby, lay in the middle of the road to stop traffic, jumped onto cars, and destroyed and damaged property." "At one stage, there was almost a battle on the seafront with missiles of all descriptions being thrown," reported the *London Times*. The police intervened and arrested more than a hundred rioters, whom the *Times* called a "collection of uncivilized youths with no respect for persons, property, or the comfort of other people." Explaining the incident, Labour's chief front bench spokesman, Fred Willey, observed that the "general complaint of those who took part was that there was nothing for them to do. They came from housing estates with far too few social amenities and were expected to spend their time in amusement arcades."

On May 17, 1964, trouble broke out in the Kent resort of Margate and at Brighton. More than 800 Mods, arriving "on scooters bristling with headlights and badges," fought 200 leather-jacketed Rockers. The *Daily Express* painted a terrifying picture: "There was dad asleep in a deck chair and mum making sandcastles with the children when the 1964 boys took over the beaches at Margate and Brighton yesterday and smeared the traditional scene with more bloodshed and violence." Fumed Dr. George Simpson, Margate Court Chairman, said: "These long-haired, mentally unstable petty little sawdust Caesars seem to find courage, like rats, by hunting only in packs." By Tuesday, May 18, when the clashes subsided, at least forty youths had been arrested, the *Daily Mirror* informed its readers. "And there was blood on the sand."

Many of these warring youths, having time and lacking direction, turned to music. When the British draft ended, "music was a way out," explained Beatles drummer Ringo Starr. "People were picking up instruments instead of guns. There were so many kids, so many bands, so many places to play." During the early 1960s in Liverpool, a large port city in England, 350 bands spouted up. "Had not the government stopped the draft there would have been no Dave Clark Five, no Beatles, no Stones," recalled Dave Clark who would start his own band in London.

Skiffle, a mixture of Dixieland jazz and country blues, first attracted British youths. The music originated from British Dixieland, or traditional jazz, which reached the height of its popularity with a group that included banjo/guitar player Tony "Lonnie" Donegan and the co-owners of the Marquee Club, trombonist Chris Barber and Harold Pendelton. "We discovered that our trumpet player, Ken Coyler, had a weak lip which gave out on him, so he needed an occasional rest," remembered Pendelton. To solve the problem, Chris Barber formed a small band within his larger outfit, composed of guitar, bass, a washboard strummed with a thimble and a suitcase played with a whisk broom. Barber, remembered Pendleton, "called it his skiffle group."

Soon Barber's novelty skiffle act became more popular than his traditional jazz band and engendered an accessible, participatory musical style. According to Barber, "the way Lonnie [Donegan] did it was a way that anyone could join in with, and they did it with homemade guitars, tea chest and broom handle string bass and all this stuff. Just singing any kind of song." In 1956, Lonnie Donegan climbed the chart with skiffle versions of two Leadbelly songs, "Rock Island Line" and "John Henry," and started a skiffle craze in Britain among poor youths who launched bands with homemade instruments and little musical schooling. "Skiffle bands sprung up everywhere because the kids didn't have to learn how to play difficult instruments like the trombone or trumpet or clarinet. Anybody could skiffle," Pendelton added. "Out of this skiffle craze, the new rock groups like the Beatles began to emerge. The Beatles began as a skiffle group."

The Early Beatles

The four rowdy, working-class Rockers from Liverpool, who banded together as the Beatles during the skiffle craze, changed rock-and-roll history. Formed in 1958, the Quarry Men, as they first called themselves, then the Silver Beatles, and finally just the Beatles, started their musical careers as a skiffle band. They graduated to rock and roll at Liverpool's Casbah, a club operated by the mother of drummer Pete Best. In August 1960, they traveled to Hamburg, Germany, returned to Liverpool, and in February 1961 started a regular lunch-time engagement at the dingy, stone-walled Cavern Club. Two years later, the Beatles became the rage of England, and by 1964, they skyrocketed to international stardom.

The Beatles came from working-class families. Abandoned by his father and mother, John Winston Lennon grew up with his aunt Mimi Smith and as a boy joined a Rocker gang. Paul McCartney, the son of a cotton salesman, lived in a half house with a bare-brick wall. The youngest of the Beatles, George Harrison, was the son of a bus driver and apprenticed to an electrician at age 16. Drummer Ringo Starr (b. Richard Starkey) was raised in a working-class family. When her husband deserted the family, Ringo's mother worked as a barmaid to support her child. At age 15, Ringo landed a job as a messenger boy for the British Railways.

The four Liverpool youths adopted a Rocker image. To his aunt, Lennon seemed to be "a real Teddy boy." Lennon insisted, "I wasn't really a Ted, just a Rocker." Paul and George spent hours styling their pompadoured hair and choosing the clothes that fit Rocker fashion, especially tight trousers. As a band, the Beatles affected a Rocker image, wearing black-and-white cowboy shirts with white tassels dangling from the pockets, leather jackets, and pointed cowboy boots.

The quasi-western attire indicated a major musical influence on the Beatles: American rockabilly. Although first drawn to music through skiffle and covering Chuck Berry tunes such as "Rock and Roll Music" and "Roll Over Beethoven," the early Beatles modeled their sound after Elvis Presley. "Nothing really affected me until

Elvis," John Lennon remembered. "I had no idea about doing music as a way of life until rock-'n'-roll hit me. …It wasn't until 'Heartbreak Hotel' that I really got into it."

McCartney felt that Presley "was the biggest kick. Every time I felt low I just put on Elvis and I'd feel great, beautiful." "Elvis was the one who actually turned my head around," added Ringo Starr. When Malcolm Evans, a bouncer at the Cavern club and later a road manager for the Beatles, first heard the group at the Cavern Club, he felt that they "sounded a bit like Elvis."

The Beatles idolized other rockabilly stars as well. In 1959, as a Silver Beatle, George Harrison changed his name to Carl Harrison after one of his heroes, Carl Perkins. On tour with Perkins in 1964, John Lennon told the rockabilly star, "We've got all your records! We slowed 'em down from 45 to 33 rpm [to learn them]." After telling the Beatles that they sounded "a lot like the old Sun Records," remembered Perkins, John jumped off the couch, put "both arms around me and kissed me on the jaw." At another point during their early years, the foursome called themselves the Foreverly Brothers in honor of the Everly Brothers. *Variety* spotted the influence years later. "Malarkey," read one story. "The Beatles are dishing up a rock-and-roll style that was current in this country ten years ago and that is still typical of such groups as the Everly Brothers." The name the group eventually adopted reflected the rockabilly connection. As John told a reporter, "I was looking for a name like the Crickets [Buddy Holly's band] that meant two things. From Cricket I went to Beatles. …When you said it, people thought of crawly things; when you read it, it was beat music."

Brian Epstein Shapes the Beatles

This Rocker band, playing an English brand of rockabilly influenced by R&B and skiffle music, achieved fame through the efforts of manager Brian Epstein. Epstein, born in September 1934 into a wealthy family, was raised in a five-bedroom house in Childwall, one of Liverpool's most exclusive residential areas. He began a successful career as a salesman in two of his father's stores: a furniture shop and the North End Music Enterprises record stores. "I enjoyed selling, watching people relax and show trust in me," he explained.

In November 1961, Epstein saw the Beatles perform at the Cavern Club located around the corner from his office. On December 10, 1961, he signed the group to a management contract, getting a 25 percent share of their net revenues. As he told it, "I suppose it was all part of getting bored with simply selling records. I was looking for a new hobby," he explained. The Beatles "were also getting a bit bored with Liverpool." He wanted to mold the Beatles so "they'll be bigger than Elvis."

To make the band more palatable to the general public, Epstein changed their Rocker image. When he first saw them at the Cavern Club, he thought that the group, wearing leather jackets, looked "scruffy." "They smoked as they played and they ate and talked and pretended to hit each other." "First I got them into trousers and sweaters and eventually into suits," bragged Epstein. Besides changing their appearance, the manager forced the band to play a pre-planned set list rather than a spontaneous choice of songs. He engineered the ouster of original drummer Pete Best and in August 1962 replaced him with veteran Ringo Starr. After Epstein finished molding the four Liverpudlians, noticed Malcolm Evans, "the image of the Beatles was so good and nice."

To sell the band, Epstein connected with other professionals in the music business. After being rejected by nearly every British label, in May 1962 he approached George Martin, an executive with the Parlophone branch of the Electrical Music Industry (EMI), who "was looking for a new act." In September 1962, Martin, hoping to create a "vibrant" sound for the group, recorded the Beatles' first British release, "Love Me

Beatles at Cavern Club, February 2, 1963.

Keystone Pictures USA/Alamy Stock Photo.

Do" and "P.S. I Love You." Epstein enlisted the services of Tony Barrow, a publicity man for Decca Records. By May 1963, the manager had set up the machinery to make the Beatles a national sensation.

The Toppermost of the Poppermost

As with many working-class youth, the Beatles initially wanted money and fame. In 1961, remembered George, they had the "idea of getting to the top. When things were a real drag and nothing happening, we used to go through this routine: John would shout, 'Where are we going, fellas?' We'd shout back, 'To the Top, Johnny.' Then he would shout, 'What Top?' 'To the Toppermost of the Poppermost, Johnny!'"

The Beatles soon achieved their goal. They first became well known in Liverpool. By late 1962, admirers hung around the dark, dank but popular basement Cavern Club to catch a glimpse of the band. "It was terrible, the mad screams when they came on. They went potty," remembered Maureen Cox, Ringo's first wife. News spread quickly. More than 5,000 squealing teens mobbed a Beatles performance and caused a riot in Manchester. At Newcastle-upon-Tyne, more than 4,000 diehards lined up in front of a concert hall at 3:00 A.M. to secure tickets for an evening Beatles show.

British television helped propel the Beatles into the spotlight much like American television had benefitted Elvis. "Television was the key media, massive," contended Sean O'Mahony, publisher of the *Beatles Book Monthly*. "One little airing and you could sell an awful lot of records very quickly." In early 1963, Beatles music publisher Dick James called television host Philip Jones, who produced James's radio sing-alongs, and convinced the TV personality to include the Beatles on his influential variety show, *Thank Your Lucky Stars*. On January 19, 1963, the program launched the foursome and their new song, "Please Please Me."

On October 13, 1963, the band gained national exposure when it headlined at the London Palladium on a show called *Sunday Night at the London Palladium*. More than 15 million television viewers watched thousands of young Londoners claw at each other to get a glimpse of the Beatles. "From that day on, my job has never been the same again," insisted press agent Tony Barrow. "From spending six months ringing up newspapers and getting no, I now had every national reporter and feature writer chasing *me*."

Less than a month later on November 4, the Beatles increased their visibility with a Royal Command Variety Performance. At this charity event, they performed four songs for an audience that included show-business luminaries, music tradesters and the Queen Mother and Princess Margaret. Before their last number, "Twist and Shout," a nervous John asked the crowd for their help. "Will the people in the cheaper seats clap your hands," he requested. Looking toward the royal box, he added: "and the rest, if you'll just rattle your jewelry." The following Sunday, 26 million Britons witnessed the escapade while sitting in front of their television sets.

By December 1963, Beatlemania had engulfed Great Britain. Manufacturers started to offer Beatles products, with one firm in Peckham selling Beatles sweaters designed especially for Beatles fans. The Beatles Fan Club swelled to more than 800,000 members, and the foursome sold a million copies of two singles that featured "I Want to Hold Your Hand" and "She Loves You." The band's first British album, *Please Please Me*, topped the British chart for more than six months. By the end of 1963, the Fab Four had sold 11 million records and $18 million worth of Beatles goods. The Fab Four even wrote three songs for a ballet entitled *Mods and Rockers*.

British public opinion generally responded favorably to the Beatles. The *Daily Mirror* argued that "you have to be a real sour square not to love the nutty, noisy, happy, handsome Beatles." Although Conservative politician Edward Heath first criticized the Beatles' language as "unrecognizable as the Queen's English," he later told an interviewer: "Who could have forecast only a year ago that the Beatles would prove the salvation of the corduroy industry" as thousands emulated the band in its trouser style. Prime Minister Sir Alec Douglas-Home called the group "our best export" and "a useful contribution to the balance of payments." Even the Queen Mother complimented the Beatles. "So young, fresh, and vital. I simply adore them," she cooed.

Amid such praise, Brian Epstein questioned his marketing tactics. He feared overexposure. Though excited over the initial success, he wondered about the longevity of the Beatles. "By a stringent watch on their bookings and press contacts we just averted saturation point. But it was very close," he confided.

The band members started to doubt the value of stardom as they began to pay the price of success. Ringo Starr complained about the loss of friendships and the diminishing control he exercised over his own life. "There were so many groups in Liverpool at one time that we often used to play just for each other, sitting in on each other's sessions, or just listening." But when the Beatles became popular nationally, "it broke all the community up." Moreover, Ringo felt slighted when George Martin replaced him with session drummer Andy White on "P.S. I Love You." "Nobody said anything. What could the others say, or me? We were just lads, being pushed around." From his perspective, John believed that the band had relinquished too much control. In Liverpool, he told an interviewer, the Beatles "felt embarrassed in our suits and being very clean. We were worried that our friends might think we'd sold out—which we had, in a way."

The Beatles Invade America

Despite their doubts, the Beatles prepared for even greater success in America. Epstein paved the way for the British invasion, convincing Capitol Records to spend $50,000 on a crash publicity program. The company plastered 5 million "The Beatles Are Coming" stickers on buildings, fences, and telephone poles in every state and printed a million copies of a four-page tabloid about the Fab Four. Capitol executives pressed 1 million units of a promotional, 7-inch Beatles interview record, which gave radio listeners the impression that the Beatles had personally contacted every disc jockey in the country. They also convinced many of the major weekly publications to run stories about the British foursome before their arrival: *Time* covered the group in its November 15, 1963, issue in an article titled "New Madness"; *Newsweek* did so three days later; and on January 31, 1964, *Life* published a color spread entitled "Here Come the Beatles." By February 7, 1964, Brown Meggs, director of eastern operations for Capitol Records, told the *New York Times* that, "I have been on full-time Beatles duty since—the date is indelibly imprinted on my mind—January 6, when I returned from vacation. All this came at once." Voyle Gilmore, a vice president of Capitol, summed up the efforts of his company in an understatement: "There was a lot of hype."

Radio also plugged the Beatles. During February 1964, one record executive in a company that had no Beatles releases complained that "stations are playing our records like spot commercials between Beatles tunes." Explained Brown Meggs of Capitol, "What sells records is radio. The Beatles got unbelievable radio play. There wasn't a single market in the country in which airplay wasn't simply stupendous."

By the time the Beatles arrived in New York City on February 7, 1964, Beatlemania had swept the United States. Entering the charts at number eighty-three, by January "I Want to Hold Your Hand" replaced a song by young crooner Bobby Vinton in the number-one slot. The song remained in the top position for seven weeks.

The mop tops received a tremendous boost from television when they appeared on the *Ed Sullivan Show*. Late in 1963, Ed Sullivan, the square-faced, stocky show business impresario, had witnessed a near riot at the London airport, where more than 15,000 screaming fans descended upon the terminal, delaying the Queen and Prime Minister Sir Alec Douglas-Home in order to welcome the Beatles back from a trip abroad. Impressed, Sullivan told the *New York Times*, "I made up my mind that this was the same sort of mass hit hysteria that had characterized the Elvis Presley days." He hurriedly located Brian Epstein, the dapper, brilliant manager of the group, and for less than $20,000 booked the Beatles for three appearances on his show.

On February 9, 1964, Sullivan showcased the Beatles. Packed into the studio from which *The Ed Sullivan Show* was broadcast were 728 wild teenagers who had battled 50,000 others for tickets to the show that featured their heroes. When Sullivan introduced the foursome—"and now, the Beeeatles!"—the room erupted. Girls with checkered skirts and Macy blouses let out primal screams and pulled their hair, thrusting themselves toward the front of the stage or leaning perilously over the balcony. Some simply fainted. Few noticed that one of the microphones had

Beatles land in New York City, February 7, 1964.

Trinity Mirror/Mirrorpix/Alamy Stock Photo.

gone dead. All eyes fastened on Paul, bobbing back and forth as he played a left-handed bass guitar; Ringo, smiling as he brushed the drum skins; John, yelling the lyrics over the din; and a rather dour, flu-stricken George, the youngest, skinniest member of the group, just looking down at the neck of his lead guitar. The screaming intensified with teenage girls fainting and swooning. The show, ending amidst the wails, had been phenomenally successful. It had been witnessed by more than 73 million people across the country, who constituted more than 60 percent of all television viewers.

By February 24, when the Beatles appeared on the third Sullivan show segment, the entire nation had been swept away by the four Liverpudlians. Headlines in the staid *Billboard* told the story: "The U.S. Rocks and Reels from Beatles Invasion"; "Chicago Flips Wig, Beatles and Otherwise"; "New York City Crawling with Beatlemania"; and "Beatle Binge in Los Angeles." "Great Britain hasn't been as influential in American affairs since 1775," Billboard informed its readers. "The sensational impact of the Beatle on England's former colonies has had an explosive effect."

Americans purchased all types of Beatle merchandise. In the nine days during the Beatles' brief visit, Americans bought more than 2 million Beatles records and more than $2.5 million worth of Beatles-related goods. They acquired blue-and-white Beatles hats; Beatles T-shirts and beach shirts; Beatles tight-fitting pants; Beatles pajamas and three-button tennis shirts; Beatles cookies; Beatles egg cups; Beatles rings, pendants, and bracelets; a pink plastic Beatles guitar with pictures of the four lads stamped on it; and a plethora of Beatles dolls, including inflatable figurines, 6-inch-tall hard rubber likenesses, painted wooden dolls that bobbed their heads when moved, and a cake decoration in the form of the Beatles. Others snapped up Beatles nightshirts, countless Beatles publications, Beatles ice-cream sandwiches covered with a foil Beatles wrapper, Beatles soft drinks, and Beatles wigs, which Lowell Toy Company churned out at the rate of 15,000 a day. Seltaeb (Beatles spelled backward), the American arm of the Beatles manufacturing company, even planned for a Beatles motor scooter and a Beatles car.

The "cute and safe" Beatles, appealing to a vast audience, continued their fantastic successes after their initial invasion of America. In March 1964, John Lennon released his book *In His Own Write*, which nudged Ian Fleming's latest James Bond thriller from the top of the best-seller list and won Lennon an invitation to the prestigious Foyles Literary Lunch on Shakespeare's 400th birthday. Some compared the book to James Joyce's classic *Finnegan's Wake*. On July 6, 1964, the Beatles premiered a full-length motion picture, *A Hard Day's Night*. "The idea was to make it as quickly as possible and get it out before their popularity faded," admitted director Richard Lester, because United Artists Films "felt the Beatles probably wouldn't last the summer." The timing was superb. Even historian and John F. Kennedy speechwriter Arthur Schlesinger, Jr. lauded the movie as "the astonishment of the month" by a band that embodied the "timeless essence of the adolescent effort to deal with the absurdities of an adult world." During its first six weeks, the film earned $5.6 million.

In August 1964, the Beatles returned to the States for a victorious tour. Immediately following a tour of the Netherlands, Australia, New Zealand and Britain, it started at the Cow Palace outside San Francisco on August 19 and ended a month later in New York with a charity benefit.

In Seattle, on August 21, a typical explosion of mayhem erupted over the second coming of the Beatles. When the foursome arrived in town, they faced screaming, clawing teenagers. Escorted by a police motorcade, the band stopped for a fourteen-minute press conference and then sped to Room 272 of the Edgewater Inn, which had been secured with barbed wire and sawhorse barricades. While in their room, Ringo, George, Paul, and John sorted through hundreds of letters from their fans, ate a few of the cookies and pieces of cake that Beatles diehards had baked, and fished from a window that overlooked Elliot Bay.

The Beatles emerged from the hotel to play an afternoon and an evening show, running from the Edgewater Inn lobby and jumping into a limousine bound for the Seattle Coliseum. Marty Murphy, a 25-year-old switchboard operator at the Edgewater Inn, rode with the Beatles, dragged into the car by Brian Epstein, who desperately needed help with two terrified Beatles secretaries. "When we got to the barricade," she related, teenage girls "had their faces pressed up against the car, all bent out of shape. They were crying, screaming, 'Touch me! Touch me!' They were saying that to me, and they didn't even know who I was." Eventually, the limousine reached the Coliseum. When the Beatles leapt onstage and started to play, remembered police officer Noreen Skagen, she could barely hear the group above the deafening roar and delivered the foursome to the stage by using a flying wedge of police officers. "The entire audience charged the stage when the Beatles were ready to leave. We were constantly dragging hysterical youngsters who had gone berserk," she related. "It was hysteria. The girls were in love. They would say, 'I have to talk to them! You don't understand!'"

After the evening performance, the police bundled the Fab Four in blankets, put them on stretchers, and carried them through the crowd to a Red Cross van, which escaped the rabid hordes of fans, who demanded their heroes. About the entire episode, the *Seattle Times* reported: "Seattle seethed with uncontrollable hysteria, terrifying noise, and danger in a real-life nightmare last night. This was the Beatles' show. For thirty incredible minutes, those in the jam-packed Seattle Center Coliseum had the feeling of being sealed in a crazed capsule pitching through the chasms of space." A similar hysteria gripped other cities on the four Beatles' tours of America, which by August 1966 had reaped more than $56 million.

The intensity and magnitude of Beatlemania in America can be attributed, at least in part, to the postwar baby boom. By 1964, the number of American youth between the ages of 12 and 17 had grown amid the postwar baby boom to more than 21 million, an increase of more than 67 percent from 1950. These teens, especially the girls, searched for an identity and collectively latched onto the Beatles as a symbol of unity. As one Beatles fan told a reporter as she stood vigil in 1964 outside of a hotel where her heroes resided, "I'm here because everyone else is here." Though youths had idolized Elvis Presley, the mass hysteria of Beatlemania could only have occurred during the mid-1960s, when the majority of baby boomers were old enough to become interested in music. "We were just the spokesmen for a generation," explained Paul McCartney.

Teenage girls who had just reached puberty and hysterically vented their hormones especially vaulted the Beatles to fame and fortune. Girls generally picked one of the Beatles as their favorite and swooned over and dreamed about them. One young Beatle fan singled out John for his sexy body and became obsessed with him. In her dreams, she and John made love and skipped in an idyllic countryside. When the stalkers of John discovered he had been married and had a child, they wished "his bride would drop dead." In 1964, a psychologist explained Beatlemania as a "release of sexual energy." "The Beatles belonged to every teenage girl," possessively insisted on 12-year-old fan from Liverpool. In 1964, when 11 million teenage girls accounted for more than half of the $650 million spent on record sales, they clutched the Beatles in a locked and loving embrace, which led to the sensational success of the Fab Four.

The Cute and Safe Beatles

A few adults disapproved of the new rage. After the *Sullivan* show appearance, the *New York Times* described the Beatles vocals as "hoarsely incoherent." Ray Bloch, orchestra leader on the *Sullivan* program, prophesied that the band "wouldn't last longer than a year," and actor/playwright/singer Noel Coward said, "I've met them. Delightful lads. Absolutely no talent."

Most media commentators, however, welcomed the clean-cut, well-tailored Beatles and their aristocratic manager. *Time* wrote that "the boys are the very spirit of good clean fun. They look like shaggy Peter Pans, with their mushroom haircuts and high white shirt collars, and onstage they clown around endlessly." *Newsweek* probably best captured the majority opinion. The magazine labeled the Beatles "a band of evangelists. And the gospel is fun. They shout, they stomp, they jump for joy." The band, continued the magazine, "appeal to the positive, not negative …. They have even evolved a peculiar sort of sexless appeal: cute and safe. The most they ask is: 'I Want to Hold Your Hand.'"

The fun-loving Beatles seemed a perfect antidote to the pessimism that had engulfed America after John F. Kennedy's death a few months earlier. "We had lost Kennedy [in November 1963], and the kids seemed to sense we were missing something in America, something the Beatles were ready to give us," reasoned Murray "the K" Kaufman, the radio announcer for New York station WINS who accompanied the Beatles during their first tours of the United States.

The Mersey Beat

In the mid-1960s, the Beatles, who had conquered the American music market by appealing to the baby-boom generation, paved the way for other British groups, some of them linked to Brian Epstein. "The biggest thing the Beatles did was to open the American market to all British artists," contended British promoter Arthur Howes, who planned the early Beatles tours of England. "Nobody had ever been able to get in before the Beatles. They alone did it." By February 1965, *Variety* told its readers, "Britannia ruled the airwaves. The advent of the [Beatles] now has shattered the steady, day-to-day domination of made-in-America music here and abroad." During 1964, British rock bands sold more than $76 million worth of records in the United States.

Some of the British groups had grown up with the Beatles in Liverpool. In 1959 Gerry Marsden, a truck driver, formed a band called the Pacemakers. Under the watchful eye of manager Brian Epstein, who signed the group in June 1962, Gerry and the Pacemakers established a following at the Cavern Club in Liverpool, frequently playing on the same bill as the Beatles. In early 1963, they climbed to the top of the British chart with "How Do You Do It?" a song first earmarked for the Beatles and ended the successful year with an appearance on the British television show *Sunday Night at the London Palladium.* On May 10, 1964, Gerry and the Pacemakers debuted in America on *The Ed Sullivan Show*, which promoted the group's best-selling U.S. single, "Don't Let the Sun Catch You Crying." They capped their career in 1965 by starring in the movie *Ferry 'Cross the Mersey* and scoring with a Top-Ten single of the same name.

Billy J. Kramer and the Dakotas, another Epstein act, rose from their working-class backgrounds to stardom. Billy J. Kramer (b. William Ashton), a worker for the British Railways, teamed with a Manchester combo, the Dakotas, on the advice of Epstein, who signed the Liverpudlian in late 1962. "The marriage of the zing singing of Billy J. to the true-beat accompaniment of the Daks has proven a brilliant stroke on the part of Epstein," observed *The Big Beat*, an English fanzine. Billy J. Kramer hit the British chart in May 1963 with "Do You Want to Know a Secret?" a track from the Beatles first album, and the same month toured the United Kingdom with the Beatles. Two months later, he followed with the British chart-topper "Bad to Me," a song written by John Lennon specifically for Kramer, and a Top-Ten hit in the United States. Within a year, the group hit the British Top Ten with two Lennon/McCartney originals.

The Searchers, another Liverpool group, rode the crest of the Beatles' success. Formed in 1961 and named after a John Wayne movie, the group began performing regularly at Liverpool clubs such as the Cavern, the Casbah, and the Hot Spot, eventually becoming the house band at the Iron Door. "We copied such people as Buddy Holly,

Eddie Cochran, and Gene Vincent," related John McNally, one of the founders of the band. In June 1963, they topped the British singles chart with a remake of the Drifters' "Sweets for My Sweet" and followed later in the year with the British chart-topper "Sugar and Spice." After an April 1964 appearance on *The Ed Sullivan Show*, and amid Beatlemania, the Searchers scaled the U.S. charts with their best-selling record, a remake of "Needles and Pins."

Along with the Beatles, these Liverpool groups delivered the "Mersey sound." Alexis Korner, a British blues innovator, found that "there was a certain brashness about the Liverpool music, which stamped it almost immediately—they played it the way they speak English, you know!" He characterized the Mersey sound as "a guitar sound: lead guitar, rhythm guitar, bass guitar, and drums was the basic Liverpool setup."

Groups from the Northern part of Great Britain invaded America with a sound similar to the Mersey beat. From Manchester, a dingy, smoke-stacked industrial center much like Liverpool, came Freddie Garrity and the Dreamers. Becoming popular on English television for their comedy act, in 1963, the band nearly topped the British chart with "I'm Telling You Now." In March 1965, after the group appeared on the U.S. television programs *Hullabaloo* and *Shindig*, they promptly topped the U.S. chart with the same song.

The Hollies proved to be more long lasting than most Manchester beat bands. The group was started by Graham Nash and singer-guitarist Allan Clarke, who first met in grammar school and later formed the Two Teens. After a few name changes, the duo added three other members in 1962 and labeled themselves the Hollies after their musical hero, Buddy Holly. "We were Buddy Holly crazy," recalled Nash, who, as with other Merseybeats, looked to the rockabillies for inspiration.

The group followed the path blazed by the Beatles. They performed at the Cavern Club in Liverpool, where EMI producer Ron Richards saw the band and signed them. Amid Beatlemania in 1964 and 1965, the Hollies hit the British Top Ten with "Just One Look" and "I'm Alive" and followed with several other chartbusters, including the Beatles' composition "If I Needed Someone." The Beatles "opened the door for the rest of us," insisted Graham Nash of the Hollies. In 1966, the group performed on such American television shows as *Shindig, Hullabaloo*, and *The Smothers Brothers Show* and toured America to the wild screams of teenage girls. "If we wiggled a leg or reached forward to touch a girl's fingertips, the volumes of the screams would be unbelievable," explained Nash. Plugged by live concerts and American television, the Hollies crossed over to the American Top Ten with "Bus Stop" and "Stop Stop Stop."

Herman's Hermits, another Manchester band, capitalized on the beat music craze. Formed in 1962 with Peter Noone as the front man, the band signed two years later to EMI Columbia by producer Mickie Most, who noticed the facial resemblance of Noone to John F. Kennedy. "When Most finally agreed to help us," recalled Noone, "he found this Carole King [and Gerry Goffin] song, 'I'm into Something Good,'" which featured Noone backed by such session musicians as Jimmy Page and John Paul Jones, later of Led Zeppelin. "Once we recorded it, and I heard it on the radio, I said, 'That's it, my life's complete.' Then we did some TV shows, and in three weeks we were number one. It was unbelievable." In 1965, Herman's Hermits followed with a string of upbeat hits including a revival of the turn-of-the-century tune, "I'm Henery the Eighth, I Am."

The Dave Clark Five (DC5), from the Tottenham section of London, initially posed the most serious threat to the commercial dominance of the Beatles. Teaming together to raise money for Dave Clark's soccer team for a trip to Holland, the band found inspiration in Little, Richard, Elvis Presley, and many of rock's originators. In 1964, the Five journeyed to America for a spot on *The Ed Sullivan Show*, which scheduled the first of nearly twenty DC5 appearances for May 31. "The power of the man and his show were unbelievable," raved Clark, one of the few drummers who fronted a band. "Within the course of seven days, we were household names."

After publicity from *The Ed Sullivan Show*, the DC5 hit the charts on both sides of the Atlantic with their jubilant sound. They scored with "Glad All Over," "Bits and

Pieces," and other jumpy, light-hearted gems. The liner notes on their American debut album predicted that the Tottenham sound of the Dave Clark Five would quickly over-throw the reign of the Beatles. In 1965, they copied the Fab Four by releasing a film, titled *Catch Us If You Can*, and charted with a song of the same name. All told, the group sold 50 million records, placing eight singles in the U.S. Top Ten.

The Beatles and the Mersey beat in general churned out a buoyant, danceable music very unlike the serious-minded protest of early Bob Dylan. "Records are for enjoyment," insisted Clark. "There's no message in our music; it's just for fun." "In the early days, we didn't care about lyrics as long as the song had some vague theme," agreed John Lennon. Gary Smith, the producer of the television show *Hullabaloo*, a showcase for many of the Mersey beats, identified the basic reason for the Mersey sound as "the desire to escape." It provided a way "to get away for a moment, to get away from Vietnam and civil rights, reality."

The Monkees

Two American producers took advantage of the Mersey beat craze by creating the Monkees, a prefabricated American version of the Beatles. Observing the success of Richard Lester's Beatles film *A Hard Day's Night*, Bob Rafelson and Bert Schneider, the son of then-president of Columbia Pictures, Abe Schneider, formed Raybert Productions. In January 1966, they placed an ad in the *Hollywood Advertiser* for "four insane boys, age seventeen–twenty-one, want spirited Ben Frank types" for "acting roles in new TV series." In a month the duo auditioned 437 hopefuls, including folk rocker Stephen Stills.

The producers picked four photogenic, energetic, largely inexperienced applicants: Robert Michael Nesmith, an unknown folk singer; Mickey Dolenz, who as a child had played Corky in the TV children's series "Circus Boy," and more recently had played in a California garage band; Greenwich Village folk singer Peter Thorkelson, shortened to Tork; and David Jones, the most experienced of the four, who had appeared on Broadway

From left to right, Davy Jones, Peter Tork, Micky Dolenz, and Michael Nesmith, 1965.

Everett Collection Historical/Alamy Stock Photo.

as the Artful Dodger in *Oliver!*, had played a drug-crazed husband on the TV program *Ben Casey*, and had released an album of pop songs, some of which he performed on the same *Ed Sullivan Show* on which the Beatles had debuted. When he witnessed the reaction to the performance of the Fab Four, Jones exclaimed, "I want to be part of that!"

In late 1965, Rafelson and Schneider secured $225,000 from Jackie Cooper, the former child actor who headed the television subsidiary of Columbia Pictures, for a pilot TV series. "It all went great," Rafelson told *Time*. "NBC bought the series twenty-four hours after it saw the pilot and sold it to two sponsors seventy-two hours later."

The producers quickly groomed their new product for the airwaves. They hired underground film director James Frawley to provide intensive acting lessons for the group. "At first they were embarrassed, they were stiff, and they were a little raw," Frawley told the *Saturday Evening Post*. "We would roll over on the floor, sometimes, and do animals .... It was like a training period to free them physically, to start to use their bodies in a new way."

Rafelson and Schneider also shaped the Monkees musically. Besides enlisting the help of songwriters Tommy Boyce and Bobby Hart, the team approached former Brill Building music publisher Don Kirshner, the president of the music division of Columbia Pictures/Screen Gems TV and its new record label, Colgems. "The boys didn't relate," explained Kirshner at the time. "I was looking for a driving, exciting, frantic young sound. There was no sound to the Monkees." Having little time to develop and record twenty-two songs for an album and five TV shows, he "brought in Goffin and King, Mann and Weil, Sedaka and Greenfield, the Tokens and Neil Diamond and created songs for the group. On most of the records I did with the Monkees, Carole King and Neil Diamond would sing background." Studio musicians such as Glen Campbell, Leon Russell, and James Burton would play the instruments. "The music had nothing to do with us," complained Michael Nesmith.

Though prefabricated, the look and sound of the Monkees sold. After their television debut on September 12, 1966, the group attracted 10 million viewers every Monday night and received 5,000 fan letters a day. Just as they launched their television show, the group hit the top of the singles chart with "Last Train to Clarksville" and three months later did the same with "I'm a Believer." In October 1966, the Monkees scored with a number-one, self-titled album, and within the next year released three more chart-topping LPs. During less than a three-year period from 1966 to 1968, the band sold more than $20 million in Monkees merchandise, including shirts, slacks, raincoats, sweaters, comic books, trading and playing cards, dolls, lunch boxes, stuffed animals, games, wool hats, bubblegum, shoes, charms, guitars, and puppets. "We're advertisers," enthused Mickey Dolenz. "We're selling a product. We're selling Monkees."

The successful Monkees had been patterned after the Beatles. Before releasing the Monkees debut LP, the band's label spent $100,000 on an ad campaign that involved seventy-six advance men, who distributed thousands of posters proclaiming "The Monkees Are Coming" and provided preview records to 6,000 disc jockeys. The name of the group had been calculatedly misspelled, as had the Beatles, and the first Monkees single included several "no-no-no" choruses to substitute for the Beatles' "yeah-yeah-yeah" chants. The group's management even published a *Monkees Monthly* magazine, similar to the many fanzines dealing with the Beatles, such as *Beat Monthly* and *Beatles Monthly*. "The teens have bought the Monkees," a Raybert official proclaimed in early 1967. "They're the American Beatles." *Newsweek* called the band members "direct videological descendants of the Beatles," and *Time*, in early 1967, commented that "less than a year ago, a team of wily promoters ran the Beatles through a Xerox machine and came up with the Monkees."

During the mid-1960s, the Beatles and their American counterpart faced competition from another group of bands. Coming from London and its suburbs, groups of British youths adopted American electric blues and its underdog image to blast out a siren call to teens across the Western world. Headed by the Rolling Stones, these bands formed the second prong of the British invasion.

Chapter 8
The British Blues Invasion and Garage Rock

"We wanted to sell records for Jimmy Reed, Muddy [Waters] and John Lee Hooker. We were disciples."

—Keith Richards

On June 10, 1964, the Rolling Stones reverentially approached the studio of Chess Records at 2120 South Michigan Avenue in Chicago. They had dreamed about this day, when they could enter the hallowed inner sanctum, where their blues heroes such as Muddy Waters had recorded electric-blues hits. The Rolling Stones hoped that they could replicate the magic of the old Chess releases if they recorded at the epicenter of Chicago blues.

As they knocked on the door, the band was met by 22-year-old Marshall Chess, son of owner Phil Chess and nephew of Leonard Chess, the other co-owner. Marshall led the awestruck blues fanatics on a tour of the facilities. He first took them to his father and uncle who mumbled a few words to the band. When the Stones left, Leonard asked Phil, "Who are they?" Phil thought that they "looked like freaks" with their long hair and could barely understand their thick British accents.

The Stones followed Marshall to the recording studio, where Buddy Guy wailed "My Time After While" into the microphone for an upcoming release. The Rolling Stones stood against the wall in rapture, intently listening to the singer/guitarist in near disbelief.

After hearing Guy finish his song, the Rolling Stones walked down the hall and readied themselves for their recording. Within a few minutes they carted their instruments and amplifiers into the studio and started to record "It's All Over Now." Phil Chess monitored the session and engineer Ron Malo who had balanced sound for many of the Chicago greats manned the control booth. According to a wide-eyed Bill Wyman, bass player for the Stones, "Chuck Berry wandered in while we were recording 'Down the Road Apiece,' and he said to us: 'Wow, you guys are really getting it on.'" They also encountered their musical god, Muddy Waters, who gave them words of encouragement. At the urging of Leonard Chess, Willie Dixon, bassist and the author of many essential blues standards, met the Stones and suggested that they wax some songs by Chess artists.

The Rolling Stones returned the next day to complete their recording. In the two-day session, they finished sixteen songs including the Muddy Waters gem "I Can't Be Satisfied" and the Chuck Berry hit "Reelin' and Rockin.'" They also pleased the Chess brothers by naming one of their originals "2120 South Michigan Avenue" to honor Chess studios and its prodigious output. When the Stones finished on June 11, Marshall Chess loaded Stones multi-instrumentalist and blues diehard Brian Jones with a stack of Chess records and escorted the group out of the building. By the time they left, the Rolling Stones had fulfilled their wildest dreams. To Bill Wyman, it "was more than a thrill. It was like God had arrived. The clouds open and Boom!" The British blues invasion of America had begun.

The British Blues Explosion

English groups playing American electric blues formed a second flank of the British invasion, led by the Rolling Stones. "By 1962 it became clear to me that the music scene was in a real rut, and a new twist was needed. Blues was the answer," recalled Giorgio Gomelsky, the first manager of the Stones.

The British fascination with American blues and the seeds of the Stones' success began during the late 1950s, when American bluesmen finally were allowed to perform in England. When the British Musicians Union ended its ban on American musicians in 1956, skiffle innovator Chris Barber and his bandmates invited American blues artists to England. "Muddy Waters came out on stage [in 1958] and played an electric guitar. This was the first electric guitar anyone in Britain had ever seen," remembered Harold Pendelton. "When we opened the Marquee Club in 1960, skiffle was on the way out so we were able to occasionally feature a rhythm and blues group." Within a few years, the club introduced John Lee Hooker, Otis Spann, Sonny Boy Williamson, James Cotton, and many other blues artists to England.

After hearing American bluesmen, British teens became converted to the music. "Blues are bustin' out all over," heralded *Melody Maker* in late 1962. Two months later, the magazine described the decline of skiffle and meteoric rise of rhythm and blues. "The number of clubs that have suddenly sprung up is nothing short of fantastic," it noted. Nightspots such as the Marquee, the Crawdaddy, the Ealing Club, and the Flamingo catered to teens clamoring for Chicago-style blues. On any given weekend in a forty miles radius around London, 300,000 teens flocked to R & B club to hear electric blues. By late 1963, *Melody Maker* referred to London as the "new Chicago!"

British youths, especially in the London area, welcomed the blues as part of their general interest in American culture. "American culture was really something special to us," related drummer Jim McCarty who played with the Yardbirds. "Loads of films and TV shows, and that cool thing about America." He felt that the United States "really looked abundant" to British teens who lived in a country, which still suffered the after-effects of World War II. Like other aspects of the American experience, American blues seemed hip. Guitarist Eric Clapton likewise exhibited a passionate interest in American culture. "The first books I bought were about America. The first records were American. I was devoted to the American way of life without ever having been there," he explained. He wanted to learn about "red Indians and the blues."

Guitarist Alexis Korner and harmonica player Cyril Davies, two members of the Chris Barber band, helped popularize American blues among British youths. "Alexis and Cyril Davies were the only ones really playing blues in London at that time," remembered Rolling Stones drummer Charlie Watts, who originally played with them. In 1956, they opened the Barrelhouse Blues Club that featured such blues stalwarts as Big Bill Broonzy. By January 1962, the two formed Blues Incorporated and played a blues set laced with modern jazz at the Marquee Club, when Barber's skiffle group took a break. A few weeks later, they landed a regular Saturday night job at the Ealing Club, a crowded basement venue, which attracted youths such as Keith Richards, Mick Jagger, Charlie Watts, and Brian Jones, who occasionally performed with Korner and Davies. "Blues Incorporated was showing us that even we white chaps could make reasonable R & B," insisted Ian Whitcomb who at the time played in a blues band.

John Mayall's Bluesbreakers provided another breeding ground for blues fanatics eager to perform their favorite music. In 1963, Mayall, a 30-year-old art director, moved to London into the emerging British blues scene after being encouraged by Alexis Korner. A self-proclaimed "blues freak" who was "totally obsessive and totally oblivious to whatever else was going on," the multi-instrumentalist blues enthusiast founded the Bluesbreakers with a lineup, which included a series of guitarists who would spread the gospel of the blues. Mayall first enlisted the help of Bernie Watson from the Cyril Davies R&B All-Stars. In April 1965, blues purist Eric Clapton joined the Bluesbreakers. "Modern Chicago blues became my new Mecca," asserted Clapton. When Clapton left a year later, Mayall tapped Peter Green (b. Peter Greenbaum) who split in 1967 with the Bluesbreakers' rhythm section—bassist John McVie and drummer Mick Fleetwood—to form Fleetwood Mac. The Bluesbreakers then hired Mick Taylor who stayed for two years before joining the Rolling Stones.

The Bluesbreakers and Blues Incorporated inspired a landside of other youths who picked up electric guitars to play the blues. In 1963, at least 140 blues bands sprouted in the greater London area. Another twenty blues-based groups surfaced on the Southern coast. "You had this feeling of being in a clan of people who were sharing information and musical abilities, who were into the blues," explained Giorgio Gomelsky.

The Rolling Stones Emerge

The Rolling Stones represented one of the bands of blues zealots, which formed amid the British blues explosion. Initially like the Beatles, Richards, Jagger, and Jones started with an interest in American rockabilly. Mick Jagger sang in several bands, which played Buddy Holly tunes, guitarist Keith Richards remembered. "Buddy Holly was in England as solid as Elvis. Everything that came out was a record smash number one." Richards himself listened to Elvis, Little Richard, and Jerry Lee Lewis. When the movie *Blackboard Jungle*, featuring the music of Bill Haley and the Comets, showed in London, Richards found that "people were saying 'Did ya hear that music, man?'" Members of the Stones soon uncovered the blues roots of rockabilly. Keith Richards heard "[Big Bill] Broonzy first…. Then I started to discover Robert Johnson and those cats." The multi-instrumentalist Brian Jones, initially the impetus behind the group, one day heard "Elmore James, and the earth seemed to shudder on its axis…. The blues was real. We only had to persuade people to listen to the music, and they couldn't help but be turned on to all those great old blues cats." When Jones saw Muddy Waters perform, recalled Jones's friend Richard Hattrell, "It was as if Brian had found his mission in life. He got himself electrified and he never stopped practicing." Mick Jagger similarly idolized Chuck Berry, Bo Diddley, Muddy Waters, and Fats Domino.

In London, Jagger and Richards discovered their mutual fascination with the blues. "I get on this train one morning and there's—Jagger—and under his arm he has four or five albums," recalled Richards. "He's got Chuck Berry, Little Walter, Muddy Waters," the two talked about their passion for Chicago blues and in a few weeks, with friend Dick Taylor, they formed a band called the Glimmer Twins, based upon Chicago electric blues. Remarked Dick Taylor: "We'd sit around and listen to Mick's records, and then our little skiffle group would try to imitate what we were hearing."

In July 1962, Keith Richards, Mick Jagger, and Brian Jones, along with Dick Taylor and drummer Tony Chapman, formed the Rolling Stones and moved into a rundown apartment in the downtrodden district of King's Road. They debuted on July 12 at the Marquee Club in London as a replacement for Blues Incorporated and landed a steady gig at the Crawdaddy Club in Richmond, owned by Giorgio Gomelsky and named after a then-recent Bo Diddley song, "Doing the Craw-Daddy." By January 1963, modern jazz aficionado Charlie Watts replaced Chapman as drummer and bassist Bill Wyman (b. Bill Perks) joined when Taylor went back to school and several months later launched the blues-driven band, The Pretty Things, solidifying a lineup that would remain intact for over forty years. "We wanted to sell records for Jimmy Reed, Muddy, John Lee Hooker," explained Keith Richards. "We were disciples—if we could turn people on to that, then that was enough. That was the total original aim." The "translation" of American blues "into a British sound was our blueprint," added bassist Wyman (Wyman, Stone Alone, p. 77).

The material chosen by the early Stones showed their Chicago blues orientation. For their first single, recorded in early 1963, they covered Chuck Berry's "Come On" and Muddy Waters' "I Wanna Be Loved." Their first American album, *England's Newest Hitmakers*, included Slim Harpo's "I'm a Kingbee," "Carol" by Chuck Berry, Willie Dixon's "I Just Wanna Make Love to You," and Jimmy Reed's "Honest I Do." Subsequent albums exposed teenage record buyers to Chicago blues classics such as "You Can't Catch Me" (Chuck Berry), "Little Red Rooster" (Willie Dixon), "Mona" (Bo Diddley), and "Look What You've Done" (Muddy Waters). The Stones recorded many of these cuts at the Chess studio in Chicago. The band even took its name—the Rolling Stones—from a track on Muddy Waters' debut album, "Rollin' Stone."

By April 1963, the *Record Mirror* characterized the Stones as "genuine R&B." "As the trad scene gradually subsides," the magazine informed its readers, "the hip kids throw themselves around to the new jungle music like they never did in the more restrained days of trad. And the combo they writhe and twist to is called the Rolling Stones."

The Stones Turn Raunchy

On May 6, 1963, Andrew Loog Oldham, a former employee of fashion queen Mary Quant and publicity man for Bob Dylan and the Beatles, became the manager of the Stones. He helped propel the blues-based group to fame by creating a raunchy, crude, offensive image that contrasted sharply with the reputation of the cute and clean-living Beatles.

At first, the band appeared like most other British invasion bands. On July 7, 1963, when debuting on the influential British television show *Thank Your Lucky Stars*, the Stones wore checkered suits with black velvet collars, matching ties and trousers, and blue leather waistcoats. The show required such formal dress, and Oldham told his band that they needed to make the compromise. Oldham instructed the group, sounding like his one-time boss, Brian Epstein.

Oldham quickly changed his strategy and manufactured opposite counter-image to the neat, smiling Beatles. He portrayed the Stones "as a raunchy, gamy, unpredictable bunch of undesirables. I decided that since the Beatles had already usurped the clean-cut choirboy image with synchronized jackets, I should take the Stones down the opposite road." He rejected matching clothing and fabricated "an unclean appearance" to attract the sensationalist-hungry press. "I wanted to establish that the Stones were threatening, uncouth and animalistic," said Oldham. "It was perfect, just perfect," he told Jagger after a press conference at which the Stones had given flippant and insulting replies to journalists. "They're going to plaster your pictures and your terrible, terrible statements all over the papers. Those dirty Rolling Stones, that's what you are. The opposite of those nice little chaps, the Beatles. … We're gonna make you famous." To refine the image, Oldham engineered a few other changes. He downgraded piano player Ian Stewart to roadie. "Well, he just doesn't look the part, and six is too many for [fans] to remember the faces in the picture," Oldham told Richards at the time. The manager shaved a few years off the ages of each Stone in their official biography, making them teens again. He then convinced his label, Decca Records, to blitz the media. As one ad read in *Billboard* on May 16, 1964, "They're great! They're outrageous! They're rebels! They sell! They're England's *hottest* … but *hottest* group." "The Rolling Stones aren't just a group, they're a way of life," insisted Oldham (Wyman, Stone Alone, p. 203).

The Stones reinforced the image of sixties rebellion. "We've become a figurehead for all the kinds who would like to rebel against authority," remarked Brian Jones. "We're expressing something they cannot say or do." "The Rolling Stones became the archetypical rebels," summarized Bill Wyman (Wyman, Stone Alone, p. 219, 160).

The media soon picked up on the cue. In March 1964, *Melody Maker* carried an article headlined "Would You Let Your Sister Go with a Rolling Stone?" and described the band as "symbols of rebellion … against the boss, the clock, and the clean-shirt-a-day routine." The Stones, it continued, looked like "five indolent morons, [who] give one the feeling that they really enjoy wallowing in a swill-tub of their own repulsiveness." *New Musical Express* labeled the group as "the caveman-like quintet." The British *Daily Express* characterized the band as "boys any self-respecting mother would lock in the bathroom." In 1964, *Newsweek* interviewed Keith Richards, who told the magazine that he hoped "to be sitting in a country house with four Rolls-Royces and spitting at everyone."

Success

The raunchy Rolling Stones soon achieved success in England, ironically through help from the Beatles who considered the Stones their friends. On a chance meeting, George Harrison suggested to Dick Rowe, the head of Artists and Repertoire for Decca Records, that he sign the Rolling Stones. In early May 1963, after witnessing their performance at the Crawdaddy Club, Rowe inked a three-year deal with the band. Four months later, the Beatles gave the Stones one of their unrecorded songs, "I Wanna Be Your Man," which reached the number-twelve slot on the British chart. "To us the Beatles were always the door opener," contended Keith Richards.

Jump-started by the Beatles, the Stones took off. After signing with Decca, the Stones appeared on various British television shows such as *Thank Your Lucky Stars, Ready, Steady, Go!* and *Top of the Pops*. In March 1964, the Stones accentuated the Bo Diddley beat on a remake of Buddy Holly's "Not Fade Away" to reach number three. By May, the group received 100,000 advance orders for its first British album, which immediately topped the chart on its release. During concerts, the Stones were mobbed by teenage girls and pulled off the stage.

Rolling Stones performing on *Ready, Steady, Go!*, 1964.

Pictorial Press Ltd./Alamy Stock Photo.

The British success of the blues-based Stones probably stemmed from their youth and good looks, appealing to the growing legion of U.K. baby boomers. "The Stones were the first people into the blues in England. Alexis Korner and Cyril Davies were, but the Stones were the first ones who were young," recalled Giorgio Gomelsky, the first manager of the Stones. "I like to think we became popular," agreed Charlie Watts, "because we played music to dance to, which was a massive appeal to the young people. In addition, we weren't bad looking."

The Stones initially had more difficulty igniting the youth in the United States despite a major promotional campaign by their record label. During their first U.S. tour, which started in early June 1964, the Stones received scant notice. On June 3, they appeared on a segment of *The Hollywood Palace* television show, which was hosted by crooner Dean Martin. After the Stones chugged through their versions of "I Just Want to Make Love to You" and "Not Fade Away," a twisted-faced Martin, eyes rolling upward, asked the audience, "Aren't they great?" "They're off to England to have a hair-pulling contest with the Beatles," he joked. "Their hair is not long, it's just smaller foreheads and higher eyebrows." When a trampolinist finished his comedy act, Martin added: "That's the father of the Rolling Stones. He's been trying to kill himself ever since." To a distraught Brian Jones, Dean Martin "was just a symbol of the whole tour for us."

On the remaining dates of the tour, the band mostly played to empty seats. In San Antonio, Texas, the crowd clamored for an encore by a trained monkey rather than one by the Rolling Stones. "We all wanted to pack up and come home," confessed Bill Wyman. The colorful Keith Richards remembered, "Nebraska, we really felt like a sore pimple in Omaha." When they arrived in the city, a motorcade of twelve policemen escorted the band to the auditorium. The Stones, initially ebullient over the police escort, soon became dejected when they found an audience of 600 in the 15,000-seat hall. In Detroit, less than a thousand fans attended the Stones concert held in a venue that seated 13,000. Mick Jagger vowed to "never get involved in this kind of tour again."

The Ed Sullivan Show helped the Stones conquered America on their second tour, which began on October 24, 1964. During the 1950s and 1960s, Ed Sullivan provided the means for teens across the United States to hear rock and roll. He had helped promote Elvis Presley, had fostered Beatlemania, and had provided the springboard for British invasion groups such as Gerry and the Pacemakers, the Searchers, and the Dave Clark Five. "The power of the man [Sullivan] and his show was unbelievable," enthused Dave Clark, who appeared on the show seventeen times. "He was responsible for the success of the British invasion."

On *The Ed Sullivan Show* of October 25, 1964, American teens were introduced to the Stones as a raunchy, hip alternative to the Beatles. After the appearance by the Stones, the host publicly proclaimed: "I promise you they'll never be back on our show." Privately, remembered Mick Jagger, "Ed told us it was the wildest, most enthusiastic audience he'd seen any artist get in the history of his show. We got a message a few days later saying: 'Received hundreds of letters from parents complaining about you, but thousands from teenagers saying how much they enjoyed your performance.'" Sullivan hosted a return engagement by the Stones on May 2, 1965.

An antagonistic American press also helped publicize the Rolling Stones. *Newsweek* pegged the Stones as a "leering quintet" obsessed with pornographic lyrics. *Newsweek* magazine printed the letter of one concerned woman, who wrote: "We like the Beatles because they have rhythm, enthusiasm, and a good sound. After listening to the groans, pants, and frankly dirty words of the Rolling Stones and a few other sick groups, one begins to wonder where they dig up a DJ to play such garbage."

Such adult criticism of the band predictably pushed rebellious American teenagers into the Stones' camp. Beatle George Harrison noticed that "it's become the in thing for adults to say the Beatles are good or the Beatles are funny, it's in for adults to like us. So the real hip kids—or the kids who think they are—have gone off us. The in thing for those kids now is to be a Stones fan, because their parents can't stand the Rolling Stones." Agreed Sean O'Mahony, publisher of the *Beatles Book Monthly*, "The Stones and the Beatles had quite different fans. The Beatles were thugs who were put across as nice blokes, and the Stones were gentlemen who were made into thugs by Andrew [Loog Oldham]."

Throughout the remaining dates of their second American tour in 1964, the Stones played to enthusiastic crowds. Keith Richards at the time felt an "energy building up as you go around the country. You find it winding tighter and tighter, until one day you get out halfway through the first number and the whole place is full of chicks screaming." A performance seemed like the Battle of Crimea with "people gasping, tits hanging out, chicks choking, nurses running around," added Richards. "It was unbelievable. You'd get chicks flying out of the balconies like, 'I love youuu. .' Crash, broken ribs and wore." Ian Stewart, who by this time traveled with the band as a roadie, added, "There sure as hell weren't any empty seats this time. Wherever we went, it was bedlam."

The Stones' success coincided with a new, less blues-dominated sound. "I was convinced they couldn't make it as a top group by just playing old rhythm and blues tunes," recalled Andrew Loog Oldham. "The entire teenage population of the British Isles could not be expected to relate to the needs and wants of middle-aged blacks." "We had all witnessed with our own eyes and ears how easy Lennon and McCartney had knocked off 'I Wanna Be Your Man,' and I felt that Mick and Keith could do the same for us once they got the hang of it."

Encouraged by Oldham, Richards and Jagger pushed aside the versatile Brian Jones and concentrated on their own material, which combined pop conventions with Chicago-style blues. "Andrew literally forced Mick and me to start writing songs," reminisced Richards. "Andrew presented the idea to us, not on an artistic level, but more money." At one point, the dictatorial Oldham locked Jagger and Richards in a room the size of a small kitchen and instructed them to write. "When I came back I expected a song, and they'd better have one if they expected me to bring them any food," recollected Oldham. When the manager returned, the duo had produced a song for their dinner, "Tell Me (You're Coming Back)." "It's a very pop song, as opposed to all the blues songs and Motown covers, which everyone did at the time," mentioned Jagger. "One thing I can never thank Andrew Oldham enough for—it was more important to the Stones than anything and probably his main achievement," asserted Richards, "was that he turned Mick and me into songwriters."

The Jagger–Richards songwriting team quickly became prolific. By their fourth LP, *Out of Our Heads*, which was recorded in mid-1965, the band had moved toward the R&B-influenced, hard rock songs of Jagger–Richards, such as the rebellious, chart-topping "Satisfaction" which, according to Mick Jagger, dealt with "my frustration with everything. Simple teenage aggression." "It was the song that really made the Rolling Stones," explained Jagger, "changed us from just another band into a huge, monster band."

By the 1966 *Aftermath*, Jagger–Richards compositions, such as the murky incantations of "Paint It Black" and the misogynist venom of "Under My Thumb" and "Stupid Girl," had almost totally replaced R&B covers. "That was a big landmark record for me," explained Jagger. "It's the first time we wrote the whole record and finally laid to rest the ghost of having to do these very nice and interesting, no doubt, but still cover versions of old R&B songs."

As well as writing their own material, the Stones changed visually. Rather than stand in a stationary position, front man Jagger danced around the stage in choreographed moves. "I used to aspire to be like James Brown in his moves, and so I copied a lot of James Brown's moves in the early days," he explained. Together with their new songs, by the end of the 1966, the Rolling Stones vied with the Beatles for the rock-and-roll crown.

The Who

The Who made a similar transition from the Chicago blues to their own compositions. As the Detours, the band covered American blues such as Jimmy Reed's "Big Boss Man," Bo Diddley's "I'm a Man," and Willie Dixon's "I Just Wanna Make Love to You." The group, changing its name to the High Numbers, reworked bluesman Slim Harpo's "Got Love If You Want It" for its first single, "I'm the Face."

Pete Meaden, the archetypical Mod and a freelance publicist who had worked with Andrew Loog Oldham, first managed and reshaped the R&B cover band. To distinguish the leather-clad boys from other blues cover bands in Britain, Meaden grafted a Mod image onto the group. He "had this dream of getting a group together that would be the focus, the entertainers for the Mods; a group that would actually be the same people onstage as the guys in the audience … an actual representation of the people." "Our Mod image was engineered by our first manager, a very bright boy named Peter Meaden," recounted singer Roger Daltrey. "At the time in England, 90 percent of the bands resembled either the Rolling Stones or the Beatles. If anything, we were similar to the Stones. … The Mod look was very clean-cut, Ivy League, fashion conscious, which was exactly opposite from the Stones."

The band quickly adopted the clean-cut Mod style. "The original idea was for Roger [Daltrey] to dress up as a sharp top Mod, a face; and the rest of the band to be in T-shirts and Levis, boxing boots and the current 'in' clothes of a typical street Mod, a ticket," remarked Richard Barnes, an early confidant of the band. "Pete Meaden introduced The Who to the very hub of this exclusive group," taking them to the prime Mod handout, Scene Club in London's Soho. Guitarist Pete Townshend even "practiced the complicated steps to the two main Mod dances, the 'block' and the 'bang.' He rehearsed the Mod way of walking and tried to pick up the correct way of standing around."

In 1964, Meaden promoted the reworked blues single of the High Numbers as a Mod anthem. He titled the song "I'm the Face," a reference to a sharply dressed, top Mod. His press release called the record "the *first authentic* Mod record, a hip tailored-for-teens R&B-oriented shuffle rocker … with a kick in every catch phrase for the kids of the fast-moving crowd." In the summer of the same year, Meaden negotiated with filmmakers Kit Lambert and Chris Stamp, the brother of actor Terence Stamp, to feature the group in a film about the Mods.

After working on the film, the band fired Meaden and hired as managers Lambert and Stamp, who reinforced the Mod image of the group. Bankrolled by their new

The Who in London, 1964.

Pictorial Press Ltd./Alamy Stock Photo.

managers, the band members went to Carnaby Street, the district in London, which featured the most modern styles of clothing. "We weren't into clothes, we were into music," contended drummer Keith Moon, but "Kit thought we should identify more with our audience. Coats slashed five inches at the side. Four wasn't enough. Six was too much. Five was just right." The band, influenced by the Pop art movement that Townshend had encountered in art school, returned with garb that would become their trademark: bull's-eye T-shirts, and pants, shirts, and jackets cut from the British flag. The group renamed themselves The Who and played for sixteen consecutive Tuesdays at the new London Marquee Club, a Mod hangout owned by Ziggy Jackson.

To complete the reshaping of The Who, Pete Townshend began to write original material for the band on the advice of the managers. He first penned "I Can't Explain." Though "Roger in particular wanted the band to be a blues-based band and thought that 'I Can't Explain' was too pop sounding," mentioned Richard Barnes, Townshend followed with "Anyhow, Anyway, Anywhere." As his third song, he wrote "My Generation," which became the battle cry of the Mods. "That's my generation, that's how the song 'My Generation' happened, because of the Mods," Townshend explained.

The members of The Who grew up in the same working-class neighborhoods as other London Mods. Roger Daltrey, lead singer and organizer of the group, Pete Townshend, and bassist John Entwistle were raised in Shepherd's Bush, a dilapidated suburb of West London. Before The Who gained notoriety, band members worked as manual laborers—Daltrey for five years as a sheet metal worker, and Townshend and Entwistle at various odd jobs.

Keith Moon, the ebullient madman of the group, who met an untimely death in 1978, grew up in Wembley and joined the band when he wandered into the Oldfield Hotel one day to listen to their show. Standing out with his "dyed ginger hair and a ginger cord suit," Moon asked the band if he could play with them during one number. In the words of the drummer, "they said go ahead, and I got behind this other guy's drums and did one song—'Road Runner.' I'd several drinks to get me courage up and when I got onstage I went arrgggGhhhh on the drums, broke the bass drum pedal and two skins, and got off. I figured that was it." After Moon's antics, Roger unexpectedly asked the drummer to join the band.

The Who's sound captured the anger and rebelliousness of the English Mods. Daltrey screamed the lyrics of a song, backed by Townshend's crashing chords, the thumping bass of Entwistle, and Moon's propulsive drumming. Townshend, who wrote most of the band's material, felt that The Who's brand of rock and roll "is a single impetus and it's a single force which threatens a lot of crap which is around at the moment in the middle class and in the middle-aged politics or philosophy." Townshend's guitar-smashing antics and Moon's destruction of his drum kit accentuated the defiant spirit of the band. The R&B-influenced group became the most popular band among British Mods. "The groups that you liked when you were a Mod were The Who," bragged Pete Townshend.

The British Blues Onslaught

Other British bands, enamored with Chicago blues, gained the allegiance of British and American teens. The Yardbirds learned about the power of the blues from the Rolling Stones. In 1963, singer Keith Relf and drummer Jim McCarty "went to see the Rolling Stones because they started playing in Richmond, which was quite near … and we gradually listened to more of this R&B stuff, got more records," recollected McCarty. That year, McCarty's band, which included guitarists Chris Dreja and Top Topham, merged with Relf and bassist Paul Samwell-Smith, both of whom wanted to play more R&B like their heroes Jimmy Reed, Howlin' Wolf, and Chuck Berry.

The Yardbirds first performed as a backup band for Cyril Davies, and in 1963, replaced the Rolling Stones as the house band at the Crawdaddy Club, owned by the first manager of the Stones, Giorgio Gomelsky. In June 1964, they debuted on record with a cover of Chicago blues harmonica man Billy Boy Arnold's "I Wish You Would" and first charted in Britain a few months later with Don & Bob's R&B standard, "Good Morning Little School Girl." On a December 1963 tour of England, booked by Gomelsky, the band backed Sonny Boy Williamson and a few months later played at the Rhythm and Blues Festival in Birmingham. "A lot of the basis of our act was rearranged rhythm and blues," commented Dreja.

The Yardbirds featured a series of guitar wizards steeped in the blues. When lead guitarist Top Topham left for college in 1963, the band hired blues purist Eric Clapton, who "grew up loving black music." Clapton left the group in 1965, when he felt that the hit "For Your Love" sounded too pop, which he held in contempt. "I went back to Skip James and Robert Johnson—I spent years in that field and then I came back to the city blues, worked around there for a while, and I guess that's where my heart really still is," explained the guitarist. When the Yardbirds recorded "For Your Love," Clapton felt "that we had completely sold out." After the departure of Clapton, the Yardbirds added the more rockabilly-influenced Jeff Beck. "We still played the blues—Jeff could play a great blues—but at the same time we were always looking to something new, something fresh," remarked McCarty. In June 1966, Jimmy Page, who would later help invent heavy metal with Led Zeppelin, joined the group. By July 1968, when they disbanded, the Yardbirds had scored such blues-inspired hits in Britain and America as "Heart Full of Soul."

From the Muswell Hill region of London, a northern working-class suburb, came the Kinks. The band formed in late 1963 by R&B enthusiasts Ray and Dave Davies, Peter Quaife, and Mick Avory, who had briefly played with the Rolling Stones. In February 1964, they unsuccessfully debuted with Little Richard's "Long Tall Sally." By August of the same year, the group topped the British chart and entered the U.S. Top Ten with "You Really Got Me," which defined power-chord rock. The song featured multi-note barre chords played loudly in a staccato fashion up and down the neck of the guitar through a distorted amplifier, when lead guitarist Dave Davies slashed the speaker of his amplifier with a razor blade. Two months later, the Kinks followed with the crunching "All Day and All of the Night" before turning toward a softer, music-hall style. Although charting in America, the group met disaster when the American Federation of Musicians instituted a four-year ban on them for unprofessional conduct during their first American tour in June 1965.

Spencer Davis, a teacher and blues enthusiast, launched an R&B-based band. In August 1963, he joined with drummer Peter York and the Winwood brothers, Steve and Muff, to start the Spencer Davis Group, which opened with a remake of John Lee Hooker's "Dimples." "We were really heavily into the blues, blues singers and blues writers," remembered Davis. "Basically what we used to do was more or less copy—or do our own arrangements of—blues and rhythm 'n' blues records, which at the time were fairly unheard of," agreed Steve Winwood. Within two years, added Winwood, "we had an idea that we no longer wanted to actually copy, [we wanted] to write; we felt we could contribute ourselves toward the material." In 1965 and 1966, the band members scored on both sides of the Atlantic with their own blues-drenched compositions such as "Gimmie Some Lovin'" and "Somebody Help Me."

In 1962, a budding jazz pianist (b. Manfred Lubowitz) teamed with Mike Hugg to become the Mann–Hugg Blues Brothers. After greeted by wild receptions at the London Marquee Club, the duo added three more members to emerge as Manfred Mann and the Manfreds or, in the United States, as simply Manfred Mann. In early 1964, the band scored in Britain with "5-4-3-2-1," the theme of the popular British rock television show *Ready, Steady, Go!*, and by August topped the U.S. charts with a remake of the Jeff Barry/Ellie Greenwich song "Do Wah Diddy Diddy." The band subsequently covered R&B standards such as "Smokestack Lightnin'" by Howlin' Wolf, and Willie Dixon's "(I'm Your) Hoochie Coochie Man."

The Animals, a group of poor youths from a mining town in northern England, named for their wild stage behavior, played a convincing brand of British R&B to both British and American fans. In 1962, jazz organist Alan Price joined with lead guitarist Hilton Valentine, bassist Bryan "Chas" Chandler, drummer John Steel, and Eric Burdon, who had become captivated by Chicago blues after witnessing a Muddy Waters performance. Price was pushed in the direction of rhythm and blues by the new musicians, especially Burdon, who in a book of his lyrics had written the word *blues* in his own blood. "We were all crusaders tryin' to carry the spear forward of belief in rhythm and blues and blue music and get the kids to listen to the original stuff," contended Burdon. During their first two years, The Animals attracted a following at the Club-a-Go-Go in their hometown of Newcastle-on-Tyne. After moving to London in 1964, the band reworked the folk-blues number "The House of the Rising Sun" into a number-one, million-selling hit on both sides of the Atlantic. They then revived a series of other blues songs and in September 1964 triumphantly toured the United States.

George Ivan Morrison and his group, Them, were equally dedicated to American R&B. Raised in Ulster by parents who were blues and jazz enthusiasts, Van Morrison grew up listening to John Lee Hooker, Muddy Waters, and Sonny Boy Williamson. At age 15, he dropped out of school to join the band The Monarchs, which headlined at the R&B Club in Belfast. In 1963, Van Morrison formed a group called Them, who charted in Britain and America with "Here Comes the Night." Though hardly cracking the U.S. chart with "Gloria," a song that Van Morrison attributed to a blues club that he had joined, the band defined a sound that would be emulated by thousands of garage bands in the United States during the next few years.

American Garage Rock

The British blues invasion of America prompted young American teens to embrace their blues heritage. The British covers of American originals initially offered notoriety for some blues pioneers among a white audience. "We still have mostly Negro adults at our gigs," remarked B. B. King in 1966, "but I've noticed in the last year or so I've had a lot [more] of the white kids come than ever before." When the British bands came over," he added, "they made the U.S. as a whole aware of the blues." Muddy Waters noticed the same trend: "The Rolling Stones came out named after my song, you know, and recorded 'I Just Wanna Make Love to You' and the next thing I knew [white youths] were out there. And that's how people in the States really got to know who Muddy Waters was." During the mid-1960s, the sound of Chicago blues ironically had been introduced to American youths by British bands.

British blues groups compelled a generation of American youths to buy electric guitars and drums, form bands, practice in their garages, and sometimes produce gutbucket, primal, proto-punk regional hits. From 1964 to 1966 after the Stones and other British blues invasion acts toured the United States, garage bands coalesced in nearly every part of the country.

Los Angeles and other parts of California nurtured several prominent garage groups. Assembled by former folkie Sean Bonniwell in 1966, the Music Machine exploded on the scene with the hard-hitting anthem "Talk Talk." The group, referred to as "the American Rolling Stones" according to Bonniwell, "really wanted that bottom power punch." In 1965, the Stones-influenced Seeds blasted forth from Los Angeles around Sky Saxon (b. Richard Marsh). They delivered garage-rock anthems such as "Pushin' Too Hard." The same year, the Los Angeles–based Electric Prunes joined with Rolling Stones engineer Dave Hassinger to hit the chart with "I Had Too Much to Dream Last Night." The band also charted with the Bo Diddley–inspired

"Get Me to the World on Time." "We loved Bo Diddley," explained singer James Lowe. Just like the Rolling Stones, he "grew up on that beat, I ate to that beat."

In San Jose near San Francisco around 1965, the Chocolate Watchband started performing with vocalist Dave Aguilar and Sean Tolby on guitar. The British blues–influenced group quickly became a regional sensation with "The Blues Theme." On stage, the band, according to Aguilar, covered "Muddy Waters to the Yardbirds or an occasional very obscure Stones song." They also selected the Chuck Berry song "Come On." "Hell, if it worked for the Stones, it might work for us," reasoned the lead singer. Ed Cobb, the manager of the Chocolate Watchband, also refashioned the Los Angeles pop group the Standells into a garage band with the 1966 classic "Dirty Water." San Jose yielded the Count Five, a Yardbirds-inspired outfit that in 1966 hit the Top Five of the national chart with the churning, raucous "Psychotic Reaction."

In the Midwest, bands seemed to be coming from nearly every garage. Chicago, the epicenter of electric blues, listened to the Shadows of Knight, which modified the British blues for the Windy City. "The Stones, the Animals and Yardbirds took the Chicago blues and gave it an English interpretation," observed the group. "We've taken the English version of the blues and re-added a Chicago touch." In late 1965, they remade Them's "Gloria" for a Top Ten national hit.

Detroit spawned a series of garage bands that added a touch of soul to the British blues. With earth-shattering shrieks and flying-knee drops in concert, Mitch Ryder (b. William Levise, Jr.) and the Detroit Wheels delivered a gut-bucket, propulsive sound. He scaled the chart with such raves as "Devil with a Blue Dress On." Question Mark and the Mysterians played a more straightforward, Stones-influenced style. After topping the regional chart, the Latino band scored a national number-one smash in 1966 with the rowdy, organ-powered "96 Tears."

A more original, wilder, and definitive garage band sound emanated from the Seattle area. Getting together well before the Rolling Stones, the Wailers met at an officers' club outside Tacoma, Washington. They originally listened to blues and early rock and roll. "We used to go to the Evergreen Ballroom to see R&B shows," remembered bassist Buck Ormsby. "We'd go see Little Richard and the Upsetters every time they came through, and we were the only white guys there." Soon the band played covers of the songs that they liked. "There were all these old ballrooms left over from the big band era, and we just sort of took them over," continued Ormsby. "When we had a dance up there at the Spanish Castle [the subject of Jimi Hendrix's 'Spanish Castle Magic'], we had like two or three thousand kids. We were doing Freddie King songs like 'Stumble' and 'San-Ho-Zay' before anybody had ever heard of them." In 1959, the Wailers hit with the original "Tall Cool One," appearing on *American Bandstand* and the *Alan Freed Show* to promote the record.

In 1960, the Wailers, unhappy with their record contract, launched their own label, calling it Etiquette. They released what would become the all-time classic garage single, "Louie Louie." The group followed with the raw abandon of *The Fabulous Wailers at the Castle*. Though having some early local competitors, the Wailers took a pivotal role in transforming an instrumental rhythm and blues into the nitty-gritty sound of the garage. The group provided an inspiration to such soon-to-be stars as the Rolling Stones, Pete Townshend of the Who, and the Kinks.

Buck Ormsby sought other local bands for his label, finding the Sonics in a Tacoma garage practicing in 1963. They started playing "'The Witch' and I went, 'Man this is it! Let's go record that!,' " enthused Ormsby. The Sonics acknowledged their debt to the Wailers. "Overall, the Wailers were our biggest influence always!" confessed bass player and Sonics leader Andy Parypa. "Other influences were people like James Brown and Freddie King, [organist] Bill Doggett was a big influence on all the Seattle groups." The group took these influences, revved them up and distorted them, adding the bloodcurdling screams of Gary Rosalie for vocals. In songs such as "The Witch," "Psycho," and "Strychnine," the band defined garage rock and presaged heavy metal and punk with its nearly uncontrollable music. "It's raw, it's forceful, it's energetic," explained Parypa about his band's sound. "I mean the Sonics were savage!"

Other Northwest bands commercialized the Tacoma crunch of the Sonics. Formed in Portland, Oregon, in late 1963, the Kingsmen spent $50 to cut a demo audition tape of "Louie Louie" in a Portland recording studio. Jerry Dennon, the owner of Jerden records, bought the song and rushed it to market. By the end of the month, the Kingsmen version of the Northwest classic became a number-two national hit and raised the ire of adults who imagined obscene lyrics in the obscured vocals of Jack Ely. The governor of Indiana even banned the record from the state, and the Federal Bureau of Investigation investigated the band. With their newfound fame, a revamped Kingsmen lineup scored again with two covers, Barrett Strong's "Money" and the Olympics's "Big Boy Pete," which they titled "Jolly Green Giant."

Paul Revere and the Raiders, an Idaho band coming together in 1959, scored even greater success as they built upon the sound of the Wailers and Sonics. "It was the Wailers who really inspired everybody," remembered Paul Revere (b. Paul Revere Dick). "Everyone wanted to be like the Wailers." Sporting Revolutionary War costumes after 1963, the band offered a slightly more accessible version of Northwest garage rock and hit regionally with "Louie Louie."

In 1964, the band opened for the Rolling Stones and attracted the attention of Columbia Records. In early 1965, they just missed the Top Ten with "Just Like Me," characterized by singer Mark Lindsay as "a rip-off. Sounded to me like the Kinks and the Stones." By June 1965, with the help of Beatles publicist Derek Taylor, the Raiders achieved national stardom, becoming the house band for the weekday, Dick Clark–inspired television show *Where the Action Is*. Within a year, they hit the Top Ten with "Kicks" and "Hungry." "We were in the right place at the right time with the right name with the right costumes, just in time for the British invasion, just in time [when] Dick Clark happened to have a television show where he needed something visual, colorful with three-cornered hats," explained Revere.

By the mid-sixties, garage bands played in nearly every major American city. The Litter covered the songs of the Yardbirds in Minneapolis; the Human Beinz sang their hit "Nobody But Me" in Youngstown, Ohio; the Moving Sidewalks wailed their "99th Floor" in Houston, Texas; the Strangeloves from Brooklyn snarled their "I Want Candy"; and the Mojo Men covered the Stones' "Off the Hook" in San Francisco. Throughout the country, hundreds of garage bands scored regional and sometimes national hits with the raw, many times British-inspired, blues-based rock, which paved the way for later developments such as punk and grunge.

Chapter 9
Motown: The Sound of Integration

"This organization is built on love."

—Berry Gordy

"This organization is built on love," 35-year-old Berry Gordy, Jr., the founder of Motown Records, told *Newsweek* in early 1965. "We're dealing with feeling and truth."

Gordy, sounding much like Martin Luther King, Jr., created a music empire that exemplified the peaceful integration advocated by King and reflected the progress of the civil rights movement. The African-American-owned and operated Motown was established a year before the first sit-in demonstration and achieved moderate success during the civil rights strife of the early 1960s. The Detroit-based company, using the assembly-line techniques of nearby auto factories, became a major force in popular music from late 1964 to 1967, when civil rights partisans won a series of significant legislative victories. At a time when the civil rights of African Americans began to be recognized, Motown became the first African-American-owned label that consistently and successfully groomed, packaged, marketed, and sold the music of African-American youths to the white American masses.

Motown: The Early Years

Berry Gordy, Jr. started his career in the music industry as a producer and songwriter. Born in Detroit on November 28, 1929, Gordy became interested in songwriting as a youth. "I did other things," he remembered. "I was a plasterer for a while in my father's business, took a job on an automobile assembly line. But I always wrote songs." In 1957, Gordy had his first success with the song "Reet Petite," which was recorded by Detroit-born Jackie Wilson, who at one time replaced Clyde McPhatter as the lead singer of the Dominoes. The next year he penned the million-selling "Lonely Teardrops" for Wilson and established the Jobete Music Publishing Company. At the same time, Gordy produced records such as the Miracles' "Got a Job."

In January 1959, the same year that Don Kirshner started Aldon Music, Berry Gordy borrowed $800 from his family, rented an eight-room house at 2648 West Grand Boulevard, and founded the Motown Record Corporation, which would issue records under a variety of labels. "If I ever get this house and get it paid for," Gordy told his sister Esther at the time, "I'll have it made. I'll live upstairs, I'll have my offices down in the front part, and I'll have a studio out back where I can make demonstration records or masters to sell to record companies."

Gordy initially recorded rhythm-and-blues artists on Tamla Records. He signed blues belter Mable John, the gospel-trained sister of bluesman Little Willie John. Gordy scored a minor hit with the first Tamla release, R&B singer Marv Johnson's "Come to Me." Later during his first year of operation, he cowrote and released "Money," which was recorded by Barrett Strong and climbed to the number-two position on the R&B chart. In September 1959, the Motown founder recorded "Bad Girl" by

19-year-old William "Smokey" Robinson and the Detroit-born Miracles, a song that reached number ninety-three on the pop chart with the help of national distribution by Chess Records.

Gordy became convinced by Smokey Robinson that Motown should distribute its own records. "When I started," Gordy told *Black Enterprise*, "we licensed our singles to other companies such as United Artists. Smokey Robinson gave me the idea to go national with my own product; my attorneys and other people said it was madness, that I shouldn't do it because a hit would throw me into bankruptcy since [we were] undercapitalized." In 1960, Gordy cowrote and distributed "Shop Around" by Smokey Robinson and the Miracles, which hit the top of the R&B chart and the number-two slot on the pop chart to establish Motown as an important independent company.

Throughout the next four years, Berry Gordy continued to produce hits by capitalizing on the girl group craze. In 1959, 16-year-old Mary Wells approached the Motown founder with a song she had written for Jackie Wilson. Unable to write music, she sang the song to Gordy, who immediately signed the teenager and released her version of "Bye Bye Baby," which hit the Top Ten on the R&B chart in 1960. Two years later, Wells teamed with Smokey Robinson, who by now wrote and produced for Tamla, and hit with "The One Who Really Loves You," "You Beat Me to the Punch," and "Two Lovers," all of which hit the Top Ten on the pop chart. After a few minor hits, in 1964 Wells topped the pop chart with her signature song, "My Guy."

Gordy charted with the Marvelettes. "We were discovered at a talent show in Inkster [Michigan]," recalled Wanda Young, who established the group with Gladys Horton. "One of our teachers arranged an audition for us with Motown, even though we didn't even win the contest." In 1961, the group signed with the label and released "Please Mr. Postman," written by Marvelette Georgia Dobbins, a song that became Motown's first number-one hit. The next year, the Marvelettes hit the Top Twenty with "Playboy." In November 1962, the group toured the South in a bus and five cars as part of the first Motortown Revue and, according to Katherine Anderson of the Marvelettes, "did what we could to play for integrated audiences."

Berry Gordy, Jr., encouraged by his success with the Marvelettes, recorded another group of girls from Detroit—Martha and the Vandellas. Martha Reeves, influenced by the gospel sound of Clara Ward and jazz singer Billie Holiday, joined with Annette Sterling and Rosalind Ashford to sing as the Del-Phis while in high school and recorded the unsuccessful "I'll Let You Know" for Chess. In 1961, Reeves accepted a job at Motown as a secretary and, by July 1962, convinced the company to use her group. The persistent trio sang backup vocals on a number of Motown hits, including "Hitch Hike" and "Stubborn Kind of Fellow" by Marvin Gaye, a romantic balladeer who had sung in the doo-wop group the Moonglows and in 1961 had joined Motown. In late 1963, amid the girl-group explosion, Martha and the Vandellas hit the chart with the million-selling, Top-Ten "(Love Is Like a) Heat Wave" and "Quicksand." The next year, they recorded the memorable "Dancing in the Street," which neared the top of the pop chart and, along with hits by Mary Wells and the Marvelettes, positioned Motown as a major source of the girl-group sound.

Civil Rights in the Great Society

The civil rights movement, which became more visible in the 1950s and escalated during the early 1960s, resulted in significant achievements during the mid-1960s that coincided with the Motown heyday.

On July 2, 1964, Congress passed the most sweeping civil rights legislation since the Civil War. The Civil Rights Act established a sixth-grade education as a minimum voting requirement and empowered the attorney general to protect the voting rights of all citizens. It forbade discrimination in public places such as restaurants, hotels, bathrooms, and libraries; created an Equal Employment Opportunity Commission and a Community Relations Service to help communities solve racially based problems; banned discrimination in federally funded programs; and authorized technical and financial aid for school desegregation. Also in 1964, Congress ratified the Twenty-Fourth Amendment to the U.S. Constitution, which outlawed the poll tax in federal elections.

The next year, Congress enacted the Voting Rights Act, after violence erupted in Selma, Alabama. Early in 1965, Sheriff James G. Clark forcibly resisted a voter registration drive in Dallas County, Alabama, where no African Americans had voted in years. He collected a posse wielding whips, clubs, and canisters of tear gas to disperse peaceful demonstrators, two of whom were murdered. Martin Luther King, Jr. and 3,200 equal rights partisans, protected by the Alabama National Guard, marched 50 miles from Selma to Montgomery to protest the blatant discrimination and violence. "No tide of racism can stop us," King exhorted 25,000 listeners in Montgomery after the completion of his five-day march.

Disturbed by the events in Selma, President Lyndon Johnson proposed greater voting safeguards for African Americans and, in the words of the civil rights anthem, promised Congress that "we shall overcome." Congress responded with a law that banned unfair literacy tests used in the South to disenfranchise African Americans and authorized the attorney general to dispatch federal examiners to register voters in areas, where local examiners discriminated on the basis of color. By the end of the year, nearly 250,000 African Americans had registered to vote for the first time.

President Lyndon Johnson also promised a Great Society "where the city of man served not only the needs of the body and the demands of commerce but the desire for beauty and the hunger for community." In his State of the Union address on January 4, 1965, he encouraged America to ask "not only how much, but how good; not only how to create wealth, but how to use it; not only how fast we are going, but where we are headed."

To achieve his humanitarian goals, Johnson pushed through Congress a series of bills designed to eradicate economic inequality. In 1964, Congress passed the Economic Opportunity Act, which declared a "war on poverty." It created the Office of Economic Opportunity, which included a Job Corps for high school dropouts; a Neighborhood Youth Corps for unemployed teens; Volunteers in Service to America (VISTA), which was a domestic version of the Kennedy-established Peace Corps; the Head Start Program for disadvantaged children; and the Upward Bound Program, which prepared the poor to attend college.

President Lyndon Johnson signs the Civil Rights Act.

Library of Congress Prints and Photographs Division [LC-DIG-ppmsca-03196].

Throughout 1965, Congress continued to legislate reforms. It enacted the Criminal Justice Act, which provided the indigent with adequate legal representation. Congress passed the Food Stamp Act to provide groceries to needy families and ratified the Housing Act, which authorized $1 billion for the urban renewal of inner cities. It passed the Elementary and Secondary Education Act, which earmarked more than $1.3 billion for the improvement of school districts that had desegregated. Congress created Medicare, which provided medical and hospital insurance to the aged. Coupled with civil rights legislation, the new laws of the Great Society provided African Americans with hope for a better future.

The Sound of Integration

In 1964, Berry Gordy, Jr. assembled the parts of a music machine to create a distinctive Motown sound, which reflected and furthered the integration of African Americans into white America. Gordy had always supported the peaceful integrationist program of Martin Luther King, Jr., who once paid a brief visit to the Motown offices. In 1963, he released a recorded version of King's "I Have a Dream" speech along with talks by other civil-rights leaders, delivered on the steps of the Lincoln Memorial at the end of the march on Washington, D.C. He also recorded another album of King's speeches, *Great March to Freedom*, which captured the civil rights leader in freedom rally at Cobo Hall in Detroit. "Motown was a very strong backer of Martin Luther King's total program," asserted Motown producer Mickey Stevenson. Gordy who considered himself a "very, very close friend of Dr. King's" "felt closely connected to Dr. King and liked his philosophy." He added that "I saw Motown much like the world Dr. King was fighting for with people of different races and religions, working together harmoniously for a common goal."

Gordy, the son of an African-American entrepreneur, who hoped for the upward mobility of African Americans, specially groomed and cultivated streetwise teens from Detroit to make them acceptable to mainstream America. In 1964, he hired Maxine Powell, who formerly had operated a finishing and modeling school, to prep his performers. "The singers were raw. They were from the streets," remembered Powell. "They were a little crude: some were backward, some were arrogant." "I always thought of our artists as diamonds in the rough who needed polishing. We were training them for Buckingham Palace and the White House, so I had my work cut out for me," she related.

Martin Luther King, Jr. at a White House conference, 1963.

Library of Congress Prints and Photographs Division [LC-DIG-ds-00836].

Powell transformed the Motown artists into polished professionals. She taught them to speak in a nonthreatening manner, schooled them about correct posture, appearance, and a positive attitude, and chose their clothes. "I had to *force* these lessons," Powell concluded.

A few months after adding Maxine Powell to the staff, Berry Gordy, Jr. hired choreographer Cholly Atkins. Atkins, a well-known dancer during the 1930s and 1940s who had performed in the Cotton Club and the Savoy Ballroom, taught the Motown groups to move gracefully. "My method for the Motown artists was that I always wanted them coming from someplace and going to someplace," he said. Within a year, boasted Atkins, "we had the best-looking artists in the record business."

Atkins worked with Maurice King, who served as the executive musical director. King, who had arranged shows at Detroit's Flame Show Bar for years and had worked with jazz artists such as Billie Holiday and Dinah Washington, taught the Motown acts about stage patter. "My rehearsals were conducted like a class, a noninterrupted class," he recalled. "When we were through with them, they could play any supper club in the country and shine." By the mid-1960s, Berry Gordy, Jr. had assembled a Motown team that took poor African-American youths from Detroit and taught them to talk, walk, dress, and dance like successful debutantes and debonair gentlemen. Though such black entertainers as Duke Ellington had exuded charm and dignity before, the Motown artists set the standard among blacks for fashionable dress and behavior during the Sixties. The Motown team "wanted young blacks to understand that you do not have to look like you came out of the ghetto in order to be somebody other blacks and even whites would respect when you made it big," contended one Motown staffer.

Berry Gordy, Jr. combined the polished image of the Motown acts with a gospel-based pop music that appealed to the American mainstream. "Blues and R&B always had a funky look to it back in those days, and we at Motown felt that we should have a look that the mothers and fathers would want their children to follow. We wanted to kill the imagery of liquor and drugs and how some people thought it pertained to R&B," explained Motown producer Mickey Stevenson. "I did not like blues songs when choosing material for our artists, and Berry agreed with that," continued Stevenson. "We enjoyed John Lee Hooker and B. B. King just as much as the next guy, but we would reject anything that had a strong blues sound to it."

In place of blues and R&B, Gordy favored a distinctive music grounded by an insistent, pounding rhythm section, punctuated by horns and tambourines and featuring shrill, echo-laden vocals that bounced back and forth in the call-and-response of gospel. Building upon his experience with girl groups, he produced a full sound both reminiscent of and expanding upon Phil Spector's wall of sound. Aiming for the mass pop market, Gordy called the music "The Sound of Young America" and affixed a huge sign over the Motown studio that read "Hitsville U.S.A."

The Supremes on the Assembly Line

The Supremes fulfilled Berry Gordy's dream of a polished African-American act that sang gospel-tinged pop to both African Americans and whites. Born in Detroit and meeting in the low-income Brewster housing project, Diana Ross, Mary Wilson, Florence Ballard, and Betty Travis began singing together in high school "when groups were becoming very popular with teenagers," recalled Wilson. They sang as the Primettes at sock hops, and in 1960 they won the first prize at the Detroit/Windsor Freedom Festival talent contest. Late that year, after pestering Motown staffers for a few months, the group, which included Barbara Martin, who replaced Betty Travis, signed to Motown. On the advice of Berry Gordy, Jr., the group changed their name, when Motown songwriter Bradford, "came up with three names, put them in a hat on little slips of paper. Florence picked the Supremes."

The newly signed act had little success initially. In December 1960, the Supremes recorded "I Want a Guy," which attracted so little attention that Barbara Martin quit the group. During the next three years, the vocalists recorded more than forty songs, of which only twelve were released and met with limited success.

Around 1964, when Mary Wells left the company, Motown polished the Supremes into a dazzling act. It sent the girls to Maxine Powell, who taught them about proper etiquette and attire. "We spent only about six months working with Mrs. Powell, but anything we learned would be incorporated the same day," recalled Mary Wilson. "We would be out eating something, and if one of us accidentally picked up her chicken with her fingers, the other two would say, 'remember what Mrs. Powell said'." The company also provided the group with lessons from music director Maurice King and choreographer Cholly Atkins.

In 1964, the Supremes, groomed by the Motown organization, scaled the charts. After cracking the Top Thirty with "When the Lovelight Starts Shining Through His Eyes," the group recorded "Where Did Our Love Go," which was released just fifteen days after the passage of the momentous Civil Rights Act. In the summer, Gordy secured a spot for the Supremes on Dick Clark's Caravan of Stars tour. "We need Dick Clark for the white people," Gordy asserted. "I gotta have that tour." Prepped by Gordy and promoted by Clark, the Supremes' "Where Did Our Love Go" topped both the pop and R&B charts by the end of the year. On December 27, 1964, the Supremes made their first of twenty appearances on *The Ed Sullivan Show*, which had introduced Elvis Presley and the Beatles to the American public. The Supremes, appearing in sleek, light-blue chandelier gowns, embodied the Motown image of the slick, cultivated African-American entertainer and became overnight pop stars.

Berry Gordy, using methods practiced in the Detroit auto factories, ensured the continued success of the Supremes by assembling the parts of a hit-making machine that included standardized songwriting, an in-house rhythm section, a quality-control

The Supremes Stop in the Name of Love, 1965.

INTERFOTO/Alamy Stock Photo.

process, selective promotion, and a family atmosphere reminiscent of the paternalism fostered by Henry Ford in his auto plant during the early twentieth century. "I worked in the Ford factory before I came in the [record] business, and I saw how each person did a different thing," Gordy reasoned. "And I said, 'Why can't we do that with the creative process?' It was just an idea of coming in one door one day and going out the other door."

The songwriting team of Brian Holland, Lamont Dozier, and Eddie Holland, Jr., joining forces in 1962, perfected the formula of success that they discovered with their composition "Where Did Our Love Go." From late 1964 to early 1967, they wrote a series of number-one hits for the Supremes, which included "Baby Love," "Come See About Me," "Stop! In the Name of Love," "Back in My Arms Again," "I Hear a Symphony," "You Can't Hurry Love," "You Keep Me Hangin' On," and "Love Is Here and Now You're Gone." After the success of "Where Did Our Love Go," remembered Lamont Dozier, "we knew we had stumbled onto a sound. You'll notice that we patterned 'Baby Love' and 'Come See About Me' right after the first hit. In fact, all the Supremes' big hits were really children of 'Where Did Our Love Go.'"

Lamont Dozier explained the creative process of the team. He took credit as the "idea man" for the songs. Brian Holland crafted the melodies and served as the recording engineer. Then, Eddie would finish the song and teach it to the vocal group. "You might say that we had our own little factory within a factory," Dozier concluded. "We were able to turn out a lot of songs that way."

The different singles sounded remarkably similar because of the in-house rhythm section known as the Funk Brothers, who played on most of the Supremes' recording sessions. In 1964, Earl Van Dyke, a former bebop jazz pianist who had toured with R&B singer Lloyd Price, assumed leadership of the studio band. He orchestrated the other studio musicians who included drummer Benny Benjamin, Robert White or Joe Messina on guitar, and bassist James Jamerson, who had backed Jackie Wilson and the Miracles. Along with a few other musicians who joined them occasionally, the Funk Brothers forged the trademark percussive beat of the Motown sound.

Berry Gordy, Jr. maintained the consistent quality of Motown material by conducting weekly meetings that scrutinized possible releases. "The quality control meetings on Fridays were real intense," remarked Motown songwriter Ron Miller. "All of the writers, producers, and many of the executives gathered in Berry's office, and he would play everyone's songs. And then he went around to everyone there and asked them for their opinion. It was brutal." Sometimes, Gordy even invited teens off the street to rate the latest songs. More often than not, he chose the selections of neighborhood critics.

Berry Gordy, Jr. carefully promoted the songs, which were released through a marketing strategy that kept the slick Motown image intact. Besides spots on *The Ed Sullivan Show*, he snagged appearances for the Supremes on mainstream television programs such as *The Tonight Show, Hollywood Palace*, a special presented by African-American crooner Sammy Davis, Jr., and the Orange Bowl Parade. For concerts, Gordy favored posh settings such as the Copacabana in New York, which hosted the Supremes for three weeks in July 1965; the Yale University prom of 1965, which featured jazz great Duke Ellington as well as the Supremes; and exclusive Las Vegas hotels such as the Flamingo, where the Supremes performed in 1967. He even asked established entertainers such as Sammy Davis, Jr. and Broadway star Carol Channing to write liner notes for the Supremes' albums.

Gordy retained control of the successful group by creating a family atmosphere at the company. In 1965, like a watchful father, he limited each Supreme to a $100 weekly allowance and funneled the remainder of their $300,000 profit for the year into a joint bank account. The Motown owner refused to allow the girls to date and, to fend off possible suitors, gave each girl a diamond ring. "They're Christmas presents from Gordy," Florence Ballard told *Newsweek* about her ring in 1965. "Someone saw mine the other week," chimed in Mary Wilson. "He said, 'Oh, you're engaged.' I said, 'Yeah. To Motown.'" "Gordy is like a father to us," cooed Diana Ross. "When we're on the road he's always calling and bugging us about taking vitamins, wearing warm clothes and getting to bed on time."

The Motown Stable

Berry Gordy, Jr.'s paternal, production-line approach produced other successful performers such as the Temptations. In 1957, the 18-year-old, Detroit-raised, gospel-schooled Otis Williams started a street-corner, gospel-drenched doo-wop group, the Distants, with a few friends, including Elbridge Bryant and teenager Melvin Franklin who released "Come On" on Warwick Records. Three years later, the Distants joined forces with Eddie Kendricks and Paul Williams to become the Elgins. In 1960, between sets at a local club, Williams walked into the bathroom of the Stevens Community Center in Detroit, where he by chance met Berry Gordy, Jr., who complimented the group and signed them to Motown. Renamed the Temptations after Gordy signed them, from 1961 to 1963 the group released seven singles, which met with only moderate success.

By 1964, Berry Gordy shaped the Temptations into the Motown image and placed them on the charts. He replaced their processed hair styles with carefully cropped Afros, discarded their casual clothes for top hats and tails, inserted such standards as "Old Man River" into their repertoire, and added the precise choreography of Motown dance master Cholly Atkins to their stage show. After Gordy's grooming, in 1964 the Temptations enjoyed their first U.S. hit, "The Way You Do the Things You Do," which peaked at number eleven. When lead singer David Ruffin replaced Elbridge Bryant in March 1965, the refurbished Temptations recorded the Smokey Robinson composition "My Girl," an answer to the Mary Wells hit "My Guy," which topped both the pop and R&B charts. During the next eighteen months, the group remained on the charts with a series of songs, including "Since I Lost My Baby" written by Smokey Robinson and "Beauty Is Only Skin Deep," and "(I Know) I'm Losing You," all by Eddie Holland and Norman Whitfield who, with Robinson and the Holland-Dozier-Holland team, constituted the legendary Motown songwriting production crew.

This Motown team revived the careers of other former doo-woppers, the Four Tops. The group—Levi Stubbs, Renaldo Benson, Lawrence Payton, and Abdul Fakir—grew up together in Detroit during the late 1940s. In 1954, they banded together as the Four Aims and in 1956 released "Kiss Me Baby" on Chess Records. The vocal group subsequently backed jazz vocalist Billy Eckstine and in 1960 signed with Columbia to record the unsuccessful "Ain't That Love." In 1962, the group signed with Riverside Records and recorded "Where Are You?" which also failed to chart. "We were working," recalled Abdul Fakir, "perfecting our craft and just out there hustling. Guess you could say we were getting ready for the Chairman."

In 1963, Chairman Berry Gordy signed the group and refined their act. He, dressed them in tuxedos, and within a year paired them with the songwriting team of Holland-Dozier-Holland. Gordy sent them to the Motown finishing school and dance classes, offered musical direction, and engineered a marketing blitz, which promoted the group as a slick act for both white and African-American audiences. "Our pop sound [and] our visual performance, especially the dancing, was such that people were comfortable with us," explained Levi Stubbs. "Because of Motown the music merged, black-and-white music was brought together and solidified. The mixture was a turning point in our country—the music melted together, and that was great for social relations."

In 1964 after the Motown make-over, the Four Tops achieved success. The vocal quartet neared the Top Ten with "Baby I Need Your Loving," a smooth, gospel-flavored composition written by Holland-Dozier-Holland. They continued to climb the charts with the Holland-Dozier-Holland team, reaching the number one pop spot with "I Can't Help Myself (Sugar Pie, Honey Bunch)" and "Reach Out I'll Be There" as well as Top-Ten chartbusters such as "Standing in the Shadows of Love," and "It's the Same Old Song."

The successful integration of Motown's version of R&B pop into the white mainstream of rock and roll did not come easily. The Motown tours throughout the American South consistently met opposition. As the tour reached the South, remembered the Temptations' Otis Williams, "These white guys drove by in a car, called us the 'n' word, shot at us and the [Four] Tops and other Motown acts." Though no one was hurt, the Temptations felt the degradation of segregation. In another instance, the Revue went to Georgia. The Four Tops left the bus and walked into a waiting room for whites only. "This big cop comes in, seven feet tall with his gun out, and says, 'I don't know where you niggers are from, but segregation still exists,' [Quotation reproduced exactly from the original source]" related Levi Stubbs. Dragged by the scruffs of their necks, the downcast Four Tops moved to the waiting room designated for "colored."

Despite the roadblocks, Berry Gordy, Jr. persisted and established a music empire. He built eight record labels, a management service, and a publishing company. From 1964 through 1967, Motown placed fourteen number-one pop singles, twenty number-one singles on the R&B chart, forty-six more Top-Fifteen pop singles, and seventy-five other Top-Fifteen R&B records. In 1966, 75 percent of all Motown releases hit the charts. The next year, Motown grossed $21 million by selling 70 percent of its records to whites. "It is no coincidence," observed a British newspaper columnist in 1965, amid a Motown tour of England, "that while 10,000 Negroes are marching for their civil rights in Alabama, the Tamla-Motown star is on the ascendant." Berry Gordy, Jr., putting into action the program of peaceful integration, created one of the most commercially successful African-American-owned enterprises and certainly the most successful African-American-owned record company.

In the process of empire building, Berry Gordy furthered the aims of the civil rights movement. Mary Wilson of the Supremes felt that "we were heroes to the people." "Blacks didn't have too many heroes in those days, but we gave people pride in themselves," she contended. For songwriter Lamont Dozier, Motown did "more for race relations than any politicians or laws being implemented at the time." The Motown sound represented that "one common denominator that could get around all obstacles, all hatreds or stupid prejudices." Motown had helped racially integrate America.

Chapter 10
Acid Rock

"We have a private revolution going on."
—A handbill distributed from the Blue Unicorn,
a coffeehouse in the Haight

In 1967, a reporter approached Marty Balin, one of the founders of the Jefferson Airplane, a group that took off in San Francisco during the mid-1960s. He asked the singer/guitarist to describe the emerging lifestyle in San Francisco around him. "The one word I can think of is love, even though that sounds like a cliché, but that's where it's at, it's uninhibited, coming-out emotion," Balin responded. "Even the philosophy of the day is being changed by what's happening now," he added.

Balin had accurately and hopefully described the emergence of a new counterculture. In the wake of the British invasion, thousands of middle-class, college-educated youths clustered around San Francisco Bay to demonstrate to the country, and eventually to the world, that love could replace war, sharing could replace greed, and community could supersede the individual. These San Francisco visionaries strove for nothing less than a total transformation of American society that they demanded immediately. Jim Morrison, lead singer of the Doors, screamed that he wanted the new world *now*.

A new hybrid of rock and roll reflected and helped propagate the new way of life. Named after a strange new drug, LSD, acid rock broadcast the word of hippiedom from the epicenter, San Francisco, to the hinterlands. Unlike the working-class British invaders and the Motown groups from the poor sections of Detroit who used music to entertain, West Coast bands such as the Jefferson Airplane, the Grateful Dead, Quicksilver Messenger Service, and countless others (1500 by one count) led a youth movement that consciously withdrew from America's nine-to-five, work-centered society and tried to create an alternative community built upon love. From 1965 to 1967, the vanguard of rock and roll had a mission.

The Beats

The social upheaval of hippiedom had its origins with the Beats who had wandered from their homes in New York City to San Francisco's North Beach more than a decade earlier. In 1951, Jack Kerouac, a Columbia University football star-turned-writer, planted the seeds of the Beat Generation, when he bummed around the country with the ever-energetic, ever-adventuresome Neal Cassady and told of their travels in his book *On the Road*. That same year, poet Lawrence Ferlinghetti left New York for San Francisco and after two years opened the prime beatnik haunt in North Beach, City Lights Bookstore. In 1953, Allen Ginsberg migrated to San Francisco on the advice of his friend Neal Cassady. Two years later, he organized the first public appearance of the Beat Generation—a poetry reading at the Six Gallery, at which he premiered his controversial poem *Howl*, which the San Francisco Police Department first declared obscene, then banned and confiscated. In 1957, Kerouac published *On the Road* to critical acclaim.

Allen Ginsberg signing an anti-draft petition, 1968.

Library of Congress Prints and Photographs Division.

The Beats formulated a countercultural philosophy based on tenets of Eastern religion. Their metaphorical name—Beat—suggested the quest for beatitude that could be discovered in Zen Buddhism. It also referred to the patron saints of the movement, the drifters who shed the trappings of institutional society and gathered in places such as New York City's Bowery. Although appearing "beat down" and downtrodden to "straights," the bums symbolized the freedom that the avant-garde so dearly cherished. Finally, the term alluded to the beat of jazz, especially bebop artists such as Charlie Parker and Dizzy Gillespie and the cool jazz of Miles Davis, Lennie Tristano, and Gerry Mulligan who the Beat writers considered cultural heroes.

Congregating in San Francisco and New York City's Greenwich Village, the countercultural literati lambasted traditional American values. In his once-banned Naked Lunch (1959), William S. Burroughs, the literary genius who had inherited the Burroughs adding-machine fortune, wove together powerful, graphic images of a decaying society: "A heaving sea of air hammers in the purple brown dusk tainted with rotten metal smell of sewer gas." Ginsberg penned antiestablishment poems such as the stream-of-consciousness America (1956), which blasted the Cold War and referred to emerging suburbia as "dark" America.

In place of traditional bourgeois values, the Beats sought fundamental change through cultural relativism. "We love everything," explained Kerouac. "Billy Graham, the Big Ten, rock-and-roll, Zen, apple pie, Eisenhower—we dig it all."

Believing that no value was absolute, the Beats emphasized individual feelings. As one Beat argued, "I stay cool, far out, alone. When I flip it's over something *I* feel, only me." Ginsberg contended that the Beats wrote to encourage a "liberating insolence of recognizing one's own feelings and acting on one's own feelings rather than acting on Madison Avenue feelings of careerism."

Such an ethos, revolving around the individual rather than a structured career-oriented, consumer-based society, led to experimentation with sex and drugs, especially marijuana and amphetamines, which Kerouac mentioned in *Dharma Bums* and Ginsberg glorified in his poetry. "They had no interest in building a greater America, in fighting Communism, in working at a career to buy $100 suits and dresses, color television sets, a house in the suburbs, or a flight to Paris," observed writer Burton Wolfe. "Some brew, a few joints, a sympathetic partner in the sack," he argued, "this was all there was."

The Beats, blatantly challenging institutional values, suffered attacks from more traditional quarters. Right-wing FBI director J. Edgar Hoover, turning literary critic in 1959, reviewed Lawrence Ferlinghetti's poem *Tentative Description of a Dinner Given to Promote the Impeachment of President Eisenhower* and concluded that "it appears that Ferlinghetti may possibly be a mental case." One month later, the Alcoholic Beverages Commission declared North Beach a "problem area" and refused to issue any more liquor licenses there. Other, more violent critics bombed the women's restroom at the Co-Existence Bagel Shop, a favorite gathering spot for the San Francisco Beats that, along with The Place, closed down shortly thereafter. By the end of 1959, Eric "Big Daddy" Nord (b. Harry Pastor), a West Coast Beat poet, actor, and nightclub owner, told a courtroom that "the Beat Generation is dead. I don't go to North Beach anymore."

The Beats Reemerge in New York

Some of the Beats reappeared on the cultural scene to parent the psychedelic movement during the mid-1960s. On the East Coast, at St. Mark's Place in Greenwich Village in 1965, Beat poets Tuli Kupferberg, Ken Weaver, and Ed Sanders, the editor of *Fuck You: A Magazine of the Arts*, started the Fugs. "We used to read at the Metro, on Second Avenue," recalled Kupferberg. "After the readings, we'd go to the Dom, on St. Marks Place…where lots of young people would go…Ed Sanders got the idea it might be good to try to combine some of our poetry with rock music."

The band caricatured American society by using the verse of William Blake in "How Sweet I Roamed from Field to Field" and the prose of William S. Burroughs in "Virgin Forest." In the liner notes on the Fugs' second album, released in 1966, Allen Ginsberg characterized the group as symbols of the counterculture, which constitutes "everybody who makes love with their eyes open, maybe smokes pot and maybe takes LSD and looks inside their heads to find the Self-God Walt Whitman prophesied for America." "Now every ear can hear," added the poet, "and every eye shall see."

To some extent, Ginsberg's prophecy came true. Although none of their albums were best sellers, the Fugs appeared on the cover of *Life* and *Look* magazines and snagged a spot on the David Susskind television show. They used their national forum to propagate a philosophy, which fused the Beat sensibility with a hope for political change. Buoyed by "the tide of expectations created by the Kennedy era still in place," explained Ed Sanders, the band believed that there might be "some permanent change, that the country might become a social democracy. There'd be no homelessness, that there was an expectation the economy would be adjusted so everyone could partake in the largess of America."

The Velvet Underground who many times shared a bill with the Fugs drew inspiration from the same Beat source. In 1964, at a party in New York City, songwriter/guitarist Lou Reed met musical prodigy and classically trained John Cale who had been performing with an avant-garde ensemble, and they decided to form a band. "When I first met Lou, we were interested in the same things," recalled Cale. "We both needed a vehicle. Lou needed one to carry out his lyrical ideas and I needed one to carry out my musical ideas." They enlisted the help of guitarist Sterling Morrison and drummer Angus MacLise, who the following year was replaced by Maureen Tucker, and began playing at local clubs.

Pop art innovator Andy Warhol (b. Andy Warhola) helped the band achieve notoriety. Rather than continue with his own rock group of fellow artists such as Jasper Johns, in July 1965 he agreed to manage the band after meeting Reed and Cale through mutual friends and added Hungarian chanteuse Nico (b. Christa Paffgen) to the lineup. Warhol named the band the Velvet Underground, after Michael Leigh's novel about sadism and masochism. He showcased the band at his Factory club and added them to his mixed-media extravaganza, the Exploding Plastic Inevitable. "He was the catalyst," remarked Reed about Warhol.

Reed who wrote the lyrics for the band derived his ideas from Beat sources. The songwriter who had studied at Syracuse University with Beat poet Delmore Schwartz crafted songs that dealt with the down-and-out themes of Beat fiction—heroin addiction in "I'm Waiting for the Man" and the rushing "Heroin," and cocaine in "Run, Run, Run." In a self-titled Velvet album, Reed led the listener through the adventures of a girl named Candy who roamed the cultural underground assisted by her junkie boyfriend. The sexual and drug-related themes of the Velvet Underground, Reed later mentioned, were "only taboo on records. Let's keep that in mind. Movies, plays, books, it's all there. You read Ginsberg, you read Burroughs."

The Haight-Ashbury Scene

The Beats resurfaced in San Francisco to inspire the hippies, as *San Francisco Examiner* writer Michael Fallon first called them in September 1965. On October 16, 1965, the Family Dog, a small commune in San Francisco, organized one of the first public hippie gatherings, held at Longshoremen's Hall near Fishermen's Wharf. Colorfully clothed free spirits danced freely to the music of the Jefferson Airplane and the Great Society. Amid the revelry whirled a long-haired, bearded Allen Ginsberg.

Three weeks later, on November 6, Allen Ginsberg appeared at the Appeal, a benefit rock concert for the San Francisco Mime Troupe, an avant-garde theater group managed by Bill Graham. He brought his Beat friends, San Francisco poet Lawrence Ferlinghetti and the Fugs, who flew in from New York for the event and mingled with hundreds of free-minded participants who lived in the surrounding Haight-Ashbury district near San Francisco State College. At the end of the evening, Ginsberg chanted as the Hashbury hippies cleaned the Mime Troupe loft.

Beat writer Ken Kesey, author of *One Flew Over the Cuckoo's Nest* (1962), and his band of free spirits, known as the Merry Pranksters, played a pivotal role in the origins of the hippie culture. On January 8, 1966, the writer rented the Fillmore Auditorium, then owned by African-American entrepreneur Charles Sullivan, to spread the gospel of a new way of life. Kesey spiked the punch with LSD, a concoction that became known as the Kool-Aid acid test, to replicate the experience he had created with the Pranksters at his ranch in nearby La Honda, California. Amid a flashing, astonishing light show, costumed youths wildly danced with each other and batted balloons in the air. The women adorned their faces with day-glo poster paint interspersed with jewel-like baubles, and the men painted a "third eye" on the foreheads.

Two weeks later on January 21 through 23, Kesey, along with Zach Stewart and ecologist Stewart Brand, hosted the Trips Festival, which attracted more than 6,600 people. For the event, they enlisted the services of the Grateful Dead and Big Brother and the Holding Company, set up five movie screens on which they projected a mind-boggling combination of colors and shapes, and staged another acid test. At the festivities, Kesey stalked the floor dressed in a space helmet and a jumpsuit and periodically composed free-form poetry on an overhead projector.

Neal Cassady played a central role in the event and served as a forged link between the Beats and the hippies. Cassady, the Beat High Priest who had appeared in Kerouac's *On the Road* as Dean Moriarty and had inspired the Indian character in Kesey's *Cuckoo's Nest*, served as the main announcer at the event, scat singing, dancing, and delivering rapid-fire commentaries as preludes to the performances. At one point in a typical display of physical dexterity, he stood on the balcony and swung out over the crowd by a cord, terrifying everyone below that he might slip and fall to his death. Cassady also sat at the helm of the psychedelic bus, a 1939 International Harvester that had been painted in day-glo colors with free-form squiggles, which took Kesey and the Merry Pranksters on a symbolic trip across the country. He especially influenced the Grateful Dead, the premier psychedelic band. "There's no experience in my life yet that equals riding with Cassady in like a '56 Plymouth or a Cadillac through San Francisco or from San Jose to Santa Rosa," remembered Jerry Garcia, lead guitarist for the Dead. "He was the ultimate *something*—the ultimate person as art."

Grateful Dead in concert: From left to right: Jerry Garcia and Bob Weir, early 1970s.

Mark Goff.

Other Beats helped organize the "First Human Be-In," which took place in Golden Gate Park Stadium on January 14, 1967. Allen Ginsberg, painter Michael Bowen, playwright Michael McClure, and poets Lenore Kandal and Gary Snyder helped stage the multicolored community gathering, which attracted 20,000 people on an unseasonably warm day. Early in the morning, Ginsberg and Snyder opened the proceedings by conducting an ancient Hindu blessing ritual, the dakshina, around the Polo Field to ensure its suitability for the coming pilgrimage. Throughout the day, hippies in wild attire danced on the grass to the sounds of the Grateful Dead, the Jefferson Airplane, and Quicksilver Messenger Service. Poets read constantly in fifteen-minute intervals, and acid-king Timothy Leary preached from the stage. Throughout the day, Ginsberg chanted, and periodically Gary Snyder joined him. The celebration ended, when Gary Snyder blew on a conch shell, the ritual instrument of the Yamabushi sect of Japanese Buddhism, and Allen Ginsberg led a chant of "Om Shri Maitreya" to the Coming Buddha of Love.

When news of these remarkable events spread to the burgeoning ranks of college-age baby boomers, the psychedelic ranks in San Francisco swelled. "Like, wow! There was an explosion," remarked Jay Thelin, co-owner with his brother Ron of the Psychedelic Shop, which served as a briefing center for hippie initiates to the city. "People began coming in from all over and our little information shop became sort of a clubhouse for dropouts and, well, we just let it happen." By 1967, 50,000 hippies resided in or near the Haight-Ashbury district of San Francisco.

The Hippie Culture

Many who flocked to the Haight were baby boomers who came to San Francisco during a period of almost unrivaled economic prosperity. In 1966, at the beginning of the influx to the Haight, the U.S. economy posted a healthy 6.5 percent growth rate, the highest rate since 1951. Unemployment stood at less than 4 percent, and inflation stood at less than 3 percent. By any measure, youth experienced a bright present.

Many of the Haight hippies had grown up in educated, middle-class homes. Most of the hippies who lived in San Francisco at the time, wrote journalist Hunter Thompson in 1967, "were white and voluntarily poor. Their backgrounds were largely middle class; many had gone to college." According to a report by San Francisco State sociologist H. Taylor Buckner, 96 percent of the Haight hippies were between the ages of 16 and 30, 68 percent had attended college for a time, and 44 percent had a father who had earned a college degree.

The hippies, as with the Beats, criticized the bourgeois values with which they had been raised. "The standard thing is to feel in the gut that middle-class values are all wrong," remarked one hippie. "It's the system itself that is corrupt," added another. "Capitalism, communism, whatever it is. These are phony labels. There is no capitalism or communism. Only dictators telling people what to do." The hippies, remarked Peter Cohan of the Haight, "are the fruit of the middle class, and they are telling the middle class they don't like what has been given them."

The hippies, raised in an age of relative affluence, attacked the materialistic American culture that had been formed and embraced by their Depression-bred parents. "I have no possessions," remarked Joyce Ann Francisco of the *San Francisco Oracle*, the preeminent psychedelic newspaper, which was published by Ron Thelin in the Haight. "Money is beautiful only when it is flowing. When it piles up it's a hang-up." The residents of the Haight, noticed historian Arnold Toynbee, when he toured the district during the spring of 1967, "repudiate the affluent way of life in which making money is the object of life and work. They reject their parents' way of life as uncompromisingly as Saint Francis rejected the rich cloth merchants' way of life of his father in Assisi."

Many hippies challenged other dominant values. Morning Glory, a long-haired, 22-year-old hippie, felt that the "human body is a beautiful thing. It should be displayed. I want people to see what I look like, and I want to see what they look like without a bunch of clothes covering them up. Nude, everybody is in the same bag, the same economic class."

Such a freewheeling attitude toward nudity, coupled with the use of the birth control pill by more than six million women in 1966, six years after its introduction to the general public, led to a rejection of sexual taboos. As early as 1965, Haight residents launched the Sexual Freedom League to confront traditional standards concerning sex. Within two years, hundreds of youths engaged in premarital sex with many partners, continuing a trend that had intensified with the Beats. "The '60s will be called the decade of the orgasmic preoccupation," predicted Dr. William Masters, a gynecologist and the director of the Institute for Sex Research at Indiana University. "Young people are far more tolerant and permissive regarding sex."

To distinguish themselves from, and many times to antagonize, the middle-class American mainstream, male hippies generally wore their hair long. "As for bad vibrations emanating from my follicles, I say great," wrote one youth, "I want the cops to sneer and the old ladies to swear and the businessmen to worry."

By challenging authority, the hippies hoped to create an atmosphere that engendered freedom of individual expression. "We have a private revolution going on," read a handbill distributed by the Blue Unicorn, a coffeehouse in the Haight. "A revolution of individuality and diversity that can only be private."

Hippies turned to mind-expanding drugs to enhance their individual potentials. Most rolled marijuana or the more expensive hashish into joints or smoked the weed Indian style in pipes. In 1965, Haight residents organized the legalize marijuana movement (LEMER), which held meetings at the Blue Unicorn. By the end of the decade, more than 96 percent of the hippies in the Haight had smoked marijuana, and more than ten million youths across the nation had tried the drug.

Another drug, the hallucinogen LSD (lysergic acid diethylamide), defined the hippie experience. Synthesized by Swiss scientist Albert Hoffman in 1938 and legal in the United States until late 1966, "acid" fragmented everyday perception into a multitude of melting shapes and vibrant colors. "The first thing you notice is an incredible enhancement of sensory awareness," related Timothy Leary, the ex-Harvard professor who edited the *Psychedelic Review*, organized the LSD-based League for Spiritual

Discovery, and became the most visible popularizer and high priest of acid. "Take the sense of sight. LSD vision is to normal vision as normal vision is to the picture of a badly tuned television set.... The organ of the corti in your inner ear becomes a trembling membrane seething with tattoos of sound waves. You not only hear but *see* the music emerging from the speaker system like dancing particles, like squirming curls of toothpaste."

Timothy Leary contended that the drug experience resulted in altered, introspective states that expanded individual consciousness. In September 1966, comfortably lying on a mattress in his headquarters, a sixty-four-room mansion in Millbrook, New York, he outlined the various states of consciousness. "The lowest level of consciousness is sleep—or stupor, which is produced by narcotics, barbiturates and our national stuporfactant, alcohol," he began. "The second level of consciousness is the conventional wakeful state, in which awareness is hooked to conventional symbols: flags, dollar signs, job titles, brand names, party affiliations." To reach the third level, he believed that the symbols of the wakeful state needed to be turned off through marijuana. On the fourth and highest level, the cellular level, Leary recommended mescaline and LSD to "take you *beyond* the senses into a world of cellular awareness. During an LSD session, enormous clusters of cells are turned on, and consciousness whirls into eerie panoramas for which we have no words or concepts." Leary advised readers to "turn on, tune in, and drop out."

Many heeded Leary's advice. "Grass and LSD are the most important factors in the community," remarked Ron Thelin. "You should acquaint yourself with all of the consciousness-expanding drugs. I turn on every Sunday with acid, and I smoke grass every day, working continuously with an expanding consciousness." Gabe Katz of the *San Francisco Oracle* agreed, "The only way to understand is to turn on. The chemicals are essential. Without them you can ask a million questions and write a million words and never get it." On October 6, 1966, when legislation outlawing LSD took effect, hundreds of residents in the Haight staged a "Love Pageant" to assert the "inalienable rights" of the "freedom of the body, the pursuit of joy, and the expansion of consciousness." In 1966, an official from the Food and Drug Administration estimated that more than 10 percent of all college students had ingested LSD and more than 90 percent of youths in the Haight had taken the drug. Many of the hippies obtained LSD from chemist Augustus Owsley Stanley III, the grandson of a Kentucky senator and sound man for the Grateful Dead, who produced and distributed an estimated fifteen million acid tabs. He sometimes dispensed them free at events such as the Trips Festival.

Many hippies considered the use of drugs, especially LSD, a revolutionary act. "Turning on, tuning in and dropping out means to conduct a revolution against the system," believed Jay Thelin. "We have all that we need to do this within ourselves."

With their newfound consciousness, the hippies embraced the beliefs of past, less technology-driven civilizations, real or imagined, to create a counterculture. Some followed the example of the Beats by looking for salvation in the mysteries of the Orient. One San Francisco free spirit expounded that "society feeds us machines, technology, computers and we answer with primitivism: the *I Ching*, the *Tibetan Book of the Dead*, Buddhism, Taoism. The greatest truths lie in the ancient cultures. Modern civilization is out of balance with nature." Many hippies adopted the teachings of Zen popularizer Alan Watts. Others joined Hare Krishna, when in January 1967 the International Society for Krishna Consciousness moved to the Haight, and Allen Ginsberg declared that a Hare Krishna mantra "brings a state of ecstasy."

Others turned to pure pastoral fantasy. Many hippies carried well-worn copies of J.R.R. Tolkien's anti-industrial *Lord of the Rings* trilogy. They avidly read the pastoral fantasies of A.A. Milne's *Winnie the Pooh*, Lewis Carroll's *Alice's Adventures in Wonderland*, Kenneth Grahame's *The Wind in the Willows*, and C.S. Lewis's *Chronicles of Narnia*.

Attempting to recapture a lost innocence, some hippies embraced the popular stereotype of the noble American Indian. They slipped into moccasins and sported fringed deerskin jackets, headbands, feathers, and colorful beads. Many hippies painted their faces and bodies for festive occasions as did Native Americans during ceremonies. In September 1965, the Committee Theater in the Haight staged a multimedia extravaganza with teepees, ceremonial tapes of Indians drumming and 360-degree slide shows called "America Needs Indians," and a few months later took their show to the acid tests. In January 1967, organizers of the Human Be-In at Golden Gate Park called the event a "Pow Wow" and a "Gathering of Tribes," advertising it with a poster that pictured a Plains Indian on horseback clutching a blanket in one hand and an electric guitar in the other.

Residents of the Haight created a cult of Indian-based tribalism, even though Native Americans such as Robert Costo, president of the American Indian Historical Society, believed that the hippies practiced a "certain insidious exploitation of the Indian which is the worst of all." "For one of the yearly Tribal Stomp dances at the Avalon, we gave everyone a little leather thong with a little Indian bell and a long white turkey feather tied to it," recalled Chet Helms, manager of the dance hall. "I can't tell you how effective that thematic favor was. It made everyone a member of the tribe."

Adhering to the notion of tribalism, some banded together in communal living arrangements. At Drop City near Trinidad, Colorado, twenty-two midwestern hippies built and lived in geodesic domes constructed from automobile hoods. Roughly 40 miles from San Francisco near Sebastopol, more than fifty hippies communally farmed the 31-acre Morningstar Ranch. Morningstar founder Lou Gottlieb, who had played in the folk group the Limeliters, envisioned the Ranch as "an alternative society for those who can't make it in the straight society and don't want to.... for people who are technologically unemployable and for other people it would be a retreat where they could come and recreate, I mean really re-create themselves." Gottlieb wanted to promote "a whole different culture based on noncompetition." In the Haight itself, reported a San Francisco State sociologist, more than 25 percent of the hippies lived with ten or more people.

Some hippies, believing in a noncompetitive, tribalistic society, shared their resources with others. The Diggers, most of them former members of the San Francisco Mime Troupe, who named themselves after a seventeenth-century sect of English agricultural altruists, provided free food, shelter, and transportation to needy hippies in the Haight-Ashbury district. A Digger leaflet distributed at the October 1966 "Love Pageant" advertised "free food, every day, free food, it's free because it's yours." The Prunes in Cleveland, the Brothers in Seattle, and the Berkeley Provos participated in the same activities in their cities.

Even the shopkeepers in the Haight exhibited a community spirit. On November 23, 1966, the *San Francisco Examiner* told its readers that "the hip purveyors of painting, poetry, handcrafted leather and jewelry along Haight Street, having been blackballed by the Haight Merchants' Association, have formed their own Haight Street Merchants' Association, HIP for short." Once organized, HIP established a job cooperative to cope with the incoming hippies and provided free legal advice. Psychedelic Shop owners Jay and Ron Thelin additionally devoted over one-third of their shop's floor space to a "calm center," where hippies could meditate, talk, or sleep.

The hippies cultivated clothing styles that reflected the elements of their counterculture. In 1966, when Janis Joplin migrated to San Francisco to eventually become the lead singer for Big Brother and the Holding Company, she noticed the emerging fashions in the Haight. The young women in the Haight, she wrote home, favored the "beatnik look." "Pants, sandals, capes of all kinds, far-out handmade jewelry, or loose-fitting dresses and sandals." "The younger girls," Janis continued, "wear very tight bell-bottoms cut very low around the hips and short tops—bare midriffs," which reflected the ongoing sexual revolution and contributed to the doubling of the sale of

Levi Strauss jeans from 1963 to 1966. The young men donned colorful, acid-inspired attire highlighted by "tight low pants in hounds tooth check, stripes, even polka dots!" "Very fancy shirts—prints, very loud, high collars, Tom Jones full sleeves. Fancy print ties." The hippies had created a fashion that exemplified a counterculture influenced by the Beats, accessed by LSD, and based upon a loose-knit community of individuals that focused on self-expression.

The belief in general change and hope for the future underlay the hippie world view. Chet Helms, the manager of the Avalon Ballroom, captured the sentiment. "For me and most of the people I knew in the Haight-Ashbury, the whole '60s thing was not about dropping out but rather commitment on the part of the people, and the belief in possibility." "The climate of the '60," he asserted, "made me feel things could be changed, that it was worth changing."

By the mid-1960s, hundreds of newspapers were established to promulgate the countercultural ethos. In 1964, Art Kunkin started the *Los Angeles Free Press*, an underground newspaper modeled after the *Village Voice* in New York. In late 1966, the *San Francisco Oracle* published the first of thirteen issues, unveiling a non-news, art-oriented format and a psychedelic look of vibrant, random colors and swirling typefaces perfected by hip artist Rick Griffin. Remembered *Oracle* editor Allen Cohen: "We were going to fill our newspaper with art, philosophy, poetry and attend to this change of consciousness that was happening in the Haight-Ashbury and, we hoped, the world." The *Oracle* staff wanted to "serve as vehicles for the forces that were emerging" and "aid people on their [LSD] trips." *The East Village Other*, a New York City-based underground paper founded in late 1965, trumpeted the seven-hilled San Francisco to be "the Rome of a future world founded on love." By 1967, when the Underground Press Syndicate (UPS) was founded, four other major underground tabloids printed stories about sex, drugs, and revolution: *The Paper* in East Lansing, Michigan, the *Berkeley Barb*, the *Seed* in Chicago, and the *Fifth Estate* in Detroit. Two years later, more than 500 underground newspapers printed stories about the counterculture that reached nearly 4.5 million readers.

Acid Rock: The Trip Begins

A legion of rock bands, playing what became known as "acid rock," stood in the vanguard of the movement for cultural change. The *San Francisco Oracle* defined rock music as a "regenerative and revolutionary art, offering us our first real hope for the future (indeed, for the present)."

"Rock-and-roll," announced *Rolling Stone*, which had been established in late 1967 by Berkeley dropout and budding journalist Jann Wenner and well-known music critic Ralph Gleason, "is more than just music. It is the energy center of the new culture and the youth revolution." Ray Manzarek, keyboard player for the Doors, felt that acid rock had a mission to "change the world" and spread the message of "love to a new world." In January 1966, handbills distributed to promote the Trips Festival hinted that "maybe this is the ROCK REVOLUTION."

Not surprisingly, psychedelic music had its basis in Dylanesque folk. "I began as a folk musician. I went to New York and I heard Dylan when he was at Gerde's," mentioned Marty Balin (a.k.a. Martyn Buchwald), who had played in the Los Angeles folk group the Town Criers. After hearing Dylan, Balin decided to form a band in San Francisco where he saw Paul Kantner walking into a folk club. "I said, 'That's the guy.' I just knew it. He had a twelve-string [guitar] and a banjo and he had his hair down to here and an old cap," recalled Balin. In July 1965, the duo asked a few other musicians to join their band including lead guitarist Jorma Kaukonen, who had studied with the folk-blues master Reverend Gary Davis. The group searched for a "name that would imply a whole different way of looking at things," recalled Kaukonen. They settled on the Jefferson Airplane.

The Grateful Dead, another major exponent of acid rock, grew from folk roots. "When the whole folk music thing started, I got caught up into that," remembered Jerry Garcia, lead guitarist for the Dead. "When Joan Baez's first record came out I heard it and I heard her finger picking the guitar,... I got into finger style, the folk-music-festival scene, the whole thing." Garcia then traveled throughout the South and recorded bluegrass bands on his tape recorder, hunting for authentic folk styles. He formed a jug band, "and from the jug band it was right into rock-and-roll." "I was sort of a beatnik guitar player," he proudly asserted. Bob Weir, the rhythm guitarist for the band, "did the whole folk-blues coffeehouse thing" and joined the jug band Mother McCree's Uptown Jug Champions. He often played with and learned from Jorma Kaukonen. "Here on the West Coast, the guys that are into rock-'n'-roll music have mostly come up like I have...up through folk music," concluded Jerry Garcia. In early 1965, folkies Garcia and Weir joined with blues enthusiast Ron "Pig Pen" McKernan, drummer Bill Kreutzmann, and bassist Phil Lesch to establish the band the Warlocks, which was renamed the Grateful Dead later that year.

Other acid rockers rose through the ranks of folk. Guitarist Peter Albin, an impetus behind Big Brother and the Holding Company, had organized folk concerts during the early 1960s and had been a member of a folk group playing "Kingston Trio-type music." James Gurley, another member of Big Brother, began worked in a bluegrass band. Janis Joplin, eventually the blues belter for Big Brother, had sung in various North Beach folk clubs such as the Coffee Gallery, sometimes backed by Jorma Kaukonen. David Freiberg, the unofficial leader of Quicksilver Messenger Service, learned guitar in 1963 amidst the folk craze, and one-time fellow band member, drummer Dino Valenti, had worked for several years as a folk singer in Greenwich Village. In 1964, Country Joe McDonald "came to become a folk singer with the beatniks in San Francisco" and formed a jug band with Barry Melton shortly before he teamed up with the Fish to deliver his politically minded brand of psychedelic rock. Likewise, lead guitarist Robby Kreiger of the Doors—which formed in late 1965 with Kreiger, John Densmore on drums, singer Jim Morrison, and Ray Manzarek—had started a jug band during his stay at the University of California at Santa Barbara and named the folk blues as a major influence.

Psychedelic music, though based in folk, featured a loud, experimental sound. Unlike the acoustic strummings of early Bob Dylan, the acid rockers amplified their message. "The thing about being loud was great," enthused Jerry Garcia. The San Francisco bands also favored extended, acid-inspired guitar improvisations, sometimes distorted by guitar effects, which combined folk music with blues riffs, avant-garde jazz and traces of Indian ragas. "LSD, it made me want to hear longer sounds and be freer musically," asserted Garcia. Improvisation, noticed Avalon-Ballroom proprietor Chet Helms, "was a general characteristic" of the San Francisco bands.

Such eclectic experimentation fully utilized the long-play (LP) format of the 12-inch, 33 1/3-rpm record. Introduced by Columbia in 1948, the LP had been used in the pop field to market collections of three- to four-minute songs. During the psychedelic era, rock artists improvised on songs that sometimes lasted an entire side, using the LP medium as classical and jazz musicians had done years earlier. Paralleling the rise of the avant-garde in jazz during the mid-1960s, the psychedelic sound exemplified the freewheeling, experimental bent of the counterculture.

Rock-and-Roll Revolution

The new sound of experimentation came from middle-class youths. Grace Slick, the daughter of a Chicago investment banker, attended the exclusive Finch College where, in her words, she became a typical suburbanite. Fellow Airplane member Jorma Kaukonen was the son of a foreign service official and graduated from the University of

California at Santa Clara; Airplane drummer Spencer Dryden had moved to Hollywood with his father, an assistant film director. Jim Morrison, the son of a rear admiral, had enrolled in the Theater Arts Department at UCLA, where he met keyboardist Ray Manzarek. John Cipollina, the guitarist for Quicksilver Messenger Service, had become interested in music through his mother, a concert pianist, and his godfather, Jose Iturbi, a well-known classical pianist. Peter Albin of Big Brother and the Holding Company grew up in suburban San Francisco, the son of a magazine editor–illustrator.

These middle-class youths wanted to overturn the social order in which they had been raised. Jim Morrison, heavily influenced by Jack Kerouac, professed an interest "in anything about revolt, disorder, chaos. It seemed to me to be the road toward freedom—external revolt is a way to bring about internal freedom." He told the *New York Times*: "When I sing my songs in public, that's a dramatic act, but not just acting as in theater, but a *social* act, real action." Paul Kantner of the Jefferson Airplane hoped for "a whole turnaround of values." Chet Helms, the transplanted Texan who opened the 1,200-seat Avalon Ballroom in the Haight and who became the manager of Big Brother and the Holding Company, "was very interested in the scene's potential for revolution. For turning things upside down, for changing values."

As with the hippies in general, the psychedelic rockers challenged restrictive, middle-class values, especially those dealing with sex. The Fugs, always forthright, belted out "Boobs a Lot," "Group Grope," and "Dirty Old Man." Their name itself raised the eyebrows of the sexually inhibited. Reveling in the same theme, the Doors hit the chart with "Love Me Two Times," "Hello, I Love You," "Love Her Madly," and their biggest hit, "Light My Fire." Morrison, who referred to himself as an "erotic politician," faced legal charges, when he supposedly exposed himself on stage in Florida. The outspoken Grace Slick who delivered such songs as "Somebody to Love," confessed that "it doesn't matter what the lyrics say, or who sings them. They're all the same. They say, 'Be free—free in love, free in sex'." Marty Balin of the Airplane added, "The stage is our bed and the audience is our broad. We're not entertaining, we're making love."

Many psychedelic bands renounced the competitive, corporate structure of American society in general and of the recording industry in particular. Jerry Garcia of the Grateful Dead resented "being just another face in a corporate personality. There isn't even a Warner 'brother' to talk to. The music business and the Grateful Dead are in two different orbits, two different universes." Paul Kantner of the Jefferson Airplane complained that the record companies "sell rock-and-roll records like they sell refrigerators. They don't care about the people who make rock or what they're all about as human beings." Max Weiss, owner of Fantasy Records in the Bay Area, characterized the San Francisco bands as "absolutely noncommercial."

Opposed to a faceless commercialism, bands such as the Grateful Dead and the Airplane staged free concerts. "We'd rent flatbed trucks and a generator, show up early in the morning, set it up and start playing until the cops shut us down," explained Dead manager Rock Scully. "It was an outgrowth of a need of the community and since the community was supporting us in the ballrooms it was our way of paying them back," he reasoned. "The concept of doing free shows for people really made a lot of sense to a lot of San Francisco bands like the Dead, us and Big Brother," added Jorma Kaukonen, guitarist for the Jefferson Airplane.

The emphasis on sharing shaped the group concept of the psychedelic bands. David Getz, drummer for Big Brother and the Holding Company, recalled that the groups tried "to consciously avoid making anyone the star, focusing more on the inter-action between the audience and the band, and trying to create something together." Acid master Owsley Stanley agreed. "All the bands were tribal and tribal meant you agreed amongst yourselves as to who was momentarily the leader of the team."

Most San Francisco rock groups felt an intense camaraderie with one another. "All of the bands were very close," remembered Mickey Hart of the Grateful Dead. "We'd be over at each other's houses, see each other all-day long, party at night. There were no hassles about who was going to open the show or close the show. It seemed like when we played with one of our sister bands, our compadres, we always played a little better for each other."

The cooperative feeling within bands sometimes extended to their living arrangements. The members of the Grateful Dead lived communally in the Haight district in an old, downtrodden Victorian house at 710 Ashbury Street. "It was sort of a community center," remembered Rock Scully. "People would drop acid and sit around philosophizing about the world," added Chet Helms about the Dead residence. Quicksilver Messenger Service roomed together in a house near the Dead headquarters. For a time, the Jefferson Airplane lived together in the Haight at a three-story 1904 building at 2400 Fulton Street, and the members of Big Brother and the Holding Company roomed communally in a Victorian house at 1090 Page Street.

Many acid rockers discovered the cooperative alternative to a competitive society through LSD. "Along came LSD and that was the end of that whole world. The whole world just went kablooey," related Jerry Garcia. "I suddenly realized that my little attempt at having a straight life and doing that was really a fiction and just wasn't going to work out."

As well as demonstrating the hollowness of self-centered mainstream values, acid helped Garcia realize the interconnected relationships in the world. "To get really high is to forget yourself," he asserted. "And to forget yourself is to see everything else. And to see everything else is to become an understanding molecule in evolution, a conscious tool in the universe."

As the avenue to understanding a new social order, mind-expanding drugs became the centerpiece of acid rock. They inspired the names of many West Coast bands: the Loading Zone, Morning Glory, the Weeds, the Seeds, and the Doors, the last name taken from a phrase of poet William Blake, which had been quoted by Aldous Huxley in a book about a mescaline experience, *The Doors of Perception*.

Many San Francisco bands extolled psychedelic drugs in their songs. The Jefferson Airplane delivered the Haight-Ashbury anthem, "White Rabbit," which used the drug-infused imagery of Lewis Carroll's *Alice's Adventures in Wonderland* to instruct listeners to alter their consciousness through drugs. Grace Slick felt that "*Alice in Wonderland* is blatant. Eat Me! She gets literally high, too big for the room. Drink Me! The caterpillar is sitting on a psychedelic mushroom smoking opium." The singer wanted to use the images in children's stories to show that "you [can] take some kind of chemical and have a great adventure." By 1970, Vice President Spiro Agnew complained that much of "rock music glorified drug use."

Drugs defined the purpose of some psychedelic bands. According to Jerry Garcia, "The Grateful Dead is not for cranking out rock-and-roll, it's not for going out and doing concerts or any of that stuff, I think it's to get high."

Light shows at dances in the Haight simulated the LSD experience. The projection of light through liquid pigments in motion to create ever-changing, expressionistic light shows had been revived in 1952 by San Francisco State professor Seymour Locks who wanted to reintroduce theater experiments from the 1920s by Igor Stravinsky that projected images behind dancers and actors in his ballet "The Rite of Spring." Through the efforts of beatnik art student Elias Romero, who witnessed some of Locks's first shows, hipsters such as Bill Ham, Tony Martin, and Ben Van Meter learned the craft and adapted it to the hippie subculture. By 1966, dances in the Haight, normally held in the Avalon Ballroom, the Straight Theater, or the Fillmore Theater, featured light shows of melting colors that mimicked an LSD experience.

The poster art advertising the gatherings captured on paper the acid-inspired, swirling designs of the light shows. The posters recycled motifs and the lettering of Art Nouveau artists such as Alphonse Mucha and built upon the eye-dazzling, vibrant images of Op Art, which peaked in 1965 at an exhibit at the Museum of Modern Art in New York City called "The Responsive Eye." Fused to the LSD experience, this combination of influences resulted in psychedelic posters, which featured a unique graphic style of thick, distorted letters that melted together against vibrant, multicolored, pulsating backgrounds that could only be easily deciphered by members of the hippie tribe. They were crafted by Haight artists such as Wes Wilson, Stanley Mouse (b. Miller), Alton Kelley, Victor Moscoso, Bonnie MacLean, Lee Conklin, and Rick Griffin, who also designed album covers for the Grateful Dead and Big Brother and the Holding Company. "When I started doing posters," explained Wes Wilson, "I think I selected my colors from my visual experiences with LSD." Poster artist Lee Conklin likewise "made it my mission to translate my psychedelic experience onto paper." The San Francisco graphic rock art, contended Chet Helms, signaled that "the joyless headlong rat-race to the top was supplanted by the joyful, sensuous curves and gyrations of the dance, expanding in all directions."

Bill Graham (b. Wulf Grajonca), a politically minded, 35-year-old émigré, who as a child had fled Hitler's Holocaust, helped organize the psychedelic groundswell in San Francisco. In 1965, after staging two benefit concerts as the manager of the San Francisco Mime Troupe, Graham decided to concentrate his efforts on the concert scene, first coordinating the Trips Festival for Ken Kesey and his Merry Pranksters. By March 1966, Graham secured a three-year lease on the Fillmore Auditorium, which became a popular dance hall in the Haight. He also managed the Fillmore house band, the Jefferson Airplane, and later the Grateful Dead. Although never "a great fan of high volume rock-and-roll, and a lot of it was nonsensical to me," Graham took pride in his organizational abilities. "I was always, 'Well, I took your ticket and you came here expecting something, and I want you to have that,'" he recalled. "I want the food to be hot and the drinks to be cold." Marty Balin of Airplane asserted that "Bill Graham was the star of the sixties. In the beginning there was great talent, but there were no sound systems. No microphones. Graham came along and changed it. He made the performers a stage. He was what Alan Freed was to the fifties."

Chet Helms who operated the Avalon Ballroom, a refurbished swing-era venue with gilded booths, red flocked wallpaper and majestic columns, operated much like Bill Graham. Coming from the folk scene in Austin, Texas to San Francisco, he took the fluid hippie scene and helped organize it. "Helms is definitely an organizer," asserted Grace Slick of the Jefferson Airplane. "Instead of running a bank, he runs the Avalon." Helms opened the Avalaon Ballroom through an organization, the Family Dog, and featured mainly weekend, thematic concerts with light shows synchronized to the music. He considered the ballroom "a sanctuary" for the "evolving rites of passage that fit our lives."

The acid-inspired music, organized by Graham and Helms, reached youths across the country through airplay on FM radio. During the 1940s, the Federal Communications Commission (FCC) encouraged AM radio stations to create counterparts on FM frequency bands. In 1964, after issuing a moratorium on new AM licenses, the FCC decided that at least half of the airtime on FM stations in cities of 100,000 or more people had to be original programming.

Psychedelic music appeared in the expansion of FM. Not produced for the Top-Forty play list of AM radio, the meandering psychedelic sounds first aired through the freewheeling San Francisco station KMPX on the programs of disc jockeys such as Larry Miller and Tom Donahue. "Somewhere in the dim misty days of yore, some radio station statistician decided that regardless of chronological age, the average mental age of the audience was twelve and a half, and Top Forty AM radio aimed its message directly at the lowest common denominator," sniped Donahue. To eradicate the "rotting corpse stinking up the airwaves," the San Francisco jockey used FM radio to air songs that lasted more than three minutes, began to spin entire albums, discontinued the breakneck delivery of Top-Forty disc jockeys, and played songs by the new groups in the Bay Area. When confronted by an unhappy owner and a strike at KMPX, Donahue and his staff took their hip format to KSAN, which poster artist Alton Kelley described as a "community drum." Soon FM stations in other parts of the country adopted Donahue's format and broadcast psychedelia across the airwaves.

Promoted by FM radio, acid rock scaled the charts. In June 1967, the Jefferson Airplane, the first Haight band signed by a major label, hit number three with *Surrealistic Pillow*, an album that included the guitar of Jerry Garcia in the background. That same year, the Grateful Dead cracked the charts with its self-named debut LP. By the next year, Quicksilver Messenger Service charted with its first album. The Doors, probably the best-selling West Coast band, in early 1967 neared the top of the chart with its self-named debut album and later the same year hit the Top Five with *Strange Days*. In late 1968, they topped the chart with *Waiting for the Sun*. The Doors also scored with singles such as "People Are Strange," and "Touch Me," as well as the chart-topping "Light My Fire" and "Hello, I Love You."

The Beatles jumped on the psychedelic bandwagon. In August 1966, the Beatles released *Revolver*, which included the song "Tomorrow Never Knows" that John Lennon wrote based upon Timothy Leary's *The Psychedelic Experience: A Manual Based on the Tibetan Book of the Dead* (1964). The next year, the lovable, mop-topped Beatles released two influential number-one albums: *Sgt. Pepper's Lonely Hearts Club Band*, which included the cryptic "Lucy in the Sky with Diamonds," reputedly LSD for short; and *Magical Mystery Tour*, a soundtrack to a movie modeled after Ken Kesey's travels in his psychedelic bus. Later that year, the bubbly Paul McCartney admitted that he had taken LSD. In the summer of 1967, the Beatles studied transcendental meditation with Maharishi Mahesh Yogi, and George and Pattie Harrison, wearing heart-shaped granny glasses and paisley frocks, took a ceremonial tour of the Haight district.

Other established bands followed the Beatles into psychedelia. In December 1967, the Rolling Stones released *Their Satanic Majesties Request*, a psychedelic album featuring a wild three-dimensional cover, and Mick Jagger joined the Beatles in transcendental meditation. Eric Burdon of the Animals shunned the blues for vibrantly colored shirts and love beads and sang such odes to hippiedom as "San Franciscan Nights" and "Monterey." Even Dick Clark changed with the times to mastermind the movie *Psyche-Out*, which starred a young Jack Nicholson and music by the pop psychedelic band the Strawberry Alarm Clock.

By 1967, acid rock had spread to youths throughout the country. Philadelphia hippies danced at the Electric Factory. Adherents to the counterculture flocked to acid rock shows at the Tea Party Ballroom in Boston, the Kinetic Playground in Chicago, and the Grande Ballroom in Detroit, where Russ Gibb, inspired by Family Dog concerts in San Francisco, coordinated the events and Gary Grimshaw designed flowing psychedelic posters. In New York, hippies frequented the Electric Circus and the Fillmore East, which Bill Graham had designed as an East Coast counterpart to the San Francisco original. Acid rock had become a national phenomenon.

Psychedelic London

The counterculture developed on the other side of the Atlantic in swinging London. In 1966, Michael Hollingshead brought 6,000 tabs of acid to England that he obtained from Timothy Leary, with a mission to turn on London. He opened the World Psychedelic Centre (WPC) in Chelsea and started his work. The same year, Nigel Waymouth opened the alternative clothing store "Granny Takes a Trip," stocked with velvet jackets, Native American–styled garb, and wild-colored shirts and trousers. "It was a rebellion against conventional outfits," Waymouth contended. "Why can't things be more androgynous? Why can't men wear flowered jackets with their long hair?"

The communication network for the growing London counterculture emerged at the same time. In March 1966, photojournalist John "Hoppy" Hopkins and Rhaune Laslett started the London Free School, modeling it after the American "free universities," which had sprung up across the United States as alternatives to traditional college curricula with such classes as the history of rock and roll. They hoped to "connect traditional disciplines in a relevant 'modern' manner." In 1966, to help finance the Free School, Barry Miles and Hopkins launched the underground newspaper *International Times*, later just called *IT*, which, according to Peter Jenner who helped with the publication, "was all about enlightenment and freeing your head from all the old hang-ups."

Locally grown acid rock burst on the London scene. In late 1966, Joe Boyd, an American who had landed a job at the London branch of Elektra Records, met "Hoppy" Hopkins. After witnessing Fillmore shows in San Francisco and looking for a way to raise money for the fledgling *International Times*, Boyd joined with Hopkins to stage concerts. Leasing a club on Friday nights after 11:00 P.M., the duo established the UFO club on London's Tottenham Court Road that featured light shows, poetry readings, well-known rock acts such as Jimi Hendrix, and avant-garde art by Yoko Ono. They hired the Art Nouveau–inspired Michael English and Nigel Waymouth as poster artists, who called themselves Hapshash and the Coloured Coat and designed sinuous, vibrant silkscreen posters that advertised many of the UFO happenings. "We felt like we were illustrating an ideal," remembered Waymouth. "We were trying to give a visual concept of what we were experiencing, which was like hallucinations."

The UFO also featured local house bands such as Pink Floyd. Named after country bluesmen Pink Anderson and Floyd Council, the band began by playing R&B music at the Marquee Club. Fueled by the psychedelic energy of front man Syd Barrett and the vision of their co-manager Peter Jenner, Pink Floyd quickly embraced an airy acid rock complemented by a light show of exploding colors. In 1966, they played at a benefit for the London Free School, performed at an abandoned railroad engine shed called the Roundhouse to launch the *International Times*, and on December 23 played the first show at the UFO. "It's definitely a complete realization of the aims of psychedelia," bass player Roger Waters told the *Sunday Times* about their performance at the Roundhouse. In 1967, they debuted with the first British Top-Twenty acid-rock single "Arnold Layne," cracked the Top Ten with "See Emily Play," and by the summer introduced a spacey electronic sound to the British Top Ten with *Piper at the Gates of Dawn*, named after a chapter in the children's novel *The Wind in the Willows*. On April 29, 1967, with several other bands, they spearheaded the 14-Hour Technicolor Dream event at Alexandra Palace that attracted more than 10,000 members of the London counterculture, who came to support the underground *International Times*, which had been raided by police on alleged obscenity charges.

The Soft Machine, another free-flowing UFO band, epitomized English psychedelia. The outfit, "all middle-class kids from literary backgrounds" according to cofounder Kevin Ayers, rejected the aspirations of their parents. Prodded by coleader Daevid Allen, they read the American Beats, lifting their name from a William Burroughs novel. The group lived together communally and developed a hippie ethic. "It was just to be nice to each other, and don't step on other people's toes and infringe on their freedom," explained Ayers.

By the end of 1967, many London teens fully adopted the hippie culture. Youths experimented with acid tests, rallied for an underground newspaper, opened alternative clothing shops, listened to their own psychedelic bands, and crowded into their own version of the Fillmore. Most important, they accepted a new way of looking at the world. "The whole movement was about a change in attitude from aggression to peace," insisted Steve Howe, who played at the UFO with the band Tomorrow before becoming the guitarist for Yes. "It was a very euphoric time."

The Decline of Hippiedom

The counterculture had a short-lived heyday, falling victim to its own drug-based logic. Many hippies, initially using drugs to increase awareness and open alternative realities, became wasted addicts. As some youths repeatedly tried to delve deeper and deeper into their consciousnesses with LSD, they became isolated and detached from their own bodies. In the street vernacular, these hippies "burned out." Others became hooked on drugs that seemed to promise freedom. By 1967, many Haight residents became methamphetamine or "speed" addicts who, according to Dr. Ellis D. ("LSD") Sox, the San Francisco public health director, cost the city $35,000 a month for treatment. "You had a lot of people talking to posts," remembered Travis Rivers, then owner of the Print Mint, which sold psychedelic posters in the Haight. "They were ripping one another off, because it costs a lot of money once you get strung out on speed."

Some of the major figures in the Haight drug culture fell prey to the guns of gangland. On August 3, 1967, John Kent Carter, a dealer known as "Shob," was found murdered with his arms hacked off at the elbows. Three days later, William "Superspade" Thomas ended up in a sleeping bag with a bullet through his head at the bottom of a cliff in Marin County.

The saga of Alexander "Skip" Spence provides a moving testimony to the perils of drug experimentation. Alexander ("Skip") Spence was the original drummer for the Jefferson Airplane, composing "Blues from an Airplane." When he quit the Airplane to form the pathbreaking psychedelic band Moby Grape, he began to overindulge in psychedelics and suffered a mental breakdown. "Acid was like heaven, a moment of God, inspiring, tragic. I must have taken it a hundred times, a thousand times," confided Skip. One day, Spence reached too high. He woke up in a hospital: "An overdose where I died and was brought back to life." Before his untimely death at age fifty-two in 1999, the scraggly, unwashed ex-rock star lived in San Jose, where he spent his $7-a-day allowance from the state. At night, when he did not confine himself to the psychiatric ward of a San Jose hospital, Spence stayed alone in a dingy, rundown room in the Maas Hotel. Sometimes he spoke to Joan of Arc. Once in a while he was visited by Clark Kent, who the drummer/guitarist found to be "civilized, decent and a genius." And on a few thick, intense, San Jose summer nights, Spence met his "master," who materialized with startling revelations. Asserted Spence, delivering his own epitaph, "I'm a derelict. I'm a world savior. I am drugs. I am rock-and-roll."

A drug-fueled, somewhat naive psychedelic worldview left the hippies prey to enterprising businessmen who commercialized it for profit. During early 1967, more than twenty shops opened in the Haight-Ashbury district to cater to the tourist traffic. The Pall Mall Lounge marketed "love burgers," and one store sold hippie costumes to weekenders: scraggly wigs for $85 and beards for $125. Even the Greyhound Bus Company started a "Hippie Hop" in San Francisco, advertised as "the only foreign tour within the continental limits of the United States." The commercialization of the Haight became even more pronounced with a CBS television special and a *Time* magazine article about the District. "Haight Street is no longer fun," complained Tsvi Strauch, an original hippie proprietor in the Haight. "Many of us are getting away from it because of all the plastic hippies and tourists that are fouling up the whole scene. They've made a mess of it."

Many of the original hippies, disgusted with the exploitation of their ideal, left the scene. On October 4, 1967, Jay Thelin closed the Psychedelic Shop, a hub of the Bay Area counterculture, and posted a sign on the front door: "Be Free—Nebraska Needs You More." Two days later, a procession of original hippies in the Haight district, including the Grateful Dead, loaded a coffin full of beads, peace signs, flowers, and other symbols of their lifestyle and publicly burned it, announcing the "death of hippie, loyal son of media." That same day, the Fugs coordinated a similar procession in the East Village in New York City, memorializing the hippie culture. "The tourist buses started coming through. Then they [hippies] left," summarized one Haight resident. "The kids went out to the country. Bolinas, Santa Rosa, Healdsburg, Auburn, Santa Cruz. Basically, they all left the city and it became a very different situation." "The idyllic time was over."

Monterey and the Commercialization of Psychedelic Rock

Acid rock, the music of the counterculture, became subsumed by the recording industry. Though complaining about the corporate structure of the music industry, most psychedelic rockers readily signed contracts with the major record labels that marketed the psychedelic sound. The Grateful Dead and Quicksilver Messenger Service chose Warner Brothers. Big Brother and the Holding Company switched from Mainstream Records to Columbia. The Doors went with Elektra Records. The Jefferson Airplane inked a deal with RCA. "We plunder the unsuspecting straight world for the money and means to carry out our program and revolutionize its children," rationalized Paul Kantner of the Airplane in the *San Francisco Express Times* on November 13, 1968.

The major labels employed innovative promotional strategies to reach a national audience with their bands. "We found we couldn't sell the Grateful Dead's records in a traditional manner," said Joe Smith, at the time the president of Warner-Reprise. "The cult was important. Free concerts where you handed out fruit and nuts were important" as well as exposure on the underground club circuit, the campuses, and FM radio. Some companied hired "freaks" to serve as intermediaries between the groups and the label to better control the bands. Such marketing of the counterculture by the major labels led to successful albums by the Jefferson Airplane, the Grateful Dead, Quicksilver Messenger Service, Big Brother, and especially the Doors. Bill Siddons, manager of the Doors, complained that "It's funny, the group [is] out there on the stage preaching a revolutionary message, but to get the message to the people, you gotta do it in the establishment way."

The Monterey International Pop Festival, held from June 16 to June 18, 1967, exemplified the corporate assimilation of psychedelic bands into the mainstream. On one hand, the festival held outside San Francisco seemed to epitomize the flowering hippie world view. It included many of the psychedelic mainstays: The Jefferson Airplane, Big Brother, and Quicksilver. A few days before the event, the Grateful Dead reluctantly agreed to perform. All the bands played for free, and all proceeds had been promised to charities such as a Harlem-based music instruction program. The Diggers orchestrated free soup and accommodations at some of the communes in the Bay area. The Dead arranged free camping at Monterey Peninsula College for concert goers, and Owsley Stanley passed out free tabs of acid backstage.

Despite its hippie gloss, the Monterey International Pop Festival had been planned and engineered by the record business. Lou Adler, then head of Dunhill Records that had scored with the pop-folk sounds of the Mamas and the Papas, teamed with Mamas-and-Papas front man John Phillips to plan the festival. They set up headquarters in the Renaissance Club in Los Angeles and established a board of directors that included Paul Simon, Rolling Stones manager Andrew Loog Oldman, Mick Jagger of the Stones and Beach Boy Brian Wilson. As a theme for the event, Phillips composed the sugary "San Francisco (Be Sure to Wear Flowers in Your Hair)" and enlisted unknown singer Scott McKenzie to sing the tune, which neared the top of the chart on both sides of the Atlantic. Adler concocted the tag line "Music, Love and Flowers" to market the event. The board of directors, assisted by Beatle Paul McCartney, diversified the bill, adding The Who, Simon and Garfunkel, the Byrds, Jimi Hendrix, Scott McKenzie, and a bevy of other non-psychedelic groups. The record executives wanted to package the

"San Francisco sound and sell it, Los-Angeles-style, to the world," complained Sam Andrew of Big Brother and the Holding Company.

During the festival, the record moguls took center stage. "Back stage the sharks are busy scheming and maneuvering. All those L.A. record types. Man, are they scary," cautioned Dead manager Rock Scully. They catered to Brian Jones, clothed in flowery attire as he mixed with the crowd, and members of the Monkees who appeared, though did not perform. During the set by the Grateful Dead, festival planners sent Mickey Dolenz of the Monkees on stage in an Indian war bonnet to make an announcement.

Festival organizers negotiated film rights for the concert. Bob Rafelson, a film director and one of the originators of the Monkees, suggested to D. A. Pennebaker that he film the three-day concert, and Pennebaker stalked the grounds with his 16-mm cameras to visually document the bands and search for the ideal hippie. In the midst of the performances, John Phillips asked the bands to sign an agreement that they could appear in the movie. The completed film, released in December 1968, netted profits for the concert planners who had not compensated the performers for the film or the concert. "All the money has mysteriously disappeared," sarcastically blurted Rock Scully. "Adler & Co. claim that their accountant ran off with it to Mexico."

By the end of the Monterey festival, the businessmen had overtaken over acid rock. "The forces of darkness have ripped us off," contended Rock Scully. "They've stolen out music, stolen the San Franciscan *vibe* for crissakes!" "Monterey was the beginning of the end," lamented Chris Darrow of the psychedelic band Kaleidoscope.

By the end of 1967, acid rock and the counterculture it exemplified had been drawn into the competitive society it attacked. "When the Summer of Love happened, that was it," recalled Bill Thompson, a manager of the Jefferson Airplane. "It had all started happening in the summer of 1965 and it was over by the summer of 1967." The psychedelic baby boomers, armed with flowers and a hopeful spirit, soon confronted race riots and the M-1 rifles of National Guardsmen, who turned the brightly colored hopes of hippiedom into a dark nightmare of war-torn cities and campuses.

Chapter 11
Soul Music: Fire from the Streets

"Soul is sass, man."

—Claude Brown, 1968

Four o'clock on a muggy, steamy Sunday morning in Detroit, July 22, 1967. A crowd of young African Americans clustered around a pack of police squad cars on the corner of Twelfth Street and Clairmount, the heart of the city's West Side ghetto. As 200 African Americans pressed against one another to get a better view of the action, blue-shirted, white-faced policemen herded eighty-two captives into paddy wagons. The arrested African Americans had been accused of drinking liquor after hours at the United Community League for Civic Action, which hosted a party for two returning veterans from Vietnam. After finishing their job by 5:00 A.M., the policemen jumped into squad cars, revved the engines, and started to move out of the area. Someone in the crowd flung a full wine bottle through the air, shattering the windshield of the car driven by Sergeant Arthur Howison of the Tenth Precinct. Howison slammed on the brakes and leapt onto the street. He was pelted first by a few stones and then by a barrage of rocks and bottles. The police officer ducked back into the car and sped off, followed by the angry mob.

The crowd, recently incensed by the killing of African-American veteran Danny Thomas by a band of white thugs, multiplied as it made its way down Twelfth Street until it had grown to 3,000 agitated men, women, and youths. Someone grabbed a brick from the pavement and hurled it through the window of a grocery store. People swarmed toward the jagged opening. They poked out the rest of the glass in the window frame with sticks, jumped into the store, and gathered armloads of meat, bread, and canned goods. One man struggled with an entire side of beef.

Around daybreak, the discontent spread. Some teens overturned a line of garbage cans and set the trash on fire. Another man threw a homemade firebomb into a shoe store that already had been sacked. Summer breezes fanned the flames, which spread to adjoining buildings. Within a few hours, columns of fire engulfed East Detroit and spread across Woodward Avenue into the western part of the city. Williams' Drug Store and Lou's Men's Wear, along with hundreds of other buildings, disappeared in the blaze. "It looks like 1945 in Berlin," reported a dejected Mayor Jerome Cavanaugh, who had been credited with the idea for the Model Cities Program and just a year earlier boasted that *Look* magazine had named Detroit the All-American City.

The rioting and looting continued during the next four days. Enraged African Americans ravaged thousands of stores, searching for food, clothing, furniture, and liquor. They spared only storefronts that had been marked "Soul Brother" or "Afro All the Way." Fires set by the rioters gutted 19 square miles of Detroit, causing an estimated $40 million in damage. "Man, this is crazy," one older African American told *Newsweek*. "We're burnin' our own houses up. Where are these poor people going to live now?" "This is madness. Why do they have to burn our houses?," echoed another homeowner. …"And there's not a house burning in Grosse Point [a white, middle-class suburb of Detroit]." But other African Americans in the Motor City, unemployed and confined to dilapidated slums, were impatient for reforms promised by the Civil Rights Act of 1964, and predicted more trouble. Said one 22-year-old youth: "We're tired of being second class. We've been asking too long. Now it's time to take. This thing ain't over. It's just beginning."

The authorities responded to the rioting with brutal armed force. During the first day of trouble, Mayor Cavanaugh unleashed his 4,000-man police force on the ghetto. When police proved inadequate, Michigan Governor George Romney mobilized 7,300 state troopers and National Guardsmen armed with tear gas, grenade launchers, M-1 rifles, submachine guns, M-48 tanks, and Huey helicopters. "I'm gonna shoot anything that moves and is black," vowed one young Guardsman. The next day, President Lyndon Johnson airlifted Task Force Detroit, a 4,700-man paratrooper unit commanded by Lieutenant General John L. Throckmorton, who had served as a deputy to General William Westmoreland in Vietnam. All told, a 16,000-man army marched into Detroit to quell the tumult. The city had become an armed camp divided into war zones, cordoned off by barbed wire and patrolled by helmeted troops in khakis.

After the fires had been stamped out and the smoke had cleared, the authorities counted 43 dead, 2,250 injured, and 7,200 arrested, the worst civil disorder in twentieth-century America. Most of the casualties were African-American men. On national television, President Johnson pleaded that the "violence must be stopped—quickly, finally, and permanently. There are no victors in the aftermath of violence. … We have endured a week such as no nation should live through: a time of violence and tragedy."

The cause of the Detroit riot stemmed from the abject poverty of African Americans in the inner city, which stood in stark contrast to the promise of the Civil Rights Act. Despite low national unemployment, nearly 30 percent of Detroit rioters were unemployed, and many others held low-skilled, low-paying jobs. Only a small percentage owned their own homes, and most lived in fear of being robbed or beaten on the streets and wanted to move from their neighborhoods. After playing an active role in the civil rights movement, some Detroit rioters despaired of change through nonviolence. The Detroiters, remarked civil rights leader Roger Wilkens, "saw Congress pass those laws in 1964 and 1965. When they looked around, they saw that nothing, absolutely nothing, was changing in their lives."

During 1967, the Detroit riot sparked other disturbances. In the last days of July, looters sacked stores in the African-American neighborhoods of Phoenix, Hartford, Passaic, Poughkeepsie, and South Bend. The next month, four nights of violence ripped Milwaukee, leaving four dead and more than 100 injured. African Americans in nearby Chicago took to the streets, and riots scarred Providence and Wichita. During the first eight months of 1967, race riots tore apart more than 131 cities and left a trail of 83 dead, thousands injured, and blocks of charred rubble. One government report estimated that 41 percent of the cities with populations of more than 100,000 had experienced racial violence. The press called it the "long hot summer."

On April 4, 1968, another wave of violence swept the country after the murder of Dr. Martin Luther King, Jr., who had become increasingly convinced of the need for economic as well as racial equality and had just begun to organize the Poor People's Campaign. "When White America killed Dr. King," sneered African-American militant Stokely Carmichael, "she declared war on us. … We have to retaliate for the deaths of our leaders. The executions of those deaths are going to be in the streets."

Carmichael proved to be prophetic. A few hours after the King assassination, Washington, D.C., burst into flames. More than 700 fires burned in the national capital, the worst conflagration in the city since the British set fire to it during the War of 1812. President Lyndon Johnson activated nearly 15,000 troops—more than twice the size of the U.S. garrison that defended Khe Sanh in Vietnam—to quiet the violence. In three days of rioting, the death toll reached ten, and property damage exceeded $13.3 million.

Martin Luther King, Jr. and Malcolm X, 1967: The two wings of protest.

Library of Congress Prints and Photographs Division [LC-USZ6-1847].

Other African-American populated urban areas exploded after receiving news about the King assassination. In Kansas City, six rioters died and sixty-five were injured. Chicago's riot, quelled by 5,000 federal troops and 6,700 National Guardsmen, left 11 dead, 91 injured, and miles of burned-out buildings. By the end of the week, 168 cities had erupted into violence; 5,117 fires had been started; almost 2,000 shops had been ransacked; $40 million worth of property had been destroyed; and 46 people, mostly African Americans, had died. It took almost 73,000 U.S. Army and National Guard troops to subdue the disturbances.

Black Pride

During the late 1960s, many African Americans rioted to dramatically reassert their collective identity after decades of discrimination and called their sense of self *soul*. "Soul is sass, man," African-American author Claude Brown wrote in 1968. "Soul is arrogance. Soul is walkin' down the street in a way that says, 'This is me, muhfuh'. … Soul is that uninhibited, no, *extremely* uninhibited self-expression that goes into practically every Negro endeavor. That's soul." Black became "beautiful" without the requirement of becoming part of the white mainstream.

The emphasis on black pride arose within the context of the decolonization of Africa. The Gold Coast provided the spark, which ignited an African liberation movement. During the 1950s, the Convention People's Party headed by Kwame Nkrumah united the various sections of the country. He worked with British authorities who in late 1956 agreed to independence for the country, which became known as Ghana on March 6, 1957.

African liberation efforts spread like wildfire. On January 1, the Republic of Cameroon declared its independence from France. Within the year, a dozen more African nations revolted from British, French, and Dutch colonial rule to declare their sovereignty. Between April and June, Senegal, Togo, Mali, and the Congo overthrew their colonial masters. In August, Benin, Niger, Burkina Faso, Chad, the Central African Republic, and Gabon shed their French shackles. On October 1, 1960, Nigeria established its own coalition government. Within another five years, eleven more countries overthrew their colonial masters and changed their names from Nyasaland to Malawi, from Northern Rhodesia to Zambia and from Southern Rhodesia to

Kwame Nkrumah with President John Kennedy, March 8, 1961.

Abbie Rowe. White House Photographs. John F. Kennedy Presidential Library and Museum, Boston.

Zimbabwe. Between 1957 and 1966, thirty-one countries heralded their independence from France, Britain, or Belgium.

The African liberation movement triggered a militant African-American pride and self-determination. Firebrands such as Malcolm X, Stokely Carmichael, and H. Rap Brown preached a doctrine of African-American autonomy. Carmichael, who coined the term *"black power,"* had joined the Student Non-Violent Coordinating Committee, had been a Freedom Rider, and reluctantly had worked for change through nonviolent tactics. Radicalized by the struggle of African nations to shed their colonial rulers, he increasingly viewed the struggle of African Americans within a colonial context and adopted the tenets of militants such as Malcolm X, who preached a doctrine of political and economic equality without whites rather than integration. After the assassination of Martin Luther King, Jr., Carmichael and others completely abandoned nonviolence for a militant stance. "If America don't come around, we're going to," threatened H. Rap Brown.

The Black Panther Party of Self-Defense directly confronted the white-dominated power structure with its brand of black nationalism. Founded in October 1966 by Huey P. Newton and Bobby Seale, the Party initially sought to protect African-American neighborhoods in the Oakland area. They developed a ten-point program of "land, bread, housing, education, clothing, justice and peace." Their first, overarching tenant stated, "We want freedom. We want power to determine the destiny of our black Community." As uniforms, the new organization chose blue shirts, black pants, black leather jackets, and black berets and carried loaded shotguns.

The Black Panthers became increasingly militant. On May 2, 1967, they invaded the California State Capitol in Sacramento to protest a selective ban on weapons. Five months later, police arrested Huey Newton for the death of a police officer. Newton at first denied the allegation and then proudly confessed to his crime. H. Rap Brown, the Panther Minister of Justice, called Newton "our only living revolutionary." "He has paid his dues," he continued to a "Free Huey" crowd. "How many white folks did you kill today?" Sounding like his revolutionary counterparts in Africa, James Forman, the Panther Minister of Foreign Affairs, screamed that "we serve notice on our oppressors that we as a people are not going to be frightened by the attempted assassination of one of our leaders." He called for "30 police stations blown up, one Southern governor, two mayors and 500 cops, dead."

H. Rap Brown, 1967.

Library of Congress Prints and Photographs Division [LC-U9-17744-28].

The rhetoric of the Black Panthers resonated with many African Americans. By 1968, the group had offshoots in 19 different cities, including Los Angeles, New York, and Boston, with a membership of 10,000. *The Black Panther newspaper,* edited by Eldridge Cleaver, reached 250,000 readers.

African-American writers coalesced in the Black Arts Movement to display the importance of the African-American perspective. The roots of the movement lay in the Umbra Workshop in Manhattan's Lower East Side, which, starting in 1962, brought together young African-American writers. The Harlem Writers' Guild did the same further uptown. In 1965, respected African-American writer LeRoi Jones, who two years later changed his name to Amiri Baraka, founded the Black Arts Repertory Theater/School and gave the movement a name. In his poem "Black Art" (1966), he called for "poems that kill" and aligned himself squarely with black power. Magazines such as *Freedomways* and the *Liberator* spread the gospel of the movement, and publications such as the *Black Dialogue* and *Journal of Black Poetry* provided a forum for aspiring African-American authors, playwrights, and poets. According to African-American writer Ishmael Reed, "There would be no multi-cultural movement without Black Arts." "Blacks gave the example that you don't have to assimilate," he continued. "You could do your own thing, get into your own tradition and your own culture."

Most African Americans embraced black pride through cultural attributes such as food and fashion. Emphasizing the value of their heritage, African Americans referred to food that they had been forced to eat during slavery as "soul food"—chitterlings (pig intestines), ham hocks, collard greens, black-eyed peas, candied yams, and sweet potato pie. Rather than a reminder of past enslavement, the

Eldridge Cleaver, *Soul on Ice*, 1968.

Library of Congress Prints and Photographs Division [LC-U9-20018-9A].

food distinguished African Americans from their former oppressors and signaled solidarity with one another.

African Americans championed a distinctive look. By the late 1960s, some prominent African-American men sported the colorful, loose-fitting, pull-over Dashiki garment, and women wore corresponding kaftan robes, mimicking the fashion of West Africans. Rather than straighten or "conk" their hair, African Americans proudly wore full Afros. "We saw more and more sisters begin to wear natural hairdos, and more and more brothers begin to wear their hair in the new natural styles," related one African American in Detroit. Calling themselves soul brothers and soul sisters, African Americans emphasized the importance of their own culture through their language, dress, food, and actions.

Many blacks in the United States even favored a new word to define themselves, "Afro-American," which focused on their African heritage rather than the term "Negro," which conjured memories of the segregated past. By 1967, Lerone Bennett, Jr., the senior editor of *Ebony* magazine, discovered "a large and vocal group" that undertook "an aggressive campaign for the use of the word 'Afro-American' as the only historically accurate and humanly significant designation of this large and pivotal portion of the American population. This group," he observed, "charges that the word 'Negro' is an inaccurate epithet which perpetuates the master-slave mentality in the minds of both black and white Americans." Black-power adherents, he mentioned, used the word "African-American." Unlike early twentieth-century bluesman Big Bill Broonzy who "never heard a black man or woman say, 'I'm proud to be black,'" many African Americans shouted the slogan, "Black is beautiful."

Hoping to refurbish the image of themselves and their culture, African Americans emphasized black pride by spotlighting African-American accomplishments. They focused on neglected contributions of Blacks in the American Revolution and other wars, science, and all professional fields. African Americans especially stressed the pioneering efforts of Blacks in popular music and referred to the blend of rhythm and blues and sanctified church music "soul music."

From R&B and Gospel to Soul

Soul music reflected the focus on African-American self-worth. Unlike Motown music only a few years before that had stressed integration of the races, soul stressed the importance of a distinctive African-American culture. It embodied the newfound African-American consciousness, which boasted pride in being black.

The term *"soul"* had been extensively used by African-American jazz musicians before the summer of 1967. Though first defined in 1947 by Babs Gonzales (b. Lee Brown) in his dictionary of jazz slang, the word had been applied to jazz amid the decolonization of Africa and the early civil rights movement. In early 1957, vibraphone player Milt Jackson released *Plenty, Plenty Soul*. The same year, pianist Red Garland recorded *Soul Junction*, and sax man Lou Donaldson produced *Swing and Soul*. The next year, John Coltrane wailed on *Soultrane*. In 1959, organist Shirley Scott waxed *Soul Searching* and followed it the next year with *Soul Sister*.

During the late 1960s, African Americans applied the soul moniker to artists who had achieved prominence in R&B. James Brown, "Soul Brother Number One," started his rise to fame in 1953, when he formed the Famous Flames, an R&B group, which specialized in numbers by such rhythm-and-blues acts as the Clovers, the Dominoes, and the 5 Royales. The next year, after attending a Little Richard concert, he rushed to the studio with his band to record a demonstration disc of "Please, Please, Please" and convinced Little Richard to use his fledgling rhythm-and-blues group as a back-up band. By early 1956, he signed with the R&B label, King Records, which released "Please, Please, Please." Two years later, Brown reached the top of the R&B chart with "Try Me" and in 1960 reworked the 5 Royales' "Think" for a hit.

By October 1962, when he recorded the album *Live at the Apollo*, Brown solidified a band and vocal group known as the James Brown Revue and perfected a stunning stage act, built upon the wild antics of Little Richard. In a typical performance, the singer leapt on stage wearing skin-tight black pants, a half-unbuttoned, dark-blue satin shirt, and a purple cape. Without missing a beat, his head jerking to the music, he suddenly jumped into the air, landed in a perfect split, and bounced back to his feet. Before the audience recovered, Brown was twirling in midair.

Ray Charles (b. Ray Charles Robinson), considered the "Genius of Soul" during the 1960s, initially gained fame in R&B. As a teen, Charles traveled from Tampa, Florida, to Seattle to play cocktail-swing piano. In 1949, he cut his first disc, "Confession Blues," which nearly topped the R&B chart. During the next few years, the pianist followed with a series of R&B Top-Ten entries.

Wilson Pickett had roots in early R&B. One day in 1959, as Pickett lounged on his porch strumming a guitar and singing, Willie Schofield, a member of the R&B group the Falcons, happened to pass by. According to Pickett, Schofield walked up to him and said, "'Man, you got a good voice,' and invited me to come to the next rehearsal. That's when I found I could sing rhythm and blues." Pickett joined the Falcons and added lead vocals to their 1962 Top-Ten R&B hit "I Found a Love."

Otis Redding, recognized as "The King of Soul" by some, initially drew his inspiration rhythm and blues. In October 1962, Redding, vocalist for Johnny Jenkins and the Pinetoppers, traveled to the Stax studio in Memphis for a recording session. The band had thirty minutes left in the studio and Redding asked if he could do a song. He first belted

Ray Charles, 1965.

Granamour Weems Collection/Alamy Stock Photo.

out a tune, which sounded like the songs of his idol, Little Richard. "The world doesn't need another Little Richard," snickered Stax President Jim Stewart. Otis followed with a ballad, "These Arms of Mine." Stewart recorded the song and gave co-publishing rights to disc jockey John Richbourg at WLAC in Nashville who played it over and over for six months. By the time Redding waxed his second song, "Pain in My Heart," the singer had become known to the R&B fans and nearly hit the rhythm-and-blues Top Ten.

Most soul artists, as with rhythm-and-blues performers of the 1950s, started their careers in the African-American church, where they learned and performed gospel music. During the late 1920s and early1930s, an ebullient, hip-shaking gospel emerged to replace the more sedate spiritual hymns, which dated to the days of slavery. Thomas Dorsey, one of the originators of gospel music, described spirituals as an overlay of the blues on spirituals. In 1932, after joining a Pentecostal church, he "tried to get into the gospel songs, the feeling and pathos and the moans of the blues." "And the folks started to flocking," he enthused.

Gospel underwent a transition after World War II with the emergence of the upbeat, swinging gospel quartet, epitomized by the Chicago-based Soul Stirrers. These post-war quartets featured a continuous four-part harmony punctuated by the melody that passed from singer to singer who pleaded to the Lord in different musical registers. This technique emphasized the cries of the soloists rather than a steady group sound to lay the groundwork for sixties soul.

Most of the "soul" artists, performing in an animated, secularized postwar gospel style with stabbing vocals that asserted their conviction and purpose, began in gospel groups. Wilson Pickett had sung in the gospel group the Violinaires before joining the Falcons; he described his style as "a gospel melody." Eddie Floyd, who in 1966 hit with the archetypical soul of "Knock on Wood," had helped start the Falcons, which had been established as a gospel group before drifting toward R&B by the time Pickett joined. Percy Sledge had sung with his cousin's gospel group, the Singing Clouds.

Other soul singers had a similar background. Garnet Mimms, who charted in 1963 with the Top Five "Cry Baby," had sung with Philadelphia gospel groups such as the Evening Star Quartet and the Harmonizing Four and had cut his first record with the gospel troupe, the Norfolk Four. As a youngster, Dave Prater, who later teamed with Sam Moore as Sam and Dave, had sung and recorded with the gospel group, the Sensational Hummingbirds. Sam Moore, the son of a Baptist minister, had been a member of the gospel group, the Mellonaires.

Solomon Burke had especially close ties to the church. "I was born upstairs while church was going on downstairs," he recalled. "People shouting and having a good time. …It's just a normal reaction to me, to hear that rhythm, to hear that beat." Beginning at age 7, he worked as a boy preacher, nicknamed the Wonder Boy Preacher, and then served as pastor of his grandmother's Solomon's Temple congregation of the United House of Prayer for All People sect. He fronted the Gospel Cavaliers quartet and hosted a gospel radio show. When he recorded, Burke demanded a pulpit in the recording studio from which he sang. "Solomon would stand up there in front of the pulpit, and we'd have church," recalled record producer and singer Don Covay.

Otis Redding had learned about music in the church. The son of a minister, Redding had sung in the Mount Ivy Baptist Church choir as a young boy. "By the time he was a kid," recalled Rodgers Redding, Otis' brother, "he was singing in a gospel group in church."

James Brown had a similar experience. As a wayward youth, he witnessed hand-clapping, singing, and exuberant preaching, when he attended church with a crippled man. "I watched the preachers real close," he recalled. He later modeled some of his stage act on the rantings and outfits of Bishop "Daddy" Grace. During the 1940s, James Brown played organ and drums for various gospel outfits, including Sarah Byrd's group, the Gospel Starlighters. Later, he regularly featured gospel performers in the first part of his show and started his act with "a little preaching before I sang." "Really, gospel is what got over me," concluded Brown.

Ray Charles's music reflected his religious upbringing, having sung as a youth in the Shiloh Baptist Church in Greenville, Florida. He replaced the Pilgrim Travelers' "I've Got a New Home" with "Lonely Avenue" and shortened "Nobody But You, Lord" to "Nobody But You." He changed the gospel standard "This Little Light of Mine" to "This Little Girl of Mine," switched "I've Got a Savior (Way Over Jordan)" to "I've Got a Woman," and exulted in gospel screams in "Hallelujah, I Love Her So." "Now I'd been singing spirituals since I was three and I'd been singing the blues for just as long," explained Charles. "So what could be more natural than to combine them?" Added bluesman Big Bill Broonzy about Ray Charles, "He's cryin', sanctified. He's mixing the blues with the spirituals. He should be singing in a church."

Aretha Franklin, the 5-foot-5-inch dynamo dubbed "Lady Soul," had a direct connection to the church. Her father, the Reverend Clarence L. Franklin, served as the pastor of Detroit's 4,500-member New Bethel Baptist Church and recorded more than seventy albums of fiery, passionate, gospel-drenched sermons. Two white-uniformed nurses commonly stood guard at the aisles of New Bethel Baptist to aid parishioners, who were overcome by the emotionally draining orations of the minister. As a youth, Aretha came into contact with gospel greats such as James Cleveland and Mahalia Jackson, and at the funeral of an aunt, she witnessed Clara Ward belt out a powerful rendition of "Peace in the Valley." At that moment, the minister's daughter later recollected, "I wanted to become a singer." Aretha learned gospel from James Cleveland, who had sung with the Caravans before assembling his own choir: "He showed me some real nice chords and I liked his deep, deep sound," explained Franklin. "What he was feelin', I was feelin', but I just didn't know how to put it across. The more I watched him, the more I got out of it." Soon, Aretha joined a family-organized traveling gospel troupe, before signing with Columbia Records. The soul of Aretha Franklin had matured in the church.

Atlantic Records distributed most of the gospel-based R&B, which became known as soul music. The company had been established in 1947 by Ahmet Ertegun, a son of the first Turkish ambassador to the United States. An avid jazz and blues record collector, he auctioned 15,000 78-rpm discs and borrowed $10,000 from his family dentist to start Atlantic Records with fellow record collector Herb Abramson, who had been a part-time producer for National Records and had helped establish Jubilee Records. Abramson's wife, Miriam Bienstock, acted as the business manager for the fledgling company.

Atlantic Records, starting as a jazz label, slowly shifted its focus to rhythm and blues. In early 1949, Atlantic scored its first hit with the R&B song "Drinkin' Wine, Spo-Dee-O-Dee," by Granville "Sticks" McGhee. The same year, they signed R&B vocalist Ruth Brown who by 1954 scored with five number-one rhythm-and-blues hits. By the mid-1950s, Atlantic produced a variety of jazz and R&B artists, hitting the rhythm-and-blues charts with performers such as former Drifter Clyde McPhatter, Big Joe Turner ("Shake, Rattle, and Roll"), LaVern Baker ("Tweedle Dee"), and Chuck Willis ("C. C. Rider").

Atlantic achieved crossover success with Ray Charles. In June 1952, it bought Ray's contract for $2,500. Working with Wexler, Charles scored a series of number-one R&B hits, including "I've Got a Woman" and "Drown in My Own Tears."

Charles teamed with two sax players to perfect a soul-drenched sound. Idolizing Louis Jordan and traveling with blues outfits, the Texas-born David "Fathead" Newman joined the Charles outfit in 1954 to unleash earthy, gritty wails to accompany his leader. Wexler considered Newman to be the pianist's "alter ego on tenor." In 1958, saxophonist Hank Crawford connected with the Ray Charles band. After attending Tennessee State University in Nashville, he formed a combo and then enlisted in the Charles outfit, where for the next five years he integrated sanctified gospel into the band to complement his leader.

With the addition of the two saxophones as the civil rights struggle intensified, the sound of Ray Charles crossed over into the mainstream. In July 1959, he reached the pop Top-Ten with "What'd I Say." For the next four years, Charles repeatedly hit the pop charts with such number-one blockbusters as "Hit the Road Jack" and "Georgia on My Mind." In 1960, he scored his first Top-Ten album with *Genius Hits the Road* and the next year neared the top of the chart with *Genius + Soul = Jazz*. Soon, the public referred to Charles as the "High Priest of Soul" and "Brother Ray."

Building on their success with Ray Charles, who as early as 1959 had been promoted as a "soul brother" by the company, Atlantic produced more soul acts. In late 1960, Ertegun signed Solomon Burke, who in 1965 topped the R&B chart and neared the Top Twenty with "Got to Get You Off My Mind." The year that Burke scaled the charts, Atlantic Records lured Wilson Pickett from the Double LL label. For the next two years, Atlantic had success with Pickett, who charted with "In the Midnight Hour," "634-5789," "Land of a 1,000 Dances," and "Mustang Sally." Percy Sledge, an Alabama farm boy who had chopped cotton as a youth, joined the Atlantic stable and in 1966 topped the singles chart with "When a Man Loves a Woman."

Atlantic also distributed the music of artists on Stax Records. In 1958, banker and country fiddler Jim Stewart and his older sister Estelle Axton teamed on the venture, the Memphis-based Satellite Records and recording studio, which they renamed Stax three years later. The new label initially recorded local talent such as African-American disc jockey Rufus Thomas and his daughter Carla, who in 1960 dueted for the regional hit "Cause I Love You," when the label assigned joint-publishing credit to influential Nashville disc jockey John Richbourg. Later in the year, Carla recorded Stax's first national hit with the Top Ten "Gee Whiz (Look at His Eyes)." After the success of the Thomas duo, the label signed other African-American artists such as William Bell (b. William Yarbrough). "We just didn't sit down and say, 'We're going on with the black music,'" mentioned Stewart. "It just happened." In 1960, after their initial successes, Stax signed a five-year agreement with Atlantic to distribute its records.

Stax gave artists who recorded at its studio on McLemore Avenue a distinctive sound, which was created by the Stax house band, Booker T. Jones and the MGs. The band originally consisted of several high school friends, including Packy Axton, Estelle's son. By 1962, the band solidified into a racially integrated rhythm section: keyboardist Booker T. Jones; drummer Al Jackson, Jr.; guitarist Steve Cropper, who drew his inspiration from 5 Royales' guitarist Lowman Pauling; and bassist Lewis Steinberg, who in March 1964 was replaced by Donald "Duck" Dunn. The band, who in 1962 hit with its own number-three smash, "Green Onions," played with the Memphis Horns, anchored by Andrew Love and Wayne Jackson, to back virtually every artist who recorded at Stax, including Wilson Pickett, Percy Sledge, Otis Redding, and Sam and Dave who scored with the signature "Hold On, I'm Coming" (1966).

The gospel-based rhythm and blues, recorded by Atlantic and Stax, became known as soul music during the mid-1960s, when many African Americans rediscovered a sense of self-esteem. In 1965, station WOL in Washington, D.C., attracting primarily African-American listeners, began to call itself "soul radio," local disc jockey Fred Correy labeled himself "Soulfinger," and *Soul* magazine began publication. In 1965 and 1966, Otis Redding perfected his style with several albums, culminating in *Otis Blue (Otis Redding Sings Soul)*, which included the hit "Respect."

During the mid-sixties, amid the movement for black pride, African Americans supported soul acts. Otis Redding broke attendance records at shows in Harlem and Watts, and in 1966 grossed $250,000 on a month-long rhythm-and-blues tour. He earned enough money to start Jotis Records and helped to promote the career of Arthur Conley, who in 1967 neared the top of the chart with "Sweet Soul Music," which Redding cowrote. James Brown bought a bright-red Corvette Stingray racing car, a Lear jet, an English-style mansion surrounded by a moat, several apartment buildings, and a wardrobe of 150 suits and 80 pairs of shoes with the money he amassed from the sale of records to an audience, which, except for crossover interest in his *Live at the Apollo* album, consisted almost exclusively of African Americans.

During the mid-1960s, while white youths listened to the Beatles, acid rock, or British blues-based bands such as the Rolling Stones, African Americans took pride in a punchy, testifying soul sound performed by fellow African Americans. "It's SOUL, man, SOUL," exclaimed African-American disc jockey Magnificent Montague in *Billboard*. "Now what is soul? It's the last to be hired, the first to be fired, brown all year-round, sit-in-the-back-of-the-bus feeling."

Funk

James Brown, a prime exponent of gospel-drenched soul, perfected a new African-American-based style called "funk," which merged rhythm and blues with African polyrhythms and reflected the quest for black self-awareness. From 1955, when he began to record secular music, to his breakthrough *Live at the Apollo* album eight years later, Brown sang a mixture of gospel and spirited rhythm and blues. In the summer of 1964, with the single "Out of Sight," he unveiled a new genre that featured bursts of dominant, repeating, overpowering rhythm accented by phrase-shouting vocals and the staccato punch of horns. As the distinctive feature of funk, he laid down an intense groove by using drum-like, bass-guitar lines to ground the music. Over the bass rhythms, Brown layered a percussive guitar, horns that delivered powerful "rhythm hits" and his frantic vocals, punctuated with hollers and well-placed grunts. Unlike soul music and most other rock-and-roll, he deserted chord changes for a single-chord mode to further focus on the complicated rhythmic patterns. Finally, James Brown emphasized the first beat of a four-beat measure rather than the dominant second and fourth beats of traditional rock-and-roll. "I changed the upbeat to the downbeat," he explained, "Simple as that, really." The

James Brown in funky action, 1967.

Philippe Gras/Alamy Stock Photo.

resulting music constituted a new sound that harkened to the polyrhythms of Africa and captured the black nationalism of the era.

In 1965, James Brown hit the national Top Ten and topped the R&B chart with the million-selling funk of "Papa's Got a Brand New Bag (Part 1)." Later in the year, Brown released the equally successful funk single "I Got You (I Feel Good)." In 1967, Brown offered the single-chord funk of "Cold Sweat (Part 1)," which hit the top of the R&B chart and number seven on the pop chart. The same year, Brown epitomized the quest for African-American respect, when he started recording his *Say It Loud—I'm Black and I'm Proud*. "I will never get too big to remember I'm still a soul brother," he exclaimed. After 1967, Brown completed his transition to funk when he hired musical director Albert Ellis and new musicians such as bassist Bootsy Collins, drummer Clyde Stubblefield, saxophonist Maceo Parker, guitarist Jimmy Nolan, and horn man Fred Wesley. His new sound paved the way for other funksters such as Dyke and the Blazers with their hit "Funky Broadway" (1967) and Tower of Power with their debut *East Bay Grease (1970)*.

As Brown shifted from more traditional R&B and gospel to funk, he recalled, "I got the name 'Soul Brother Number One.' The word 'soul' by this time meant a lot of things—in music and out. It was about the roots of black music, and it was a kind of pride thing, too, being proud of yourself and your people. Soul music and the civil rights movement went hand in hand, sort of grew up together."

Black Soul in White America

During the late 1960s, the inner-city tumult made many Americans, especially those raised during the civil rights era, more aware of and interested in African-American culture. Though causing a white backlash in some quarters, the 1967 riots in Detroit and other cities allowed many whites to better understand the plight of African Americans. Discrimination "hurts them real bad. I'd probably be rioting right with them," a Texas salesman lamented. Mrs. Margaret Lamb, a widow from Owensboro, Kentucky, felt the same way. "It makes you wonder that they do as good as they do the way people treat them sometimes. You see things that make you wonder why they put up with it."

Sympathizing with African Americans, many young whites supported an African-American outlook. Radicalized students, protesting the war in Vietnam, embraced the ideology of militant Black Power groups such as the Black Panther Party for Self-Defense. "We had captured the imagination of the white radical left in this country to a point that its whole identification became connected with what the Black Panther Party was doing, how it was personifying things," boasted Panther cofounder Bobby Seale.

The students successfully lobbied for ethnic studies and black history classes, which fostered a greater awareness of the contributions of African Americans to fields such as history, psychology, science, literature, and anthropology. In 1968, students at San Francisco State University engineered a five-month strike for a black studies program. Activists at other universities such as the University of California at Berkeley occupied buildings to demand that the curricula include courses about black culture.

African-American soul records crossed over into white America with Aretha Franklin. In August 1960, Aretha signed with John Hammond, the talent scout for Columbia Records who had discovered Count Basie and Bob Dylan. Mitch Miller, the Columbia executive who had assailed rock during the 1950s, gave Franklin voice and dance lessons, hooked her up with Bob Mersey, the musical arranger for pop singer Barbra Streisand, and assigned her such pop material as the show tune "If Ever I Would Leave You" and Al Jolson's "Rock-a-Bye Your Baby with a Dixie Melody." By late 1966, a dissatisfied Aretha had found only moderate commercial success after nine albums with the label. "Things were kinda hungry then," she admitted.

In January 1967, when her contract with Columbia expired, Franklin signed with Atlantic Records. Within a few weeks, Aretha recorded *I Never Loved a Man (the Way I Love You)*, which included the single "Respect." In early 1967, "Respect," an R&B hit for Otis Redding two years earlier, took on added importance. The song, belted out by the Detroit native Aretha Franklin, hit the streets just a few months before the ghetto of the Motor City exploded into flames. To whites, it seemed to epitomize the renewed self-pride that African Americans had discovered. The chart-topping song sold more than 1 million copies in ten months and brought African-American soul into white America. The album reached number two on the chart.

Aretha Franklin, 1960s.

Anthony Wallace/Associated Newspapers/ Daily Mail/Rex/Alamy Stock Photo.

Aretha continued her crossover success. During the next two years, she charted with the million-selling singles "(You Make Me Feel Like a) Natural Woman" and "Chain of Fools" and hit the Top Five with her next three albums. *Ebony* magazine characterized the summer of 1967 as "'Retha, Rap [Brown], and Revolt." In 1968, Aretha won the Best Female Vocalist of the Year award, and on February 16, Detroit Mayor Jerome Cavanaugh declared Aretha Franklin Day. In July 1968, Aretha solidified her reputation among whites as the soul spokeswoman with her rendition of "Think," which ended with the singer crying for her freedom.

After the crossover triumph of Aretha and the 1967 riots, other soul singers attracted greater mainstream interest. In 1967, Wilson Pickett hit the Top Ten with a remake of Dyke and the Blazers' "Funky Broadway" and spent eight weeks on the album chart with *The Best of Wilson Pickett*. In 1968, James Brown reached the Top Ten with "Say It Loud—I'm Black and I'm Proud (Part 1)." In late 1967, Sam and Dave scored a crossover hit with the number-two "Soul Man." "Soul Man was written when there was a lot of racial unrest in the country. There was uprising in various cities, people burning buildings—Watts, Detroit," recalled Isaac Hayes who cowrote the song with Dave Porter. After hearing a newscast that reported rioters bypassed black businesses with "Soul" emblazoned on them, Hayes realized the power of "the word *soul*." "Wow, soul. Soul. Soul man. 'David, I got one,'" he exclaimed to Porter.

Otis Redding crossed over into the white mainstream before his untimely death on December 10, 1967, when his twin-engine Beechcraft plane plunged into icy Lake Monoma outside of Madison, Wisconsin. He won posthumous accolades for the chart-topping "(Sittin' On) The Dock of the Bay." The King of Soul, who had received little attention from the white audience during his lifetime until he electrified youths at the June 1967 Monterey Pop Festival, hit the Top Five with the album *Dock of the Bay*.

The Soul Clan hit the charts amid soul fever. Formed in 1966, the artist collective included Otis Redding, Wilson Pickett, soul singer Joe Tex, organizer Solomon Burke, and soul songwriter and singer Don Covay. After Redding's death, his protégé Arthur Conley joined. The Soul Clan hoped to raise money to refurbish ghetto housing, encourage the building of schools in the inner cities, and help with the development of black-owned restaurant franchises. In 1968, Clan members collaborated on an album and charted in the summer of 1968 with "Soul Meeting."

Atlantic Records, which produced many of the soul artists including those in the Soul Clan, reaped financial rewards of its roster. By July 1967, the company sold more records in two months (2.6 million) than it did for the entire year in 1950.

By 1968, black soul had permeated white America. Considering "all the commercial yardsticks used in the trade," asserted *Time* in 1968, "soul has arrived."

Chapter 12
Guitar Heroes and Heavy Metal

"The aggression I play is the aggression I know. And it's obviously aggression a lot of people have."

—Ozzy Osbourne

On November 2, 1968, the Minneapolis Auditorium hosted the "Experience," a trio headed by black guitarist Jimi Hendrix. The group's manager, Chas Chandler, had hired more than twenty police officers and ten security guards to encircle the stage and keep the surging audience at bay. After unleashing several of his hit songs such as "Foxy Lady" and "Are You Experienced," the guitarist launched into a gut-wrenching version of the blues, "Red House." The band let loose a deafening, earth-shaking roar from the stacks of nine Marshall amplifiers and the dozens of speaker cabinets behind them. The stage looked like a "wall of speakers with three midgets playing in front of them," recalled bassist Noel Redding.

As a finale, Hendrix picked the American national anthem, "The Star Spangled Banner." He hurled himself into "an atonal, quavering improvisation—barely touching upon the melody of the anthem," wrote the *St. Paul Pioneer Press*. The stunned audience watched silently.

The Hendrix had rendered a new version of the anthem to punctuate his concerns over racial inequality and the Vietnam War. One of the few black rock-and-roll musicians, Hendrix a few months earlier played on behalf of a Black Power group and joined a benefit concert to commemorate the death of Martin Luther King, Jr. In 1968, he wrote such songs as "Peace in Mississippi," "Long Hot Summer," and "Housing Burning Down," the last a composition describing the 1965 Watts riot. "We made the guitar sound like it was on fire," mentioned Hendrix. The next year, Hendrix delivered "Machine Gun." At a concert, Hendrix dedicated the song to "all the troops fighting in Harlem, Chicago, and, oh yes, Vietnam."

Hendrix and his music reflected the turbulent times by combining booming volume with a furious stage presence. On June 18, 1967, at the Monterey Pop Festival, where he made his major debut in the United States and attracted acclaim, he ended his set with a thrashing version of the Troggs' "Wild Thing." As the final notes of the song blasted from a column of nine amplifiers and eighteen speakers, Hendrix doused his guitar with lighter fluid and set it on fire. "The Experience's destruction is inevitable rather than accidental, the surfacing of a violent streak," commented *Newsweek*. "The people who dig me," explained the guitarist, "want to feel something inside, something real—revolution, struggle, rebellion."

Hendrix hoped that his staged assault would provide the catharsis to defuse the violence around him. "It's best to have violence onstage," he instructed a journalist in early 1969. "We try to drain the violence out of their system." "We can play violent music, and in a way it's like watching wrestling or football for them—it releases their violence," he concluded. In the tumultuous Sixties, Hendrix served as a mirror for the times.

Jimi Hendrix Experience, 1968.

Odile Noel/Lebrecht Music and Arts Photo Library/Alamy Stock Photo.

Escalating Conflict in Vietnam

The war in Vietnam triggered much of the angst and disturbances, which Hendrix mirrored. The war pitted the United States against South Vietnamese peasants, or Viet Cong, who had been stripped of their land after World War II and allied with the communist-led North Vietnam. By 1963, President John Kennedy had commissioned more than 16,000 military advisors to help the South Vietnamese train their troops. Worried about the threat of communism in Southeast Asia, American officials slowly increased the U.S. commitment in Vietnam. In 1965, after Congress passed the Gulf of Tonkin Resolution that gave the president authority to conduct military operations in Southeast Asia without declaring war, the number of American troops skyrocketed from 23,000 to 184,000. By 1966, President Lyndon Johnson increased ground troops in the region to 385,000, including young black men who comprised more than 26 percent of the troops.

By 1968, the United States had shipped 542,000 troops to the war-torn country. The U.S. government also embarked on a bombing campaign to quell the North Vietnamese National Liberation Front Army. Between 1965 when the bombing started and 1968, it dropped more than a million tons of bombs, rockets, and missiles during such campaigns as Operation Rolling Thunder and Operation Flaming Dart. The Chief of Staff of the United States Air Force Curtis LeMay vowed to "bomb them [North Vietnamese] back into the Stone Age."

Campus Unrest

Youths, clustered in major universities such as the University of California at Berkeley, protested against the war. On April 15, 1967, in New York's Central Park, more than 100,000 demonstrators gathered for the Spring Mobilization to End the War in Vietnam. On the same day, 75,000 San Francisco protesters showed their support for the same

A Marine moves a Viet Cong suspect near Da Nang, 1965.

Department of Defense. Department of the Navy. U.S. Marine Corps. 9/18/1947/National Archives and Records Administration.

cause. Others organized a draft resistance movement and burned their draft cards, urging others to undermine the selective service system. Sometimes the protests included a dash of humor. On October 21, 1967, Abbie Hoffman, a civil rights organizer, and his friend Jerry Rubin, a founder of the Vietnam Committee at Bekeley and a co-conspirator with Rubin in the Youth International Party (Yippie), attempted to levitate the Pentagon to display their disdain of the Vietnam War.

The Yippies, who merged left-wing politics with a psychedelic lifestyle, teamed with Beat poet Allen Ginsberg and Ed Sanders of the Fugs and coalesced outside the Pentagon. Standing with 150,000 adherents, the leaders chanted "in the name of the lives of the dead soldiers in Vietnam who were killed because of a bad karma, in the name of the Tyrone Power pound cake society in the sky—out demon out, out demon out." Organizers of the event dropped 10,000 flowers on the Pentagon, many of which eventually ended in the barrels of the rifles of the military police who had been sent to disperse the protesters. Unsuccessful in their attempt to levitate the building, the exorcising demonstrators were dispersed by the police, who arrested 647 protesters. "We wanted to be stoned, wasted, and free," asserted Ray Mongo, cofounder of the Liberation News Service, who had been arrested at the event. "We were proud of being individuals."

In early 1968 after the Viet Cong launched the Tet offensive on thirty-six provincial capitals and the United States expanded aerial bombardment and defoliation efforts, student protests against the war turned more serious and violent, when students at Columbia University occupied university buildings to protest the war. "Columbia was seen as part of a power structure linked to the same forces that were waging war in Vietnam," contended Allen Young of the Liberation News Service. "We viewed the disruption of university life as a necessary step." Authorities responded to the student protests with a show of force. In early May 1968, at 2:30 A.M., a thousand New York City policemen approached the Morningside Heights campus of Columbia University. They moved onto the campus in police vans and squad cars, sealed off the entrances to the university, and, on orders from Police Commissioner Howard Leary, marched toward five buildings that student rebels occupied to protest the university's affiliation with the Institute for Defense Analysis. As they attempted to dislodge student militants, the police encountered resistance. At Fayerweather Hall, they clubbed and kicked angry students and newsmen such as columnist Walter Winchell. By mid-morning, the police had dispersed the students from the buildings, arresting 698 and

Student Protest against the Vietnam War, October 1967.

Library of Congress Prints and Photographs Division [LC-DIG-ds-07432].

injuring 120. To noted anthropologist Margaret Mead, who taught at Columbia for forty-eight years, the police action signaled "the end of an epoch."

The protest at Columbia sparked trouble at other colleges and universities. More than 500 students at Princeton demonstrated in support of students at Columbia. At Stony Brook in New York, 50 student militants staged a seventeen-hour sit-in to express their sympathy. In Philadelphia, 200 Temple University students picketed university buildings in the wake of the Columbia protests. By mid-June, as the inner cities burst into violence, almost 40,000 students engaged in 221 major demonstrations at 101 colleges and universities.

In August, student dissent intensified at the National Democratic Convention in Chicago, where the ineffectiveness of the flower-power approach became evident. To protest the war in Vietnam, 10,000 young, peaceful reformers traveled to the Windy City for the opening of the convention on August 26. They were organized by David Dellinger of the National Mobilization Committee to End the War in Vietnam, Tom Hayden and Rennie Davis, cofounders of the Students for a Democratic Society (SDS), and Jerry Rubin of the Yippies. To recruit demonstrators, Rubin announced, "The Democratic Party is dying. While it dies, we will celebrate the Festival of Life. Come to Chicago!" He promised "making love in the parks...singing, laughing, printing newspapers, making a mock convention, and celebrating the birth of FREE AMERICA in our own time."

As hopeful students flooded into Chicago armed with backpacks and flowers, Chicago Mayor Richard Daley readied the city for battle. The mayor, who the previous year had recommended that looters be maimed and arsonists be killed during a race riot, heavily barricaded the Amphitheater, the site of the convention. He activated

6,000 National Guardsmen, requested and received 6,000 federal troops armed with bazookas, barbed wire, and tanks, and placed 12,000 Chicago policemen on twelve-hour shifts. After encountering stiff resistance from the organized students, Daley planned a strategy of confrontation that, according to the subsequent *Walker Report*, created a "police riot." By the time Democrats left on August 29, Daley's police force had injured 198 and arrested 641 protesters. Violence at the Chicago convention and the subsequent trial of eight protest leaders radicalized many hip students who once believed in the power of example. "I saw the power of flowers wilt, first by gas, then when the guy next to me—a hardened street hippie out of *A Clockwork Orange*—lobbed a trash can through the windshield of a trapped squad car," remembered Abe Peck of the *Seed*, a Chicago underground paper.

Events at Columbia University and the Chicago convention changed the mood of students from a hope-filled ebullience to a dark, protective aggression. "The scene has changed," wrote Steve Dreyer in the Austin *Rag*, "as people realized that you can't build a 'community' of beautiful people in a rotten, capitalist society. And it occurred with Columbia and Chicago—with the death (and co-optation) of 'do your own thing' and with the beginning of the revolutionary consciousness." Steve Diamond of the Liberation News Service agreed: "Nobody wanted to know about communal living in the country, about organic food. It was 'Be in the city, in the streets fighting the man.'" In January 1969, *The Rat*, an underground newspaper in New York City, told its readers that "the revolution has come. It's time to pick up your gun."

In 1969, campus violence escalated. In May, 3,000 students at the University of California at Berkeley tried to remove a chain-link fence that university officials had erected around a grassy lot known as People's Park, which students recently had renovated. Ronald Reagan, then governor of California, calling the action "a deliberate and planned attempt at confrontation," activated 2,000 National Guardsmen, who gassed the unsuspecting students from a helicopter and with shotguns killed one onlooker, wounded thirty protesters, and arrested 800 others. *Time* magazine called the reaction a "crushing repression."

More of the 7.8 million university students across the country marched in protest. In 1969, disturbances occurred at state universities in Maryland, Delaware, and Minnesota. Student militants faced the police in major confrontations at San Francisco State, Duke University, Queens College in New York, Dartmouth College, and even at Harvard University, the bastion of academic respectability. At the University of Wisconsin at Madison, students protested the war in Vietnam by building 435 crosses, which they planted in rows on the lawn of the main administration building. The organizer of the demonstration wanted to show that "students really are faced with death."

The war in Vietnam became very personal for American youths with the draft. On December 1, 1969, federal officials held the first lottery drawing to draft men into the armed forces since the Korean War. No longer a distant, philosophical problem, the war became an immediate concern for young men who feared death in combat. The draft helped further mobilize students who now protested to protect their lives. By the end of 1969, millions of worried students had taken to the streets, and more than 100,000 militants had banded together in 350 chapters of the radical SDS.

In 1969, a few thousand youths joined the violent Weathermen, bent on destroying the "system." Started in June when the Students for a Democratic Society fragmented into competing factions, the Weather Underground Organization borrowed their name from a Bob Dylan lyric, in the song "Subterranean Homesick Blues." They vowed to stop the war in Vietnam by any means possible. The group demanded "the full participation and involvement of masses of people in the practice of making revolution," according to their founding manifesto, and vowed to engineer "a movement with a full willingness to participate in the violent and illegal struggle." "In an all-out civil war over Vietnam and other fascist U.S. imperialism, we were going to bring the war home," exclaimed organizer John Jacobs, "and we were going to kick ass." The Weathermen circulated the slogan "Elections Don't Mean Shit—Vote Where the Power Is—Our Power is in the Streets," and Jacobs promised that "we will burn and loot and destroy. We are the incubation of your mother's nightmare."

The White Blues

Radicalized by a war in Vietnam, militant American youths abandoned the folk-based, airy sounds of acid rock and turned to the angry, slashing, piercing, and distorted blues of American and British guitar heroes. Faced with police clubs and tear gas, they embraced the music of an oppressed race. "The blues are bigger now than ever—ten times bigger," John Lee Hooker noticed in late 1968. "You know why it's bigger? Because all the college kids are digging it now."

The militant, dark mood of youth sparked a late-1960s electric blues revival. Young, white blues performers raised in the American South gained popularity. Johnny Winter, growing up in Beaumont, Texas, had played the blues since childhood. After launching a number of blues-rock outfits with his brother Edgar, he traveled to Louisiana and then to Chicago, where he backed local blues greats. He returned to Texas, played the Georgia-Florida blues circuit, and produced a demo tape that included blues standards such as Howlin' Wolf's "Forty-Four," Sonny Boy Williamson's "Help Me," and Muddy Waters' "Rollin' and Tumblin'." In 1968, after *Rolling Stone* magazine mentioned Winter in an overview of the Texas blues scene, the guitarist snagged a contract with Columbia Records and the next year neared the Top Twenty with his debut. "I'd been put down for years for singing the blues and suddenly everyone liked me and wanted to hear me," shrugged Winter at the time.

The Allman Brothers delivered electric, Deep-South blues combined with a dash of jazz. Raised in Florida, brothers Duane and Gregg Allman became young blues fanatics. Late-night radio station WLAC "would play those [blues] tunes and we'd head to the record store, man. We'd run in yelling, 'Who is this guy Lightnin' Hopkins?'" Gregg reminisced. By the time Duane graduated from high school in 1964, the duo had spearheaded blues bands up and down Daytona Beach and had recorded a commercially unsuccessful version of Willie Dixon's "Spoonful." In 1967, they moved to Los Angeles and signed with Liberty Records as Hourglass. After two LPs, Hourglass disbanded, and Duane moved to Muscle Shoals, Alabama, providing background guitar for Wilson Pickett, Aretha Franklin, and Percy Sledge.

In 1969, Duane Allman formed a new blues band with brother Gregg, Dickey Betts on second guitar, Berry Oakley on bass, and drummers Butch Trucks and Jaimoe Johanson. "Duane and Gregg were students of the urban blues," recalled Betts. He and Oakley "may have been influenced by the blues and were students of it," the guitarist continued, but "we would go *sideways* with it. When we all came together, we gave each other a new foundation." In 1969 on their self-named debut, the band featured a several blues-based originals alongside such standards as Muddy Waters' "Trouble No More." Their next effort paid homage to their blues heroes with "Hoochie Coochie Man" written by Willie Dixon and made famous by Waters. By their 1971 breakthrough *At Fillmore East*, which included Blind Willie McTell's "Statesboro Blues," they became leaders of the blues-rock movement.

Canned Heat, a Los Angeles-based blues band named after the Tommy Johnson song "Canned Heat Blues," promoted the blues. In 1965, the band came together around guitarist Alan Wilson and singer Bob "The Bear" Hite who had "a mission in his life to propagate the blues" according to drummer Fito de la Parra. Initially, the group had trouble finding work. "Nobody would hire us because we were blues," complained Hite, who in the 1960s rabidly collected more than 70,000 blues records. In 1967, they signed with Liberty Records and released their self-named debut, composed mostly of blues standards. The next year, the group neared the Top Ten with the 1928 Henry Thomas blues tune "Going Up the Country" and reached the Top Twenty with two more albums. In 1971, Canned Heat recorded an album with one of their idols, John Lee Hooker. At the turn of the decade, reported *Time* magazine, "the pop scene has become a roaring, pulsating paradox of sound—the white man singing the black blues."

Amid the white-blues frenzy, some of the electric blues originators attracted crossover attention. In 1967, B.B. King played the Fillmore auditorium, which had been an African-American venue before entrepreneur Bill Graham transformed it into a hippie concert hall. When King took the stage, he saw cheering white youths who gave him a standing ovation. In 1963, "the last time we played there it was 95 percent black. This time it was 95 percent white," King recalled. "I wanted to cry." Other blues pioneers such as Muddy Waters, John Lee Hooker, and Albert King (b. Albert Nelson) experienced that same feeling at the Fillmore, which regularly featured older blues artists. "My days of paying dues are over," insisted Albert King. "Now it's my time to do the collecting."

Jimi Hendrix: The Sound and the Fury

Some guitar heroes such as Jimi Hendrix, rather than pay tribute to their blues idols, updated the blues by featuring an ear-splitting volume, an array of electronic gadgetry, sometimes sobering lyrics and intricate, improvised solos to perfectly capture the rage, fury, and pain of the late 1960s.

Jimi Hendrix, a poor, part-African American, part-Cherokee from a broken home in Seattle, became the prototype for the sixties blues-based guitar hero. Hendrix based his music on the blues. The music "is some sort of blues—that's all I'm really singing about. It's today's blues," he contended. Billy Cox, the bassist who became friends with Hendrix during their Army days in the early sixties and joined his band after the break-up of the Experience in 1969, characterized Hendrix as "a blues master." The guitarist idolized such blues icons as Muddy Waters, Howlin' Wolf, B.B. King, and Albert King.

Unlike many other rock guitarists, Hendrix began his professional career in R & B bands. In November 1961, Jimi and Billy Cox joined the King Kasuals during their stint in the 101st U.S. Airborne Division as paratroopers. The King Kasuals, mentioned Cox, played "blues and R & B." When discharged from the Army after breaking his foot on a jump, Hendrix traveled to New York City, where in March 1964, he hooked up with the R & B singing group, the Isley Brothers, and then bolted to R & B singer Gorgeous George Odell. While with Odell, he backed established blues and R & B stars who headlined the shows. In December 1964, the vagabond Hendrix landed a six-month gig with Little Richard and the Upsetters. Subsequently, he played with R & B sax men King Curtis and Lonnie Youngblood as well as Curtis Knight and the Squires.

When Hendrix founded his own group, he adopted many of the trappings used by his previous rhythm-and-blues employers. On the cover of his 1967 debut, *Are You Experienced?*, he and his band mates decked themselves in outrageous garb. Hendrix wore bright yellow hip huggers and a white vest over a red, pink, and yellow paisley shirt, which had two openings around the chest that let two red eyeballs peek out. Around his neck, Hendrix sported a vibrant orange tufted scarf. Bass player Noel Redding favored a double-breasted, yellow felt sport coat with flowers emblazoned on it, and drummer Mitch Mitchell had white-and-blue-striped trousers, a yellow scarf, and a white, red, and yellow tie-dyed shirt. The group stood against a backdrop of blood-red trees. Though many attributed the style to the burgeoning white hippie culture on the West Coast, Hendrix had assimilated the sartorial approach of the flamboyant Little Richard who performed in frilled shirts and headbands and Gorgeous George Odell who designed and sewed his own stage costumes.

Musically, Hendrix ramped up the volume of his rhythm-and-blues past and assaulted his listeners through stacks of amplifiers. On the advice of guitarist Pete Townshend of The Who, electronics wiz Jim Marshall worked on a more powerful amplifier that defined the Hendrix sound. He designed a huge 100-watt amp that could be stacked to generate a deafening roar, which resulted in overtones through feedback, when a guitarist played closely to them. In 1966, Hendrix visited Marshall's shop in London and agreed to exclusively use the new mega-powered amplifiers, which he stacked on top of one another to blast his audiences.

In addition to mountains of amplifiers and speakers that gave him a thundering volume, Hendrix championed many new electronic gadgets, some of which engineers built exclusively for him to make his music more menacing, distorted, and complex. Hendrix favored the wah-wah pedal, first introduced in late 1967, which altered frequency to give the music a crying effect. For the guitarist, the wah-wah generated a feeling of "loneliness and that frustration and the yearning for something. Like something reaching out." Jimi took advantage of the fuzz box, prominently heard on the Rolling Stones' "(I Can't Get No) Satisfaction," which clipped sound to distort it and make it appear gritty and harsh. He utilized the Univibe, a device initially developed for pianos, which layered an uncertain, swirling, wobbly feel to the music by shifting phase. "We wanted to have the music itself warped," Hendrix expounded. He also used the Whammy bar on many of his guitars to achieve further pitch-bending distortion.

Hendrix worked with acoustic engineer Roger Mayer to develop several effects. They developed the Octavia, which produced a sound an octave higher than the notes played to produce a doubling effect. "It can be thought of as producing multiple mirror images of the sound," instructed Mayer. First featured on "Purple Haze," the gadget gave Hendrix the ability to experiment with sound patterns by using the Octavia in conjunction with other effects at ear-shattering volume. In the studio, Jimi and Mayer took "two tape machines and slowed one down slightly, and then they mixed them back together. As one machine slows down, you get a slight time difference between the two."

In less than two years after his debut album, Hendrix reflected the times by shedding his showy demeanor. In place of extravagant stage garb and an act that sometimes included making mock love to an amplifier with his guitar, Hendrix became more serious. "I was beginning to feel that too many people were coming to see 'the freak' and not to listen to the music," explained Jimi. "I lost the rings one by one, cut my hair, got rid of the baubles and changed my clothes because I felt too loud, visually." "I don't want to be a clown anymore," he insisted.

The guitarist became more overtly political. Abandoning his apolitical stance, he contributed $5,000 to the Martin Luther King, Jr., Memorial Fund and $6,000 for poverty students. In September 1969, Hendrix staged a free concert for the Harlem United Block Association and, in January 1970, performed at a benefit concert for the Vietnam Moratorium Committee. He publically championed the Black Panthers who he felt needed to harass the establishment and dedicated a song to them.

Hendrix likewise expanded upon the more sobering strains of his music. In his debut, he delivered the somber blues of "Manic Depression," "Purple Haze," and "I Don't Live Today," the last dedicated to his fellow Native Americans, alongside the pop of "Fire." By October 1968, when he released his masterpiece, *Electric Ladyland*, he abandoned all pretext of pop for swirling, dark soundscapes.

By 1970, Hendrix pioneered a harsh, explosive, ripping style of electric blues, which served as a soundtrack for a tumultuous time. He delivered songs such as "Machine Gun," which combined Hendrix's guitar explosions with a growing awareness of social problems. "Jimi told me that what he was trying to express in ['Machine Gun'] was that at every moment there are terrible things going on all over the world—war, destruction, and terror, and that he wanted to open people's eyes," confided Monika

Danneman, Hendrix's girlfriend at the time of his death. "Lots of young people now feel they're not getting a fair deal," explained Hendrix. "So they revert to something loud, harsh, almost verging on violence; if they didn't go to a concert, they might be going to a riot."

Amid the serious-minded Sixties, the innovative, hard-edged music of Jimi Hendrix sold to the masses. "We could sell two million Jimi Hendrix albums," boasted Warner Brothers executive Mo Ostin. The Experience's first album *Are You Experienced?* remained on the *Billboard* chart for 106 weeks, peaking at number five. The follow-up, *Axis: Bold As Love*, again hit number five. In October 1968, the complex *Electric Ladyland* reached the top spot on the chart.

Guitar Rage of the Metal Pioneers

Cream stood in the vanguard of the metal pioneers, who delivered a loud, aggressive 1960s blues. The Cream power trio—Eric Clapton, Jack Bruce, and Ginger Baker—had individually started in various British blues units: Drummer Ginger Baker had joined Blues Incorporated and had powered the Graham Bond Organization; Jack Bruce had played his bass with Baker in Blues Incorporated and the Graham Bond Organization, leaving to join John Mayall and Manfred Mann; and Eric Clapton, idolizing blues legends Robert Johnson and Muddy Waters, had perfected piercing guitar improvisation in the Yardbirds and John Mayall's Bluesbreakers before joining Cream. In June 1966, Ginger Baker approached Clapton about forming a group that, upon the guitarist's insistence, included Jack Bruce on bass and vocals.

Cream based their sound on their blues roots. They first released the album *Fresh Cream*, which included Muddy Waters' "Rollin' and Tumblin'," "I'm So Glad" by Skip James, and "From Four Until Late" by Robert Johnson. In late 1967, the group followed with *Disraeli Gears*, their U.S. breakthrough, which contained several blues-based originals such as their signature "Sunshine of Your Love." The next year, they followed with the number-one *Wheels of Fire*, recorded at the Fillmore West, which included the Hendrix-inspired "White Room" and the biting "Politician." After hearing the group, Rose Clapp, Clapton's grandmother who had raised him, felt that Eric had "always been a lonely boy and his music still gives me that feeling about him." Clapton, though wearing paisley, saw blues as his lifeblood and felt "pretty contemptuous of the West Coast rock-and-roll scene as exemplified by the new bands like Jefferson Airplane, Big Brother and the Holding Company and the Grateful Dead." "Rock is like a battery that must always go back to the blues to get recharged," the guitarist asserted.

Cream played their blues at a near-deafening level. Like Hendrix, Eric Clapton regularly practiced in Jim Marshall's shop and bought the new Marshall stacks to deliver a thunderous blues. Baker wailed away at breakneck speed on the drums, using two bass drums to further pump up the volume, and Bruce played a six-string bass as he interchanged solos with the guitar master Clapton, who at one point had been referred to as "God" by British blues fanatics. The roar sometimes even overwhelmed the band. At one concert, remembered Ginger Baker, "Eric and I stopped playing for two choruses. Jack didn't even know. Standing in front of his triple stack Marshalls [amplifiers], he was making so much noise he couldn't tell." The blaring music benefited from the electronic devices that Hendrix had employed. Clapton especially favored such guitar effects as the Vox wah-wah pedal ("White Room" and "Tales of Brave Ulysses") and occasionally a fuzz-tone effect. He played closely to his Marshall stacks to get the distorted feedback so important to his harsh, gritty electric blues.

Jeff Beck, another guitar hero who had been a veteran of the Yardbirds, produced a hard-edged blues. After splitting from the Yardbirds in late 1966, Beck formed his own group, which included blues shouter Rod Stewart. The guitarist, though dressed in paisley shirts and bell-bottomed, multicolored pants, reworked blues standards such as Willie Dixon's "You Shook Me" and "I Ain't Superstitious" in a tumultuous, shattering style. "We used to take things like John Lee Hooker and Muddy Waters and all the great bluesmen and play them our way," related Beck. "We wanted to mess with them a bit." Though using fewer effects than some of his proto-metal counterparts, Beck managed to deliver a hard-edged sound. He characterized his second LP, the Top Twenty *Beck-Ola*, a 1969 collection of blues-drenched originals and rock standards such as "All Shook Up," as "heavy" music.

The Motor City Five delivered an aggressive, radicalized blues and directly intersected with the student protest movement. Formed by five high-school friends in Detroit in 1964, the MC5 took off in 1966 while attending Wayne State University, where they met their manager, John Sinclair. The MC5 roomed together above the office of the underground newspaper the *Fifth Estate*. Believing in cooperation, the band started "trans-love energies," which guitarist Wayne Kramer described as "a communal association that provided all the services that we, as a band, needed." Playing a James Brown–type, free-jazz-influenced, blues-based music, the MC5 adopted as a "three-point program" the slogan "dope, rock-'n'-roll, and fucking in the streets."

During the late 1960s, the MC5 became radicalized politically. According to Kramer, they expanded their three-point plan "into a ten-point program that got more overtly political, like Free Economy, Free All Political Prisoners, and the rest of the agenda of the day." The MC5 Social and Athletic fan club morphed into the White Panther Party, and the band played to the rioters at the 1968 National Democratic Convention in Chicago. By 1969, asserted manager John Sinclair, the group was "totally committed to the revolution, as the revolution is totally committed to driving people out of their separate shells and into each other's arms."

In early 1969, the MC5 released their first album, *Kick Out the Jams*, which included songs such as "Motor City Is Burning" and was recorded live at the Grande Ballroom in Detroit. To open the album, they enlisted the services of Brother J. C. Crawford, who delivered one of the most rousing exhortations in rock history: "Brothers and sisters, I want to see a sea of hands out there, let me see a sea of hands. I want everybody to kick up some noise. I want to hear some revolution out there, brothers, I want to hear a little revolution!" The crowd, clapping when Crawford had begun, became more agitated. "Brothers and sisters, the time has come for each and every one of you to decide whether you are going to be the problem or whether you are going to be the solution," he continued, using a Black Panther slogan. "You must choose, brothers, you must choose. It takes five seconds, five seconds of decision, five seconds to realize your purpose here on the planet….I want to know, are you ready to testify? *Are you ready?*" screamed Crawford to a wild crowd that was jumping on the auditorium chairs. "I give you a testimonial—the MC5." The band launched into a near-deafening version of a twelve-bar blues called "Rambling Rose."

The debut album, though selling well, included the incendiary word "motherfuckers" that led to a clamp-down on the group. "They were arresting clerks in stores for selling the record. Certain chains refused to carry our record," bitterly remembered Sinclair, who himself was jailed several times on trumped-up charges, "and our contract with Elektra [Records] lasted only six months." Nevertheless, the band forged ahead, equating their brand of rock and roll as "not only the weapon of cultural revolution" but "the **model** of the revolutionary future."

Heavy Metal Thunder

Some British rockers built upon the sound generated by radicalized Sixties '60s guitar heroes to create a loud, churning, monstrous blues that became known as *heavy metal* and reflected the militant mood of the times. Using blues as their foundation, they interspersed brilliant guitar solos that were enhanced by guitar effects between chunky, distorted power chords to achieve a sinister sound of militancy.

Though the term heavy metal had been common for decades in chemistry, the first appearance of it in rock came with the band Steppenwolf. The group, coalescing around German-born vocalist/guitarist John Kay (b. Krauledat), provided a tumultuous, politicized rock. In early 1968, they released their self-named debut, which scaled the chart when the director of the cult film classic *Easy Rider* included two of their songs on the movie soundtrack. One song, "Born to Be Wild," became an anthem for the late 1960s and included the phrase "heavy-metal thunder" that characterized the band's sound. "We play fairly intense, fairly aggressive music," contended Kay, "and when I sing and spit out my lyrics, so to speak, it tends to come out in a sort of intense, and to some people, somewhat intimidating or frightening, kind of way." During the next two years, Steppenwolf placed four more albums of hard-driving proto-metal in the Top Twenty, culminating their efforts with the anti-war statement *Monster*, which included the song "Draft Resister."

If Steppenwolf coined a name for the new music, Led Zeppelin, led by guitarist extraordinaire Jimmy Page, helped to define heavy metal. Page, a poor youth from the London working class, had played brilliant session guitar for a wide variety of performers, including the Rolling Stones and the Who, before joining the Yardbirds. He even appeared on the Kinks' "You Really Got Me," one of the songs which first popularized the power chord. After the Yardbirds disbanded in July 1968, Page enlisted the help of session bassist John Paul Jones, drummer John Bonham, and vocalist Robert Plant, who had earned the moniker "wild man of the blues from the Black Country" for his work with groups such as the Delta Blues Band and the Crawling King Snakes. The foursome toured briefly in Scandinavia as the New Yardbirds before changing their name to Led Zeppelin.

In 1968, Led Zeppelin entered the studio to record their debut, which showcased their blues foundation. On the album, the group unveiled amplified blues versions of Willie Dixon's "You Shook Me" and "I Can't Quit You Baby," and a reworked version of Howlin' Wolf's "How Many More Years," called "How Many More Times." By early 1969, Led Zeppelin hit the Top Ten in Britain and the United States with the album, and later in the year reached the top of the chart with their second effort, which featured their signature, Willie Dixon–inspired "Whole Lotta Love." Though the band later incorporated Celtic and British folk elements into their music, "we always had some blues on our albums," asserted Page.

Led Zeppelin's Robert Plant and Jimmy Page.

Jim Summaria.

The group delivered their blues at an ear-splitting volume. Page favored Marshall amplifiers, stacking them on top of one another. Drummer John Bonham added to the magnitude of sound. "Besides being one of the best drummers I have ever heard," related Page, Bonham "was also one of the loudest. He was the reason we had to start buying bigger amps."

Page refined the sound with a series of guitar effects. On the first album, the guitarist employed a Supro amplifier, a wah-wah pedal and a Tone Bender fuzz box/distortion unit. He also pioneered a "backward echo" on "You Shook Me," and on "Dazed and Confused" rigged an old EMT reverberation unit to achieve a dense effect with heavy diffusion.

Zeppelin added other elements to the mix to create a unique sound. Jimmy Page banged out power chords between complex improvisations and played off Bonham's hard drumming and Jones' insistent, driving bass lines. The high-pitched, screeching vocals of Robert Plant completed the Led Zeppelin sound, adding an element that had been missing from proto-metal. The new sound alternated between a high-volume blues and acoustic numbers to give the electric songs an added effect. "Ultimately," explained Page, "I wanted Led Zeppelin to be a marriage of blues, hard rock and acoustic music topped with heavy choruses—a combination that had never been tried before." "I've never been so turned on in my life," recalled Robert Plant of the thirty-hour recording session for their first LP. "Although we were all steeped in blues and R&B, we found out in the first hour and a half that we had our own identity." The resulting music became known as "heavy metal."

Black Sabbath perfected the loud, aggressive blues that characterized heavy metal. Formed in 1967 as Earth, four poor toughs from industrial Birmingham initially churned out blues covers. "When we were Earth, we were doing lots of blues stuff, from Howlin' Wolf, Muddy Waters, John Lee Hooker," remembered bassist Terry "Geezer" Butler. "And a lot of the English blues band stuff, like Cream, John Mayall. Eventually [the blues covers] translated into much heavier stuff."

In early 1969, the band changed its name from Earth to Black Sabbath and pounded out a hard-driving, militant sound on its 1970 debut. As with the other metal bands, they played a roaring music. "It used to drive us mad to think that we were up there working so hard, playing our guts out while [the audience] were sitting around chattering," explained drummer Bill Ward, "so we turned up the volume louder and louder, until it was impossible for anyone to have a conversation."

In addition to the loud, power-chord, guitar-driven aspects of their music, the band employed the tritone, which resulted in an otherworldly, sinister sound. The tritone, the interval between the fourth and fifth notes, created a dissonance that led to a confrontational, almost evil music. Vocalist John "Ozzy" Osbourne called the tritone "the Black Sabbath riff, which was the scariest riff I've ever heard in my life." Guitarist Tony Iommi described the rationale for the evil-sounding guitar lick. "I just wanted to create something that was startling, something that would really take you aback."

The band complemented their sinister sound with their demonic lyrics. Prompted at least in part by Geezer Butler's fixation on religious imagery, Black Sabbath fastened on a preoccupation with demons and a hellish otherworld that had tormented pre-war bluesmen such as Robert Johnson, who had recorded "Me and the Devil Blues." The band borrowed their name from the title of a 1963 Boris Karloff movie and chose "Evil Woman," backed by "Wicked World," as their first single. They followed with songs such as "Electric Funeral," "Children of the Grave," and "Sabbath, Bloody Sabbath." "If we come across doomy and evil, it's just the way we feel," confessed guitarist Tony Iommi.

Ozzy Osbourne gave a more vivid, expansive explanation for the band's gloomy theme: "Now you consider everyone's all jolly and tip-toein' around, stoned on acid, havin' Woodstock and all love, peace, sex, drugs and rock-'n'-roll, and all that's great," he told an interviewer. "But for us guys that were livin' in this *hole* in the world, it

Black Sabbath. Ozzy on far right, 1974.

Jim Summaria.

wasn't that way. And Tony [Iommi] thought 'wouldn't it be interesting to put this horror vibe to a musical thing.' And then we started to write doomy music, we used to call it. This death music. Doom music." Such "doom music" struck a chord among youth, who propelled the first six Black Sabbath albums to the British Top Ten and the Top Thirty in the United States.

Black Sabbath, one of the leading heavy metal pioneers, crafted an evil-sounding music, which matched the militant rage of 1960s youth. "I don't profess to be a messiah of slum people," insisted Ozzy, "but I was a back-street kid, and that little demon is still in there, shoving the hot coal in. The aggression I play is the aggression I know. And it's obviously aggression a lot of people have." The group recorded songs such as "War Pigs" and "Iron Man" on their second album *Paranoid* (1970), which embodied the intense anti-war sentiment of the era.

Deep Purple turned to heavy metal midway through their career. Funded in 1967 by two London businessmen, the band charted with a series of remade pop songs such as Joe South's "Hush" and Neil Diamond's "Kentucky Woman." In September 1969, they recorded a *Concerto for Group and Orchestra* with the Royal Philharmonic Orchestra.

After *Concerto* failed to sell in the United States, virtuoso guitarist Ritchie Blackmore steered the band toward a loud, pulsating, and dangerous sound on the British Top-Five effort *Deep Purple in Rock* (1970). "I always played every amp I've ever had full up, because rock-and-roll is supposed to be played loud," Blackmore explained. "I also got my amps boosted," he intimated about the music. "I know Jim Marshall personally, and he boosted them for me." The guitarist used the tremolo bar on his guitar to give the music a pitch-bending, vibrating effect because "I liked the way Hendrix used the tremolo." He also favored the fuzz box, which had first been introduced to rock by surf bands during the late 1950s. The band, steeped in guitar effects, continued to mine explosive, roaring chunks of sound on their next six efforts, including their classic *Machine Head* (1972), all of which hit the British Top Ten and the upper reaches of the American chart.

Woodstock, Kent State, and the End of an Era

The intense mood of American youths, reflected by their interest in high-volume, distorted electric blues, changed at the turn of the decade as the fervent hope of Woodstock turned into dark fear at Altamont and Kent State. The Woodstock Music and Arts Festival in Bethel, New York, held from Friday, August 15, to early Monday morning, August 18, 1969, seemed to herald a new era. Organized by John Roberts, a young millionaire who had graduated from the University of Pennsylvania; Joel Rosenman, a Yale Law School graduate and the son of a prominent Long Island orthodontist; Michael Lang, organizer of the Miami Pops Festival; and Artie Kornfeld, a seasoned songwriter and manager, the Woodstock Festival demonstrated a growing sense of empowerment among the swelling ranks of youths.

The ebullient mood among the youth had been at least partly engendered by the recent moon landing. On July 20, 1969, just a few weeks before Woodstock, Neil Armstrong and Buzz Aldrin landed on the moon. The next day, Armstrong became the first human to set foot on the moon, proclaiming "one small step for [a] man, one giant leap for mankind." "Americans had walked on the moon for the first time so we all had this sense that we could do anything," recalled one concertgoer. "Eliminate greed, pull off a huge peaceful gathering with no violence."

Many in the audience wanted change through peace, love, and community. "There had been so much conflict over the past year, with violent confrontations occurring on college campuses, in urban ghettoes, and at demonstrations across the country," remembered organizer Michael Lang. "At Woodstock we would focus our energy on peace, setting aside the onstage discussion of political issues." He wanted to prove that "peace and understanding were possible." The poster for the event proudly proclaimed "three days of peace and music."

Another group of Woodstock attendees took a more overt political stance by asserting their opposition to the war in Vietnam. "Woodstock signified the coming together of all tribes," remarked guitarist Carlos Santana, who played a mixture of Latin rhythms and the blues to the 450,000 mostly white educated youths who journeyed to the festival. "It became apparent that there were a lot of people who didn't want to go to Vietnam, who didn't see eye to eye with Nixon."

The music at the festival reflected the two countercultural visions of late-Sixties youth. The acts included an assortment of soothing, swirling sounds from folk rockers such as Joni Mitchell and John Sebastian to psychedelic bands such as the Grateful Dead. "When I heard that Pete Townshend had kicked Abbie Hoffman off the stage,

Woodstock opening with Swami Satchidananda, 1969: The dawn of a new era.

Mark Goff.

I was delighted, because I have always thought that rock and radical politics are a bad mix," asserted Dead guitarist Bob Weir about the festival. As a counterpoint to the Dead, Woodstock featured defiant performances by Country Joe McDonald and Jimi Hendrix. Dressed in an army-fatigue shirt and jeans, Country Joe took the stage at Woodstock without his band. "I was hanging around, and I was just filling time, singing a few country and western songs and folk songs," remembered the singer. "Then I did the [anti–Vietnam War song,] 'Feel-Like-I'm-Fixing-to-Die-Rag'—the F-U-C-K cheer—the rest is history. From the first response to 'Give me an *F*,' when they all stopped talking and looked at me and yelled, *F*, I knew there was no turning back."

Jimi Hendrix played the final set of the festival around 8:30 A.M. on Monday. Taking the stage with a group of musicians called the Electric Sky Church, he launched into a series of heavy, ripping electric blues. Near the end of his performance, the guitar hero delivered a powerful version of "The Star Spangled Banner," which featured screaming-rockets and exploding-bombs induced by his Whammy bar and sounded like a heaving, wounded monster about to die. In his rendition of the national anthem, Hendrix captured the militant spirit of 1960s youth who felt alienated, detached, and at the same time enraged toward their country.

The festival at Altamont Speedway near San Francisco, held on December 6, 1969, dashed the sense of power that Woodstock had engendered among many youth. Drawn by a free concert staged by the Rolling Stones, who wanted to repeat their successful Hyde Park performance, more than 300,000 fans flocked to the site. During the event, hundreds required treatment for drug overdoses, including one youth who jumped off of a freeway overpass after ingesting some LSD. Horrified, powerless spectators watched the San Francisco contingent of the Hell's Angels motorcycle gang, hired to keep order in exchange for $500 worth of beer, stab to death an 18-year-old African American from Berkeley, one of four deaths at the concert. "Altamont was the end of the sixties," contended Bill Thompson, manager of the Jefferson Airplane. "It was December 1969, and that was the end. Of the whole feeling."

U.S. government officials torpedoed any remaining hope among America's youth. They used the Counter Intelligence Program (COINTELPRO) of the Federal Bureau of Investigation, first established in 1956 to combat communism, to harass and disperse anti-war militants and Black Panthers who by 1970 had allied with the students. COINTELPRO conducted vigilante operations, broke in unannounced on student activists, planted false stories about demonstrators in major publications such as *Newsweek,* burglarized the offices of the underground press and even funded right-wing, armed groups to monitor and bully anti-war leaders.

In May 1970, government tactics turned lethal at Kent State University. When President Richard Nixon announced that American troops had been sent into Cambodia, students at Kent State University in northeastern Ohio took to the streets. On May 2, they hurled bottles at police cars, smashed store windows, and doused trees with gasoline, setting them on fire. The next day, 1,500 protesters firebombed the one-story ROTC building on the Kent State campus.

The authorities responded swiftly and decisively to the disruptions. Mayor Leroy Satrom asked Ohio Governor James Rhodes to activate the National Guard. Rhodes, who described the students as "worse than the [Nazi] 'brownshirt' and the Communist element ... the worst type of people that we harbor in America," responded with 900 troops armed with M-1 rifles, submachine guns, and canisters of tear gas. On the third day of trouble, Guardsmen chased a mob of students to a knoll near Taylor Hall. Suddenly, without warning, sixteen National Guardsmen each knelt on one knee and leveled their guns at the crowd. Asserted journalism professor Charles Brill, who witnessed the action: "They all waited and they all pointed their rifles at the same time. It looked like a firing squad." The soldiers pumped thirty-five rounds from their M-1 rifles into the protesters standing 75 feet away. "It's about time we showed the bastards who's in charge," sneered one Guardsman. "It's like all sound blows away, you go into slow motion, everything seems unreal," said Gerald Casale, a student at Kent State who later became a member of the band Devo. "Then someone started screaming her name, and I looked over, and Alison [Krauss] is lying face down with an exit wound in her back and red blood streaming down the sidewalk.... And slowly everybody started moaning." All told, the gunfire killed four students, including Alison Krauss, and wounded ten others. "My God! My God! They're killing us," screamed one Kent State freshman.

On Thursday, May 14, only eleven days after the deaths at Kent State, authorities confronted students at Jackson State University, a historically black college. When several students protested racial discrimination by pelting motorists and igniting fires, seventy-five policemen tried to disperse the disrupters. Suddenly, the police squad opened fire on Alexander Hall, a women's dormitory, and killed two students and injured twelve others.

The murders at Kent State and Jackson State caused a swift reaction in colleges and universities across the nation. Students sacked the treasurer's office at the University of South Carolina; they bombed the ROTC buildings at the universities of Utah and Idaho; and 124 students were arrested in a fight with state troopers at the University of Colorado. Protesters occupied the ROTC building at the University of Nebraska, and a half-million-dollar fire blazed at Colorado State. Three weeks of rioting ravaged the University of California at Berkeley campus, and in a riot at the University of Maryland, state troopers injured 138 and arrested 200. Students at the University of Wisconsin, chanting "we're gonna open up a second front in Madison," took over the Army Mathematics Research Center and were responsible for at least twenty major fire bombings. More than 75,000 students marched on Washington, D.C., gathering in front of the White House, and more than 200 colleges and universities shut down for at least one day, most of them for the rest of the academic year. In May and June 1970, more than 508 protests rocked college campuses and drew support from two-thirds of the students.

After the initial outbursts of violence, a sense of helplessness enveloped many American youths. Said one student at the post–Kent State demonstration in Washington, D.C.: "The people here understand that we are surrounded by fully armed troops and that if we start anything, we'd be destroyed." "I thought that the war was just escalating, was never going to stop," recalled one youth in the underground paper *South End*. "They had put up with us protesting, marching in the streets, but now they were just going to kill us." Kent State "changed me," summarized Jerry Casale. "For me it was the turning point. I saw it clearly from there on." "Just shoot a few and it changed the whole world. Everybody straightened up and went home," Casale lamented. For the first time in a decade, rebellious youths who had hoped for a better world felt that they had reached a dead end.

Government actions after Kent State deepened the despair of radicalized youths, making future protests seem dangerous and potentially deadly. President Richard Nixon openly called the college demonstrators "bums ... blowing up the campuses." Authorities refused to prosecute the National Guardsmen who killed the Kent State students, despite an F.B.I. investigation that found the shootings "not necessary and not in order." Even though the President's Commission on Campus Unrest found the fusillade at Jackson State "an unreasonable and unjustified overreaction," the government failed to prosecute any of the police offers who shot the students. To further squelch student protests, in 1970 Congress passed the Omnibus Crime Act, which prescribed the death penalty for anyone convicted of a fatal bombing.

During the next few months, shocking news of the deaths of several prominent rock figures aggravated the hopeless mood of youth. Jimi Hendrix passed away on September 18, 1970, a victim of complications from an overdose of sleeping pills. On October 4, at the Landmark Hotel in Hollywood, authorities confirmed the death of Janis Joplin from an overdose of heroin. On July 3, 1971, Jim Morrison of the Doors

Woodstock crowd in the rain: Reality hits a generation.

Mark Goff.

died of a heart attack in a bathtub in Paris. By the beginning of the 1970s, many youths who only a few years earlier had vowed to work for sweeping social change listened to the guns of Kent State and retreated to the cerebral music of jazz rock, classical rock, the confessions of singer-songwriters and the soft sounds of a nonpolitical, country-tinged folk revival.

Chapter 13

Soft Sounds: Country Rock, the Singers-Songwriters, and Sweet Soul

"[Country rock is] a symptom of a general cultural reaction to the most unsettling decade that the U.S. has yet endured. The yen to escape the corrupt present by returning to the virtuous past—real or imagined—has haunted Americans, never more so than today."
—*Time* Magazine, 1970

Back to the Country

Confronted by the harsh, complicated realities of an unwanted war in Vietnam and events at Kent State, some youth moved to a country music that extolled simple living and rural traditions. "Country rock," observed *Time* in 1970, was a "turning back toward easy-rhythmed blues, folk songs, and the twangy, lonely lamentations known as country music." The new musical blend, continued *Time*, was a "symptom of a general cultural reaction to the most unsettling decade that the U.S. has yet endured. The yen to escape the corrupt present by returning to the virtuous past—real or imagined—has haunted Americans, never more so than today." *Rolling Stone* labeled country rock the "music of reconciliation."

Country music had always been part of the rock-and-roll gumbo, beginning with Chuck Berry and Elvis Presley. But unlike Berry and the rockabillies, who fused a jumping, gut-bucket R&B with old-style country, seventies country rock merged a mellow folk rock with bluegrass and country swing. "In the late '69 and early '70s, there was a movement afoot that was attempting to merge American country and bluegrass music with contemporary rock and roll," explained Chris Darrow who toured with Linda Ronstadt. "It was commonly called country rock and many tried to push that concept over."

Dylan and California Country Rock

Bob Dylan, the most visible protest singer of the 1960s, led youth back to the country. In 1968, Dylan began to lean toward a country sound on *John Wesley Harding*, which reinterpreted and glorified the Texas outlaw John Wesley Hardin and neared the top of the chart. In April 1969, Dylan made his country influences more obvious on the million-selling *Nashville Skyline*, recorded in the country music capital of Nashville,

Tennessee. The album featured a duet with former rockabilly and country music giant Johnny Cash on "Girl from the North Country." On June 7, Dylan appeared with Cash on a television special filmed at the Grand Ole Opry.

Dylan continued his country direction with the film *Pat Garrett and Billy the Kid*. Released in 1973, the film told the story of the clash between sheriff Pat Garrett and legendary Western outlaw Billy the Kid (b. William Bonney). It featured country singer/songwriter Kris Kristofferson and cast Bob Dylan as a mysterious stranger named Alias. The movie helped to introduce the theme of the rock star as cowboy outlaw and reinvigorated the career of Dylan who contributed the soundtrack and neared the Top Ten with "Knockin' On Heaven's Door."

As Dylan embraced country, the Byrds, the folk-rock group that had risen to fame on Dylan compositions, looked to country music for inspiration. Prodded by new Byrds singer-guitarist Gram Parsons, who idolized country icon Merle Haggard, the group released the country-flavored *Sweetheart of the Rodeo* (1968). "Gram reminded me how much I loved country music," remembered Byrd Chris Hillman. "We'd always played a little country with the Byrds, but with two of us in the band, the obvious thing was to bring out that influence in our music." Counterbalanced by the more rock-oriented Roger McGuinn, the Byrds fastened upon a country-rock sound with the album. Although achieving only moderate commercial success with their new direction, the band signaled the way back to the country. "It's sort of a backlash from the psychedelic scene, which I'm personally saturated with," explained McGuinn at the time.

The Band, Dylan's sometime backup group, achieved popularity with its country-based sound. In 1961, guitarist Jaime "Robbie" Robertson, pianist Richard Manuel, drummer Levon Helm, bassist Rick Danko, and organist Garth Hudson coalesced as the Hawks under rockabilly singer Ronnie Hawkins. In 1965, after being noticed by Dylan's manager Albert Grossman, the group backed and toured with Dylan. By 1967, they moved close to the reclusive singer in Woodstock, New York and recorded dozens of traditional songs and country-influenced Dylan compositions, which eventually surfaced in 1975 as *The Basement Tapes*.

The Band, as they were now called, recorded a debut at Woodstock in their large, pink-colored house and in 1968 released the countrified *Music from Big Pink*, which captured the laid-back signature of country rock with several originals interspersed among three recent Dylan compositions. "Everybody was getting real loud, psychedelic, flashy; and we went the other way," reasoned Band leader Robbie Robertson. The next year, they hit the Top Ten with a heavily country-influenced, self-named LP, which included the hit "Up on Cripple Creek." By late 1970, the group reached the Top Five in the United States with their third album *Stage Fright*. The Band, wrote *Time*, perfected a rock hybrid that "comes on mainly as country music full of straight lines and sentiment."

Bob Dylan and the Band, 1974.

Jim Summaria.

Poco offered a similar brand of country rock. In late 1968, when the folk-rock group Buffalo Springfield splintered into the trio Crosby, Stills, and Nash and a solo career for Neil Young, Springfield guitarist Richie Furay established a country-rock outfit with his friend Jim Messina. "Richie and I were riding in a cab in Nashville," remembered Messina. "We talked about forming a new band that would be an extension of what we'd been doing with the Springfield, but more country and rock than folk and rock." The duo invited steel guitar player Rusty Young, bassist Randy Meisner, and drummer George Grantham to join them. After two moderately successful efforts, in 1971 the group neared the Top Twenty with the live album *Deliverin'*, which relied heavily on traditional country instruments such as steel guitars, and dobros. "I think the most dominating thing was the fact that we had this country sound," Furay remarked about the album. "We were pioneering the country-rock sound at this time with the introduction of the steel guitar, the high, countryish harmonies and all."

The Arizona-born Linda Ronstadt served as the focal point for several other 1970s' country rockers. In December 1964, the singer journeyed to Los Angeles to join the folk trio the Stone Poneys. Though selling few copies of their debut, the group scored with "Different Drum" (1967) before disbanding. Not an immediate commercial success, the country-minded Ronstadt continued to frequent the Troubadour club in Los Angeles. "We all used to sit in a corner of the Troubadour and dream," she reminisced. "It was where I made all my musical contacts." At the Troubadour in April 1971, Ronstadt recruited a new band, including guitarist Glenn Frey and drummer Don Henley. Henley saw Ronstadt in a "little Daisy Mae kind of dress. She was barefoot and scratching her ass." He thought, "I'm in heaven." Ronstadt and her new bandmates quickly recorded an album, which included country standards such as "I Fall to Pieces" and "Crazy Arms." "I was fighting to do country all along," insisted the singer.

Linda Ronstadt in action, August 1978.

Carl Lender.

The singer soon reached the charts with a new label and manager. In 1972, entrepreneur David Geffen bought Ronstadt's contract and featured her on his newly established label, Asylum Records. The next year, the singer hired as her manager Peter Asher, who had started in the music business as half of the folk-rock duo Peter and Gordon. Helped by her team, the singer released *Don't Cry Now*, which remained on the chart for fifty-six weeks and cracked the Top Fifty. In 1975, she followed with the country-rock, number-one *Heart Like a Wheel*, which included country and rockabilly classics such as the Everly Brothers' "When Will I Be Loved" and "I Can't Help It (If I'm Still in Love with You)" by Hank Williams. Having set her pattern, during the next two years Ronstadt recorded a number of top-selling albums that combined sensitive ballads with smooth renditions of country-tinged songs.

Linda Ronstadt professed conservative political beliefs, which had become prevalent during the early 1970s. She hoped for a "real resurgence of patriotism in this country." After campaigning for liberal candidates, the singer felt that "I really didn't know what I was talking about. Who knows who should be president and if anybody should have an interest in determining those things, shouldn't Standard Oil" "You can say what you want about big multinationals running the country and stuff," she blurted, but "they are in a better position to decide what's going to be good for the economic climate of the country and for the rest of the world." "Rock and politics ought to stay separate," she concluded.

Ronstadt's one-time tour band, splitting from the singer in August 1971, achieved stardom as the Eagles. Frey and Henley formed the Eagles with bassist Randy Meisner, who had played for Poco, and guitarist Bernie Leadon, who had been a member of the Flying Burrito Brothers. "Glenn [Frey] said we needed to get those guys [Meisner and Leadon] because they could play the kind of country rock we were all so interested in," observed Henley.

The Eagles immediately hit the charts. In early 1972, the group recorded their self-named debut album, which neared the Top Twenty and included the hits "Take It Easy," "Peaceful Easy Feeling," and "Witchy Woman." The next year, they recorded *Desperado*, a concept album about the Dalton gang, a band of outlaws in the 1890s American West. "We grew up wanting to be the cowboys," enthused Leadon. "So much so that we actually wanted to act that out. The album was our chance to do that: a dream come true." The album cracked the Top Fifty and eventually sold two million copies. "The whole thread between outlaw rock and rock star that we were trying to get across with the album was working," commented Don Henley. In 1975, the Eagles topped the chart with *One of These Nights* and scored their first million-selling single, "Best of My Love," which exemplified their trademark soft, country-influenced rock.

Jackson Browne, writing songs for the Eagles and Linda Ronstadt, epitomized the country-tinged, West Coast tunesmith of the 1970s. According to the singer, he initially gravitated toward the civil-rights protest folk of Dylan.

Browne, as did Dylan himself, deserted social protest for an intensely personal, country-flavored folk. After traveling to New York City, where he wrote songs recorded by the Byrds, he signed with the newly established Asylum Records. In 1972, with the help of former Byrd David Crosby and country guitarist Clarence White, the singer-songwriter released his first LP, which contained the Top-Ten hit "Doctor My Eyes." Later in the year, to promote the album, he toured with the Eagles. As he toured, Browne hit the chart as a co-composer of the Eagles' hit "Take It Easy," which he wrote with former roommate Glenn Frey. He continued to compose hits for the Eagles, who charted with Browne's "James Dean." By the second half of the decade, he charted as a solo artist with two Top-Five albums of highly personal compositions. By mid-decade, a soft country rock twanged from the airwaves and attracted youths who had abandoned their militant stance of a few years earlier.

Seventies Singers-Songwriters

During the early seventies amid the retreat from protest, confessional singers-songwriters strummed their acoustic guitars to offer another form of a softer, more calming form of rock, which delved into personal loneliness and confusion.

The genre arose in part due to the disintegration of the American family. During the 1970s, as the number of women in the workforce doubled, many baby boomers questioned the institution of matrimony. In one study, conducted in 1971 among college students, more than 34 percent of the respondents believed that marriage was obsolete. Two years later, according to a Rutgers University student survey, 30 percent of the seniors felt that marriage no longer presented a viable option.

Not holding marriage as sacrosanct, many Americans, especially the baby boomers, divorced their partners at an increasing rate. In 1955, only 377,000 women divorced their partners. Twenty years later, 1,036,000 women filed for divorce. Adjusting for the population growth, the rate climbed 54 percent, most of the increase coming during the late 1960s and early 1970s with more liberal divorce laws and changing perceptions toward marriage.

Divorcing or not marrying, many baby boomers lived the sometimes lonely life of an unmarried young adult. By 1978, more than 1.1 million Americans lived in single households, an increase of 117 percent in one decade. To find companionship, they populated singles bars, singles resorts, and singles housing complexes.

During the early 1970s, singers-songwriters sang ballads about the emotional traumas of divorce, lost love, and loneliness in a plaintive, confessional style, which updated the folk tradition. James Taylor, the prototype of the easygoing, sensitive 1970s folkster, grew up in Chapel Hill, North Carolina, and spent his summers on Martha's Vineyard off Cape Cod, listening to records by the Weavers, Woody Guthrie, and Pete Seeger. He began playing with his friend Danny Kortchmar as a folk duo, James & Kootch, who won a local hootenanny contest. In 1966, he joined Kortchmar's band the Flying Machine, which performed in Greenwich Village coffeehouses before disbanding a year later. Taylor, exhausted and suffering from a heroin addiction, in 1968 traveled to England, where he recorded his first LP for the Beatles-owned Apple Records. When his vinyl debut failed to crack the Top Fifty despite backing work by Paul McCartney and George Harrison, the singer returned to the United States.

Taylor rebounded from his setback. After appearing at the Newport Folk Festival, he secured a contract with Warner Brothers through manager Peter Asher. In early 1970, he recorded the album *Sweet Baby James*, which reached the Top Five and remained on the chart for more than two years. It included the soul-baring "Fire and Rain" about the suicide of a friend of Taylor's as well as such country-based themes as "County Road" and the Stephen Foster standard "Oh, Susanna" (1848). The next year, the singer followed with *Mud Slide Slim and the Blue Horizon*, which neared the top of the charts in the United States and Britain and included the Carole King–written chart-topper "You've Got a Friend" and "Love Has Brought Me Around," both soft, reassuring ballads appropriate for the millions of divorced and unmarried baby boomers. "I wish I weren't so self-centered or self-referred all the time with the stuff I write," he later complained, "but for some reason that's the window I utilize, hopefully in an open-ended way."

Other singers-songwriters of the seventies, many of them associated with James Taylor, penned self-revelatory paeans of loneliness and confusion. Carole King, the Brill Building sensation of the early 1960s, became intrigued by the New York folk scene after she divorced husband-collaborator Gerry Goffin. She backed the Flying Machine, an early band led by James Taylor, and in 1968, with Danny Kortchmar, formed the short-lived band The City.

In 1971, King again vaulted to the top of the chart. Aided by Kortchmar and James Taylor, she released the number-one *Tapestry*, which stayed on the chart for six years and sold more than 20 million copies. It included her own version of "You've Got a Friend" as well as tales of lost love such as "So Far Away" and "It's Too Late."

From across the Atlantic, Cat Stevens (b. Steven Demetre Georgiou) wooed audiences with a series of personal, soft-spoken melodies. After a series of moderately successful albums, in 1970 he hit the Top Ten with *Tea for the Tillerman, which included the Top-Twenty "Wild World" about an ex-girlfriend of Stevens*. He followed with the number-two *Teaser and the Firecat* and in 1973 topped the chart with *Catch Bull at Four*.

Carly Simon had an intimate connection with both Cat Stevens and James Taylor on her road to success. Daughter of the cofounder of Simon & Schuster publishers, Carly left the exclusive Sarah Lawrence College to perform and record as a folk duo with her sister Lucy. After the singing sisters ended their short-lived recording career, Carly eventually met Jac Holzman, owner of Elektra Records, who signed her to his label and in 1971 released the singer's solo debut, which reached number thirty on the album chart. The next year, she scored with her second LP, *Anticipation*, which included the Top-Twenty single of the same name, as well as "Legend in Your Own Time" that were both written for Cat Stevens, her boyfriend at the time. In late 1972, Carly Simon topped the charts with the single "You're So Vain" and the album *No Secrets*, and on November 3, she married James Taylor in her Manhattan apartment. In 1974, the husband–wife team dueted on the Top-Five single "Mockingbird."

Joni Mitchell, collaborating with a number of the seventies' singers-songwriters, strummed her way to the top. Born Roberta Joan Anderson, she began to play acoustic folk in her native Canada. In 1964, she performed at the Mariposa Folk Festival, and the next year, after moving to Toronto, she met and married Chuck Mitchell, who played with her as a folk duo in local coffeehouses. In 1966, Mitchell moved to Detroit, where she became a sensation on the folk scene. She began to make appearances in New York City where she met folk artists such as Judy Collins, who hit in 1968 with Mitchell's "Both Sides Now."

Mitchell soon started her rise to fame. In 1968, she signed with Reprise Records and released her debut album, which was produced by ex-Byrd David Crosby and included on guitar Stephen Stills, formerly of the folk-rock band Buffalo Springfield. The next year, she delivered *Clouds,* which neared the Top Thirty and earned her a Grammy for the Best Folk Performer of the Year.

During the early 1970s, Mitchell delivered three confessional albums, which focused on the pain of broken relationships and epitomized the sensitive singer-songwriter ethos. In 1971, she enlisted the support of Stephen Stills on bass and James

Joni Mitchell in concert, 1972.

Pictorial Press Ltd./Alamy Stock Photo.

Taylor on guitar, the latter who had asked Mitchell sing background vocals on "You've Got a Friend." With their help, she crafted the archetypical singer-songwriter work, the Top-Fifteen *Blue*, which featured tales of lost love such as "The Last Time I Saw Richard," "This Flight Tonight," and the title song. "I made the decision in my emotionally disturbed period, which was when *Blue* was, that I wanted everything to be transparent," she later recalled. "I had to show what I was going through." She identified her "grand theme" as "Where is my mate? Where is my mate? Where is my mate?" Before moving toward a more jazz-oriented approach, she continued with the self-revelatory *For the Roses* (1972), which neared the Top Ten, and the near number-one *Court and Spark* (1974). "When I think of Vietnam or Berkeley, I feel so helpless," Mitchell told *Time*. "I just write about what happens to me."

Crosby, Stills, and Nash, entangled with Mitchell on professional and personal levels, rode the singer-songwriter wave to success. In mid-1968, after the breakup of the folk-rock group Buffalo Springfield, Stephen Stills began to practice with ex-Byrd David Crosby (b. David Van Courtland) and Graham Nash, formerly of the Hollies. A year later, the trio released a self-titled, Top-Ten album, which blended floating harmonies and acoustic guitars. It featured the Top-Twenty-Five "Suite: Judy Blue Eyes" about the breakup of Stills and folkster Judy Collins and the escapist "Wooden Ships." "We hit upon the idea of these wooden ships that would take people who thought like us from all this madness," explained Crosby. As their album scaled the chart, the group asked ex–Buffalo Springfield guitarist Neil Young to join. In March 1970, the foursome released *Déja Vu*, which topped the chart and included paeans to lost love as well as their best-selling single, "Woodstock," written by Joni Mitchell who had become romantically involved with Graham Nash. For the album cover, the band posed as characters from the Old West, an image that described their country-tinged music. The group's live effort, *4 Way Street* (1971), which included the politically charged "Ohio" about the killings at Kent State and the anti-South diatribe "Southern Man," represented anomalies to the otherwise personal, harmony-filled seventies folk of the band.

In the early 1970s, rock had turned from a politicized heavy metal to airy ballads of unrequited love. In 1971, Robert Hilburn, music critic for the *Los Angeles Times*, observed that rock music "has shifted during recent months from the loud desperation and exaggeration of such per-formers as Janis Joplin and Jimi Hendrix to reflective, more reassuring gentleness." He concluded that the soft sounds of country rock and the singers-songwriters perfectly fit a generation aching "to recover some of the balance shattered during the troubled, riot-torn, confrontation-bent late 1960s."

Sweet, Sweet Soul Music

A highly orchestrated, lush soul music produced by labels such as Philadelphia International replaced the fervent screams of sixties soul singers for respect. At the beginning of the seventies, a mellow soul drifted across the airwaves to complement the soft sounds of country rock and the lamentations of singers-songwriters to highlight the change in rock music from angry protest to a soothing palliative.

Stevie Wonder reinvigorated the sweet soul sound. A product of Detroit's Motown, in 1963 Steveland Morris had topped the chart as a teenage phenomenon with the jumping, harmonica-driven "Fingertips (Part 2)" to earn the Wonder moniker. After a series of minor hits and three more Top-Ten singles, including "Uptight (Everything's Alright)" (1966), Wonder turned from the Motown sound toward softer ballads such as the number-two "For Once in My Life" (1968) and the Top-Five "My Cherie Amour" (1969). In 1971, when Wonder turned 21 and received $1 million from his trust fund, he renegotiated his contract with Motown to secure nearly complete artistic freedom with autonomous production and publishing companies.

Enjoying artistic control, Wonder crafted sensitive, largely personal songs. In 1972, his *Talking Book* reached the Top Five on the strength of two number-one singles, the smooth ballad "You Are the Sunshine of My Life" and the funkier "Superstition." The next year, after recovering from an auto accident, he delivered another Top Five effort, the million-selling *Innervisions*, and in 1974 he topped the chart with *Fulfillingness' First Finale*. By 1976, when he again hit the number-one slot with *Songs in the Key of Life*, the singer/composer/multi-instrumentalist had snagged three consecutive Album-of-the-Year awards by softening and helping redefine soul for the 1970s.

If Stevie Wonder first popularized a silky 1970s soul, producers Gamble and Huff perfected it. Meeting on an elevator in the Schubert Building, where both men worked for Philadelphia songwriting companies, they joined the Motown-inspired band, the Romeos. In 1966, after visiting Motown Records in Detroit, Kenny Gamble and Leon Huff established several record companies in quick succession: Gamble Records; Huff Records; Neptune; and Excel Records. Not meeting much success with their own companies, the duo worked with other labels such as Mercury to compose and produce several silky and orchestrated singles such as the Top-Ten "Expressway (To Your Heart)" by the Soul Survivors and Jerry Butler's number-four "Only the Strong Survive" (1969). Encouraged by their songwriting triumphs, Gamble and Huff intensified their resolve to create a winning record company. In 1971, with the distribution help of CBS Records president Clive Davis, the duo launched Philadelphia International Records, which set the tone for seventies soul.

Philadelphia International first charted with the O'Jays. The group formed in 1958 and signed with Imperial in 1963, but failed to find much chart success through the 1960s. By 1972, when the O'Jays signed with Philadelphia International Records, the group consisted of Eddie Levert, Walter Williams, and William Powell. Using the Gamble and Huff formula of smooth, sometimes orchestrated harmonies, the O'Jays immediately registered with the number-three "Back Stabbers" and a Top-Ten album of the same name. During the next three years, they followed with a string of hits, including their crowning achievement, the number-one "Love Train" (1973).

Gamble and Huff shaped Harold Melvin and the Blue Notes. Established in the mid-1950s as a doo-wop quartet, the group floundered in roadhouse bars and Las Vegas supper clubs during the 1960s. In the early 1970s, after drummer Teddy Pendergrass assumed lead vocalist duties and Lloyd Parks joined to make the Blues Notes a quintet, the group signed with Gamble and Huff. They scored with soft, Top-Ten pop ballads such as "If You Don't Know Me By Now" (1972) and the Top-Ten album *Wake Up Everybody* (1975).

Philadelphia International Records even charted with its house band, MFSB. Standing for Mother, Father, Sister, Brother, the nearly 40 person MFSB provided the rhythm background and sometimes the lush backdrop for the label's artists. Asked to create a theme song for the television show *Soul Train*, the band hammered out an instrumental with the vocal help of the Three Degrees for a number-one smash. Gamble and Huff labeled the song "T.S.O.P" (1974), The Sound of Philadelphia, accurately defining the soul of the 1970s.

Philadelphia International soon became a force within the music business. Within its first nine months of operation, the label sold 10 million singles and 2 million albums. By 1975, Gamble and Huff grossed more than $25 million annually, making their enterprise the second-largest African-American-owned business in the United States, second only to Motown.

Thom Bell, a former songwriter and producer for Gamble and Huff, offered his own lush arrangements of strings, French horns, and light percussion to challenge his former partners. Working as a producer for Atlantic Records during the early 1970s, Bell applied his soothing trademark sound to the Spinners. Started in 1954 by several Detroit toughs, the group struggled for sixteen years with only one Top-Twenty single, the Stevie Wonder–produced "It's a Shame" (1970). In 1972, with new lead singer Phillipe Wynne, the group moved to Atlantic Records and recorded with composer/producer Thom Bell. Immediately, they scored with the lush "I'll Be Around" and followed with hits such as the number-one "Then Came You" (1974) with torch singer Dionne Warwick and the Top-Five "The Rubberband Man" (1976).

Thom Bell also hit with the Stylistics. Banding together in 1968 as a union of two Philadelphia vocal groups, the Stylistics signed to Atlantic in 1971. Led by the falsetto of Russell Thompkins, they hit the chart with the smooth, string-drenched "Betcha by Golly, Wow" (1971) and "You Make Me Feel Brand New" (1974).

Most Gamble and Huff and Thom Bell acts sang about personal relationships against the soothing backdrop of strings and horns. Though occasionally tackling civil-rights issues in such songs as the O'Jays "Ship Ahoy," sweet-soul music mostly revolved around love songs. It featured such tunes as the number-one "Me and Mrs. Jones" (1972) by Billy Paul; the Stylistics' Top-Ten "You Are Everything" (1971); the O-Jays' "The Love I Lost (Part 1)" (1973); and "Could It Be I'm Falling in Love" (1972) by the Spinners. During the first half of the 1970s, a soft, lush, romantic, and non-confrontational soul drifted across the airwaves to signal the shift in attitude among young Americans.

Chapter 14
Rock Turns Serious: Jazz Rock and Progressive Music

"These days nobody wants to hear songs that have a message."
—Vocalist Robert Lamm of the group Chicago

"We know that people and movements are fallible," concluded one college senior from American University in the early 1970s. "We're afraid to believe too much in anything or anyone."

In the aftermath of Kent State, most youths of the Woodstock generation agreed with the cautious sentiments expressed by the college senior from American University. Sent to a war in a faraway land and attacked by National Guardsmen at home, they abandoned hope for a revolution in values and turned inward.

Economic conditions caused further concern. From 1969 to 1970, unemployment in the United States increased from 3.5 to 6.2 percent. In the same year, the buying power of the dollar declined by nearly 6 percent, and the government cut public spending and imposed credit restrictions. Throughout the country, the fear of a major recession gripped many Americans.

Music reflected the somber, conservative mood as many deserted a hard-driving rock. "The fading out of ear-numbing, mind-blowing acid rock [and metal]," *Time* contended in early 1971, "is related to the softening of the youth revolution. Its decline is variously viewed as a symptom of either progress toward harmony and thoughtfulness or a tragic slide from activist rage to a mode of 'enlightened apathy.'" "The times you live in have to do with what you produce, and you can either control that or not," insisted drummer Tony Williams who helped pioneer a jazz–rock fusion. "The '70s for a lot of people were a reaction to the '60s."

Rather than the swirling sounds of psychedelia, the punchy rhythms of soul, or the wrenching, angry metal, rock became introspective and strove for legitimacy. Built on the yen for experimentation fostered during the hippie era, it fused with more established musical forms such as jazz and classical to become more acceptable to the mainstream. During the early 1970s, rock and roll became an apolitical, intensely serious experience.

The Jazz–Rock Fusion Begins

Rock and roll has always been a union of diverse types of music. At its inception, it was concocted from an amalgam of electric R&B and country, first joined together by Chuck Berry, Elvis, and the rockabillies. During the mid-1960s, when Bob Dylan plugged an electric guitar cord into an amplifier, rock merged with folk for what critics called folk rock. Later in the decade African Americans transformed gospel-based R&B into soul and funk. The psychedelic bands, dedicated to experimentation, merged fifties' rock with blues, folk, and exotic-sounding world music such as the Indian raga. At the turn of the decade, performers continued to weld rock with other musical forms such as jazz.

The first rumblings of a fusion of jazz and rock came from two Columbia Records acts: Blood, Sweat and Tears and Chicago, a name later shortened to Chicago. Organized in 1967 by guitarist/keyboard man Al Kooper (b. Alan Kuperschmidt), a former member of the Blues Project who in 1965 backed Bob Dylan, when he went electric, Blood, Sweat & Tears delivered a blues-based music complemented by the horns of jazzmen such as trumpeter Randy Brecker and saxophonist Fred Lipsius. "When I first came to New York in 1967," intimated Brecker, "I joined the original Blood, Sweat & Tears. By then, jazz was already on the wane and you had to pay attention to pop and rock if you wanted to be part of a larger picture."

In April 1968, after other members forced Kooper out of the group, the band recruited David Clayton-Thomas, who added gritty, booming pop vocals to the jazz rock for the top-selling *Blood, Sweat and Tears*, which included the number-two hits, "Spinning Wheel," "And When I Die," and "You've Made Me So Very Happy." The group followed with two more top-selling albums, both featuring Clayton-Thomas on vocals and jazz horn men such as saxophonist Joe Henderson and trumpeter Lew Soloff. Blood, Sweat & Tears, boasted drummer Bobby Colomby, combined "jazz concept solos" with rock and roll.

James William Guercio, who had produced the first top-seller for Blood, Sweat & Tears, successfully promoted and managed another jazz–rock unit, Chicago. Formed in 1967 as the Big Thing by DePaul University classmates—guitarist Terry Kath, drummer Danny Seraphine, trombonist James Pankow, trumpeter Lee Loughnane, and saxophonist Walter Parazaider—the band changed its name to the Chicago Transit Authority as a nod to their hometown. In April 1969 amid the student revolts on campus, the band released a politically charged, jazz–rock album that included protest chants from the 1968 Democratic National Convention. Within a year, the record sold more than a million copies.

In early 1970, after a legal dispute, the band shortened its name to Chicago and released a second album, which nearly topped the chart. Though this album was less focused on anti-war sentiments than its predecessor, the liner notes called for a swift end to the Vietnam War and pledged the support of the group to the cause of revolution in all forms.

By 1971 after Kent State, the band followed the mainstream sentiments of youth by dispensing with radical politics and fusing their sound with a pop sensibility to achieve long-standing commercial success. They reached the number-two slot with *Chicago III*, and during the next four years topped the album chart five times.

Robert Lamm of Chicago, 1974.

Jim Summaria.

Miles Ahead

Trumpeter Miles Davis, another act on Columbia Records, provided the framework for many jazz–rock experiments. Davis had played with Charlie Parker at the inception of bop during the mid-1940s, had helped spearhead the cool jazz movement, and released a commercial version of modal jazz with *Kind of Blue* (1959) with saxophonist John Coltrane.

Davis became interested in rock after hearing Jimi Hendrix. First listening to Hendrix on the suggestion of his then-wife Betty Mabry, Miles became intrigued by Hendrix's use of electronic instruments and gadgets and felt that "Jimi Hendrix came from the blues, like me. We understood each other right away because of that."

In 1968, Miles and Jimi kindled a friendship and jammed, mostly at Miles' home. "He influenced me, and I influenced him," contended Davis. By October, Davis and Hendrix developed such a mutual respect for one another that they asked Beatle and bass player Paul McCartney if he would record with them and drummer Tony Williams. McCartney, out of town on vacation, never responded, and the album never materialized. During the last days of August 1970, Miles and Hendrix each played at the Isle of Wight outdoor festival. Miles and Jimi planned to meet in London, when the concert concluded on August 30, to discuss a joint album. Stopped by traffic jams, Hendrix never appeared at the meeting, and a joint Davis-Hendrix studio collaboration never took place.

Influenced by Hendrix, Miles slowly mixed electronics into his sound. "Musicians have to play the instruments that best reflect the times we're in, play the technology that will give you what you want to hear," recalled Davis. "I was moving more and more to using electronic instruments to make up the sound that I wanted."

By using electronic instruments, Davis hoped to reshape jazz and jump-start his career. "Jazz seemed to be withering on the vine," observed Davis. "I wanted to change course, *had* to change course for me to continue to believe in and love what I was playing," intimated the trumpeter. "I wasn't prepared to be a memory yet," he declared.

By late 1967, Davis began his experimentation with electronics. Early in the year during a recording session for *Miles in the Sky*, he convinced pianist Herbie Hancock to play an electric piano. Later the same year, Chick Corea (b. Armando Corea) played electric piano on the Miles Davis album *Filles De Kilimanjaro*. Davis then hired Austrian Joe Zawinul as a second keyboardist, who played both organ and the mellow-sounding Fender Rhodes electric piano. Near the end of 1968 and into the next year, Miles took his outfit into the studio and ratcheted his use of electric instruments to a new level. In the title cut of *In a Silent Way*, written by Joe Zawinul, Davis "wanted to make the sound more like rock." He characterized the song as "a classic and the beginning of fusion."

With a new record in the racks, the band delved more heavily into the electronic sound on tour. In concert, Davis "was using the wah-wah on my trumpet all the time so I could get closer to that voice Jimi had when he used a wah-wah on his guitar," admitted Miles.

When they returned to New York City, the electrified band clustered together in the Columbia studio on 52nd Street for another recording. In three days, starting on August 19, 1969, the group waxed *Bitches Brew*. Coaxing the music from his band like a conductor, the trumpeter merged jazz and rock together into a new hybrid.

Columbia Records, Davis' label, took advantage of the emerging jazz rock by marketing *Bitches Brew* to the youth market. Columbia president Clive Davis hoped to take the trumpeter who generally sold approximately 60,000 copies of an album into a new sales category, where top artists moved a million discs. The Columbia executive believed that Miles could attract "a younger market" by playing at such youth-oriented auditoriums as the Fillmore. On March 6 and 7, 1970, Miles Davis appeared at the Fillmore East. The next month, Miles played the Fillmore in San Francisco along

Miles Davis, 1969.

Philippe Gras/Alamy Stock Photo.

with the Grateful Dead. "We went into the *Bitches Brew* shit and that really blew them out," recalled Davis. Within the span of a year, Davis and his electric group reappeared twice at the Fillmore West and one more time at the East Coast venue. The Fillmore shows, insisted Davis, "were good for expanding my audience."

Armed with a fresh sound and a broadened audience, Miles Davis sold more albums. *Bitches Brew*, released on March 30, 1970, reached number thirty-five on the *Billboard* chart, the best chart position of a Miles Davis record. The album hit the number-one position on the jazz chart and achieved the goal of Columbia president Clive Davis by selling more than 2 million copies. Jazz, armed with electric instruments, again entered the mainstream of American music.

The Offspring of Miles: Fusion Explodes on the Scene

During the early seventies, several jazz–rock groups, mostly spearheaded by Miles Davis sidemen, exploded on the scene. Musicians who worked with Miles revered their leader and continued in his direction. "Billy Cobham, an uncredited drummer on *Bitches Brew*, described Miles as a big, black pot of notes" who served "as the foundation of a lot of what's going on right now."

The alumni of the late-sixties Miles Davis bands felt that the electric instrumentation of rock offered a means to extend the jazz idiom. "Technology had progressed and when it progresses there's a point where new musics can be formed," insisted drummer Lenny White played on *Bitches Brew*. "Music is a reflection of the times," he believed. "Now there's a new kind of music where you improvise more, like the traditional jazz music, but you use different instruments."

Tony Williams, the powerful drummer who at the age of twenty-three split with Miles less than a year before *Bitches Brew*, embraced the electric possibilities of rock in his pioneering band, Lifetime. Williams became interested in jazz on visits to jazz clubs with his father and as a teen played with such jazz luminaries as saxophonist Jackie McLean. When the young drummer heard Jimi Hendrix's first record, "all that electricity" excited him. "My drumming became more aggressive and that was the direction I wanted to follow," he explained. "The energy of the music is happening, but it's rock and roll," concluded Williams. In 1969, the drummer joined with electric guitarist John McLaughlin and organist Larry Young to form Lifetime, which displayed the band's dual stylistic interests and helped launch the jazz–rock fusion.

In 1971, John McLaughlin split with Lifetime and launched the Mahavishnu Orchestra. Before his work with Miles Davis and Tony Williams, guitarist McLaughlin had been part of the British blues scene as a member of the Graham Bond Organization and Alexis Korner's band. For the Mahavishnu Orchestra, McLaughlin recruited drummer Billy Cobham, Czechoslovakian keyboardist Jan Hammer, and violinist Jerry Goodman who had been a member of the rock group, The Flock. The band, featuring McLaughlin's screaming electric guitar, wove intricate jazz improvisations against a rock background.

Just as the Mahavishnu Orchestra organized, three Miles Davis sidemen— saxophonist Wayne Shorter, Austrian keyboardist Joe Zawinul, and Czech bassist Miroslav Vitous—launched Weather Report. Along with drummer Alphonse Mouzon, the band delivered an improvisational fusion of traditional jazz mixed with the electric explorations of rock.

Weather Report introduced the synthesizer, which replicated the full span of orchestral sounds through technology. Simultaneously developed in 1963 by Robert Moog and Don Buchla, the original synthesizer consisted of a series of modular circuits that emitted electrical signals, which could be converted into sound through loudspeakers or headphones. The pitch, timbre, amplitude, and spatial location of the sound could be altered by patching different modules together in different configurations to develop a rich, orchestral variety of soundscapes. Once patched together, the

Drummer Tony Williams.

Brian McMillen.

modules could be physically accessed through a keyboard played by a musician. By 1967, such rock bands as the Monkees, the Doors, the Rolling Stones and the Beatles experimented with the instrument on a limited basis. By 1970, when Robert Moog offered the less expensive, smaller Minimoog that dispensed with the clumsy patch chords, synthesizers became a staple among rock-and-roll musicians.

In the aptly named second effort by Weather Report, *I Sing the Body Electric* (1972), Joe Zawinul welcomed the new technology. The synthesizer, contended the keyboardist, "replaced all the many, many instruments you find, for instance, in a symphony orchestra, which a small group of musicians (for example, a quintet like Weather Report) could never accomplish before." "It produces an incredibly full and versatile sound," maintained Zawinul. "It's like a dream world." "I've heard orchestra sounds my entire life, and now I can do it myself because of a machine," he added.

In 1972, the Italian-Spanish pianist Chick Corea formed Return to Forever. After a brief foray into Latin music, the group turned to jazz rock. For *Light as a Feather*, the leader hired electric bassist Stanley Clarke who "as a kid, grew up listening to Hendrix, James Brown, Miles Davis, John Coltrane." By 1974, he replaced guitarist Bill Connors with Al Di Meola, then a teenager at the Berklee College of Music who idolized the Beatles. The next year, Chick Corea supplemented his electric piano with the synthesizer, played by both himself and Stanley Clarke. "I like the synthesizers because I like having the ability to bend a note, modulate a tone, and do things with timbres that the piano doesn't offer," Corea contended.

Larry Coryell, an admirer of Miles Davis and Jimi Hendrix, established The Eleventh House. In 1973, he hired drummer Alphonse Mouzon who recently left Weather Report, along with Mike Mandel on keyboards and bassist Danny Trifan. He also lured into the band trumpeter Randy Brecker who had been part of Blood, Sweat & Tears and Dreams, an early fusion group, which included Billy Cobham and his brother Michael on saxophone. "We love the Beatles but we also love Coltrane," disclosed Larry Coryell. "We love the Rolling Stones, but we also love Miles."

Donald Fagen and Walter Becker, the cofounders of Steely Dan, dished out a brand of jazz–rock. "I met Walter in college and we had very similar musical interests," remembered electric keyboardist Fagen, who became proficient on piano after dissecting Thelonious Monk and Red Garland records. "We kind of combined the [rhythm and] blues thing—which was much simpler but very direct and emotional—with the jazz stuff we knew into a big mess." The two jazz fanatics first joined rock revival bands "to pay the bills." By 1973, the duo, aided by such jazz stalwarts as bop saxophonist Jerome Richardson and ex-Basie trumpeter Snooky Young, hit the Top Twenty with their jazz–rock debut *Can't Buy a Thrill*, which, according to Fagen, "used devices that I think had formerly been used only by jazz people."

Carlos Santana added Latin rhythms to the jazz–rock amalgam. Raised in Tijuana, Mexico, Santana moved to San Francisco and, in October 1966, founded the Santana Blues Band. By 1968, the group added jazz and Latin influences to their electric blues. "If I would go to some cat's room," remembered the guitarist about his band mates, "he'd be listening to Sly [Stone] and Jimi Hendrix; another guy to the Stones and the Beatles. Another guy'd be listening to Tito Puente and Mongo Santamaria. Another guy'd be listening to Miles [Davis] and [John] Coltrane." In late 1969, Santana released their first, self-named album, which featured their trademark Latin and jazz rhythms mixed with an electric blues base and became the first in a string of top-selling releases. "I think the most effective thing we were doing was mixing blues with African rhythms," asserted Santana. "There's another name for this mix—Latin music. All those African beats come through the clave rhythms that became part of the Santana DNA."

Reflecting the gains made by the civil rights movement, most of the newly created jazz–rock outfits followed the example of their leader Miles Davis who did not care whether his sidemen were "black, white, blue, red or yellow" and featured inter-racial line-ups. Weather Report consisted of two white former Miles Davis sidemen who had been born and raised in Europe—keyboardist Joe Zawinul and Miroslav Vitous—and two African Americans—ex-Miles saxophonist Wayne Shorter and drummer Alphonse Mouzon. For the Mahavishnu Orchestra, white British guitarist John McLaughlin selected, white violinist Jerry Goodman, Irish-born bassist Rick Laird, Czech-born keyboardist Jan Hammer, and African-American drummer Billy Cobham. To form Return to Forever, Chick Corea recruited white guitarist Al DiMeola to his otherwise African-American group.

These inter-racial outfits, steeped in jazz, felt that they legitimized the more straight-forward rock. In 1970, James Pankow, the trombonist for Chicago, declared that "people are listening to better music in general. Rock 'n' roll is no longer 1-4-5 [time]; it's no longer simple music. It's becoming a legitimate music form." Miles Davis, an originator of the jazz–rock hybrid, contended that most top-selling "rock musicians didn't know anything about music." "They didn't study it, couldn't play different styles—and don't even talk about reading music," the trumpeter asserted. Given the sad state of proficiency among rock musicians, Miles concluded that "if they could do it—reach all those people and sell all those records without really knowing what they were doing—then I could do it, too, only better."

James Pankow.

Carl Lender.

Focused on a complex music, fusion bands mirrored the social environment by displaying little interest in social protest. Robert Lamm, the lead singer for Chicago best exemplified the attitude. "These days nobody wants to hear songs that have a message," he asserted.

Not focused on changing social values, jazz–rock bands generally saw no problem with financial success. "When I hear people talk about commercialism versus artistic something, it sort of makes me think that there is possibly some sort of weird computation behind that," snarled electric bassist Stanley Clarke. "I sell records, so my music is commercial." Larry Coryell provided an even more blunt description of his financial aspirations. "I want to be a star and make a lot of money," he asserted. "I have a large family and a lot of debts to pay off."

Many fusion outfits reached their commercial goals after the success of *Bitches Brew*. "After we recorded *Bitches Brew*," maintained Joe Zawinul, "Columbia was immediately interested in [Weather Report]." The label offered a contract to the group and snagged the Mahavishnu Orchestra and Return to Forever.

During the early seventies, jazz–rock groups hit the charts. In 1973, *Birds of Fire* by the Mahavishnu Orchestra made it to number-fifteen slot. The same year, drummer Billy Cobham entered the Top Thirty and climbed to the number-one position on the jazz chart with *Spectrum*, which included rock guitarist Tommy Bolin. He duplicated his feat with two follow-ups, *Crosswinds* and *Total Eclipse*. In 1974 Return to Forever approached the Top Thirty with *Where Have I Known You Before,* and Weather Report cracked the Top Fifty with *Mysterious Traveller*. Steely Dan scored with the Top-Ten *Pretzel Logic*, which included the Top-Five "Rikki Don't Lose That Number." The next year, electric bassist Stanley Clarke released the Top-Forty album *Journey to Love*, which included guitar work from ex-Yardbird Jeff Beck who also experimented with jazz-rock in his solo efforts. By the mid-seventies, jazz rock had been firmly established among young rock fans.

Progressive Rock

The seventies' quest for legitimacy in rock surfaced with British musicians who merged rock sounds with classical music and sometimes added escapist, fantasy-laden lyrics. Some called the classical-rock hybrid progressive rock to indicate the progress that rock had made from its simple twelve-bar blues beginning to a more complex, high-brow form.

Two English R&B bands, the Moody Blues and Procol Harum, represented forerunners of the classical-rock movement. Formed in 1964, the Moody Blues initially delivered high-powered British R&B, even backing Sonny Boy Williamson and Little Walter on their UK tours. In late 1964, they topped the British chart and hit the U.S. Top Ten with "Go Now!," a cover of an American R&B song by singer Bessie Banks. "At that time, there were only two bands in Birmingham playing the blues, us and the Spencer Davis Group," explained vocalist and harmonica player Ray Thomas, a founder of the Moody Blues.

With a reconstituted lineup, the band shifted from R&B to an atmospheric, classically driven sound, which showcased Mike Pinder's Mellotron, a tape-replay keyboard capable of reproducing the sounds of violins, trumpets, cellos, and other orchestral instruments. The Mellotron-driven band scaled the chart with *Days of Future Passed* (1967), which featured the London Festival Orchestra and included lead singer/guitarist Justin Hayward's composition "Nights in White Satin." Hayward called the album "a little rock opera." "Rock musicians are creating a new field for serious music," heralded the *Guardian*. Six more albums of orchestrated rock, highlighted by obscure, fantasy-filled lyrics, followed. In 1972, as youths abandoned harsh, political heavy metal, the Moody Blues scored with the chart-topping *Seventh Sojourn*.

Procol Harum presaged the flowering of 1970s' classical rock. The band had its roots in an R&B group called the Paramounts, which enjoyed limited success. After guitarist Robin Trower left the Paramounts, eventually to form a Hendrix-style power trio, vocalist Gary Brooker and lyricist Keith Reid joined the classically trained organist Matthew Fisher, guitarist Ray Royer, bassist Dave Knights, and drummer Bobby Harrison to start Procol Harum. In 1967, the group topped the British chart and reached the U.S. Top Five with "A Whiter Shade of Pale," a surreal poem by Reid set to music adapted from Bach's *Suite No. 3 in D Major*. After several commercially disappointing follow-ups, in 1972 Procol Harum rode the crest of the classical-rock wave for their greatest success with *Procol Harum Live: In Concert with the Edmonton Symphony Orchestra*, which included an orchestral version of hit "Conquistador."

Jethro Tull made the transition from blues bashers to classical rockers. Rising from the remains of an earlier blues band, flautist Ian Anderson and bassist Glenn Cornick joined with guitarist Mick Abrahams and drummer Clive Bunker to form Jethro Tull, named after an eighteenth-century English agriculturalist. In 1968, they delivered the blues-drenched *This Was* to modest success and a year later moved away from the blues with new guitarist Martin Barre. In 1971, the band released the Top-Ten *Aqualung*, which abandoned the blues for a rock-folk sound. The next year, Jethro Tull merged English folk, rock, and obscure lyrics with classical flourishes for the number-one *Thick as a Brick* and the next year followed with the classical rock of the chart-topping *A Passion Play*.

Other rock acts strove for high-culture legitimacy by creating rock operas. The British blues band The Pretty Things, led by crack guitarist Dick Taylor, started the trend. In late 1968, the band abandoned the blues for the commercially unsuccessful rock opera *S.F. Sorrow*, which told the tale of protagonist Sebastian F. Sorrow from cradle to grave. A few months later in May 1969, mod mainstays The Who released *Tommy* to rave reviews. Charting the life of a deaf, dumb, blind pinball wizard, the rock opera captured the attention of rock fans and critics alike. The band performed the opera in top houses throughout England and the United States, and the album hit the Top Five in both countries. The *Sunday Telegraph* referred to *Tommy* as a "libretto as intricate as anything in classical opera." "Overnight we became snob rock," lamented John Entwistle, the band's bassist. During late 1969 as a rock opera frenzy swept rock and roll, the Kinks, the originators of the power chord, produced a rock opera named *Arthur (or the Decline of the British Empire)* for Granada Television.

King Crimson, fueled by the ideas of Robert Fripp, forged a direct connection to the classics and served as a prototype for 1970s classical rock. In late 1968, the band formed around Fripp, who combined his interest in classical composers Anton Dvorak and Karlheinz Stockhausen with screaming Hendrix-like rock solos. "Well-educated university graduate types were coming in as musicians and band members," reasoned Chris Blackwell, owner of Island Records. "So you were starting to have a different input in the music. Robert Fripp really represented that type of new performer." The group neared the top of the British chart with its debut, *In the Court of the Crimson King*, which included the symphonic sounds of the Mellotron and featured mythical, escapist, fantasy-based lyrics similar to the motifs that appeared on the albums of other classical-rock bands. The next year they followed with the commercially successful *In the Wake of Poseidon*, which included "The Devil's Triangle," based on Gustav Holst's orchestral suite *The Planets*, and continued their fascination with deep-sea mythology.

Genesis used King Crimson as a role model. Meeting at secondary school, the band members started as songwriters who idolized Fripp and his mates. "King Crimson appeared on the scene, and we thought they were just magnificent," explained singer Peter Gabriel. After several unsuccessful albums, Genesis gathered a following based on their theatrical stage shows that harkened back to ancient legends and an intricate, melodic sound that was accentuated by Mellotron player Tony Banks. Sometimes appearing in long medieval gowns and wearing masks, the costumed Peter Gabriel wooed audiences, and from 1972 to 1974 the band hit the British Top Ten with three albums of classically tinged rock.

Banding together backstage at the Fillmore in San Francisco, former King Crimson guitarist Greg Lake, classically trained pianist Keith Emerson, and drummer Carl

Peter Gabriel of Genesis in full costume, 1974.

Jim Summaria.

Palmer made their major debut as Emerson, Lake and Palmer on August 29, 1970, at the Isle of Wight Festival. That year, they reached the Top Twenty with their first album, embellished with classical motifs and songs written by ex–King Crimson lyricist Pete Sinfield. In 1971, the trio released a live version of Russian composer Modest Mussorgsky's composition *Pictures at an Exhibition*, which reached the Top Ten. In 1974, the group charted with the three-record set, *Welcome Back My Friend to the Show That Never Ends*, which included "Toccata" by Bach. "We didn't play the blues, and we really didn't play rock-and-roll. We played classical adaptations," related Carl Palmer. "I think all of us in the band appreciate classical music an awful lot."

As with other classically oriented rock groups, Emerson, Lake, and Palmer featured fantasy-laden concept albums. In 1971, they released the top-selling *Tarkus*, which revolved around the concept of a mechanized armadillo that battled a mythical beast, the Manticore. "What I write is a figment of my imagination and it has to be fairy-tale-like," confessed Greg Lake. To reinforce the otherworldly aspect of their music, the band staged a theatrical rock extravaganza with more than 35 tons of equipment. "You have to exaggerate some points theatrically to express what you're doing musically," explained Keith Emerson. "I'd rather give entertainment than preach," summarized guitarist Lake of the band's approach.

Pink Floyd, a British psychedelic band, moved increasingly toward classical structures during the 1970s. In early 1968, when vocalist-guitarist Syd Barrett became incapacitated because of excessive LSD use, the group hired guitarist David Gilmour, who led the band toward a more subtle, classically based experimental sound evident on several atmospheric albums, which all hit the Top Five in England. "Syd moving out meant that we had to start writing," explained bassist-vocalist Roger Waters. "In fact, his leaving made us pursue the idea of the extended epic and a more classically constructed idea of music."

Keyboardist Richard Wright who admired French Romantic composer Louis-Hector Berlioz and German classicist Carl Orff signaled the intentions of the group to use classical structures and players in their work. In early 1970, he proclaimed that Pink Floyd wanted to "write a complete work for the orchestra and ourselves." By September, the band had been commissioned to write a ballet for dancer Rudolph Nureyev with a 108-person orchestra at their disposal. The next year, the group played at the Montreux Classical Musical Festival. "This is what we like," enthused Wright. "A lot of people who normally listen to classics will be able to hear us, and a lot of young people will probably be hearing a symphony orchestra for the first time. It will be good for both."

By their 1973 masterpiece *The Dark Side of the Moon*, which took nine painstaking months to produce and sold more than thirteen million copies, Pink Floyd had perfected a Wagnerian electronic sound that provided a backdrop for epic tales of alienation, paranoia, and madness. Rather than a political statement so popular a few years before, "*Dark Side of the Moon* itself is an allusion to the moon and lunacy," explained guitarist David Gilmour. "The dark side is generally related to what goes on inside people's heads, the subconscious and the unknown."

Yes, a band formed in 1968, featured neoclassical structures and three-part harmonies. After adding guitarist Steve Howe and classically trained pianist Rick Wakeman, the group recorded the Top-Five *Fragile* (1971), their U.S. breakthrough, which contained the hit "Roundabout." "That kind of using the classical structure as a basis to make music, rather than pop music, that's where we were heading when we did *Fragile*," explained Yes founder Jon Anderson. The group followed with the Top-Five *Close to the Edge*, which showed the influence of Finnish classical composer/violinist Sibelius and consisted of three extended cuts and a four-movement title suite. Starting with *Fragile*, the Yes albums highlighted the fantasy-style artwork of Roger Dean that reinforced the escapist lyrics of the classical rockers.

By 1974, *Time* gushed over "the complex, educated sounds" of groups such as Yes. "Thus do barriers fall," the magazine concluded, "and such often enclosed worlds as rock music get a little sunshine in." The screaming guitars of protest had given way to rock mixed with heavy doses of music more palatable to the mainstream.

Chapter 15
The Era of Excess

"You can't make a revolution if you have to make a living."
—John Sinclair, 1977

"It's a very selfish decade," Tom Hayden, the cofounder of the radical Students for a Democratic Society (SDS), complained to *Newsweek* magazine in 1977. "It's all me. People who experienced profound disappointment trying to change the system are jogging and growing vegetables and concentrating on brightening their own corners of the world."

During the mid- and late 1970s, many former radicals of the 1960s turned inward for fulfilment. One winter day in 1973, Rennie Davis, the other founder of SDS, closed his eyes, saw the bright light of the mythic "third eye" in his forehead, and "suddenly I was in a place no words could describe. I felt such a peace—it humbled me and shattered all my assumptions about life." Having experienced transcendental Consciousness Four, he joined the spiritual sect of the guru Maharaj Ji and began selling life insurance for John Hancock in Denver. Four years later, Davis described his life as "light and music and vibration."

Jerry Rubin, the radical yippie who practiced his guerrilla theater of the absurd during the late 1960s, underwent a similar rebirth. In 1970, Rubin questioned his radical beliefs, and by 1977 lived in a Manhattan high-rise apartment, feasted on vitamin pills and health food, jogged regularly, and attended seminars about money consciousness. He hoped to be "as Establishment as I can possibly get."

John Sinclair, the head of the White Panther Party who exhorted MC5 fans to join the revolution, became disillusioned with radical politics after a prison term and parenthood. The "Left, man, I'm just not interested anymore," Sinclair, dressed in a suit and tie, told *Newsweek*. "You can't make a revolution if you have to make a living."

The "Me" Decade

An end to the war in Vietnam, disillusionment with politics, and a sometimes booming economy helped transform sixties' radicals into seventies' yuppies. After escalating during the sixties, the war in Vietnam ground to a halt. In January 1973, the United States signed the Paris Peace Accord, a formal peace treaty with North Vietnam, and left behind 56,555 dead American soldiers. Six months later, Congress ended the military draft. By April 30, 1975, the United States had withdrawn all troops and military advisors from Vietnam and Cambodia, an action that satisfied one of the last major demands of college-age radicals.

As the war in Vietnam ended, Richard M. Nixon, who had first attracted national prominence for his strident, anticommunist stance during the McCarthy hearings, was reelected to the presidency by voters in forty-nine of fifty states. He defeated George McGovern, the liberal senator and former college history professor who had been championed by radicalized college-age youths. Coupled with an end to the war, the reelection of Nixon deflated the rage and blunted the resolve of college radicals. As Rennie Davis contended, "Suddenly that collective energy was gone. The war was over and Nixon had just been reelected. People just found themselves living lives— settling in, getting a job because you had to buy food and pay the rent."

A new crop of college students in the mid-1970s, the last of the baby boom generation, focused their energies on immediate, material concerns. The students, a senior from Boston University told *Time* in late 1974, were "seeking tangible, not spiritual, returns from their investment in a university." Oriented toward financially rewarding careers, they enrolled in business administration and engineering classes, bypassing the history, English, and philosophy courses so popular only a few years earlier. "The mood here is, 'I'm here for me,'" remarked senior Steve Ainsworth, editor of UCLA's *Daily Bruin*. During the 1970s, *Time* magazine characterized baby boomers in general as "the Self-Centered Generation."

A growing economy allowed the baby boomers to indulge themselves. Although beset by a temporary economic downturn and inflated prices after the Vietnam War, Americans enjoyed increased real disposable income, which during the 1970s rose by 28.5 percent, and allowed many baby boomers who graduated from college and entered the white-collar workforce to satisfy their fantasies. Having money to spend, baby boomers embraced the full array of new consumer products introduced during the 1970s. They bought automatic garage door openers, hot tubs, food processors, air-conditioned cars, snowmobiles, and ten-speed bicycles.

Many self-indulgent boomers sought pleasure through drugs, which only a few years earlier had been considered weapons to break down barriers and change the social order. "Drugs have become co-opted by the consumer society," asserted LSD guru Timothy Leary in 1976. "Drugs are now just another thing people can buy to make themselves feel one way or another."

Baby boomers indulged in the more expensive, ego-enhancing cocaine, a drug introduced to the U.S. market in 1886 by John Styth Pemberton, who mixed it with caffeine for a syrup he called Coca-Cola. As early as 1973, more than 4.8 million Americans had sampled the drug, which *Time* magazine labeled "tyrannical King Coke." "Why the fad?" asked the magazine. "For one thing, smoking pot has become commonplace, even passé, and some people look for new thrills."

Some baby boomers sought excitement in their personal relationships, especially through open sexual relations, which had continued to expand since the 1960s. Singles, a category that doubled to 1.3 million during the decade, spent $40 billion a year to meet ready partners. More than a few married boomers discussed open marriage, engaged in wife swapping, and joined free sex clubs such as the Sandstone in Los Angeles, which sought the "membership of stable couples, young middle-class sensualists who believed that their personal relationships would be enhanced, rather than shattered, by the elimination of sexual possessiveness."

Some homosexuals became more open and vocal about their sexual orientation. In June 1969, when homosexuality remained illegal in every state except Illinois, gays at the Stonewall Inn in Greenwich Village resisted police arrest and rioted. Spurred by the protest, gays banded together in the Gay Liberation Front and published newspapers such as *Come Out!*, which called for gay power. In December 1969, gays founded the Gay Activist Alliance and the *Gay Activist* to highlight gender politics. At the turn of the decade, homosexuals read other newspapers such as *Gay Sunshine, Gay*, and *Gay Power*. By the late 1970s, the Institute for Sex Research discovered that 6 percent of single men considered themselves homosexual, and another 5 percent had at least one homosexual experience after age nineteen. Among single women, 5 percent considered themselves lesbians, and another 13 percent had at least one homosexual encounter as an adult.

Many of these homosexuals, especially men, practiced unrestrained sex. Though 50 percent of gay men enjoyed a steady relationship at the time of the Institute study, gay men confessed to having sex with a stranger 80 percent of the time, 30 percent admitted to "cruising" in parks, and 28 percent contended that they had engaged in sex with more than 1,000 different partners. As with the heterosexual population, many gays became absorbed by their own search for pleasure.

The baby boomers, preoccupied with their own needs, chased the dream of self-perfection. They aimed at "changing one's personality—remaking, remodeling, elevating, and polishing one's very self...and observing, studying, and doting on it," wrote Tom Wolfe in his influential essay "The Me Decade." Some trekked to Big Sur, California, where they paid $200 a week to attend the Esalen Institute, which, in the words of Tom Wolfe, promised "lube jobs for the personality." Others flocked to Oscar Ichazo's Arica or Werner Erhard's EST sessions to purge themselves through abuse and self-deprivation. A few expelled personal demons and discovered themselves through primal-scream therapy. Unlike the hippies, who informally met with friends to discuss changing the social system, the seventies' baby-boom generation paid money for encounter sessions that delved into the individual psyches of the participants. In their material possessions, their intimate relationships, and their self-explorations, baby boomers of the 1970s became obsessed with their own desires and sometimes excessive cravings.

Elton John

Elton John mirrored the extravagance of the era, serving as the transitional figure from the early 1970s sensitive singer to the mid-1970s excessive rock star. One of the most commercially successful of the 1970s acoustic solo acts, although atypical, pianist John (b. Reginald Dwight) was raised in England and as a teen joined the blues group Bluesology. In 1967, he auditioned for Liberty Records and, at the suggestion of the label, teamed with songwriter Bernie Taupin. Two years later, John released his debut album, and in 1970 charted with a Top Five, self-titled effort, which featured a gospel-influenced piano sound and the sensitive ballads of Taupin. Throughout the 1970s, he crafted six singles that became number-one hits. Between 1972 and 1975, the singer recorded six number-one albums and became the first act since the Beatles to place four albums in the Top Ten simultaneously.

Unlike the subdued singer-songwriters of the 1970s who generally strummed their guitars with few flourishes, Elton John developed a wild stage act that included handstands on the piano and kicking over the piano bench. "I'm pretty much making up for lost time," he told an interviewer. "Not having had a real teenage life, I'm living those thirteen to nineteen years now. Mentally I may be twenty-eight, but somewhere half of me is still thirteen."

John complemented his antics with extravagant costumes. Many times he wore sequined, gaudy jumpsuits, platform shoes, and pink boas. He sported his trademark outrageous glasses, owning more than 200 pairs, including mink-lined glasses, diamond-inlaid spectacles, and a pair with fifty-seven tiny light bulbs that spelled ELTON. "I love...to wear great, feathery costumes—and I do it," revealed the singer. "It's like an actor getting into his costume for his part." Though specializing in sensitive ballads such as "Your Song," played on an acoustic piano, John reflected the theatrical extravagance that characterized the "me" generation of the mid- and late 1970s. He confessed, "If I do it, I do it to extreme excess."

Heavy Metal Theater

A theatrical, glittery, sometimes androgynous heavy metal, exemplified by David Bowie, epitomized seventies rock-and-roll excess. Born David Jones, a teenaged Bowie rejected the sixties' counterculture. "I hated the whole togetherness, peace and love thing," he recalled. "It was conceited, flabby, *suffocating*." After joining several commercially unsuccessful bands and changing his name to avoid confusion with Davy Jones of the Monkees, in 1967 he took mime and dance lessons from theatrical fringe artist Lindsay Kemp. In 1969, amid the furor over the first moon landing, Bowie released "Space Oddity," which hit the Top Five in Britain.

Bowie changed his image at the turn of the decade. After backing Marc Bolan, who had begun a glitter-rock craze in England as T-Rex, the singer affected an androgynous image by appearing in a dress publicly as well as on the album cover of *The Man Who Sold the World*. In January 1972, Bowie declared his bisexuality to the British music paper the *New Musical Express*, reflecting the 1970s trend toward openness about different sexual orientations.

Expanding on his image, Bowie created the bisexual, space-age, glittery persona of Ziggy Stardust. On August 16, 1972, at the Rainbow Theater in London, he materialized from a cloud of dry ice, adorned by a tight-fitting, glimmering jumpsuit, high-topped, sequined hunting boots, and orange-tinted hair. He had shaved his eyebrows and wore red eye shadow. "The only thing that shocks now is an extreme," explained the singer about his space-age character. "Unless you do that, nobody will pay attention to you. Not for long. You have to hit them on the head." "We were coming out of the whole hippie thing, which was very much a dressed-down thing, denimy, T-shirts, grungy," suggested Mick Rock, Bowie's photographer at the time. "David was technicolor compared to this gray/blue/brown world. He was also sexual—a very decadent thing that would come to influence even brick layers."

The shocking image of Ziggy Stardust sold to the seventies' boomers. After having only limited success with his previous albums, Bowie sold more than 1 million copies of *The Rise and Fall of Ziggy Stardust and the Spiders from Mars*, which featured a hard-rocking band anchored by guitarist Mick Ronson. The next year, he topped the British chart and hit the Top Twenty with *Aladdin Sane* and charted with previous albums such as *Hunky Dory*.

The heavy metal androgyny of Ziggy Stardust gave direction to the careers of other bands such as Mott the Hoople. Begun in 1969 as a hard-rock outfit led by singer Ian Hunter, Mott the Hoople initially released four poor-selling albums and then disbanded. On the eve of their dissolution, in March 1972, they met David Bowie, a long-time fan of the group, who offered them one of his songs, "All the Young Dudes." The heterosexual band, agreeing to wear 9-inch platform shoes, heavy mascara, and sequined costumes, recorded the hard-rocking song, which hit the charts in both Britain and the United States and became a gay-liberation anthem. Reinforcing their image with songs such as "Sucker" and "One of the Boys," in 1974 the group neared the Top Twenty with *The Hoople* and *Mott the Hoople—Live*.

Iggy Pop revitalized his career by following the advice of David Bowie. A young Iggy (b. James Osterberg) traveled from his native Michigan to Chicago, where he briefly played drums for electric-blues artists. Upon returning to Ann Arbor in 1967, he formed the Stooges, who debuted at a Halloween party, and during the next three years they recorded two slashing, hard-driving, proto-punk LPs that failed to chart. Disconsolate, Iggy moved to Florida, where he cut lawns for a living.

In 1972, on a trip to New York, Iggy met Bowie and manager Tony DeFries, who persuaded Pop to reform the Stooges under DeFries's management and Bowie's guidance. The Stooges, continuing their trademark live performances, unleashed wild theatrical shows. "Iggy had gone beyond performance—to the point where it was really some kind of psychodrama," observed John Sinclair, manager of the MC5. "It exceeded conventional theater. He might do *anything*. That was his act." In April 1973, Iggy and the Stooges released *Raw Power*, which showcased the thrashing guitar of James Williamson and on the cover pictured a shirtless Iggy with bleached-blonde hair, heavy makeup, dark red lipstick, eye shadow, and silver-lamé, skin-tight, studded pants. Though disbanding within a year after the album's release, the Stooges served as a model for late 1970s punk, and Iggy became a collaborator with Bowie, writing "Jean Genie" for the singer.

Lou Reed also collaborated with Bowie for a new direction. After quitting the Velvet Underground in August 1970, the New Yorker went into seclusion at his parents' home in Long Island. In 1972, Reed met Bowie, who encouraged him to pursue a solo career. He began to perform with bleached-blonde hair, makeup, and black fingernail

A pleading Ian Hunter of Mott the Hoople, 1973.

Jim Summaria.

polish. In August 1972, Reed recorded the Bowie-produced album *Transformer*, which on the cover pictured a prominent New York drag queen and included the Top-Twenty "Walk on the Wild Side," a song about a transvestite that became Reed's first pop hit. In 1974, he earned his first and only Top-Ten album with *Sally Can't Dance*.

The New York Dolls adopted the Bowie-defined image of heavy metal androgyny. Formed in 1971 and fronted by guitarist Johnny Thunders (b. John Genzale) and singer David Johansen, the group began playing locally at clubs such as the Mercer Arts Center. In 1973, they released their first album, which included thrashing, driving, proto-punk anthems such as "Personality Crisis." On the cover, done in gray and shocking pink with the band's name written in lipstick, the group posed with heavy makeup, jewelry, and ruby lipstick. Johansen, with a shoulder thrust forward, stared wistfully into the mirror of his powder box. The other group members looked straight ahead, attired in 6-inch heeled boots, skin-tight leather or spandex pants, and provocative blouses. In one concert, the band assaulted traditional gender roles by appearing in cellophane tutus and army boots. "We liked dressing up, which was kind of like a thing that was happening in the Village anyway," explained Johansen, "like mixing and matching and going to thrift stores and wearing man-tailored jackets that were made for Marlene Dietrich."

On stage, the New York Dolls delivered a wild, extreme heavy metal act. They "were totally outrageous" remarked rock photographer Bob Gruen "The Dolls blew up more equipment than anybody because they were just over the top. They did everything to the fullest, to the maximum."

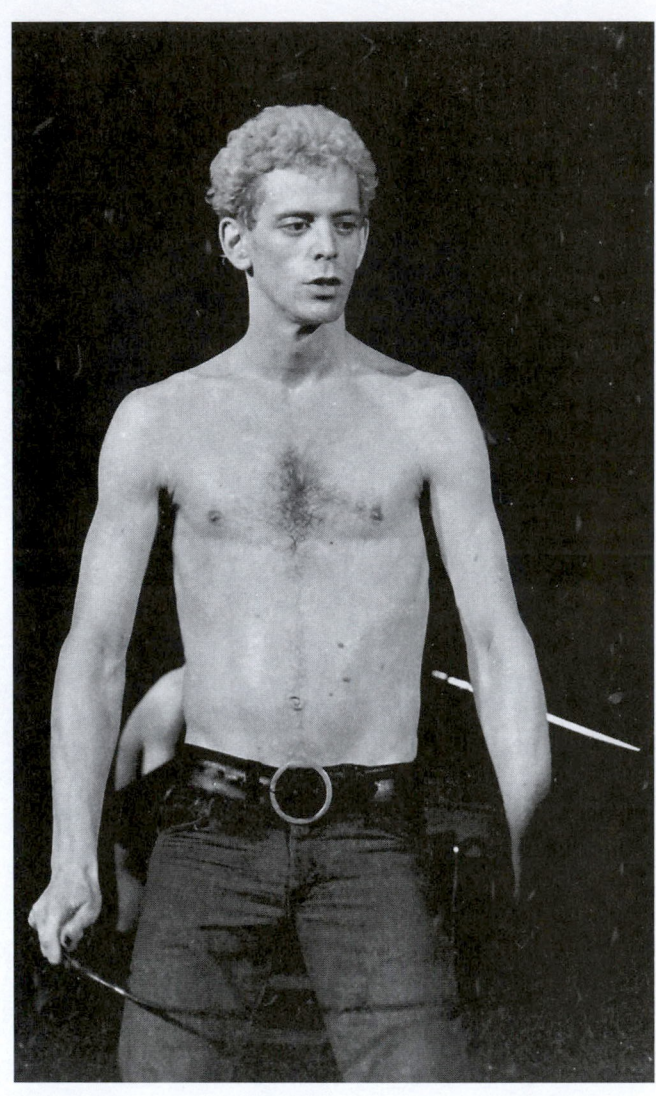

Lou Reed walks on the wild side, early 1970s.

Mark Goff.

Kiss tried to outdo the New York Dolls, their cross-town rivals. "In 1972 there was only one impressive band in New York and that was the New York Dolls," remembered Gene Simmons (b. Chaim Witz), the impetus behind Kiss. "I was impressed mostly by their stage presence, and the fact that they didn't look like other American bands." He added: "We were extremely jealous of the New York Dolls and we were going to do them one better."

To grab attention, the band, according to Simmons, "decided to put on bizarre makeup. What came out for me was an expression of the superhero/horror/science fiction sort of genre that I'd always admired... [Guitarist] Paul [Stanley's] was kind of the rock star, Eddie Cochran, I-wanna-be-Elvis routine—magnified. [Guitarist] Ace [Frehley] had his space stuff and [drummer] Peter [Criss] his cat stuff." Like cartoon characters, the face-painted group dressed in skin-hugging, bejeweled, spandex pants, platform shoes, and black, glittering, leather shirts. Coached and bankrolled by ex-television producer Bill Aucoin, Kiss assaulted their audiences with rockets, police lights, snow machines, smoke bombs, and levitating drum kits.

Neil Bogart (b. Neil Bogatz), a record entrepreneur who signed Kiss to his Casablanca label, engineered a barrage of promotion for the band. He arranged appearances on television shows from Dick Clark specials to *The Mike Douglas Show*. Bogart inked deals with the publishers of *Creem* and *Circus* magazines to feature the band on their covers and to give away boxes of Kiss albums to subscribers. Bogart

David Johannson of the New York Dolls in shocking pink, 1973.

Jim Summaria.

created the KISS Army by inserting a recruiting postcard in their albums, and developed 150 different types of Kiss-related items, including Kiss dolls and a Marvel Kiss comic book. By 1978, the band grossed more than $100 million annually and waxed 3 million selling albums to become one of America's hottest acts.

As with their counterparts, Kiss avoided any political messages. Some bands "get heavily into politics and political issues, which we try to stay clear of," explained Ace Frehley. "We're just entertainers." "The basic premise of behind Kiss is that we are there to give people a couple hours of pure escapism," echoed Simmons.

Alice Cooper matched Kiss with overtly sexual, heavy metal, apolitical rock theatrics. Born Vince Furnier, Cooper formed his first band with a group of high school friends. On Halloween 1967 at the Cheetah club in Los Angeles, the group followed the Grateful Dead and the Jefferson Airplane, with Cooper wearing Janis Joplin's gold lamé pants, high-heeled boots, and black mascara. "Everyone was taking acid, and peace and love, but when they got us, we were anything but peace and love," explained Cooper. "We were more sensational. We were the *National Enquirer* of rock-'n'-roll." In the audience, Shep Gordon, the manager for Frank Zappa, attentively watched the spectacle. Gordon told Zappa that Alice Cooper had emptied the club in a few minutes with their act, and an interested Zappa auditioned the group. Zappa signed the band to his Straight Records, which released two largely unnoticed albums.

The band slowly generated more attention through sensationalist tactics. In 1971, they released the hard-rock album *Love It to Death*, which included the hit "Eighteen" and on the cover showed Cooper's thumb suggestively thrusting through a 3-inch-wide ring. Late the same year, they released the Top Twenty-Five *Killer*. Having more money and encouraged by new manager Shep Gordon, the group attracted an even larger audience through an elaborate show that included throwing live chickens into the crowd, axing off the heads of dolls, staging mock executions in fake electric chairs, Cooper draping himself with a live boa constrictor, and beating fans over the heads with 6-foot-long, inflated phalluses.

By 1973, when they released the number-one *Billion Dollar Babies*, the group had become one of the preeminent practitioners of rock theater. On a tour that grossed more than $6 million in a few months, they simulated a beheading, a hanging, an electrocution, a dismemberment, and a transformation of Cooper into a bloodsucking vampire. "I didn't feel that people went to rock shows to be preached to," sniffed Cooper. "I go to shows to escape. I hated the idea of going to something, and having people tell me what I should do about Vietnam. What we were doing was saying, 'Go have fun.'" The bandleader added: "I would like to think that Alice Cooper opened the door to theatrics. We were sort of the band that drove the stake through the heart of the love generation."

Queen nearly rivalled Alice Cooper in extravagance. Formed in 1970 by guitarist Brian May and drummer Roger Taylor, the band featured vocalist Freddie Mercury (b. Farrokh Bulsara), who named the band. "I'd had the idea of calling a group Queen for a long time," he asserted. "It was a very strong name, very universal and very

Freddie Mercury of Queen.

Carl Lender.

immediate; it had a lot of visual potential." Sometimes Mercury favored dresses, tights, and black nail polish, modeling his demeanor after one of his idols, pop singer Liza Minnelli. In other shows, Mercury wore leather storm-trooper outfits that emphasized the gay connotation of the band's name. The *New York Times* referred to Mercury's act as "strutting and preening, by turns campy and almost militaristic." "Of all the more theatrical rock performers, Freddie took it further than the rest," explained David Bowie, who collaborated with Queen on the 1981 hit "Under Pressure." "He took it over the edge. And of course, I always admired a man who wears tights."

Queen produced a dramatic music equal to its theatrical stage shows. After securing a following in Britain during 1973, the band neared the U.S. Top Ten with Sheer Heart Attack (1974). The next year, the band delivered *A Night at the Opera* (1975), which included the operatic heavy metal of "Bohemian Rhapsody" and followed with four more Top-Five efforts including *News of the World*, which featured the militaristic thump of "We Will Rock You" and the dramatic-sounding, self-important "We Are the Champions." By the end of the decade, Queen had fashioned a sound and an act that reflected the extravagant "me" generation. "It's just pure escapism," asserted Mercury. "People should escape for a while, and then they can go back to their problems."

Art Pop in the Arena

The extravagant stage antics of mid-seventies rock fit well with the venue that became the staple of the "Me Generation": the arena. During the folk boom and the surf craze, acts generally played in small, intimate clubs. British invaders graduated to 1,000- to 5,000-seat auditoriums, and only amid the height of Beatlemania did the Fab Four perform at such places as Shea Stadium. Psychedelic bands played at local halls such as the Fillmore and the Avalon ballrooms, where light shows could be projected on the walls and the bands mingled with the fans. By the mid- to late 1970s, as rock performances became bigger business, shows moved to large sports arenas, where smoke-bomb explosions, fake decapitations, and outlandish costumes appeared apropos to thousands of cheering fans. Like the gladiator contests in ancient Rome, the event had moved to the Coliseum.

These arenas, separating the audience from the performer, gave rise to a new genre of art rock, sometimes disparagingly called arena rock. Suitable for a larger-than-life, flashy era, mostly American-bred bands fused elements of British art-rock with simplified R&B rhythm sections in slickly produced, hook-laden, and melodramatic ballads about lost love and bygone eras sung by high-pitched vocalists. During the late 1970s, stadiums offered the setting for bands, which attracted thousands of fans and sold millions of records of smooth, escapist music.

Kansas exemplified American art-rock that filled an arena with operatic-sounding ballads. Hailing from Topeka and the surrounding area, band members such as guitarist Richard Williams found inspiration in early seventies art-rock groups such as Yes and King Crimson "with more of a heavy American rhythm section." Robbie Steinhardt, violinist for the group, described Kansas as "apolitical," and vocalist/guitarist Kerry Livgren contended that "Kansas has always been on the weightier side of popular music," similar to the original art-rockers. Signed in 1973 by music mogul Don Kirshner who had created the girl groups and the Monkees, Kansas patiently played small venues until late 1976, when they reached the Top Five with *Leftoverture* and the single "Carry On Wayward Son." They repeated their success with *Point of Know Return* (1977), which included the philosophical musing of "Dust in the Wind." By the end of the decade, Kansas had sold more than 11 million discs to young, white, largely male devotees with a sound that one fan called "daydreaming music."

The Chicago-based Styx delivered showy guitar solos sandwiched between melodramatic classical introductions and grand finales. They complemented the music with reflective lyrics about love and deliverance. "The essence of Styx is about escapism," asserted guitarist James "J.Y." Young. After several chart failures, the group hit the Top Ten in 1977 with *The Grand Illusion, which sold three million copies on the strength of such songs as "Come Sail Away."* In quick succession, they added three more Top-Ten efforts, including the chart-topping *Paradise Theater (1981).*

Journey, a San Francisco band led by former members of Santana, turned from a jazz-tinged art rock to a more bombastic and commercially successful music. In early 1978, they added vocalist Steve Perry and enlisted the help of Queen-producer Roy Thomas Baker, who layered harmonies on top of one another for the platinum pop of *Infinity.* The band continued to deliver powerful, slick ballads of lost love for million sellers such as "Lovin', Touchin', Sqeezin'."

Amid the arena-rock craze, Boston found dizzying commercial success. The brainchild of basement-studio wizard Tom Scholz who had graduated from Massachusetts Institute of technology, the band merged "the power and emotion of classical music into rock and roll" and used a full array of production techniques for a flowing, textured concoction. The group filled coliseums with smooth, expansive Wagnerian ballads of two top-sellers, including their 1976 self-titled debut, which sold 17 million copies.

Supertramp, one of the few British arena bands, grafted art-rock soundscapes onto snappy hooks for a hit record about American culture. In 1969, keyboardist Rick Davies joined with bassist/vocalist Roger Hodgson to form the kernel of the band. Initially, the group delivered standard progressive rock with a British musical-hall flavor. "Supertramp has always been rich in musical 'colors,'" asserted Hodgson. After struggling with their initial releases, in 1979 the band and a forty-man crew dragged fifty-two tons of equipment worth $5 million dollars to large arenas to promote *Breakfast in America* which reached number one and sold 18 million copies.

The Electric Light Orchestra switched from British art rock to art pop. Formed in 1970 by Roy Wood, the band initially adhered to an art-rock sound. Wood thought, "Wouldn't it be great to get a band together and instead of advertising for a guitarist, advertise for a French horn player or cellist?" "There must be young people around that play those instruments and that like rock-'n'-roll," he reasoned. The first ELO album (1972) included string-drenched tracks such as "10538," which included Wood's Chinese cello. The second effort featured a classical rendition of Chuck Berry's classic, "Roll over Beethoven" with a violin trio.

The band slowly abandoned the combination of rock and roll and classical music for more hook-driven, orchestral ballads, which conquered arenas across the globe. By 1975, after Wood left and his colleague Jeff Lynne took over leadership, ELO hit the Top Ten with their fourth release, the polished *Face the Music,* and the rock ballad "Evil Woman." "I always write the lyrics *last*. They're not very deep," contended Lynne who wrote most of the songs. He never constructed the songs "for putting a message over." The group ceaselessly toured arenas with a 140-man crew, seven trucks and their own stage, lighting and sound gear. By the end of the decade, the Electric Light Orchestra racked up three Top-Five albums and sold millions of discs. By the end of the seventies, radio-friendly, art-pop snagged listeners and led them to immense stadiums, which resonated with art pop's full-blown, enveloping sound.

Rumours

The arena allowed Fleetwood Mac to attain mega-success with tales of excess in *Rumours.* During summer 1967, blues guitar hero Peter Green (b. Peter Greenbaum) and drummer Mick Fleetwood formed the band with guitarist Jeremy Spencer and bassist John McVie. When Green left the outfit in 1970, the group slowly abandoned their blues roots for a more folk-based sound.

In 1974 after a flurry of personnel changes, Fleetwood Mac stabilized with a new direction. In January, Mick Fleetwood hired guitarist Lindsey Buckingham who favored a more pop sensibility rather than the blues. "I was more interested in songs," he explained. "A 12-bar [blues] gets boring to me after the first couple of choruses." Buckingham brought his personal and musical partner Stephanie "Stevie" Nicks into the group.

Armed with a folk-based, sometimes acoustic sound and Nicks' distinctive vocals, the band assaulted the charts. In 1975, Fleetwood Mac hit number one with a self-named album, which sold 5 million copies. The album, wrote *Newsweek*, "carries no message but is infectiously easy to listen to and understand." In 1977, playing to arena crowds, the band bared their souls with tales of extravagance in *Rumours*. "Go Your Own Way" chronicled the breakup of the Nicks-Buckingham eight-year relationship; "Don't Stop" described keyboardist Christine McVie's separation from her husband bassist John McVie; "You Make Loving Fun" dealt with an affair of Christine's; Buckingham wrote "Second Hand News" about his new personal relationships after Nicks left him; and Stevie Nicks' "Gold Dust Woman" referred to the band's experience with cocaine. The album took nearly a year to record, explained Nicks, because they "were trying to speak to each other in a civil tone, while sitting in a tiny room listening to each other's songs about our shattered relationships." *Rumours*, capturing the era of excess, sold more than 45 million records.

Funk from Outer Space

During the mid-1970s, George Clinton covered funk with heavy metal glitter. Funk, the stripped-down gospel blues that featured an insistent rhythm, punchy horns, and repetitious, drum-like vocals, had been unveiled by James Brown. "I emphasized the beat, not the melody, understand?" explained Brown. "Heat the beat, and the rest'll turn sweat." "Funk," observed bassist William "Billy Bass" Nelson, "comes from James Brown. And James Brown got it from the blues."

Sly Stone (b. Sylvester Stewart) combined funk with rock and roll. As a child, Stewart moved with his family from Texas to San Francisco, where he sang in gospel groups and studied trumpet. During the flowering of hippiedom, he landed jobs as a disc jockey on station KDIA and as a producer for Autumn Records, where he mixed the psychedelic music of the Mojo Men and the Great Society, which included Grace Slick. In late 1966, Stewart formed the racially integrated Sly and the Family Stone with his brother Freddie on guitar; his sister Rosie, who added gospel-inflected vocals; trumpeter Cynthia Robinson; bass player Larry Graham, Jr., who had played with the Drifters, John Lee Hooker, and several gospel groups; and Jerry Martini on saxophone and Greg Errico on drums.

Sly and the Family Stone combined their rock and funk influences with a psychedelic sensibility to top the charts. Though flopping with their debut, the band hit with "Dance to the Music" (1967). The next year, Sly and the Family Stone topped the chart with "Everyday People." In 1969, the band delivered the number-two "Hot Fun in the Summertime" and the chart-topper "Thank You (Falettinme Be Mice Elf Agin)," and neared the Top Ten with the politically charged *Stand!*, which included "Don't Call Me Nigger, Whitey" [Title reproduced exactly from the original source]. "It was just a recognition of all the racial tensions that were happening," recalled Martini. In 1971, after an appearance at Woodstock, the group topped the chart with the funky *There's a Riot Goin' On* by appealing to both black and white audiences.

George Clinton took Sly's funk rock into the extravagant mid-1970s. In 1955, a fifteen-year-old Clinton started the Parliaments, a doo-wop group that performed on the streets of New Jersey. Eight years later on the urging of Clinton, who had landed a job as a staff writer for Berry Gordy, Jr.'s Jobete Music, the group relocated to Detroit,

George Clinton poster.

Mark Arminski.

where they recorded unreleased tracks for Motown. In 1967, amid the soul explosion, the Parliaments finally hit the Top Twenty with "(I Wanna) Testify."

On the road to promote the hit single, Clinton changed the direction of his band. The leader, forced to use the equipment of a rock band, bought Jimi Hendrix's *Are You Experienced?*, a Cream album, and Sly's *A Whole New Thing*. He gave them to guitarist Eddie Hazel, and bassist Billy Nelson. After fusing hard-rock sounds to their funky base, Clinton created a stage show similar to the onstage antics of fellow Detroiters Iggy and the Stooges. "It was like the Stooges!" Clinton remembered. "I had a head with a dick shaved onto it right down the middle with a star on one side and a moon on the other and bald all around that. I was crawling all around on the floor sticking my tongue out. We were James Brown on acid."

Clinton solidified the funky rock sound of his band. Threatened with a lawsuit over the name Parliament, he renamed the group Funkadelic and added ex–James Brown sidemen such as bass player William "Bootsy" Collins, trombonist Fred Wesley, and saxophonist Maceo Parker. In addition, "We had doo-wop, Motown, Jimi Hendrix, rock-'n'-roll white groups," he recalled. By the mid-1970s, when he regained the right to the Parliament name, Clinton had created a hard funk-rock amalgam with Parliament and, to some extent, with Funkadelic, which he continued as a more rock-oriented outfit.

In tune with the times, Clinton changed his stage image. "I knew the psychedelic thing was all but gone," he reasoned, "so I went with glitter." Touring to promote his breakthrough *Mothership Connection* (1976), Clinton and his band appeared Bowie-like, garbed in leather spacesuits, Gogglelike sunglasses, and jewel-studded boots. He hired Jules Fisher, who had designed overblown stage sets for Bowie and Kiss, to create a huge spaceship that descended to the stage from a denim cap. "Black [audiences] have never experienced a really loud group, let alone all these theatrics," enthused Clinton. "You cannot make sense and be funky." Several years earlier, he already had instructed his listeners to "Free Your Mind and Your Ass Will Follow." The funk-rock master had accurately gauged the rock audience, who bought millions of Top-Twenty Parliament albums such as *Mothership Connection* (1975) and *Funkentelechy vs. the Placebo Syndrome* (1977).

Disco

Disco, based upon a simplified version of George Clinton's funk with flourishes of sweet-soul music, epitomized the excessive, self-absorbed seventies. It started in New York City at African-American, Latin, and gay all-night clubs such as the Sanctuary, the Loft, and the Gallery, where disc jockeys spun unrelenting, funky, pounding beats mixed with the orchestrated soul sounds of Philadelphia. Disc spinners such as Francis Grosso, David Mancuso, and Nicky Siano carefully sequenced records to bring dancers to a fever pitch. "Dancing at the Loft was like riding waves of music, being carried along as one song after another built relentlessly to a brilliant crest and broke," recalled one scenester. To further increase the intensity on the dance floor, DJs such as Walter Gibbons remixed songs to emphasize the heavy beat and played two of the same record simultaneously to achieve a wobbly sound.

The resident disc jockeys hoped to create an underground community centered around the music. "I view the whole scene as a spiritual congregation," DJ David Rodriguez observed. "You've got hundreds of people in a room, and their bond is the music."

Though broad in appeal, disco initially became associated with gay clubs in New York City and the gay liberation movement. By the mid-1970s, the music represented "a symbolic call for gays to come out of the closet and dance with each other," explained Nat Freedland of Fantasy Records. It allowed gays, who many times owned prominent New York discos and worked as the disc jockeys and lighting crews, to demonstrate their solidarity through music.

Gays danced to a persistent beat. Disco incorporated the antiseptic, rock-steady, electronic beat of European synthesizer groups such as Kraftwerk, who, according to group founder Ralf Hutter, created a "rhythmically more primitive" and "industrial music" based on the sterile environment in Dusseldorf, Germany. Rather than the funk emphasis on the first beat of a four-bar measure (**1**-2-3-4) or the two-beat rhythm of most rock (1-**2**-3-**4**), disco stressed every beat with equal weight (**1**-**2**-**3**-**4**) by incorporating insistent, thumping bass lines. Many times, the pounding beat steamrolled along at 125 beats per minute. Disc jockeys called it "four to the floor." Gloria Gaynor, one of the first disco recording stars, disclosed the genesis of the disco beat. "It was kind of hard for white people to get into R&B music because the beat is so sophisticated and hard for the kind of dancing that white people are used to doing," she explained. "This clearly defined beat that is so apparent in disco music now makes it easier [for them] to learn to do our kind of dancing."

Unlike the guitar-driven rock of the sixties, disco sometimes used synthesizers or electric pianos and prominently featured lavish, orchestrated productions similar to the sweet-soul sound. Soaring, often reverberated vocals further distinguished disco from hard rock.

The highly orchestrated and syncopated disco, spun by DJs rather than performed by live rock musicians, allowed the participants to assume primary importance. "A few years ago, I went into clubs, and I realized people needed mood music," remarked Neil Bogart, then president of Casablanca Records, the label that released many disco singles. "They were tired of guitarists playing to their amplifiers. *They* wanted to be the stars." "It's like an adult Disney World. We really give people a chance to get off on their fantasies," explained Steve Rubell, co-owner of one of the premier discos, Studio 54 in New York City. "I think the theater atmosphere has a lot to do with it. Everybody secretly likes to be on stage, and here we give them a huge space to do it all on." The audience-focused disco became a perfect music for many self-obsessed baby boomers.

During the mid- to late seventies, disco emerged from the New York gay underground into the mainstream. Twelve-inch singles especially made for disco, first popularized in late 1974. "Never Can Say Goodbye" by Gloria Gaynor, reached the Top Ten. A few months later, the acknowledged queen of disco, Donna Summer (Gaines), almost topped the pop chart with the suggestive "Love to Love You Baby," which was punctuated by Summer's seductive sighs and groans. The same year, Van McCoy and the Soul City Symphony topped the chart with "The Hustle," which inspired a line dance of the same name. In 1975, KC and the Sunshine Band, formed by Harry Casey and Richard Finch, hit the number-one slot on the singles chart with "Get Down Tonight" and "That's the Way (I Like It)," and the next year followed with the smash "(Shake, Shake, Shake) Shake Your Booty."

The Village People, named after a gay enclave in Greenwich Village in New York City, brought disco to the masses with a humorous portrayal of gay culture. The group consisted of a costumed band of actors and singers portraying stereotypes of the rugged American male. The band, manufactured by French producer Jacques Morali, hit the chart in 1978 with the million-selling anthems "Macho Man" and "Y.M.C.A." The albums that contained the two songs each sold more than 33 million copies.

Even established artists turned to disco. In 1978, blues shouter Rod Stewart who lent his vocals to the Faces and the Jeff Beck Band unabashedly released the disco tune "Da Ya Think I'm Sexy?" which reached number one. The next year, Beatle Paul McCartney hit the Top Five with the disco-based "Goodnight Tonight." By 1980, blues bad boys, the Rolling Stones, released the disco-influenced "Emotional Rescue." In 1978, *Billboard* categorized more than 20 percent of songs on the singles chart as disco. "Disco will be the major force in the music marketplace for some time," predicted Nat Freedland of Fantasy Records.

Near the end of the decade, disco became a national craze at least partially due to the movie *Saturday Night Fever*. In mid-December 1977, producer Robert Stigwood, owner of RSO records, released the movie, which showed the transformation of a poor, trouble-ridden, Italian teenager, played by John Travolta, into a white-suited disco star. He built the soundtrack of the film around songs written and performed by one of his groups, the Bee Gees, who scored with three number-one singles such as "Stayin' Alive." By 1978, the record executive had achieved a major success. The film, which cost $3.4 million to make, eventually grossed more than $237 million, and the soundtrack sold more than 20 million copies worldwide.

Discomania spread across the country in the wake of *Saturday Night Fever*. In New York, more than 1,000 discos opened their doors for business. The Holiday Inn motel chain added more than thirty-five discos on its premises. A lavish disco even opened in the small town of Fennimore, Wisconsin (population: 1,900). High school students went to disco proms and disco roller-skating rinks. One disco in Dubuque, Iowa, provided a disco wedding service complete with smoke-machine effects. Throughout the country in 1978, more than 36 million Americans danced on the floors of 20,000 discos.

The disco subculture encapsulated the narcissism of the mid- and late 1970s. Studio 54, once the baroque Fortune Gallo Opera House and later a CBS studio, featured theatrical lighting, flashing strobes, and more than 450 special effects, including plastic snowfalls and 85-foot backdrops. Zorine's in Chicago offered members rooms of mirrors, twisting staircases, balconies, and secret nooks for sexual encounters. In Los Angeles, Dillion's offered a four-floor pleasure dome. Pisces in Washington, D.C., spotlighted old movie sets, a 1,000-gallon, shark-filled aquarium, and exotic flora. Richard Himmel, a partner in Zorine's, described the discos as "pure escapism."

The clothing of the dancers reflected glittery opulence and a freewheeling attitude toward sex. Men sported gold chains, gold rings, patent leather platform shoes, tight Italian-style pants, and unbuttoned shiny satin shirts. Women wore low-cut, backless, sequined gowns, spiked heels, long gold necklaces, and gold lamé gloves. "The new boogie bunch dress up for the occasion—with shoulders, backs, breasts, and midriffs tending to be nearly bare," observed *Time*. In a disco, where the participants became the stars, remarked fashion photographer Francesco Scavullo, "the dress becomes your dancing partner."

The dances, notably Le Freak, which was popularized by a 1978 number-one song of the same name by premier disco group Chic, exhibited an unrestrained sexuality. The exotic dance consisted of two people spreading their legs, bending backward, and thrusting their pelvises against each other in time to the music. Disco, reasoned Nile Rodgers, who cowrote "Le Freak," "was the most hedonistic music I had ever heard in my life. It was really all about Me! Me! Me! Me!"

The freewheeling disco culture involved the use of drugs, especially cocaine. When asked about drug use at Studio 54, co-owner Steve Rubell replied, "We look the other way. Anyway, so many people are taking pills these days how do I know if it's an aspirin or something else?" As one of its special effects, Rubell's club displayed a man in the moon with a spoon uplifted to his nose.

The discos, trading in excess, lured celebrities to their doors. Studio 54 hired socialite Carmen D'Alessio to entice her rich and famous friends to the club. "It's all the celebrities," explained Rubell. "You have to have them first. They draw business in." Among his guests, he catered to Cher, actress Farrah Fawcett, actor Warren Beatty, comedian/moviemaker Woody Allen, and David Bowie. Pisces in Washington, D.C., attracted stars such as Elizabeth Taylor and actor Gregory Peck. In Los Angeles, Pip's enticed actors Paul Newman, Peter Falk, and Tony Curtis as well as singers Dean Martin and Frank Sinatra. "Studio 54 was like going to a movie," remembered on club goer. "It was all about who was there."

By the end of the decade, disco became a lucrative business. Besides discothèques and record sales, it involved products such as spandex pants, magazines such as *Discothekin'*, disco dresses slit to expose the thighs, more than 200 disco radio stations from Los Angeles to Miami, and undersized disco purses. Discos such as Studio 54 netted yearly profits of millions. "The profits are astronomical," enthused Steve Rubell. "Only the Mafia does better." By 1979, disco, a mirror for the excesses of the rock generation, was an industry that generated $5 billion in gross revenues.

Corporate Rock

The record business, buttressed by the increasing number of materialistic, disco-crazed baby boomers, consolidated into a few highly profitable international companies, which dominated the marketplace. During the 1950s, American business in general started to consolidate. By 1955, the fifty largest corporations controlled 27 percent of the national market and sold more than $86 billion of manufactured goods, a figure equal to more than one-fourth of the gross national product. The merger trend to persisted until by 1970 the market share of the 600 largest companies increased to 75 percent, and the share held by the top 200 corporations rose to more than 60 percent. The 102 giants on top of the corporate pyramid, holding assets of $1 billion or more, controlled 48 percent of the U.S. market and made 53 percent of the profits.

The record industry followed the pattern of consolidation. Though influenced by a number of viable independent companies such as Chess and Sun during the 1950s, by 1973 the record business was almost completely controlled by seven majors: CBS, Capitol, MCA, Polygram, RCA, A&M, and Warner Communications. The top four companies accounted for more than 52 percent of all record and tape sales, and the leading two—CBS and Warner-Elektra/Asylum-Atlantic—sold 38 percent of the total product manufactured by the industry.

These companies, as with other American conglomerates during the decade, had interests in fields other than music. MCA owned Universal Films, various television stations, Arlington and Mount Vernon cemeteries, a bank in Colorado, and the Spencer Gifts novelty chain. RCA, the twentieth largest corporation in the country, operated NBC television and radio and owned the Hertz Rent-A-Car company, Banquet Foods, the Cushman and Wakefield real estate firm, and Random House and Alfred Knopf publishers. It also served as a prime defense contractor.

These giant corporations built rock and roll, which by 1975 accounted for 80 percent of all record sales, into a multibillion-dollar enterprise. In 1955, before Elvis hit the scene, record companies sold $277 million worth of product. By 1973, in the United States alone, the industry grossed $2 billion, which surpassed the gross revenues of Broadway ($36 million), professional sports ($540 million), the film industry ($1.3 billion), and network television ($1 billion). By 1978, the record industry sold more than $4 billion in records and cassette tapes.

Many companies posted healthy profits. In the summer quarter of 1978, MCA made a profit of more than $5.5 million, CBS cleared $48.5 million, and Warner netted $19.8 million. "Records are where the big money is in the entertainment business these days," observed *Forbes* in July 1978.

The vast sums of money came from the baby-boom generation, which by the late seventies had all reached record-buying age. Rather than accounting for sales in the thousands, the more than 78 million boomers who had been born between 1946 and 1964 purchased millions of copies of a title. In 1978, more than a hundred records went platinum or sold more than a million, and many sold in excess of 3 million. "We all want to be double platinum, triple platinum, quadruple platinum. We're all in this platinum derby," enthused Jerry Moss, co-founder of A&M records with Herb Alpert of Tijuana Brass fame. "It may be time to move to titanium," suggested *Fortune* magazine in 1979.

Profits came from around the world. In 1973, record companies sold more than $555 million worth of records and tapes in Japan; $454 million in West Germany; $441 million in the Soviet Union; $384 million in the United Kingdom, controlled largely by the British Electrical Manufacturing Industries (EMI); and even $16 million in Poland. By the end of the decade, the corporate rock establishment had penetrated nearly every world market to amass excessive profits in an excessive age.

Some seventies rock stars eagerly embraced the international music business. Gene Simmons of Kiss equated a "successful rock-and-roll band" with "a well-oiled machine. It's a good business." "This is not an ivory-tower age," echoed Greg Geller, Columbia Records talent scout. "There's some recognition that we're involved in commerce." For Alice Cooper, "The idea all along was to make $1 million. Otherwise the struggle wouldn't have been worth it . . . I am the most American rock act. I have American ideals. I love money."

Many rock stars realized their financial goals. In 1973, *Forbes* estimated that at least fifty rock superstars earned between $2 million and $6 million a year, with each musician accumulating from three to seven times more than the highest-paid executive in the United States.

Many successful 1970s stars invested their earnings. The Bee Gees, one of the largest draws of the 1970s, established their own merchandising company, which sold "things like nice T-shirts," according to Barry Gibb, who with his twin brothers Maurice and Robin started the band. "We deal in jewelry but only real gold plate. We're doing a little electronic piano with Mattel Toys that'll be available soon." They also marketed "a cute Andy Gibb doll" to promote the career of their younger brother. Alice Cooper financed films such as *Funny Lady* and *Shampoo* for tax shelters and invested in art, antiques, and tax-free municipal bonds. Ted Nugent, the guitarist who scaled the charts during the 1970s with a heavy metal sound and Neanderthal costumes, owned a mink farm and a trout operation. Said Bob Weed, Nugent's financial manager, "all of this fits in with Ted's plan for acquiring land. Sure, we're involved in some oil and gas-lease tax shelters, but when I tell him about property, that's something he understands." Rod Stewart, the blues singer turned disco star, adopted a similar investment strategy. "I've always said that Rod isn't a rock star. He's a growth industry," remarked Billy Gaff, Stewart's manager. "Rod is essentially very conservative. He doesn't invest in football clubs or crazy movie- or record-financing schemes. The tax shelter scams are all a little scary, so we stick to art and real estate." By the end of the decade, rock and roll had become a big business dominated by millionaires who provided extravagant entertainment to self-absorbed baby boomers. Soon it would be challenged by the rebellious music of a new generation.

Chapter 16
Punk Rock

"You don't sing about love to people on the dole."
—Johnny Rotten, 1977

On November 28, 1976, the *London Times* declared, "Punk rock is the generic term for the latest musical garbage bred by our troubled culture. It features screaming, venomous, threatening rock sounds." The next month, Bernard Brook Partridge, a member of the Greater London Council, articulated the sentiments of the establishment toward punk rock, when he rhetorically asked, "What is punk music? It's disgusting, degrading, ghastly, sleazy, prurient, voyeuristic and nauseating." A few months later, Anthony Burgess, author of the futuristic *A Clockwork Orange*, dismissed punk rock as "caged simian gibber," and "British youth, like American and French and Upper Slobovian youth, needs a good kick in the pants and a bit of solid education," he sniffed.

A new generation of rock-and-rollers elicited this outrage. Punk originated with a small group of literary, Beat-influenced musicians in their twenties such as Patti Smith and Richard Hell, who congregated in New York City's seedy Bowery. Within a year, the pained posture of an artistic punk had been transformed into an anarchic, sometimes political rage by enraged British teens who felt that they had nothing to lose. Opposed to the excessive seventies corporate rock, they created a minimalistic, angry music that threatened their materialistic elders. In 1976, a new generation had arisen to lay claim to a rebellious rock-and-roll heritage.

New York Punk

CBGB's, a small bar in the Bowery section of New York City, served as the birthplace of punk rock. Established in December 1973 by ex–U.S. Marine Sergeant Hilly Kristal, the bar first catered to Bowery bums. "When I first opened it as Hilly's on the Bowery," recalled the proprietor, "I ran it for a while as a derelict bar, and bums would be lining up at eight in the morning when I opened the doors." After a few months, Kristal changed the name of his bar to CBGB-OMFUG, which stood for "country, bluegrass, blues, and other music for uplifting gourmandizers."

Bands such as Television played regularly at CBGB's. Formed in late 1973, the band drew inspiration from the New York avant-garde of Andy Warhol, the Velvet Underground, the New York Dolls, Iggy Pop and the free-jazz improvisations of John Coltrane and Albert Ayler. Television originally included bassist Richard Hell (b. Richard Meyers), who had traveled to New York City to become a real writer like his French symbolist and surrealist heroes; guitarist Richard Lloyd; drummer Billy Ficca; and vocalist-guitarist Tom Verlaine (b. Tom Miller), who renamed himself after the French symbolist poet. After debuting at the New York Townhouse Theater, the group convinced Andy Warhol associate Terry Ork to manage them. Through the efforts of Ork in early 1974, the group landed a permanent job at CBGB's.

Terry Ork, persuading his artist friends to hear Television, created an avant-garde scene at CBGB's. "He brought in a lot of theater and poetry people from this area, since he lived around here and knew them all," remembered Hilly Kristal. "He was very excited about the whole thing, and he excited me about it ... the whole scene wouldn't have happened without him."

David Byrne, Tina Weymouth, and Chris Franz—fellow students at the Rhode Island School of Design—traveled to New York and in late 1974 began to play informally together as the Talking Heads, a name found in an issue of *TV Guide*. They reacted against the corporate art rock of Emerson, Lake and Palmer who took "something from a standard high art and try to make it palatable for the masses," reminisced vocalist David Byrne. The Talking Heads attempted to reflect "a proletarian view of art" without the obsession with technical virtuosity. Living in an apartment only a few blocks from CBGB's, the Talking Heads auditioned for Hilly Kristal with their stripped-down music and in June 1975 performed at the bar. In 1977, the group invited keyboardist Jerry Harrison to join them and released their debut album, which included the eccentric minor hit "Psycho Killer." "The Heads were great and Television were great, but on a sort of intellectual level," recalled Kristal. "The Heads were so quirky and weird that they set much of the stylistic tone. Not punk, but a transition period."

Patti Smith brought national attention to the literary, avant-garde rock that CBGB's featured. The daughter of a New Jersey factory worker, Smith herself worked in a factory until moving to New York City. Once in town, she met photographer Robert Mapplethorpe and playwright Sam Shepard and started to write a William Burroughs–Arthur Rimbaud style of poetry. She regularly read her work at the Mercer Arts Center and published two books of poetry, *Witt* and *Seventh Heaven*.

Patti Smith in concert.

Cameron Garrett.

A diehard fan of Jimi Hendrix, Bob Dylan, and Jim Morrison and a former writer for the rock magazine *Creem* who wanted to "keep alive the rock 'n' roll traditions," Patti Smith combined her poetry with rock music. In early 1971, she read her poems at St. Mark's Church in New York, accompanied by guitarist/rock writer Lenny Kaye, who had assembled the sixties' proto-punk record compilations, *Nuggets*. "I had this little poem called 'Ballad of a Bad Boy,' which ends in a stock car crash," she related. "And I was thinking that it would be really cool not only to deliver this emotionally, but to illustrate this car crash sonically, with feedback or some Hendrix style of guitar playing." Smith slowly assembled a rock band.

By March 1974, she had invited pianist Richard Sohl to help Kaye provide an improvisational rock backdrop to her readings. "Of course it was still more of an art thing," Kaye pointed out. "It wasn't even a club circuit. We played with Television." Three months later, Smith recorded the independently produced single "Hey Joe/Piss Factory," which convinced Sire Records to sign the fledgling group. After club dates on the West Coast, Smith added guitarist Ivan Kral and drummer Jay Dee Daugherty to form the Patti Smith Group. "As soon as we [added Kral and Daugherty], we became more of a rock band," observed Lenny Kaye.

In early 1975, the Patti Smith Group brought attention to the emerging scene at CBGB's during a stint at the club. "What happened was that [as] we played there more and more people came down," recalled Lenny Kaye. "CBGB's became not only a place for them to come and check us out, but it sort of got into the New York consciousness." Kristal added that "Patti's stay here was one of the most memorable seven-week periods the club ever had. Clive Davis [of Arista Records, which signed Smith in January 1975] came a number of times, and a lot of the record people came, but mostly it was newspapers and a lot of people on the periphery of theater and the arts. Those first dates put us on the map." A few months later, the Patti Smith Group released their debut *Horses*, produced by former Velvet Underground leader John Cale, which combined rock history with avant-garde poetry in songs such as "Gloria" and the William Burroughs–inspired "Land of a Thousand Dances." The 1976 follow-up *Radio Ethiopia* featured hard-driving improvisational numbers such as "Pumping (My Heart)" and "Ask the Angels."

Like other New York punks, the poet adopted the Beat-inspired, populist stance of the Sixties. She admired "all the great sixties guys" who had "a political consciousness." With her music, Smith was "determined to make us kids, us fuck-ups, us ones who could never get a degree in college, whatever, have a family, or do regular stuff, prove that there's a place for us." Neither a hippie nor a punk, Smith later "thought one could call us a sacrificial bridge between the two. We anticipated the future and sort of encapsulated the past."

Smith hoped that her music and poetry would serve as a wake-up call for her generation. Like the Revolutionary rebel Paul Revere, she wanted "to take up arms, the arms of our generation, the electric guitar and the microphone." "CBGB was the ideal place to sound a clarion call," she added. "It was a club on the street of the downtrodden that drew a strange breed who welcomed artists yet unsung."

Richard Hell developed an image for the emerging artistic, do-it-yourself New York rock scene. As a member of Television, Hell created a minimalist, plebeian image that characterized punk rock and contrasted starkly with the glittery image of David Bowie. He cut his hair in a short, spiky style and wore ripped T-shirts. "My look was a sort of a strategy," explained the bassist. "I wanted it to look like do-it-yourself. Everything we were doing…had that element, from having ripped up clothes to not knowing how to play instruments. The whole thing was partly a reaction to the hippie stadium music." "I wanted the way we looked to be as expressive as the material on the stage," he continued. "It was all of a piece. The ripped T-shirts meant that I don't give a fuck about stardom and all that or glamour and going to rock shows to see someone pretend to be perfect. The people wanted to see someone they could identify with. It was saying, 'You could be here, too.'"

Richard Hell's empowering do-it-yourself attitude surfaced in his songs. He delivered the New York punk anthem "Blank Generation," which he wrote in 1975 and recorded two years later with the Voidoids after leaving Television. "To me, 'blank' is a line where you can fill in anything. It's positive," he explained. "It's the idea that you have the option of making yourself anything you want, filling in the blank. And that's something that provides a uniquely powerful sense to this generation."

The Ramones added a buzz-saw guitar attack and a fifties' sensibility to the populist stance and ripped T-shirt fashion of Richard Hell to complete the transition from the minimalist avant-garde to an unadulterated punk rock. Banding together after playing at a private party in late 1974, Johnny Cummings, Dee Dee Colvin, Jeffrey ("Joey") Hyman, and Tommy Erdelyi adopted the surname Ramone. They first performed in public at CBGB's, appearing in black-leather motorcycle jackets, black-pegged pants, torn jeans, and ripped T-shirts to emulate their rockabilly idols such as Elvis and Eddie Cochran.

The Ramones cared little for the artistic avant-garde. On one European tour with the Talking Heads, remembered then-manager Danny Fields, "the Ramones were like Archie Bunker at the Vatican. They were not amused. They hated the food and just looked for hamburgers everywhere." On a Talking Heads–planned side trip to Stonehenge, the Ramones refused to leave the bus. "It's really nothing to see," explained Dee Dee. "It's not like going to see a castle."

The proletarian Ramones delivered a thrashing sound borrowed from the New York Dolls. "What really kicked it off was seeing the New York Dolls in clubs around Manhattan," recalled Dee Dee Ramone. "It was so inspiring to see a bunch of young

Joey Ramone.
Cameron Garrett.

people playing rock-and-roll that we wanted to do it, too." Tommy added that "subconsciously it struck me, if there's going to be a new direction in music, it's not going to be through virtuosity."

Unlike the more expansive, poetic art groups, which looked to literary and free-jazz sources for inspiration, the Ramones perfected hyper-charged, two-minute punk anthems derived from bubblegum roots of sugary pop bands such as the Bay City Rollers. They sped through eight-song, seventeen-minute sets at CBGB's without a break In 1976 on their first self-titled LP, the band zoomed through three-chord ditties such as "Blitzkrieg Bop," "Beat on the Brat," and "Now I Wanna Sniff Some Glue" at breakneck speed. After attending a Ramones concert, writer Norman Mailer raved that "for me it was like I was an old car and I was being taken out for a ride at 100 miles an hour."

The Ramones shared a common theme with the artists bands at CBGBs. "Even though the Ramones played hard and raunchy," explained Tommy Ramone, "there were a lot of similarities: the minimalism." "Rock-'n'-roll was a hodgepodge of Pink Floyd and ELP and all this crap," related Joey Ramone who voiced the prevailing anticorporate rock attitude of most New York bands. "What we did was we stripped it right down to the bone and we disassembled it and reassembled it and put all the excitement and fun and spirit, raw energy and raw emotion and guts and attitude back into it."

In mid-1975, CBGB's Rock Festival Showcase Auditions brought international attention to the emerging New York punk scene. Featuring the Ramones, the Talking Heads, and Television, the festival attracted major U.S. and British music and mainstream journalists. "The coverage of the festival started making things happen," maintained Hilly Kristal. "The record companies started coming down, mainly Sire Records, but also others."

The New York scene, which coalesced around CBGBs, soon received a name. In January 1976, writer Legs McNeil launched *Punk* magazine with John Holmstrom as editor and cartoonist. "I came up with the name 'punk,'" bubbled Legs McNeil. The magazine gave it "visual definition," added Holmstrom. "*Punk* was like the print version of the Ramones." The *New York Rocker*, established a few months after *Punk* by Alan Betrock, helped promote the New York punk explosion.

Promoted by the press, the Ramones unveiled their thrashing attack in England. In 1976, they released a British version of their debut, which gave English punks direction. "I heard the Ramones' first record and I thought that it was fucking brilliant," remembered Billy Idol, who started the British punk band Generation X and was a member of the Bromley Contingent that followed the Sex Pistols. "Every song was under two minutes and it was like revolution! We were playing normal speed until we heard the Ramones, and because of them, [we] revved everything up. Everybody did."

On July 4, 1976, the Ramones brought their live show to British youths. They celebrated the U.S. Bicentennial by performing in London at the Roundhouse, which, contended Hilly Kristal, "started the whole thing going. All the other groups saw them and realized they could do it too." Joey Ramone felt that "we were responsible for the whole punk revolution. We signed to Sire in 1975 and our first album came out in 1976." "That's sort of what inspired the English [punk] bands to start up," he boasted. Though somewhat overstating his influence, Joey and the other Ramones mirrored and, to some extent, shaped the music that exploded from Britain later the same year.

The Sex Pistols and British Punk

British youths, confronting an uncertain future, infused New York punk with a venomous anger. Between 1974 and 1977, unemployment in Britain shot up from less than 3 percent to more than 6 percent. In 1975, the rate of inflation ran rampant at a staggering 24.2 percent and hovered at more than 15 percent for the next two years. To cope with the crisis, a beleaguered British government suspended wage increases and in 1976, borrowed L3.6 billion from the International Monetary Fund.

The economic instability especially affected British youths who in 1977 faced an unemployment rate of 36 percent. "It's not much fun to be young today. If you think otherwise, take a look at yesterday's jobless figures," instructed the *Daily Mirror* on June 22, 1977. "Is it any wonder if the youngsters feel disillusioned and betrayed? A brave new generation of talent and purpose is turning sour before our very eyes."

Guided by manager Malcolm McLaren, the Sex Pistols combined the desperate rage of unemployed British teens, the do-it-yourself attitude of the New York avant-garde, and the buzz-saw guitar attack of the Ramones to create British punk. The transition from a literary New York scene to an explosive, politically charged British punk began in early 1975, when clothing-store owner McLaren traveled to New York City to manage the fashion-conscious New York Dolls. Returning six months later when the Dolls disbanded, McLaren agreed to manage the Swankers, a group of lower-class London schoolmates, which consisted of Paul Cook, Steve Jones, and Wally Nightingale, who were joined by Glen Matlock, assistant clerk in McLaren's shop, called Sex. He suggested the group move Jones to guitar and dispense with Nightingale, who appeared too clean-cut.

As a lead singer, McLaren proposed Richard Hell, who in 1975 played with ex–New York Doll Johnny Thunders in the Heartbreakers and who had impressed the store owner during his brief stay in the States. "I just thought Richard Hell was incredible," enthused McLaren. "Here was a guy all deconstructed, torn down, looking like he just crawled out of a drain hole, looking like he was covered in slime, looking like he hadn't slept in years, looking like he hadn't washed in years, and looking like no one gave a fuck about him. And looking like he didn't give a fuck about you!" He wanted to import "the image of this distressed, strange thing called Richard Hell. And this phrase, 'the blank generation.'"

Confronted with opposition from the Swankers over an American addition to the band and having no money for a plane ticket for Hell, McLaren asked John Lydon, nicknamed Rotten, to come to a pub near the manager's shop. In August 1975, wearing an "I Hate Pink Floyd" T-shirt, a green-haired Lydon successfully auditioned for the band by singing along to Alice Cooper's "School's Out," which played on the jukebox. "It really didn't take off "till John got involved," remarked bassist Matlock. "We knew what we wanted, but we didn't have the gift of gab. John did. He put his words out on sort of a gut-level sensibility."

Johnny Rotten fit the band's image better than Richard Hell because of his age. In 1976, Richard Hell and Tom Verlaine were 27, Patti Smith was 30, Johnny Ramone was 25, and Joey Ramone was 24. Like their fellow British punks, the Swankers had barely finished school: Johnny Rotten, Glen Matlock, and Paul Cook were 20, and Steve Jones had just turned 21.

Finding themselves in the dire financial situation of most British teens, the Swankers had few options other than forming a band. Johnny Rotten characterized the group as "a collection of extremely bored people. I suppose we'd come together out of desperation. There was no hope as far as any of us were concerned. This was our common bond.... There was no way out, [and] quite literally no."

By 1975, Malcolm McLaren had the ingredients for his new rock-and-roll band. "I was taking the nuances of Richard Hell, the faggy pop side of the New York Dolls, the politics of boredom and mashing it altogether to make a statement," he related. The manager renamed the band the Sex Pistols: "It came about by the idea of a pistol, a pinup, a young thing, a better-looking assassin—a sex pistol," he explained.

The Sex Pistols combined the energy of the New York Dolls, Iggy Pop, and the Ramones for an aggressive, pumping sound. Playing their first show in November 1975 at St. Martin's School of Art in London, the group featured a frenzied attack anchored by guitarist Steve Jones. "I'd wake up in the morning," related Jones, "and play along with an Iggy Pop record and the New York Dolls' first album. I would listen to them over and over again and play guitar to them." Johnny Rotten agreed that "*Funhouse* by Iggy and the Stooges was my kind of music. Our sound was pretty damn close to that."

Besides adopting the sound of American punk, the Sex Pistols created an onstage image that at least partly derived from the Stooges and New York punks. Like Iggy Pop, they taunted, shouted, and spat at the audience, blurring the distinction between the artist and the fan. Band members appeared in ripped, graffitied shirts and pants, black boots, and leather jackets that flashed with metal studs and zippers. Like Richard Hell, they cut their hair in a short, spiky style. To reinforce their image, in February 1977, the band fired bass player Glen Matlock because of his personality clash with Rotten and replaced him with Sid Vicious (b. John Ritchie) who, like Iggy, mutilated himself onstage with broken beer bottles.

The rebellious band offered their furious music to disenfranchised youth. "The millionaire groups were singing about love and their own hang-ups," sneered Rotten. "That's stupid. You don't sing about love to people on the dole." "Groups like the Who and the Stones are revolting," he insisted. "They have nothing to offer the kids anymore."

The Sex Pistols even rejected their arty New York predecessors who at least on some level provided them with inspiration. A day after Patti Smith played the Roundhouse in London, the Sex Pistols performed in a small club on Oxford Street. "Before they even play the first song," remembered Jay Dee Daugherty of the Patti Smith Group, "John Rotten says, 'Did anyone go to the Roundhouse the other night and see the hippie [Patti Smith] shaking the tambourine? Horses, horses, HORSESHIT.'"

The Sex Pistols substituted an angry anarchism for the poetic leanings of the New York avant-garde and the theatrical excess of seventies' superstars. In late 1976, they recorded their first single, "Anarchy in the U.K.," which warned of impending chaos in Britain. The band next blasted royalty in "God Save the Queen," releasing the single to coincide with Queen Elizabeth's Silver Jubilee in June. The Sex Pistols followed with other songs such as their adaptation of Richard Hell's "Blank Generation" called "Pretty Vacant" and "Holidays in the Sun," which described the hopeless plight of many British youths. "There'll always be something to fight—apathy's the main

John Lydon a.k.a. Johnny Rotten of the Sex Pistols.

Cameron Garrett.

thing," asserted Rotten. "The Pistols are presenting one alternative to apathy and if you don't like it, that's just too bad. Anarchy is self-rule and that's better than anything else." Rotten later observed that "the Pistols projected that anger, that rock-bottom working-class hate."

An outraged, threatened establishment aimed a barrage of criticism at the anarchistic Sex Pistols, reminiscent of the outcries against Elvis Presley in 1956. On April 10, 1976, the British music paper *Melody Maker* told its readers that "the Sex Pistols do as much for music as World War II did for the cause of peace." A vicar of the Anglican Church, his face muscles tightened and his head raised high, planted himself outside a club, where the Sex Pistols were scheduled to play, and warned concertgoers: "Keep out of there! They're the devil's children." Almost every local government in Britain banned the Pistols, publications refused to print ads publicizing the band, and in June 1977, a month after the release of "God Save the Queen," royalists attacked both Johnny Rotten and Paul Cook with razors, knives, and iron pipes.

The record industry offered little help to the Sex Pistols. EMI first signed the band for a £40,000 advance. After packers in the record plant refused to handle "Anarchy in the U.K.," and drunken band members had been prodded into using profanities on the live BBC TV broadcast of the Bill Grundy-hosted *Today* show, the company criticized the Pistols for their aggressive behavior and terminated the band's contract. In a ceremony outside Buckingham Palace on March 10, 1977, A&M Records signed the Sex Pistols but six days later, terminated the agreement. Two months later, Virgin Records offered a deal to the band and in October released the British version of *Never Mind the Bollocks—Here's the Sex Pistols*. The police promptly descended on record shops, which displayed the discs, and arrested shopkeepers on the grounds of obscenity until a month later, when a British court reluctantly ruled in favor of the Sex Pistols.

Despite opposition, the Sex Pistols' records topped the charts. "God Save the Queen," even though banned by British radio, sold 150,000 copies in five days and shot to the number-two spot on the chart. "Pretty Vacant" hit the number-six slot, and "Holiday in the Sun" reached number eight. In November 1977, the band's first and only studio album topped the British chart.

As well as a new rock sound, the Sex Pistols created an alternative do-it-yourself culture for British youths. Carefully cultivated by manager and fashion-monger Malcolm McLaren, they wore clothes that appeared disheveled, dirty, and menacing. "We'd take brand new T-shirts, make them look old, stamp on them, throw them around in the garden … cut them up, dye them the grungiest colors so they went from being clean white to dirty gray," remembered McLaren. They stenciled such slogans as "Destroy" and "Anarchy" in bold letters on the refashioned shirts. Within months, McLaren saw his antifashion statement, borrowed in part from New York punks, spread to British teens, who sported ripped T-shirts with stenciled slogans, spray-painted pants, studded leather, and spiked hair. "They wear with snarling pride the marks of the downtrodden," wrote Anthony Burgess about British teens in 1977. "Hair is cropped because long hair holds lice. Clothes are not patched, since patching denotes skill and a seedy desire for respectability; their gaping holes are held together with safety pins."

McLaren contacted the politically minded Jamie Reid, a friend from his days at Croydon Art College, to create posters and record-cover art for the Sex Pistols that provided punk culture with a graphic style. Much like the swirling, psychedelic poster art had reflected the acid rock of hippiedom, Reid's cut-and-paste, ransom-note style captured the threatening anger of British punk. "The Pistols were just the perfect marriage between the images I was creating and the music," remembered Reid. "Because we had no money, I was cutting up newspapers and doing collage. It was from there that the look for punk came." An outgrowth of twentieth-century collage agit-prop art, including early Russian Revolutionary artists such as Kazimir Malevich, Vladimir Tatlin, and Alexander Rodchenko, Reid's graphic design style of sharp, piercing lines against stark backgrounds helped define the look of a generation.

The low-tech, do-it-yourself (DIY) culture extended to the music. Though guitarist Steve Jones and Paul Cook could play their instruments well, Sid Vicious had little proficiency on the bass and band members led their fans to believe that they could hardly tune their instruments. Jones recalled upon meeting Rotten that he "looked the part, with his green hair, but he couldn't sing. Then again, we couldn't play so it was okay." The DIY ethos encouraged others to form bands without much technical expertise and exploded the rock-star-virtuoso image of the highly gifted, guitar god that had been dominant for more than a decade.

By 1977, the Sex Pistols and their manager had unleashed a revolutionary culture on an unsuspecting Britain and, eventually, the Western world. "Getting into the Sex Pistols wasn't like, 'Oh, I like this new band.' It really was a lifestyle choice," explained Mark Perry, the editor of the influential, photocopied punk fanzine *Sniffin' Glue* and later a founder of the band Alternative TV. "If you got into the Pistols, you changed your life. That's how dramatic it was."

The British Punk Legion

Driven by the forces of a do-it-yourself cultural change that had been created by the Sex Pistols, some British youths followed the Pistols by launching punk bands. After hearing the Sex Pistols at the 100 Club in London, Joe Strummer (b. John Mellor) quit his pub-rock band, the 101ers, and joined with guitarist Mick Jones and two other musicians to form the Clash. "When I saw the Pistols it just knocked my head right off," revealed Strummer. "I mean, they couldn't play great but they were just going, 'So what!'" "As soon as I saw the Sex Pistols, you just knew this was it — it had happened," echoed Jones.

The Clash quickly rivaled the Pistols for the punk crown. On July 4, 1976, with the help of manager Bernie Rhodes, a regular at Malcolm McLaren's boutique, the band first performed when they backed the Sex Pistols in Sheffield. That December, they joined the Pistols' "Anarchy in the U.K." tour. A few months later, the Clash signed with CBS Records, in March 1977 debuted with the single "White Riot," and followed a month later with their first, self-named LP.

Prodded by manager Rhodes, the band churned out a series of pointed political diatribes unlike the general anarchic message of the Pistols. "Bernie would say, 'An issue, an issue. Don't write about love," remembered Strummer. Their British Top-Twenty debut included punk anthems such as "I'm So Bored with the U.S.A.," "Career Opportunities," and "London's Burning." In late 1978, the Clash followed with the sobering *Give 'Em Enough Rope*, which hit the number-two slot in Britain with such punk gems as "Tommy Gun." "You write about what affects you," explained Strummer. The Clash sang about the "dissatisfaction among the young people, the way that everyone seemed to be going nowhere."

Like the Sex Pistols, the politicized Clash met with resistance from established, right-wing organizations. In 1977, the *British Patriot News*, the magazine of the right-wing National Front, warned its readers about the Clash and instructed its readers to remove Clash gig posters to discourage youth from attending the concerts. During their first tour of Great Britain, the band confronted police who repeatedly stopped their tour bus for no reason, and arrested and fined them for forgetting to return hotel keys. In the United States, Epic Records executives at first refused to issue the group's debut *The Clash*, branding it too crude for American consumption. The company released the album more than two years later in an altered format.

The Damned began their career backing the Sex Pistols. Formed in 1976 by Dave Vanian, Brian James, Captain Sensible (b. Raymond Burns), and Rat Scabies (b. Chris Miller), the New York Dolls-influenced group performed on the Pistols' "Anarchy in the U.K." tour. Trying to "play as fast and as loud and as chaotically as possible," according to bassist Captain Sensible, in October 1976 the band released the first British punk single, "New Rose." Nearly four months later, they hit the streets with the first British punk LP, *Damned, Damned, Damned*, which climbed to number thirty-six on the English chart.

Siouxsie and the Banshees started as part of a group of Sex Pistols fans living near Bromley in London. On September 20, 1976, at the 100 Club Punk Festival headlined by the Pistols, Siouxsie Sioux (b. Susan Ballion), Sid Vicious, Marco Pirroni, and Steve Havoc (b. Steve Severin) jumped on the stage and performed an extemporaneous, twenty-minute punk version of "The Lord's Prayer." At the end of the year, Siouxsie appeared with the Sex Pistols on the British television show *Today*, and later the next year the fledgling band backed Johnny Thunders in concert. On June 9, 1978, the Banshees signed with Polydor Records and in two months released their first single, "Hong Kong Garden," which hit the number-seven spot on the British singles chart. They quickly recorded *The Scream*, which by the end of the year climbed into the British Top Fifteen.

Generation X arose from two Bromley Contingent fans, Billy Idol (b. William Broad) and Tony James. In late 1976, the band performed at 150-person-capacity Roxy, which became a punk hangout. Within a year, the Generation X released the single "Your Generation," an answer to the Who's baby-boom anthem "My Generation." In March 1978, the group released their first LP, which charted at number twenty-nine in Britain.

The Buzzcocks banded together after witnessing a Sex Pistols show in Manchester. Although a Stooges fan, guitarist Pete Shelly (b. Pete McNeish) confessed that "we just weren't moving in any kind of musical world. We *needed* to see the Sex Pistols." "The idea that you could make your own record was revolutionary," added bassist Steve Diggle. Within weeks after the Manchester show, the Buzzcocks snagged their first gig, supporting the Sex Pistols. Later in the year, they participated in the "Anarchy in the U.K." tour. By January 1977, they released the EP *Spiral Scratch*, which featured such punk gems as "Boredom," and early the next year reached the Top Fifteen with *Another Music in a Different Kitchen*.

Marion Elliot, soon to become Poly Styrene, also grabbed the punk banner after a Sex Pistols show. "The Pistols," she remembered, "sparked me to realize that there was something happening that was a little bit more of my generation. I thought, 'Oh, if they can get a band together, I should be able to do that too.'" In 1976, Poly Styrene formed X-Ray Spex and blasted consumer culture with the ranting "Oh Bondage, Up Yours!" "It was about being in bondage to material life," she explained. "A call for liberation. I was saying, 'Bondage? Forget it, I'm not going to be bound by the laws of consumerism.'" By 1977, X-Ray Spex and a raft of other outfits had followed the Pistols to create a punk movement.

Ska, Reggae, and Radical Punks

Reggae, the music of the downtrodden in Jamaica, became popular among the punks who challenged the prevailing racist attitudes in Britain. It served as an essential element of the Jamaican Rastafarian religion, which emerged as early as the 1930s, when the rotund Marcus Garvey urged Jamaican blacks to return to the Ethiopian kingdom of Haile Selassie, who was considered the Lion of Judah. Garvey's back-to-Africa message appealed to many unemployed Jamaicans, who comprised approximately 35 percent of the working-age population during the 1960s and congregated in the slums of West Kingston.

Trapped in a poverty-stricken existence, many Jamaicans adhered to Rastafarianism's coherent set of beliefs. They worshipped Haile Selassie, who embodied the second coming of Christ and became God, or Jah, to the Rastafarians. Rastas carried the Ethiopian colors—yellow, green, and red. From their perspective, the

Rastafarians considered Western society as the corrupt Babylon and ate organic, or I-tal food, followed Old Testament kosher laws, and abstained from meat, salt, tobacco, and alcohol consumption. By 1935, many Rastas sported a plaited hairstyle known as dreadlocks, which were inspired by East African warriors and smoked ganja, or marijuana, to reach a higher level of consciousness; by the late 1960s, reggae, which combined African and indigenous Jamaican rhythms, replaced the westernized R&B–based rock-steady to serve as the music of the countercultural religion. Peter Tosh (b. Winston McIntosh), one of the founders of reggae, explained that "reggae, the word, means 'king's music,' and I play the King's music. The King put many princes on earth, and the music is given to those who praise Him."

Reggae originated in the slums of the Jamaican capital. "When I came to Kingston at about sixteen years of age," Tosh remembered, "Nine out of ten singers found themselves in poverty in Trenchtown, the ghetto. It was me, Bob Marley, [Neville] 'Bunny' Livingstone, Joe Higgs, the Maytals—we'd sit around every night and just sing." The singers joined with producer Clement "Sir Coxsone" Dodd, "and that was the start of recording for me and Bob and Bunny," Tosh explained.

Tosh and his friends initially developed a music called ska. It combined Jamaican folk mento, calypso beats from Trinidad, jazz-like horn sections, and Western rhythm and blues. Ska featured a prominent walking bass with accents on the upbeat, giving the music a happy feeling. In 1963, calling themselves the Wailing Wailers, Tosh, Bob Marley and Bunny "Wailer" Livingston worked with Sir Coxson Dodd to hit the Jamaican chart with "Simmer Down," a song about gang violence. A year later, they recorded another ska song, "Rude Boy," which immortalized the outlaws of Kingston's shantytown and reached the number-one spot. Changing with the times, the Wailers next recorded a series of songs with a rock-steady beat, a style slower than ska and heavily indebted to the soul music that was exploding from urban America.

The Wailers abandoned ska and rock-steady for a new style that was rooted in Rastafarianism and became known as reggae. The music, played at a very slow tempo, featured rhythmic accents on the offbeat, syncopated and prominent bass lines, and an emphasis on the third beat of a four-bar measure for a laid-back easy feeling.

The Wailers benefited from the success of the film *The Harder They Come*. Released in 1972, the movie chronicled gang life in Trenchtown and featured the music of Jamaican star Jimmy Cliff. The film became an international hit and created a worldwide market for reggae music. Chris Blackwell of Island Records, who had helped promote *The Harder They Come*, became attracted to the image of the Wailers and signed the band. The Wailers "all had this fuck you–type attitude," related Blackwell, "just like *The Harder They Come*." In 1973, the group released two reggae LPs, *Catch a Fire* and *Burnin'*, the second including "I Shot the Sheriff," a song covered by Eric Clapton. Two years later, the Wailers cut *Natty Dread*, a testament to the Rastafarian culture.

The Wailers, along with other reggae groups, lambasted the racism and capitalism that Britain had imposed on Jamaica. Burning Spear (b. Winston Rodney), using a Rastafarian dialect, contended that everyone should "be equal or I-qual and get an equal share." "These things come through the music," he insisted. Lee Perry, who produced bands such as the Wailers, claimed that reggae "denounces the very heart of the system on which much of the capitalist world is built." Not just venting idle rhetoric, reggae groups such as Bob Marley and the Wailers actively backed the government of socialist Prime Minister Michael Manley. At a 1976 rally for the prime minister, Marley barely escaped an assassination attempt.

By mid-decade, Bob Marley gained international fame. "Bob really broke strong in England in 1976 or '77," remembered Blackwell. "He did a concert in London that really broke him. It was also big in America." The recorded album of the 1975 concert, titled *Live!*, hit the Top Forty in Britain. Marley, who by this point had split with Peter Tosh and Bunny Wailer, reached the Top Ten in the United States and the Top Fifteen in Britain with *Rastaman Vibration* (1976).

Discontented British punks, attracted to Marley's rebel image, championed the activist reggae bands. "I was heavily into reggae," recalled Johnny Rotten. In 1976, the Clash remade Junior Murvin's reggae hit "Police and Thieves." "You see, there wasn't enough good punk records around. So, to supplement it, we filled it out with a lot of reggae records," explained Mick Jones of the Clash. "It was like punk's other 'chosen music.'" Many British youths supported reggae bands who played alongside the punks on concert bills "Everybody loved reggae music," commented Chrissie Hynde about the English punks.

Some British youths revived ska—the light, happy Jamaican music that predated reggae—and fused it with the radical message and energy of punk. "We liked them [punk and ska] both," recalled Jerry Dammers of the racially integrated Specials, one of the most influential of the new ska groups. "I was aiming for revolution, of racial harmony, of peace and unity," he continued. "I wanted to overthrow the establishment while having a hell of a lot of fun." In 1979, the band borrowed £700 to record "Gangsters," a tribute to the Prince Buster ska classic "Al Capone" (1964) that was released on the group's 2-Tone label. They followed a few months later with a debut album, which reworked such older Jamaican songs as "Monkey Man" by Toots and the Maytals, "Too Hot" by Prince Buster and "A Message to You, Rudy" by Robert "Dandy" Livingstone into a British Top-Five entry. "We combined black music with punk," explained vocalist Neville Staples. "We just mixed the two cultures."

The Selecter, idolizing the same ska roots as the Specials, delivered a radical punk message on the Specials' 2-Tone label. Living in Coventry, as did the Specials, and featuring the vocals of Pauline Black, the band chronicled the tense racial and political situation in Britain with singles such as "Three Minute Hero" and "Too Much Pressure." "2-Tone came to light exactly when Margaret Thatcher and Ronald Reagan came to power," explained Black. "We had two years before they sucked both countries dry, which the music scene reflected."

The English Beat, the other major Seventies ska band, produced a similar sound for a similar purpose. Guitarist Dave Wakeling rediscovered ska because "it said what a terrible world this was—with a smile on its face." In 1979, the Birmingham group created its own Go Feet label and released its near top-selling debut, which included "Stand Down Margaret," which was aimed at Conservative Prime Minister Margaret Thatcher who had been elected only a few months before.

Rock Against Racism united many British punk bands, which fought against the racism rampant in Britain by embracing ska and reggae. The organization arose after an August 14, 1976, concert in Birmingham at which a drunken Eric Clapton stammered about Britain becoming "overcrowded" with "black wogs and coons." "Musicians were coming out with the 'Blame the Blacks bit,'" recalled one organizer. "Bowie and Clapton were the last straws—how dare they praise Hitler or want to repatriate the race that had created the music they profitably recycled? We loved music,

Margaret Thatcher, the Iron Lady and Prime Minister of England.

Library of Congress Prints and Photographs Division [LC-DIG-ppmsca-09786].

hated racism and thought it was about time rock-and-roll paid back some dues." Rock Against Racism fought "back against the creeping power of racist ideas in popular culture" and attacked the right-wing, neo-Nazi National Front. By early 1978, the co-alition had organized fifty-six chapters.

The antiracist group appealed to punkers such as the Clash. "If you wanna fuckin' enjoy yourself, you sit in an armchair and watch TV," goaded the Clash's Mick Jones, "but if you wanna get actively involved, rock-'n'-roll's about rebellion." More specific about his political agenda, Clash vocalist Joe Strummer asserted that "we're hoping to educate any kid who comes to listen to us, just to keep 'em from joining the National Front when things get really tough." To back their words with action, on April 30, 1978, the Clash headlined an Anti-Nazi League Carnival in London that attracted more than 80,000 fans.

The Clash headlined several Rock Against Racism shows. In June 1978, the Clash, the Tom Robinson Band, and Sham 69 played to 100,000 young punks who attended a Rock Against Racism concert. Tom Robinson, who had formed his band in early 1977 and had hit the Top Five in Britain with "2-4-6-8-Motorway," shouted to the audience that the National Front must be confronted "at school and at work." "If we can keep a few kids from joining the National Front, or keep a kid from being beaten up, we've achieved something," he proclaimed. "Through my lyrics," agreed Morgan Webster of Sham 69, "I want to show the National Front that they're fucking assholes." Joe Strummer of the Clash declared that "we're against any racism." By the end of summer 1978, more than 250,000 youths had rocked against racism in thirty-six concerts held across England.

The Punk Independents

Independent labels with a do-it-yourself (DIY) ethic distributed the politicized punk. "Punk was always about having control, seizing the means of production, instead of waiting for the record company idiots to make the decisions," insisted Pete Shelley of the Buzzcocks.

Created from a record shop owned by Geoff Travis, Rough Trade Records put the do-it-yourself ethic into action. "Punk gave everyone on the scene the impetus to do things for themselves," asserted Travis. "If that hadn't happened, perhaps we wouldn't have started." In 1977, the new label began pressing discs and distributing records from smaller punk independent labels to "provide an alternative to the music establishment so that a record could be available that otherwise wouldn't," according to staffer Allan Sturdy.

Rough Trade organized as a cooperative. The twenty-five employees at the company all made the same amount of money and democratically made decisions about the discs to record and distribute. They split profits equally between the company and the artist, kept prices as low as possible, and funneled their share of the net revenues back into the company. "It was a cooperative collective from the beginning," explained Travis. "There weren't bosses and a hierarchy."

The collaborative workers at Rough Trade supported bands, which attacked racism. It first distributed the debut LP of the politically minded Belfast band Stiff Little Fingers, who delivered charged anthems such as "Alternative Ulster," "Suspect Device," a reworked version of Bob Marley's "Johnny Was," and "White Noise," the last lambasting Britain's racism toward blacks, Pakistanis, and the Irish. The label subsequently featured punks prominent in Rock Against Racism events.

Rough Trade leveled its sights on sexism by backing women punk bands who played instruments as well as serving as vocalists. It released discs by all-female bands such as the Slits and the reggae-influenced Raincoats as well as the gender-integrated Delta 5, who screamed for sexual and racial equality. "Women were relatively empowered by punk," contended Geoff Travis. "We just had respect for women. We didn't see any reason why women couldn't be equally good at making music as their male counterparts."

The collaborative ethic of Rough Trade spread. In 1978, Tony Wilson and Alan Erasmus launched Factory Records, a cooperative venture in Manchester. The same year, Bob Last and his partner Hilary Morrison opened Fast Product in Edinburgh. Graduate Records appeared in Dudley, England. Some punk bands, though lauding the independents, signed with major labels for better distribution of their records. Tom Robinson, facing the contradiction between his leftist politics and the money-making goals of his label, EMI, asserted that one has "to use the capitalist media to reach the people." Mick Jones of the Clash rationalized the band's contract with CBS Records as a way to "reach a few more people. If more kids started hearing the record, maybe they'd start humming the songs, they'll read the lyrics and learn something from them." Clash vocalist Joe Strummer described the contradiction: "We're trying to be the greatest group in the world, and that also means the biggest. At the same time, we're trying to be radical—I mean, we never want to be *really* respectable—and keep punk alive," he lamented.

The Decline of British Punk

Businesses on both sides of the Atlantic undermined punk by selling punk style without its substance. As early as June 1977, Saks on Fifth Avenue and Bonwit Teller sold gold safety pins at prices up to $100, and British designer Zandra Rhodes designed a collection of gowns for Bloomingdale's that incorporated stylized and strategically placed rips and glitter-studded safety pins at $345 to $1,150 a dress. The June 1980 issue of *Mademoiselle* offered its readers the choice between "punk or prep" fashion in a four-page spread. By 1982, Richard Hell lamented that "punk was intended to be a whole kind of consciousness. But then it got corrupted into being simply a style or a fad."

Some seventies rock acts assimilated and homogenized the punk image. Linda Ronstadt appeared with spiked hair on the pink-and-black album cover of *Mad Love* (1980). Billy Joel, the piano man who nearly topped the charts in 1977 with *The Stranger*, posed in a leather jacket with a rock in his cocked arm for the cover of his *Glass Houses* (1980) album. Even Cher, the folk singer turned disco queen, surfaced in full punk regalia with cropped hair as the lead singer of the short-lived punk/heavy-metal band, Black Rose. In 1979, Sandy Pearlman, producer of The Clash's second album, complained that "no one's really very scared of punk, especially the record companies. They've sublimated all the revolutionary tendencies this art is based on."

Some aggressive British punk rockers abandoned the buzz-saw guitar sound for different styles of music. In 1979, Tom Robinson felt that punk had become predictable and opted for the electronic pop of Sector 27. The Clash, always interested in Jamaican rhythms, moved further and further from the boisterous sound of their first album. By the triple album *Sandinista* (1980) and *Combat Rock* (1982), they sounded very little like the snarling punks of 1976. "We've become the people we'd set out to destroy," Joe Strummer finally admitted.

Even the Sex Pistols deserted punk rock. On January 14, 1978, after completing an American tour, the group was disbanded by Johnny Rotten, who felt that the band had extended rock to its outer limits and had been "packaged and sold as a commodity." "The Pistols finished rock-and-roll. That was the last rock-and-roll band. It's all over now," he snarled. "Rock-and-roll is shit. It's dismal. Granddad danced to it." Paul Cook and Steve Jones played briefly with Johnny Thunders before starting more pop-oriented ventures. On February 2, 1979, Sid Vicious, the archetype of the punk image, died from a drug overdose in New York City.

British punk, though beginning to disintegrate by 1978, left a legacy by shattering the monopoly of corporate rock. "Imagine in your mind an ELP [Emerson, Lake and Palmer] number," suggested Joe Strummer of the Clash. "Then imagine punk rock like a blow torch sweeping across it. That to me is what punk rock did." "I did it. I did it," boasted Johnny Rotten. "I made doors open. I made it easier for up-and-coming bands. It was a Rolling Stones–type of monopoly of the entire business. Record companies would not sign new acts. I opened that up."

Postpunk Depression

A depressingly conservative British political climate molded the outlook of postpunk bands. On May 4, 1979, Margaret Thatcher brought the Conservative Party to power and instituted a series of punitive economic policies. She deregulated the financial sector, privatized government-owned industries, and established tax cuts for the rich and regressive taxes for everyone else. Nicknamed the "Iron Lady," Thatcher reduced expenditures on education and social services and in 1979 passed the Vagrancy Act, which gave police broad powers to stop and search anyone suspected of wrongdoing. As a reaction to these measures, in 1981 riots engulfed many British cities and by the next year unemployment rose in the United Kingdom to 12 percent, a rate not experienced since the Great Depression of the thirties.

To punkers, Thatcher's election signaled an even gloomier future than had been previously envisioned. In 1979, explained bassist Jah Wooble (b. John Wardle), "Thatcher came in, and I just thought 'This is such bad news.' You just knew great changes for the worse were gonna come. This person was going to attack a lot of the culture of the country. She was the contract killer."

In such a dire atmosphere, many postpunk bands delivered a cold, dissonant, minimalistic music. Johnny Rotten reclaimed his original surname, Lydon, and started the "antirock-and-roll" band Public Image Ltd. (PiL). Extending the minimalistic tendencies of the punks, PiL produced a dissonant, bass-heavy, jagged electronic sound perfected on *Metal Box* (1979). "I've grown very far away from human beings," Lydon asserted. Rather than people, the ex-Pistol found solace in "machines. Lots of buttons on record players. Knobs and gadgets, electrical equipment of any kind." "With PiL," related bassist Jah Wobble, "there's a great darkness."

Throbbing Gristle abandoned rock music for synthesizer drones, tape samples, and depraved performances to paint a picture of a society in decline. Formed in late 1976 from a performance art group, Genesis P-Orridge (b. Neil Megson), his girlfriend/guitarist Cosey Fanni Tutti (b. Christine Newby), tape manipulator Peter "Sleazy" Christopherson, and keyboardist Chris Carter constructed an "alienation sensation," which reflected a "dystopian view of life." "I was drawn to William Burroughs and Anthony Burgess and his Clockwork Orange ideas," asserted the beat-inspired P-Orridge, "because that was what the world looked like to me." The band debuted with a show that featured tape loops, synthesizer improvisations, gloomy lyrics, and a bevy of strippers that Nicholas Fairbairn, a Tory member of Parliament, deemed it "a sickening outrage, sadistic, evil." In late 1977 the band released its first album *Second Annual Report* on its own Industrial Records.

Cabaret Voltaire from the industrial sludge of Sheffield expressed their vision of social disintegration through a harsh, intense electronic sound. Banding together in 1973, Chris Watson, Stephen Mallinder, and Richard H. Kirk named themselves after the experimental Parisian Dadaist performances of pre-1920s France. Using the cut-up technique of writer William Burroughs and sound poet Brion Gysin, the trio produced tape samples, slide shows, distorted vocals, and electronics to deliver a chilling, minimalist, disjointed primitivism. "We thought we'd never get a record deal," reasoned Richard H. Kirk. "There's no point in trying to be commercial, so let's go and upset people." The group released their debut *Extended Play* (1978) on Rough Trade. The next year after the demise of the Sex Pistols, the group gained notoriety with its first full-length album, the experimental din of *Mix-Up*.

Joy Division offered a more accessible sound of gloom. In 1976, friends Peter Hook and Bernard Sumner (b. Albrecht) decided to form a band. "We were both twenty-one when we started and had never played an instrument before in our lives. It was straight after seeing the first Sex Pistols gig in Manchester. We thought they were so bad, but yet it was so exciting. God! We could have a go at that," recalled Hook. "It was the same for other people all over the country." A few months later, Hook, Sumner, and their friend Stephen Morris met singer Ian Curtis who, according to Hook, "introduced us to Lou Reed and the Velvet Underground, to Iggy Pop and the Stooges and the Doors."

By 1977, the foursome produced a droning, Velvet Underground–inspired sound punctuated by Curtis's gloomy lyrics that captured, in the words of guitarist Sumner, "the death of optimism." They named themselves Joy Division after the prostitute wing in a Nazi concentration camp. The band joined the newly established Factory Records owned by local television host Tony Wilson, who in 1979 used his life savings to finance the group's first LP, *Unknown Pleasures*. The next year Joy Division hit the British Top Twenty with the single "Love Will Tear Us Apart" and started to gain momentum just as Ian Curtis hanged himself on May 18, 1980, on the eve of an American tour. The posthumous *Closer* reached the British Top Ten.

The Fall, another Manchester outfit, joined the downbeat postpunkers. Formed during 1976 after witnessing a Sex Pistols concert, the band named itself after an Albert Camus existentialist novel (*The Fall*) and aimed to create "music for the people that don't want it." They banged out a Velvet Underground–inspired raw, edgy, repetitive sound exemplified by the song "Repetition." Guitarist Martin Bramah characterized the number as "our mission statement. It was just a riff and a beat." "If we were feeling particularly abused," he related, "we'd just play 'Repetition' till the audience either walked away or got really violent." In early 1979, the group released its first full-length album, the ominous-sounding *Live at the Witch Trials*.

The Cure reflected the post-punk pessimism. Formed in 1976, the band debuted with the single "Killing an Arab" (1978), inspired by a passage in the Albert Camus novel *The Stranger*. In May 1979, they released their first LP, the pop-oriented *Three Imaginary Boys*. The band turned to pessimistic themes such as "The Funeral Party" and "The Drowning Man" on subsequent albums such as the Top-Twenty *Faith*. In April 1982, the Cure released the downbeat, gothic classic *Pornography*, which reflected the deep pessimism of many postpunk bands. "I suppose doing an album like *Pornography* and coming to those depths and coming out of it proves that something can come out of nothing," observed singer-lyricist-guitarist Robert Smith. "Nihilism took over," added bassist/keyboardist Simon Gallup.

Bauhaus gave Gothic rock, as it came to be called, its theme song. Forming in 1978 from the remains of the punk band Submerged Tenth, Bauhaus quickly released the brooding single "Bela Lugosi's Dead." Written initially as a joke by lyricist and singer Peter Murphy, the song captured the postpunk gloom of many youths and created a following for the band. By 1982, they hit the British Top Five with *The Sky's Gone Out*.

The Gang of Four deserted punk for an edgy, brittle, funk-oriented sound, based upon the Velvet Underground and reggae. Formed in 1977 in Leeds, they crafted a staccato guitar-driven beat to reflect sobering postpunk realities. "There's almost nothing in the Gang of Four that relates to what purists would describe as punk," explained guitarist Andy Gill. "For a start it's funky, it's stripped down, it's simple. Power chords aren't part of the repertoire." To reflect a downbeat mood, he wanted music "which was empty, full of gaps" and "not warm. We were *against warmth*." The band used their sound to blast social ills in such song as "(Love Like) Anthrax" and "Damaged Goods" in their 1979 debut *Entertainment!*

The Cure.

Cameron Garrett.

Across the Atlantic in New York City, provocative bands such as Teenage Jesus and the Contortions used funk underpinnings to deliver a dissonant, minimalist music. Born in Milwaukee, James Chance (b. James Siegfried) migrated to New York City at the end of 1975 to become part of the avant-garde jazz scene. There, he met Lydia Lunch (b. Koch), who waitressed at CBGB's, and joined her arty band Teenage Jesus and the Jerks as a saxophonist. Lunch described the sound of the band as "pretty atrocious—tight, horrible, painful to play and to listen to." "Teenage Jesus was fast and stabbing," she added. When Lunch no longer wanted a sax in her group, Chance assembled the Contortions, which combined the free jazz of Albert Ayler with James Brown-like funk. In 1978, a number of like-minded bands gathered at the Artists Space in New York. Their performances led to the *No New York* record, produced by Brian Eno, which included four bands that practiced together in the same loft on Delancey Street: the Contortions, Teenage Jesus, the noisy DNA, and Mars that featured surrealistic lyrics and China Burg on atonal slide guitar. Other journalists, using part of the album title, termed the movement No Wave.

The New Wave

Refocused punk bands offered a bright, pop alternative to the dissonant postpunk drone. Sire Records President Seymour Stein who signed the Talking Heads and the Ramones labeled the bouncy punk as "the new wave" because "punk was too tough to digest as a word for the record industry in conservative America." "New wave was watered down, that was a completion corruption of everything," a bitter Johnny Rotten snapped. "That's when everyone tried to be nice again."

The Police crested with the bubbly new wave. In January 1977, Stewart Copeland and Gordon Sumner, nicknamed Sting because he often wore a black-and-yellow striped jersey, met at a jazz club and began rehearsing with guitarist Henri Padovani. The next month, the trio released the punk single "Fall Out," and in March toured with Johnny Thunders and the Heartbreakers. "All I could see in punk was a very direct, simple image of power and energy," recalled Sting, who had been enamored of jazz as a youth. "I could easily ally myself with that, and forget about changes, chords with flatted fifths, forget all that."

The Police quickly changed musical direction. They replaced Padovani with guitarist Andy Summers and in April 1978 released the single "Roxanne," which blended the energy of punk with a reggae-influenced, jazz-tinged sound. "I'm an opportunist," admitted Sting. "I saw this vacuum between punk, which was unschooled, and the horrible corporate rock on the other side. I saw this thing in the middle that was clean and simple. That's what 'Roxanne' is."

The new pop sound of the Police led to superstardom. The album *Outlandos D'Amour* (1978), which included "Roxanne," hit the Top Ten on the British chart. "Message in a Bottle" and "Walking on the Moon," singles from the band's second album, both topped the U.K. chart. In 1980, *Zenyatta Mondatta* hit the top of the British chart and became the group's first Top Ten effort in the United States. The next year,

The Police, kings of the New Wave.

Cameron Garrett.

Ghost in the Machine climbed to number two in America and again topped the chart in Britain, yielding hits such as "Every Little Thing She Does Is Magic." *Synchronicity* (1983) provided the band with its first number-one album on both sides of the Atlantic, making the Police a pop phenomenon. "I don't think pop music is a pejorative term," Sting observed. "I want to be proud of being a pop singer when I turn forty." "My power is in selling records," he added.

Elvis Costello rode the new wave. The son of bandleader Ross MacManus, Declan MacManus played at local folk clubs under his father's stage name, Costello. In 1976, he signed to Stiff Records, owned by Jake Riviera, who suggested that he rename himself Elvis. Though Costello released political diatribes such as his debut "Less Than Zero," which attacked Oswald Mosley, a 1930s British fascist who inspired the creation of the National Front, he became popular when he adopted a more pop sensibility on such songs as his reworking of the Sam and Dave's "I Can't Stand Up for Falling Down." "What I really wanted to do was approach the music with the same attitude, the same attack as punk, without sacrificing all the things I liked about music—like, say, tunes," Elvis remembered.

Billy Idol channeled his punk energy into a bouncy pop. After quitting Generation X in 1980, the singer hired ex-Kiss manager Bill Aucoin and recorded pop songs such as "White Wedding" and "Hot in the City," which fused the persistent beat of punk with snappy melodies. In 1983, he released the Top-Ten, million-selling album *Rebel Yell*.

The Cars rode the punk-pop hybrid to success. Banding together in Boston in 1976, the group hit the Top Twenty two years later with a shiny, upbeat debut. "We knew there was a scene called punk," mentioned vocalist/guitarist Ric Ocasek. "We were certainly liking the rawness of the music that was coming out of that. And we also liked pop." The Cars continued to ride up the chart with four Top-Ten albums, which Ocasek called "disposable pop."

Chrissie Hynde jumped on the new wave with a combination of hard-edged punk and soul. After attending Kent State University in Ohio, she journeyed to London, where she modeled, sold leather handbags, and wrote for the rock paper *New Musical Express*. In 1974, Hynde worked part-time for Malcolm McLaren in his clothing shop Sex. Two years later, she tried unsuccessfully to form a band with guitarist Mick Jones, who had just joined the Clash. Hynde then briefly played guitar for the Malcolm McLaren–managed band Masters of the Backside, which eventually became the Damned. In 1978, Chrissie Hynde formed the Pretenders with bassist Pete Farndon, James Honeyman-Scott on guitar, and Martin Chambers on drums. During the next three years, the band released two top-selling albums, which expanded the sound of punk by infusing it with elements of soul. "I didn't quite fit into the London punk scene because I'd been listening to too many Bobby Womack albums," Hynde maintained.

Adam Ant (b. Stuart Goddard) transformed punk energy into pop hits. In 1977, after leaving Hornsey Art College and attending a Sex Pistols concert, he formed a series of punk and postpunk bands, including the Ants. By early 1980, Adam reformed the Ants and adopted a different image. He abandoned the ripped T-shirts and safety pins of punk for foppish scarves, embroidered, double-breasted jackets, skin-tight leather pants, and sashes and replaced punk's enraged blasts with an upbeat, drum-based sound. During the next three years, Adam and his Ants hit the chart with three Top-Five albums, which were promoted by videos of the photogenic group. In 1985, Adam disbanded the group to concentrate exclusively on his acting career.

Ant dropped the political rage of punk along with his new video-friendly image. "Who wants politics in music," he rhetorically asked. "I find politics the single most uninspiring, unemotional, insensitive activity on the planet." Within a few short years, Adam Ant had been transformed from an angry punk into an apolitical video star, who became popular on MTV, an American music channel that irrevocably changed rock music into a visual medium.

Chapter 17
American Hardcore

"I feel pain every day of my life. When you see me perform, it's that pain you're seeing coming out."

—Henry Rollins, Black Flag

On July 1, 1981, hordes of punks lined up on Hollywood Boulevard in anticipation of the premier of the film the *Decline of Western Civilization*, which focused on the California hardcore punk scene. They expected to see on-screen their favorite bands such as the hardcore icons Black Flag from Hermosa Beach, the more cerebral Los Angeles punk-pioneers X and the Germs, which bridged the two extremes. The punkers had heard rumors that the film showcased action at some of their favorite clubs such as the Fleetwood, where angry young, suburban, testosterone-fueled males beat each other mercilessly in a blood sport to display their manhood.

Without warning, the police descended upon the crowd. They blocked Hollywood Boulevard to cordon off the area and formed a line across the street from the punks. Jittery from confrontations with hardcore fans for the past several years, the officers, armed in SWAT gear, goose stepped toward the moviegoers. Unprovoked, they attacked the hardcore punks by shoving their batons into them. The police seemed intent on "trying' to eradicate punk rock," according to spectator Lisa Francher. The incident typified a violent hardcore punk, which dominated sunny Southern California during the late seventies and early eighties.

Stirrings in Los Angeles

During the late seventies, the desperate, angry, and extreme version of punk fittingly arose in Hollywood, the smog-filled, make-believe fairyland steeped in excess and corruption. Los Angeles punk surfaced with bands such as X, which fused the hyperactive roar of English punk with lyrics that described a society, which had degenerated beyond repair. By late 1977, X featured the thunderous drumming of Don Bonebrake, the rockabilly tinged, Ramones-influenced guitar of Billy Zoom (b. Tyson Kindell), and the Charles Bukowski–beat-inspired lyrics of John Doe (b. John Duchac) and poet Exene Cervenka. "I saw the Ramones. That made me decide to play the kind of music we play now in X," Zoom explained.

On their 1980 debut, *Los Angeles*, released by the independent Slash Records, which had evolved from the punk-rock fanzine of the same name, X applied the energy of the Ramones to tales of despondency such as "Nausea" and "Sex and Dying in High Society." "In 1979 or '80, people realized everything was fucked up, and they couldn't do anything about it, and they didn't want to," recalled Doe. "I only want to sing these songs about desperation," chimed Cervenka.

X set the desperate tone for other Los Angeles punk bands. The Germs, first performing at the Orpheum Theater in Los Angeles in 1977, featured the staccato fuzz guitar of Pat Smear (b. George Ruthenberg) and the barking vocals of Darby Crash (b. Paul Beahm). In concert and on their first LP (*GI*), they sang sobering songs such as "We Must Bleed." "The Germs were much darker than most of the other bands," explained John Doe. Germs followers ceremoniously burned themselves with cigarettes.

Exene of X in action, 1982.

Cameron Garrett.

"Self-destruction is a means of showing, if you're cutting up your body and marking or whatever, it's your own, it's one thing that you can call completely and totally your own," reasoned one Germs fanatic. On December 7, 1980, Crash symbolically committed suicide as a tribute to his hero, Sid Vicious.

X and the Germs, the leaders of the scene, were joined by other punk outfits such as the Weirdos, the Zeros, and the Zippers, which played to the growing throngs of discontented youths in Los Angeles at clubs like the Orpheum and the Masque. A 1977 advertisement for a show at the Masque captured the desperation of the bands and their followers. The poster promised "a spectacle of simulated London street desperation in the promised land, filtered through a rock & roll sensibility of carbonated freeway fury and terminal-swimming pool despair."

Orange County Hardcore

By 1978, Los Angeles punk had moved from the city into the suburbs and had turned from self-destruction to violent attacks. Former surfers and skateboarders from Huntington Beach and Costa Mesa looked for fights, at shows by suburban punk bands such as Black Flag and the Minutemen. "We were riled up and protesting against what was going on socially and musically," explained one-time Black Flag singer and Circle Jerks leader Keith Morris. "We reacted in a very aggressive, energetic, hateful, spiteful manner. Because we're from SoCal and we've grown up surfing and skating and skiing, we have a bit of aggressiveness to us." The up-and-down pogo dance of London and Los Angeles gave way to bodies slamming against each other near the stage in a slam pit, which eventually became known as the "mosh pit." Youths rushed and jumped on the stage and dove off onto the slamming masses below. "Right around the time of our first album, around '81," explained Lee Ving (b. Lee Capallero) of the Los Angeles hardcore band Fear, "it changed from the pogo bullshit into the real slam stuff."

The pace of the music changed from Hollywood's fast tempos to the hyperkinetic, blinding speed of hardcore kids hell-bent on violence. "The focus changed from Hollywood toward the beaches, and the idea of speed and the slam pit had its birth," Lee Ving remembered. "We started playing as fast as you could fucking think and the crowd would go berserk, pounding the shit out of each other in the pit." The new version of punk, added Ray Farrell of the aptly named hardcore label SST, "replaced the arty stuff [of Hollywood] with an injection of extreme energy, to the point of where being a faster band was the equivalent of playing a faster solo in the 70s." Though disdained by most of the original Los Angeles punk bands such as X, this new suburban punk, known as hardcore, muscled out its urban counterpart.

Generally young middle-class male suburbanites fueled the hardcore explosion. "When the hardcore thing really took off, it became more of a macho testosterone over-drive thing, the stage diving and the slam pits," remembered Keith Morris. "Most girls didn't want to have anything to do with it." Ray Farrell agreed that "hardcore made it more like a sporting event than music—with like the worst jocks you've ever seen. It excluded women … because it was violent."

The hardcore ethos of violence led to a new punk fashion. Rather than the Mohawk haircuts of British punk, hardcore youths shaved their heads to avoid someone grabbing their hair in the mosh pit. They favored tattoos of the names and logos of their favorite bands and sometimes pierced themselves in various parts of their bodies. Keeping some of the original punk style, the hardcore wore T-shirts, worn-out jeans, combat boots, and leather jackets, which sometimes had rows of pointed studs. As a total look, the hardcore youth dressed like they were preparing for war. As vocalist Jack Grisham of the Long Beach hardcore band T.S.O.L. (short for True Sounds of Liberty) maintained, "we were into the combat thing—we'd go to an Army Surplus [store] and get black combat gear. We'd go on missions."

These violent young males many times came from dysfunctional families nestled in the ultraconservative conclave of Orange County, California. Mike Ness, leader of the Fullerton band Social Distortion, grew up in a welfare home plagued by alcohol abuse. Jack Grisham from T.S.O.L. confessed that "we all came from broken families." Mugger, a roadie for Black Flag, characterized hardcore fans as "kids whose families didn't care about them … and they just got crazy. It was basically a full-on white suburban rebellion."

Tony Cadena, the singer–songwriter of the Adolescents, typified the youth that joined the hardcore ranks. He grew up in the "very suburban right wing, white middle-class stifling environment" of Orange County. "There was no father in my family," he confessed. "We were dysfunctional, a welfare family living in an upward middle-class neighborhood. Punk came along at just the right time. It gave me a chance to reject everything I couldn't have anyway." "It was the final fuck you," he sneered.

Black Flag, named for the symbol of anarchy, emerged as the prototypical band for the violent, angry hardcore scene by fusing punk energy with themes of desperation. The group found its inspiration in the early New York punks. Guitarist Greg Ginn first became interested in music when he read about "CBGB's and thought, 'maybe this is something that is going to open it up again.' That's when I started getting interested in having a band." Singer Dez Cadena echoed that "I hooked up with people who were getting into the Dolls, the Stooges, MC5, and all of a sudden we read about these bands playing CBGB's."

Unlike lower-class British punks, the band consisted of suburbanites from middle-class, sometimes dysfunctional, families. Henry Rollins (b. Henry Garfield), who joined Black Flag in the summer of 1981 and wrote many of the group's lyrics, contended that "I've always been privileged, I've got it all going for me." But as with many of the band's fans, Rollins confessed that he was "a classic product of a typical dysfunctional family. I don't know jack shit about love, or about feeling a relationship with a blood relative. That shit means nothing to me."

Black Flag delivered songs about personal dysfunction over a thrashing, fuzzy, chaotic, speed-guitar sound. In 1978, the band recorded *Nervous Breakdown*; three years later, it released *Damaged*, which included the hardcore anthem "Rise Above" and such despair-ridden songs as "Depression" and "Life of Pain." "Pain is my girlfriend; that's how I see it," related Rollins. "I feel pain every day of my life. When you see me perform, it's that pain you're seeing coming out … People hurt me, I hurt myself—mentally, physically." In contrast to the politicized British punk, explained Rollins in 1983, "There are no songs telling you to do anything. There are no political songs, there are no songs that speak out on some topic." Black Flag founder Greg Ginn summarized that "we were an extrapolation of the blues."

Henry Rollins of Black Flag.
Cameron Garrett.

If political at all, Orange-County hardcore professed right-wing extremism. Some of the bands sported Nazi armbands and mouthed reactionary slogans. "You guys always bitch at me for wearing Nazi armbands," blurted bassist Roger Rogerson to his Jewish band mates in the Circle Jerks. "Well, it's a white people's country, and it you don't like it, you can go back to your country."

The Los Angeles media promoted such pain-filled, sometimes hateful music. Rodney Bingenheimer, calling himself Rodney on the ROQ, played punk and then hardcore on his regular show at radio station KROQ that was broadcast from 8:00 P.M. until midnight on Sundays. In 1981, filmmaker Penelope Spheeris released *The Decline of Western Civilization*, which documented the seamier sides of the lifestyle and live performances of hardcore bands. Punk fanzines such as *Slash, Flipside*, and *Maximum RocknRoll*, patterned after English predecessors such as *Sniffin' Glue*, served as bibles of the new scene.

Local independent record companies appeared to record and distribute hardcore. In 1980, Lisa Fancher, a former employee at the Los Angeles–based Bomp! Records, established Frontier Records. She recorded the Circle Jerks, a group of young, middle-class teens from the suburbs, which included Keith Morris. Fancher recalled, "No one wanted to put out the Circle Jerks' LP *Group Sex*," Fancher recalled. "I said, 'I'll do it.'" "It's what made everything else fall into place for me," she explained. After the Circle Jerks, Fancher signed the Adolescents and T.S.O.L. In 1983, Fancher recorded the Suicidal Tendencies single "Institutionalized" and their first album, which, according to the label owner, sold more than a half million copies.

Other labels in California specialized in hardcore. Posh Boy, launched by Robbie "Posh Boy" Fields in 1978, recorded the Southern California hardcore of Agent Orange, Red Cross (later Redd Kross), the initial T.S.O.L. release, and compilations overseen by Rodney Bingenheimer. Brett Gurewitz, bassist for the less frenetic hardcore outfit Bad Religion, started Epitaph to record his own band and, within a decade, hit the Top Ten with Offspring, who sold seven million copies of *Smash.*

In 1979, two founding members of Black Flag, guitarist Greg Ginn and drummer Chuck Dukowski (b. Gary McDaniel, renamed in honor of beat poet Charles Bukowski), opened the label SST to record their band. They enlisted the help of Ginn's brother, Raymond Pettibon (b. Raymond Ginn), who crafted stark, graphic-novel-like artwork with the hint of impending violence for the band's logo, posters and album covers to provide a fitting graphic element to the music. Almost immediately, SST pressed the music of other local hardcore punkers such as San Pedro's Minutemen, which debuted with the extended-play *Paranoid Time* (1980).

Regional Hardcore

Ginn and Dukowski documented the burgeoning national hardcore scene, which spread from California to other urban areas across the nation. They recorded Husker Du from Minneapolis. When guitarist Bob Mould "heard the first Ramones' record," he said "This is something." In 1979, he joined with drummer Grant Hart and bassist Greg Norton in Husker Du, which played loud, fast songs of alienation, reflected in the title of their 1983 studio debut *Everything Falls Apart*. As with Black Flag, Husker Du delivered songs of personal angst. "I don't write about politics because I'm not an expert," commented Bob Mould in 1985. "We're sort of like reporters in a way. Reporters of our own mental state."

In Minneapolis, Husker Du shared the hardcore spotlight with the Replacements, which drew their inspiration from the punk that blasted forth from Southern California. "We were spawned by power-pop and hardcore, which were both offshoots of punk, so we were a product of that environment," pointed out singer Paul Westerberg. In May 1980, Westerberg dropped off a demo tape at the Oarfolkjokeopus record store for manager Peter Jesperson, who since 1978 had co-owned Twin/Tone Records. "I know it sounds like a fairy tale," remembered Jesperson, "but I knew how special it was the minute I heard it." The band signed with the label, which late the next year released the hyperactive *Sorry Ma, Forgot to Take Out the Trash*. Westerberg characterized the follow-up, the extended-play *Stink*, as an "excursion into hardcore to try and compete with Husker Du."

Hardcore contingents arose in other cities. In Washington, D.C., Ian MacKaye and his band mates carried the hardcore banner. In 1978, MacKaye converted to punk, when he heard the Clash and the Sex Pistols. "It scared the shit out of me. Just the anger of it. That was revolutionary music," he recalled. "Not just revolutionary, but *shockingly* revolutionary." Hooked on punk, singer MacKaye formed the Teen Idles and, with friend and soon-to-be Black Flag singer Henry Rollins, carefully listened to Black Flag singles and religiously devoured such California fanzines as *Slash* and *Flipside*. In the fall of 1980, MacKaye and Teen Idles drummer Jeff Nelson established the label Dischord to release their first single. They decided to document the expanding Washington, D.C., hardcore community by recording Rollins's band, SOA [State of Alert] and following with the first single of their renamed band, Minor Threat. Dischord continued to record local hardcore outfits such as Government Issue. "We thought, 'This is so cool, we'll do a little label, and everyone will get their own seven-inch.'"

Minor Threat, musically as aggressive as their Los Angeles hardcore counterparts, eschewed drugs, wanton sex, and alcohol to inspire the "straight-edge" movement. MacKaye and his band mates tried "to get away from a really corrupted music, you know, basically your heavy-metal bands that were into heroin, cocaine, just a lot of drinking. We just drank a lot of Coke and ate a lot of Twinkies." Nathan Strejcek, who played in the Teen Idles, explained that "since we weren't allowed to legally drink, we said, 'Fine, we don't want to,' just to piss the lawmakers off. This is where we established a new place in modern society for ourselves … clear-minded thinking against the most evil of all, the adults!"

Hardcore Politics in San Francisco

The premier hardcore band in San Francisco, the Dead Kennedys, were older than the teens in the hardcore scene and cared more about leftist politics than abstention from the rock-and-roll lifestyle. Leader Jello Biafra (b. Eric Boucher) had attended the University of California at Santa Cruz. By 1980, when he was 22, Biafra had become enamored of a politicized British punk. As he told it, "punk was an outbreak of new talent that … opened the door to a whole new generation of people who had ideas to replace the bankrupt swill."

The Dead Kennedys, formed in June 1978, embraced the message of British punk by merging a buzz-saw guitar sound with lyrics, which lambasted U.S. imperialism, the Moral Majority, and the creeping fascism among some hardcore youths, who wore Nazi armbands. In 1979, on their own Alternative Tentacles label, they released their first single "California Über Alles," which criticized California Governor Jerry Brown and other "Zen fascists." On their first LP, *Fresh Fruit for Rotting Vegetables* (1980), the Dead Kennedys blasted U.S. involvement in Southeast Asia in "Holiday in Cambodia" and tackled the issue of poverty in "Let's Lynch the Landlord" and "Kill the Poor." The band continued to deliver social commentaries such as "Terminal Preppie" and "Nazi Punks Fuck Off!" until they disbanded in 1986, amid a controversy over censorship of the album cover to *Frankenchrist*. "I think what we are witnessing in this country is the slow but inevitable fall of an empire that got too comfortable," declared Biafra.

The Dils, a band that garnered a following in San Francisco alongside the Dead Kennedys after they moved from Los Angeles, embraced a politicized version of punk. "We believed in punk-rock revolution," explained guitar/vocalist Chip Kinman. "Punk rock to change the world." The Dils delivered two hard-hitting singles, "I Hate the Rich" and "Class War," which embodied their philosophy and contrasted starkly with many of the Los Angeles hardcore punkers. "San Francisco was the more serious punk town, into punk revolution," Kinman mentioned. "Whereas L.A. was more into the nihilistic punk-rock vibe. It was a constant battle with those two towns, and the philosophies."

San Francisco hardcore became disillusioned with the embittered generation of suburban punks around Los Angeles who exhibited a violent, nihilistic aggression. "[We] had talked for years about how great it would be for us to get our music to younger kids and how once they saw the energy they'd automatically like it," Jello Biafra explained. But "when younger people did start coming to shows in droves, they brought the arena rock mentality with them, including fights, jumping off the stage just to see if you could hit people."

By the mid-1980s, the hardcore aggression that Biafra criticized had dissipated. Some bands left the scene quickly, such as the Adolescents who released only one album in 1981 and then disbanded. In late 1985, the Minutemen folded when guitarist D. Boon died in a car crash. Even the premier hardcore band, Black Flag, played their final show on June 27, 1986. In 1984, Husker Du switched from punk to a less frantic, even sometimes folk-based Zen Arcade. "Hardcore is basically music for young people," Bob Mould explained. "We were growing up and [Zen Arcade] showed a lot of that." Hardcore aggression gave way to a video channel, which featured slick, smartly dressed rock stars and changed rock music forever.

Chapter 18
I Want My MTV

"Video will be the way to keep time with the future."
—*Time* magazine, December 26, 1983

"Increasingly, and perhaps irreversibly, audiences for American mainstream music will depend, even insist, on each song being a full audiovisual confrontation," observed *Time* in 1983. "Why should sound alone be enough when sight is only as far away as the TV set or the video machine?" "Video will be the way to keep time with the future," concluded the magazine.

MTV, a music television channel established only two years earlier, was the subject of the *Time* article. During the early 1980s, it replaced radio among a generation of teens born during the 1960s, who had no personal recollection of Elvis, the Beatles, or Vietnam, and who sought their own musical identity. MTV helped create the visual rock of Duran Duran and pop metal and played a major role in the mania over Michael Jackson. During the 1980s, MTV designed and delivered rock to the TV generation.

MTV and the Video Age

In the 1980s, Americans became obsessed with a video technology that had first been introduced to the mass market with the television set. By the end of the decade, 98.2 percent of all American households watched television, most had at least two sets, and 85 percent owned a color TV. Americans purchased videocassette recorder-players, which were first mass marketed in 1976 by the Victor Co. of Japan (JVC). In 1981, Americans purchased 1.3 million videocassettes, a 69 percent increase from the previous year, and spent $9.2 billion on video products. Four years later, they purchased more than $15 billion in video hardware and accessories. By the end of the decade, more than 97 million Americans owned VCRs and bought more than 480 million prerecorded and blank videocassettes for their machines.

American teenagers who had been raised on television embraced the video craze. The youths, on average, watched television three to four hours a day. By high school graduation, they had spent more time watching television than sitting in the classroom. In a 1981 survey of eighth graders, the teens named TV personalities as their Top Ten role models. They even stared at television sets in their schools, which had become increasingly equipped with instructional TV.

Accustomed to the television screen at home and at school, American teens became entranced by video games. They first played Space Invaders at the turn of the decade. By 1981, the TV generation dropped more than 25 billion quarters into video game machines at local arcades, which grossed more than the combined television revenues of baseball, football, and basketball, or the combined income of all of the casinos in the country. Teens, mostly male, spent an average of $4.30 per week on coin-operated video games, and in 1981 spent the equivalent of 75,000 years playing Pac-Man, Asteroids, and other video games.

By the early 1980s, teens enjoyed video games at home. In 1982, the Atari Corporation, owned by Warner Communications, grossed approximately $1.3 billion on sales of 25 million Atari 2600 home video computer systems and millions of Space

Invaders and Missile Command game cartridges. By the end of that year, more than 8 percent of all households owned home video games.

Warner Communications applied video technology to rock and roll. Aided by the advent of stereo TV and the deregulation of the airwaves, which encouraged the growth of cable television, on August 1, 1981, Warner and American Express invested $20 million to launch Music Television (MTV). They broadcast a Vee-Jay-hosted format of three-minute video clips, which focused primarily on Warner artists and initially appeared on 300 cable outlets in 2.5 million homes. The music channel cost little to operate because record companies begrudgingly provided video content to the station for free to better market their acts.

Music Television, headed by 28-year-old Robert Pittman, targeted its programming to young people under 25 years old, who had been neglected by radio. "Where is the Woodstock generation? They're all old and bald," reasoned Pittman. Recycling the fifties ad campaign for the once-popular breakfast cereal Maypo into "I Want My MTV," he stalked the "TV babies," who seldom read newspapers, books, or even the rock press.

The New Romantics

MTV attracted the TV generation with young, visually exciting bands from the dance clubs of England. Opened as a reaction to the austerity of punk, English dance clubs such as the Blitz in Covent Garden provided working-class youths with escapist entertainment. "Most kids who actually live there are *sick* of the street," contended Gary Kemp, the founder and guitarist of Spandau Ballet, a prominent dance-club band who played at the Blitz. "They want to be in a club with great lights, and look really good and pick up girls." The Blitz, explained Martin Rushent who produced records by some of the English dance bands, "became just the hippest place on earth."

As with its American counterpart, English disco focused on a fashion-conscious audience. "Discos are always parties because you have to make your own visual entertainment," commented Kemp. "The most important thing in a club is the people, not the music they listen to. You become the most important person. *You* become the visual aspect of the evening, rather than the band." He hoped that his band could provide the soundtrack for "people who want to go out and dance and look good."

Gary Kemp linked the excessive concern over fashion to British culture. "The attitude behind it has always been there; Mods, skinheads, and the soul kids—just kids who want to dress smart and enjoy themselves."

The music played at the clubs, a combination of a steady disco beat and the atmospheric sounds of the electronic synthesizer, originated with groups such as Roxy Music. Formed in early 1971 by singer Brian Ferry and named after the popular chain of Roxy cinemas in England, the band wore stylish, sometimes flamboyant, futuristic costumes designed by Anthony Price. A reporter from the *Music Scene* spotted Brian Eno, a member of the group, "traveling the Underground wearing heavily applied brown eye shadow, thick mascara, lipstick, black glitter beads, pearly nail varnish, and violent purple streaks in his blonde hair."

Unlike most seventies glam rockers who delivered hard rock, Roxy Music featured the synthesizer, which in the hands of Eno added an almost ethereal element to the music. In 1972, the band released its debut, self-named album, which reached the Top Ten in Britain. The next year, Roxy Music refined its distinctive style with the synthesizer-drenched *For Your Pleasure*, which reached the British Top Five, and in 1974 topped the British chart with *Stranded*. By 1976 after several personnel changes, Roxy Music disbanded.

Ultravox continued the tradition of Roxy Music to become the direct precursor of the New Romantic movement. Brought together in 1976 by John Foxx (b. Dennis Leigh), who had dabbled in tapes and synthesizers while in school, the extravagantly bedecked band recorded two albums of electronica, which were punctuated by the violin and keyboards of Billy Currie. In 1978, the band enlisted the help of producer

Conny Plank, who had worked with experimental electronic groups such as Can and Kraftwerk to release *Systems of Romance*, which offered listeners a sparse, crystalline, electronic sound that defined the electro-pop of the New Romantics.

In early 1979, keyboardist Billy Currie joined fashion-conscious Steve Strange (b. Steven Harrington), synthesizer player James "Midge" Ure, and some members of the group Magazine to form a side project, which they called Visage. As with Ultravox, the band emphasized outrageous fashion. "Fashion," commented Strange, "has been missing from the scene since the early seventies with Bowie and Roxy, so what we're part of is just an upsurge in fashion."

Visage expanded the Ultravox sound by featuring two synthesizers and guitars supported by a heavy, repetitious drumbeat. "We were trying to get away from the obvious disco sound," explained Strange. "I messed around with synthesizers and found sounds which were really different from the traditional guitar and bass. We wanted to create a danceable beat. I know you can do that with drums and a bass, but it was a new sound that we wanted to use."

Gary Numan (b. Gary Webb) popularized the sound of electro-pop that Ultravox and Visage had developed. First joining the punk-influenced Tubeway Army, he soon abandoned the guitar for the synthesizer, donned futuristic outfits, and, in May 1979, released the synthesizer dance number "Are 'Friends' Electric?" Two weeks later, Numan and his band, which included Billy Currie, appeared on the British television show *Top of the Pops*, and by the end of July, the single and the album *Replicas* hit the top of the British chart. "Gary Numan just released "Are 'Friends' Electric?" when everyone thought synthesizer bands were just junk or something or that anyone who used a synthesizer was just a bit of a joke," remembered Midge Ure. "At the time it was very unfashionable, but six months later because of Gary Numan it became very fashionable to be a synthesizer band."

Gary Numan with synthesizer.

Cameron Garrett.

The ease of mastering the synthesizer contributed to its popularity. "In some ways it's quite strange that synthesizers were so hated in the punk era," remarked Andy McClusky of the successful electro-pop band Orchestral Manoeuvres in the Dark, which formed in 1978. "They're the ideal punk instrument if you believe in the ethic of 'anybody can do it.' Someone who's been playing synth for ten minutes can easily sound as good as someone who's been playing for years, provided the ideas are there." Andy Fletcher of the all-synthesizer band, Depeche Mode, confessed that "we couldn't hardly play at all then; we can't play very well now. In pop music nowadays you don't need technical ability, you need ideas and the ability to write songs."

By the beginning of the 1980s, portable synthesizers had become relatively inexpensive. Unlike the cumbersome, sometimes stationary Moog models of the previous decade, easy-to-handle portables could be purchased for as little as $100 to $300. "Synthesizers suddenly got cheaper," explained Phil Oakey of the Human League about his band's switch to the electronic keyboard.

The electro-pop sound of the synthesizer, easily attainable and affordable, embodied the digital, push-button 1980s. "Not a day goes by when you don't press a button, whether it's for a cup of coffee or to turn on the stereo or video," observed David Ball of the two-man synthesizer group Soft Cell. "People are so surrounded now by electronics, of course there's electronic music."

MTV Goes Electro-Pop

MTV, searching for videos of new bands to air on its twenty-four-hour-a-day format, promoted the electro-pop of the fashion-obsessed New Romantics. "New Romantics were all about looking at themselves in the mirror, so they absolutely adored the idea of someone sticking a camera in front of them," maintained video director Julien Temple.

Duran Duran led the MTV-friendly electro-pop bands. Begun in 1978 as a duo and named after a character in the science fiction movie *Barbarella*, within two years the group became a quintet that featured an airy-sounding synthesizer, the insistent drumbeat of disco, and a pop sensibility for what keyboard player Nick Rhodes (b. Nick Bates) dubbed "entertainment music." In 1982, the band hit the Top Ten when their second album *Rio* received heavy MTV airplay. "The band was a natural for music television," noted *Rolling Stone* magazine. "They may be the first rock group to ride in on a video wave." The group promptly re-released their first album to rave reviews and became teenage heartthrobs on both sides of the Atlantic with the Top Ten album *Seven and the Ragged Tiger* (1983). "Videos are incredibly important for us," asserted Rhodes. "It's a way of expressing a song in visuals. It gives another dimension." He added that "MTV was instrumental in breaking us in America." Norman Sammick, senior vice president of Warner Communications, put it more bluntly: "I think Duran Duran owes its life to MTV."

The music channel helped other electro-pop bands such as The Human League reach the record-buying American public. The group, formed in Sheffield in 1977, first produced icy, dense electronic music modeled after European outfits such as Kraftwerk. In 1980, vocalist and synthesizer wiz Philip Oakey disbanded the Human League because of its reliance on taped music during concerts, and with Adrian Wright and four new members reformed the band. The next year, the revamped group hired producer Martin Rushent, who infused the band's synthesizer-based music with a toe-tapping, pop sensibility. "I wanted to make a pop electronic album," remembered Rushent. "Not a DAF or a Kraftwerk, but something that was accessible to everybody. The Human League just walked through the door at the right time." The producer replaced the traditional keyboard synthesizer with a Roland Microcomposer sequencer, added the flawless beat of a drum machine, and in 1981 produced *Dare*, which included the single "Don't You Want Me" that immediately topped the British chart.

After MTV placed "Don't You Want Me" in heavy rotation in 1982, the song became a number-one single, and the album hit the number-three position in the United States.

MTV lifted other wildly garbed, British electro-pop bands up the American charts. Through repeated showings of selected videos, it successfully promoted Soft Cell, which scored with a remake of the obscure soul song "Tainted Love" (1981) that stayed on the chart for forty-three weeks. The next year with the help of the music channel, A Flock of Seagulls reached the number-three slot with "I Ran (So Far Away)." In 1983, MTV marketed the Thompson Twins' club hit "Hold Me Now" and the Top Five "True" by the London quintet Spandau Ballet. The next year, MTV lifted Depeche Mode's (translated: "fast fashion") "People Are People" into the Top Twenty.

MTV refurbished the career of David Bowie, the seventies' icon who had helped lay the groundwork for electro-pop. Bowie, the king of glitter rock who served as a model of fashion for the foppish New Romantics, abandoned a hard, guitar-based rock sound for the synthesizer around 1976, when he released a collection of techno-pop songs, *Station to Station*. The next year, he began a three-album collaboration with synthesizer wunderkind Brian Eno, who produced a sometimes-fragile, sometimes-dense synthesizer sound that he had pioneered as a member of Roxy Music. In 1983, at the height of New Romantic success, the ever-visual Bowie recorded *Let's Dance*, which, with the help of MTV and a world tour, neared the top of the American chart and hit the number-one spot in Britain.

By 1983, the electro-pop sound, largely introduced to America by videos on MTV, had swept across the United States. It dominated the charts, filtered throughout mainstream pop, and captivated the TV generation. Pursuing the new sound, devotees bought an unprecedented number of synthesizers rather than guitars, which declined in sales by 37 percent in one year. MTV, created in the decade of technology, sold a visually interesting, electro-pop dance music to a generation raised on glitter rock, disco, and television.

MTV successfully marketed electro-pop through a new type of television programming known as the MTV style. It aired brief, glitzy, extremely fast-paced clips, which focused on fashion rather than content. "With the creation of MTV," explained Robert Pittman, president of music channel, "we changed the form of TV to fit the form of music, as opposed to trying to fit music into a narrative structure." Nick Rhodes, the keyboardist for Duran Duran more bluntly asserted that "I don't think videos have to make sense. They only have to be really cool-looking."

To hook their young viewers, especially teenage boys, the music channel videos many times featured scantily clad women with large breasts and toothy smiles. MTV aired such clips as Duran Duran's video "Girls on Film," which prominently highlighted two models in skimpy lingerie who fought and oil-rubbed a sumo wrestler amid the backdrop of the band, which performed the song. "It had glamour, it had polish, it had sex, it had good-looking boys, it had girls sliding on poles. It was a dirty film," confessed director Kevin Godley. "In hindsight, it had the ingredients that became MTV-able."

Ironically, MTV opened the music business to women. At first, video production held little interest to record companies, which focused on vinyl and radio. Because labels had "a lot of women in less glamorous, lower-paying jobs," recalled producer John Diaz, "they put women in charge of videos." "The record business was a man's world," explained RCA video producer Susan Silverman. "Video was the one area we could take over. We went in and fucking kicked ass." Women such as Debbie Newman and Debbie Samuelson at CBS, Liz Heller at MCA, and Siobhan Barron at Limelight oversaw video production for clips broadcast on the music channel.

MTV, airing rapid-fire, sex-filled clips of new bands for a neglected youth market, experienced a meteoric increase in viewers. Initially broadcast to 2.5 million households in late 1981, within two years the music channel reached more than 17 million homes on 2,000 cable affiliates. The average MTV viewer was less than 23 years old and watched the network for one hour a day on weekdays and ninety minutes on weekends. "They're watching it," raved MTV vice president Les Garland in early 1983, "not in front of their homework, not as background. They're watching it!"

Attracting the under-23-year-old bracket, MTV appealed to many corporate sponsors that manufactured products for the youth market. "MTV is very attractive," asserted Joseph Ostrow, executive vice president of the ad agency Young & Rubicam. "It allows you to target very discreetly to a particular segment of the population. For youth-oriented companies, that's terrific." During its first year of operation, MTV convinced more than 125 companies to spend $1,500 for a thirty-second spot and grossed $20 million. By 1984, revenues had jumped to $73 million.

Music Television provided a much-needed boost to a formerly radio-dependent U.S. record industry that in 1978 peaked with roughly $4 billion in gross revenues before declining 11 percent the next year. The network created a style of music for youth that radio had neglected. "Groups are chalking up huge sales on songs [through MTV] that have never been played on radio," boasted Les Garland. In 1983, *Billboard* estimated that exposure of mostly new bands on MTV resulted in sales increases of 15 to 20 percent. "We were there for the industry," explained John Lack, executive vice president of Warner. "We found we could help a business in trouble and it's worked, and they've responded. Ask anyone at CBS or RCA or Arista."

MTV and Michaelmania

MTV continued to support the U.S. recording industry by promoting a Motown-style revival, which followed naturally from electro-pop. Though using synthesizers, the New Romantics created a discolike dance music that had its foundation in the slick, fashionable Motown. As a youth, Steve Strange of Visage frequented northern soul clubs, which featured Motown-type bands. "Our direction came from the soul/disco/dance side, not rock," agreed Gary Kemp of Spandau Ballet.

As the synthesizer craze faded, MTV capitalized on the renewed interest in Motown by airing videos of former Motown star Michael Jackson. Growing up in Gary, Indiana, during the 1960s, Jackson and his siblings Tito, Jermaine, Jackie, and Marlon practiced songs and dance steps at home. "When I found out that my kids were interested in becoming entertainers, I really went to work with them," recalled father Joe Jackson. He rehearsed with them for two to three hours a day for three years before any public performances. "When the other kids would be out on the street playing games, my boys were in the house working—trying to learn how to be something in life," he noted. Under the strict and sometimes harsh tutelage of Joe Jackson, the boys entered and won talent contests in Indiana and Illinois and played at Chicago clubs. "This was on weekends," remembered the elder Jackson. "I had a Volkswagen bus and I bought a big luggage rack and put it on the top and had everybody on the inside of the bus."

Joe Jackson approached Motown about his family musical act. In 1967, he sent Berry Gordy a tape, which the label owner kept for three months before sending it back. Two years later, the persistent father convinced Gordy to sign the Jackson 5, who had impressed Gladys Knight, when she performed on the same bill as the boys at a civic Soul Weekend in Gary.

Berry Gordy, following his formula for success, groomed the boys. "We provide total guidance," a Motown vice president explained. "We provide their material, set their basic sound, and work out the choreographic routines." The company gave special attention to the 10-year-old Michael, who was taught to mimic James Brown's frenzied dancing and the romantic pleadings of Smokey Robinson. In late 1969, Motown featured Michael on the first Jackson 5 release, "I Want You Back," which by January 1970 hit the number-one slot on the singles chart and sold more than 2 million copies. "We're labeling it soul-bubblegum," declared Berry Gordy.

The Jackson 5 kept churning out the hits. They followed their first smash with thirteen Top Twenty singles, including the number-one hits "ABC," "The Love You Save," and "I'll Be There." By March 1976, when they left Motown, the Jackson 5 had received a commendation from Congress for their "contribution to American youth," had inspired a Saturday morning network television cartoon show, and had become the most successful African-American pop vocal group by selling more than 100 million records worldwide.

The Jackson 5, Gordy's crossover dream, appealed to all races, genders, and ages. "The Jacksons' music," proclaimed Joe Jackson, "is a type of music that the young kids like, and as you know, the older people like, too. It's music to send a message to all the people whether they're black or white. It's music for rejoicing, whether you're black or white. It's music for the whole world."

When the Jackson 5 signed with Epic Records, the group changed their name to the Jacksons and continued to produce hits. Using the songwriting team of Kenny Gamble and Leon Huff, they scored with the Top Ten "Enjoy Yourself" and then charted with their own material. In 1978, the brothers nearly hit the Top Ten with *Destiny*.

Michael Jackson enjoyed a successful solo career as well. In 1971 and 1972 he hit the chart with the Top Ten singles "Got to Be There," a reworking of "Rockin' Robin," and the number-one "Ben." In 1978, he played the scarecrow in the movie *The Wiz*, an all-African-American version of *The Wizard of Oz*, which starred Diana Ross. While filming the movie, Jackson met producer Quincy Jones, who arranged the music for the soundtrack. The next year, assisted by Jones, Jackson recorded *Off the Wall*, which sold 8 million copies and included the chart-topping singles "Don't Stop 'Til You Get Enough" and "Rock with You."

In 1982, Jackson again teamed with Quincy Jones on *Thriller*. Trying to appeal to both African-American and white audiences, he chose as the first single "The Girl Is Mine," a duet with former Beatle Paul McCartney, a choice that ensured a wide audience. He then released "Beat It," which included an Eddie Van Halen guitar solo that assured play on rock radio stations.

To further market his product, Jackson approached MTV with slick videos of several songs on the album. MTV had never played videos with African Americans in them. The music channel at first hesitated and then begrudgingly played "Billie Jean" in medium rotation. Inundated by a positive response, MTV placed the video in heavy rotation and the next week added "Beat It" to their playlist. On December 2, 1983, MTV aired the premiere of Jackson's 14-minute, horror-themed video of the title track, which cost more than a million dollars to produce, when most MTV videos had a budget of $50,000.

For the videos, the singer perfected dazzling choreography unlike most other rock acts. Gene Kelly, a popular dancer during the 1940s, attended a screening of the "Thriller" video and raved about Jackson's "native histrionic wit. He knows when to stop and then flash out like a bolt of lightning." "I think he's terrific," enthused Bob Fosse, the director-choreographer who became known for his work on the movie *Cabaret* and the Broadway smash *Pippin*. "Clean, neat, fast with sensuality that comes through…. It's the style. That's what Michael Jackson has." Even Fred Astaire, probably the best-known dancer in American history, visited the "Thriller" set and complimented Jackson: "My Lord, he is a wonderful mover."

Video provided an ideal medium for Jackson, who had been trained at Motown. "Rock videos have transformed the music industry, providing a showcase for Jackson in much the same way as musical comedy did for Fred Astaire in the 1930s," *Maclean's*, the Canadian counterpart to *Time* magazine, told its readers in 1984. "Videos have revived the demand for old-fashioned entertainment skills, an ideal situation for Jackson, who has been perfecting his act from the age of five."

MTV broadcast the visually stunning, expertly choreographed Jackson videos to help create Michaelmania. Though Jackson's records had always sold well, *Thriller* sold at an amazing rate after it was promoted on MTV. At the height of the mania, it sold 1 million copies every four days. The album stayed on the Japanese chart for sixty-five weeks, sold on the black market in the Soviet Union, and even topped the chart in South Africa. "Jackson, you might say, bridges the apartheid gap," observed one record executive.

Crazed fans around the globe snapped up Michael Jackson paraphernalia. They bought posters, buttons, and T-shirts. Michael Jackson fanatics purchased *Thriller* caps, key chains, duffel bags, bubblegum cards, an 11-inch Michael Jackson doll that could be twisted into various dance poses, and replicas of the single, white sequined glove that Jackson wore onstage. They even bought a video that chronicled the making of the video for the song "Thriller."

When the mania subsided in early 1985, Jackson had achieved singular success. He had released seven of the ten songs on the album as singles that reached the Top Ten. The 25-year-old singer had sold 40 million copies of *Thriller* worldwide, topped the U.S. charts in both 1983 and 1984, and won 150 gold and platinum awards, as well as a record-breaking eight Grammy awards. "Jackson," asserted *Time* in March 1984, "is the biggest thing since the Beatles. He is the hottest single phenomenon since Elvis Presley."

Michael Jackson, the most important rock star of the early 1980s, ostensibly epitomized the growing conservatism in America. He did not smoke, drink, or take drugs. He even refused to utter the word *funky*, preferring *jelly* instead. A devout adherent of the Jehovah's Witnesses, the singer attended meetings at a Kingdom Hall four times a week and regularly fasted on weekends. "Such pop superstars as Elvis Presley, Bob Dylan or the Beatles have traditionally posed a sexual or political challenge to the status quo," contended *Maclean's* magazine, "but Michael Jackson is by contrast an establishment figure, perfectly in tune with the conservative America of Ronald Reagan." In 1984, Jackson received a public service award from the president, a former actor, who himself had become one of the most popular U.S. presidents through his use of video.

Jackson amassed a fortune from his success. By the end of 1984, he had earned more than $30 million from the sales of *Thriller* and had grossed another $50 million from the burgeoning industry of Michael Jackson products. The singer increased his personal net worth to $75 million in 1985 and became one of the richest men in America.

Michael Jackson in full concert costume, 1988.

Trinity Mirror/Mirrorpix/Alamy Stock Photo.

If *Thriller* transformed Michael Jackson into an icon, the album boosted the status of MTV. "Michael Jackson was the reason MTV went from big to huge," explained John Sykes, a founding executive at the music channel. "He put us at the center of the culture. Bob Pittman thought that Jackson "brought people to MTV for the first time, and it made them stay and watch it again and again. Now everybody was into MTV." As jazz trumpeter and *Thriller* producer Quincy Jones observed, "MTV and Michael rode each other to glory."

The Jackson Legacy

The wild success of the Michael Jackson–MTV collaboration paved the way for other fashion-conscious, Motown-influenced artists, including British bands such as Culture Club, who climbed the charts with the help of MTV. Formed in 1981 by singer Boy George (b. George O'Dowd), the group dressed in outlandish costumes. "I used to dress up from the age of thirteen or fourteen, and George is the same," related the group's guitarist Mikey Craig. "Dressing up in different styles and going to the clubs is a big thrill for kids. You follow the fashion changes and get caught up in it."

The extravagantly bedecked, video-ready Culture Club played, in the words of Boy George, "imitation soul." In 1982, they released the soul-pop album *Kissing to Be Clever*, which included the warm, bouncy, Top Ten "Do You Really Want to Hurt Me" and "I'll Tumble 4 Ya." Scaling the charts on the coattails of Jackson's *Thriller* the next year, the group produced the number-two *Colour by Numbers*, which employed signature Motown riffs. "'Plagiarism' is one of my favorite words," admitted Boy George. "Culture Club is the most sincere form of plagiarism in modern music—we just do it better than most."

The Eurythmics scored with an updated Motown sound. Formed in 1980 by Dave Stewart and the photogenic, classically trained Annie Lennox, the duo first recorded electronic experimental music that failed to chart. Amid Michaelmania in 1983, the twosome earned international acclaim for *Sweet Dreams (Are Made of This)*, which featured the sultry, Motown-influenced vocals of Lennox over the insistent beat of a drum machine. "I identify my vocal style very much with black soul music," explained Lennox at the time. "Not with blues, but with 1960s soul. It really struck a chord in me, and I can't get away from that." Stewart added that "what she really loved was Tamla/Motown material." During the next two years, the duo followed with two Top Ten, soul-tinged albums.

Wham!, another sharply dressed duo from Britain, hit the charts with African-American-inspired dance music. Wham!'s Andrew Ridgeley and George Michael (b. Georgios Panayiotou) met as young teens and frequented local clubs, dancing to the soundtrack of *Saturday Night Fever*. "There was disco before *Saturday Night Fever* but after that it all caught fire," George Michael recalled. "It revolutionized dance music. And us."

In 1982, the two friends formed Wham! and released several successful singles. In late 1984, amid the furor over Michael Jackson, Michael and Ridgeley released a second album, *Make It Big*, which, after being promoted through videos aired on MTV, yielded three number-one singles in the United States and Britain, including "Wake Me Up Before You Go-Go." When Wham! disbanded in 1986, George Michael continued to offer spunky dance hits on the multi-million-selling *Faith* (1987), which yielded four number-one singles.

On the other side of the Atlantic, Madonna combined a decadent sex appeal with African-American dance rhythms to attain stardom. Born of Italian-American parents near Detroit, Madonna Louise Ciccone bonded with the Motown sound at an early age. "Motown was everywhere," she remembered about her neighborhood. "Stevie Wonder and Diana Ross and the Jackson 5, that's what I grew up on." Madonna won a dance scholarship to the University of Michigan but, after her freshman year, she left school to pursue a career as a dancer in New York City. She briefly studied at the Alvin Ailey Dance Theater and moved to Paris, where she danced with the revue of disco star Patrick Hernandez. In 1979, Madonna formed a band with drummer Steve Bray, and the next year she gave a tape of the band to Mark Kamins, a disco disc jockey who helped Madonna land a record contract with Sire.

Madonna used MTV to quickly gain notoriety. In 1983, the singer/dancer released her first self-named record, which presented her breathy vocals over a disco beat. A few months later, Madonna landed a spot at MTV's first Video Music Awards (VMA). She appeared in a wedding gown and writhed around the floor of the Radio City Music Hall. At one point, the entertainer shoved the microphone up into her pelvic area. "People were stunned and speechless that Madonna behaved in such a shocking fashion," recalled Liz Rosenberg, Madonna's press agent. Nick Rhodes from Duran Duran, who witnessed the scene, concluded that "afterwards, everyone knew she was going to be a *big* star."

Propelled by the VMA performance, provocative videos of her songs, and a trashy, sex-queen image, Madonna scaled the charts. In 1984, she attained national stardom with the number-one *Like a Virgin*, on the cover of which Madonna suggestively lounged in a lace corset and wore a belt emblazoned with "boy toy" on the buckle. Based upon her MTV success, the next year she snagged a leading role in the feature-length movie *Desperately Seeking Susan*.

The success of Michael Jackson's brand of Motown dance music reignited the careers of African-American soul-pop performers. "It inspired black artists not to look at themselves in a limited way," noted producer Quincy Jones. "Before Michael, those kinds of sales had never happened for a black artist. Michael did it. He did it for the first time."

Motown artist Lionel Richie followed Jackson to the top of the charts. In 1968, Richie joined with five other freshmen at the African-American Tuskegee Institute in Tuskegee, Alabama, to form the Commodores. Four years later, the band signed with Motown and for two years served as the opening act for the Jackson 5. In 1974, the Commodores released their first album to a mediocre response. After two more albums, Lionel Richie convinced the group to record his softer, soul-pop ballads such as "Three Times a Lady" and "Sail On," which hit the top of the singles chart.

Richie had even more success as a solo act with the assistance of MTV. In 1982, the Motown performer released his first solo album, which contained the chart-topping single "Truly." Though initially rejected by MTV, the next year he recorded *Can't Slow Down* in the midst of Michaelmania, and MTV gladly broadcast "All Night Long (All Night)," which hit the top of the chart and transformed Lionel Richie into *Billboard*'s Top Artist of 1984. "Michael had broken down the door," asserted the singer, "and from then on I was on MTV."

MTV helped the youngest member of the Jackson family, Janet Jackson. In the early eighties, before the success of *Thriller*, Janet Jackson released two commercially unsuccessful albums. In 1986, promoted by a series of videos and amid the Motown-influenced craze that had been created by her brother, Janet Jackson hit the top of the chart with *Control*. "Janet's a video artist," reasoned Roger Davies, who managed the singer.

Whitney Houston achieved similar success through video. The daughter of Cissy Houston, who had anchored the Aretha Franklin backup group the Sweet Inspirations, Whitney performed in a gospel choir at age eight. She continued her singing career by backing dozens of artists in the studio, including Jermaine Jackson and appeared as a model in fashion magazines such as *Glamour, Cosmopolitan*, and *Seventeen*. In 1983, Houston signed with Arista Records, which, as Motown had done with its young talent, groomed the young singer.

In 1985, Houston released her first, self-named album, which featured upbeat ballads in the Motown tradition. As the first two singles from the LP climbed the chart, she filmed a video of "How Will I Know," which, according to Peter Baron, Arista's associate director of video production and promotion, "helped build her image. She's become a superstar in a year." The singer had three consecutive number-one singles and sold 25 million copies of the album, which made it the biggest-selling debut in history.

Prince grafted rock guitars and overtly sexual lyrics onto a soul-pop sound for an innovative hybrid of the Michael Jackson formula for success. Born in Minneapolis to a bandleader father, Prince Rogers Nelson taught himself piano, guitar, and drums by age 14 and began to play a mixture of rock, funk, and soul. "I never grew up in one particular culture," Prince related. "I'm not a punk, but I'm not an R&B artist either— because I'm a middle-class kid from Minnesota, which is very much white America."

In 1976, Prince met Minneapolis sound engineer Chris Moon, who suggested sexually explicit lyrics. "It was amazing to see," recalled Moon. "Here was this very quiet kid, but once he'd discovered the notion of sex as a vehicle for his writing, it was as if a door unlocked for him." Within a year, Prince signed with Warner Brothers and recorded four moderately successful albums.

Prince attained stardom through video and film. In 1982, he released *1999* and filmed a video of the song "Little Red Corvette," one of the first clips by an African-American artist aired on the music channel, which slowly lifted the single to the Top Ten. In 1984, Prince starred and performed in a quasi-autobiographical film *Purple Rain*, which grossed $80 million and won an Oscar. Through constant promotion by MTV, Prince sold 14 million copies of the soundtrack and scored with the number-one "When Doves Cry" and the number-two "Purple Rain." In 1985, Prince followed with the number-one *Around the World in a Day*. As with other African-American and white soul-pop artists in the wake of the mania over Michael Jackson, Prince rode the video wave to prominence.

Pop Goes the Metal

MTV ensured its preeminent place among the cable networks during the decade by creating a craze for pop metal bands. As it had done with electro-pop and soul-pop, the music channel delivered a visually exciting, largely inoffensive heavy metal to post–baby boomers.

Van Halen served as the archetype for the metal bands of the 1980s. The sons of a jazz musician, Alex and Eddie Van Halen grew up in the Netherlands, where they received extensive classical music training. In 1965, they moved with their family to Pasadena, California, where they discovered and played rock and roll. By 1974, the Van Halen brothers joined with bassist Michael Anthony and singer David Lee Roth to form a band, which for three years performed at Los Angeles bars such as Gazzarri's on Sunset Strip in West Hollywood.

The members of Van Halen each contributed a different element to their unique sound. "I think the only true rocker of the bunch is Al," related guitarist Eddie Van Halen. "He's the only one who listens to AC/DC and all that kind of stuff. Dave will walk in with a disco tape, and I'll walk in with my progressive tapes, and Mike walks in with his Disneyland stuff." At home, Eddie preferred the "progressive stuff" and "a lot of Chopin, piano. Very little rock-and-roll."

Unlike the blues-rooted heavy-metal artists of the late sixties and early seventies, the eclectic Van Halen presented a more polished, smooth sound. The band favored a variety of tempos; rapid-fire, arpeggio guitar solos much shorter than the extended guitar breaks of the original heavy-metal groups; and fast-paced, light bass lines. Van Halen many time spotlighted three-part harmonies that reinforced the hooks in the songs and, according to bassist Michael Anthony, added "a more sophisticated pop element that most metal bands weren't able to replicate." In addition, Van Halen featured frequent falsetto screams by the photogenic, acrobatic David Lee Roth, who added a wry sense of humor to the lyrics. "Van Halen is entertainment," contended singer Roth. "Van Halen is entertainment delivered at maximum impact, but it's entertainment."

The band started a slow rise to fame. In 1976, the group recorded a demo tape financed by Gene Simmons of Kiss, who spotted them at the Starwood club in Los Angeles. A year later, they signed a contract with Warner Brothers and in early 1978 released their first album, which hit the Top Twenty and sold more than 2 million copies. Van Halen followed with four Top Ten albums. After Eddie Van Halen received acclaim for his guitar work on Michael Jackson's "Beat It," the band neared the top of the chart with *1984* after receiving constant support from MTV.

Def Leppard perfected the pop metal that Van Halen originated. Raised in the factory town of Sheffield in the midlands of England, vocalist Joe Elliott, guitarists Steve Clark and Pete Willis, and bass player Rick Savage worked in blue-collar jobs before founding the band. They drew their inspiration from a combination of heavy-metal and pop groups. "We always loved the heavy bands of the early seventies, obviously Zeppelin, Uriah Heep, Deep Purple even, but other than that we also were very influenced by what was happening in the pop charts," related bassist Rick Savage. "I suppose if you analyzed it, it was some sort of cross between the two forms." He added that "We always want to have that commercial aspect that's pleasing on the ear, while the seventeen-year-olds can still get off on the power of it."

In 1981, the band joined with producer Robert "Mutt" Lange, who helped Def Leppard refine their pop-metal. "I heard those vocal harmonies and thought, 'Wow, an English band doing that stuff,'" remembered Lange. "Since they had the looks and they had the riffs I knew that with me as an extra member, so to speak, we could pull the songs together." By 1983, after Phil Collen replaced guitarist Willis, Def Leppard had perfected its sound. The group featured tight vocal harmonies and dramatic guitar work accentuated by Lange's production. Joe Elliott called the sound "nice, youthful, melodic rock-'n'-roll."

The band members penned catchy, unobtrusive lyrics. "Because the whole idea of Def Leppard is escapism," asserted Rick Savage, "we hate singing about unemployment and such, and we hate bands that do sing about it. Everybody knows it's tough. A band can't change anything. Who wants to go to one of our shows to hear how bad life is?" Joe Elliott echoed that "it's all wine, women and song. Nothing annoys me more than records about politics this, Greenpeace that. Someone has to be the opposite, and that's us. All we are is total escapism."

The apolitical band members visually transformed themselves for video. Vocalist Elliott dyed his hair blonde, and the group dressed in glam outfits. "We're all fucking posers," admitted Rick Savage. "We all want to go on stage, pose, wear dinky white boots, tight trousers and have all the girls looking at our buttocks." By the end of their makeover, gushed Joe Elliott, "we couldn't wait to make videos."

MTV promoted the photogenic, escapist pop metal of Def Leppard through performance videos. Offering heavy rotation to clips of such songs as "Photograph," the music channel broadcast the band to its young viewers. Coupled with constant touring, the band successfully marketed *Pyromania* (1983), which sold more than 9 million copies. "1983 was our year," enthused Cliff Burnstein, comanager of the group.

The music channel contributed to the success of other pop-metal bands, some of which favored the outlandish costumes, puffy hair, and the antics of seventies glam rockers. In 1981, Motley Crue played a West Coast version of video-ready glam rock. Nikki Sixx (b. Frank Feranna, Jr.) on bass, vocalist Vince Neil (b. Vince Neil Wharton), guitarist Mick Mars (b. Bob Deal), and drummer Tommy Lee (b. Tommy Lee Bass) began performing together around Los Angeles. Setting fire to their extravagant clothing and chain sawing mannequins on stage, the band gained a loyal following for their theatrical heavy metal.

The flamboyantly garbed band identified Kiss as its major influence. "When I first saw Kiss I stood in line for six hours at the Paramount Theater in Seattle, Washington," recalled Nikki Sixx. "I was sitting in the front row, and when they took the stage I knew then that I wanted to have a band that was nothing less than what I saw. The theater bug bit me. Rock 'n' roll from then on had to have an element of theater to excite me."

The band climbed the chart through MTV. In May 1983, Motley Crue signed to Elektra Records. Five months later, they released *Shout at the Devil*, which, through heavy rotation on MTV entered the Top Twenty. By the end of 1984, the readers of *Hit Parader* and *Circus* magazines voted the band Rock Act of the Year. The glam rockers followed with the Top Ten *Theater of Pain* (1985).

Ratt came from the same Los Angeles heavy-metal scene. Banding together in 1982 around guitarist Robbin Crosby and singer Stephen Pearcy, the group played an escapist pop metal. "We have more melody in our music," noted Crosby as he compared the group to heavy-metal pioneers such as Led Zeppelin. "We talk about love and sex and reality and fantasy—just down-to-earth, fun stuff."

The group members affected a glam image to increase their popularity. "When we first got together, we were a real heavy-metal band—black leather, studs, the whole thing," admitted Robbin Crosby. To differentiate themselves from other metal outfits, Ratt, "started wearing more fashionable clothes," continued Crosby. "Started dressing real sharp. But it's more of a mass appeal kind of thing."

The band proved its popular appeal with the help of MTV. In 1984, Ratt released *Out of the Cellar* with accompanying videos for the music channel. By the next year, the group had cracked the Top Ten and had sold more than 2 million copies of their debut. The next year, the band repeated its success with million-selling *Invasion of Your Privacy*.

MTV boosted the career of Bon Jovi. Formed in 1983 by singer Jon Bon Jovi (b. John Bongiovi) and quickly signed to Mercury Records, the pop-metal band, described itself as "just a good-time entertainment band." Despite extensive touring to promote its first two LPs, it failed to crack the U.S. Top Thirty. Three years later, the group released *Slippery When Wet* and filmed videos for several of the songs, which MTV aired ceaselessly. By late 1987, Bon Jovi had sold more than 12 million copies of its chart-topping album. "The success of such current hot groups as Bon Jovi," observed *Time*, "is largely traceable to the saturation airplay given their videos on MTV."

Guns N' Roses at least partly owed its success to MTV. Launched in March 1985 by vocalist William "Axel" Rose and guitarist Izzy Stradlin, the band favored a mixture of heavy metal and theatrical pop. Rose cited the Sex Pistol's *Never Mind the Bullocks* and *Queen II* as his favorite albums. Other group members idolized Aerosmith, the mid-seventies hard rockers who, in the words of their guitarist Joe Perry, took "the emotional power of the blues and cut it with an accessible pop sensibility."

Within a few months of their formation, Guns N' Roses landed a contract with Geffen Records and started their rise to the top. On July 21, 1987, they released *Appetite for Destruction* and a video of "Welcome to the Jungle," which David Geffen convinced MTV to place the single in rotation. The next year, the band topped the chart with "Sweet Child o' Mine," which MTV heavily promoted. "So they had two songs being played regularly on MTV. And it just took off," recalled the band's manager Doug Goldstein. Later in the 1988, Guns N' Roses hit the Top Ten with "Paradise City," which MTV featured on its daily heavy-metal program, Headbangers Ball that premiered on April 18, 1987. By the end of 1988, Axl Rose and his band mates sold more than 14 million copies of *Appetite for Destruction* and had become superstars.

The MTV-based success of acts such as Guns N' Roses opened the doors for a pop-metal explosion during the late 1980s. "The majors are now going nuts. Everyone's out there trying to sign up a metal band," reported Bob Chiappardi, co-owner of the metal-oriented Concrete Marketing. The major labels signed acts such as Poison, Kix, Kingdom Come, and dozens of others. Established pop-metal acts continued to sell. In 1986, Van Halen topped the chart with *5150* and followed with the number-one *OU812* (1988), both of which benefited from videos that received continual play on MTV. After a four-year hiatus, Def Leppard topped the charts with *Hysteria*, which sold more than 5 million copies. In 1989, Motley Crue topped the chart with *Dr. Feelgood* (1989).

MTV aired sexist videos to sell the pop-metal bands, which found their target audience among teenage boys. It featured a blonde, skimpily clad bombshell in the video for "Cherry Pie" by the band Warrant. "There was so much pressure to sell sex," confessed lead singer Jani Lane. The music channel prominently featured Whitesnake singer David Coverdale's girlfriend and actress Tawny Kitaen who posed suggestively in the band's clips. "The hair metal bands loved MTV and they had a huge number of fans," snapped Judy McGrath, eventually chairwoman and CEO of MTV networks, "but their videos promoted the objectification of women."

MTV, using sex to sell its acts, rose to a prominence through the success of pop-metal and electro-pop bands and the unparalleled achievements of Michael Jackson. "At any one time, 130,000 homes are watching MTV, according to Nielsen," observed Len Epand of Polygram Records. "If the video is in power rotation—fifteen or sixteen plays a week—and that audience tunes in ten times, that's 1.3 million people hearing the record and deciding whether they like it or not. If they like it, they'll buy it." The director of marketing for RCA video productions, Laura Foti, added that "there isn't a national radio station. That's where MTV comes in. That's where they have their power: immediately showing everyone in the country this new band." Joe Jackson, the new-wave singer who hit the chart in 1979 with *Look Sharp*, complained about the dominance of MTV: "Things which used to count, such as being a good composer, player, or singer, are getting lost in the desperate rush to visualize everything. It is now possible to be all of the above and still get nowhere simply by not looking good in a video, or worse still, not making one."

The marketing clout of MTV and its ability to air the label-produced videos for free translated into profits. In the first half of 1984, after the *Thriller* hysteria started to abate, MTV registered $8.1 million in profits from sales of $30.3 million. In 1986, after Viacom International purchased the network from Warner Amex for more than a half million dollars, it grossed $111 million and turned a profit of $47 million. Though by the late eighties, when its ratings declined, MTV tied with the USA Network and the Cable News Network for first place among the cable channels.

The video stars promoted by MTV became extremely wealthy. In 1991, Michael Jackson, the jewel of MTV, signed a contract with Sony that gave Jackson half of all profits from his albums after he received artist, publishing, and songwriting royalties with a $5 million per-disc guarantee. Madonna funneled her $25 million annual salary into antiques, gold coins, Japanese art, and porcelain. "Madonna is well diversified," observed her business manager Bert Padell. Bon Jovi and his band mates invested in money-market funds and municipal bonds. Duran Duran, one of the first successes on the music channel bought rare art and real estate to shelter earning.

MTV, broadcast on more than 5,000 cable outlets to more than 46 million viewers in 1989, had helped define eighties rock and roll. It fostered and successfully promoted electro-pop and pop metal and created a frenzy over Michael Jackson's *Thriller*. To a large extent, the music network replaced radio as the preeminent trendsetter in rock, and CBS Records President Walter Yetnikoff proclaimed that "MTV has been a shot in the arm for the record business." As *Billboard* noted in its wrap-up of the decade, "MTV is singularly responsible for one of the most basic changes in the current music fan's vocabulary: Where somebody might have said ten years ago, 'Yeah, I've heard that song,' that same person now might likely say, 'Yeah, I saw that video,' or, even more revealing, 'Yeah, I saw that song.'" During the eighties, MTV packaged and delivered rock and roll to the TV generation.

Chapter 19
The Promise of Rock and Roll

"In the '80s, which is a barren era, we look back at the '60s as a great reservoir of talent, of high ideals, and of the will and desire to change things."

—Bono

"I'm a romantic," Bruce Springsteen confessed to a reporter in 1980. "To me the idea of a romantic is someone who sees the reality, lives the reality every day but knows about the possibilities, too. You can't lose sight of the dreams. That's what great rock is about to me, it makes the dream seem possible." Rock and roll, added Springsteen, is "a promise, an oath."

The romanticism of Bruce Springsteen, rooted in sixties' idealism, became prevalent from the mid-eighties into the nineties. It appealed to baby boomers who during the sixties protested against the war in Vietnam and now confronted a severe economic recession. The return to a sixties sensibility resulted in numerous benefit concerts, which revived the careers of some sixties rockers and revitalized the rock industry. It influenced a nineties country-rock boom, which captivated the baby-boom generation. Baby boomers embraced a sixties-inspired, cause-oriented rock that provided a stark contrast to the entertaining, glossy, sexy images on MTV.

Trickling Down with Ronald Reagan

The return to sixties ideals occurred around mid-decade, when the policies of President Ronald Reagan drove the country into a dire economic recession and increasingly stratified the American people into rich and poor. Taking office in January 1981, Reagan hoped to roll back the innovative social programs of Franklin Roosevelt's New Deal through conservative economic policies and subsidies to businesses. Using "trickle down" logic, he believed that government aid to corporations would lead to increased profits for business, which would in turn reinvest new revenues into expanded operations that would translate into higher wages and increased employment. Misunderstanding the basic profit motive of capitalism, for eight years Ronald Reagan offered corporate incentives, slashed domestic programs, and padded the military budget to force the nation into an economic tailspin.

A determined Reagan tried to decrease the involvement of the federal government in social welfare programs. During his tenure as president, he cut spending for such programs as job training, college loans, food and medical aid, disability services, and childcare centers for working mothers. Opposed to any programs that sought to provide equality to disadvantaged groups, in 1981 Reagan lashed out against affirmative action by ending the requirement for contractors on federally funded projects to adhere to affirmative action laws. During his administration, he reduced efforts by the Justice Department to enforce laws that prohibited job discrimination and encouraged fair housing.

Farm workers protest against Ronald Reagan, 1981.

Library of Congress Prints and Photographs Division [LC-DIG-ds-02975].

While abandoning poor, disadvantaged Americans, Reagan catered to the interests of business. He crushed the trade unions by first targeting air traffic controllers. In the summer of 1981, when the Professional Air Traffic Controllers Organization (PATCO) declared a strike, Reagan threatened that if the strikers did not report for work within 48 hours, they would forfeit their jobs and would be terminated. Two days later on August 5, 1981, Reagan fired 11,359 controllers.

In addition to neutralizing unions to benefit businesses, the president pushed through the Economic Recovery Act (1981), which provided a series of tax breaks to businesses and wealthy individuals. The act further stratified American society by cutting the highest tax rate from 70 to 28 percent and effectively decreased the taxes of the wealthiest 1 percent of Americans by 6 percent while increasing the taxes of the poorest 1.6 percent of wage earners by 10 percent.

Just as Reagan cut taxes for the rich and lowered governmental revenue, he escalated spending for the military to defeat the Soviet Union, which he called the "evil empire." From 1980 to 1988, Reagan ballooned defense spending from $134 billion to $290 billion.

The twin policies of tax reduction for corporations and high tax-bracket Americans and skyrocketing funding for the Pentagon dramatically increased the national debt. When Reagan assumed the presidency, the United States had a national debt of approximately $995 billion. By September 1984, the debt increased to $1.6 trillion, and near the end of the Reagan presidency in late 1989 the United States had a debt load of nearly $3 trillion.

Reagan's Darwinian, free-market policies led to a crisis in the domestic banking industry. Intent on deregulating banks and savings and loans, he supported a new law that gave savings and loans the ability to expand their portfolios into lending for risky real estate deals just as the real-estate market soften. Caught with billions of dollars in bad loans, many banks failed. In 1983, 49 banks crashed and another 540 banks teetered on the brink of closing. Between 1980 and 1983, 118 savings and loans with assets of $43 billion became insolvent. Fearing the effect of the banking debacle on the economy and his popularity, Reagan eventually spent $160 billion to rescue savings and loans and in 1984 engineered a $4.5 billion bailout for the Continental Illinois National Bank and Trust Company, the seventh largest bank in the United States. Despite these government subsidies, the insolvency of the banking industry persisted until the end of Reagan's second term with the Financial Institutions Reform Act (1989).

Reagan's pro-business stance led to economic distress for many average Americans. In 1981, when Reagan took office, the unemployment rate stood at 7.2 percent. Within two years, it had swelled to 10.8 percent and remained in double digits for nearly a year, only falling when Reagan revised the formula to calculate the unemployment rate by ignoring workers whose benefits had expired. Excepting for 1988 and 1989, the Reagan legacy of high unemployment persisted until 1994, when Democrat Bill Clinton took office.

By the midpoint of the Reagan years in 1984, the economy stood in shambles, and many Americans struggled to survive. According to a Census report, nearly 66 million Americans in 36 million households were forced to rely on government benefits in the third quarter of 1983. Of the total, which represented nearly 30 percent of the U.S. population, 42 million Americans used food stamps, welfare, subsidized housing, or Medicaid to meet their most basic needs.

Many baby boomers who expected the prosperity of their youth to continue especially felt the effects of the recession. "When we grew up in the '50s and '60s, we were told the world would be our oyster," explained Richard Hokenson, a demographer at a New York firm. "Now life's turned out to be more of a struggle than we were told it would be." In 1984, *U.S. News and World Report* referred to the baby boomers as "the disillusioned generation, people in their 20s and early 30s who wonder whatever happened to the American dream."

The Boss

Bruce Springsteen, nicknamed the Boss, sang about Americans who felt the hard times. The son of a bus driver, Springsteen grew up in Freehold, New Jersey. At age 14, he learned guitar, which, as with many other rockers, provided Springsteen with solace. "Music saved me," he remarked. "From the beginning, my guitar was something I could go to. If I hadn't found music, I don't know what I would have done."

Armed with a guitar, Springsteen joined a series of bands beginning in his high school years. Working with a variety of local musicians, in 1971 Springsteen finally formed the ten-piece Bruce Springsteen Band, which included David Sancious on keyboards, bassist Garry Tallent, Steve Van Zandt on guitar, drummer Vini Lopez, keyboardist Danny Frederici, and Clarence Clemons on saxophone.

Working as a solo act by early 1972, the Boss signed a contract with manager Mike Appel, who arranged an audition with Columbia Records talent head John Hammond. "The kid absolutely knocked me out," recalled Hammond, who had discovered Bob Dylan, Aretha Franklin, and Count Basie. "I only hear somebody really good once every ten years, and not only was Bruce the best, he was a lot better than Dylan when I first heard him." Within a week, Hammond signed Springsteen to the label.

Springsteen initially failed to fulfill Hammond's expectations. In January 1973, he and a reformed version of the Bruce Springsteen Band released a folk-tinged debut, *Greetings from Asbury Park, N. J.*, which, though touted by Columbia as a masterpiece by the "new Dylan," in the first year sold only 12,000 copies, mostly to fans on the

Jersey shore. The band toured to promote the album, mismatched as an opening act for the group Chicago. In May 1973, Springsteen made a disastrous appearance at the CBS Records Annual Convention in San Francisco. "It was during a period when he physically looked like Dylan," recalled Hammond. "He came on with a chip on his shoulder and played too long. People came to me and said, 'He really can't be that bad, can he, John?'" At the end of the year, Springsteen and his group, renamed the E Street Band after a road in Belmar, New Jersey, released *The Wild, the Innocent and the E Street Shuffle*, which sold only 70,000 copies in nearly a year.

The next year Springsteen received some encouragement. In April 1974, at Charley's, a small bar in Harvard Square in Cambridge, Massachusetts, the guitarist was spotted by *Rolling Stone* journalist Jon Landau, who wrote: "I saw the rock-and-roll future and its name is Bruce Springsteen." Springsteen remembered that "at the time, Landau's quote helped reaffirm a belief in myself. The band and I were making $50 a week. It helped me go on." Within a year, he hired Landau to coproduce his third album, *Born to Run*.

Springsteen displayed his many influences on *Born to Run*. Besides the obvious Dylan elements that surfaced in his rapid-fire lyrics and harmonica playing, he borrowed the dramatic stylings of Roy Orbison, the wails of Little Richard, and the operatic sweep of Phil Spector that he labeled "the sound of universes colliding." The Boss adopted the pounding piano of Jerry Lee Lewis, the intensity of R&B exemplified by the honking sax of Clarence Clemons, and Chuck Berry's chugging guitar sound and his preoccupation with girls and cars. "I was about 24 and I said, 'I don't want to write

Bruce Springsteen rocks Milwaukee, October 2, 1975.

Mark Goff.

about girls and cars anymore,'" recalled Springsteen, who cherished his own 1957 yellow Chevy convertible, customized with orange flames. "Then I realized, 'Hey! That's what Chuck Berry wrote about!'" Within one record, Springsteen incorporated many aspects of the history of rock and roll to produce a signature sound.

Executives at Columbia Records launched a nearly unprecedented promotional campaign to market *Born to Run*. They spent $40,000 on radio spots in twelve major geographic regions to promote Springsteen's first two albums, and in mid-August, Columbia Records and manager Mike Appel organized an exclusive performance by Springsteen at the Bottom Line in New York City, reserving almost 1,000 of the 4,000 tickets for the press and radio disc jockeys. After releasing *Born to Run* in September 1975, they spent an additional $200,000 to advertise the record in the press and on the radio and $50,000 for television spots. "These are very large expenditures for a record company," admitted Bruce Lundvall, then vice president of Columbia. To further plug their artist, the Columbia brass engineered cover stories in the October 27 issues of both *Time* and *Newsweek*.

The promotional blitz had mixed results. *Born to Run*, though hailed by the critics and reaching the number-three slot, sold fewer than 1 million copies in the first year after its release. The title cut from the album peaked at number twenty-three on the singles chart. *Darkness on the Edge of Town*, Springsteen's follow-up, released in 1978 after a lengthy legal dispute with Appel, stalled at number five on the chart. A single from the album, "Prove It All Night," failed to crack the Top Thirty.

After his thirtieth birthday in 1979, Springsteen changed along with other baby boomers. "I'm a different person now," he shrugged late 1980. "When you're in your 30s or late 30s, the world is different. At least it looks different."

Springsteen's music reflected his changed attitude. Rather than focusing exclusively on cars, girls, and images of street toughs, his music dealt with the plight of average Americans trapped by circumstances. The transition started with *Darkness on the Edge of Town*. In addition to Beach Boys–like paeans such as "Racing in the Street," the album included songs such as "Factory" that, in the words of the Boss, described people "who are going from nowhere to nowhere." The double album *The River* (1980) continued to combine car-and-girl-oriented songs such as "Cadillac Ranch" and "You Can Look (But You Better Not Touch)" with the title song, which told about a factory worker who lost both love and his job because of a collapsing economy.

The stark, acoustic album *Nebraska* (1982) completed the transition. It chronicled the alienation of aging baby-boom Americans who had abandoned their sixties idealism. "I think what happened during the seventies was that, first of all, the hustle became legitimized," Springsteen asserted. "*Born to Run* was a spiritual record in dealing with values. *Nebraska* was about a breakdown of all those values….It was kind of about a spiritual crisis, in which man is left lost. It's like he has nothing left to tie him to society anymore. He's isolated from the government. Isolated from his job. Isolated from his family."

In 1984, Springsteen fused his vision with the infectious rock and roll of the E Street Band to create his masterpiece *Born in the U.S.A.* He sang in "Downbound Train" about a lumber worker who lost his job and his wife, when hard times hit. In the brooding "My Hometown," the Boss detailed the bleak changes affecting a town located in the depressed heartland of industrial Middle America. Springsteen made a powerful statement in the title song, wailing about the dead-end fate of a working-class Vietnam veteran ten years after the war. In "Glory Days," he sang about the aimlessness of an ex–high school baseball star and a divorced ex–prom queen.

The album dealt with the loss of innocence experienced by an aging baby-boom generation, which faced the grim realities of the Reagan era. "I think *Born in the U.S.A.* kind of casts a suspicious eye on a lot of things. That's the idea. These are not the same people anymore and it's not the same situation," the Boss remarked. "It certainly is not as innocent anymore. But, like I said, it's ten years down the line." "I wanted to make the characters grow up," he explained.

Despite an unadorned realism, Springsteen sought a renewed commitment to sixties social consciousness. "We've abandoned a gigantic part of the population—we've just left them for dead. But we're gonna have to pay the piper some day," he insisted. "I live great, and plenty of people do, but it affects you internally in some fashion, and it just eats away at whatever sort of spirituality you pursue." Springsteen pledged a return "to the social consciousness that was part of the '60s," which during the next decade seemed to become "old-fashioned." "I wanted the band to come out to be an alternative voice of America that was being presented by the Reagan administration," the Boss explained. "There's people who the trickle down theory of economics ain't trickling down to," he proclaimed to screaming fans at a concert in Greensboro, North Carolina during the *Born in the U.S.A.* tour.

The Boss backed his words with action. On September 23, 1979, on his thirtieth birthday, he performed at Madison Square Garden in New York City in a concert organized by Musicians United for Safe Energy (MUSE), which protested against the proliferation of hazardous nuclear power plants. A year later, he played six benefit concerts for down-and-out Vietnam veterans.

Springsteen intensified his benefit appearances on the *Born in the U.S.A.* tour. He donated money to Washington Fair Share, which forced the cleanup of an illegal landfill in Washington State. "This is 1984 and people seem to be searching for something," he told the sellout crowd at the Tacoma Dome. In Oakland, California, he urged listeners to donate to the Berkeley Emergency Food Project, and in New Jersey, he donated $10,000 to a soup kitchen. He sent money to unemployed steelworkers, striking copper miners, and food banks across the country. The Boss united with Peter Gabriel, formerly of Genesis, to tour in support of Amnesty International, which sought to free political prisoners around the world. Springsteen, who donated more than $200,000 to the charity, told one sellout crowd on the tour, "The great challenge of adulthood is holding on to your idealism after you lose your innocence." "One of the things I can do is play benefits and help people out that need help, people that are struggling," he contended in December 1984.

Born in the U.S.A., reflecting Springsteen's social awareness, appealed to many baby boomers who had protested the war in Vietnam and during the sixties had hoped for a better world. Snapped up by thirty-something baby boomers, the album reached the top of the U.S. and British charts. The LP yielded seven Top-Ten singles and by the end of the decade had sold 11 million copies.

The Benefits

Benefit concerts given by other rock performers demonstrated the reawakened interest in improving the world. Bob Geldof launched the first major benefit of the Eighties. Geldof, the leader of the British rock band the Boomtown Rats, saw a graphic BBC television report about the devastating effects of famine in Ethiopia. Moved by the catastrophe, on November 25, 1984, he contacted thirty-five fellow rock musicians and recorded the single, "Do They Know It's Christmas?" The Geldof called the effort Band Aid. "If you don't like the music, buy the record and throw it to the rubbish. You don't need to like the music, but we need you to buy the records to save lives," he pleaded. He wanted to "draw attention to a monstrous human crime, a moral and intellectual absurdity. It worked," he enthused. Geldof and his fellow musicians donated the $84 million proceeds directly to the starving victims in Ethiopia.

Spurred by their British counterparts and joined by Geldof, several American superstars started United Support of Artists for Africa, or simply USA for Africa. On January 28, 1985, nearly forty rock luminaries such as Motown artists Michael Jackson, Diana Ross, Lionel Richie, and Stevie Wonder, R&B giant Ray Charles, Bob Dylan, and Bruce Springsteen got together in the A&M studios in Los Angeles to record the single,

"We Are the World." The song became a blockbuster hit and raised American awareness of the plight of thousands of starving Ethiopians. The nonprofit group asked their listeners to buy the single, the record album, and other USA-for-Africa merchandise such as T-shirts and sweatshirts to support the cause.

Not content with his successes and those of his American counterparts, Bob Geldof hatched another venture to aid Ethiopia and dubbed his effort Live Aid. He planned two coordinated televised concerts, one in Philadelphia's JFK Stadium and the other in London's Wembley Stadium. He captured the imagination of artists of all types, including Crosby, Stills and Nash, the Beach Boys, David Bowie, Santana, The Who, Elton John, ex-Beatle Paul McCartney, singer Mick Jagger of the Rolling Stones, and folk legends Bob Dylan and Joan Baez. He also attracted heavy metalers Judas Priest and Black Sabbath, blues rocker Eric Clapton, Robert Plant of Led Zeppelin, and blues legend B. B. King. Besides his own band, the singer snagged such new acts as U2, Dire Straits, and Madonna. He even convinced the rap group Run-D.M.C. to participate. Airing on July 13, 1985, broadcast of the two concerts lasted more than seventeen hours, reached 140 countries and 1.5 billion people, and generated more than $140 million in pledges. "I think Live Aid and Band Aid were the beginning of an awareness," observed Jackson Browne, the seventies singer/songwriter who helped organize the MUSE benefit concert.

Steve Van Zandt, nicknamed Little Steven, organized rock-and-rollers against racism in South Africa. In late 1985, after leaving the E Street Band for a solo career, he established Artists United Against Apartheid, an organization that lashed out against the brutal discrimination toward blacks in South Africa. He and his compatriots targeted the $90 million, white-only Bophuthatswana resort, Sun City, which had hosted Rod Stewart, Linda Ronstadt, and Queen. Little Steven released an album, a book, and a video to combat apartheid, enlisting the support of rock luminaries such as Springsteen, Pete Townshend, Ringo Starr, Bob Dylan, Keith Richards, and Lou Reed. Taking the civil rights movement into the international arena, Little Steven donated nearly a half-million dollars to causes, which supported the anti-apartheid struggle. "I hope next year and the year after there will continue to be some measure of reality in music," declared Van Zandt. "That's vitally important."

The anti-apartheid furor among rock musicians peaked with Paul Simon's *Graceland*. After participating in USA for Africa, the former folk rocker traveled to South Africa to record with South African musicians. "To go over and play Sun City, it would be exactly like going over to do a concert in Nazi Germany at the height of the Holocaust," Simon reasoned. "But what I did was go over and essentially play to the Jews." He hoped the record, which featured the South African choir Ladysmith Black Mambazo, would serve as a "powerful form of politics" that would attract people "to the music, and once they hear what's going on within it, they'd say, 'What? They're doing *that* to these people?'" In 1986, *Graceland* topped the British chart and climbed to the number-three slot in the United States.

Children of the Sixties

The renewed interest in social causes shaped a number of new bands, notably U2. Formed in Dublin by schoolmates Bono (Paul Hewson), The Edge (David Evans), Adam Clayton, and Larry Mullen, Jr., in March 1978 the band won a talent contest sponsored by Guinness Harp Lager. After two years of local gigs, it released the debut single "11 O'Clock Tick Tock," which failed to chart. The group recorded two albums, *Boy* (1980) and *October* (1981), which attracted critical attention but sold only moderately.

U2 infused its music with a political message. In October 1982, during a concert in Belfast, Northern Ireland, Bono introduced the song "Sunday Bloody Sunday," which condemned the long-standing political troubles in Ireland and called for peace. A few months later, the band released *War*, which combined anthem-like rock with various strands of punk. "Punk had died," recalled The Edge. "We couldn't believe it had happened, and *War* was designed as a knuckle buster in the face of the new pop." "We loved the Clash's attitude early on and Richard Hell and the Voidoids, the Pistols," the guitarist continued. "We wanted love and anger. We wanted a protest record, but a positive protest record." Right for the times, *War* topped the British chart and neared the Top Ten in the United States.

The band continued to demonstrate its commitment to sixties ideals. Though beginning to replace hard-driving guitars with more ethereal, echo-laden sounds engineered by producer Brian Eno, U2 dedicated its 1984 hit "Pride (In the Name of Love)" to Martin Luther King, Jr. In July of the same year, Bono sang "Blowing in the Wind" in a duet with Bob Dylan at a Dylan concert in Ireland. U2 contributed to Band Aid, played at the Live Aid spectacular in Wembley Stadium, appeared on the anti–Sun City project, and performed on Amnesty International's twenty-fifth anniversary tour. In 1986, the band raised funds for the unemployed in Dublin and performed in San Francisco for Amnesty International's "A Conspiracy of Hope" tour.

By 1987, when it hit the top of the charts on both sides of the Atlantic with *Joshua Tree*, U2 had become spokesmen for change. As Bono remarked that year, "in the '80s, which is a barren era, we look back at the '60s as a great reservoir of talent, of high ideals and of the will and desire to change things." "We were part of creating this kind of positive protest movement in the Eighties…[based] on the idealism of the Sixties," Bono later remembered. He focused on "this journey of equality, which had come through the civil-rights movement in the United States" that now extended internationally. "Their concerts are revivifying as anything in rock, with a strong undertow of something not often found this side of Bruce Springsteen: moral passion," *Time* magazine gushed in 1987. "Without sermonizing, they have become a rallying point for a new and youthful idealism."

The sixties spirit inspired R.E.M., which delivered a socially conscious message through jangly, folksy rock. Formed in 1980 in Athens, Georgia, by vocalist Michael Stipe, guitarist Peter Buck, bassist Mike Mills, and drummer Bill Berry, the group perfected a Byrds-influenced, guitar-driven sound. Starting in 1983, they released four albums that garnered a cult following and moderate sales. In 1987, the band entered the mainstream with the Top-Ten *Document*, which directly confronted President Ronald Reagan through such songs as "Welcome to the Occupation" and "Exhuming McCarthy." The next year, they followed with *Green*, which lambasted the Vietnam war in "Orange Crush" and blasted Reagan's foreign policy in "World Leader Pretend." R.E.M. lobbied for Greenpeace, voter registration, a clean environment, and human rights causes. "In the late '80s, I was influenced and politicized to the point that I felt like I wanted to try to make some of these things [songs] topical," remembered Michael Stipe. "Our political activism and the content of our songs was just a reaction to where we were, and what we were surrounded by, which was just abject horror." The singer needed to be politically active during "the dark ages of our country with Reagan."

Classic Rock and the Compact Disc

A return to sixties-style protest, coupled with the advent of the compact disc, led to a nostalgic rebirth of sixties rock. *Billboard* noted that "one of the more notable trends of the late '80s was the commercial success of many bands that made their commercial debut more than twenty years ago." *Time* added in late 1989: "And, as the fairy tales say, it seemed that it might be time again for legends. Twenty years later, there was suddenly on every side the familiar sound of the '60s."

Radio helped promote 1960s rock. Largely ignoring the younger generation, which preferred the rapid-fire video bites of MTV, it programmed oldies for baby boomers who still purchased the greatest number of records and served as the prime target of most advertisers. In 1988, of the roughly 10,000 stations in the country, more than 500 radio stations broadcast oldies exclusively. The next year, contended Ken Barnes, editor of the trade magazine *Radio and Records*, at least 40 percent of all radio programming fell into the "classic rock" or "oldies" categories. In early 1990, oldies station WCBS-FM grabbed the number-one spot in the New York market. Radio, observed CBS Records president Al Teller, seemed to be "chasing the yuppie generation to its grave."

Along with oldies radio, the compact disc revived an interest in classic rock and rescued a troubled music industry. Introduced to the mass market in late 1982, it provided record buyers with a high-quality, digital, durable, long-lasting format. The compact disc, commonly called the CD, contained millions of digitally encoded pits, which held musical information that could be converted into almost noise-free sound through a low-powered laser beam. Less than 5 inches in diameter, the polycarbonate plastic disc only warped at temperatures over 220 degrees Fahrenheit, could not easily be scratched like a vinyl record, and produced up to seventy-five minutes of music with a dynamic range of 90 decibels.

The silver platter quickly became more popular than its vinyl counterpart. During its first two years on the market, the CD appealed primarily to jazz and classical music buffs, who appreciated its expanded dynamic range. As the price of compact disc players plummeted from about $900 in 1983 to less than $150 in 1987, and as the cost of a compact disc declined from $18 to $14 during the same period, the convenient CD sold to rock fans. In 1985, 16.4 million CDs were purchased worldwide. Three years later, more than 390 million compact discs were sold internationally and accounted for sales of more than $6 billion, compared to 295 million vinyl LPs that sold for $2.8 billion. Cassette tapes, which became the most popular format for music during the late seventies and registered even greater sales after the introduction of the portable Walkman cassette player in 1981, outperformed both formats with sales of more than $6.7 billion for 787 million units sold. However, by 1990, the CD even outsold the popular cassette.

At the end of the decade, many industry executives predicted the demise of the vinyl LP. "I assume the death knell has been sounded, and there's not much we can do about it," mused Joe Smith, president of Capitol Music-EMI. "It's gasping for breath," agreed Russ Solomon, founder and president of the Tower Records chain. "We'd like to hold on, but unfortunately the world is not going that way." Bob Sherwood, senior vice president of Columbia Records, predicted that "our little flat friend, the record, is what drove the business for a long time, but we're going to be out of the business."

Industry predictions became reality. In 1989, the Camelot Music chain of 338 stores dropped vinyl albums from its inventory. Other retailers, such as the 85-store Disc chain, the 119-store Hastings Books and Records, and the 60-store Music Plus group, severely limited vinyl selections. By 1992, vinyl records, which only ten years earlier had accounted for more than 42 percent of music sales, shrunk to 2.3 percent of the U.S. music market. "The LP went bye-bye," confirmed Stan Goman, senior vice president of retail operations for Tower Records, in 1990.

The new compact-disc format and the disappearance of vinyl encouraged many baby boomers to replace their old, scratched LPs with CDs, which sometimes included bonus tracks. In early 1990, *Billboard* observed that "if the CD did anything in the '80s, it convinced consumers that they needed to buy their favorite albums all over again." *Time* magazine called the compact disc "the technology most likely to bring Elvis back to life. With revolutionary speed, music lovers are replacing their favorite old scratched-up 45s and 33s with shiny compact discs." By 1992, previously released rock and roll accounted for more than 40 percent of record sales.

A slumping U.S. recording industry was revitalized by the geometric growth in sales of compact discs that was created in part by baby boomers who rebought the music of their youth. After hitting a high point in 1978 with revenue of $4.13 billion, the U.S. record industry experienced a sharp decline. In 1979, it sold only $3.67 billion in records and tapes despite a high rate of inflation and slashed 2,500 music-industry jobs. During the next four years, the industry stabilized, but by 1983 it reported only $3.81 billion in total sales despite price hikes, MTV, and the phenomenal success of Michael Jackson.

The U.S. record industry experienced a boom after the introduction of the CD, which cost about 90 cents to manufacture, including packaging. The United States record trade was dominated by six corporations—Time-Warner (WEA), Sony/CBS, Bertelsmann Music Group (BMG), MCA-Matsushita, N.V. Philips of Holland, and Thorn-EMI (CEMA)—which by 1990 sold more than 93 percent of the records in the United States. By 1986, it exceeded its previous gross-revenue record by shipping $4.65 billion worth of CDs, records, and tapes. A year later, the industry sold $5.57 billion, and in 1988 it generated more than $6.25 billion in records, tapes, and discs sales. In 1989, the industry registered $6.57 billion in sales of more than 800 million units, bolstered by a 38 percent increase in CD shipments compared to the previous year. The next year, sales peaked at $7.5 billion and continued to rise meteorically until 1992, when the industry realized revenue of more than $9 billion.

The phenomenal increase in revenues resulted from the soaring sales of compact discs. CDs cost approximately the same to produce as records but carried a price tag of $14 compared to $9.98 for records and cassettes. In addition, the companies had no production costs for already-recorded music reissued from their vaults. The combination of higher prices and in many cases no recording costs contributed to rising gross revenues for the American market. Internationally, the record industry grew at the same dizzying pace. After a drastic downturn from 1979 to 1986, by 1988 the industry sold more than $14 billion and a year later nearly $17 billion in records, tapes, and CDs. Japan, dominated by the Sony/CBS giant, increased sales to $2.4 billion in 1987, a 10 percent gain from the previous year. By 1989 in West Germany, dominated by BMG, which had purchased RCA during the decade, sales exceeded $1.82 billion. At the end of the eighties, the United Kingdom, the fourth largest market in the world, had sales of $1.5 billion annually.

The increased sales translated into profits. In 1988, Warner Communications, the largest company in the field, posted sales of $2.04 billion and profits of nearly $319 million. The next year, after merging with Time Inc., Warner generated music revenues of $2.54 billion and profits of nearly $500 million. In 1987, CBS earned $202 million in profits on $1.75 billion in total sales. The next year, EMI, the British conglomerate, sold $1.2 billion in music-related products for a profit of $70.3 million. BMG showed remarkable growth by building sales to $1.1 billion in 1989 and increasing profits to $85.4 million. "The ultimate shot in the arm the record industry was craving, the CD allowed companies to rake in the bucks on a product that, in some cases, was one step away from actually being deleted," observed *Billboard* in late 1989. From the mid- to late 1980s, the baby-boom generation repurchased the music of their youth and tuned in to the socially charged rock of artists such as Bruce Springsteen and U2 to revitalize the music industry.

Chapter 20
Country Boomers

"The nation's seventy-six million baby boomers continue to determine America's musical preferences, and what America currently prefers is country."

—*Time*, 1992

During the final years of the 1980s and the first years of the next decade, baby boomers flocked to a sometimes issue-oriented version of country rock. They listened to a music that melded the socially oriented rhetoric of Springsteen with an updated country-rock sound from the 1970s, which captured the increasing economic stability and the lingering issue-oriented proclivities of the baby-boom generation.

The baby boomers looked for a sound that reflected their situation. In 1990, the average baby boomer had already turned 30 and possibly some kids. Many of them finished their education and had a steady job. The challenging economic climate of the mid-1980s eased considerably by 1988, when unemployment dropped from nearly 8 percent to just above 5 percent and remained stable for three years. In 1990, of the young boomers between the ages of 25 and 34, only 5.1 percent could not find work. Of the more typical, older members of the baby-boom generation, unemployment stood at less than 4 percent. Amid better times, the boomers favored country rock.

The Country Rock Rebirth

During the first four years of the decade, more than 21 million Americans, mostly baby boomers, became country music fans. By 1994, many of the Americans who listened to country music fit the baby-boom profile: 42 percent owned a house, 40 percent had a college education, and 36 percent lived in households with incomes of more than $60,000 a year. "By their sheer demographic weight, the nation's seventy-six million baby boomers continue to determine America's musical preferences," observed *Time* in 1992. "And what America currently prefers is country."

These country boomers caused an upsurge in country music. In 1985, only sixteen country releases sold more than 500,000 copies. Seven years later, fifty-three country discs went gold, and nearly thirty sold more than 1 million copies. In 1992, sales of country discs and tapes reached $660 million, more than a 50 percent increase from the previous year. In 1980, approximately 1534 radio stations played country music; twelve years later, more than 2600 stations catered to country listeners. On television, The Nashville Network (TNN) grew from 7 million viewers at its inception in 1983 to 54.5 million subscribers in 1992, and from 1990 to 1992, the magazine *Country America* doubled its subscriptions to almost 1 million readers.

A new breed of young country artists born during the baby boom popularized a neo-traditional genre that delivered the populist message of country with a rock beat. Raised on rock and roll as well as country, singers such as Steve Earle, Travis Tritt, Dwight Yoakam, and Clint Black started the trend toward baby-boom country by producing an energized, hard-hitting country rock with an outlaw image that grabbed the attention of baby boomers.

Steve Earle hoisted the country-rock banner. Growing up near San Antonio, Texas, during the late 1950s and early 1960s, Earle wrote songs in Nashville during the 1970s for artists such as Carl Perkins. In 1986, he released an album of heartland rock gems in his major label debut, *Guitar Town*, which appealed to country and rock audiences and cracked the popular chart. He followed with progressively rock-oriented *Copperhead Road* (1988), which neared the Top Fifty and included collaboration with the punk-folk band the Pogues.

Dwight Yoakam had similar success as a neo-traditionalist country-crossover artist. A diehard fan of the Bakersfield honky-tonk style of Buck Owens, Yoakam unashamedly identified his rock roots. "I listened to country and to rock, everything from Haggard to the Grateful Dead. I was interested in country rock, because it suggested there might be a place I could go." Rejected by the Nashville tastemakers, the singer traveled to California to deliver his distinctive blend of honky-tonk rock as an opening act for punk bands such as X. In 1987, Yoakam struck a chord with the million-selling *Hillbilly Deluxe*. In 1990, he again hit platinum with *If There Was a Way*, which crossed over to the rock audience.

Riding an outlaw image up the charts, Travis Tritt melded traditional country with the music of his youth, the southern rock stylings of Lynyrd Skynyrd and the Allman Brothers. In 1991, he hit the Top Twenty-Five with *It's All About to Change*. The next year, Tritt scored with the country rock of *T-R-O-U-B-L-E*, and its roaring "Blue Collar Man," which included guitar work from Gary Rossington of Lynyrd Skynyrd. The singer called his songs "country music with a rock-'n'-roll attitude."

Clint Black used the same combination of country and rock for success. Raised in Houston, Black started to collect records at the age of 8 and became enthralled with "the rock stuff that my older brothers had exposed me to." He then listened to singer-songwriters of the 1970s such as James Taylor and the country-flavored sound of Jackson Browne. By the late 1980s, Black signed with ZZ Top manager Bill Ham and released the country-rock breakthrough *Killin' Time* (1989) that scaled the country and pop charts. The next year, he hit the Top Twenty with *Put Yourself in My Shoes*, which signaled mass acceptance of country in its new form. In 1990, country music "reclaimed the sound of its glory," the *New York Times* told its readers, "in spiffy rented cowboy garb for an audience that has expanded into the suburbs."

Garth Brooks

The popularity of the neo-traditionalists presaged the mega-breakthrough of Garth Brooks, who owed a musical debt to rock and reflected the social concerns of the baby boomers. The son of a former country singer, Colleen Carroll Brooks, the college-educated Garth drew his inspiration from rock and roll. After attending a Queen concert, Brooks became convinced that he wanted to perform. "My ears are still ringin' from that concert," he enthused. "I was thinking, one day I'm going to feel this feeling—only it's gonna be me up there on that stage." "I don't even remember the music. But I know what I saw," the singer added. Brooks hoped to duplicate "the seventies-arena-rock thing" in country music.

Folk rock also shaped Brooks. He listened to "a sixties wave of singers" such as Peter, Paul, and Mary, "that kind of music. It was very warm, but you had to step inside it to see what was going on. From that moment on, that's the kind of music I was attracted to. Off that, I went to James Taylor."

Brooks combined folk rock and 1970s theatrics with his country roots for superstardom. In 1989, he released a self-titled debut, which sold well and reached the Top Fifteen. The next year, the singer hit the Top Five with his breakthrough *No Fences*, which included singer-songwriter Billy Joel's "Shameless" and eventually sold more than 17 million copies. Brooks followed with the blockbuster number-one *Ropin' the Wind* (1991), which became the first country album to hit the top of the pop chart, and

Garth Brooks in concert, April 1994.

Associated Newspapers/Alamy Stock Photo.

in two years sold 10 million copies. During the next two years, he hit the Top Five with a Christmas album and topped the chart with *The Chase* (1992) and *In Pieces* (1993). In the span of a few years, Brooks sold more than 30 million discs and tapes. He had reached the top of the chart with three albums, topped the chart with sixteen of his eighteen singles, sold more than a million copies of each of his long-form videos, and won a Grammy, four People's Choice awards, six American Music awards, and nine Country Music Association awards.

Garth Brooks addressed the current social concerns of his audience. Unlike past country messages that distanced the music from baby-boom culture (Merle Haggard's "Okie from Muskogee" 1969) or pledged blind allegiance to the government (Lee Greenwood's "God Bless the USA" 1984), he supported racial, religious, and gay rights in "We Shall Be Free" and chose antiwar songs such as "Last Night I Had the Strangest Dream" for his concerts. In "The Thunder Rolls," he sang about the effects of domestic violence and released a graphic video of the song to make his point. In 1992, after the riot in Los Angeles, Brooks performed a benefit concert that raised nearly $1 million to help rebuild the inner city. "Tolerance is an important issue to me," Brooks emphasized. "Hiding your head in the sand isn't going to make real life go away." During the early 1990s, Garth Brooks fashioned a rock-based country that explored socially relevant issues to create music for baby boomers.

Brooks was the perfect star for aging boomers who embraced him as one of their own. Born in 1962, Brooks was 28 years old when he became a massive success. As with many educated boomers, Brooks graduated from college by earning a degree in advertising from Oklahoma State University. At the time of his breakthrough, he professed devotion to his wife and his children. Like many boomers, he subsequently divorced but publically apologized for the indiscreet actions that led to the break-up. Balding and slightly overweight, Brooks looked like the typical baby boomer as well as reflecting their attitudes. "Three years ago, would you have thought that the largest-selling artist in the Nineties would be going bald and have an eating problem and be doing fiddle and steel-guitar music?," Brooks joked in 1994.

A concert by Brooks at Brendan Byrne Arena in East Rutherford, New Jersey, epitomized baby-boom fascination with nineties country rock. Far from the Old South, nearly 20,000 faithful fans assembled to watch their new hero. According to the *New York Times*, "an audience that mixed couples in their 30s and 40s with teenagers" donned cowboy hats, pointed snake-skin boots and frilled shirts to bring rural America to suburbia. They listened to rock-inflected country songs, and even several rock songs such as Bob Seger's "Night Moves" during a stage show borrowed from wild arena rockers such as Queen and Kiss. The audience witnessed Brooks appear on stage "via elevator while lights flash and twirl and recorded rumbles and explosions are heard." After the spectacular entrance, they applauded Brooks as he stalked the stage from one side to another like a caged leopard and, as a finale, swung out across the arena by an overhead cable. For baby boomers reveled in Garth Brooks who delivered the familiar showmanship of the excessive 1970s along with a countrified music. The *New York Times* labeled him the "suburban cowboy" who seemed "in touch with country's roots, but adopts these traditions to address the urbanized realities of the present." "I think there's a very good comparison between Nineties country and Seventies rock & roll," asserted Brooks.

Brooks unlocked the gates for other country rockers, none more successful than Shania Twain. Twain (b. Eilleen Edwards) grew up near Ontario, Canada, on the Mattagami Indian Reservation and supported her siblings by singing at a resort after the tragic death of her parents in 1987. In 1995 after meeting and marrying rock producer Robert "Mutt" Lange, who had produced such heavy metal acts as AC/DC and Def Leppard, Twain released the mega-hit *The Woman in Me*, which fused country fiddles and steel guitars with Lange's trademark slick, hard-rock sound. "Country audiences are capable of stretching, and we can take them with us," Twain insisted. The album sold more than 12 million copies. Two years later, Twain sold even more discs with the radio-friendly *Come On Over* to extend the crossover success of Garth Brooks.

The country boom even spread to a group of bands labeled alternative country or Y'alternative epitomized by Uncle Tupelo. The brainchild of singer-songwriters Jeff Tweedy and Jay Farrar, the group solidified in 1987 to combine their country and punk rock roots. In 1990, they issued their influential debut *No Depression*, which overlaid punk madness on top of a country twang. After three subsequent albums, the band splintered when Tweedy formed Wilco and Farrar put together Son Volt.

During the early 1990s, various strands of country rock reigned supreme on the charts. "A lot of people turned to country because it's more like [early] seventies rock-and-roll," observed Neil Young, who twenty years earlier had released a series of revelatory country-tinged folk-rock discs and in 1985 cut the unadulterated country album *Old Ways*. "Pop and rock have just changed their name to country."

Chapter 21
The Generation X Blues

"We had to grow up with this idealization that was never going to fucking come true."

—Courtney Love of Hole

Kurt Cobain, the leader of Nirvana, suffered through a difficult, unstable childhood. At the age of 8, his mother initiated an acrimonious divorce from her husband. "It just destroyed his life. He changed completely," his mother disclosed about the split, "and he became very inward." The young boy scrawled, "I hate Mom, I hate Dad, Dad hates Mom, Mom hates Dad, it simply makes you want to be sad" on his bedroom wall.

Kurt lived with his mother for a year before moving in with his father. After a period, he stayed with his paternal grandparents and three sets of aunts and uncles. Lonely and abandoned, Cobain convinced his mother to give him a room in her home, which she shared with her new husband. At one point, his overstressed mother pointed a gun at his head and threatened to kill him. When Cobain quit high school, he left his mother and moved in with friends.

Cobain's childhood experience left an indelible scar on his psyche. In 1994, he confessed that he had "lacked love" his entire life. He sometimes blamed his childhood on himself and expressed it in such Nirvana songs as "Negative Creep." On April 5, 1994, Kurt Cobain tragically shot and killed himself in his Seattle home.

Many post-baby-boomers felt the pain of broken homes and tough economic times that Cobain experienced. Cobain explained that "my story is exactly the same as 90 percent of everyone my age. Everyone's parents got divorced, their kids smoked pot all through high school." He observed that "the majority of bands you interview would have divorced parents. I think there's a universal display of psychological damage that everyone my age has acquired."

Facing an unstable family life and grim economic prospects, the post–baby-boom generation created and listened to an angry rock, which displayed their rage and alienation. During the mid-1980s to the early 1990s, they vented their frustration over their bleak prospects through thrash, death metal, industrial music, and grunge.

Generation X

A new generation created a raging rock. The post-baby boomers, tagged Generation X by the press, were born between 1965 and 1981 and had a very different experience than their baby-boom parents. By the early to mid-1980s, the first wave of Gen X had become youths who created and listened to music that reflected a harsh situation.

The post–baby-boom generation in the United States faced a grim economic reality. In 1992, the average American worker earned $391 a week, $18 less than the average worker brought home in 1979 after adjusting for inflation. As wages declined, unemployment rose. During much of the 1950s and 1960s, the unemployment rate vacillated between 3.5 percent and 5 percent. In 1984, the rate of unemployment stood at 7.5 percent. By 1992 unemployment rose precipitously to nearly 20 percent, including the 13 percent of nonworking Americans whom the government classified as underemployed or discouraged workers. Many of the remaining jobs shifted from manufacturing to the service sector, which did not pay well and accounted for more than three-quarters of all new jobs. In late 1992, Lawrence Mishel, chief economist at the Economic Policy Institute contended that "the economy is failing nearly every American."

Post–baby boomers, nearly 50 percent of the population by the early 1990s, especially felt the economic squeeze. In 1992, 20 percent of teens no longer in school could not find jobs. More than 11 percent of young men and women between the ages of 20 and 24 were officially unemployed nearly double the unemployment rate among the baby-boom generation.

Generation X found little stability in their families. During the seventies, baby boomers separated from their partners in record numbers and left their children in single-family households. In 1970, single-parent households accounted for only 11 percent of homes with children. By 1992, homes headed by one parent comprised more than 26 percent of the total.

The turbulent American family caused frustration, pain, and fear among Generation X. "The bottom line is that most of us come from broken homes," explained Jesse Malin, vocalist for D Generation. "We have this self-destructive thing: We'd get a kick out of breaking up the band. And we do it with a lot of relationships, with girlfriends and everybody, because that was our first impression from when we were seven years old: seeing people split."

To add to their personal problems, many youths suffered abuse, often within the family. In 1991, reported the National Committee for the Prevention of Child Abuse, 2.7 million children, or 4 percent of all youths under age 18 in America, endured physical and sexual abuse. The finding represented a 40 percent increase in abuse after only six years.

Overall, Generation X faced somber challenges. "I do think that having no family structure, having no sense that there's shelter from the storm, drives people insane," contended Elizabeth Wurtzel, author of the autobiographical *Prozac Nation: Young and Depressed in America* (1994). "The level of uncertainty we function under in a personal realm is daunting. And, obviously, economically, things are very uncertain. So altogether, this is not a pretty way to live."

Confronted with few economic prospects and a painful, sometimes brutal home life, many youths turned to violence. As children, most post–baby boomers witnessed violent actions daily on television. According to the American Psychological Association, in the 1980s the average sixth grader had watched 8,000 murders and 100,000 other acts of violence. In the 1980s and 1990s, some youths followed the celluloid images by carrying guns. "For youth today, I don't care where you live, what class you are, or whether you're white, black, or Hispanic, it's cool to carry a gun," complained Colonel Leonard Supenski of the Baltimore County Police Department. "Owing to a lot of things, primarily the entertainment industry, it's a macho thing to do." In 1990, more than 4 percent of all high school students surveyed by the Centers for Disease Control and Prevention carried a gun, especially the semiautomatic 9-millimeter pistol, at least once during the previous month.

Youths used the guns that they carried. In the Seattle city school system, 6 percent of high school juniors confessed to carrying a gun into school, and one-third of the gun-toting students fired their weapons at another person. In the United States during 1987, almost 1,500 youths aged 10–19 died from gunshot wounds, which were usually inflicted by another youth. Two years later, nearly 2,200 youths died as a result of gun violence.

Many gun-carrying youths banded together in urban gangs across the country. By 1985, nearly 45,000 Los Angeles youths had formed more than 450 gangs, which represented an increase of 25 percent in gangland activity in just five years. By 1992, in Los Angeles, 150,000 disgruntled youths joined more than 1,000 gangs. Though highly visible due to press coverage, the Los Angeles gangs reflected a national trend. Seeking security in an insecure world, eighties' youth started gangs in such disparate locales as Davenport,

Iowa; Chicago; New Haven; Jackson, Mississippi; and Portsmouth, New Hampshire. By 1994, gangs roamed the streets in 187 U.S. cities. "The kids are all on the edge," warned Chicago social worker Sharon Brown. "Brush against them, and they're ready to fight."

The desperate generation, which followed the baby boomers, gravitated toward loud, aggressive, angry music. In 1992, Jonathan Poneman, co-owner of Sub Pop Records, noticed that "a lot of people our age and younger have been brought up with these notions of Reagan-era-fueled affluence." "Then when you suddenly see a lot of those dreams subside because of this particularly brutal recession, and class warfare, race warfare, it makes you very angry, very fearful, very alienated. And those are qualities that lead to an unusually rebellious, passionate rock."

From the New Wave of British Heavy Metal to Thrash Metal

The alienated Generation X flocked to such harsh rock and roll as thrash, death metal, industrial, and grunge. The aggressive, dissatisfied youth of the 1980s listened to a speedy thrash metal, which originated with the New Wave of British Heavy Metal (NWOBHM). The NWOBHM stemmed from conditions that helped foster English punk. Poor British youths with no apparent future formed bands to express their frustration through a violent, explosive sound.

In 1976, Diamond Head formed. The band consisted of four working-class youths from Stourbridge in the West Midlands near Birmingham—an area that had produced original heavy metalers Black Sabbath and Led Zeppelin's Robert Plant and John Bonham. "We started on June 26th, 1976. It was the last year of our school, about to leave to get jobs or go on the dole, whatever," recalled lead guitarist Brian Tatler.

Near the same time, other heavy metal bands arose with names that indicated a dark militancy: Saxon, Venom, Tygers of Pan Tang, Angel Witch, and Iron Maiden. These bands owed a musical debt to seventies' heavy metal. Iron Maiden favored the Led Zeppelin sound. Venom and Angel Witch leaned more toward Black Sabbath. Diamond Head first learned Black Sabbath's "Paranoid." Though adopting the blues-based style of original heavy metalers, NWOBHM adherents delivered a harsh-sounding, fist-pumping music that shared the spirit of British punk. "What people were looking for in punk is what they are looking for in heavy rock," observed Saxon vocalist Biff Byford. "We were the ones breaking down the barriers between band and audience, and we were doing it with complete honesty and no b.s." As with British punkers, NWOBHM bands dressed in leather jackets with spikes, denim jeans, and tennis shoes, but wore their hair shoulder length like their heavy metal heroes rather than the short-cropped hair of punk.

Disc jockey Neil Kay helped popularize the new wave of heavy metal. Kay constantly promoted the albums of struggling bands such as Iron Maiden at his heavy metal club, London's Soundhouse. In May 1979, he helped stage a concert, which featured many of the new metal acts and prompted Alan Lewis and Geoff Barton, editors of the British music magazine *Sounds*, to coin the phrase "New Wave of British Heavy Metal." In August 1980, the British television show *20th Century Box* aired a special on the new music.

Heavy metal magazines such as *Kerrang* helped to create an underground of metal fans who spread the word. "The number one source [of support] is fanzines," contended Bret Hartman, manager of A&R at MCA. "Getting demos with good songs is the bottom line, but the sources to expose the band are word of mouth, fanzines, and magazines, especially for metal." Metal fans, remarked Roadrunner Records executive Michael Schnapp, "print fanzines, they talk to each other all the time on the phone, they are pen pals; you have that family type of atmosphere."

By the turn of the decade, the new metal bands offered records to the swelling ranks of the metal underground. In 1979, Saxon debuted and during the next three years provided fans with four more British Top-Twenty albums. The next year, Diamond Head, mirroring the do-it-yourself punk attitude, released their first album on their own Happy Face label. In 1980, the Tygers of Pan Tang entered the British Top Twenty with *Wildcat* and Angel Witch cut its debut. The next year, Venom released *Welcome to Hell*.

AC/DC, the blues-powered Australian band that formed in 1973 and struggled for popular acceptance during the mid-1970s, benefited from the exposure given to the NWOBHM. In 1979, amid the growing furor over the NWOBHM, the band hit the British Top Ten and the Top Twenty in the United States with *Highway to Hell*. The next year, AC/DC topped the British chart and reached the Top Five in the United States with *Back in Black*. In 1981, they topped the U.S. chart with *For Those About to Rock (We Salute You)*.

During the early 1980s, Iron Maiden, a commercially successful NWOBHM band, gained a following. In early 1979, the band distributed by mail order their first effort, *The Soundhouse Tapes*, which DJ Neal Kay plugged constantly. Early the next year, the group unveiled their self-named, major-label debut, which hit the British charts. Iron Maiden continued to chart with *The Number of the Beast* (1982), which topped the British chart, and the million-selling *Piece of Mind* (1983). At the end of 1983, readers of *Kerrang* voted the latest two Iron Maiden efforts as the best two heavy-metal albums of all time.

Motorhead stood at the vanguard of the new metal explosion. Banding together in 1975, the group consisted of guitarist "Fast" Eddie Clarke, drummer Philthy Animal (b. Phil Taylor), and bassist and vocalist Lemmy Kilmister (b. Ian Kilmister), a former member of Hawkwind and an ex-roadie for Jimi Hendrix. The trio played a fast, aggressive, loud brand of metal fueled by amphetamines. After a self-named debut in 1977, they continued their vinyl output with *Overkill* and *Bomber*, which suggested the destructive intent of the music. In 1980, the band hit the British Top Five with *Ace of Spades*. The next year, as the NWOBHM swept across the United Kingdom, Motorhead topped the chart with the live album *No Sleep 'til Hammersmith*.

Ian "Lemmy" Kilmister of Motorhead, 1975.

Jim Summaria.

Metallica combined the different elements of the NWOBHM with California hard-core punk to create a new genre called "thrash" or "speed metal," which swept across Britain and the United States during the mid-1980s. The band initially grew from a passion for metal that drove Danish-born Lars Ulrich. In 1980, Ulrich, the son of a professional tennis player, moved to Los Angeles with his parents. "I got very pissed off being in L.A., so the summer of '81 I just upped and went back to Europe," related Ulrich. "I'd go hang out with Diamond Head for a while, and then try and find Iron Maiden, or try and find Motorhead." After returning to the United States, the drummer started to assemble a band that resembled the heavy metal he had heard in Europe. Ulrich placed an ad in a Los Angeles newspaper and found guitarist/vocalist James Hetfield, a devoted Black Sabbath and Motorhead fan, who turned to music to escape the pain of a father who deserted him. "Music wouldn't lie to me, or *leave* me," he bitterly attested. The duo added lead guitarist Dave Mustaine and bassist Ron McGovney, Hetfield's roommate, to complete the Metallica lineup.

The band first mimicked the NWOBHM. "When we started doing clubs," recalled Hetfield, "we were doing mostly covers of the new wave of British metal bands, and because nobody had heard these records [in the United States], all the bangers thought we were doing our own songs." Prodded by California crowds who were moshing to West Coast punk, Metallica began to speed up the already fast, loud, propulsive metal music. "When we started writing our own songs, they weren't fast at all," explained James Hetfield. Then "we got a little more pissed off at the crowd and how people weren't appreciating our stuff. So they gradually got faster and faster as we got more aggressive. Instead of going, 'Please like us,' we were like...'AAAHH! Fuck you!'"

The speeded-up sound of Metallica became known as thrash or at times speed metal. In addition to intense guitar speed referred to as shredding, the music featured low-register guitar tuning, high-pitched virtuoso guitar solos, and pounding double-base drumming. "Metallica really created a form of music," contended Brian Slagel, the metal enthusiast who founded Metal Blade Records. "When they came out, there was no speed metal or thrash metal. They were doing something new." *Rolling Stone* magazine called the new sound "a marvel of precisely channeled aggression."

Metallica, which eventually included bassist Cliff Burton and guitarist Kirk Hammett, who replaced McGovney and Mustaine, snagged a record contract through the metal underground. The band recorded a demo tape of its songs that Ulrich, an avid metal tape swapper, sent through the underground. "All we wanted to do was to send it out to the traders, get mentioned in some fan magazines," mentioned Ulrich. "The cool thing about the metal scene is that you could pass out ten copies of your tape to people who were really into it and within a week know that 100 people would have it, and another 100 a week later." In 1982, the tape landed in the hands of John Zazula and his wife Marsha, New Jersey record store owners who had recently launched the label Megaforce. By the next March, Metallica had signed with Megaforce and had traveled to New York to record *Kill 'Em All*, originally titled *Metal Up Your Ass*. In 1984, they cut *Ride the Lightning* for Megaforce.

The band attracted a national following by mid-decade, when seminal California punk bands such as Black Flag and the Dead Kennedys disbanded. In early 1986, they released *Master of Puppets* and embarked on a six-month tour behind metal legend Ozzy Osbourne. Osbourne "told us, 'Man, you guys remind me of Sabbath in their early days—hungry, all the energy,'" enthused James Hetfield. With little radio play and virtually no support from MTV, which characterized thrash metal as "very polarizing music," Metallica slowly climbed to the U.S. Top Thirty. As the metal army grew, the band hit the Top Ten on both sides of the Atlantic with...*And Justice for All* (1988). They topped British and U.S. charts with *Metallica* (1991), which sold more than 9 million copies. "It's a cultlike audience," claimed Geoff Mayfield, director of retail research for *Billboard*. "A record like *Metallica* can sell without airplay and without MTV."

Metallica delivered a somber, angry message. "*Puppets* was about manipulation, *Ride the Lightning* was about death and dying, and *Justice* talked about the American dream and how that doesn't always work out anymore," explained James Hetfield. "Our music," agreed Kirk Hammett, "it's grim, based in reality. Our music mirrors modern life as much as Motown's mirrored the romance of falling in love. It says, 'You're being manipulated, man, by the big corporations, by the media.'"

Capturing the alienation and frustration of post–baby-boomers, Metallica paved the way for a legion of thrashers. In 1988, Megadeth, fronted by ex-Metallica guitarist Dave Mustaine who listed Motorhead as a major influence, hit the Top Thirty with *so far, so good…so what!* The same year, Anthrax, the New York thrash band influenced heavily by Iron Maiden, AC/DC, and the Ramones, hit the Top Thirty with *State of Euphoria*. Slayer, fronted by shredder Kerry King, joined the thrash pantheon by hitting the Top Forty in 1990 with *Seasons in the Abyss*. "The thing is," explained vocalist/bassist Tom Araya, "we apply all our anger to our music and lyrics."

Megadeth, Anthrax, and Slayer played together on the 1991 Clash of Titans tour to wild-eyed, enthusiastic throngs of metalers. "I tend to think of that tour as the pinnacle of the thrash movement in general," fondly remembered David Ellefson, the bassist for Megadeth, "because it proved to everybody how big the whole thing really was." By the beginning of the 1990s, even *Time* magazine admitted that "heavy metal is white hot."

Death Metal and Grindcore

Within a few years, some bands revved up speed metal and fused it with violent, slasher-type lyrics, nearly incomprehensible growls, and abrupt tempo, key, and time signature changes to create an even more aggressive music called death metal. Ironically, the genre started in California and Florida, two of the sunniest states in America.

The genre first sprang from California with the band Possessed. On their 1985 debut, *Seven Churches*, the group introduced the standard death metal growl and took thrash metal guitar to a new level of speed. Bassist/vocalist Jeff Beccera even coined a new term for "the heaviest thing on the face of the planet." As he explained, "I figured speed metal and black metal were already taken, so what the fuck? So I said death metal."

If Possessed jump-started the sound, the band Death perfected it. The brainchild of guitarist and vocalist Chuck Schuldiner, Death started in 1984 in sunny Orlando, Florida, and helped popularize the genre in their debut *Scream Bloody Gore* (1987). "Our main goal was to bash out the most brutal riffs ever with the most brutal guitar sound ever," reasoned Schuldiner.

Two other Florida bands helped shape death metal. Fronted by guitarist Trey Azagthoth, Morbid Angel came together in Tampa during 1984. "We used to go out of our way to shock people," explained guitarist Richard Brunelle. Given their goal, the group initially found no interested labels. According to vocalist David Vincent, "the letters of rejection that we got from various labels from our first few demos were amazing. One label went so far as to write us a letter back saying that we do for music what King Herod did for babysitting." The band eventually landed on Earache, an influential metal label that signed many death-metal bands, and pounded out their debut, *Altar of Madness* (1989).

Obituary, coming from Tampa and founded in 1985, signed to the extreme-metal label Roadrunner. The group released *Slowly We Rot* (1989), which featured the low-pitched growls of John Tardy who became one of the premier death-metal vocalists.

Once death metal rose from the roots of thrash, the groups of death-obsessed headbangers multiplied. Also from Florida, vocalist and bassist Glen Benton fronted Deicide, which delivered a hard and heavy slice of death metal. "I've always seen this kind of music as a progression from rock and roll, from early on to where it is now," reasoned Benton. "You're getting kids who in the early Eighties were getting into thrash and from there, slowly, they just get more aggressive and aggressive and aggressive."

Coming from Buffalo, New York, Cannibal Corpse offered the most vividly violent, gory lyrics imaginable to become the most extreme form of the genre. "Everyone wants to be the fastest and the heaviest, and that kept the scene moving forward in a faster, heavier direction," recalled bassist Alex Webster. "When those guys [fellow band mates] wrote, it presented such a violent image to me, I felt I had to match it with the lyrics," added Chris Barnes. "And I was able to pull from my imagination some sick qualities of mankind and put it down on paper." He ended up with such songs as "Butchered at Birth."

During the early 1990s, death metal peaked in popularity. In 1990, Deicide produced the best-selling death-metal album of all time with their self-named debut. The next year, Death toned down their gory lyrics and honed their guitar prowess to deliver *Human*, which hit the chart and even garnered some MTV airplay on *Headbangers Ball*. "I always believed that the *Ball* needed to play death," remembered Riki Rachtman, a former host of the show. In 1992, Morbid Angel signed to Giant Records and the next year released *Covenant*, which entered the *Billboard* Heatseekers chart and snagged a spot on the television show *Beavis and Butt-Head* with the song "God of Emptiness." In 1992, Obituary hit the Heatseekers chart and cracked the British Top 100 with *The End Complete*.

Guitarist James Murphy described the sudden popularity of death metal: "I was playing in Paris with Obituary in 1991 and as we tried to walk through the crowd, people were diving for us and ripping hunks out of our clothes and hair just to get a piece of us. I just thought, 'This is like death metal Beatlemania.'"

A few bands took heavy metal to even greater extremes, when they combined the gutteral growls of death metal with the speed of thrash and the energy of hardcore punk to create a style called grindcore. The British band Napalm Death headed the grindcore movement. After producing a series of militant efforts on the Earache label, the band finally hit the chart amid the death metal craze. They inked a distribution deal with Columbia Records through Earache and charted with *Harmony Corruption* (1990) and *Fear, Emptiness and Despair* (1994), which summed up the mood of Generation X. They reached their commercial apex when their song "Twist the Knife (Slowly)" from *Fear, Emptiness and Despair* hit the Top Ten as part of the soundtrack to the movie *Mortal Kombat* (1995).

Carcass, a grindcore project fronted by former Napalm Death guitarist Bill Steer, signed with Sony Records and climbed the chart in America and the United Kingdom with several albums of harsh music. "I think cheezy music weakens us," contended Steer. "We're to take music to its heaviest, most ludicrous extremities." Along with Napalm Death, Carcass defined the extreme metal of grindcore.

Death metal and grindcore, as with other extreme musical styles of the period, exemplified the anger and hopelessness of a generation. Openly embracing violence and death, the bands reflected the aggression and depression of youths during the late 1980s and early 1990s. Morbid Angel guitarists Azagthoth and Brunelle openly slashed their arms with razor blades on stage. Deicide's Glen Benton burned a three-inch cross into his forehead. Some of the album titles clearly displayed the hopelessness of a generation: *Entangled in Chaos* by Morbid Angel; *World Demise* by Obituary; and *Gallery of Suicide* by Cannibal Corpse. Others such as *Butchered at Birth* and *Bloodthirst* by Cannibal Corpse showed the violent bent of youth.

Not confined to song titles, violence surfaced at death metal and grindcore concerts. Like their hardcore punk counterparts, death metalers formed mosh pits in front of the stage and pummeled each other throughout the shows. Sometimes, the mosh pit jostling led to serious consequences. "I've seen people killed. I've seen people with their heads completely fucking cracked open and their brains laying out," remembered Glen Benton of Deicide. "I've seen fingers snapped back. I've seen broken arms. I've seen fucking gashes in faces and heads—I've seen it all," he asserted.

Benton attributed the violence to broader social trends operative during the 1990s. "Society is becoming more and more violent," he contended. "You can't let your 10-year-old kid go off with his buddies to go see a movie or even ride his bike around the block. You just can't. Things are getting worse," he concluded.

Benton blamed the growing violence on the breakdown of the family. "We live in the age of divorce, where 80 percent of the kids at school come from divorced households," he observed. Youth seemed "lost" without a stable family, and social values seemed to be breaking down. By the early 1990s, Generation X headbanged to the extreme metal of death and grindcore to relieve their frustrations.

The Industrial Revolution

Industrial music, the wild buzz-saw abandon of thrash metal combined with harsh, dissonant vocals and electronic samples and synthesizers, also reflected and captured the mood of alienated youths during the late 1980s and early 1990s.

The industrial sound of the eighties had its roots in the postpunk pessimism that enveloped England in the wake of the Sex Pistols. Post-Pistols bands such as John Lydon's PiL, Cabaret Voltaire, and Throbbing Gristle combined taped music, synthesizer moans, and distorted vocals to reflect the grim life of postindustrial England.

By the mid-1980s, industrial music surfaced on the other side of the Atlantic with outfits such as Skinny Puppy and Foetus. Originating in Vancouver, British Columbia, Skinny Puppy owed its sound to multi-instrumentalist cEvin Key (b. Kevin Crompton), lyricist/droner Nivek Ogre (b. Kevin Ogilvie), and producer Dave "Rave" Ogilvie. After a synthesizer-based debut, the outfit enlisted the help of sample master and synthesizer player Dwayne Goettel to churn out a harsh, dissonant industrial music on efforts such as *Cleanse Fold and Manipulate* (1987) and the overtly political *VIVIsectVI* (1988).

The various incarnations of Foetus, the brainchild of Jim Thirlwell, enhanced the cacophonic din with tinges of melody. On mid-1980s releases such as *Hole*, the band used automatic weapons, symphony orchestras, clanging metallic objects, and tape samples to capture the intense chaos of the times.

Other American outfits such as Ministry and Nine Inch Nails added a thrashing heavy metal guitar to the mix to make industrial music more accessible to the masses of disenchanted youths. The brainchild of Wax Trax label co-owner Al Jourgensen, Ministry abandoned funky dance music in 1986 for a sound labeled "aggro": sheets of guitar music broken by tape samples and angry vocals. By 1988, the group perfected their sound on the genre-breaking *The Land of Rape and Honey*, which added guitars to an industrial clamor to bring it into the mainstream. "Guitars and sequencers just seemed a natural combination," recalled Jourgensen. The next year, Jourgensen combined forces with Skinny Puppy's Dave Ogilvie on the guitar-steeped *The Mind Is a Terrible Thing to Taste* to complete the marriage between thrash metal and industrial samples. By 1992, Ministry hit the U.S. Top Thirty with *Psalm 69: The Way to Succeed and the Way to Suck Eggs*.

Trent Reznor (b. Michael Trent Reznor), a Pennsylvania farm boy, classically trained pianist, and former synthesizer-band member, created Nine Inch Nails (NIN) just as Al Jourgensen introduced industrial music to the heavy-metal masses. Formed in 1988, NIN became the most popular embodiment of industrial music. Reznor first added guitars to his industrialist mix in *Pretty Hate Machine* (1989), which encapsulated the doomy negativity of nineties youth. According to Oliver Stone, who commissioned Reznor to record the soundtrack to the film *Natural Born Killers*, NIN reflected "that

Nine Inch Nails concert poster, September 2, 1995.

Mark Arminski.

agony, that pain, that overwhelming sense of suffering." Though at first selling slowly, in 1990 *Pretty Hate Machine* reached the Top Seventy-Five. By the 1991 Lollapalooza tour, Reznor had become an underground rock icon.

Reznor followed with the Top Ten extended-play *Broken* (1992), characterized by the industrial mastermind as "just one big blast of anger. Not necessarily a well-rounded record—just one ultra-fast chunk of death." In 1994, the gloom spread with NIN's aptly titled *The Downward Spiral*, which debuted at number two on the chart. "When I'm writing songs," explained Reznor, "I deliberately try to explore incredibly black emotions—combining personal experience with imaginative projection—to see how far I can get. I often end up bumming myself out pretty good." By the mid-decade, the commercial success of NIN encouraged a spate of other industrialists such as Marilyn Manson (b. Brian Warner), who signed to Reznor's fittingly named label Nothing and neared the top of the chart with *Antichrist Superstar* (1996).

Grunge

Grunge, growing in the Seattle offices of the independent Sub Pop Records, combined hardcore and metal to top the charts and help define the desperation of a generation. In 1979, Bruce Pavitt moved to Olympia, Washington, to attend the experimental Evergreen State College, where he worked at the alternative radio station KAOS and started the fanzine *Subterranean Pop*. After graduating in 1983, he relocated to nearby Seattle, where he wrote a column for the local music paper *The Rocket* and landed a job as a disc jockey on the University of Washington radio station KCMU, hosting a show called *Sub Pop U.S.A.*

In 1986, after unsuccessfully launching a record store, Pavitt expanded his concept of regional-band cassette compilations, which accompanied his *Subterranean Pop* fanzine, into a record label. "I could always see that the real essence of the punk work was the Dead Kennedys putting stuff out themselves," reasoned Pavitt, "and people taking control of their own culture."

To inaugurate the label, Pavitt released a collection of local Northwest bands, *Sub Pop 100*, and in June 1987 followed with an extended play by local punk band Green River, *Dry as a Bone*. He became convinced that "there was a kind of unique sound happening in Seattle" and "wanted to focus my attention on Seattle and help the scene out." After the initial releases, in early 1988 Pavitt joined with fellow KCMU jockey Jonathan Poneman to launch Sub Pop Records as a joint venture. In an early catalog, the label owners referred to their music as "ultraloose GRUNGE that destroyed the morals of a generation."

Sub Pop scored its first success with Soundgarden. In 1987, Pavitt and Poneman borrowed money to record *Screaming Life* by the band, which included vocalist Chris Cornell and guitarist Kim Thayil. The band fastened upon a new sound, which Poneman characterized as "a bastardization of the '70s revisionist guitar thing, with a healthy dose of punk-rock aesthetic. It wasn't orthodox metal, and it wasn't a bunch of people moshing in the pit either." The Soundgarden sound melded guitars tuned down low to D with elements of Led Zeppelin, Black Sabbath, post-seventies punk, the MC5, and the avant-garde jazz of Ornette Coleman for a nervous, angry, tense feeling. Bass player Ben Shepherd simply characterized the music as "dark, black and blue. Like the overcast days of Seattle."

Attracting fans with their musical hybrid, Soundgarden attracted the attention of other record labels and left Sub Pop. "Sub Pop did not have the money to make another record for us," related Kim Thayil who had been a childhood friend of Bruce Pavitt and had introduced Pavitt and Poneman. In 1988, the band recorded *Ultramega OK* with SST, the company owned by Black Flag members Greg Ginn and Chuck Dukowski, and the next year released *Louder Than Love* on A&M Records.

Encouraged by its success with Soundgarden, Sub Pop signed other grunge bands, including Nirvana, which became the pacesetter of the new music. Nirvana vocalist and guitarist Kurt Cobain grew up in Aberdeen, Washington. The musical impetus behind the band, Cobain first became enraptured with the Beatles and then seventies metal bands such as Led Zeppelin and Black Sabbath. By his teens, remembered the singer, "I was looking for something a lot heavier, yet melodic at the same time, something different from heavy metal, a different attitude."

Soundgarden in Seattle, 1986.

Cameron Garrett.

Cobain found his niche with punk rock. He became friends with Buzz Osborne, leader of the Aberdeen punk band the Melvins. When he heard the Melvins for the first time, recalled Cobain, "it just blew me away, I was instantly a punk rocker. I abandoned all my friends, 'cause they didn't like any of the music. And then I asked Buzz to make me a compilation tape of punk-rock songs, and I got a spiky haircut." Osborne also took Cobain to his first rock concert, a show by Black Flag.

By the mid-1980s, Cobain decided to start a band that would showcase his musical influences. He joined with fellow Aberdeen resident and bassist Krist Novoselic, another fan of the Melvins. Cobain observed that his band "sounded exactly like Black Flag, totally abrasive, fast, punk music. There were some Nirvana elements, some slower songs, even then. And some heavy, Black Sabbath–influenced stuff. I can't deny Black Sabbath. Or Black Flag."

In 1987, Cobain, Novoselic, and drummer Aaron Burckhard, named themselves Nirvana and signed a record contract with Sub Pop. In late 1988, Cobain, Novoselic and new drummer Chad Channing released the 7-inch single "Love Buzz/Big Cheese." The next spring, they released their first album, *Bleach*, recorded for $606.17, which combined hardcore and metal influences.

The group added a new musical dimension as they entered the studio to record their second Sub Pop album. Working on the songs that would become *Nevermind*, Nirvana added a melodic, Beatlesque element, which had shaped Cobain, Novoselic, and Dave Grohl, the last in the long succession of Nirvana drummers. "We might as well just play Beatles covers for the rest of our careers," joked Novoselic. "They started it, they did it best, they ended it." Grohl agreed, "When it comes down to pop, there's only one word—the B word, Beatles." Cobain enthused at the time that "I had finally gotten to the point where I was mixing pop music and the heavy side of us in the right formula."

As Nirvana moved toward a pop/metal/punk hybrid, Sub Pop grabbed media attention for the Seattle scene. From its inception, Sub Pop tried to market the Northwest music scene. "We're using a precedent set by Tamla/Motown and Stax, where you have the scene that is being born in a particular region and then you just have a machine that you use to refine and perfect your product," Poneman admitted. "All of a sudden there are all these bands coming out of this part of the world, there's good press, it's romantic."

To popularize a regional scene, the Sub Pop owners tried to create a consistent look and sound for their bands. They hired photographer Charles Peterson, who shot the label's album covers. "I developed a style, which was down in the front with a camera in one hand and a beer in the other," the photographer explained.

Producer Jack Endino at least somewhat standardized the sound of the Sub Pop bands for Poneman and Pavitt. Using "cheap amps, cheap guitars, multiple distortion boxes and a general sort of rowdy approach," he captured "screaming thrashing guitars,

Nirvana at a Sub Pop Festival, August 26, 1989.

Cameron Garrett.

loud bashing drums, wailing screaming singers and a general loud intent." The goal, Endino explained, "was to be loud and aggressive, and still have a sense of humor."

Sub Pop helped to create a downtrodden punk/metal fashion unique to the Northwest. It signed bands who dressed in faded flannel shirts or T-shirts, ripped jeans or baggy shorts over long johns, and worn Doc Marten boots. The mostly male band members favored long hair underneath woolen caps, which had become a trademark among heavy-metal fanatics. In 1992, Poneman wrote the copy for an eleven-page *Vogue* fashion spread that featured the Northwest grunge look. "When nobody wants to look like they have money, what better champions of hobo chic than the upwardly spiraling grunge rock elite?" he asked. "If you look at it in context," justified Pavitt, "everything was Spandex and hairspray and we were trying to create something that was the polar opposite to that."

Sub Pop marketed their acts through a singles-of-the-month club. It introduced bands to the metal/punk underground by a subscription service, which was modeled after the cassette compilations Pavitt had included in his *Subterranean Pop* fanzine. For $20, the label sent to subscribers six limited-edition singles such as "Room a Thousand Years Wide" by Soundgarden.

To promote their bands, the label also courted the press. In 1989, Sub Pop paid for a visit from journalist Everett True who wrote for the British music magazine *Melody Maker*, which subsequently called Sub Pop the "life force to the most vibrant, kicking music scene encompassed in one city for at least ten years." Within a year, the label attracted the attention of the national press. In August 1990, Billboard declared that "at long last, Seattle is suddenly hot." In November, the *New York Times* referred to Seattle as "America's latest music mecca," and articles about Sub Pop appeared in the *Los Angeles Times*, the *Wall Street Journal*, and other newspapers and magazines across the country. By the end of 1990, Sub Pop developed an image of Seattle as the site of an exciting, emerging music scene. "Bruce and I like to compare what's going on here in Seattle with what happened in San Francisco in 1967," Poneman told the *Seattle Post-Intelligencer*. "People are moving out here to become part of a scene," added Pavitt. "No matter how silly it sounds, Seattle has become a mecca."

Two new companies helped shape the hip Northwest aura. In 1981, Microsoft, started during the mid-1970s by young Northwest computer whizzes Paul Allen and Bill Gates, III, signed a contract with IBM to develop an operating system called DOS (disk operating system). In 1983, the fledgling business located near Seattle launched the word processing application, Word, and two years later released the graphical extension of MS-DOS called Windows. In another year, the company perfected a suite of word processing, spreadsheet, and database applications, which it called Microsoft Works and then Microsoft Office. By the early 1990s, when Sub Pop packaged grunge, Microsoft had become the dominant force in computer operating systems and applications, cornering 90 percent of the market and hoisting the Pacific Northwest to a leading role in emerging digital technology.

As Microsoft drew international attention to Seattle, a coffee company shone a spotlight on the Emerald City. Starbucks, established by three friends in 1971, grew to six stores in Seattle by the mid-1980s. In 1987, the trio sold their expanding business to competitor Howard Schultz who aggressively opened forty additional stores within two years. By 1992, when the company went public, Starbucks had 140 outlets valued at more than $73 million and made Seattle synonymous with the coffee shop.

Television and film solidified the image of Seattle as a trendy and exciting hub of popular culture. In April 1990, David Lynch premiered the ABC television show *Twin Peaks*, which was filmed in Snoqualmie and North Bend, Washington, and popularized an image of flannel-clad, coffee-drinking Northwesterners. *Northern Exposure*, starting as a replacement series in 1990 and quickly becoming one of the most popular shows on television, extolled the virtues of the Northwest and was filmed a few miles outside Seattle. In early 1991, director and former *Rolling Stone* writer Cameron Crowe started to film the movie *Singles* about the punk/metal Seattle scene that included the music of Northwest bands and featured band members in cameo roles. The film revolved around a fictional Seattle grunge band, which recorded the single "Touch Me I'm Dick," patterned after "Touch Me I'm Sick" by the garage-rock Seattle grunge outfit Mudhoney. By early 1992, when *Singles* aired in theaters across the country, the national media had embraced Seattle as the newest hip locale. "Now you get people going, 'Oh, it's about Seattle? How trendy,'" gushed Cameron Crowe.

Just as the media lionized the Northwest, Nirvana signed to a national label and became a national phenomenon. By 1990, the band realized that Sub Pop had fallen into financial difficulties and searched for a new label. In August, the group signed to David Geffen's DGC label, which paid Sub Pop $75,000 for the Nirvana contract.

The band released their major label debut *Nevermind* on September 24, 1991, amid the Northwest frenzy. Even before MTV placed the video of "Smells Like Teen Spirit" in heavy rotation, the album went gold, and in January 1992 Nirvana hit the top of the chart in the United States and the Top Ten in Britain. The band appeared on *Saturday Night Live* and was featured in *Rolling Stone, Spin*, and many other music publications. Within a year, Nirvana had sold 10 million copies of the record and entered the chart at the number-one position with their follow-up, *In Utero*.

Pearl Jam followed Nirvana to the top of the chart. The band had been established in Seattle by hardcore/British heavy metal fans Jeff Ament and Stone Gossard who had been members of Green River, the first band to record for Sub Pop. They added Black Sabbath–influenced guitarist Mike McCready, vocalist Eddie Vedder, and eventually drummer Dave Abbruzzese to complete the lineup. In late 1991, Pearl Jam released their first album, *Ten*. After waiting twenty weeks to crack the Top 200, the band nearly topped the chart in the wake of Nirvana's success and eventually sold 30 million copies of the album. Matching Nirvana's track record, in 1993 the group entered the chart at number one with *Vs*.

Other Northwest metal/punk bands scored similar successes. In 1992, Alice in Chains, described by the band's guitarist Jerry Cantrell as "not entirely metal, not entirely grunge, but all of the above," released the foreboding Top Ten album *Dirt*, which contained such songs as "Hate to Feel" and "Down in a Hole." "There's some pretty disturbing things that we write and sing about," explained Cantrell. "We live in a time when everything is falling apart." Two years later, the band topped the chart with the more pop-sounding, extended-play *Jar of Flies*. In early 1994, Soundgarden, the first Seattle band to land a major label deal, topped the chart with *Superunknown*. Mudhoney, formed by Mark Arm and Steve Turner who had played in Green River, delivered *Every Good Boy Deserves Fudge* (1991), which became Sub Pop's biggest seller after Nirvana's *Bleach*. By early 1994, Seattle bands dominated the album chart.

The Northwest bands played music for a post–baby-boom generation. "There's millions and millions of people in their 40s who think they're so fucking special," railed Kim Thayil of Soundgarden. "They're this ultimate white-bread, suburban, upper-middle-class group that were spoiled little fuckers as kids 'cause they were all children of Dr. Spock, and then they were stupid, stinky hippies, and then they were spoiled little yuppie materialists. They thought they had a monopoly on rock-'n'-roll," Thayil sneered, "and all of a sudden they realize they don't. It belongs to someone else now."

Seattle bands articulated the fears and frustrations of their many post–baby-boom fans. For most of his childhood, Eddie Vedder believed that his biological father was a distant family friend and fought constantly with his stepfather, who masqueraded as his biological father. After his real father died of multiple sclerosis, a teenaged Vedder discovered the truth and "had to deal with the anger of not being told sooner." To purge his feelings of parental neglect, he wrote such songs as "Jeremy." "I think the Seventies and Eighties were a really weird time for parenting, especially in the middle class," reasoned Vedder. "Was that the 'Me Generation' or something? Parents were looking for their things, which meant a lot of kids got left behind."

Soundgarden similarly mirrored the concerns of Generation X. Chris Cornell's lyrics "deal with inner struggles he's gone through, but a lot of people can relate to them," remarked Soundgarden and Pearl Jam drummer Matt Cameron about the band's songs. "I think the angst this generation is experiencing is very valid, and I think it's a pretty important change that this generation of bands is actually dealing with those issues." Cornell noted that "I guess the music industry didn't predict that this generation of songwriters was going to plug in so accurately and so unanimously to the group of people who were buying records. It's a representation of the generation that wasn't being accurately represented."

The marketing tactics of Sub Pop reflected the mood of a new generation. On June 9, 1989, the label dubbed a showcase of Sub Pop bands at the Moore Theater in Seattle as a "Lamefest" and billed the event as "Seattle's lamest bands in a one-night orgy of sweat and insanity!" The record-company owners followed with three more annual Lamefest events. They sold Sub Pop T-shirts emblazoned with the word "loser." "That shirt really hit home," explained Poneman. "There were an incredible number of young people out there who weren't making it. It was a real anti-yuppie statement." Guitarist Kurt Danielson of the Northwest grunge band Tad defined "the loser" as "the existential hero of the 90s."

Sub Pop Lamefest poster by Frank Kozik, master of gallows humor.

Frank Kozik.

Nirvana poster by Frank Kozik.

Frank Kozik.

The poster art of the grunge era reflected the desperate mood of youth. Artists such as Derek Hess, Ward Sutton, and Coop drew cartoonish images of a society in decline. Frank Kozik, probably the most well-known poster artist of grunge, pictured naive, happy cartoon characters shooting heroin or tormenting one another. "I prefer gallows humor, black humor," explained Kozik.

Grunge Spreads

The sound and spirit of grunge spread to nearby Olympia with the riot grrrls. A loosely bound group of Northwest bands, the riot grrrls built upon the foundation laid by such earlier punk icons as Patti Smith, Siouxsie Sioux, and Exene Cervenka of X to deliver an angry heavy-metal/punk music that demanded female empowerment.

In 1991, the riot grrrls surfaced, when Kathleen Hanna, Allison Wolfe, Molly Neuman, and Tobi Vail launched the *Riot Grrrl* fanzine. They addressed neglected issues such as rape, domestic abuse, patriarchy, and discrimination against females. "Because in every form of media we see ourselves slapped, decapitated, laughed at, objectified, raped, trivialized, pushed, ignored, stereotyped, kicked, scorned, molested, [and] silenced," the riot grrrls wanted to "create mediums that speak to US."

Prodded by the 1991 International Pop Underground convention sponsored by K Records in Olympia, Washington, the riot-grrrl originators started bands as a platform for change. Hanna and Vail launched the heavy-metal/punk Bikini Kill with Kathi Wilcox and Billy Karren. Wolfe and Neuman established all-female Bratmobile. Bikini Kill immediately released *Revolution Girl Style Now* on their own label. In 1993, they collaborated with the riot-grrrl-band Huggy Bear on *Yeah, Yeah, Yeah, Yeah*, which neared the Top Ten in Britain and included "Rebel Girl."

Other riot-grrl bands formed to disseminate their feminist message. Sleater-Kinney, a band near Olympia, signed to Chainsaw records and later to Kill Rock Star Records, an Olympia-based label, which signed many riot-grrrl acts. In 1992, 7 Year Bitch of Seattle released their debut on the local label, C/Z Records. The Los Angeles-based heavy-metal punk female band L7, formed in 1985 and inspired by Motorhead and the Stooges, joined the movement and in 1992 hit the chart with *Bricks Are Heavy*.

Hole, headed by sometime Northwest resident Courtney Love, became the most successful female-dominated, heavy-metal/punk group. Like most of her generation, Love suffered through a scarring childhood, when her parents divorced. She moved from a boarding school in New Zealand, to a free school in England and to Eugene, Oregon, where she lived with her mother's therapist. "You know how in most family homes they'll be pictures of the kids at the head of the stairs," she asked. "There's not a picture of me."

After high school, Love turned to music. After a few several forays into rock, in 1989 the vocalist/guitarist started Hole with lead guitarist Eric Erlandson. She recruited two women, drummer Patty Schemel and bassist Jill Emeroy for the band. "Generally, I sought the female most of my life," she insisted. In 1991, the band created the harsh punk of *Pretty on the Inside*. Three years later with Kristen Pfaff on bass, Hole neared the Top Fifty in the United States and the Top Ten in Britain with the grunge-based aggression of *Live Through This*, which sold 2 million copies. By 1993, reported the *New York Times*, "more women are taking up instruments than ever before, and a new round of artists has emerged to challenge the usual virgin-Vixen-bimbo stereotypes."

As Northwest grunge enveloped the music industry, the angst spread to nearby San Francisco as Green Day popularized California hardcore by grafting snappy melodies onto punk's speedy, muscular sound and its message of frustration. Formed in 1989 by singer/guitarist Billie Joe Armstrong and bass player Mike Dirnt, the band signed with the pop-punk label Lookout. After releasing their debut and adding drummer Frank "Tre Cool" Wright III to complete its lineup, the band delivered a soundtrack for the alienated Generation X with *Kerplunk*.

Sighted by the major labels during the grunge-band signing frenzy, in 1993 Green Day inked a deal with Warner-Reprise. Early the next year, the group released *Dookie*, which offered listeners lyrics of hopelessness over a snappy, bright nineties punk sound. The threesome snagged listeners with the cynical "Welcome to Paradise," the despondent "Longview," the apathetic "Burnout," and the self-deprecating "Basket Case." "I think it's a sign of the times to be way more self-destructive, way more apathetic," reasoned Armstrong. "Basically it's yet another generation falling down the shithole. I just think about the whole American culture and go, Why?" With help from MTV and an appearance at Woodstock 1994, the album sold 15 million copies worldwide.

Green Day opened the floodgates for a spate of other Southern California pop-punk bands that reflected the feelings of their generation. In early 1993, the metallic-tinged skate punk of Offspring hit the Top Five with *Smash*. "Punk was really abrasive,

Hole at the Edge, March 14, 1995.

Mark Arminski.

and a lot of the topics the songs dealt with were alienation, not fitting in, and being disillusioned with what American values were supposed to be," asserted singer/guitarist Bryan "Dexter" Holland. "Nowadays, it seems like mainstream America is identifying with those kinds of feelings."

Rancid cracked the chart amid the pop-punk explosion. The Northern California quartet grew up in broken homes and poverty. "I remember my mom trying to raise two kids on her own in the eighties and Ronald Reagan being in power, and having her hours cut so she could barely make the fucking rent," Lars Frederiksen bitterly recollected. "I remember eating fucking Raisin Bran for Christmas dinner." Though banding together in 1991 and debuting two years later, the politicized group first charted in 1994 with *Let's Go* and the next year with…*And Out Come the Wolves*. "As long as America is the way it is, punk is never going to die," explained Rancid frontman Tim Armstrong. "Kids are always going to be going through shit, and will be using guitars as vehicles to express how fucked up they feel."

Grunge's Demise

By mid-decade, rock-and-roll bands expressed the disillusionment that gripped many post–baby boomers and ultimately sowed the seeds of grunge's demise. "We had to grow up with this idealization that was never going to fucking come true, and it turned us into a bunch of cynics—or a bunch of drug addicts," complained Courtney Love who fronted the grunge band Hole and married Kurt Cobain.

The grunge community embraced heroin, which seemed to offer an escape from a hopeless situation. "For a long time in Seattle, it seemed like everyone was doing heroin," remarked Nils Bernstein, a publicity man for Sub Pop.

The combination of drugs and despondency led to the deaths of musicians and the end of grunge. Early nineties' overdose deaths of Mother Love Bone singer Andrew Wood, Hole bass player Kristen Pfaff, and guitarist Stefanie Sargent of the all-female Seattle punk band Seven Year Bitch emphasized the effects of harrowing heroin. On April 5, 1994, Kurt Cobain, probably the most important figure in Northwest grunge, shot and killed himself in his Seattle home and highlighted the angry desperation of a generation. "I think there's gonna be more and more people who just give up hope," predicted Chris Cornell. "I mean, that's the way I feel. I'm successful in what I do, but I don't really have a clue where I'm going or how I fit into the rest of society." The anger, frustration, and disillusionment of a new generation had become lethal.

Chapter 22
Post-Grunge Party

"It's all about escapism—a pint in one hand, your best mate in the other, whoever that may be, and just having a good time."

—Noel Gallagher

During the mid-1990s, as the economy improved and as the desperation of grunge diminished, youth turned to a brighter, more pop sound on both sides of the Atlantic. In Britain, Britpop enveloped the United Kingdom and invaded America. The United States offered its own party music with the long, varied improvisations of the jam bands that played to hordes of fans at open-air festivals.

An improved economy helped brighten the spirits of youth on both sides of the Atlantic. In the United States during 1994, the unemployment rate dropped precipitously to approximately 5 percent under the administration of Bill Clinton. It continued to decrease and stabilized at nearly 4 percent for nearly seven years. Simultaneously, inflation plummeted to approximately 2 percent, and the Gross National Product (GNP) expanded at a healthy 4 percent for five years. Similarly, starting in 1993 an economic upturn in Britain blunted the hopelessness of British youths. By 1997, double-digit unemployment dropped to 6.5 percent, and inflation increased at a 3 percent rate. Within this rosy economic context, American and British youth abandoned grunge and hardcore techno for British pop and jam bands.

Britpop

During the mid-1990s, British bands played a new version of British pop called "Britpop" by the press. Building upon the success of the mid-1980s popdom of the Smiths, groups such as Suede, Pulp, Blur, and Oasis dominated the British charts. They projected a pro-British, anti-grunge attitude as part of a nationalistic Cool Britannia movement, which arose from the growing support for the New Labour party of Tony Blair and proclaimed the virtues of all things British, including music, fashion, and art.

The Smiths inspired many of the Britpop bands. The group, formed by guitarist Johnny Marr and singer Steven Morrissey, or just Morrissey, successfully combined Morrissey's morose lyrics with Marr's upbeat guitar work. In 1984, the band hit the number-two slot on the British chart with their self-named debut and the same year reached the Top Ten with *Hateful of Hollow*. The next year, they hit the top of the chart with *Meat Is Murder*. In 1986, they followed with the near chart-topper *The Queen Is Dead* before disbanding.

Suede, banding together in 1989, jump-started the Britpop mania. Inspired by the Smiths, vocalist Brett Anderson and guitarist Bernard Butler took the name of the band from a Morrissey single, "Suedehead." In early 1993, they topped the British chart with a dark, guitar-based debut. In April, a posing Anderson appeared on the cover of the British magazine *Select* with a British flag in the background and a headline that read "Yanks Go Home!" Coming out just as economic times brightened, Suede set the stage for a number of fashion-conscious bands who played mid-1960s British invasion rock and prided themselves on being English. Pulp, another band that had been featured in the April issue of *Select*, rode the British pop wave started by Suede.

Led by vocalist/guitarist Jarvis Cocker, the group made its recording debut in 1983 to lukewarm reviews. As the Britpop craze took hold, their version of British-invasion rock climbed the English chart. In 1994, Pulp hit with the Top Ten *His 'N' Hers* and the next year topped their competition with *Different Class*.

Launched in 1989, Blur initially mined the sound of the late-1980s Manchester scene but changed its musical direction toward a more guitar-pop sound. As Justine Frischmann, the leader of the Britpop band Elastica and one-time girlfriend of Blur singer Damon Albarn, recalled after a tour of the United States, "it occurred to us [she and Albarn] that Nirvana were out there, and people were very interested in American music, and there should be some sort of manifesto for the return of Britishness." Newly armed with an English sensibility, Blur hit the chart with two successive number-one albums, *Parklife* (1994) and *The Great Escape* (1995). The band paved the way for a spate of British guitar-based popsters such as Menswear, the Boo Radleys, and Supergrass.

In 1994 during the Britpop explosion, Oasis rose from obscurity to international stardom. Headed by lyricist/guitarist Noel Gallagher and his brother Liam, the group burst on the scene with the number-one *Definitely Maybe*, which sold 500,000 copies in a day and holds the record for the fastest-selling debut in history. The next year, the Manchester outfit again topped the chart with *(What's the Story) Morning Glory?* Unlike the other British pop bands, Oasis crossed over into America by hitting the Top Five with *Morning Glory*, which also topped charts in Europe and Asia. In 1996, they played a two-night set in Knebworth to 250,000 cheering fans who had vied for tickets with more than 2.6 million other adherents.

The more experimental pop of Radiohead attained success. Fronted by singer Thom Yorke and featuring a three-guitar lineup, the band debuted with *Pablo Honey* (1993), which neared the Top Thirty on both sides of the Atlantic and featured the grunge-like, angst-ridden hit, "Creep." During the mid-1990s, Yorke and his band mates rejected "all the ugly, male, sleazy, semen-smelling rock bullshit" and moved

Oasis concert poster, March 3, 1996.

Mark Arminski.

toward a sonically layered seriousness laced with techno textures. In 1997, the band released their masterpiece, the eclectic, progressive pop of *OK Computer*, which topped the British chart and neared the Top Twenty in the United States. The album, explained Thom Yorke, joined the band's "electronica fetishes" within "a live band context" for a new guitar-driven, ethereal pop.

From 1994 to 1997, Britpop swept Britain and invaded America. Blur, Oasis, and other Britpop bands derived their sounds from many borrowed sources, including the Beatles who spearheaded the first, most successful British invasion. Radiohead, one of the most stylistically diverse acts, incorporated aspects of the Beatles, U2, and Pink Floyd. They also cited jazz great Miles Davis and Italian film composer Ennio Morricone as important to their music. Noel Gallagher of Oasis mentioned the Smiths as a major influence. "When the Smiths came on the *Top of the Pops* for the first time, that was it for me," he confessed. "From that day on, I wanted to be Johnny Marr." He also paid homage to the ultimate British pop band, the Beatles. The guitarist called the Beatles more than "an obsession. It's an ideal for living." Blur bassist Alex James identified the same Beatlesque influence. "We made a very deliberate attempt to embrace classic British songwriting values and imagery," he explained.

The Britpop bands proudly displayed their British-invasion roots as a reaction to American grunge. "Grunge? People in shorts and socks and pumps with guitars and stickers jumping up and down screaming," Liam Gallagher sniffed. "Not having it. Far too smelly for me." His brother Noel added that "the grunge thing was all about eating your parents and all that shite." Though he enjoyed some grunge bands, Graham Coxon, guitarist for Blur, said he would take his "Walkman to his bunk on the tour bus and listen to it in secret, because we had to be proud of being British at that point." "If punk was about getting rid of hippies," added Blur singer Damon Albarn, "then I'm getting rid of grunge."

Unlike the starkly realistic grunge, Britpop encouraged British youths to enjoy better times. As Noel Gallagher described it, "we just came along and it was like, if fuckin' 'cow' rhymes with 'now,' and it goes with a good tune, you know, who cares?" "It's all about escapism," he explained, "a pint in one hand, your best mate in the other, whoever that may be, and just having a good time."

The fun-loving Britpop peaked by mid-decade. In August 1995, the *New Musical Express* described the furor over the self-consciously British bands: "In a week where news leaked that Saddam Hussein was preparing nuclear weapons, everyday folks were still getting slaughtered in Bosnia, and [boxer] Mike Tyson was making his comeback, tabloids and broadsheets alike went Britpop crazy." In February 1996, British Labour leader Tony Blair exclaimed that "it's been a great year for British music. A year of creativity, vitality, energy, British bands storming the charts." "British music," he concluded was "back once again in its right place, at the top of the world."

By 1997, the girl power of the Spice Girls joined the male-centered Britpop to ensure the dominance of British pop for another year. Just like the Monkees had been assembled nearly twenty-five years earlier, in 1994 the quintet resulted from a magazine advertisement for volunteers who were "street smart, extrovert[ed], ambitious and able to sing and dance." The next year, the five young women—Geri "Ginger Spice" Halliwell, Melanie "Scary Spice" Brown, Victoria "Posh Spice" Adams, Emma "Baby Spice" Bunton, and Melanie "Sporty Spice" Chisholm—signed with veteran music entrepreneur Simon Fuller and started to work on their debut.

The Spice Girls presented a feminist outlook sprinkled with a rave flavoring for their young fans. They projected the collective persona of scantily clad nineties feminists, who spouted a philosophy of "girl power, an equalization of the sexes" to an army of preteen and teenage girls. "Girl power is about being able to do things as well as the boys—if not better—and being who you 'wannabe.'" The group also included an element of rave culture with their constant lip service to "positivity" and their smiley demeanor.

The message of the Spice Girls empowered many young girl fans. In a survey about the group conducted in 1997, most of their young female fanatics felt that "girl power" meant that "girls can do everything that boys can do. That we're as good as boys, and sometimes better." "I think it's really cool for girls to see people they want to grow up to be," asserted Carla DeSantis, publisher and editor-in-chief of the feminist *Rockrgrl* magazine.

Adored by masses of "tweens" and teenage female fans, the Spice Girls became one of the most visible musical phenomena of the 1990s. Featuring a bright, bouncy R&B sound on their debut *Spice*, they quickly scaled the charts. Their hit "Wannabe" became the first number-one single in Britain by an all-female band and topped the charts in thirty-one countries, including the United States, when it reached American shores in January 1997. They sold 7 million copies of their album in the United States and 31 million worldwide. The Spice Girls followed with the album *Spiceworld*, a movie of the same name, and a book, *Girl Power*, that sold 200,000 copies in a day. By the end of 1997, the Spice Girls had earned nearly $70 million, and the two Spice Girls albums amazingly still charted in the United States for another year. Remembering another British invasion by mop-tops from Liverpool, the press referred to the pop delivered by the first British female teen idols as the "Spice Girls revolution."

Though abandoning the guitar-driven, sixties-derived sound of Britpop for an even more pop-oriented confection, the Spice Girls held the banner of Cool Britannia high. They extolled the virtues of their homeland, and Geri Halliwell wore a Union Jack mini-dress as her trademark. Until Halliwell suddenly departed the group in May 1998, the Spice Girls represented the most commercially successful flank of the second British invasion.

Jam Bands

As youths danced to British pop, Americans offered an alternative rooted in the past. During the mid-1990s, Jam bands topped the chart by harkening back to a sixties-style tribal community, epitomized by the Grateful Dead. They incorporated a multiplicity of influences, and played long, winding, languid improvisational solos, which gave them their collective moniker and reflected a generation, which experienced good times.

Phish and the Dave Matthews Band, two of the most well-known jam bands, attributed their sounds to a diversity of musical sources. Guitarist Trey Anastasio, launching Phish in 1983 at the University of Vermont, melded such diverse influences as progressive rock, Miles Davis, and jazz guitarist Pat Metheny in his extended guitar solos. Dave Matthews, a South African immigrant to the United States who ironically settled in grunge-friendly Seattle, delivered a concoction of jazz, blues, rock, and folk. "I got into different kinds of music," explained Matthews who cited the Beatles, Led Zeppelin, Joan Baez, Cat Stevens, Bob Marley, and jazz pianist Keith Jarrett as sources of inspiration.

Many sixties-influenced jam bands not surprisingly mentioned Jerry Garcia of the Grateful Dead as a stimulus for their musical gumbo. "Jerry Garcia has been a huge influence on me," explained Anastasio of Phish. "I think there was more of an 'overall ingesting' of Garcia's style." Widespread Panic, the jam band organized by guitarist Michael "Panic" Houser, started by playing Grateful Dead covers in its hometown of Athens, Georgia.

Like the Grateful Dead and other San Francisco bands from the mid-to-late sixties, the jam bands toured incessantly. Blues Traveler and the Dave Matthews Band constantly toured to build their following. Widespread Panic generally played 250 shows a year. "They're like us," Jerry Garcia explained as he spoke about the jam bands. "They're following the Grateful Dead tradition of screw the record companies, screw MTV, just go out and play for real humans. And it's working for them."

Much like the Dead, jam bands created a sense of community with their audiences. Phish bolstered their popularity through audience-friendly tactics at concerts such as the "Big Ball Jam," which involved the band throwing a beach ball into the concert going throngs and composing a song by adding a new note each time the ball bounced. The band affectionately referred to fans as "phans," "phriends," "phamily," and, in a tribute to Deadheads, "Phishheads." "I think our fans look at us not as idols or icons, but more as family members," explained bassist Dave Schools of Widespread Panic.

The jam bands promoted themselves and fostered camaraderie among fans by allowing the audience to freely tape their many shows and trade them with one another, much like the Grateful Dead had done. John Hermann, the keyboardist for Widespread Panic, explained the rationale in equalitarian terms. "The minute that you play a note, it doesn't belong to you anymore," he pointed out. "It belongs to everybody else."

The democratic spirit extended to interaction among band members. Similar to the sixties San Francisco groups which contended that all of the members contributed equally to success, jam bands of the nineties prided themselves on being leaderless. "That's one of the things about this band that everybody likes," contended Carter Beauford, drummer for the Dave Matthews Band. "There isn't a leader. Each one of us can express ourselves musically without being choked by a leader." Even the name the Dave Matthews Band arose accidentally rather than by design. Early in the band's career, one venue simply assumed that the group called itself by the guitarist's name and advertised the "Dave Matthews Band." "It was sort of too late to change when we started thinking that this could focus unfairly on me. People sort of made that association but it's really not like that," clarified Matthews.

Jam bands exhibited a socially conscious ethos, especially a concern for the environment, which reflected the general attitude of their sixties forebearers. The Dave Matthews Band first performed at Earth Day in 1991 and generously contributed to causes such as Farm Aid to promote the importance of organic farming. In 1995, Phish challenged its audience to a game of chess and asked the fans to signal their moves through Greenpeace, one of the band's favorite causes. The group also established nonprofit foundations such as the Touring Branch, the Vermont Giving Program, and the Water Wheel.

Jam bands coalesced at sixties-style rock festivals. In 1992, Blues Traveler harmonica whiz John Popper established H.O.R.D.E. (Horizon of Rock Developing Everywhere) as an outdoor venue for jam-band music. In addition to his group, Popper recruited the jam-band royalty of Phish, Widespread Panic, and the Dave Matthews Band, as well as a spate of less known jammers to H.O.R.D.E. Though H.O.R.D.E. ended in 1998, its music-festival successors Coachella and Bonnaroo showcased music for a generation that expressed a jubilant hope rather than a sobering grunge cynicism.

During the mid-1990s after the death of Grateful Dead icon Jerry Garcia and amid a booming economy, jam bands hit the mainstream. On August 9, 1995, Jerry Garcia passed away from a heart attack. He represented a central figure of the sixties spirit by staging free concerts, showing a distain of the corporate establishment, and extending musical boundaries. Band mates and Deadheads mourned Garcia's death and hoped to save the thirty-year community, which Garcia had helped build.

Many Deadheads and their younger counterparts embraced the jam bands. Though Phish had formed a dozen years before, the band scored their first Top Ten

Coachella poster, 2007.

Emek Studios.

effort with *Billy Breathes* (1996). That year, they moved from clubs to massive festivals such as the two-day Clifford Ball, which attracted nearly 80,000 people.

The Dave Matthews Band, though organized in 1991 in Charlottesville, Virginia, first scaled the chart in 1994 with *Under the Table and Dreaming*, which nearly cracked the Top Ten and proved to be the first among many top-selling albums. The group neared the top with the mega-selling *Crash* (1996) and *Live at Red Rocks 8.15.95* (1997). In 1998, it hit the top spot with *Before These Crowded Streets*.

Blues Traveler ascended the chart at the same time. Formed in 1987 in New Jersey by John Popper, the band moved to New York City, played in local clubs, and toured constantly. It featured the jam-band trademark of extended guitar improvisations. By 1994, Blues Traveler reached the *Billboard* Top Ten with *four* and neared the top with *Straight On till Morning* (1997).

Widespread Panic followed their jam band compatriots to commercial success. In 1997, the group snagged one of their highest chart positions with *Bombs & Butterflies*. It also became one of the Top Twenty concert attractions in the country without radio play, MTV, or much major record label help. During the mid-to-late nineties, Widespread Panic and other jam bands created a community of white, mostly middle-class devotees who streamed by the thousands onto fairgrounds to participate in shared cultural celebrations. The jam bands, backing environmentalism and embracing a wide-ranging, sometimes meandering musical style, contrasted sharply with the rapid-fire raps which sounded from destitute urban areas of the hip-hop nation.

Widespread Panic poster.

Jeral Tidwell/www.humantree.com.

Chapter 23
The Hip-Hop Nation

"Rap is today's rock and roll."
—Hale Milgrim, President, Capitol Records, 1990

African-American youth, facing greater hardships than their white counterparts on both sides of the Atlantic, responded with a hard-edged hip-hop music to chronicle their plight and to generate community support. They created an adaptable vehicle that constantly changed and merged with other music to become an innovative, distinctive, nearly ubiquitous sound during the late eighties, the nineties, and into the twenty-first century.

African-American Reality

African Americans generally experienced hard times despite gains made by the civil rights movement. By 1980, more than 31 percent of African Americans lived in poverty, nearly three times the percentage of impoverished whites. Six years later, 14 percent of African-American families earned less than $5000 a year and more than 30 percent had a yearly income of less than $10,000.

African-American youths especially confronted forbidding economic prospects. In 1987, more than 34 percent of African-American teens were unemployed, compared to 17 percent of white teens. Of the African-American teens between the ages of 20 and 24, more than 21 percent could not find jobs, compared to less than 10 percent of their white counterparts. By 1992, nearly 40 percent of African-American teens and 24 percent of African Americans in their early twenties found themselves on the unemployment rolls.

Many of these poor, unemployed youths lived in single-parent, single-income households, usually headed by a mother. In 1964, roughly 25 percent of African-American children lived in female-headed homes. Abetted by a welfare system that rewarded fatherless families, in 1984, the number of female-headed, single-parent African-American families skyrocketed to more than 50 percent, compared to 14 percent among white families. By 1992, the number of fatherless families increased to 59 percent among African Americans.

Searching for the support provided by a stable family, many African-American youths joined gangs such as the notorious warring Crips and Bloods in Los Angeles. By the mid-1980s in Los Angeles, 24,000 young African Americans belonged to more than 260 gangs. By 1992, the membership among the Bloods and Crips numbered around 40,000.

Many of the new gang members found the intimacy that they sought. "There's a lot of admirable qualities in gang membership. A guy will look at you and say, 'If something happens to you, I'll be the first one to die.' There's a lot of love," suggested rapper Ice-T (b. Tracy Marrow). "The gang was like your family," disclosed rap pioneer Afrika Bambaataa (b. Kevin Donovan) who had been a member of the Black Spades in New York City. "Sometimes a gang is more your family than a real family is, and that's what a lot of people don't understand," added B-Real (b. Louis Freese) of

Cypress Hill. "Why do you want to be in a gang? Well, because my homeboy loves me more than my fuckin' mother or father does."

Many gangs warred against one another. Unlike gangs in previous decades that wielded clubs, knives, and chains, gang members during the eighties and nineties carried guns for protection. As rapper Coolio (b. Artis Ivey, Jr.) explained about the need for a gun, "They say on the radio and TV that you have a choice, but it's bullshit. If you're getting your ass whipped every day, you've got to have some protection."

Gang members, sporting some of the most modern handheld weaponry available, contributed to a dramatic growth in street violence and death. From 1986 to 1989, the number of African-American teen homicide victims increased from under 1,000 to more than 1,600. By 1992, homicide became the leading cause of death among African-American teenagers. "The other day I was looking at an old picture from back when I used to play Pop Warner football," remembered rapper and one-time Crips member Snoop Dogg (b. Cordozar Calvin Broadus, Jr.), who was later be charged with murder, "and like of twenty-eight homies on the team, twelve are dead, seven are in the penitentiary, and three of them are smoked out."

The proliferation of "crack," an inexpensive type of cocaine popular in the inner cities, intensified the violence. Surfacing in 1974 around San Francisco, freebase cocaine resulted from a heated mixture of ether and cocaine into a powder. By the end of the decade, freebase cocaine turned into crack, when drug dealer and ex-tennis pro "Freeway Rick" Ross added baking soda to the mix and let it harden. Crack became increasingly inexpensive, when the U.S. government under Ronald Reagan allowed military operatives to help Contra counter-revolutionaries in Nicaragua smuggle the drug into large American metropolitan areas in exchange for Contra cooperation in selling weapons to Iran. By the mid-1980s, crack cocaine became an epidemic in the inner cities.

Without many options, some inner-city African-American youths sold crack. "When a nigga sells drugs around here," observed rapper OMB of the group OFTM [Operation from the Bottom], "he ain't selling for no big thing, 'cause his family is starving, he's starving, so he's gotta make some kind of move to get what he gotta get, and I mean dope [crack] is the most popular and quickest way he can get money." "Everybody was either selling it or using it," agreed rapper Jay-Z (b. Shawn Carter) about his neighborhood. "When I was growing up in the Eighties, crack was everywhere—there were Uzis in the projects. I heard shootings my whole life. It was not a big deal."

As crack sales became more competitive and lucrative, gangs dominated the scene, and violence escalated. "When this whole crack thing came on, people really started getting smoked," recalled Senen "Sen Dog" Reyes, a former member of the Bloods gang and a rapper for Cypress Hill. "That was like in 1985, 1986, crack shit hit big out in L.A." "And that's part of the deterioration of the gangs, yunno, the drug element that comes in." The violent, economically bleak conditions that faced inner-city African-American youth led to a sense of despair. "We not living no American Dream," remarked rapper Kam (b. Craig Miller). "We in a nightmare. Like I said, this is hell for us. Anything else would be an improvement, you know what I'm saying, we can't get no lower, we can't get no farther back."

Old School

Hip-hop music arose from and chronicled the African-American desperation in the inner cities, many times decrying poverty, drugs, and gang-inspired violence. The ghettos of New York City, especially the impoverished Bronx, served as the breeding ground for hip hop. In 1978, residents of the Bronx experienced on average 33 fires per day, a declining population, dilapidated homes without running water and a lack of police protection. Of the inhabitants, 40 percent collected welfare, 30 percent stood in unemployment lines, and 25 percent could not read.

During the early seventies, as disco became popular in New York, some disc jockeys in the Bronx and Harlem spun records from their sizeable collections at parties to entertain their friends who could not afford admission to a disco. Rather than use an entire song, record spinners such as the Jamaican-raised Kool Herc (b. Clive Campbell) played, or sampled, short fragments, usually the percussion breaks, which dancers requested. Starting in 1974, Kool Herc used his booming, state-of-the-art sound system called the Herculords to blast "funky percussion breaks and he just kept that beat going" over and over in loops, recalled Afrika Bambaataa who began spinning records a few years after Herc. "It might be that certain part of the record that everyone waits for." "They always wanted to hear breaks after breaks after breaks after breaks," added Herc.

The rap pioneers sampled all types of music. As Afrika Bambaataa explained, "the music itself is colorless 'cause you can't say, I don't like R&B, I don't like heavy metal, when half the shit that's out comes from all the different styles of records that's out there." Bambaataa used snippets from such a diverse set of influences as the German electronic group Kraftwerk to the heavy metal of Led Zeppelin.

Though having eclectic tastes, rappers generally favored polyrhythmic funk over the more simplistic disco. "We was against the disco that was happenin', we had the funk back 'cause they weren't playing James [Brown], Sly [and the Family Stone], or Parliament no more," remarked Bambaataa. "How the funk came back on the scene was through hip-hop, through the street," agreed Jazzy Jay (b. John Byas), a member of one of Bambaataa's groups. "All of them—James Brown, George Clinton, Parliament, all that—that was almost dead. Disco was in, everybody was hustling, and the disco deejays were taking over. Well, what happened, the kids just rebelled. They wanted something that they couldn't hear on the radio."

Some jockeys altered their samples to create new sounds. Kool Herc added special effects to samples of funky music. Following the lead of his fellow Jamaican, reggae producer King Tubby (b. Osbourne Ruddock), he removed most vocals from the track to create a "dub" version of the song and then supplemented it with echo and reverberation effects. Using a special stylus, other spinners such as the teenaged Grand Wizzard Theodore (b. Theodore Livingston) rotated, or scratched, the records back and forth to produce a unique rhythmic pattern. Kool Herc sometimes mixed the beat with two turntables by quickly fading one song into another. Through these methods,

Afrika Bambaataa, hip-hop pioneer.

Mika Vaisannen, Mika-Photography.

jockeys wove together intricate polyrhythms into a staccato sound that mimicked the short, abrupt changes that had become commonplace on commercial television.

Building on the African oral history tradition and copying Jamaican U-Roy (b. Ewart Beckford) who spoke, or toasted, to the dubs of King Tubby, Kool Herc talked along with the halting, polyrhythmic sounds. Afrika Bambaataa remembered that "Herc took phrases, like what was happening in the streets, what was the new saying going round the high school like 'rock on my mellow,' 'to the beat y'all,' 'you don't stop,' and just elaborated on that."

Soon other disc jockeys such as pioneers Bambaataa and DJ Hollywood (b. Anthony Holloway) who played disco records at the Apollo Theater during breaks, rapped to their sampled music. As time went by, these raps became more elaborate, with the DJ sometimes including a call-and-response "conversation" with the regulars in the house. Bambaataa summarized that "we just took the Jamaican style and put it to American records."

To achieve greater dexterity and creativity with the funk-based music, some disc jockeys enlisted the help of friends to rap, or emcee (MC), for them. Kool Herc asked his high school friend Coke La Rock to accompany him, "saying little poems on the mike, or saying something in a joke-ified manner." Lil Rodney Cee of the rap duo Double Trouble observed that "the first MC that I know of is Cowboy [b. Robert Wiggins], from Grandmaster Flash and the Furious Five. He was the first MC to talk for Grandmaster Flash [b. Joseph Saddler] and say how great Flash was—you know, 'the pulsating, inflating disco shaking, heartbreaking, the man on the turntable.'" Grandmaster Flash then enlisted the help of Mel Melle (b. Melvin Glover). "I was just trying to take off from where Coke La Rock had left it," Melle remembered.

By 1977, the Bronx in New York City had been divided into quadrants: The South Bronx belonged to Grandmaster Flash; in the Southeast, Afrika Bambaataa held sway with his anti-violence, self-defense organization, the Zulu nation, which organized under the motto "Peace, Love, Unity and Having Fun"; Kool Herc reigned in the West; and in the North followers flocked to DJ Breakout and DJ Baron.

By the end of the 1970s, the number of disc jockeys and their friends who rapped to the funky samples of effect-laden music multiplied. "After myself, Herc, and Flash, crazy amounts of DJs started springing up everywhere," recalled Bambaataa. "They always wanted to challenge or battle somebody. It was no joke .... If you lost, you could kiss your career goodbye."

Most of the DJs displayed their skills on the streets of New York by wiring their increasing elaborate sound systems to the base of a street lamp that they had broken. "Block parties was a way to do your thing, plugging into the lamp post," Jazzy Jay

Grandmaster Flash at the turntables.

Mika Vaisannen, Mika-Photography.

remembered. "It's like we'd rather see them doing that . . . than to be beating each other upside the head like they used to in the gang days." Despite the danger of electrocution, jockeys took the chance. "Playing music was more important than our lives," reasoned Charlie Chase, the DJ for the Cold Crush Brothers.

A few of the dedicated disc jockeys, ready for sonic battle, performed at prominent disco clubs. By September 2, 1976, Grandmaster Flash, nicknamed for his speed on the turntable, had progressed from parties, parks, and small clubs to the Audubon Club in Harlem that held a maximum of 3,000 patrons. "The pinnacle of a DJ group's career, before it was recording, was who can make it to the Audubon," recalled the Grandmaster. "Once you played there you were famous throughout the five boroughs" of New York City. By the late 1970s, popular jockeys such as Afrika Bambaataa found jobs at well-known downtown discos. After playing the Mudd Club, Bambaataa performed at Negril. Bambaataa then moved to the Danceteria. "Then it got too big for Danceteria," he related. "Finally, we made home at the Roxy. It started slow, building at the Roxy, and [soon] Friday nights always [attracted] three thousand, four thousand."

A youth culture partly based on disco arose around rappers such as Grandmaster Flash and Afrika Bambaataa. "Not only did our fans want to talk like we did," remembered Kurtis Blow (b. Kurtis Walker), a onetime collaborator with Grandmaster Flash, "but they dressed like we did, and seemed to be trying to live out the fantasies we were kicking in our raps." Calling themselves break boys (or just b-boys for short) and fly girls, the hip-hop fanatics in the inner cities of New York, Philadelphia, and Baltimore initially wore disco-like heavy gold chains and oversized gold rings.

They extended disco by perfecting break dancing, a complex form of dance in which the dancers simulated fights by sudden moves such as pop ups, freezes, head spins, flips, and backspins. They learned their moves from funk master James Brown. "Our immediate influence in b-boying was James Brown, point blank," contended well-known dancer Crazy Legs (b. Richard Colon). Eventually crews of break dancers competed with one another. Rock Steady Crew, probably the most famous break dancing team, boasted more than 500 members at one point and battled such dancers as the New York City Breakers and the Dynamic Rockers. By the mid-1980s, break dancing hit the mainstream in the films *Flashdance* (1983) and *Breakin'* (1984).

In reaction to the extravagance of disco, the poor, urban rappers grafted a street element to their counterculture, which they called hip-hop after a common phrase chanted at many Bronx dance parties. They adopted a low-brow fashion that included baseball caps with upturned bills, Adidas or 69er Pro Keds tennis shoes, and T-shirts. Mimicking the rappers, b-boys and fly girls used a street language that reflected their everyday concerns and included words and phrases such as "chill" (calm down), "sweat" (hassle), "dope" (great), "posse" (gang), "def" (good), and "wack" (bad).

Using subway trains and building facades as their canvases, individual artists such as Fab 5 Freddy (b. Fred Brathwaite), FUTURA 2000, Dondi White, and Lee Quinones, the latter who appeared in the film *Wild Style* (1982), and such groups as the Vanguards, Magic, Inc., and the Nod Squad used cans of spray paint to perfect a low-budget form of hip-hop visual art called graffiti. "Graffiti writing is a way of gaining status in a society where to own property is to have identity," explained Hugo Martinez who in 1972 organized the artists in United Graffiti Artists association. By 1980, graffiti entered art galleries through the efforts of graffiti-style painters such as the young Jean-Michel Basquiat and Keith Haring.

"For a culture to be really a complete culture, it should have a music, a dance and a visual art," explained Fab 5 Freddy. "Then I realized, wow, all these things are going on. You got the graffiti happening over here, you got the break dancing, and you got the DJ and the MCing thing. In my head, they were all one thing."

The hip-hop culture engendered a sense of community and self-worth among the poor African Americans in New York. "I'm wearing my suede Pumas. I got the whole thing with my Gazelle spectacle frames and Kangol hat with my gold watch going on.

In short, I'm fresh," explained hip-hop performer KRS-One (Lawrence Parker). "In this community, I can *win*. Now, if I step out of this community dressed like this, not only will I be thrown up against the wall and asked what drugs I got, but I also can't get a job and I'm ridiculed in school. So this community, the block parties, was an escape."

Like the eighties heavy-metal underground, the hip-hop community spread, when a growing number of fans bought and traded tapes of their favorite performers. "Cassette tapes used to be our albums before anybody recorded what they called rap records," Bambaataa pointed out. "People started hearing all this rapping coming out of boxes. When they heard the tapes down in the Village they wanted to know, 'Who's this black DJ who's playing all this rock and new wave up in the Bronx?'" Jazzy Jay added that "we had tapes that went platinum before we were even involved with the music industry."

Independent companies eventually heard the tapes and recorded the new music. In 1979, Sylvia Robinson, a former R&B vocalist who during the Fifties had been half of the Mickey and Sylvia duo, listened to several hip-hop tapes that her children played at home. "Hey, if my kids like this, all the kids around the world will like this!" she reasoned. With her husband Joe, she started Sugarhill Records and recorded "Rapper's Delight" by their studio creation the Sugarhill Gang, which reached the Top Five on the R&B chart and cracked the national Top Forty.

Grandmaster Flash and the Furious Five, the next Sugarhill signing, infused rap with a social awareness. The group was comprised of disc jockey Flash, Cowboy, Melle Mel and his brother Kid Creole (Nathaniel Glover), Scorpio (Eddie Morris), and Rahiem (Guy Williams). In 1980, following in the path of African-American performers such as the Last Poets ("When the Revolution Comes" and "White Man's Got a God Complex") and Gil Scott-Heron ("The Revolution Will Not Be Televised"), they released the socially charged "Freedom." Two years later, the group recorded "The Message," a bleak tale of life on the streets, which hit the charts in Britain and the United States. In November 1983, before fracturing into different factions, they produced the anti-cocaine "White Lines (Don't Do It)."

Afrika Bambaataa joined the recording spree with "Planet Rock." He transformed the electronic sounds of Kraftwerk to "make something real funky with a hard bass beat." Like his fellow hip-hip jockeys, he believed the song told "the truth what black people, brown people, red people, white people, yellow people did to better civilization on this planet so-called Earth." Bambaataa backed his meagae with action by raising money to combat sickle cell anemia and build a community center.

The Second Wave

Leading a second wave of hip hop that replaced the Old School sound, Run-D.M.C. brought inner-city hip hop to the masses of American teens by combining it with guitar-based rock. In 1982, the group banded together after graduating from St. Pascal's Catholic School in New York City. Two years later, disc jockey Jam-Master Jay (b. Jason Mizell) and rappers D.M.C. (b. Darryl McDaniels) and Joseph "Run" Simmons who had worked as a disc jockey behind Kurtis Blow released their first LP, which after a year on the chart became the first gold rap album.

The group followed its initial success with rock-infused hip hop. Run-D.M.C. waxed *King of Rock*, which reached number fifty-two on the chart through the use of the heavy-metal guitar of Eddie Martinez. "Run-D.M.C. used to rap over rock records a lot," recalled Jam-Master Jay. "I used to mix rock tunes, and have the guitar come in a little bit, and then play the drum over and over again. *Toys in the Attic*, Aerosmith, that was the best."

The band secured airplay on MTV for "Rock Box," which became the first rap video aired on the network. Russell Simmons, the manager of the band and brother of

Run, excitedly informed the group that MTV had called. "We didn't know what MTV was," confessed Run. After the group secured rotation on the music network, they saw an explosion in album sales. "MTV came along just as everything was rolling," explained Run. "We took the beat from the street and put it on TV."

Through its heavy-metal rap on MTV, Run-D.M.C. appealed to white teens. "Does the band have white crossover fans?" asked Bill Adler rhetorically, who helped manage the group. "I'll tell you, a typical letter we get is from someplace like North Dakota. They say, 'I'll bet I'm the only white person ever to write to you, but I love Run-D.M.C.' All the white people think they're alone, but they're not."

Run-D.M.C. increased its white audience by collaborating with Aerosmith, a mid-1970s, Rolling Stones–influenced, hard-rock outfit that neared the top of the chart with *Rocks* (1976) and rebounded with two number-one albums during the nineties. In 1986, Run-D.M.C. combined the polyrhythms of hip hop with hard rock to nearly top the singles chart with a remake of Aerosmith's "Walk This Way," which featured Aerosmith's Joe Perry on guitar and Steven Tyler helping with vocals. Run-D.M.C. sold more than 3 million copies of the Top-Five *Raising Hell*, the album that included the hit single and, according to Darryl McDaniels, "put rap into a lot of people's living rooms." Hip-hop promoter Van Silk explained that "it was what took rap to the next level. 'Walk This Way' was the door opener." By the end of the year, observed Fred Durst, who a decade later headed the rock/rap outfit Limp Bizkit, "all the white kids jumped on the rap thing hard, dude. Suddenly everybody's walking around trying to rap like D.M.C."

If Run-D.M.C. introduced rap to white teens, the Beastie Boys opened the floodgates. Originally members of fledgling New York City punk bands, the white, middle-class threesome—Adam "MCA" Yauch, Michael "D" Diamond, and Adam "King Ad-Rock" Horovitz—met Rick Rubin who had partnered with Run-D.M.C. manager Russell Simmons to establish Def Jam Records. In October 1984, the Beastie Boys signed with Def Jam and the next year toured with Run-D.M.C. Only a few months after Run-D.M.C. scored with "Walk This Way," the trio released *Licensed to Ill*, which featured raps over Led Zeppelin and AC/DC heavy-metal riffs and the solos of guitarist Kerry King of Slayer. One of the fastest-selling albums in history, *Licensed* sold 10 million copies, largely on the strength of the Top-Ten, heavy-metal/rap anthem "(You Gotta) Fight for Your Right (To Party!)," and brought rap into the white rock mainstream. The Beastie Boys became the first rap group to top the U.S. chart and reached the Top Ten in Britain. "By making our rap records sound more like pop songs, we changed the form," boasted Rick Rubin. "And we sold a lot of records."

Gangsta

As the Beastie Boys partied, a third wave of African-American rappers highlighted the sobering conditions that confronted young, urban African Americans by graphically describing violent life in the inner cities with "gangsta rap." Schoolly D (b. Jesse Weaver, Jr.), a former member of the Parkside Killers in North Philadelphia, started the trend with the shocking description of gang warfare in "P.S.K. – What Does It Mean?" (1986). "The first record that came out along those lines was Schoolly D's 'P.S.K.,'" explained Ice-T who scored in 1991 with the Top-Ten gangsta classic *O.G. Original Gangster*. "All he did was represent a gang on his record."

Formed in 1986 by Eric "Eazy-E" Wright, N.W.A. [Niggaz wit Attitude] perfected gangsta rap. They sold 1 million copies of their debut album, *Straight Outta Compton* (1988), which included the genre-defining "Gangsta Gangsta." In 1991, the group stood atop the chart with the harsh number-one *Niggaz4Life*. Ice Cube (b. O'Shea Jackson), the rhymer who split from N.W.A. in 1990, rapped about the consequences of gang violence in his debut *AmeriKKKa's Most Wanted* (1990), "Dead Homiez," and

"The Product" on *Kill at Will* (1990). He followed the next year with the number-two *Death Certificate*. In 1992, Dr. Dre, another alumnus of N.W.A. and co-owner of Death Row Records, helped define gangsta with the slow-grooved, deep-bass, synthesizer-heavy G-funk of *The Chronic*, which included the archetypical gangsta of "Nuthin' But a 'G' Thang."

The angry gangsta rappers, though sometimes glorifying a streetwise, misogynist, gun-crazy culture, considered themselves reporters on the urban African-American beat. "I show white America about the black community, and I hold a mirror up to the black community to show them about themselves," contended Ice Cube. Ice-T rhetorically asked "if there wasn't rap, where would the voice of the eighteen-year-old black male be? He would never be on TV, he ain't writing no book. He is not in the movies." "They call it gangsta rap, I call it reality-based rap," he added. Tupac Shakur who scaled the charts with five gold gangsta rap albums similarly wondered why the "raps that I'm rapping to my community shouldn't be filled with rage? They shouldn't be filled with the same atrocities that they [white America] gave to me? The media, they don't talk about it, so in my raps I have to talk about it, and it just seems foreign because there's no one else talking about it."

The American legal system that jailed a disproportionate number of African Americans served as the focus of many gangsta rappers. In 1999, African Americans comprised 49 percent of the inmate population in U.S. jails but accounted for only 13 percent of the population. On any given day, one in fourteen (7 percent) African-American males were in prison compared to just 1 percent of Caucasian men. Put in another way, an African-American male born in 1991 had a 29 percent likelihood of spending some time in prison compared to only a 4 percent chance for their Caucasian counterparts. "You got to remember that half the people in the ghetto got somebody who's in jail," observed Ice-T.

Some African Americans landed in prison due to the racist practices of police, referred to as racial profiling. For example, during 1995 in Volusia County, Florida, African Americans accounted for nearly 70 percent of the drivers who police stopped on the roads even though they made up 12 percent of the county population. The "Driving While Black" detentions and arrests engendered a fear of uncontrolled police action among some African Americans. "When I'm alone and driving, coming from the studio, if I see a cop pull up behind me, I really am afraid that they might just decide they don't like me and pull out that backup gun they carry and shoot me," Ice-T confessed. "The only way you can run around with a gun is to be a cop."

In Los Angeles, the original home of the gangsta rap, racial profiling became institutionalized. In 1988, the city funded police chief Darryl Gates to begin the punitive Operation Hammer, which Gates envisioned as a war on gangs. After the first year of the program, police had booked more than 25,000 African-American youths, sometimes 1500 in a day, for "looking suspicious." Nearly 90 percent of those arrested were released without charge, and by 1992 the city spent $11 million annually for police brutality settlements. "Police would stop you and ask you 'What gang are you from,'" related DJ Davey D Cook. "They would get up in your face and grab your collar, push you up against the police car and choke you … [then] the police would accuse us of not cooperating. Next thing you know, you would get pushed in the back or knocked over."

Gangsta rap understandably and bluntly lashed out against racial profiling and police brutality. N.W.A. released "Fuck Tha Police." The Geto Boys penned "City Under Siege" (1990) about police harassment, and Cypress Hill included "Pigs" on their 1991 self-titled debut. Ice-T mined the same theme with the controversial "Cop Killer," which he wrote in 1990 and released in early 1992 with the heavy-metal band Body Count backing him. "I'm singing in the first person as a character who is fed up with police brutality. I ain't never killed no cop. I felt like it a lot of times," contended the rapper. The song sparked protests and a boycott of Warner Records, Ice-T's label, from police organizations throughout the country until the rapper voluntarily removed the song from the *Body Count* album.

During late April and early May 1992, the truth behind the gangsta-rap message became starkly evident, when rioting erupted in Los Angeles after the acquittal of the police officers who had senselessly beaten African-American taxi driver Rodney King. For six days, angry African Americans took to the streets in response to the decision of a nearly all-white jury who seemingly disregarded videotaped evidence of police brutality. They burned and looted buildings until they were dispersed by 2,000 National Guardsmen and 4,500 federal troops dispatched by President George Bush. When the smoke cleared, the riots had caused nearly $1 billion in damage and had resulted in 53 deaths, 2,383 injuries, more than 7,000 fire responses, and 3,100 damaged businesses. One of the worst riots in U.S. history, the disturbance in Los Angeles sparked riots in other cities such as Las Vegas and Atlanta. "When rap came out of L.A., what you heard initially was my voice yelling about South Central," remarked Ice-T. "People thought, 'That shit's crazy,' and ignored it. Then N.W.A. came out and yelled, Ice Cube yelled about it. People said, 'Oh, that's just kids making a buck.' They didn't realize how many niggas with attitude are out there on the street. Now you see them."

Young, Gifted, and Black

Besides reporting the stark realities of the African-American community, rappers such as the militant Public Enemy delivered an updated version of the late sixties soul message of African-American pride. "Black men and women are treated like bullshit," declared Chuck D (b. Carlton Ridenhour), who started Public Enemy while a student at Adelphi University on Long Island. "Our goal in life is to get ourselves out of this mess and be responsible to our sons and daughters so they can lead a better life," he continued. "My job is to build 5000 potential black leaders through my means of communication in America. A black leader is just someone who takes responsibility."

The technology of the sampler helped Public Enemy and its production group, the Bomb Squad headed by Hank Shocklee, deliver its message. In August 1987, the digital sampler, the E-mu SP-1200, came on the market. A year later, the Japanese electronics firm Akai launched the MPC (MIDI Production Center) 60, which included sixteen large rubber pads or triggers that gave a producer the means to create beats as well as record, sequence and then sample recorded material. Easy to use and affordable, the MPC 60 sampler quickly became a standard in the music industry along with the Roland TR-909, which had similar capabilities to the Akai machine.

Public Enemy in concert.

Mika Vaisannen, Mika-Photography.

Public Enemy used sampling technology to revolutionize hip hop. No longer patching together a few snippets of music, they used the machine to sample dozens of disparate sounds from multiple sources in one song and layer them on top of one another. The group also featured innovative scratching from Terminator X. Using these techniques, Shocklee's Bomb Squad changed the production of the genre. "Hank is the Phil Spector of hip hop," proclaimed Chuck D.

Public Enemy used the new production approach to broadcast their ideology of African-American self-esteem. By the end of the 1980s, they had sold more than 1 million copies of *It Takes a Nation of Millions to Hold Us Back* (1988), a pointed discourse about drugs, inner-city poverty, and African-American self-determination. They contributed the song "Fight the Power" to director Spike Lee's controversial, popular film *Do the Right Thing* (1989), which pictured life in the inner city. The next year, the group hit the Top Ten on both sides of the Atlantic with *Fear of a Black Planet*, released by Def Jam Records, which Russell Simmons, brother of Run-D.M.C.'s Joseph Simmons, and white producer Rick Rubin had launched. "We represented a combination of self-empowerment, nationalism, and militancy from the combined influences of the Black Panther Party and the Nation of Islam," explained Chuck D.

Arrested Development scaled the chart with its call for African-American self-respect. "We wanted to recognize all the bad things going on—the killings, the shootings, AIDS, and everything that's crushing the communities," insisted Speech (b. Todd Thomas) who had been a gangsta rapper before forming the group. "But we wanted to make people understand that you've got to still be alive in order to change it." In 1992, the group released its debut album, *3 Years, 5 Months and 2 Days in the Life of ...*, which included hopeful songs such as "Raining Revolution" and sold 2 million copies.

During the late eighties and early nineties, others used rap to convey a sense of African-American self-worth. The Jungle Brothers fused rap, jazz, and drum 'n' bass "to bring about peace and unity." "We always felt that spreading a message was the way to go," related the group's Mike G. (b. Michael Small). In 1990, the group embarked on the "Politics of Nature" tour, which included speaking engagements about the African-American culture. In 1989, Big Daddy Kane (b. Antonio Hardy) rapped about African-American pride in "Young, Gifted and Black" and "Ain't No Stoppin' Us Now." "You start respecting your people and you find out things that you never knew about your people," Kane remarked, "contributions to the society that Black people have made, things that Black people have created."

As African pendants replaced gold chains, female rapper Queen Latifah (b. Dana Owens) emphasized an Afrocentric "show of pride for ancestors from whom we descended" to foster a sense of unity among African Americans. In September 1990, L.L. Cool J (b. James Todd Smith III) released *Mama Said Knock You Out*. "It's about truancy, drug abuse, teenage pregnancy," he explained. "It's about knocking out all the ills of society." Eric B. (b. Eric Barrier) and Rakim (b. William Griffin) rapped about African-American pride in "In the Ghetto" (1990), and the rap duo Erick "E" Sermon and Parrish "P" Smith, known as EPMD, addressed the same topic in "So Wat Cha Sayin'." Even rap pioneer Kool Moe Dee (b. Mohandas Dewese) who had been a member of the old school Treacherous Three, which had perfected speed rapping during the early eighties, rapped about African-American unity in the Top Twenty-Five *Knowledge Is King* (1989).

Having pride in their race, some rappers warned against the damaging effects of drugs on the African-American community. De La Soul delivered the sobering "My Brother's a Basehead" (1991). "We guide a lot of kids," mentioned Queen Latifah. "When kids constantly hear rappers saying, 'don't do drugs, don't do drugs,' there's a chance it will sink in."

KRS-One, an acronym for Knowledge Reigns Supreme over Nearly Everyone, organized rappers into action. After abandoning gangsta rap, in 1988 KRS helped organize the Stop the Violence movement. The next year, he convinced a number of leading rappers such as Chuck D and Flavor Flav (b. William Drayton) of Public Enemy, and Kool Moe Dee to denounce gang warfare on the inner-city streets in "Self-Destruction," which sold a half-million copies. He donated the $500,000 in royalties to the National Urban League, which used the money to combat illiteracy. The Stop the Violence movement also sponsored a video, book and a march through Harlem to bring attention to the problem. "We wanted to reach the kids most affected by black-on-black crime" that many times resulted from "unemployment which can be the result of illiteracy," noted Ann Carli, Jive Records vice president of artist development who helped KRS-One organize Stop the Violence. "Rap records," added Carli, "can be a tool that can be used in education today; young adults will listen to rap and what rap artists have to say."

KRS-One continued his educational efforts. In 1991, with the help of Queen Latifah and Run-D.M.C., he started H.E.A.L. Yourself and released a self-help video. The rapper gave profits from the video to Human Education Against Lies, which printed and distributed books to high schools. The next year, he joined with Rutgers-educated rapper and activist Sister Souljah (b. Lisa Williamson) to advocate a ten-point program to empower African Americans. The program "addresses all areas of African American life, economics, education, culture, spirituality, defense, and everything," explained Sister Souljah. "It's not a militant message but one of truth and common sense. We have to be educated on our own ethnicity."

Many rappers followed the socially active path of KRS-One and Sister Souljah. In 1990, Michael Conception, a former gang member and Grand Jury Records president, organized several rap performers for the antiviolence rap single and video project "We're All in the Same Gang." "I hope it generates a lot of money, and we can get it to the people who really need it," Conception told *Billboard*. "If anyone can convince the black gangs, it's somebody who was in one." Female rapper Yo-Yo (b. Yolanda Whittaker) started the Intelligent Black Woman's Coalition. LL Cool J visited schools to advise students about drug abuse, and the New York hip-hop collective X-Clan organized voter registration drives and anti-crack seminars. MC Hammer (b. Stanley Burrell) who in 1990 sold 6 million copies of the chart-topping *Please Hammer Don't Hurt 'Em*, which blended rap with melodic hooks, worked with inner-city school children in his hometown of Oakland. "I make an active role model to kids," he explained. "They need people to show them there's another way." By the nineties, rappers directly faced the problems that confronted African-American youths and made efforts to change them.

The militant message of rap, though sometimes including a Black Muslim–inspired separatism, reached discontented white teens. "Rap music in the '90s is developing a more socially aware conscience. For example: Public Enemy, [the KRS-One-led] Boogie Down Productions, and X-Clan," observed Troi Torain, R&B alternative promotion director for Virgin Records. "These artists are committed to broadening the state of awareness, which is being acknowledged by more and more young people." Ernie Singleton, president at MCA Records, agreed that "now more than ever the rap market had reached a level of acceptance [among white teens]."

Television, the medium that had helped expose previous generations to rock and roll, introduced white teens to hip hop. In 1987, MTV began to air more rap videos and on August 6, 1988, premiered a special two-hour program on rap, "Yo! MTV Raps," hosted by Fab 5 Freddy. "That wall between rock and hip-hop is falling down, especially with our younger audience," explained Andy Schuon, senior vice president of MTV. "We've created an environment where Aerosmith can be programmed right next to Snoop and people will accept that." Filling a void created by radio, which seldom played rap, other networks programmed rap shows such as Fox's "Pump It Up" and the Black Entertainment Television network's "Rap City." Advertisers used hip-hop rhythms and rap rhymes in television commercials. By 1991, noticed Rick Rubin, cofounder of Def Jam Records, "rap has moved into the suburbs. Ice Cube, N.W.A.,

Public Enemy—I'd say 90 percent of their audience is white." Two years later, the leading rap magazine *The Source* contended that "hip-hop is like rock and roll was twenty-five years ago. It's a music-driven lifestyle being lived by an entire generation of young people now."

As rap moved into the suburbs, it helped to integrate America. "The black kids, they listening to the beat. The white kids are listening to the words. The kids are not only listening to it, but they're becoming allies," asserted Ice-T. "They're saying, 'Yo! This is injustice.' … They're questioning all these authoritarian hate figures, because of rap, because rap is saying, 'Yo! Check this!'"

New Jack Swing

During the late eighties and early nineties, a melodic hybrid called New Jack (or Jill) Swing further pushed hip hop into the white mainstream. The new genre replaced hard, punchy raps with smooth, romantic, hip-hop-influenced R&B vocals to update seventies soul.

Producers such as Teddy Riley and the team of Antonio "L.A." Reid and Kenneth "Babyface" Edmonds masterminded the music. In 1987, Riley produced hits with the romantic styling of Keith Sweat on the Top-Five "I Want Her," probably the first New Jack Swing single, and the multiplatinum album *Make It Last Forever*.

Former members of the teenage sensation New Edition scored some of the most notable New Jack Swing successes. Bobby Brown hooked up with L.A. Reid and Babyface, who grafted hip-hop beats onto Brown's ultra-soothing vocals for the chart-topping effort *Don't Be Cruel* (1988). The album spawned five Top-Ten singles, including the Teddy Riley collaboration "My Prerogative," and sold 13 million copies with heavy play from MTV.

The same year that Bobby Brown topped the charts, three other former members of New Edition—Ricky Bell, Michael Bivins, and Ronnie DeVoe—banded together as Bell Biv DeVoe to craft hard-edged New Jack Swing. "It's mentally hip-hop, smoothed out on the R&B tip with a pop-feel appeal to it—that's what our music is," explained Ricky Bell. Their debut album, *Poison* (1990), reached the Top Five and sold 4 million copies.

Despite the dominance of grunge and gangsta rap during the early and mid-nineties, the harmonies of Boyz II Men kept New Jack Swing alive. Meeting at their high school in Philadelphia in 1988, the quartet combined hip-hop beats with harmonies reminiscent of doo-wop and seventies soul. Discovered by Michael Bivins of Bell Biv DeVoe, they signed with the Motown label and in 1991 revitalized the near-dormant company with *Cooleyhighharmony*, which reached the Top Ten in the United States and Britain. Three years later, they followed with the chart-topping *II*, which included the smash single "I'll Make Love to You." In 1997, the foursome sold 4 million copies of *Evolution*, which led the way for a chart onslaught of a hip-hop/R&B fusion that *Rolling Stone* called a "distinctive, nonthreatening, and video-friendly" form of hip-hop.

The hip-hop harmony group Jodeci offered their mixture of R&B and hip-hop. Cedric "K-Ci" Hailey and his brother Jo-Jo joined with brothers Donald "DeVante Swing" and Dalvin DeGrate to form the group. In 1991, the foursome, gaining experience in different North Carolina gospel choirs, hit the Top Twenty with their debut *Forever My Lady* an example of hip-hop-tinged soul, which sold more than 3 million copies. After exposure on MTV, they hit the Top Five with their combination of soul and New Jack Swing, *Diary of a Mad Band* (1993).

Bone Thugs-N-Harmony offered a harder-edged version of hip-hop harmony. Raised in a tough Cleveland neighborhood, Bizzy Bone (b. Bryon McCane II), Wish Bone (b. Charles Scruggs), Krayzie Bone, and Layzie Bone (b. Steven Howse) practiced their sound in Gordon Park. Wearing baggy pants, braids, and other rap fashions, they sang about the hard realities of street life with sweet harmonies. "Growing up we loved Michael Jackson and Run-D.M.C.," explained Krayzie Bone (b. Anthony Henderson). "We couldn't decide if we wanted to rap or sing, so we did both."

In 1993, the group signed to Ruthless Records, owned by N.W.A. rapper Eazy-E. Two years later, they released the chart-topping album E. 1999 Eternal, which was dedicated to Eazy-E who had died of AIDS earlier in the year. In 1997, the group delivered their fourth album, the multiplatinum, number-one *The Art of War*. By the late nineties, *Newsweek* enthusiastically called the hip-hop singers "one of the most successful and innovative groups in rap."

Mary J. Blige rode the New Jack Swing wave with the up-tempo, soul/hip-hop of the Top-Ten *What's the 411?* (1992). Helped by the production of Sean "Puffy" Combs, she sold 3 million copies of the album and earned the title of "queen of hip-hop soul." In 1994, she followed with the triple-platinum success of *My Life*, and in 1997 resurfaced to top the chart with *Share My World*.

Lauryn Hill and her compatriots in the Fugees epitomized the success of the late nineties hip-hop gumbo. Formed in 1992 by Hill, Prakazrel "Pras" Michel, and Wyclef Jean, the threesome combined hip-hop beats, reggae, and seventies-style funk and soul. Their second album, *The Score* (1996), became one of the hits of the year by selling 23 million copies and reaching number one in the United States and number two in Britain. The Fugees' hip-hop renditions of Roberta Flack's "Killing Me Softly" and Bob Marley's "No Woman, No Cry" exemplified the evolution of hip-hop. "The Fugees created a poetic hybrid that has become hip-hop's universal amalgam," pointed out Elektra Records CEO Sylvia Rhone. "It's the new definition of pop." Lauryn Hill scored with solo efforts, when she topped the chart with a mixture of hip-hop and soul in *The Miseducation of Lauryn Hill*. "With my record, I wanted to merge the two—old school soul and hip-hop," explained the singer.

During the late nineties, other artists scaled the charts with hip-hop beats grafted onto R&B. Usher Raymond signed to Babyface's LaFace label and sold 8 million copies of *My Way* (1997). The same year, Sean "Puff Daddy" Combs who had produced hits for Mary J. Blige, Usher, Boyz II Men, and Jodeci, topped the chart with his own *No Way Out*. In 1999, TLC, the trio that had combined rap and R&B for success with *CrazySexyCool* (1994), topped the chart with the million-selling *FanMail*. In 1998, even New Jack Swing pioneer Keith Sweat reappeared in the Top Ten with the aptly titled *Still in the Game*.

Destiny's Child probably scored the biggest commercial success with the hip-hop/R&B sound. Formed in Houston by manager Mathew Knowles, the group featured Knowles' daughter Beyonce, Kelly Rowland, LeToya Luckett, and rapper LaTavia Roberson. In 1997, Destiny's Child signed to Columbia Records and the next year scored with their million-selling, self-titled debut, which featured a potent base of R&B laced with hip-hop. In the summer of 1999, they assaulted the chart with their multi-platinum breakthrough *The Writing's on the Wall*. By the time they disbanded in 2005, the group had sold more than 40 million records worldwide. Beyonce continued with a solo career marked by six number-one albums. Commenting on the shifting trend from gangsta rap to hip-hop R&B, *Newsweek* called it a transition from "raunch to romance."

The Return of *Shaft*

During the late nineties and into the twenty-first century, hardcore rappers co-existed with R&B/hip hoppers. They scaled the chart and captured the imaginations of male suburban teens with wild tales of guns, women, and drugs to revive seventies blaxploitation.

Starting in the early 1970s, filmmakers featured African-American actors in violent action movies such as *Shaft* (1971), *Superfly, The Mack,* and *Trouble Man* (all 1972) that critics termed "blaxploitation." On one hand, the films offered African Americans one of their first chances to star in leading roles and play heroes. "From 1970 to 1976, the Black actor being the winner, being the hero was really happening," asserted film star Fred Williamson who played the leading role in such films as *Black Caesar* (1973). "In my films, I was trying to say, 'Hey, we're tired of seeing the train porters, the waitresses, the maids, we're tired of seeing that.'" Issac Hayes who had co-written many soul hits such as "Soul Man" and "Hold On, I'm Coming" and in 1971 composed the soundtrack to *Shaft*, thought that "it was fun to see, at least, the brother on the screen being a hero, being a sex symbol, having the upper hand, and winning for a change." The movies, contended Jack Hill, the director of *Coffy*, "brought Black subject matter and Black characters into the mainstream of film."

Though providing African Americans with a chance to star in the movies, the blaxploitation films portrayed African-American life as violent, drug-obsessed, and ghetto-like without a hint of a stable family. The heroes toted guns, cavorted with pimps and drug dealers, and shot their opponents at will. Objecting to the recurring themes of violence, African-American leaders such as Jesse Jackson and Roger Wilkins of the NAACP (National Association for the Advancement of Colored People) lashed out against the films and called for more positive role models for African Americans. After 200 movies in the genre, in 1977 the blaxploitation craze started to ebb.

The soaring rate of incarceration of African Americans helped refocus rap on the themes of seventies blaxploitation films. In 2000, African Americans accounted for more than 60 percent of the prison population, even though African Americans only comprised 25 percent of the general population. For a young African-American man, prison life or fear of imprisonment became an everyday reality.

Similar to the thirties, when gangsters such as Al Capone and John Dillinger became national heroes to youngsters, rappers created and embodied a new gangster chic to reflect African-American incarceration. They boasted about their gats and ho's and with puffed chests challenged the world to a fight. Rather than simply report about the atrocities of the ghetto, they embraced a materialistic, misogynist, drug-infested, and violent culture and bragged about their subservient women, guns, sexual prowess, and wealth. As break dancing, graffiti, and the disc jockey faded from hip-hop culture, the rapper became the central cultural figure in hip hop and symbolized a gangster preoccupied with a macho ethos and a quick dollar.

The gangsta culture turned its violence inward with the chilling murders of two prominent gangsta rappers. During the evening of September 7, 1996, on the Las Vegas strip, gunmen opened fire on a car driven by Death Row Records President Suge Knight that had several passengers, including rapper/actor Tupac Shakur (b. Lesane Crooks). Though Knight survived a head injury, four gunshot wounds in the chest proved fatal to the 25-year-old Shakur who had scored with three consecutive number-one albums during the mid-nineties. A few months later, on March 9, 1997, the Notorious B.I.G. (b. Chris Wallace), reputedly the East Coast rival of Shakur who in 1994 ironically hit the chart with the million-seller *Ready to Die*, was murdered in a drive-by shooting.

Hardcore gangsta rap sales mushroomed after the gangland executions. The Notorious B.I.G. topped the chart with the posthumous *Life After Death* (1997) and Snoop Dogg reached number-one with *Da Game Is to Be Sold, Not to Be Told* (1998). During the same period, Master P (b. Percy Miller) hit with two number-one efforts. DMX (b. Earl Simmons) delivered five consecutive number-one albums, starting with *It's Dark and Hell Is Hot* (1998).

Eminem (b. Marshall Mathers III) repeatedly grabbed the top spot on the chart with his gangsta raps. Beginning his career as the white protégé of Dr. Dre, he topped the chart with his third effort *The Marshall Mathers LP* (2000) and followed with five more number-one discs. All told, the rapper sold 120 million albums to become one of the best-selling and most well-known rappers. His movie *8 Mile* (2002) grossed more than

$116 million and won an Academy Award for Best Original Song ("Lose Yourself"), and his record label, Shady Records, hit pay dirt with the gangsta rap of 50 Cent (b. Curtis Jackson III) on the multimillion-selling *Get Rich or Die Tryin'* (2003). During the late nineties and into the new century, the braggadocio of gangsta rap translated into multimillion sales and kept record labels profitable, much like the blaxploitation films of the early seventies had saved Hollywood by providing astounding returns on modest investments.

Gangstas preached a message of violence, misogyny, and hedonism. Popular songs such as Jay-Z's (b. Shawn Carter) infectious "Big Pimpin'" (2000), Juvenile's (b. Terius Gray) Top-Twenty "Back That Azz Up" (1998), and Eminem's "Kim" (2000) portrayed women as g-stringed, big-breasted playthings from the pages of *Playboy* who could be commanded at will, slapped around, and even killed. Gangsta lyrics transformed rappers into gun-toting, drug-dealing sex machines who roamed the streets for their next conquests and their next big deal. Through their street smarts, they grabbed women and the cash, or the "bling-bling," as rapper B.G. (b. Christopher Dorsey) insisted in a song of the same name. Almost as a capstone of the gangsta era, New Jack Swing pioneers La Face remade the film *Shaft* (2000), which promulgated the unfortunate but lasting caricature of African Americans as unsavory characters from the underworld. "What else can you rap about but money, sex, murder or pimping?" shrugged Queens, New York, rapper Ja Rule (b. Jeffrey Atkins) who first hit the top chart spot with *Rule 3:36* (2000).

Gangsta rappers hoped to parlay their commercially successful swagger into independence in a white-dominated entertainment business. Sean "Puffy" Combs, a rapper and owner of Bad Boy Entertainment, which recorded and marketed the Notorious B.I.G., urged participants at a music seminar to "focus on handling a business, creating a business plan" in order to "build up the economic power of your race and your community." His own success provided a role model to young black youth who wanted to break into the American mainstream on their own terms. "We try to continue the tradition of Black entrepreneurship," instructed Puffy. "It gives you a sense of independence" and an opportunity to "reach back into your neighborhood and provide jobs."

Jay-Z.

Mika Vaisannen, Mika-Photography.

Master P followed Puffy's advice to become a successful entrepreneur. After studying business at Merritt Junior College in Oakland, he became a $50-million-dollar industry with the successful record label No Limit, a clothing line, a property company, sports agent services, and a film company that released *I Got the Hook Up* (1998) with Master P as one of the stars. *Fortune* magazine featured Master P on a 1999 cover to celebrate his business acumen.

Other gangstas translated rap success into business empires. 50 Cent launched a new footwear line with Reebok as part of his G-Unit Clothing Company. He marketed his own line of watches and condoms and wrote an autobiography. The rapper endorsed a video game (*50 Cent: Bulletproof*), starred in a feature-length film, and endorsed the grape-flavored Formula 50 Vitamin Water drink. "50 is a promo man's wet dream," enthused manager James Cruz. "He's a conglomerate." Dr. Dre started Aftermath Entertainment and co-owned Beats Electronics, which featured a new line of headphones and speakers. Jay-Z, the Brooklyn rapper who vacillated between a hip-hop pop and the gangsta of the million-selling *Vol. 2 … Hard Knock Life* (1998), owned a fashion line (Rocawear) that in 2002 grossed $200 million, a production house (Roc-A-Fella Films), the label Roc-A-Fella Records, a sports bar, and part of the New Jersey Nets NBA basketball team. "This music is just a stepping stone," he told *Vibe* magazine. "We used this music to get our foot in the door." At the turn of the century, the *New Yorker* contended that "over the past ten years, 'corporate rock' has been upstaged by 'corporate rap.'"

Hollywood helped gangsta rappers achieve even greater monetary success and stardom. Capitalizing on the popularity of hip-hop, film producers and directors fully embraced rap stars as actors. In 1991, Warner Brothers successfully cast Ice-T as a policeman in crime thriller *New Jack City*. During the next three decades, studios hired Ice-T for dozens of other parts in film and television Directors looked to Ice Cube who appeared as a gang member in the critically acclaimed *Boyz n the Hood* (1991) and following with roles in dozens of other movies. Hollywood gave several roles to Tupac Shakur, including leads in the crime film *Juice* (1992) and the romantic drama *Poetic Justice* (1993) with Janet Jackson.

Master P.

Mika Vaisannen, Mika-Photography.

Within a few years, rap artists appeared regularly in Hollywood blockbusters. Snoop Dogg snagged roles in the award-winning *Training Day* (2001) as well as more than thirty other movies. Miramax Films gave Master P a movie contract, and DMX acted in nearly twenty movies. Universal Pictures tapped Atlanta rapper Ludacris (b. Christopher Bridges), who scored with four number-one albums, for the *2 Fast 2 Furious* series. Hollywood recruited Atlantan Andre [Benjamin] 3000 from the multi-platinum-selling OutKast to appear in more than a dozen films. During the first years of the new century, gangsta rap dominated the charts, filled the silver screen, and accounted for a billion-dollar clothing industry.

A new generation of teens caused the phenomenal growth of gangsta-rap-related business. In 1982, eighteen years after the postwar baby boom ended, the annual births in the United States started to rise and continuing on an upward trend. By 2002, the census counted more than 78 million members of Generation Y or, as some called them, the Millennials who were born between 1982 and 2001. This baby-boom echo slightly exceeded the number of baby boomers born between 1946 and 1964.

The "boomlet" children lived in an increasingly favorable economic climate. In 1993, during the height of grunge, the unemployment rate in the United States topped 7 percent. By April 1998, it had decreased to a respectable 4.3 percent, a hallmark that had not been achieved since the early days of rock and roll. Even in Britain, which had been racked by a stifling unemployment for nearly two decades, the jobless rate declined from 10.5 percent in 1993 to 5.9 percent six years later.

Teens benefited from the economic boom. Using earnings from part-time jobs and allowances, American youths during the late nineties spent approximately $109 billion a year. Unlike older Americans, they considered 90 percent of their money disposable income, which they spent on clothes and entertainment, including CDs and music concerts. The youths also influenced their parents to buy another $139 billion in goods annually to make Generation Y an economic force that determined marketing strategies and the economic well-being of countless American businesses.

Generation Y, especially white suburban males, embraced gangsta rap. "The endorsement of thugs is white people's fantasy of what they want us to be," complained Public Enemy's Chuck D. "That's what white people want to believe about us," agreed rapper Mos Def (b. Yasiin Bey), "that it's about money, cash, ho's for all of us." White teens dressed, walked, and talked like gangsta rappers and bought millions of their CDs. "Hip-hop has permeated them," observed Danny Hoch who wrote and acted in the film *Whiteboyz* (1999), which chronicled the misadventures of three white teens from Iowa who become enraptured with gangsta rap and its lifestyle. "We saw these kids throughout the country. America likes to think of itself as strip malls and apple pie and everybody eats at Denny's. And here are these kids completely attracted to hip-hop." In 1999, asserted the *Los Angeles Times*, "America's non-black youth are accepting and co-opting hip-hop as their own social and cultural movement."

By the turn of the century, whites accounted for 71 percent of all rap album sales. Even though gangsta rap promulgated a stilted, racist image of African Americans, it ironically helped to racially integrate a new generation of American teens just like rock-and-roll had done throughout its history. "If there's one music that could break down racist barriers, it's hip-hop," insisted Eminem. "When I do shows, I look out into the crowd and see black, white, Chinese, Korean people—I see all nationalities there for one thing. You don't see that shit at a country show, you don't see it at a rock show. It's hip-hop that's doing it."

Chapter 24
Metal Gumbo: From Rap-Rock to Nu-Metal

"Modern rock is the category in which we find the largest increase in the share of teenagers who rank it as one of their favorites."
—Recording Industries Association of America, 2000

As the new century unfolded, a multidimensional, metallic rock resurfaced and co-existed with hip-hop as the dominant sound. Rather than gangsta rap, some youths favored what critics termed "nu-metal," which grafted hip-hop, grunge, funk, punk, thrash, and other elements of rock history onto a heavy-metal base. Though not totally displacing rap, metal dominated the charts and became the first musical trend of the twenty-first century.

Hip-Hop Rock

During the late seventies and early eighties when unemployment and inflation soared under President Ronald Reagan, angry punk rockers and politicized rappers almost naturally joined forces. "White punk rockers started coming to black and Latino areas to hear the [rap] music" in New York City, recalled hip-hop pioneer Afrika Bambaataa. "People were scared at first," he admitted, because "they had the spikes and the hair, and the colors and all the different clothing, but when that music hit, you just see everybody tearing they ass up."

Punk rockers, thrash-metal shredders, and rock bands recorded with rappers to create a united front of a desperate generation. In February 1985, ex–Sex Pistol John Lydon and hip-hop pioneer Afrika Bambaataa started the trend toward a rap-rock fusion with their collaboration on "World Destruction." The next year, rockers Aerosmith cooperated with hip hoppers Run-D.M.C. for a rap-rock version of Aerosmith's "Walk This Way," and guitar thrash-master Kerry King of Slayer played guitar parts on the Beastie Boys' anthem, "(You Gotta) Fight for Your Right (To Party)." Thrash-metal kings Anthrax combined with Chuck D to record a thrash/rap version of Public Enemy's "Bring the Noise" (1991) and subsequently toured with the hip hoppers. "These two kinds of music have always been similar in attitude; I never understood why there wasn't more of a crossover," explained Anthrax guitarist Scott Ian. "Heavy metal and rap music are both defiant forms of music," echoed Chuck D of Public Enemy.

In 1991, Ice-T married rap and heavy metal by linking with the band Body Count. On *O.G. Original Gangster*, he used the heavy-metal band as a background for his furious rhymes about prison, drug addiction, and police abuse. Ice-T admired the "more evil sounds" of metal bands such as Black Sabbath and the "punk energy" of Black Flag and the Dead Kennedys. He chose Body Count because he "wanted a group that has the attack of Slayer, the impending doom of Sabbath, the drive of Motorhead and groove-oriented ... like what Anthrax does."

Other rappers and grunge rockers united to deliver a rap-rock sound. In 1993, on the soundtrack to *Judgment Night*, the grunge-metal outfit Pearl Jam recorded "Real

Thing" with hip-hoppers Cypress Hill. "We listen to that kind of music anyway," insisted B-Real of the rap group, "so it wasn't hard to click with them." On the same soundtrack, Slayer joined with Ice-T on "Disorder." Sir Mix-a-Lot (b. Anthony Ray), the Seattle hip–hopper who had released a rap version of the Black Sabbath classic "Iron Man" with Metal Church, rapped over the grunge band Mudhoney in "Freak Momma" on the *Judgment Night* soundtrack. "I was wondering when we'd bring rap and rock together in a big way," remarked Mix-a-Lot, "because the fans are a lot alike."

Rapper Method Man (b. Clifford Smith) of the Wu-Tang Clan saw a similar connection between rap and rock. "There was a time when I had nothing but Soundgarden in my goddamn CD player, you know?" he told a journalist. "'Black Hole Sun' was my shit!" In 1997, Method Man and his compatriots in the nine-man Wu-Tang Clan collective topped the chart with *Wu-Tang Forever*.

Faith No More, coming together in Los Angeles in 1982, added funk to the hip-hop/metal mix to create an original sound. Guitarist Jim Martin paid homage to such metal gods as Black Sabbath, Led Zeppelin, and Jimi Hendrix. "If it wasn't for Sabbath, I wouldn't be sitting here," explained drummer Mike "Puffy" Bordin. Keyboard player Roddy Bottum cited hip-hop as an inspiration. "We really liked the Run-D.M.C. thing that was going on at the time—'Rock Box' and all those big rap songs with heavy guitars." Other band members such as singer Mike Patton added funk to the metal/hip-hop mix. Characterizing the group's music as funk-rap-metal, in 1989, the band hit the Top Ten with *The Real Thing*.

The Red Hot Chili Peppers played a funk-metal-rap amalgam. Cemented by singer Anthony Kiedis and funk-master, bass player Michael "Flea" Balzary, the California band coalesced in 1983. In 1988, the Peppers added guitarist John Frusciante and drummer Chad Smith to break into the mainstream with *Blood Sugar Sex Magik* (1991), which hit the number-three slot. They followed with the Top-Ten *One Hot Minute* (1995). Inspired by diverse musicians such as Parliament/Funkadelic, Sly and the Family Stone, Run-D.M.C. and the Beastie Boys, Kiedis thought that "you can definitely make a case for us being a big part of what became nu-metal or rap metal. When I meet those bands today that are along the rap-metal vein—nu-metal or whatever you want to call it, they often say they enjoyed us when they were beginning."

The Rap-Rock Explosion

Shown the path by experimental pioneers during the eighties and into the next decade, by the late nineties an enraged rock-rap hit its stride with bands such as Rage Against the Machine, which climbed to the top of the chart with an incendiary mixture of heavy-metal riffing and hip-hop beats. Formed in 1991, the group featured guitarist Tom Morello, the son of a Kenyan Mau Mau revolutionary and the great-nephew of radical Kenyan President Jomo Kenyatta, and rapper/vocalist Zack de la Rocha, the son of a Chicano artist. "In Rage Against the Machine, I am the DJ," Morello asserted. "Scratching" the strings on a guitar like a hip-hop disc jockey scratches records on a turntable, he cited Run-D.M.C.'s DJ Jam Master Jay and Public Enemy's DJ Terminator X "as influences on my six-string instrument, giving me a different perspective."

The band quickly scored with a political version of hip hop/rock. First charting in 1992 with a confrontational, self-titled album, Rage Against the Machine delivered a Public Enemy–like song called "Take the Power Back," raged against American authority in songs such as "Know Your Enemy," and envisioned a revolution that would engulf cities from Capetown, South Africa, to Los Angeles in "Township Rebellion." Living their convictions, the group railed against the British right-wing National Front and made the video "Freedom" to protest the unjust imprisonment of Native American leader Leonard Peltier, who in 1977 had been jailed on flimsy evidence for allegedly killing two F.B.I. agents. In 1996, the band topped the U.S. chart and hit the British Top Five with *Evil*

Rage Against the Machine concert poster, 1996.

Emek Studios.

Empire, which featured Morello's rap-influenced guitar. Three years later, the rap-rock of Rage Against the Machine again hit number-one with *The Battle of Los Angeles*.

Rage Against the Machine embodied the anger and frustration of Nineties youth. In the words of Tom Morello who idolized the Clash and Public Enemy, the group capitalized "on the widespread angst and alienation caused among young people by the Reagan-Bush years." "A lot of people are really pissed," he continued, and the band provided "angry, aggressive soundtracks for young people."

Several bands kept the aggressive sound but minimized the overt political venom of Rage Against the Machine to scale the charts with their own version of a bass-heavy rap-metal. The California-based Korn, fronted by singer Jonathan Davis and formed in 1993, delivered a hip-hop and funk-inflected version of a monstrous rock sound. The band incorporated hip hop into their metal core through bassist Reginald "Fieldy" Arvizu. "He's a hip-hop fanatic," explained singer Davis. "When he plays his bass lines he gives everything a hip-hop feel. He turned the rest of us on to a lot of hip hop, too." Added Korn guitarist James "Munky" Shaffer: "We were kinda influenced by the whole hip-hop thing, so we wanted all of the tones on the verses and stuff to sound very hip-hoppish." In 1996, the group neared the top of the chart and followed with two number-one efforts, *Follow the Leader* (1998) and *Issues* (1999).

Limp Bizkit, the Florida band led by singer Fred Durst and anchored by guitarist Wes Borland, found similar success with hip-hop/heavy metal. In 1999, amid the rap-rock rage, the band topped the chart with the million-selling *Significant Other*, which included collaborations with Eminem and Method Man of the Wu-Tang Clan. The next year, Limp Bizkit followed with another chart-topper.

Limp Bizkit relied heavily on Eighties metal and hip-hop for their signature sound. Asked to describe his influences, Wes Borland pointed toward metal acts such as Metallica and Megadeth as well as "the first crossover thing that happened with Anthrax and Public Enemy." Together with his band mates, including turntablist DJ Lethal, Borland generated a hard-hitting, late nineties version of hip-hop metal.

Rob "Zombie" Straker (b. Robert Cummings), the frontman of the band White Zombie as well as a solo act during the late Nineties, drew similar inspiration from the rap-rock wellspring. After an initial foray into the art-noise, New York scene, White Zombie mixed the energy of metal, punk, and rap into a potent concoction. As Rob explained it, "I loved the power of metal guitar, but so many times, it was too stiff. I also loved rap music like Public Enemy, when it was high powered and almost seemed like metal with this insane wall of sound. That was my main inspiration, loving Public Enemy and Slayer at the same time but not wanting to sound like either of them." The sound of the band, characterized by Zombie as "rhythmic guitars locked into these heavy beats," propelled White Zombie into the Top Ten with *Astro-Creep 2000* (1995). In 1998 and 2001, amid the rap-metal craze, Rob Zombie followed with two Top-Ten solo efforts.

The Deftones launched their own rap-metal mix. Formed during 1988 in Sacramento and spending years on the road, the band finally neared the top of the chart with *White Pony* (2000), which featured turntablist Frank Delgado. "I feel like I've been playing metal the whole time! But the rap was there all along. I mean, Anthrax was doing that, like, a decade ago," mused guitarist Stephen Carpenter. "We're *all* caught up in the rap game now."

Kid Rock and his band, Twisted Brown Trucker, concocted one of the more sonically varied versions of the hip-hop/rock mixture. After a series of commercially unsuccessful efforts, Kid Rock (b. Bob Ritchie) hit pay dirt with a musical stew of sounds. The Michigan-born leader cited a variety of influences from swamp-rock icons

White Zombie concert poster.

Mark Arminski.

Off Fest poster, July 4, 2001.
Drowning Creek Studio.

Creedence Clearwater Revival to southern rock gods Lynyrd Skynyrd. He also "got into hip-hop 'cause I thought it was the best sounding music at the time that it came out," listening to pioneers such as the Sugarhill Gang, Run-D.M.C., and the Beastie Boys. "I wanted to sing on some songs. I wanted to rap on some songs. I wanted to do it all," he explained. His twin-guitar attack featured Kenny Olson with some "country pickin' or some blues-based stuff" and Jason Krause "with the pretty straightforward metal stuff," according to Kid. In 1999, the band scored with its melting pot of heavy sounds in the million-seller *Devil Without a Cause*.

Hip-hop rock carried into the new millennium with the mega-success of Linkin Park. The band, signed by Warner in 1999, tried to break down "the boundaries between different genres," according to guitarist Brad Delson. "The idea of Linkin Park is to make every part a mixture of everything, so that you can't pull apart the influences." The group especially fused hip-hop to heavy rock sounds. In addition to Delson and a rhythm section, Linkin Park included vocalist Chester Bennington, MC Mike Shinoda, and DJ Joseph Hahn. In 2000, the band released a flurry of guitar riffs, hip-hop beats, and well-timed scratches on *Hybrid Theory*, which sold more than 20 million copies worldwide. Linkin Park followed with four more number-one, multiplatinum sellers during the decade.

Nu-Metal Anthems

As the new millennium dawned and economic prospects brightened for a while, a more melodic nu-metal replaced the seething rap/metal mix. Youth listened to more straight-ahead bands such as Creed and Nickelback, which combined grunge, seventies metal, and sometimes a dash of funk or thrash.

The baby-boom-echo generation, the target audience for nu-metal, had mushroomed in size. From 1998 to 2002, the number of U.S. teens aged 14 to 17 increased by more than a half million. The number of young adults in the United States grew even more dramatically, swelling by more than 8 percent to a total of 27.5 million. Combined, the population between the ages of 14 and 24 skyrocketed by 11.5 percent to more than 42.5 million.

These youths shared the hope for bright futures. From late 1997 to 2000, the country enjoyed a wild boom, which was fueled by an information-technology bubble. Americans flocked to start-up companies with get-rich-fast dreams of well-paying jobs and stock options for anyone who learned basic computer programming. In 1997, the unemployment rate stabilized at less than 5 percent in three years dipped to 3.9 percent. At the same time, the inflation rate fell to less than 2 percent.

As youths faced rosy economic prospects, they turned to the snappy anthems of nu-metal acts such as Creed. Put together by Florida high school buddies vocalist Scott Stapp and guitarist Mark Tremonti, the band revived seventies rock. Tremonti defined the group's music as "old-school rock." He wanted "the big soaring chorus, the stomping distortion, the great melodies." "We wanna give you goosebumps," he smiled. Signed to Epic in 1997, the outfit debuted with *My Own Prison*, which rose slowly on the chart, peaked a year later, and eventually sold 6 million copies. In 1999, Creed released the multiplatinum chart-topper *Human Clay* and continued its success with the radiant, number-one *Weathered* (2001). Unlike rap/metal and grunge, Creed focused on upbeat lyrics. "I don't see any merit in wallowing in misery," Creed front man Scott Sapp disclosed. "When I'm dealing with a heavy issue or something that stirs my anger, I don't want to stay there."

Staind waved the hard-rock banner. Heralding from Springfield, Massachusetts, the group started in late 1995 by covering nineties metal and grunge songs with a sprinkling of their own material. In 1998, the group signed to Flip Records and the next year joined the Family Values Tour. In 2001, amid the nu-metal craze, Staind scored with the number-one, multimillion-selling *Break the Cycle* (2001), which according to guitarist Mushok focused on "melody." "People talk about this resurgence of rock," explained guitarist Mike Mushok in 2001, "but to me, rock never went away."

The Canadian outfit Nickelback joined the hard-rock vanguard. Learning by playing along with heavy-metal records, guitarist/singer Chad Kroeger characterized his band as four guys who "play rock-and-roll." "We're a rock band that tries to write really contagious melodies," he added. The group toured ceaselessly and released two self-financed records. In 2001, amid the nu-metal renaissance, Nickelback teamed with producer Rick Parasher of Pearl Jam fame to near the top of the chart with the hook-laden hard rock of *Silver Side Up*, which sold more than 10 million copies worldwide.

By the start of the new century, nu-metal bands had swept through the charts. "Metal is resurging back, coming out of the underground," contended Meegs Rascon, the guitarist for the gothic-looking metal outfit Coal Chamber, which hit the Top Twenty-Five in 1999 with *Chamber Music*. "Metal is like a roller coaster: It has its peaks, it goes down—and stays down for a while—but I think it's going up the big hill right now." In a 2001 story, even *Time* magazine carried the headline, "Rock at the Top," and begrudgingly admitted that upbeat nu-metal acts such as Creed "may prove to be a lesson in Rock 101 for the [new] generation."

The recording industry looked toward a rebounding hard rock as its salvation. In 2000, the Recording Industry Association of America reported that the "modern rock" category registered the greatest gain in listeners among all music genres compared to the previous year. The interest in rock, especially nu-metal acts, showed a remarkable 24 percent annual increase among teenagers, of whom 57 percent cited it as their favorite music. Internationally, rock music experienced a similar rebirth. "The year 2000 was a 'comeback' year for rock music in many markets," asserted the International Federation of the Phonographic Industry, "driven by the popularity of 'nu-metal' acts." As the century unfolded, buoyant rock-and-roll metal bands reflected the mood of a new generation.

Chapter 25
The Age of the Internet

"We've gone from selling physical product to selling downloads to selling *access*."
—Dick Huey, founder of the digital marketing company Toolshed

The Internet irrevocably changed rock and roll. Like other defining technologies such as the electric guitar, the $33^1/_3$ LP, and the compact disc, it altered the way people found, listened to, and approached popular music. By the mid-2000s, online digital files became a ubiquitous part of the music experience that allowed people to download a wide variety of musical genres and carry thousands of their favorite songs with them conveniently.

The Advent of the Internet

The Internet linked a series of networks, some first established during the sixties and expanded among academic institutions during the eighties. The intertwined networks connected governmental, business, personal, and academic computers with one another. The World Wide Web provided an open-source information site on the Internet, where people shared and accessed information freely. Identified in 1989 by English scientist Tim Berners-Lee, the Web allowed people to post, read, and share text, visual documents, and moving images of all types. The advent of search engines such as Mosaic, which the National Center for Supercomputing Applications at the University of Illinois at Urbana-Champaign perfected in 1993, permitted people to easily find content on the Web.

Once browsers such as Mosaic had been introduced to the general public, the use of the Web spread quickly. In less than a decade, the Internet became an essential part of every office and home. In 1995, only 7 percent of Americans had access to the Internet. Five years later, a majority of Americans surfed the Net.

American teenagers, a prime demographic for the record industry, went digital more quickly than the average American. By 2000, approximately 13 million, or 68 percent, of American teens spent an average of 303 minutes on the Internet per month. Seven years later, 93 percent of all teens in the United States used the Web.

Broadband access—the ability to download material from the Internet at a faster rate than a dial-up connection through a phone line—swept the United States. In 2003, only a third of active Internet users subscribed to broadband. Three years later, 68 percent of Internet-connected Americans had purchased either a Digital Subscriber Line (DSL) or the faster but more expensive broadband cable connection. These 95.5 million Americans spent an average of 30.5 hours a month on the Web, up from 25.5 hours a month just three years earlier.

An online video-game craze arose from broadband connections, which permitted Americans to play and download complex video files quickly and easily. The software game industry started in 1972, when a tavern in Sunnyvale, California, installed the first Pong game. Four years later, companies sold consoles to allow people to play games in their own homes through their television sets. Game consoles slowly evolved into computers such as Sony's PlayStation, Xbox from Microsoft, and Nintendo's GameCube and Wii to allow for more graphically rich, artificial-intelligence-based games, which in 2004 averaged $10 million each to develop.

After the turn of the century, the gaming environment changed further. In 2000, only 19 percent of gamers indicated that they played online. By 2006, a majority of gamers played on desktop computers, which featured ever-faster central processing units (CPUs) and enhanced graphical processing units (GPUs). Players bought 241 million games such as World of Warcraft and Sims 2. Including their computer consoles, they spent $7.4 billion on their hobby, which vied with the record industry for the discretionary income of young Americans.

The Download Mania and the iPod

Americans engaged in another broadband-facilitated venture that directly affected the record industry: downloading music files. Plugged-in teens logged onto central and peer-to-peer sites such as Napster, Morpheus, Freenet, and Gnutella to access their favorite music for free. In 1999, Americans racked up more than 1 billion music downloads through MP3 technology, which represented a standard, universal compression format for Internet audio files. Three years later, 60 million Americans over the age of 12—especially teens and young adults who historically accounted for nearly half of all sound recording purchases—downloaded music from the Internet. In 2006, as broadband became more widespread, 10 million people globally used peer-to-peer services at any given moment and chose from 13 billion song files. Half of these file swappers resided in the United States.

Many people who downloaded music files had no ethical concerns over accessing copyrighted material without a charge, feeling entitled to any material on the Internet. In late 2000, 78 percent of the downloaders did not consider the digital capture of copyrighted songs for free as stealing. Sixty-one percent did not even care whether a digital file had been copyrighted or not. Others rationalized away their actions. In 2007, one writer for *Time* magazine used a typical excuse. "Most of us are really criminals," he contended. "O.K., I ripped the audio of the Shins' *Phantom Limb* off a YouTube video. But on the strength of that minor copyright atrocity, I legally bought two complete Shins albums and shelled out for a Shins concert. The legit market feeds off the black market."

Some rock musicians claimed that free online music resulted in increased purchases by allowing teens to sample their music. David Draiman, lead singer of Disturbed, which scored with five number-one albums starting in 2002, told an interviewer that "I can't tell you how many kids have come up to me and said, 'I downloaded a couple of tunes off Napster and I went out and bought the album.'" Other musicians agreed with the singer. In a 2004 study, when asked about the impact of free downloading on their careers, 37 percent of the musicians indicated that it made no difference, 35 percent maintained that it helped, and 8 percent complained that it both helped and hurt their careers. Only 5 percent believed that free downloading damaged their careers.

A series of market studies verified the suspicions of the musicians. In 2002, a study found that 81 percent of downloaders claimed that their CD purchases have stayed the same or even increased since they began downloading music from the Net. Nearly half of the respondents replied that they had purchased a CD from an artist because of something they read or listened to on the Internet. In 2005, a market research firm asserted that downloaders purchased four-and-a-half times more CDs than the average music fan. Aram Sinnreich, analyst for Jupiter Media Metrix, concluded that "it is safe to say that active usage of online music content is one of the best predictors of increased consumer purchasing."

The digital-audio player (DAP) encouraged the digital-download practice. Introduced in 1998, the first DAP, called the MPMan, allowed users to download digital music files into a small handheld device for storage, organization, and play-back. The Rio PMP300 quickly followed. Though attacked by the Recording Industry Association of America (RIAA), which contended that it encouraged illegal digital downloads, the MP3 Rio player remained on the market.

The digital-audio players offered a seemingly ideal listening experience. They provided musical consumers with the ability to handpick cuts from an artist, hear songs of any length, and shuffle and reshuffle tunes at will. The players gave music lovers an easy and quick way to customize their collections and make their own compilations.

Introduced in October 2001, the iPod popularized and commercialized the use of the digital audio player. Masterminded by Apple Computer, the iPod enabled music listeners to download thousands of songs, and eventually videos, on a device that weighed 6.4 ounces. It permitted teens to download Internet files or music from physical compact discs into iTunes software developed by Apple that transferred digital audio and video files to the iPod. By 2003, sales of the digital device reached a million. Within five more years, Apple had sold more than 120 million iPods, which became a new way to store and listen to rock and roll, and more than half of American teens owned an iPod. "The iPod is the new electric guitar," enthused record entrepreneur Jimmy Iovine of Interscope-Geffen-A&M Records as he described the revolutionary impact of the new device on the record industry.

The iPod shifted the focus to individual songs. Most iPod owners downloaded single tracks and deserted the LP, which since the 1950s had become the most popular format. By 2006, more than 95 percent of digital music lovers chose songs rather than complete albums.

Free Music for the Masses

Web-based services such as Internet radio, MySpace, and YouTube added to the dizzying array of digital songs available to music fans. Internet-only radio began in 1995, when Radio HK broadcast online a program of music by independent bands. Within a few years, hundreds of stations appeared to challenge commercial radio, which had consolidated into a few giants such as Clear Channel Communications. Unlike traditional commercial radio that played a limited number of artists in a very tight programming format, Internet-only radio catered to the interests of listeners who wanted to hear non-mainstream acts. It offered almost any type of music imaginable. In 2000, Tim Westergren started the Music Genome Project, which broke down songs by 400 characteristics and permitted anyone, free of charge, to create a personal radio station based on his or her musical tastes. He wanted to "be your guide as you explore your favorite parts of the music universe." By the end of the decade, the Music Genome Project through its Pandora Radio had more than 80 million subscribers who accessed 800,000 songs for free or through an ad-free subscription.

Other online radio stations used the same business model to attract listeners. In the United States and Canada, Slacker provided a customized radio channel with both subscription and ad-supported tiers. Founded in 2007, the service boasted 2.4 million songs and millions of subscribers. MOG and its successor Beat Music service served as a subscription-based, personalized, online radio station as well as a music social network. It offered listeners 11 million songs. Though not completely replacing traditional radio, the Web gave online fans a wide access to music.

Spotify, a digital streaming service launched by Daniel Ek in April 2006, encouraged users to select music from an online database, which included millions of songs.

Most listeners opted for the free, ad-supported service rather than subscribe at $10 a month for an ad-free experience. "The end goal is to increase the entire pool of music," insisted Ek. "What we've built is the largest set of data of the most engaged music customers." By 2015, Spotify penetrated fifty-eight countries and attracted 60 million active users with a stunning number of rock styles. Three years later, it boasted 159 million regular users and 3.3 billion in revenues from advertising and 71 million paid subscribers.

MySpace allowed listeners to become familiar with a range and number of artists that would have been inconceivable in the past. Created in 2003 by eUniverse and two years later purchased by media mogul Rupert Murdoch as part of his Fox Corporation, MySpace encouraged anyone to establish an interactive "social network," which included photos, personal profiles, music, videos, blogs, and other material. "Young people don't want to rely on a Godlike figure from above to tell them what's important," proclaimed Murdock when he bought the Web-based company. "They want control over their media instead of being controlled by it." In September 2007, it had 200 million accounts.

MySpace enabled unknown and unsigned bands to air music videos in a cost-effective manner to an audience of potentially millions. In a success story, rapper Soulja Boy (b. DeAndre Way) created a MySpace site and in 2004 aired a music video, which featured his dance, the "Superman," and his single "Crank Dat (Soulja Boy)." Benefiting from the buzz on MySpace, the 16-year-old signed with Interscope Records and released *Souljaboytelleum.com,* which neared the top of the *Billboard* chart. "A year ago, I was just making songs in my house and putting them online," shrugged Soulja Boy. Similarly, teen singer Colbie Caillat posted her music on MySpace, attracted 14 million hits, and snagged a record deal with Universal Republic. In 2007, her album *Coco* hit the *Billboard* Top Five. "Labels were signing fewer acts, giving them less time to prove themselves," explained MySpace CEO Chris DeWolfe. "We saw a need to develop a community of artists to get their music to the masses." By 2007, 800,000 artists had registered on MySpace. MySpace "is the blueprint for the new record business," commented Chris Clancy, the co-head of marketing at Interscope.

YouTube offered similar exposure to unsigned artists and successfully competed with MTV as the video site of choice for rock fans. Created in 2005 and bought the next year by Google, it allowed users to upload, view, and share videos. By 2007, the site had more than 56 million videos of a variety of acts and more than 500,000 accounts. "Other video sites were making decisions on what was entertaining," insisted Chad Hurley, a founder of the site. "We removed that barrier by allowing everyone to participate and add content. It's really the users of the community that decide what's entertaining and what rises to the top." Funded by advertising, YouTube supplanted the tight playlist of MTV, which during the 2000s increasingly abandoned music videos for reality television shows. By 2012, 64 percent of all teens and young adults turned to YouTube to discover new music.

The Web significantly changed the way people discovered and evaluated rock music. For years, publications such as *Rolling Stone* had been the prime tastemakers for music among youths. The Web, presenting immediate news and information, fostered such online publications as *Pitchfork*. Started by Ryan Schreiber in 1995, the Webzine introduced and rated all types of bands to quickly vie with traditional media as the hippest place to hear about new musical trends. By 2005, *Pitchfork* drew 120,000 readers to its site. In two more years, when many printed publications failed and giants such as *Rolling Stone* shrunk due to a significant loss of advertising revenue, the Webzine doubled its readership and influence. "By the time a [printed] publishing cycle happens now, the Internet is already done with the story," explained Schreiber about the sudden transition to an online rock press.

The Web nurtured independent fledgling rock critics who no longer needed printing presses or a large capital investment to launch a publication. With the introduction of blogs, self-appointed rock experts such as Scott Lapatine swayed the musical choices of teens. Launching his initial blog, Stereogum, in 2003, he quickly became the blog-sphere's most influential music tastemaker and hired five staff writers to help him. Artist identification and development "is happening on the Internet now," Lapatine remarked, "because blogs constantly look for new bands—championing them and watching them grow." By 2008, more than 1,800 blogsters informed and debated with fans about the merits of rock artists.

Social networking sites extended the music-critic role to fans. Sites such as iLike.com and Last.fm recommended tunes to listeners based upon their preferences on Internet radio and the files on their computers and allowed like-minded fanatics to connect with each other to share their discoveries. By March 2008, iLike.com had 23 million subscribers and the British-based Last.fm snagged 21 million unique users per month.

Rick Rubin, the co-founder of Def Jam Records and then co-head of Columbia Records, described the paradigm shift caused by the Web. "Until very recently there were a handful of channels in the music business that the gatekeepers controlled," he observed in 2007. "They were radio, Tower Records, MTV, certain mainstream press like *Rolling Stone*. That's how people found [out] about new things. Every record company in the industry was built on that model ... and that's how the music business functioned for 50 years. Well, the world has changed."

The Web, offering a plethora of music, significantly changed the way people discovered, evaluated, and consumed music. Operating on the democratic principle of openness rather than controlled scarcity, it offered listeners resources to explore music, which before the Web might otherwise never have been known to them. Not only providing an abundance of music, the Web supplied rock fans with information to make decisions about their musical preferences. Once supplying listeners with information, the Web offered the means to download the songs inexpensively or for free. The technology of the Web recast the entire music experience by making it more expansive, immediate, and much less expensive to music consumers.

The New Realities of the Music Industry

Established rock acts found their world irrevocably changed by the Web, especially they way they earned money. At the turn of the century, bands collected two-thirds of their money from the sale of prerecorded music and a third from the sale of merchandise and concert tickets. By 2007, the situation had reversed. Many groups expected to make the bulk of their earnings from endorsements and products with their logos plastered on them. They especially relied on the sale of concert tickets, which by 2009 grew to a $4.6 billion industry due to the consolidation of the concert business in giants such as Live Nation and Ticketron and the development of a secondary ticket market with companies such as StubHub. "The business model has changed," maintained Irving Azoff, the manager of a multitude of major rock acts. "The order used to be: first, records; second, live; third, merchandise. Now it's: first, live; second, third-party sponsorship; third, merchandise; fourth publishing; fifth, records. So that's a big difference."

With the new focus on concerts, merchandise, and other non-album revenue sources, some artists approached physical CDs as promotional devices. Prince who had consistently made more money from concert tickets than CDs, shocked the music industry by giving away copies of his albums to concert goers. In 2004, he bundled his *Musicology* album with the price of a ticket to the shows on his tour. Three years later, he worked with the London tabloid newspaper the *Daily Mail* to send free copies of his album *Planet Earth* to their 2.8 million subscribers to promote his twenty-one shows at the London O2 arena. Prince grossed $22 million from the concerts by successfully using his CD as a promotional device for the more lucrative concert business.

Bands such as Radiohead developed a new business model by preceding the release of a physical CD by a digital version. According to singer Thom Yorke, the experimental/progressive rock act Radiohead had always supported file sharing because it served as "a nice way of spreading the word around." In a bold move, the band followed the lead of some software companies by unveiling a new "pay-what-you-want" pricing model. On October 10, 2007, Radiohead initially released their album *In Rainbows* in a digital format available only on their own Website and asked fans to decide on the price of a download. "It's up to you," read a message on their site. "Warner/Chappell fully supports Radiohead in their desire to find new ways to present their music to their fans and to the wider world," remarked Richard Manners, the managing director of their music publishing firm in the United Kingdom. "These new ways are iconoclastic in nature; they acknowledge the realities of a digital society and they challenge existing commercial assumptions." Though most fans who downloaded the album paid nothing, enough people paid for the music to make *In Rainbows* more profitable than the band's previous physical CD. Less than three months later, Radiohead licensed the album to several companies for a physical version and, within a year, sold more than a million copies of it.

A few weeks after *In Rainbow*'s digital release, Trent Reznor of Nine Inch Nails followed the Radiohead example. In late 2007, he informed readers of his Website that "as of right now, Nine Inch Nails is a totally free agent, free of any recording contract." He had "watched the business mutate from one thing to something inherently very different, and it gives me great pleasure to be able to finally have a direct relationship with the audience as I see fit." The next year, he released two albums, *Ghosts I-IV* and *The Slip*, in a free digital format as well as a physical CD version. After the release of *The Slip*, Reznor thanked his fans "for your continued and loyal support over the years—this one's on me."

By 2007, the compact disc had become a promotional device as much as an income stream for artists and companies. "I look at a CD as part of the marketing of an artist, more than an income stream," insisted Jeff Rabhan who managed several rock acts. "It's the vehicle that drives the tour, the merchandise, building the brand, and that's it."

The Reinvention of the Music Industry

Amid the download revolution, the sale of CDs, tapes, and records fell precipitously to shatter the record industry. During the nineties in the United States, the number of CD sales rose steadily. In 1991, the record industry shipped 333.3 million full-length compact discs at a value of $4.33 billion. Four years later, it shipped 723 million CDs worth nearly $9.4 billion and in 1999 sold almost 939 million silver platters for $12.8 billion. Despite illegal digital downloads, in 2000 the sale of CDs in the United States expanded to an all-time high of 942 million units worth $13.2 billion and accounted for 92 percent of all prerecorded music sales.

After the turn of the century, the sale of CDs plummeted in the United States. In 2001, purchases slipped to 881 million units worth $12.9 billion and two years later declined to 745 million units worth $11.2 billion. In 2007, CD sales dropped to 511 million units valued at just more than $7.4 billion. By 2016, the sale of CDs bottomed at 99.4 million units sold for $1.17 billion.

The international music market experienced declining revenues during the same period. In 1999, the record industry worldwide grossed nearly $36 billion. By 2003, the global-music industry revenues declined to $32.3 billion that the International Federation of the Phonographic Industry (IFPI) blamed on a global economic downturn. In 2007, even with an improved global economy, music sales continued in freefall to $29.9 billion.

Many retail outlets shuttered their doors due to plummeting sales. In December 2006, Tower Records closed its 89 stores in the United States and most of its worldwide locations. Started by Russ Solomon in Sacramento, California, Tower had been in operation for 46 years. Overall in the United States during 2006, more than 800 record stores ceased operations. Though some of their business had been siphoned off by general retailers such as Wal-Mart, specialty music stores shut down primarily due to overall declining sales in the music industry.

Faced with severely declining sales and bankrupt music outlets, major record labels searched for ways to reverse the trend. At the beginning of the century, four major companies controlled the music business and accounted for more than 80 percent of prerecorded music sales. Sony, the Warner Music Group, EMI and the Universal Music Group retained a tight grip on music manufacturing, promotion, distribution and sales. In late September 2012, when the Universal Music Group bought EMI, three major companies dominated the business.

The major labels, reeling from declining sales, blamed their troubles on illegal downloads. "Individual users are accountable for illegally uploading and downloading copyrighted works," warned Hilary Rosen, president and CEO of the RIAA. Jay Berman, the CEO and chairman of the IFPI, similarly linked "disappointing [sales] figures" to "mass CD copying." Using the same arguments that the entertainment industry had mustered against cassette and VCR taping, RIAA and IFPI contended that the digital piracy of free downloads posed a dire threat to the financial solvency of the record industry.

The music industry, attempting to protect its market share, viciously attacked free music providers on the Web. The RIAA sued file-sharing pioneer Napster, which by late 2001 capitulated, discontinued its free service, and started a subscription online music business. The music industry used a different approach against peer-to-peer online services such as Grokster, EDonkey, and Kazaa, which did not have central servers for music downloads like Napster but provided free, nearly undetectable software that allowed music fans across the globe to easily share files from their desktop computers. Unable to shut down the networks from central sites, the music companies infiltrated their enemies by planting users on the peer-to-peer sites to disrupt the networks with nonfunctioning versions of music files.

As the number of illegal downloads increased despite these tactics, the music industry realized that it could not control peer-to-peer networks and attacked individual file sharers. In 2005, the IFPI filed 2,100 lawsuits against illegal downloaders in sixteen countries. The next year, it leveled 8,000 suits against defendants in seventeen countries. From 2003 to late 2007, the RIAA filed more than 26,000 lawsuits in the United States against people who used peer-to-peer network software to download free music. It prosecuted defendants such as Jammie Thomas of Minnesota, a 30-year-old single mother of two children, who was found guilty and ordered to pay $9,250 to six record companies for each of the twenty-four songs she downloaded for a total fine of $222,000. "The case has put [file-sharing] back in the news," boasted RIAA president Carey Sherman in 2007.

In 2006, the music industry pressured the U.S. House of Representatives to pass a bill that imposed an extended prison sentence for illegal song swapping. "The Internet has revolutionized how Americans locate information, shop and communicate," argued Texas Republican Representative Lamar Smith, a sponsor of the Intellectual Property Protection Act. "We must not let new Internet technologies become a haven for criminals."

Despite efforts by the music business, the downloading continued unabated. The number of American households that downloaded music each month increased from 6.9 million in April 2003 to 7.8 million in March 2007.

The sluggish revenues of the U.S. music industry, though partly attributable to free downloads, originated from increased competition from other entertainment sectors. By 2003, movie DVDs accounted for nearly $24 billion in sales. The same year, three giants of network television—Viacom, Disney, and NBC Universal—posted $31.9 billion in television-associated revenues. Three years later, the burgeoning computer and video-game market hit the $7.4 billion gross revenue mark. In 2007, theater box office receipts from filmgoers worldwide hit an all-time high-water mark of $26.7 billion. "Music is mature," explained Eric Garland, the CEO of the media-measurement company BigChampagne in March 2008. "The growth is in TV shows, movies, and gaming."

Apple Computer, ironically not part of the music industry, offered record companies a business model to profit from the digital revolution in music consumption. Apple, the manufacturer of the iPod, launched a for-pay, music-subscriber service for iPod owners to sell more iPods. In April 2003, the company created the iTunes Store, a service that allowed listeners to download their favorite songs for 99 cents each. People "bought 45s, then they bought LPs, they bought cassettes, they bought 8-tracks, then they bought CDs. They're going to want to buy downloads," reasoned Apple CEO and founder Steve Jobs.

Apple sold tunes on its platform to consumers and groups such as college campuses, which paid the company a flat fee for unlimited use of the service to decrease illegal file sharing. By January 2005, Apple had sold more than 250 million songs in fifteen countries and reported legally downloading more than 1.25 million songs a day. Within another year, the iTunes Store had moved 1 billion songs online, "representing a major force against music piracy and the future of music distribution as we move from CDs to the Internet," according to Apple's Steve Jobs. By mid-2008, Apple had sold 5 billion songs and controlled 80 percent of the legal digital download market, with Amazon.com a distant second in market share.

Apple profited from its innovation. In a breakdown of its gross revenues from a digital download, the company estimated that 36 percent went to the iTunes Store, 30 percent to the digital distributor, 17 percent to the record label, and 17 percent to the artist. "There's no manufacturing or distributing costs" for a digital download, complained David Byrne of the Talking Heads, "but somehow the artist ended up with the exact same amount."

Witnessing the wild success of the iTunes Store, major labels slowly embraced the for-pay download business to earn royalties from their back catalogs and new acts. The companies encouraged the launching of Rhapsody and Peer Impact in the United States and online services in Australia, Europe, Latin America, and Asia. Music labels inked deals that bundled digital music with the sale of other products to maximize revenue for the music industry. In 2007, Universal Music signed an agreement with Nokia that enabled Nokia mobile phone users to have free twelve-month subscriptions to Universal's digital music catalog in the "Comes with Music" plan. Other companies collaborated with Omniphone to establish MusicStation, which permitted telephone customers to access to 1.4 million songs on their cell phones.

Promoted by the major music labels, legal downloads increased exponentially. In 2003, the legal download business accounted for less than 1 percent of the music business. Four years later, the number of digital downloads exceeded all physical formats (CDs, cassettes, vinyl, and music DVDs) sold in the United States, and legal downloads accounted for 23 percent of the U.S. music revenues and 15 percent of worldwide sales. "Steve Jobs [CEO of Apple Computer] understood Napster better than the record business did," contended record-label mogul David Geffen. "iPods made it easy for people to share music, and Apple took a big percentage of the business that once belonged to the record companies. The subscription model is the only way to save the music business."

By 2016, digital streaming by services such as Spotify, Apple Music and Soundcloud outpaced digital downloads. In the United States, streams represented a majority of total music-business revenues. "We've gone from selling physical product to selling downloads to selling *access*," commented Dick Huey, founder of the digital marketing company, Toolshed.

Eager to share in digital-streaming revenue, major record companies convinced streaming sites to pay the vast majority of royalties, on average .7 cents per stream, to them rather than to the artists that reversed the practice followed by non-online radio. They also collectively squeezed a 15 percent equity position in streaming leader Spotify that gave them an automatic percentage of any profits the company realized.

Data analytics firms further helped major labels to profit from the digital revolution. Shazam, a company established in 2002, worked with the majors to crunch data on more than 20 million daily searches of music download sites, YouTube choices, Internet radio selections, Smartphone ring tones, and other evidences of musical preferences among Americans. Such research allowed them to predict the next hits. "We know where a song's popularity starts, and we can watch it spread," confidently remarked Jason Titus, Shazam's former chief technologist. "Sometimes we see when a song is going to break out months before most people have even heard of it." Founded in 2009, Next Big Sound similarly provided major record firms with information to portend future musical trends. It scoured the Internet for Spotify listeners, relevant Instagrams and other bits of data to develop a list of the top 100 up-and-coming acts. "If you signed our top 100 artists, 20 of them would make the *Billboard* 200," boasted Victor Hu, a data scientist with the company.

Record industry leaders also grabbed music-related business to increase their bottom lines. They convinced some new acts to accept "360-degree contracts," which offered a slightly increased signing bonus in exchange for a percentage of the revenues from touring and merchandise sales. "It's a discussion you have with every new artist," explained Jeanne Meyer of EMI Records. "The record industry used to be focused on the record and all the rest was promotions. Now it's a more balanced business where you have records, TV shows, merchandise, touring revenues and so on," explained Vivendi CEO Jean-Bernard Levy.

Record-company tactics such as legal downloads, integration with record-related business, and data analytics at least partially stopped the revenue drop. In 2015, the music business remained consolidated and dominated by the Universal Music Group, Sony Music Entertainment and the Warner Music Group, which together represented 88 percent of total sales. Starting in 2010, industry sales stabilized internationally at approximately $15 to $16 billion and domestically at $7 billion. Though not approaching the profits earned during its heyday, record labels seemingly weathered the digital whirlwind of the twenty-first century.

Chapter 26
Life in Wartime

"There's a lot of fucked-up shit happening all around us, and causing a lot of frustration. The music is just a perfect expression of that."
—Adam "Nergal" Darski of the black-metal band Behemoth

On September 11, 2001, Americans experienced the horrors of an attack on the United States. In the early morning, nineteen terrorists hijacked four planes and successfully crashed two of them into the World Trade Center in New York City and another into the Pentagon outside Washington, D.C. The terrorism resulted in nearly 3,000 deaths and caused a wave of fear, which rolled across the nation. To many youths, the event defined the new millennium. "I think that the images of that day," intimated one teen, "will stay with me for the rest of my life. I cannot even begin to describe the anticipation, the dread, the uncertainty, and the sadness that I felt."

Just as planes crashed into the World Trade Center and the Pentagon, the dot com bubble burst. For several years, the wild growth of technology firms seemed to herald a new era of a knowledge economy. New start-up tech companies of all types materialized daily, launched by entrepreneurs who believed that they had just started the next Apple or Microsoft. Beginning in 2001 and through the next year, the tech dream came crashing down. The shares of tech companies listed on the NADAQ stock exchange, the main site to trade technology stocks, plunged from a high of 5,132 to near 2000 and by October 2000 wiped out $5 trillion dollars in market value of technology companies. More than 860 Internet-based technology companies failed. The dot-com recession resulted in a nearly 6 percent unemployment rate and dashed the hopes of a prosperous tech world.

American youth confronted other burdensome concerns. They faced protracted wars in the Middle East and heard scientific reports that predicted significant and perhaps irreversible global warming in their lifetimes. Rather than a buoyant hard rock, many teens turned to socially conscious singer-songwriters and a socially charged rap. A few even championed a harsh black metal in response to the problems around them.

A Never-Ending War

The U.S. invasion of Iraq helped to define the beginning of the twenty-first century. Launched by the George W. Bush administration on March 20, 2003, on the unfounded pretext of Iraq's possession of weapons of mass destruction, the war at least partly sought to secure Iraqi oil fields. Tagged "Operation Iraqi Freedom," the invasion was led by General Tommy Franks and involved 300,000 U.S. and British troops. The coalition forces quickly swept through Iraq, captured Baghdad on April 9, and within another week declared military victory.

Despite the military triumph and the discovery that no weapons of mass destruction existed in the country, insurgents who used guerrilla tactics fought a protracted war against U.S. occupational forces. On average, the rebels initiated more than seventy attacks a day against U.S. troops, contractors, and Iraqi supporters of the invading coalition. By August 2007, they had killed nearly 4,000 U.S. troops and wounded another 28,000. Of the insurgents, approximately 30,000 had been killed. Including civilians who had died violently from car bombs, aerial bombing, war-related accidents, and random blasts, the death toll stood at 1.2 million. Another 3.9 million Iraqis—16 percent of the total population—fled from their country.

As the seemingly endless conflict continued unabated, many questioned the prolonged U.S. presence in Iraq and urged withdrawal. Though more than 70 percent of Americans supported the war at the outset, within a year nearly 40 percent favored withdrawal of U.S. troops. A year later, almost half of all Americans thought that the Bush administration had made the wrong decision to invade Iraq. An Iraq Study Group Report headed by former secretary of state James Baker and former congressman Lee Hamilton concluded in late 2006 that "the situation in Iraq is grave and deteriorating," and "U.S. forces seem to be caught in a mission that has no foreseeable future." In a poll conducted the same year, 72 percent of the U.S. troops stationed in Iraq believed that the United States should withdraw within a year. Despite the casualty rate and sentiment against the occupation, in 2007 President Bush commissioned more military personnel. He initiated a "surge" strategy by increasing the tour duties of the current troops. As British forces withdrew from the country, American troop levels increased with no end to the war in sight.

American youths felt frightened and repelled by the Iraq War. In a June 2007 poll, the majority of Americans under 21 years of age identified the Iraq War as the most important issue facing their generation by more than a 2 to 1 margin. Nearly 58 percent thought that the United States never should have entered the conflict. Worried about their own safety, 42 percent of those surveyed feared that the war would lead to a reinstatement of the military draft.

Global Warming

Not only concerned about an unpopular war, American youths feared long-term environmental damage. Global warming refers to the increase in the average temperature of the earth due to heightened water vapor, carbon dioxide, methane, and nitrous oxide levels in the atmosphere that create a "greenhouse effect." Naturally occurring greenhouse gas emissions maintain an atmospheric temperature that supports humans. However, elevated levels of carbon dioxide, nitrous oxide, and methane beyond a stable point trap additional solar heat to cause increases in the temperature of the earth and the oceans and lead to an increase in extreme weather events such as hurricanes and tornados, changes in the levels of food production, the extinction of certain species, and the spread of diseases.

By the turn of the century, scientists almost universally believed that significant global warming had already occurred and would continue unabated unless the amount of human-produced carbon dioxide and methane emitted into the atmosphere decreased. They called for an end to deforestation and a reduction in the use of fossil fuels, which together had increased the atmospheric concentration of carbon dioxide by 31 percent and the amount of methane by 149 percent since the industrial revolution. Scientists found that greenhouse gas levels had especially risen at an alarming rate since 1975 and pointed toward the ongoing retreat of glaciers and a rise in the level of oceans as physical evidence of their findings.

Many world leaders heeded the scientific evidence. In 1997, more than 160 nations pledged to reduce greenhouse gas emissions in the Kyoto Protocol. Pressured by major oil companies and automobile manufacturers, the U.S. government refused to sign the Kyoto Protocol and actively manipulated scientific reports to downplay the existence of global warming. In 2002, George Bush declared that he would never impose limits on carbon dioxide emissions.

Hurricane Katrina almost instantly changed the general American sentiment about global warming. Battering and decimating New Orleans, the August 2005 hurricane seemed to indicate beyond a doubt the existence of global warming to the American public.

In a September 2007 poll, 79 percent of the respondents considered global warming a serious problem, and 61 percent had taken steps to reduce energy consumption. The same year, the *Wall Street Journal* reported that "the global-warming debate is shifting from science to economics. The biggest question going forward no longer is whether fossil-fuel emissions should be curbed. It is who will foot the bill for the cleanup."

A new generation—called the baby-boom echo, Generation Y, or the Millennials—who would suffer most from long-term environmental devastation seemed especially concerned with the deteriorating environment. Born between 1982 and 2001, the echo boomers were the sons and daughters of both the baby boomers and Generation X. These Millennials rivaled the numbers of the baby boom. By 2001, 78.2 million youths belonged to this group and totaled slightly more than the baby boomers (76.4 million) and significantly more than the previous Generation X (58.7 million). Confronted by social and economic problems, the new generation exhibited a decidedly more social bent than their parents. Rather than the Me Generation mentality of the baby boom, the echo boomers championed social causes, ethnic diversity, and environmental sustainability and embraced new technology. One pundit called them the We Generation.

When asked about the importance of global warming in 2007, 89 percent of Generation Y considered it serious. More than half of young Americans between the ages of 13 and 24 felt that global warming currently existed, and 81 percent demanded immediate action. These youths characterized global warming as "the most important problem my generation will have to deal with."

Rock Against Bush

Confronted by a terrorist attack, a declining economy, war and possible environmental catastrophe, rock musicians voiced their alarm during the 2004 Presidential election. Entering partisan politics en masse for the first time, rockers as a group opposed George W. Bush for re-election. They hoped to convince their fans to vote and sway the election toward Democratic hopeful John Kerry. Because only 32 percent of young people aged 18 to 24 voted in the close 2000 Presidential race, rock musicians reasoned that more votes from the burgeoning ranks of their young devotees would translate into victory for the Democratic Party.

Punk rockers joined together in Punkvoter. Founded by Fat Mike Burkett, the bass player for NOFX, the group characterized itself as "punk bands, musicians, and record labels who have built a coalition to educate, register and mobilize progressive voters." "Something needs to be done to unite the youth vote and bring real activism back into our society," Punkvoter contended. "It's time to engage the punk rock spirit into today's political battles," it urged. More than thirty-five independent record companies and more than 140 bands pledged their support to the Punkvoter credo.

Punkvoter took action to back their words. In April 2004, twenty-six punk bands released the compact disc *Rock Against Bush Vol. 1* and followed with a second volume in August. "It's not about 'let's be punk rock and hate the government,'" read the liner notes to the first album. "It's about 'let's be punk rock and change the government.'" By election time, more than a half million youths had purchased the first volume of the *Rock Against Bush* CD to show their support.

Hip-hop artists, already organized to achieve social justice, preached a similar message. Started in 2001, the Hip-Hop Summit Action Network (HSAN) sought "to serve as a catalyst for education advocacy and other social concerns fundamental to the well-being of at-risk youth throughout the United States." The group vowed to act as "an influential agent for social change" to "fight the war on poverty and injustice."

Rock benefit for John Kerry, 2004.

Emek Studios.

During the 2004 Presidential election, HSAN spearheaded a campaign for voter registration among black youths, supported by labels such as Def Jam Recordings, Jay-Z's Roc-a-Fella Records, and Sean "Puffy" Combs' Bad Boy Entertainment. During one event on August 14, 2003, the group registered more than 11,000 new voters. Rapper and entrepreneur Sean "Puffy" Combs launched the "Citizens Change" campaign to register his fans as voters. "We will make the difference," he urged his listeners. "We will be the deciding factor."

No Vote Left Behind began as a rock concert to raise money for the Democratic National Committee. Encouraged by their success and approached by other interested musicians, the organizers scheduled a four-day music festival in Seattle with the grunge elite, including Mudhoney, Jerry Cantrell of Alice in Chains, and Pearl Jam. "Ready for a regime change?" asked a No Vote Left Behind brochure. "Music has the power to change things—like presidents."

Music for America, formed in early 2003, described itself as a "partisan, political nonprofit, working to turn out our generation at the polls." "Culture and politics are inseparable," the group insisted, "and our peers, by participating in culture, have already been making political statements without realizing it." Music for American leaders hoped to inspire more than a million voters to participate in the Presidential election. They staged dozens of concerts throughout the country with such volunteers as Ministry and rappers the Beastie Boys.

MoveOn.org organized one of the highest profile events with several rockers who sought to influence the political process. Begun in 1998, MoveOn.org worked to "bring ordinary people back into politics." It served as "a catalyst for a new grass-roots involvement, supporting busy and concerned citizens in finding their political voice." In August 2004, the group announced a series of thirty-seven concerts scheduled for October in twenty-eight cities located in such swing states as Ohio, Wisconsin, and Michigan. It called the tour Vote for Change. MoveOn.org snagged more than twenty rock luminaries to participate such as Bruce Springsteen, Pearl Jam, R.E.M., and the Dave Matthews Band. "You can rally people to think on serious issues together, and that's what we're trying to do," explained Springsteen. The tour reached nearly a quarter of a million fans and raised $15 million dollars. MoveOn.org also released a compilation album, *Future Soundtrack for America*. Rock musicians unequivocally blamed George W. Bush for the problems that confronted them. "The real axis of evil is Bush and Cheney," snapped Chuck D of the rap group Public Enemy, which penned the bitterly satiric "Son of a Bush" and urged audiences to repeatedly chant "Fuck Bush."

Casting George W. Bush as an agent of evil, many rockers felt compelled to enter the political fray. "Frankly, I'm scared," intimated bassist Mike Mills of R.E.M. "Unlike a lot of political issues, this is literally life or death." Eddie Vedder, singer for Pearl Jam, believed that "it's hard to talk about remodeling the house when the basement is on fire." Singer-guitarist Billie Joe Armstrong of Green Day expressed the same attitude. "It was a little hipper to be apathetic [ten years ago]. Right now, it's more about facing danger." "This year," remarked Bruce Springsteen, "the stakes have risen too high to sit this election out." Sean "P. Diddy" Combs put it most succinctly: "Vote or die."

Young voters followed their rock-and-roll heroes to the polls. In the 2004 Presidential election, more than 42 percent of the population aged 18 to 24 voted. In sheer numbers, more than 20 million young Americans aged 18 to 29 cast ballots in the 2004 Presidential election, compared with less than 16 million in the previous election. Of voters in this age category, 8.2 million had never cast a ballot before. Young voters overwhelmingly favored John Kerry by a 60 to 40 percent margin. Though undermined by an overall heavy turnout for George W. Bush, youth had been politicized by rock and roll.

The Singer-Songwriters

Despite the reelection of George W. Bush, politicized American youth favored socially conscious rock acts such as singer-songwriters who railed against the Iraq War and supported environmental causes.

A growing number of college students especially listened to cerebral singer-songwriters. In 1970, 7.4 million students attended American colleges and universities. By 2004, as the baby-boom echo became older, the number of American college students mushroomed to 17.4 million.

Singer-songwriters such as John Mayer appealed to youth who sought a better country. Mayer, first inspired by blues guitar master Stevie Ray Vaughan, started playing in local Connecticut bars. In 2001, he signed with Aware Records and released the Internet-only album *Room for Squares*. Noticing the Web interest for the release, Mayer signed a deal with Sony and rereleased the album, which two years later cracked the *Billboard* Top Ten. During the next several years, Mayer garnered a large college-aged following. He toured, allowed audiences to tape and share files of his performances, and incessantly communicated with his fans through four blogs that he personally wrote. In 2003, Mayer topped the chart with *Heavier Things*.

In 2006, Mayer added a discernible blues influence to his sound and infused his music with a social message. "Waiting on the World to Change," the lead song on *Continuum*, lashed out against war, and "Belief" directly blasted the war in Iraq. He launched "Another Kind of Green" on one of his blogs to convince his fans to reverse global warming by designing, manufacturing, and selling "products that are cheap, easy alternatives to cut down on plastics."

Jack Johnson, a former professional surfer turned singer-songwriter, delivered a similar message. Starting with *Brushfire Fairytales* (2001), he crafted a mixture of blues, jazz, and soft folk to lure his listeners into songs directed against the media and its portrayal of violence ("The News" and "It's All Understood"). He followed with two near number-one efforts, *On and On* (2003) and *In Between Dreams* (2005), which attacked the war in Iraq ("Crying Shame"), war in general ("Traffic in the Sky"), American materialism ("Gone"), and the media ("Good People," "Fall Line," and "Cookie Jar"). He also lobbied for environmental issues by collaborating with local and national non-profits around the world to mitigate climate change, improve water quality, plant community and school gardens, preserve land, and develop environmental education programs. He instructed his fans to contribute 1 percent of their income to an environmentally focused nonprofit group of their choice.

Fellow singer-songwriter Ben Harper likewise voiced a call to action. Combining folk-blues with jazz and funk, Harper first hit the Top Twenty with *Diamonds on the Inside* (2003) amid the popularity of singer-songwriters. He followed with the Top-Ten *Both Sides of the Gun* (2006) and *Lifeline* (2007), the former including the Hurricane Katrina-inspired "Black Rain." By 2007, Harper featured Bob Dylan's "Masters of War" in his concerts as a potent statement against the Iraq War. "The opposite of activism is inactivity, and I would rather be active in a social way," he explained.

James Blunt mined personal experience for his antiwar songs. A former British soldier stationed in Kosovo, Blunt turned to songwriting immediately after his discharge. He nearly topped the chart with his debut *Back to Bedlam* (2004), which featured the antiwar "No Bravery," and reached the number-one spot with *All the Lost Souls* (2007). Summing up the concerns of most twenty-first-century singer-songwriters, Blunt fastened on the "remarkable state of the world, when there are important things that

Jack Johnson in concert, 2014.

Daniel DeSlover/ZUMA Press, Inc./Alamy Stock Photo.

Ben Harper concert poster, 2006.

Emek Studios.

we should be dealing with. There are wars going on. There are people dying. There's climate change."

Hip-Hop Pop with a Message

Kanye West delivered a socially charged hip-hop pop to complement the messages of the singer-songwriters. Taking the chart by storm with the mega-platinum *The College Dropout* (2004) and the subsequent number-one efforts *Late Registration* (2005) and *Graduation* (2007), West combined the beats and samples of rap with a wholesome demeanor and a social conscience to craft a successful hip-hop pop.

Kanye projected a clean-cut image, which contrasted with the gangsta rap culture of guns, baggy pants, and loose women. Raised in a middle-class suburb of Chicago by his mother who was chair of the English department at Chicago State University, he sported polo shirts, white pants, and checkered sports jackets. When he first walked into the offices of Roc-A-Fella Records, remembered Damon Dash, then CEO of the company, "Kanye wore a pink shirt with the collar sticking up and Gucci loafers. It was obvious that we were not from the same place or cut from the same cloth." "To my knowledge Kanye has never hustled a day in his life," maintained Jay-Z who gave West his break in 2001, when he allowed him to produce several of the songs on his album *The Blueprint.* Rather than brag about his sexual conquests, West told the press about a steady girlfriend and his plans for marriage. He professed a belief in God, releasing the hit single "Jesus Walks." "My [future] is in God's hands. If He wants me to make another album, then He'll give me the inspiration to do so," the rapper asserted.

"It was a strike against me that I didn't wear baggy jeans and jerseys and that I never hustled, never sold drugs," he complained.

The squeaky-clean Kanye offered crisp rhymes and reintroduced samples of soul and gospel into hip-hop to reinvigorate a general interest in rap music, which had become stultified by gangster braggadocio. Besides his own work, he scored hits as a producer for Talib Kweli ("Get By"), Ludacris ("Stand Up"), Common ("Go!," and "Faithful"), and The Game ("Dreams"). "I stopped listening to hip-hop years ago," remarked Darryl McDaniels of Run-D.M.C. "This past decade seems like hip-hop has mostly been about parties and guns and women." "When I heard [Kanye], I just stopped in my tracks," related McDaniel.

The rap sensation offered a political message. He rapped against Ronald Reagan's alleged introduction of crack cocaine into the inner cities in "Crack Music" and addressed an inequitable health care system in "Roses." West blasted the rap community for their homophobia on an MTV special in August 2005 and attacked George W. Bush at a benefit for Hurricane Katrina relief. He also addressed the human toll of the African diamond trade with "Diamonds in Sierra Leone." All told, the politically conscious, clean-cut rap innovator updated hip-hop pop for a maturing audience. "He combines the superficialness that the urban demographic needs with conscious rhymes for the kids with backpacks," observed Damon Dash.

Black Metal

More brutal, direct, and aggressive than the other socially conscious music of the time, black metal rose with a vengeance from an underground culture to prominence during the new century. It delivered a somber, edgy, furious sound, which reflected a world in decay.

Black metal sprung from the thrash of the New Wave of British Heavy Metal. In 1983, Bathory, named after sixteenth-century Hungarian serial killer Countess Elizabeth Bathory, was assembled in Stockholm by leader and guitarist Tomas "Quorthon" Forsberg. The band pioneered the black-metal sound with screeching vocals, low-fi production, a frenetic, distorted buzz-saw guitar attack, blast-beat drumming, and demonic lyrical themes. "My reason for forming Bathory was I wanted to create a mix of the atmosphere of early Black Sabbath, the energy of early Motorhead, and the pace of early [British hardcore punkers] G.B.H.," explained Quorthon. In 1984, the group unleashed a brutal self-titled debut and followed with a spate of black metal albums, which Quorthon characterized as "primitive and dark extreme metal." Together with Venom, which gave the genre its name with their second release *Black Metal* (1982), and mideighties Celtic Frost, Bathory laid the groundwork for the next generation of black metal.

Mayhem served as the hub of the second wave, which coalesced in Norway and defined nineties black metal. Coming together in 1984 in Oslo around leader and guitarist Oystein "Euronymous" Aarseth, the band took its name from the Venom song "Mayhem with Mercy." It fused the major elements of the early Bathory sound with a pagan, anti-Christian ethos and the medieval look of leather, spikes, armor, and weaponry. The group painted their faces white to emulate corpses, show their fascination with death and a disdain of the temporal world. Mayhem savagely assaulted listeners with *De Mysteriis Dom Sathanas (Lord Satan's Secret Rites)* (1994). At the same time, "Euronymous" opened a record store, Helvete, which specialized in black metal, and established a black metal record label—Deathlike Silence—with a mail-order business to promote the new music.

During the late 1980s and mid-1990s, other Norwegian black metalers arose. In 1986, Darkthrone joined forces in Kolbotn, Norway. After hearing Mayhem, the group abandoned the growling vocals and violence-obsessed lyrics of death metal and turned to black metal. The outfit began to wear corpse paint, adopted the thrash guitar and the screams of Bathory, and assumed pseudonyms. In 1993, Darkthrone released

Attila Csihar of Mayhem at the Hole in the Sky Festival, Norway, August 2011.

Christian Misje.

a landmark black metal album *Under a Funeral Moon*. Satyricon, cemented by vocalist/guitarist Satyr (b. Sigurd Wongraven) and Frost (b. Kjetil-Vidar Haraldstad), offered a satanic concoction of black metal. In 1994, they released *Dark Medieval Times* to establish themselves as a black-metal contender. "The music is rock-based but more extreme," contended Satyr on his homepage. "It is black metal pushing the boundaries that began with bands like Venom and Bathory; reinventing ourselves based on a foundation of rock-oriented black metal is our philosophy."

Changing their style to black metal on the advice of "Euronymous" in 1991, the Norwegian band Immortal emerged in corpse paint with a thrashing, screaming black metal sound. As with other black metalers, the group focused on a world plagued by war and suffering. It released a series of genre-defining albums including their debut *Diabolical Fullmoon Mysticism* (1992) and *Pure Holocaust* (1993).

Just as it rose to prominence in Norway from 1993 to 1995, the second wave of black metal unraveled through its uncontrolled aggression. In 1993, Varg Vikernes who had founded the black-metal band Burzum and had periodically played with Mayhem, stabbed "Euronymous" to death. Two years earlier, Mayhem vocalist Per Yngve "Dead" Ohlin committed suicide by a self-inflicted shotgun wound. From 1992 to 1996, black metal band members and fans put their pagan beliefs into action by setting fire to more than fifty Christian churches. By mid-1997, many black-metal notables had either been killed ("Euronymous" and "Dead"), jailed for murder (Vikernes and Bard "Faust" Eithun of the band Emperor), or incarcerated for arson (guitarist Jorn Tonsberg of Immortal and Emperor members Tomas "Samoth" Haugen and Terge "Tchort" Schei), and the Norwegian black-metal movement slowly eroded.

Black metal persisted into the twenty-first century with a worldwide underground movement. Fans traded limited-edition vinyl albums of their favorite bands and, like the hippies during the psychedelic era, deciphered intricate band logos, which featured twisted versions of art nouveau. During the nineties, black metal remained a secret society for true believers.

The Internet pushed black metal from its cult-like status into the mainstream. For the first time, the Web allowed American youths to easily learn about and hear international black metal bands through digital downloads. eBay auctioned black-metal records, and MySpace enabled fans from around the world to discuss the music among themselves and sometimes with band members. As Satyr observed as early as 1999, "the Internet [is] replacing the old correspondence of the underground, the slow mail, and now you have the Internet replacing the whole underground [communication]."

By 2003, through the help of the Internet, black metal infiltrated the American music scene. In 1994, the extreme-metal band Cradle of Filth, formed in England three years earlier, released their black-metal debut *The Principle of Evil Made Flesh*. Adopting other influences throughout the nineties, by the new century the band preached to a broad audience. The group joined the Ozzfest lineup, landed their videos in heavy rotation on

MTV, signed a deal with Sony Records, and launched a merchandising unit, Vamperotica. In 2003, Cradle of Filth cracked the *Billboard* Top 200 with *Damnation and a Day*, which guitarist Paul Allender characterized as a "black metal symphony about the expelling of Lucifer from heaven." The next year the outfit hit the Top 100 with *Nymphetamine*, and in 2006 neared the Top Fifty with *Thornography*. Singer Dani Filth (b. Daniel Davey) considered the success "a fantastic opportunity for us to reach a totally new and bigger crowd."

The symphonic black metal of Dimmu Borgir climbed the *Billboard* chart. Founded in 1993 by Norwegians Stian "Shagrath" Thoresen and Sven "Silenoz" Kopperud, the band churned out a series of albums during the 1990s. Using a number of media, Dimmu Borgir slowly attracted a sizable fan base. The group appeared on MTV and Fuse TV, communicated with their fans on their Website, and joined Ozzfest for a North American tour. In 2003, Dimmu Borgir entered the Top 200 with *Death Cult Armageddon* and cracked the Top Fifty with *In Sorte Diaboli* (2007). Despite their symphonic influence, "Shagrath" insisted that the music was "still black metal ... I mean, Dimmu Borgir is more like a second-generation black metal band."

Behemoth, a Polish band that vacillated between black and death metal, experienced mainstream acceptance. Founded in 1991, the group released several albums and toured with Satyricon. In 2007, they cracked Billboard's Top 200 with *The Apostasy*. "This genre is doing really well at the moment," observed Behemoth front man Adam "Nergal" Darski in late 2007.

A troubling conflict in Iraq and the dire prospects of global warming, coupled with the newfound accessibility of underground music through the Internet, led some American youths to an extreme music. Trying to explain the success of his band in 2007, Darski conjectured that "I think that it has a lot to do with the state of the world around us. It's not becoming a better place, unfortunately, and anytime you switch on the television or you read the news, there's a lot of fucked-up shit happening all around us, and causing a lot of frustration. The music is just a perfect expression of that." As the new century progressed, youth listened to different types of politically charged music, which mirrored the extremely precarious world around them.

Adam "Nergal" Darski of Behemoth at Motocultor a Theix, August 19, 2012.

Vassil Asjac.

Chapter 27
Country Counter-Revolution

"It's music that was rock back then but is country now."

—Blake Shelton, 2011

As the first decade of the new century came to a close, a callous, insensitive conservatism replaced the buoyant hope that defined the first years of the Obama administration. An arch-conservative wing of the Republican Party called the Tea Party dominated the media and shaped discussions of political issues.

An updated country rock reflected the new conservatism and replaced the social messages of singer-songwriters who had been popular only a few years before. Unlike the socially conscious countrified rock of Garth Brooks, the twenty-first-century country rock embodied and lauded supposedly traditional American values that the Tea Party shaped and endorsed. It rocked to the beat of conservatism by extolling a blind patriotism in the face of economic distress and never-ending war.

The End of Hope

In 2008, Barack Obama won the Presidency of the United States on a platform of hope. He promised an end to the prolonged wars in Iraq and Afghanistan, the mitigation of global warming, a more robust economy, a commitment to diversity, and regulation of big business, especially the financial industry, which had received preferential treatment from the Bush administration. Obama's carefully crafted campaign materials, especially an iconic graphic of himself with the word HOPE emblazoned on the bottom of the poster, represented a needed change in America and captured the American imagination.

By 2010, harsh realities had dashed the fervent hope for change. As the conflict in Iraq winded down, Obama renewed his military commitment to Afghanistan and entered into a new foray in Libya. Global warming appeared less frequently in Obama's speeches and the auto industry had been bailed out, much like the financial industry a few months earlier. The commitment to diversity that seemed so real with the election of the first African-American president unraveled with punitive laws enacted throughout the country aimed at Hispanic Americans and illegal Mexicans in the United States.

Most of all, the economy failed to improve. In December 2007, the United States officially plunged into "the Great Recession." Poor investment decisions and reckless lending by commercial and investment banks precipitated the economic slide. Large banks consciously lent funds at high interest rates to residential home buyers with poor credit ratings who likely could never repay their loans. The financial institutions then bundled the "sub-prime" mortgages into securities called derivatives, which were bought by naïve, greedy investors who gambled that the borrowers would repay their debts. By late 2008, the linked chain of debt created a real-estate-mortgage bubble that burst and left the banks and their investors with billions of dollars in bad debt. Established banking giants such as Lehman Brothers, Washington Mutual, and Morgan Stanley defaulted and declared bankruptcy, throwing the entire global financial structure into disarray. The U.S. stock-market indices rapidly declined to less than 50 percent of their previous levels. By the end of 2008, the American economy had lost a mind-boggling $14 trillion, and Americans watched helplessly as the value of their homes, investments, and pensions plummeted.

To stabilize the situation, President George W. Bush, offered bail-out packages to banks considered "too large to fail." On October 3, 2008, he implemented a $700 billion plan for the government to buy worthless mortgage-backed securities. "If we don't do this, we may not have an economy on Monday," warned Federal Reserve Chairman Ben Bernanke. Six weeks later, the Federal Reserve banking system earmarked another $1.2 trillion to buy financial assets and provide nearly interest-free loans to struggling financial institutions. Barack Obama took office amid the financial turmoil. He crafted a second bail-out plan to rescue the floundering auto industry with a $13 billion infusion of capital. He pledged another $800 billion to create jobs and lower taxes.

Despite Obama's efforts, the deepening economic crisis continued unabated. The residential real-estate market collapse continued, when wary buyers refused to purchase homes and banks foreclosed on indebted homeowners. In many cases, people owed more than the current value of their houses. Between 2009 and late 2011, the official U.S. unemployment rate topped 9 percent and increased to 16 percent, when discouraged and significantly underemployed workers were included. To add to the economic woes, by early 2011, inflation rose to nearly 4 percent, not including sky-rocketing food and energy prices, and the Gross Domestic Product (GDP) inched only 1 percent above the negative recession-defining mark. The few Americans who still held investments watched as the stock market jumped up and down like a yoyo on a string, responding to every bump in the fragile world economy. By early November 2011, U.S. consumer confidence plunged to minus 53 percent with unfavorable opinions expressed by 95 percent of those surveyed. "Consumer sentiment remains mired knee-deep in the big muddy of an epic housing mess, household deleveraging and a broken labor market," explained Joseph Brusuelas, a senior economist at Bloomberg.

The record industry reflected the general economic malaise. Following a pattern that had developed since the turn of the century, the U.S. recording industry experienced a precipitous decline in gross revenues. In 2000, the record industry sold $14.3 billion worth of product. By 2011, total revenues had fallen to $7 billion and crippled the largest music market in the world.

The same pattern developed throughout the worldwide music industry. From a gross revenue of $37 billion in 2000, global music revenues fell to $17 billion a decade later with the only growth registered in digital singles and albums.

The Tea Party

The radical-right Tea Party blossomed amid the downward economic spiral and the disillusionment of Americans. Not a legitimate political party, it loosely coalesced around the imagined traditional American values of rugged, common-sense individualism from frontier America, when the government did not intervene in social and personal affairs. Localized primarily in rural and suburban areas, the Tea Party idealized independent country living, Protestant Christianity, and the virtues of the male-led American family. The group fittingly named themselves after the Boston Tea Party of 1773, when wealthy Boston merchants disguised themselves as Indians and dumped tea into Boston Harbor to protest British taxes on tea.

Started in 2009 and loosely led by Texas Congressman Ron Paul and Minnesota Congresswoman Michele Bachmann, the Tea Party formed conventions across the nation. It advocated tougher restrictions on illegal immigrants and won a major victory with the punitive anti-immigrant legislation passed in Arizona. Tea Party fanatics challenged the validity of scientific reports on climate change and supported a greater reliance on domestic sources of fossil-fuel energy. The group, obsessed with common sense and Bible teachings, questioned the value of a college degree. The Tea Party took an isolationist stance internationally and demanded an end to foreign wars and stiff embargoes on non-U.S. manufactured goods.

To address economic problems, the Tea Party preached a libertarian gospel of economic prosperity through a free, unregulated market. The radical right wanted to shrink government by resisting additional legislative revenue enhancements of any kind and vociferously condemned the notion of a higher tax burden on business and the rich. The group blithely reasoned that lower taxes on business led to more jobs, increased consumer spending, and a healthier economy despite the recent failures of the banks and the auto industry.

Bankrolled by wealthy conservatives such as the billionaire brothers Charles and David Koch, Tea Party values triumphed in the mid-term elections of 2010. In a clear turn-around from the presidential election two years before, conservative Republicans appealed to Americans caught in the crossfire of economic disaster. They gained a majority in the House of Representatives by capturing 63 new seats. They snagged six new positions in the Senate and won 29 of 50 gubernatorial races. In statewide legislative elections, Republicans gained 680 seats. Republican victories marked the end of Obama dominance and signaled a sharp turn to the right.

The Country Counter-Revolution

Rock music reflected the conservative mood of the country. Unlike the pro-environment, anti-war singer-songwriters, twenty-first-century country rockers twanged about tailgate parties, beer, families, and the perfect tough-but-compliant country woman.

As the economy worsened, more and more Americans listened to country music. In 2009, a study concluded that more than 60 percent of the population listened regularly to country. Four years later, a poll by the Recording Industry Association of America found country the most popular music among all music buyers.

Americans of all ages, including youth, flocked to country rock. In 2007, a study of country radio found that nearly 20 percent of its listeners were under the age of 24. Another 38 percent came from Generation X, and the remaining country-music audience came from the over-45 age bracket. Of the predominantly white country-music devotees, the survey reported an even split between men and women and married and unmarried listeners. Sixty percent attended church services regularly and a majority felt that "you can listen to country with the whole family." Taylor Swift innocently kicked off the country craze with country-flavored songs about adolescent dramas. In 2006, she reached the Top Ten with her self-titled debut, which sold more than 5 million copies. Two years later, she solidified her position on the chart with the number-one *Fearless* and in 2010 released the multi-platinum, chart-topper *Speak Now*.

A truckload of country rockers who merged country with rock followed Taylor Swift to success. Lady Antebellum combined such rock influences as the Allman Brothers and the Eagles with the country sounds of Travis Tritt for a Top Five debut (2008) and three subsequent number-one efforts. Starting in the Atlanta folk-rock scene, Jennifer Nettles and Kristian Bush formed Sugarland and topped the chart with the country rock of *Love on the Inside* (2008). The hard-rocking Jason Aldean parroted Southern rock icons Lynyrd Skynyrd in his multi-platinum *My Kinda Party* (2010). Zac Brown Band, which broke into the chart with *The Foundation* (2008) and two years later hit with the number-one, multi-platinum *You Get What You Give*, paid tribute to country rockers The Marshall Tucker Band, a countrified Bob Dylan, and The Band

Miranda Lambert in action, 2012.
ShopKeeper Management.

and even Rage Against the Machine. Singer/guitarist Miranda Lambert who entered the Top Five with *Four the Record* (2011), cited rock to blues to country as influences. "It's music that was rock back then but is country now," shrugged Blake Shelton who hit the number-one slot with *Red River Blue* (2011).

Some country rockers expressed a Tea-Party-like ideal that diverged sharply with the early nineties socially conscious message of Garth Brooks. Jason Aldean wanted to be a redneck Romeo in the back of a jacked-up pickup in his Georgia hometown. In his double-platinum *Tailgates & Tanlines* (2011), Luke Bryan fondly recalled his country girl on the hood of his father's tractor who tangled him in knots like his grandmother's yarn. In his number-one *Chief* (2011), the hard-rocking Eric Church pleaded with his wayward "homeboy" brother to abandon his rap ways and lounge on a truck near the lake to enjoy the blue-collar life. He started concerts on one tour by appearing through a haze of smoke to belt out the song "Country Music Jesus," which implored Christ to save country music by "preaching from the book of Johnny Cash." Brad Paisley who emerged at the turn of the century with a rock-inflected country and reappeared on the chart with the number-two *This Is Country Music* (2011) tipped a cold one to his beer-swigging compatriots and summed up the twenty-first-century country-rock sentiment. "It ain't hip to sing about tractors, trucks, little towns, and mama," he explained, "but this is country music."

Some country-rock stars explicitly backed the Tea-Party platform. Trace Adkins, nearly topping the chart with *Proud to Be Here* (2011), embraced the conservative ethos of the Tea Party. "I think there are a lot of conservatives in this country that are really frustrated," he explained. "[People] don't want their conservative leaders to reach across the aisle and work with the other party. They want them to leer across the aisle and give them the finger." Through the Tea Party, "a lot of people have finally found a vehicle to express some frustrations," he contended.

Aaron Lewis, formerly vocalist and rhythm guitarist for the nu-metal band Staind, abruptly shift to Tea Party country. He converted to the radical right wing and in 2011 released the Top-Ten extended play *Town Line*, which included the single "Country Boy" that extolled old T-shirts, big orange tractors, rugged individualism, family values, and the Revolutionary war flag with the warning 'Don't Tread on Me' that had been adopted by Tea Party. One blogger called Lewis "the Tea Party's new poster child."

An old country-rock rebel, Hank Williams, Jr., vehemently blasted Obama and voiced his support of the Tea Party. In an interview preceding his Monday Night NFL

Trace Adkins entertaining sailors, 2002.

U.S. Navy photo by Photographer's Mate Airman Stephen Neel.

Football television spot, Williams compared a recent golf match between the President and Republican majority leader John Boehner to "Hitler playing golf with [Israeli Prime Minister Benjamin] Netanyahu." When the interviewer asked about the legitimacy of the comparison, the singer refused to back down and called Obama and Vice President Joseph Biden "the enemy." After having faced with a possible ouster from his role on Monday Night Football, the country star simply blurted that "some of us have strong opinions." "Every time the media brings up the Tea Party, it's painted as racist and extremist—but there's never a backlash—no outrage to those comparisons," he snapped.

Many country fans from the American heartland felt the same way as their conservative country troubadours. "God bless America, freedom, country music and the people who truly love them all!," wrote a blogger in 2011. "I like country music, it's the American way," agreed another contributor to the same country music blog. Country fan Jared Vallorani believed that "country music is a reflection of real life." He thought that it upheld the "American Spirit, supports family values and endorses Christian virtues."

By 2011, country rock had become a dominant force. New country-rock stars emerged monthly and seventies country rockers such as Lynyrd Skynyrd reentered the Top Twenty. On the *Billboard* album chart for the week of September 10, 2011, country acts snagged four of the Top-Ten positions and twelve of the Top-Thirty spots. In comparison, rock musicians hit only five slots of the Top 100. Over 50,000 fans attended the annual Stagecoach Festival in Indio, California, to watch acts such as Jason Aldean, Miranda Lambert, and Blake Shelton. Jeff Bridges won an academic award for his portrayal of a country musician in *Crazy Heart* (2009) and subsequently toured with a country-rock band. "Country music right now is the most popular American format. The most popular!," gushed Eric Church. "Look at tickets, you can look at album sales, it is *the* format."

During August 2011 in a symbolic show of force, nineties country-rock star Kenny Chesney, armed with his number-one album *Hemingway's Whiskey* (2010), joined forces with new arrivals Zac Brown Band to stage a concert for 55,000 screaming New Jersey fans at the Meadowlands Stadium. Generating the most interest in a country show since Linda Ronstadt performed in the Garden State nearly thirty years before, the two acts played to hooting and hollering New Jerseyites in cowboy hats and western-style boots. As the nation sunk in the quicksand of economic crisis, it partied to an illusory set of values reflected in country rock.

Chapter 28
The Rave Revolution and Electronic Dance Music

"Our music doesn't reflect the times, it ignores them."
—Alex Paterson of the Orb

During the eighties and early nineties, British youths confronted harsh and continuing economic conditions. In response, they followed their Mod and New Romantic forebears who jammed dance floors to escape their problems. Enjoying few prospects, they chose to blissfully scour the countryside for such American exports as house and techno music and wore ecstacy-induced smiles on their faces. By the end of the nineties and into the new century, electronic dance music spread across the world and became one of the most dominant types of popular music. Youths from across the globe, including Americans, congregated in massive festivals to create their own communities in a troubled world.

House and Techno

The house music of Chicago and the techno clubs of Detroit served as the foundation of electronic dance music, which swept the globe.

Disc jockey Frankie Knuckles (b. Frankie Nicholls) transformed disco into house music. Moving from the disco scene in New York City to Chicago in 1977, Knuckles realized that he needed to improvise because he could not find new disco records. "By '81, when they had declared disco dead, all the record labels were getting rid of their dance ... or their disco departments, so there were no more up-tempo dance records, everything was down tempo," recalled Knuckles. "That's when I realized I had to start changing certain things in order to keep feeding my dance floor." Using a tape recorder and eventually a Roland TR-909 drum machine/rhythm composer, he spliced pre-programmed rhythms into his act to boost the bass, connect one song to another, and extend parts of a song to work dance crowds to a fevered pitch. Knuckles unveiled his new sound to a young, gay, African-American audience at a three-storey Chicago club called the Warehouse, which gave this Chicago variant of funk the name "house."

In the spring of 1983, when Knuckles opened his club, the Power Plant, Chicago DJ Ron Hardy replaced him, and the owners of the Warehouse renamed their club the Muzic Box. Hardy challenged Knuckles by pushing disco into a new realm with loud, hard bass beats, and booming percussion. He excited club goers to "jack," a dance that consisted of a full-body, random, prolonged shake.

By 1984, some Chicago funksters brought house to vinyl. Jesse Saunders and Vince Lawrence recorded "On and On," for local record plant owner Larry Sherman who launched Trax Records to document the new sound. By the mid-1980s, Trax and DJ International Records posted a series of minor hits such as Farley Keith's (b. Farley

Keith Williams) and Jesse Saunders' reworking of an Isaac Hayes song into "Love Can't Turn Around" and Ron Hardy's "Sensation."

Some disc jockeys such as DJ Pierre (b. Nathaniel Pierre Jones) added the wobbly, multiple-frequency buzz of a Roland TB-303 baseline synthesizer to refine house into "acid house." Collaborating with Earl "Spanky" Smith Jr. and Herb Jackson, in 1987 DJ Pierre used the fuzzy bleeps of the Roland TB 303 for "Acid Tracks," which became a sensation after Ron Hardy introduced it to dancers at the Muzic Box. During the 1980s, when New Yorkers rapped over sampled beats, Chicago DJs established the beat-solid, instrumental house and acid house as underground phenomena.

In nearby Detroit, three turntable wizards combined house music with spacey European electronica into a concoction they called "techno." Juan Atkins, the son of a concert promoter, became enamored with the industrial, minimalistic and metallic sound of the German experimental band Kraftwerk. "I just froze in my tracks. Everything was so clean and precise," he explained. Two of Atkins' longtime friends, Derrick May and Kevin Saunderson, became equally fascinated by Chicago house during visits to the Windy City. "Some people took me to the Power Plant where I heard Frankie Knuckles play," enthused May. "Frankie was really a turning point in my life."

Looking to escape the sobering realities of the Detroit streets, the threesome joined to fuse space-age electronic music and bass-heavy house into techno, a minimalist yet romantic funk with thundering drumbeats. May described the musical marriage as "George Clinton and Kraftwerk stuck in an elevator with only a sequencer to keep them company." From the perspective of Juan Atkins, "Berry Gordy built the Motown sound on the same principles as the conveyor belt system at Ford's. Today their plants don't work that way—they use robots and computers to make the cars. I'm more interested in Ford's robots than Berry Gordy's music." He characterized himself as "a warrior for the technological revolution," and declared, "I want my music to sound like computers talking to each other."

As video game inspired Cybotron, Atkins and techno colleague Richard Davis launched the Detroit techno scene on their own Deep Space label. In 1981, they crafted "Alleys of Your Mind" and followed with "Cosmic Cars" and the *Enter* album. When the Cybotron duo split after Davis pursued a more rock-oriented direction, Atkins soloed as Model 500 with "No UFO's" on his own Metroplex label, which also featured tracks such as Eddie "Flashin" Fowlkes' "Goodbye Kiss." Saunderson, Atkins, Fowlkes, and a few others worked together on a variety of other projects. "It was real tight," remembered Fowlkes about the eighties Detroit techno scene. "Everyone was helping each other out, there were no egos, and nobody could compete with Juan because he had already done stuff as Cybotron and knew where he wanted to go. We were like kids following the Pied Piper."

A Rave New World

British youths who hoped to escape from the numbing effects of the conservative Margaret Thatcher government by dancing the night away adopted the sampled four-to-the-floor funk of house and the pristine, electronic techno. During the postpunk era, British youths experienced grim economic realities. Between 1981 and 1988 in Great Britain, the unemployment rate hovered above 10 percent, not including the "economically inactive" who had given up hope of ever finding employment. During the same period, the number of teens without jobs exceeded 20 percent. Amid double-digit unemployment, a crippling inflation rate slashed the purchasing power of the pound. Overall in Great Britain, especially among British youths, economic conditions created a sobering, sometimes hopeless attitude.

During the summer of 1986, unemployed British youths started to dance to the sounds of house and techno in Ibiza, one of the four Balearic Islands in the

Mediterranean off the east coast of Spain. "From the age of sixteen," explained clubber Marie Marden, "they left home because they didn't have careers or anything, and basically they were just thieves." The destitute youths robbed tourists by day and at night danced to a musical amalgam that included acid house and techno in clubs such as Amnesia, Pasha, and Ku.

In 1987, several party goers brought the acid house/techno scene to London. Paul Oakenfold, the head of A&R for Profile Records in Europe, hosted a 26th birthday party for himself with friends Danny Rampling and Nicky Holloway in Ibiza, where they ventured into the Anmesia club and reveled at the unrestrained dancing to the house-heavy set of DJ Alfredo Fiorito. On a mission to inform others about the driving energy at Amnesia, Oakenfold and his friends returned to London and opened clubs to replicate their Ibiza experience. He and his partner Ian St. Simon launched the dance clubs the Project, the Future, and Spectrum; Rampling opened Shoom; and Holloway started the Trip. "You'd come down and you'd dance for six hours," recalled Oakenfold about the clubs. "The idea was 'if you're not into dancing, then don't come down.'"

The new dance culture expanded quickly. By July 1988, thousands of youths flooded into the clubs. "It was like a virus," observed Kevin Saunderson, who attended some of the clubs on a trip to London. "It spread to everybody."

The dancing teens favored a fashion that resembled their Ibiza counterparts. In order to dance furiously, they wore baggy pants and T-shirts, brightly colored headbands, and casual shoes. In time, the girls sported tight-fitting lycra outfits that allowed maximum movement.

The drug ecstasy, as well as common clothing, bound together the hedonistic dance community. Ecstasy, or MDMA, had been first synthesized in Germany in 1912. Therapeutically, psychiatrists used the drug to break down barriers and to enhance intimacy and communication. Though outlawed in Great Britain by 1977, the drug became so entrenched in the house clubs of Chicago and the gay culture of New York City that sixties drug guru Timothy Leary called ecstasy the drug of the eighties before the Drug Enforcement Agency banned it from the United States in 1985. Ecstasy promised downtrodden British youths the hope of a hospitable community, which eluded them. Between 1990 and 1995, the amount of Ecstasy shipped into Britain increased by 4,000 percent, and in 1993 the drug economy grew by 500 percent to an estimated worth of £1.8 billion. "Everybody was dropping ecstasy like it was frickin' water," remembered techno disc jockey Lenny Dee (b. Leonardo Didesiderio).

Unlike the serious-minded American hippies, who twenty years earlier had used drugs to envision a new world order by expanding their collective consciousness, British youths ingested Ecstasy for pure pleasure. "In some ways it was a throwback to the '60s, but it was very much something else," commented club owner Tony Colston-Hayter. "It was totally nonpolitical. It was the ultimate leisure activity. It was about going out and having a good time."

Propelled by the hallucinatory, speedy warmth of Ecstasy's first glow, good-time British youths spouted endlessly about love and positivity and adopted the 1970s smiley face as their logo. "I liked the energy and the visual side of punk, but it was all just saying 'no, no, no,' whereas now everybody's saying 'yes, yes, yes,'" gushed keyboardist Adamski (b. Adam Tinley) in 1990, when he scored with the electronica hit "Killer." "I much prefer the positivity thing we have now."

By 1988, thousands of British teens embraced the new baggy, Ecstasy-fueled subculture and streamed into clubs. Not content with dancing until closing time, they demanded and frequented illegal after-hour venues such as RIP. Some more adventurous youths met in abandoned warehouses to dance until dawn in what became known as "raves." The press labeled the movement of pleasure-driven, dance-crazy teens as a new Summer of Love modeled after the original 1967 phenomenon in San Francisco.

The ravers danced to acid house and techno music. Sometimes, they resurrected acid house and techno pioneers. At one early rave, Juan Atkins hosted the music.

"When I first went to Europe, the first big party I played was in London for 5,000 kids at a rave in a big film studio," he remembered. "Kids were going crazy for the records."

Soon exhausting American imports, the new subculture inevitably demanded home-grown heroes. In 1988, DJ D-Mob (b. Danny Poku) and vocalist Gary Haisman delivered "We Call It Acieeed," which hit number three; "Acid Man" by Jolly Roger cracked the chart; and the British house outfit 808 State hit with their album *Newbuild* and the next year followed with their acid-house classic "Pacific State." Gerald Simpson, leaving 808 State, hit the chart with "Voodoo Ray" as A Guy Called Gerald.

Two bands, the Happy Mondays and Primal Scream, became the stars of British rave culture through the efforts of skillful DJs. Starting as a funk/rock band in 1980, the Manchester-based Happy Mondays incorporated acid house into their mix of funk, up-tempo, Motown-based northern soul and straight-ahead rock as they played in Ecstasy-infested Manchester clubs such as the Hacienda. By 1988, their sound permanently changed from a more traditional rock/funk to a rave dance machine that featured a lazy groove overlaid by seventies R&B, washes of psychedelic guitars, the rantings of vocalist Shaun Ryder, and an insistent heavy bass and drumbeat.

The Happy Mondays who had sold Ecstasy at the Hacienda mixed their guitars with dance beats of house and techno. In 1988, producer Martin Hannett helped transform the band from an ordinary-sounding dance-rock outfit to an underground rave sensation with the album *Bummed*, one of the first rave smashes. The next year, DJs Paul Oakenfold and Steve Osborne helped complete the band's transition to a house trance-dance unit with their work on the extended play *Madchester Rave On*, which hit the British Top Twenty, and *Pills 'N' Thrills and Bellyaches* (1990), which neared the top of the British chart.

Primal Scream enjoyed an even more complete makeover for rave success. Formed in 1984 by the Jesus and Mary Chain drummer Bobby Gillespie and guitarist Jim Beattie, the band initially cut several singles of jangly rock. After two harder-edged albums, the group turned to rave. "Contemporary rock ceased to excite us," explained Gillespie. "At raves, the music was better, the people were better, the girls were better, and the drugs were better." The band asked DJ Andrew Weatherall to remix their song "I'm Losing More Than I'll Ever Have." The newly ordained producer stripped most of the instrumentation from the original and replaced it with heavy bass beats and samples to create the rave classic "Loaded" (1990). Adding the programming expertise of Hugo Nicholson, Primal Scream hit the British Top Ten with *Screamadelica*, which married rock guitars with the throbbing beat of dance music to carry acid house into the mainstream.

By late eighties, British youths congregated at large-scale events in open areas with a music stage, lights, multiple DJs, huge sound systems, and vendor booths. They jumped into their cars and headed to the country to massive raves organized by groups such as Sunrise, World Dance, and Biology. On June 24, 1989, 11,000 youths crowded into an empty aircraft hangar in Berkshire at a Sunrise event called Midsummer Night's Dream. Less than two months later, on August 12, 17,000 raved traveled to the Sunrise/Back to the Future Dance Music Festival, held on a farm outside the village of Longwick. On September 30, in the pouring rain, another 4,000 youths assembled at a plowed field in Oxfordshire at the Helter Skelter Party. The retro-hippie rave scene peaked in 1992, when 40,000 rave fanatics converged at Castlemorton.

British youths felt like outlaws, when attending raves that usually were staged secretively and illegally. "We're outlaws with bandanas on our heads, dancing in the fucking street," laughed DJ Fabio.

Hardcore electronic music emerged with the growing size and commercialization of raves as well as with the continued use of Ecstasy, which left habitual users with the speedy amphetamine rush but without the communal glow. Like the transition from the Sex Pistols to American hardcore punk, the music became faster and more intense.

Hardcore electronica featured a tremoring sub-bass roar introduced by Unique 3 in "The Theme" and by LFO (short for Low Frequency Oscillation) in *Frequencies* (1991), released by Warp Records. "There were definitely loads of detailed conversations about how you could get the bass heavier," related Steve Beckett, co-owner of Warp. "The track 'LFO' was actually shaking the bar. That was when we knew we'd got it right." The four-to-the-floor house rhythm gave way to frenetic breakbeats—the percussion-only parts of a record.

Orbital, the creation of brothers Phil and Paul Hartnoll, became one of the most popular hardcore acts among the speeded-up ravers. Starting to record together in 1987, the Kraftwerk-inspired duo named themselves after the London freeway that led British clubbers to countryside raves. They first cut the bass-heavy, harsh techno of "Chime" (1989), which hit the Top Twenty. Building support with live appearances that included light shows, visuals, and electronic improvisations, the brothers added blasts of Euro-techno noise and freely sampled sounds by using computerized sequencers that had become more affordable and user-friendly during the early 1990s. By 1993, they hit the Top Thirty with *Untitled (Orbital II)*. The next year, Orbital reached the Top Five with the sonically varied *Snivilization*. Along with techno tour mates such as Moby and Richard "Aphex Twin" James the Hartnoll brothers helped move electronic music to the hardcore.

Chillin' Out

By the early 1990s, many hardcore ravers speeded out of control and left the dance floor for a somber, escapist music of lilting vocals, and atmospheric rhythms called ambient techno. The ambient scene started in the back rooms of rave clubs, where club owners furnished chill-out rooms for hardcore dancers who collapsed from exhaustion in cushy sofas and listened to liquid soundscapes laced with house music and intricate rhythms. Techno champion Mixmaster Morris of Irresistible Force characterized this "intelligent techno" as the direct "opposite of the stupid hardcore." The new sound, declared Ken Dowie of the hardcore-turned-ambient trio Black Dog, filled "a hole in music," by reintroducing a mellow emotion into the rave culture.

The KLF pioneered the soothing music. In 1986, Bill Drummond, a former A&R man for Warner Records, and guitarist Jimmy Cauty formed the Kopyright Liberation Front, or the KLF. Within four years, the duo fashioned an atmospheric techno album, the aptly named *Chill Out*, which failed to chart but provided a direction for future ambient experiments. In 1991, after nearly topping the chart with *White Room*, the KLF abruptly disbanded, publicly burned 1 million British pounds in cash, and vowed not to return until the governments of the world achieved world peace.

Before disappearing from the music scene, Jimmy Cauty joined with synthesizer wiz Alex Paterson in his project the Orb, one of the most successful of the new ambient outfits. In 1989, Paterson who had disc jockeyed at the Land of Oz, the chill-out room for Paul Oakenfold's club Heaven, joined Cauty for the extended play *Kiss*, which pieced together radio samples from New York's KISS-FM station. The same year, the duo crafted the twenty-two-minute single "A Huge Ever Growing Pulsating Brain That Rules from the Centre of the Ultraworld," which featured Cauty's samples, acid-house dance grooves, and languid, ambient soundscapes. In 1992 after recording engineer Thrash (b. Kris Weston) replaced Cauty, Paterson's the Orb hit the Top Ten with the forty-minute "Blue Room," the longest single in history to chart. On the strength of the single, *U.F.Orb* soared to the top of the chart to the glee of the growing throngs attracted to ambient techno.

Bands such as Massive Attack took the dreamy, somber sounds of ambient techno and added hip-hop and reggae rhythms and sultry melodies to create "trip hop." Originating in Bristol, Massive Attack—Andrew "Mushroom" Vowles, Grantley

"Daddy G." Marshall, and Robert "3-D" Del Naja—first performed as the Wild Bunch. According to 3-D, they would "just throw basic parties where we'd play other people's music. You'd play some track over and over, but add different vocalists and rappers and toasters on top of the music." By 1987, they formed Massive Attack and complemented the group with the smooth soul vocals of Shara Nelson.

In early 1991, Massive Attack released *Blue Lines*, which mixed ambient music, pop, hip-hop, and a trancelike soul into a beautiful but disturbing concoction. The songs consisted of a bass line or drumbeat, which expanded into a sonic landscape replete with pop melodies and samples of reverberating guitars. 3-D rapped, reggae dub legend Horace Andy lent his falsetto, and the sultry, silky vocals of Shara Nelson floated above the entire mix, giving the music a trippy, otherworldly feel. The album hit number thirteen in Britain. Though Nelson departed for a solo career after *Blue Lines*, Massive Attack recruited other divas to retain their distinctive sound for two more albums.

Tricky (b. Adrian Thaws) extended the ambient, trippy genre. He started as a member of the Wild Bunch collective and lent his raps to Massive Attack's *Blue Lines*. In 1994, he released the breakthrough single "Aftermath," which had been recorded two years earlier with his musical partner, vocalist Martina Bird. The next year, the trip-hopper recorded the brooding number-three hit *Maxinquaye*, which featured the smooth vocals of Martina over Tricky's raps, hypnotic, sullen, and disjointed rhythms, odd noises, and samples.

Portishead delivered trip hop hits. Geoff Barrow grew up in the West Coast English shipping town of Portishead and worked in the Coach House recording studio. He met Massive Attack there and began working along similar lines. By 1993, the programmer/synthesizer wizard joined with vocalist Beth Gibbons and jazz guitarist Adrian Utley to near the top of the British chart with the lilting film-noir vibe of *Dummy*, which the British rock newspaper *Melody Maker* named Album of the Year.

Ambient techno provided escapist music for teens hoping to flee an unappealing reality. "Our music doesn't reflect the times, it ignores them," asserted Alex Paterson of the Orb. "Society today is so suppressed, you can only make music that is escapist."

The Dark Side of the Jungle

The popularity of ambient techno, peaking between 1991 and 1993, gave way to a harsher version of hardcore called drum 'n' bass, which reflected a desperate mood among British ravers who confronted problems with drugs and a police crackdown.

As with most subcultures revolving around drugs, the rave scene became littered with habitual users and organized criminals. "The initial phase of taking Ecstasy, the pleasure of it is so unexpected, you just keep doing it," related journalist Jack Barron. Some ecstasy-crazy youths took handfuls of the drug in an attempt to recapture the initial warm glow of first contact. "You'd see people who were completely abusing it," related club owner Mr. C. "Seven or eight pills on a Friday, ten pills on a Saturday, and half a dozen on a Sunday." Unable to perfectly rekindle or intensify their initial high, they turned to similar drugs such as LSD and amphetamines to at least reach the frenetic speed and hallucinogenic state realized through ecstasy.

As soon as drug intake became widespread and more varied, thugs entered the scene to service a drug-addicted clientele. "You'd come out of a club at the end of the night feeling like you were going to change the world," related Ian Brown, the leader of the Stone Roses, the Manchester band that hit the Top Ten with the guitar-funk of "Fool's Gold" (1990). "The guns come in, and heroin starts being put in ecstasy. It took a lot of the love vibe out."

When drugs became big business, the police cracked down on the rave scene. As early as 1989, they combed for clues about the next rave and many times successfully blockaded disappointed ravers from their dance events. As the raves evolved to include more and more people and drug activity, police actions escalated. The anti-rave vigilance climaxed with the passage of the Criminal Justice and Public Order Act of 1994 that gave police the authority to disperse a rave, which was defined as 100 or more people listening to music "with a succession of repetitive beats." Authorities also received the power to stop and detain anyone within a mile perimeter of a rave and to order ten or more people suspected of organizing a rave to disperse with the threat of a £2,500 fine and a three-month jail sentence.

Confronted by police action and harassing legislation, the happy-go-lucky ravers turned to a somber music called drum 'n' bass. Hardcore rave units such as 4 Hero, inspired by the soundtrack to the dark futuristic film *Blade Runner*, developed the new sound by speeding up the already frenetic pace of hardcore and grafting it to jagged breakbeats and gloomy bass and sub-bass lines. Complex, computer-generated rhythms chattered over multiple bass lines, usually with one traveling at hyperkinetic speed and the other inching along at a much slower rate. Hard, fast, fractured breakbeats appeared and then disappeared from a song to create an intense, surging polyrhythmic dynamic without the aid of vocals. Originally labeled "jungle" after a dancer, Danny Jungle, the music eventually became known by its two dominant, pounding sounds: drum 'n' bass.

The music "came from the feeling of breakdown in society," drum 'n' bass pioneer Goldie explained. "It was winter, clubs were closing, the country was in decline."

The drum 'n' bass subculture bore little resemblance to the initial smiley-faced house/techno. The baggy look gave way to stylish dress, and marijuana and alcohol replaced ecstasy and speed. Some drum 'n' bass outfits such as 4 Hero, led by Dego (b. Dennis McFarlane) and Marc Mac (b. Marc Clair), who operated the influential drum 'n' bass label Reinforced Records, warned fans about the drug problems associated with the declining house/techno scene. The duo released "Mr. Kirk," which sampled a policeman telling a father that his son had died of an overdose. They delivered a similar message in "Cookin' Up Ya Brain." May be most important, fewer danced to the complex drum 'n' bass rhythms, in stark contrast to hardcore, which pulled youths to the dance floor in droves.

Drum 'n' bass became even less dance friendly as it mutated by layering atmospheric vocals on top of the scattering, complicated rhythm patterns for an "intelligent" drum-and-bass style popularized by Goldie (b. Clifford Price). First attracted to hip-hop culture, Goldie frequented the London hardcore club Rage to dance to the frantic, upbeat, hardcore sounds flying from the turntables of DJs Grooverider (b. Raymond Bigham) and Fabio (b. Fitzroy Heslop). He entered the scene as an engineer and an A&R man for 4 Hero's Reinforced Records. In late 1992, Goldie combined hardcore with heavy bass beats, deconstructed samples, and haunting vocals for the collaborative extended play *Terminator*.

U.K. Garage, another variant of the many house-techno styles, emerged from drum 'n' bass. It mixed the frenetic drum 'n' bass tempo with a sub-bass foundation, hi-hat drum work, choppy vocals, soul/gospel samples, and sometimes the urgings of an MC. During the late nineties, disc jockeys such as the Dreem Teem—Timmi Magic (b. Timothy Eugene), Mikee B. (b. Michael Bennett), and DJ Spoony (Jonathon Joseph)—perfected the style. As DJ Spoony explained, they transformed the soul-and-gospel-heavy American garage into something "a little funkier, little bit dubbier and the tempo a little faster." The Dreem Teem added an MC because "kids thought [that] if Biggie Smalls and Tupac can grab a mic, I'm gonna do it here." The end result catered to UK clubbers who "wanted a little bit more jumpin', a little more pumpin.'"

The Big Beat

During the late nineties in a style called the big beat hit the mainstream on both sides of the Atlantic, when bands such as Prodigy grafted guitars onto a blend of acid house, hardcore, and drum 'n' bass. In 1990, amid the rave craze, Liam Howlett formed the group with dancers Keith Flint and Leeroy Thornhill and reggae/house MC Maxim Reality (b. Keith Palmer). Two years later, Prodigy crafted the album *Experience*, which neared the British Top Ten and solidified its position among dance-crazy hardcore ravers. In 1997, Prodigy mixed rap and techno with heavy-metal-sounding guitars for the number–one *The Fat of the Land*. "Our sound has become harder, more guitar-oriented," pointed out Liam Howlett.

The Chemical Brothers offered big-beat for the masses. The creation of Tom Rowlands and Ed Simons, the Brothers married funky beats with house-music squeals and guitar samples for a propulsive mix. The duo hoped to capture the "funky power" of hip-hop innovators Public Enemy without the political message. Seven years after forming, they grabbed their first number-one single with "Setting Sun," which featured Noel Gallagher of Oasis on vocals. The next year after an extensive tour of the United States, the Chemical Brothers topped the British chart and reached the U.S. Top Twenty with the million-seller *Dig Your Own Hole*.

Moby turned from techno to a big-beat sound and achieved star status. Born Richard Melville Hall in Harlem, Moby immersed himself in the British techno and breakbeat scenes. In 1999, he released a guitar-driven, techno mix on *Play*, which sold 10 million copies worldwide and featured such rock collaborators as vocalist Gwen Stefani.

Fat Boy Slim, an alias of British disc jockey Quentin Norman Cook, vaulted to the top with the big beat. Fat Boy formerly played bass for the band the Housemartins, and in 1996 decided to assume the moniker Fat Boy Slim as a DJ spinning techno and house. In 1998, he released the million-selling album *You've Come a Long Way, Baby*, which on some tracks featured guitar samples and traditional song structures. "There's a little element of rock 'n' roll in all of us. We're not just studio boffins," he remarked about the big-beat scene. "There's a couple of guitars in there and that's all the Americans needed to latch on to!"

With the success of spinners such as Fat Boy Slim, select disc jockeys became pop stars. Jockeys played to ever-increasing crowds for larger and larger sums of money. "When I started DJing, the DJ was just below the glass collector in order of importance in a night club," recalled Fat Boy Slim. "Over the years the DJ got more and more important." Now, emphasized Slim in 1999, "the DJ is like the new pop star."

During the nineties and into the new century, many disc jockeys were revered by youth around the world as musical heroes. In 2004, Dutch jockey Tiesto (b. Tijs Verwest), called the greatest DJ of all time by *Mixmag*, performed at the opening ceremony of the Olympics to billions of television viewers. In a 2009–2010 fifteen-month Kaleidoscope World Tour, he attracted more than a million fans. DJ Sasha (b. Alexander Coe) once turned down $50,000 for a two-hour. When he arrived in China for a show, he received red-carpet treatment and faced a press conference with fifty microphones and dozens of cameras. In the new century, prominent DJs played beats to millions of adoring youths worldwide.

Despite the fleeting success of the big-beat sound in the United States, most American youth ignored British dance music despite the American origin of house and techno. "America is too caught up in that sort of Bruce Springsteen rock and roll tradition of driving around in a pink Cadillac with girls with big boobs," scoffed Fat Boy Slim.

Electronic Dance Music Captivates the United States

Daft Punk changed the American attitude toward techno and house. In 1993, two French music enthusiasts, Guy-Manuel de Homem-Christo and Thomas Bangalter, started Daft Punk. The duo initially focused upon house with a special nod to Primal

Scream's *Screamadelica*. In May 2006 after becoming a main attraction in Europe, Daft headlined at the Coachella Festival in Indio, California, and created an America mania for dance music that lasted more than a decade. At the festival, they performed inside a huge, glowing pyramid with flashing LED panels. To add to the visual extravaganza, they wore their customary robot headgear and gloves. "All the tastemakers were at Coachella," remembered concert promoter Disco Donnie Estopinal. "They thought rave music was dirty and gross, but they were finally able to put dance music together with the visual aspect that was apparently so important."

By 2013, Daft Punk had overtaken the United States. Collaborating with disco pioneers Nile Rodgers and Giorgio Moroder, they scored with the number-one *Random Access Memories*, which combined synthesizer squeals, progressive-rock guitar, vocals, strings, and a lilting piano. The duo urged their listeners to "Lose Yourself to Dance."

Deadamau5, otherwise known as Joel Zimmerman, mined the American interest in visually exciting dance music. He poured thousands of dollars into beat-synchronized animated graphics and light shows. Deadmau5 skipped onstage in a mouse outfit with giant ears and bulging eyes to memorialize the mouse, which had sneaked inside his home computer. In 2012 and 2014, he hit the U.S. Top Ten with albums that offered fragile, crystalline, synthesizer-power instrumentals with danceable beats.

Though used to enhance the visual aspect of their shows, the headgear of Daft Punk and Deadmau5 indicated the importance of the audience. Rather than deify musicians on a stage, the participants at a concert assumed primary importance. "We don't believe in the star system," insisted Thomas Bangalter of Daft Punk. "We don't want to run into people who are the same age as us, shaking our hand and saying, 'Can I have your autograph?' because we think we're exactly like them."

Large parties, referred to as festivals rather than raves in America, focused on the youths who attended them. In 2013, 330,000 dance fanatics moved to the beats at the Ultra Music Festival in Florida that staged wild light-show extravaganzas. The next year at the TomorrowWorld festival in Georgia, 150,000 attendees thrilled to multiple stages spaced between several lakes, plastic fish that sprayed streams of fire, and a dance floor suspended above a lake. In 2015, more than 400,000 dance fans packed into the Las Vegas Motor Speedway for the annual three-day Electric Daisy Carnival (EDC), which featured fireworks, whirling lights, and laser shows. "It's about giving people that fantasy; that storybook experience," enthused EDC-organizer Pasquale Rotella, about the festivals. "I'd like to say our headliners are the fans."

Fans at the Ultra Music Festival, 2017.

Giorgio Viera/EFE/Newscom.

The fashion statements of the festival goers intensified the fairyland atmosphere. Women wore neon tutus, underwear without outerwear, fish-net stockings, fur-topped, multi-colored boots, and sometimes science-fiction-like costumes. The shirt-less men sported bandanas, beaded masks, and body paint.

To enhance their hedonistic adventures, youth ingested drugs. Most festival partiers favored a stronger, powdered version of ecstasy called molly, short for molecule. They bought baggies of the powder from drug dealers onsite and sometimes tested their purchases at DanceSafe booths inside the festival grounds. "The EDM culture exists because kids like to get fucked up and dance," complained a concert promoter.

The disco-like festival atmosphere proved to be profitable to music entrepreneurs. "Promoters make a lot more money on the DJ shows," explained Diplo (b. Thomas Pentz), a jockey at many of the massive festivals. "A band plays for 45 minutes; DJs can play for four hours." By 2015, the dance business grossed $6.9 billion annually in the United States.

In addition to festival revenue, noted disc jockeys sold millions of their mixes in the United States. In 2011, Kaskade (b. Ryan Raddon) hit the Top Twenty with *Fire & Ice*, which included pop-styled vocals on one side and house-heavy mixes on the other. Two years later, Swedish jockey Avicii (b. Tim Berling) released the number-five *True*, which mixed a few traditional songs with heavy house and precise techno beats in such selections as "Canyons." In 2014, Skrillex (b. Sonny Moore), a former punk singer who had been promoted by Deadmaus5, debuted at number four with the harsh, hard beats, the stuttering wobble and distorted raps of *Recess*. The same year, Tiesto hit the American Top Twenty with *A Town Called Paradise*, which spliced guitars, vocals, and pianos onto a hard-edged house and techno.

Many of the leading disc jockeys became millionaires. As an annual income for 2017, Calvin Harris (b. Adam Wiles) generated an amazing $66 million. David Guetta earned $30 million; Avicii and Tiesto snagged $28 million; and Deadmaus5 brought in $16 million. Overall, fourteen disc jockeys generated more than $12 million for the year.

Pop singers who relied on electronic dance beats exploded on the scene. Lady Gaga (b. Stefani Germanotta) sang over house and techno in her million-selling debut *Fame* (2008) and used electronic beats for her next several number-one albums. Rihanna (b. Robyn Fenty), the Barbadian R&B singer who sold 230 million albums worldwide, turned to electronic dance music as the background for her two Top-Five efforts *Rated R* and *Loud*. French house disc jockey David Guetta produced hits for Rihanna ("Unapologetic," 2012), Lady Gaga ("Artpop," 2013), and Britney Spears ("Britney Jean," 2013). In 2012, Madonna, who never strayed far from electronic beats, made a surprise appearance at the Ultra Music Festival during Avicii's closing set.

EDM even incorporated trap, a version of the prevalent and ever-changing rap. Developed by rapper T.I. (b. Clifford Harris, Jr.) from Atlanta and named after drug-infested trap houses, the genre featured speedy rhythms from a Roland TR-808 drum machine, symphonic sounding synthesizers, and gangsta lyrics to replicate the menacing atmosphere of drug dealing on the streets. By the 2010s, trap infiltrated the mainstream and subsequently hit the chart with the number-two "Trap Queen" (2015) by Fetty Wap (b. William Maxwell II), Gucci Mane's (b. Radric Davis) "Rich Ass Junkie," Lil Uzi Vert's (b. Symere Woods) "XO TOUR Llif3," and Cardi B's (b. Belcalis Almanzar) chart topping "Bodak Yellow," all released in 2017. As trap seeped into the musical vocabulary in 2013, the Tomorrowland Festival included a "Trap Stage," the Ultra Music Festival featured five popular trap artists, and EDM producers such as Diplo added trap to their mixes.

By mid-decade, electronic dance music had triumphed in America. In 2016, Mark Lawrence, the chief executive for the Association for Electronic Music declared that EDM "has put dance music front and centre in North America, if not globally. The moment has come where EDM represents pop and commercial rather than the under-ground." "If you're 15- to 25-years-old now," asserted Michael Rapino, the chief executive of Live Nation Entertainment, the largest concert promoter in the world, electronic dance music "is your rock 'n' roll."

Bibliography

Chapter 1

Albertson, Chris. *Bessie*. New Haven: Yale University Press, 2003.

Allen, William Francis, Charles Pickard Ware, and Lucy McKim Garrison. *Slave Songs of the United States*. Bedford: Dover Publications, 1867.

Bruynoghe, Yannick. *Big Bill's Blues: William Broonzy's Story*. New York: Da Capo, 1992.

Calt, Stephen. "The Anatomy of a 'Race' Label – Part One." *78 Quarterly*, no. 3 (1988): 9–23.

Calt, Stephen, and Gayle Dean Wardlow. *King of the Delta Blues: The Life and Music of Charlie Patton*. Newton, NJ: Rock Chapel Press, 1988.

Corritore, Bob, Bill Ferris, and Jim O'Neal. "Willie Dixon." *Living Blues*, July/August 1988.

Grossman, James. *Land of Hope: Chicago, Black Southerners, and the Great Migration*. Chicago: University of Chicago Press, 1989.

Govenar, Alan. "Blind Lemon Jefferson: The Myth and the Man." *Black Music Research Journal* 20, no. 1 (Spring 2000): 7–21.

Handy, W.C. *Father of the Blues: An Autobiography*. New York: Collier, 1941.

Harold, Ellen, and Peter Stone. "Big Bill Broonzy." Cultural Equity. Accessed May 4, 2018. http://www.culturalequity.org/alanlomax/ce_alanlomax_profile_broonzy.php

Johnson, Charles S. *The Negro in American Civilization: A Study of Negro Life and Race Relations in the Light of Social Research*. New York: Henry Holt and Company, 1930.

Lanier, Henry, ed. *Selections from Sidney Lanier: Prose and Verse*. New York: Charles Scribner, 1916.

Lipscomb, Mance, with Glen Allyn. *I Say Me for a Parable*. New York: Norton, 1993.

Oliver, Paul. *The Story of the Blues*. Radner, PA: Chilton, 1969.

Olson, Ted. "'I Feel Like It Is a Part of Me.'" *Living Blues*, July/August 1992.

O'Neal, James, and Amy, O'Neal. "Eddie Boyd Interview." *Living Blues*, November/December 1977.

O'Neal, James, and Amy, O'Neal, eds. *The Voice of the Blues: Classic Interviews from Living Blues Magazine*. New York: Routledge, 2002.

Rowe, Mike. *Chicago Blues: The City and the Music*. New York: Da Capo, 1981.

Shapiro, Nat and Nat Hentoff. *Hear Me Talkin' to Ya: The Story of Jazz as Told by the Men Who Made It*. New York: Dover, 1955.

Shaw, Arnold. *Honkers and Shouters: The Golden Years of Rhythm and Blues*. New York: Collier, 1978.

Shaw, Arnold. *The Rockin' 50s*. New York: Hawthorn, 1974.

Smith, Willie "The Lion." *Music on My Mind: The Memoirs of an American Artist*. New York: Da Capo, 1978.

Southern, Eileen. *The Music of Black Americans: A History*. 2nd ed. New York: WW Norton, 1997.

Stearns, Marshall. *The Story of Jazz*. New York: Oxford, 1956.

Titon, Jeff. "Son House Interview." *Living Blues*, March/April 1977.

Unterberger, Richie. "Billy Boy Arnold Interview." Accessed May 4, 2018. http://www.richieunterberger.com/arnold.html.

Washington, Booker. *Up From Slavery*. New York: Modern Library, 1999.

Waterman, Dick. "Son House Obituary." *Living Blues*, January/February 1989.

Wolfe, Charles and Kip Lornell. *The Life and Legend of Leadbelly*. Boston: De Capo Press, 1999.

Chapter 2

Aldin, Katherine, and Peter Lee. "B.B. King." *Living Blues*, May/June 1988.

Berry, Chuck. *Chuck Berry: The Autobiography*. New York: Simon and Schuster, 1987.

Bertrand, Michael T. *Race, Rock and Elvis*. Chicago: University of Illinois, 2000.

"Breaking Down Barriers." *Cashbox*, January 22, 1955.

Broven, John. *Record Makers and Record Breakers: The Voice of the Independent Rock 'n' Roll Pioneers*. Chicago: University of Illinois, 2009.

Buchanan, A. Russell. *Black Americans in World War II*. Clio: Santa Barbara, 1977.

Cage, Ruth. "Horrors! Recognition Finally Comes to R&B." *Downbeat*, April 6, 1955.

Chapple, Steve, and Reebee Garofalo. *Rock 'n' Roll Is Here to Pay: The History and Politics of the Music Industry*. Chicago: Nelson-Hall, 1977.

Cohan, Lou. "Bo Diddley: The Man with the Beat." *Thunder Road*, June 1980.

Cohodas, Nadine. *Spinning Blues into Gold: The Chess Brothers and the Legendary Chess Records*. New York: St. Martin's, 2000.

Conrad, Earl. "Yesterday and Today: The Meaning of Migration." *The Chicago Defender*, April 14, 1945.

"Control the Dimwits." *Billboard*, September 25, 1954.

DeCurtis, Anthony. *Rockin' My Life Away: Writing about Music and Other Matters*. New York: Rolling Stone, 1999.

Dixon, Willie, with Don Snowden. *I Am the Blues*. New York: Da Capo, 1989.

"DJs Decry Quality Slump in Pop Singles." *Billboard*, November 12, 1955.

Dwyer, Bill. "Bo Diddley." *Blues Unlimited,* April 1970.

Escott, Colin. "John Lee Hooker: King of the One-Chord Boogie." *Goldmine*, March 20, 1992.

Finkle, Lee. "The Conservative Aims of Militant Rhetoric: Black Protest During World War II." *Journal of American History 60*, no. 3 (December 1973): 692–713.

Fuchs, Otto. *Bill Haley: Father of Rock and Roll*. Gelnhausen, Germany: Wagner/Verlag, 2011.

Gifford, Barry. "Couldn't Do No Yodeling, So I Turned to Howlin'." *Rolling Stone*, August 24, 1968.

Guzman, Jesse. *Negro Yearbook: A Review of Events Affecting Negro Life, 1941–1946*. Tuskegee: Tuskegee Institute, 1947.

Herbeck, Ray Jr. "The Birth, Growth and Strangling of Rock Radio." *Billboard*, December 2, 1978.

James, Elmore. Liner notes for *History of Elmore James*. Trip Records, TLP-8007 (2).

"JUV ASSN Gets Jock Support in Drive to Kayo 'Leeric' Platters." *Variety*, July 20, 1955.

Kiefer, Kit, ed. *They Called It Rock: The Goldmine Oral History of Rock 'N Roll, 1950–1970*. Iola: Krause, 1991.

King, B. B., and David Ritz. *Blues All Around Me: The Autobiography of B.B. King*. New York: Avon, 1996.

Kreps, Daniel. "Phil Chess, Pioneering Blues and Rock Exec, Dead at 95." *Rolling Stone*, October 19, 2016.

Larner, Jeremy. "What Do They Get from Rock 'n' Roll?" *Atlantic Monthly*, August 1964.

Lee, Alfred, and Norman Humphrey. *Race Riot*. New York: Dryden Press, 1943.

Lydon, Michael. *Rock Folk*. New York: Dial, 1971.

Marcus, Greil. "Chuck Berry." In *The Rolling Stone Interviews*, edited by the editors of *Rolling Stone*. New York: Coronet, 1971.

Mason, Bobbie Ann. *Elvis Presley*. New York: Penguin, 2003.

Miller, Mitch. "June, Moon, Swoon and KoKoMo." *New York Times Magazine*, April 24, 1955.

"Mobile Station Quotes *Variety* on Leerics, Will Not Broadcast Them." *Variety*, March 23, 1955.

Murray, Charles Shaar. *Boogie Man: The Adventures of John Lee Hooker in the American Twentieth Century*. New York: St. Martin's, 2000.

"Musical Treatment." *The Southerner*, March 1956.

O'Neal, James, and Amy, O'Neal. "Jimmy Reed Interview." *Living Blues,* May/June 1975.

O'Neal, James, and Amy, O'Neal. "Muddy Waters Interview." *Living Blues,* March/April 1984.

Palmer, Robert. *Deep Blues.* New York: Penguin, 1982.

Paulsen, Gary. "Jules Bihari!" *Blues Unlimited,* December 1969.

Penn, Roberta. "Bo Diddley: *Still Bad to the Bone.*" *The Rocket,* September 1983.

"Picker Problems." *Time,* September 14, 1936.

"President Orders an Even Break for Minorities in Defense Jobs." *New York Times,* June 26, 1941.

Puterbaugh, Parke. "Little Richard." *Rolling Stone,* April 19, 1990.

"Race Bands Save Philly from War Dough Ballroom Aches." *Billboard,* March 11, 1944.

Ressner, Jeffrey. "Pat Boone." *Rolling Stone,* April 19, 1990.

Rooney, James. *Bossmen: Bill Monroe and Muddy Waters.* New York: Dial, 1971.

"Separate Is Not Equal." *Smithsonian National Museum of American History.* Supreme Court Decision. Accessed May 4, 2018. http://americanhistory.si.edu/brown/history/5-decision/detail/slip-opinion.html.

Shaw, Arnold. *Honkers and Shouters: The Golden Years of Rhythm and Blues.* New York: Collier, 1978.

Shaw, Arnold. *The Rockin' 50s.* New York: Hawthorn, 1974.

Siders, Harvey. "Talking with a King: B. B. King." *Downbeat,* March 30, 1972.

Sitkoff, Harvard. "Detroit Race Riot, 1943." *Michigan History,* May 1969.

Sumlin, Hubert. "My Years with Wolf." *Living Blues,* September/October 1989.

Swan, L. Alex. "The Harlem and Detroit Riots of 1943: A Comparative Analysis." *Berkeley Journal of Sociology* 16 (1971–1972): 75–93.

Tamarkin, Jeff. "Boone in the U.S.A." *Goldmine,* February 22, 1991.

Unterberger, Richie. "Billy Boy Arnold Interview." Accessed May 4, 2018. http://www.richieunterberger.com/arnold.html.

U.S. Senate, 85th Congress, 2nd session. *Hearings Before the Subcommittee on Communications of the Committee on Interstate and Foreign Commerce: Amendment to the Communications Act of 1934.*

Welding, Pete. "Howlin' Wolf." *Blues Unlimited,* January 1969.

Welding, Pete. "Johnny Otis: The History of Rhythm and Blues." In *The Rolling Stone Interviews, Vol. 2,* edited by Ben Fong-Torres. New York: Warner, 1973.

Welding, Pete. "Muddy Waters—Last King of the South Side?" *Downbeat,* October 8, 1964.

White, Charles. *The Life and Times of Little Richard.* New York: Pocket Books, 1984.

"White Councils vs. Rock 'n' Roll." *Newsweek,* April 23, 1956.

Chapter 3

Aquila, Richard. *Let's Rock: How 1950s America Created Elvis and the Rock and Roll Craze.* New York: Rowman and Littlefield, 2017.

Bertrand, Michael T. *Race, Rock and Elvis.* Chicago: University of Illinois, 2000.

Broven, John. *Record Makers and Record Breakers: The Voice of the Independent Rock 'n' Roll Pioneers.* Chicago: University of Illinois, 2009.

Clayton, Rose, and Dick Heard, eds. *Elvis Up Close: In the Words of Those Who Knew Him Best.* Atlanta: Turner, 1994.

"A Craze Called Elvis." *Coronet* (September 1956), pp. 153–157.

Cronin, Peter, Scott Isler, and Mark Rowland. "Elvis Presley: An Oral Biography." *Musician,* October 1992.

Doggett, Peter. *Are You Ready for the Country: Elvis, Dylan, Parsons and the Roots of Country Rock.* New York: Penguin, 2001

"Elvis." *Hit Parade,* January 1957.

"Elvis: A Different Kind of Idol." *Life,* August 27, 1956.

"Elvis Presley: He Can't Be But He Is." *Look,* August 7, 1956.

Escott, Colin, and Martin Hawkins. *Sun Records.* New York: Quick Fox, 1975.

Fogerty, John. "Brother to Brother." *Musician,* July 1986.

"Folk Talent and Tunes." *Billboard,* December 11, 1954.

Flanagan, Bill. "Johnny Cash, American." *Musician,* May 1988.

Fricke, David. "Ricky: TV's Teen Dream Knew How to Rock." *Rolling Stone,* February 13, 1986.

Gary, Kays. "Elvis Defends His Low-Down Style." *Charlotte Observer,* June 27, 1956.

Goldberg, Michael. "The Wisdom of Solomon." *Rolling Stone,* November 22, 1984.

Goldrosen, John. *Buddy Holly.* New York: Putnam, 1979.

Goodall, Nigel. "Interview with Elvis Presley: August 28, 1956 in California." Elvis Australia. May 26, 2016. http://www.elvis.com.au/presley/interview-with-elvis-presley-august-28-1956.shtml.

Goodall, Nigel. "Interview with Elvis Presley: The February 1970 Houston Astrodome Press Conference." Elvis Australia. July 31, 2016. http://www.elvis.com.au/presley/interview-with-elvis-presley-the-1970-press-conference.shtml.

Guralnick, Peter. *Feel Like Going Home.* London: Dutton, 1971.

Guralnick, Peter. *Last Train to Memphis: The Rise of Elvis Presley.* New York: Little Brown, 1995.

Guralnick, Peter. *Lost Highways.* New York: Vintage, 1982.

Guralnick, Peter. *Sam Phillips: The Man Who Invented Rock and Roll.* New York: Little Brown, 2015.

Hilburn, Robert. "Invincible Jerry Lee Lewis." Reprinted in the *Seattle Times,* November 29, 1981.

Hopkins, Jerry. *Elvis: A Biography.* New York: Warner, 1971.

Jennings, Robert. "There'll Always Be an Elvis." *Saturday Evening Post.* September 11, 1965.

Johnson, Robert. "Suddenly Singing Elvis Presley Zooms into Recording Stardom." *Memphis Press-Scimitar,* February 5, 1955.

Kaye, Elizabeth. "Sam Phillips Interview." *Rolling Stone,* February 13, 1986.

Kiefer, Kit, ed. *They Called It Rock: The Goldmine Oral History of Rock 'N Roll, 1950–1970.* Iola: Krause, 1991.

King, B.B., and David Ritz. *Blues All Around Me: The Autobiography of B.B. King.* New York: Avon, 1996.

Larner, Jeremy. "What Do They Get From Rock 'n' Roll?" *Atlantic Monthly,* August 1964.

Laws of the State of Mississippi. Appropriations, General Legislation and Resolutions, 1959. Parts 1–555.

Loder, Kurt. "Everly Brothers Interview (1986)." In *The Rolling Stone Interviews: The 1980s,* edited by the editors of *Rolling Stone.* New York: St. Martin's, 1989.

"Lonely and Shook Up." *Time,* May 27, 1957.

Miller, Bill. *Cash: An American Man.* New York: Pocket Books, 2004.

Palmer, Robert. "Billy Burnette Rekindles the Family Magic." *Rolling Stone,* November 27, 1980.

Palmer, Robert. *Jerry Lee Lewis Rocks!* London: Omnibus, 1981.

Perry, Andrew. "Hellbound!" *Mojo,* December 2006.

Pett, Saul. "Does His Mama Think He's Vulgar?" *Nashville Tennessean,* July 22, 1956.

"Roy Orbison, 1936–1988." *Rolling Stone,* January 26, 1989.

Reder, Alan, and John Baxter. *Listen to This!* New York: Hyperion, 1999.

Richardson, Cliff. "Mixed Dancing Baffles Cops in Houstin, Texas." *Pittsburgh Courier,* August 18, 1956.

"Rock Around the Tube." *Billboard,* December 2, 1978.

"The Rock Is Solid." *Time,* November 4, 1957.

"Rock-'n'-Roll Riot." *Time,* May 19, 1958.

Roeser, Steve. "An Interview with Steve Allen." *Goldmine,* December 11, 1992.

Shaw, Arnold. *Honkers and Shouters: The Golden Years of Rhythm and Blues.* New York: Collier, 1978.

Shaw, Arnold. *The Rockin' 50s.* New York: Hawthorn, 1974.

Stern, Stewart. "Interview with the author."

Swenson, John. *Bill Haley: The Daddy of Rock-and-Roll.* New York: Stein and Day, 1984.

"Teenagers Offer Huge Disk Market." *Billboard*, November 10, 1956.

Thomas, Rufus. "Elvis and the Singing Indian." In *Elvis in Private*, edited by Peter Haining. New York: St. Martin's, 1987.

"Top Ten." *Rolling Stone*, February 13, 1986.

Weinberg, Max. *The Big Beat: Conversations with Rock's Great Drummers*. Chicago: Contemporary, 1984.

Whitmer, Peter. *Inner Elvis: A Psychological Biography of Elvis Aaron Presley*. New York: Hyperion, 1996.

"Wild Teenagers Rip Shirt Off Rock 'n' Roll Singer." *Evansville Courier*, October 20, 1956.

"Words of the Week." *Jet*, October 10, 1957.

Chapter 4

Adels, Robert. "Dialogue the Viewpoints of the Industry: Don Kirschner." *Music World*, January 18, 1975.

Alpert, Steven, dir. *Girl Groups*. 1983. MGM.

Aronowitz, Alfred. "The Dumb Sound." *Saturday Evening Post*, October 5, 1963.

Bunzel, Peter. "Music Biz Goes Round and Round." *Life*, May 16, 1960.

Buskin, Richard. *Inside Tracks*. New York: Avon, 1999.

"Challenging the Giants." *Newsweek*, December 23, 1957.

Clark, Dick. *Rocks, Rolls, and Remembers*. New York: Popular, 1978.

Clark, Dick. *To Goof or Not to Goof*. New York: Dick Clark Television Productions, 1963.

Cox, Herb. "The Heart and Soul of the Cleftones." *Goldmine*, February 21, 1992.

Dachs, David. *Anything Goes: The World of Popular Music*. New York: Bobbs Merrill, 1964.

"Jockeys on a Rough Ride." *Newsweek*, December 7, 1959.

Kiefer, Kit, ed. *They Called It Rock: The Goldmine Oral History of Rock 'N Roll, 1950–1970*. Iola: Krause, 1991.

Kiersh, Edward. *Where Are You Now, Bo Diddley?* New York: Dolphin, 1986.

Leuchtenburg, William. *A Troubled Feast: American Society Since 1945*. Boston: Little Brown, 1973.

"Phil Spector Bio." *Rolling Stone*. Accessed May 5, 2018. http://www.rollingstone.com/music/artists/phil-spector/biography.

"Rock-'n'-Roll Rolls On 'n' On." *Life*, December 22, 1958.

Schipper, Henry. "Dick Clark." *Rolling Stone*, April 19, 1990.

Shaw, Arnold. *The Rockin' 50s*. New York: Hawthorn, 1974.

Smith, Joe. *Off the Record: An Oral History of Popular Music*. New York: Warner, 1988.

Spector, Ronnie. *Be My Baby: How I Survived Mascara, Miniskirts, and Madness, or My Life as a Fabulous Ronette*. New York: New American Library, 2004.

Spitz, Robert. *The Making of Superstars: Artists and Executives of the Rock Music Business*. New York: Doubleday, 1978.

"St. Joan of the Jukebox." *Time*, March 15, 1963.

"Tall, That's All." *Time*, April 14, 1958.

U.S. Senate, 85th Congress, 2nd session. *Hearings Before the Subcommittee on Communications of the Committee on Interstate and Foreign Commerce: Amendment to the Communications Act of 1934*.

Ward, Ed. *The History of Rock and Roll, vol. 1: 1920–1963*. New York: Flat Iron, 2016.

White, Charles. *The Life and Times of Little Richard*. New York: Pocket Books, 1984.

Chapter 5

Alexander, Shana. "Love Songs to the Carburetor." *Life*, November 6, 1964.

Burt, Rob. *Surf City, Drag City*. New York: Blandford, 1986.

Cerf, Martin. "Personal Recollection by Dean Torrence." 8-page insert in the album Silver Summer, Silver Eagle Records SE 1039, 1985.

"Disneyland's History." JustDisney.com. Accessed May 5, 2018. http://www.justdisney.com/disneyland/history.html

Kiefer, Kit, ed. *They Called It Rock: The Goldmine Oral History of Rock 'N Roll, 1950–1970*. Iola: Krause, 1991.

Leonard, George. "California." *Look*, September 25, 1962.

Murphy, James. *Becoming the Beach Boys, 1961–1963*. North Carolina: MacFarland, 2015.

Nicolosi, Vince. "Jan and Dean in 1980: Still Searching for Surf City." *Trouser Press*, March/April, 1980.

"The No. 1 State: Booming, Beautiful California." *Newsweek*, September 10, 1962.

"Surf's Up." *Time*, August 9, 1963.

Walton, Samuel. "The Endless Summer of the Beach Boys." *Saturday Evening Post*, October 1976.

"A Way of Life." *Life*, September 1, 1961.

"What To Know and What To Look For." *Life*. October 19, 1962.

White, Timothy. *The Nearest Faraway Place*. New York: Holt, 1994.

Chapter 6

Alarik, Scott. *Deep Community: Adventures in the Modern Folk Underground*. New York: Black Wolf, 2003.

"Angry Young Folk Singer." *Life*, April 10, 1964.

Baez, Joan. *Daybreak*. New York: Dial, 1968.

Berkeley in the Sixties. Film transcript. Accessed May 5, 2018. http://www.newsreel.org/transcripts/berkeley-in-the-60s-transcript.pdf.

Bluestein, Gene. "Songs of the Silent Generation." *New Republic*, March 13, 1961.

"Bob Dylan Interview with Time Magazine." Video. 1965. Accessed May 5, 2018. https://www.youtube.com/watch?v=mnl5X5MQKTg.

DeTurk, David, and A. Poulin, Jr. "Joan Baez—An Interview." In *The American Folk Scene: Dimensions of the Folksong Revival*, edited by David DeTurk and A. Polin, Jr. New York: Dell, 1967.

Dunaway, David, and Molly Beer. *Sing Out: An Oral History of America's Folk Music Revivals*. New York: Oxford University Press, 2010.

"The Faculty." *Time*, June 16, 1961.

Fleming, Harold. *Encyclopedia Britannica Yearbook: 1964*, pp. 248–262.

"Folk Girls." *Time*, June 1, 1962.

"The Folk and the Rock." *Newsweek*, September 20, 1965.

"Folk Singers and Their Fans." *Look*, August 27, 1963.

Fricke, David. "Roger McGuinn." *Rolling Stone*, August 23, 1990.

Guthrie, Woody. *Bound for Glory*. New York: E. P. Dutton, 1965.

Hampton, Henry, and Steve Fayer. *Voices of Freedom: An Oral History of the Civil Rights Movement from the 1950s through the 1980s*. New York: Bantam, 1990.

Hentoff, Nat. "Profiles: The Crackin', Shakin', Breakin' Sounds." *New Yorker*, October 24, 1964.

Hinton, Harold. "Marshall U.S. Foe, McCarthy Charges." *New York Times*, June 15, 1951.

"Hoots and Hollers on the Campus." *Newsweek*, November 27, 1961.

Holzman, Jac, with Gavin Daws. *Follow the Music: The Life and Times of Elektra Records in the Grat Years of American Pop Culture*. New York: First Media, 1998.

Kennedy, John. "Inaugural Speech." American Presidency Project. Accessed by May 5, 2018. http://www.presidency.ucsb.edu/ws/index.php?pid=8032&.

Kennedy, John. "Radio and Television Report to the American People on Civil Rights, June 11, 1963." American Presidency Project. Accessed May 5, 2018. http://www.presidency.ucsb.edu/ws/?pid=9271.

Kiersh, Edward. *Where Are You Now, Bo Diddley?* New York: Dolphin, 1986.

King, Martin Luther, Jr. "I Have a Dream." Speech. Accessed May 5, 2018. http://www.let.rug.nl/usa/documents/1951-/martin-luther-kings-i-have-a-dream-speech-august-28-1963.php.

Leonard, George. "Pied Pipers of the New Generation." *Look,* January 3, 1961.

"Like From Halls of Ivy." *Time,* July 11, 1960.

Loder, Kurt. "Bob Dylan: The Rolling Stone Interview." *Rolling Stone,* June 21, 1984.

"Outrage in Alabama." *New York Times* (editorial), May 5, 1963.

Paxton, Tom. *The Honor of Your Company.* New Jersey: Cherry Lane Music Company, 2000.

Pichaske, David. *A Generation in Motion.* New York: MacMillan, 1979.

"Real Long Hair." *Newsweek,* July 9, 1962.

Ruhlman, William. "Peter, Paul and Mary." *Goldmine,* April 12, 1996.

Savio, Mario. "An End to History." Free Speech Archives. Accessed May 5, 2018. http://www.fsm-a.org/stacks/endhistorysavio.html.

Scaduto, Anthony. *Bob Dylan.* New York: New American Library, 1979.

Shelton, Robert. *No Direction Home: The Life and Music of Bob Dylan.* New York: Ballantine, 1986.

Siegal, Jules, "Bob Dylan: Rebel King of Rock and Roll." *The Saturday Evening Post,* July 30, 1966.

Smith, Joe. *Off the Record: An Oral History of Popular Music.* New York: Warner, 1988.

Stern, Jane, and Michael Stern. *Sixties People.* New York: Alfred Knopf, 1990.

"Sybil With a Guitar." *Time,* November 23, 1962.

"Take a Boy Like Me." *Time,* March 29, 1963.

Unterberger, Richie. *Turn! Turn! Turn!: The '60s Rock Revolution.* San Francisco: Backbeat, 2002.

Von Schmidt, Eric. *Baby, Let Me Follow You Down.* New York: Anchor, 1979.

"Wallace Says Birmingham 'Fed Up' with Protests." *New York Times,* May 6, 1963.

Chapter 7

"Beatles." *Time,* November 15, 1963.

"Beatles Are Just Cuddlesome." *London Times,* May 28, 1964.

"Beatles Reaction Puzzles Even Psychologists." *Science News Letter,* February 29, 1964.

Benjamin, Kent, Ken Sharp, and John Hellier. "For Nice Is the Music, For Ever and Ever, Amen: The Story of the Small Faces in Their Own Words." *Goldmine,* June 21, 1996.

Booth, Dave. "Chris Barber: The Original Sultan of Swing." *Goldmine,* July 10, 1992.

"Bugs about the Beatles: George, Paul, Ringo and John." *Newsweek,* February 24, 1964.

Davies, Hunter. *The Beatles.* New York: McGraw-Hill, 1968.

"Eight Arrested in Fresh Trouble at Clacton." *London Times,* March 31, 1964.

"Evolution." *Time,* February 17, 1967.

Fox, Margalit. "Davy Jones, Monkees Singer, Dies at 66." *New York Times,* February 29, 2012.

Garbarini, Vince, and Jock Baird. "Has Success Spoiled Paul McCartney?" *Musician,* February 1985.

Harry, Bill. "The Beatles and Royalty." Mersey Beat. Accessed May 5, 2018. http://www.triumphpc.com/mersey-beat/beatles/royalty.shtml.

Hewitt, Paolo, ed. *The Sharper Word: A Mod Anthology.* London: Helter Skelter, 2000.

Hotchner, A. E. *Blown Away: The Rolling Stones and the Death of the Sixties.* New York: Simon & Schuster, 1990.

"Interview with John Lennon and Yoko Ono." *Playboy,* January 1981.

"Keeping Hooliganism in Perspective." *London Times,* April 4, 1964.

Kiefer, Kit, ed. *They Called It Rock: The Goldmine Oral History of Rock 'N Roll, 1950–1970.* Iola: Krause, 1991.

Kiersh, Edward. *Where Are You Now, Bo Diddley?* New York: Dolphin, 1986.

"Keith Richards Interview." *Playboy,* October 1989.

Lewis, Richard Warren. "When Four Nice Guys Go Ape." *Saturday Evening Post,* January 28, 1967.

Lynskey, Dorian. "Beatlemania: 'the screamers and other tales of fandom.'" *Observer,* September 28, 2013. Accessed May 5, 2018. https://www.theguardian.com/music/2013/sep/29/beatlemania-screamers-fandom-teenagers-hysteria.

Maher, Jack. "Beatles Begin New British Artist Push." *Billboard,* February 15, 1964.

McGee, Dave. "Carl Perkins." *Rolling Stone,* April 19, 1990.

"Mr. Wilson Promises New Deal." *London Times,* March 9, 1964.

"Mods versus the Rockers." *Daily Express,* May 19, 1964.

"Monkee Do." *Time,* November 11, 1966.

Murphy, Marty. "I Took Paul and Ringo to the Space Needle." *Seattle Times,* February 12, 1984.

"97 Arrested in Rowdyism at Clacton." *London Times,* March 30, 1964.

Norman, Phillip. *Shout! The Beatles in Their Generation.* New York: Simon and Schuster, 2005.

Oldham, Andrew Loog. *Stoned: A Memoir of London in the 1960s.* New York: St. Martin's, 2000.

Phillips, McCandlish. "4 Beatles and How They Grew." *New York Times,* February 17, 1964.

Pritchard, David, and Alan Lysaght. *The Beatles: An Oral History.* New York: Hyperion, 1998.

"Remembering the Beatles." *Seattle Times,* February 12, 1984.

"Ringo Starr." *Musician,* September 1986.

Rollin, Betty. "TV's Swinging Monkees." *Look,* December 27, 1966.

"Romp! Romp!" *Newsweek,* October 24, 1966.

Schaffner, Nicholas. *The British Invasion.* New York: McGraw-Hill, 1983.

Shaw, Arnold. *The Rock Revolution.* London: Collier, 1969.

"Shindig and Hullabaloo," *Ebony,* November 1965.

Spitz, Robert. *The Making of Superstars: Artists and Executives of the Rock Music Business.* New York: Doubleday, 1978.

Strongin, Theodore. "Musicoligically." *New York Times,* February 10, 1964.

"U.S. Rocks and Reels from the Beatles' Invasion." *Billboard,* February 15, 1964.

Wienberg, Max. *The Big Beat.* Chicago: Contemporary, 1984.

Wenner, Jann. "Pete Townshend Interview." In *The Rolling Stone Interviews,* edited by the editors of *Rolling Stone.* New York: Coronet, 1971.

"Wild Ones 'Beat Up' Margate." *Daily Mirror,* May 18, 1964.

Wiener, Allen. "Starr Time: A Conversation with Ringo Starr." *Goldmine,* June 12, 1992.

Zimmer, Dave. *Crosby, Stills and Nash: The Authorized Biography.* New York: St. Martin's, 1984.

Chapter 8

"Air Pollution." *Newsweek,* August 16, 1965.

Barnes, Richard. *The Who: Maximum R & B.* New York: St. Martin's, 1982.

"Blues Is Bustin' Out All Over." *Melody Maker,* November 17, 1962.

Clapton, Eric. *The Autobiography.* New York: Random House, 2007.

Dalton, David. *The Rolling Stones: The First Twenty Years.* New York: Knopf, 1981.

Deane, Elizabeth. *Rock and Roll.* Film. Transcript to Chess Brothers segment. Accessed May 5, 2018. http://www.wgbh.org/articles/Chess-Records-the-Chicago-Blues-and-the-Rolling-Stones-8055.

Deming, Mark. "Shadows of Knight." All Music Guide. Accessed May 5, 2018. http://www.allmusic.com/cg/amg.dll?p=amg&sql=11:80q7g44ttv2z~T1.

Di Perna, Alan. "Rock Roll and Babylon." *Guitar World,* October 1997.

Escott, Colin. "An Appreciation of B.B. King The Fortunate Son." *Goldmine,* April 29, 1994.

Gilbert, Dan. "The Wailers." *Where Y'At: New Orleans' Monthly Entertainment Magazine,* May 2003.

Graham, Bill. *Bill Graham Presents: My Life Inside Rock and Out.* New York: Doubleday, 1992.

Greenfield, Robert. "Keith Richard Interview: Got to Keep It Growing." In *The Rolling Stone Interviews, Vol. 2*, edited by the editors of *Rolling Stone*. New York: Warner, 1973.

Heatley, Michael. "The Yardbirds: 'One for All and All for One.'" *Goldmine*, June 12, 1992.

Henke, James. "Eric Clapton Interview." *Rolling Stone*, October 17, 1991.

Hopkins, Jerry. "Keith Moon: So There I Was." *Rolling Stone*, October 15, 1992.

Hotchner, A. E. *Blown Away: The Rolling Stones and the Death of the Sixties*. New York: Simon & Schuster, 1990.

Kiefer, Kit, ed. *They Called It Rock: The Goldmine Oral History of Rock 'N Roll, 1950–1970*. Iola: Krause, 1991.

Kiersh, Edward. *Where Are You Now, Bo Diddley?* New York: Dolphin, 1986.

"Keith Richards Interview." *Playboy*, October 1989.

"Letters to the Editor." *Newsweek*, September 13, 1965.

Loewenstein, Dora, and Philip Dodd, eds. *According to the Rolling Stones*. San Francisco: Chronicle, 2004.

Miles, Barry. *The British Invasion*. New York: Sterling, 2009.

Oldham, Andrew Loog. *Stoned: A Memoir of London in the 1960s*. New York: St. Martin's, 2000.

Olsen, Claus. "The Sonics Interviews." http://home.subnet.dk/aerphax/Sonics/sonics2.htm.

"100 Best Singles of the Last Twenty-Five Years." *Rolling Stone*.

Pritchard, David, and Alan Lysaght. *The Beatles: An Oral History*. New York: Hyperion, 1998.

Roberts, Chris. "Trend or Tripe?" *Melody Maker*, January 5, 1963.

"Rolling Again." *Newsweek*, November 17, 1969.

Rooney, James. *Bossmen: Bill Monroe and Muddy Waters*. New York: Dial, 1971.

Ruhlmann, William. "Paul Revere's 30-Year Ride." *Goldmine*, April 20, 1990.

Ruhlmann, William. "Featuring Mark Lindsay: 'Looking for Shelter' with the Raiders' Singer/Writer/Producer." *Goldmine*, April 20, 1990.

Scaduto, Tony. *Mick Jagger: Everybody's Lucifer*. New York: McKay, 1974.

Schaffner, Nicholas. *The British Invasion*. New York: McGraw-Hill, 1983.

Schwartz, Roberta. *How Britain Got the Blues: The Transmission and Reception of American Blues in the United Kingdom*. London: Taylor and Francis, 2007.

Shapiro, Harry. *Alexis Korner: The Biography*. London: Bloomsbury, 1997.

Shaw, Arnold. *Honkers and Shouters: The Golden Years of Rhythm and Blues*. New York: Collier, 1978.

Skelly, Richard. "John Mayall: Headmaster of the British Blues School." *Goldmine*, September 3, 1993.

Smith, Joe. *Off the Record: An Oral History of Popular Music*. New York: Warner, 1988.

Unterberger, Richie. *Unknown Legends of Rock 'n' Roll*. San Francisco: Miller Freeman, 1998.

Unterberger, Richie. "Dave Aguilar Interview." Transcripts of *Unknown Legends of Rock 'n' Roll*. Accessed May 5, 2018. http://www.richieunterberger.com/aguilar.html.

Unterberger, Richie. "Sean Boniwell Interview: Parts 1 & 2." Transcripts of *Unknown Legends of Rock 'n' Roll*. Accessed May 5, 2018. http://www.richieunterberger.com/boniwell.html.

Unterberger, Richie. "James Lowe Interview." Transcripts of *Unknown Legends of Rock 'n' Roll*. Accessed May 5, 2018. http://www.richieunterberger.com/lowe.html.

Wienberg, Max. *The Big Beat*. Chicago: Contemporary, 1984.

Wenner, Jann. "Jagger Remembers." *Rolling Stone*, December 14, 1995.

Wenner, Jann. "Pete Townshend Interview." In *The Rolling Stone Interviews*, edited by the editors of *Rolling Stone*. New York: Coronet, 1971.

Whitcomb, Ian. *Rock Odyssey: A Musician's Chronicle of the Sixties*. New York: Dolphin, 1983.

Wyman, Bill. *Blues Odyssey: A Journey to Music's Heart and Soul*. New York: DK, 2001.

Wyman, Bill. *Stone Alone: The Story of a Rock 'n' Roll Band*. New York: Viking, 1990.

"The Yardbirds: Over Under Sideways Down." *Big Takeover*, February 2006.

Chapter 9

"Civil Rights." *1966 Yearbook Britannica*. New York: Britannica, 1966.

Gaye, Marvin, with David Ritz. *Divided Soul: The Life of Marvin Gaye*. New York: McGraw-Hill, 1985.

George, Nelson. *Where Did Our Love Go? The Rise and Fall of the Motown Sound*. New York: St. Martin's, 1985.

Goldberg, Michael. "Berry Gordy." *Rolling Stone*, August 23, 1990.

Gordy, Berry. *To Be Loved: The Music, the Magic, the Memories of Motown*. New York: Warner Books Inc., 1994.

Hall, Russell. "Holland-Dozier-Holland." *Performing Songwriter*, January/February 2009.

Ingham, John, and Lynne Feldman. *African-American Business Leaders: A Biographical Dictionary*. Westport: Greenwood, 1994.

Johnson, Lyndon. "State of the Union Address, January 4, 1965." ThisNation.com. http://www.thisnation.com/library/sotu/1965lj.html

Kiefer, Kit, ed. *They Called It Rock: The Goldmine Oral History of Rock 'N Roll, 1950–1970*. Iola: Krause, 1991.

Kiersh, Edward. *Where Are You Now, Bo Diddley?* New York: Dolphin, 1986.

Kubernik, Harvey. "A Conversation with Mr. Motown: Berry Gordy, Jr." *Goldmine*, March 3, 1995.

"No Town Like Motown." *Newsweek*, March 27, 1965.

Pagoda, Gordon. "Lamont Dozier." *Performing Songwriter*, June 2003.

"Recorddom's Berry Gordy." *Ebony*, February 1966.

Sharp, Ken. "The Temptations' Otis Williams." *Discoveries*, June 2006.

Smith, Joe. *Off the Record: An Oral History of Popular Music*. New York: Warner, 1988.

Smith, Suzanne. *Dancing in the Street*. Cambridge: Harvard, 2000.

"The Supremes Make It Big." *Ebony*, June 1965.

Taraborrelli, Randy. *Motown*. New York: Doubleday, 1986.

Wilson, Mary. *Dreamgirl: My Life as a Supreme*. New York: St. Martin's, 1986.

Chapter 10

Amburn, Ellis. *Subterranean Kerouac: The Hidden Life of Jack Kerouac*. New York: St. Martins, 1998.

Aronowitz, Alfred. "Doors Seek Nirvana Vote Here." *New York Times*, November 25, 1967.

Brown, Joe, ed. *The Hippies*. New York: *Time*, 1967.

Browne, David. *So Many Roads: The Life and Times of the Grateful Dead*. New York: Da Capo, 2015.

Burroughs, William S. *Naked Lunch: The Restored Text*. New York: Grove, 2001.

Chapple, Steve, and Reebee Garofalo. *Rock 'n' Roll Is Here to Pay: The History and Politics of the Music Industry*. Chicago: Nelson-Hall, 1977.

Creeley, Robert. "Poetry of Commitment." *Washington Post*, August 2, 1981.

Eisen, Jonathan. *The Age of Rock, Vol. 2*. New York: Random House, 1970.

Fitch, Vernon. *Pink Floyd: The Press Reports*. Canada: Collector's Guide Press, n.d.

Fong-Torres, Ben. "Grace Slick and Paul Kantner Interview." In *The Rolling Stone Interviews, Vol. 2*, edited by Ben Fong-Torres. New York: Warner, 1973.

Fong-Torres, Ben. "Love Is Just a Song We Sing." *Rolling Stone*, February 26, 1976.

Fricke, David. "Lou Reed Interview." *Rolling Stone*, May 4, 1989.

Ginsberg, Allen. Liner notes for *The Fugs*. ESP.

Gleason, Ralph. "The Flower Children." *Encyclopedia Britannica Book of the Year 1968*. Chicago: Britannica, 1969, pp. 790–791.

Gleason, Ralph. *The Jefferson Airplane and the San Francisco Sound.* New York: Ballantine, 1969.

Goldberg, Michael. "The San Francisco Sound." *Rolling Stone,* August 23, 1990.

Goodman, Fred. "Jerry Garcia Interview." *Rolling Stone,* November 30, 1989.

Graham, Bill. *Bill Graham Presents: My Life Inside Rock and Out.* New York: Doubleday, 1992.

Greenfield, Robert. *Dark Star: An Oral Biography of Jerry Garcia.* New York: Morrow, 1996.

Grushkin, Paul. *The Art of Rock.* New York: Artabras, 1987.

Gustaitis, Rasa. *Turning On.* New York: New American Library, 1969.

Hansen, Jay. *The Other Guide to San Francisco.* San Francisco: Chronicle, 1980.

Henke, Jim, and Parke Puterbaugh, eds. *I Want to Take You Higher: The Psychedelic Era, 1965–1969.* San Francisco: Chronicle, 1997.

Heylin, Clinton. *From the Velvets to the Voidoids: A Pre-Punk History for a Post-Punk World.* New York: Penguin, 1993.

"The Hippies." *Time,* July 7, 1967.

James, Jimmy. "Kevin Ayers Interview." Perfect Sound Forever. May 1998. http://www.furious.com/perfect/kevinayers.html

"Janis/Big Bro Disc Pegs Spirit of Mid '60s S.F. Scene." *Pulse,* April 1985.

Jones, Landon. *Great Expectations: America and the Baby Boom Generation.* New York: Coward, McCann and Geohagen, 1980.

Joplin, Laura. "Love, Janis." *Rolling Stone,* September 3, 1992.

Kubernik, Harvey. *Canyon of Dreams: The Music and Magic of Laurel Canyon.* New York: Sterling, 2009.

Kunen, James Simon as "Simon James." "A Blue Beret Always Does the Best Possible Job Within the Allotted Time." *New York Magazine,* November 11, 1968.

Leuchtenburg, William. *A Troubled Feast: American Society Since 1945.* Boston: Little, Brown, 1973.

Lydon, Michael. "Can the Doors Still 'Light My Fire?'" *New York Times,* January 19, 1969.

"Marty Balin." *Spin,* August 1990.

"Morrison." *Spin,* August 1990.

"Music. Love & Flowers." *Mojo,* July 2007.

Newman, Jason. "The Untold and Deeply Stoned Story of the First U.S. Rock Festival." *Rolling Stone,* June 17, 2014.

"Open Up, Tune In, Turn On: The Airplane." *Time,* June 23, 1967.

Peck, Abe. *Uncovering the Sixties: The Life and Times of the Underground Press.* New York: Pantheon, 1985.

Perry, Charles. "From Eternity to Hell." *Rolling Stone,* February 26, 1976.

Perry, Charles. *The Haight-Ashbury.* New York: Vintage, 1984.

Petros, George. "Ed Sanders Interview." *Seconds #27,* 1994.

Pollack, Bruce. *When the Music Mattered: Rock in the 1960s.* New York: Holt, 1983.

"Pop Records: Moguls, Money and Monsters." *Time,* February 12, 1973.

Reich, Charles, with Jann Wenner. "The Jerry Garcia Interview." *Rolling Stone,* January 20, 1972.

Rodnitzky, Jerome. *Minstrels of the Dawn: The Folk-Protest Singer as a Cultural Hero.* Chicago: Nelson-Hall, 1976.

Roeser, Steve. "Do What You Love: The Continuing Story of Big Brother and the Holding Company." *Goldmine,* September 25, 1998.

Scully, Rock, with David Dalton. *Living with the Dead.* Boston: Little, Brown and Company, 1996.

"Sex as a Spectator Sport." *Time,* July 11, 1969.

Sikes, James. "Swami's Flock Chant in Park to Find Ecstasy: Fifty Followers Clap and Sway to Hypnotic Music at East Side Ceremony." *New York Times,* October 10, 1966.

Thompson, Hunter S. "The Hippies." May 1967. Accessed May 5, 2018. https://distrito47.wordpress.com/2014/02/03/the-hippies-by-hunter-s-thompson/

"This Way to the Egress: The Doors." *Newsweek,* November 6, 1967.

"Timothy Leary Interview." *Playboy,* September 1966.

Troy, Sandy. *One More Saturday Night.* New York: St. Martin's, 1992.

Viorst, Milton. *Fire in the Streets: America in the 60s.* New York: Touchstone, 1979.

"White Rabbit." *Mojo,* December 2002.

Wolfe, Burton. *The Hippies.* New York: New American Library, 1968.

Wolfson, Jill. "Star Plunged from Highs to Depths." *Seattle Times,* November 1, 1981.

Chapter 11

"An American Tragedy: 1967." *Newsweek,* August 7, 1967.

Berkeley in the Sixties. Film transcript. Accessed May 5, 2018. http://www.newsreel.org/transcripts/berkeley-in-the-60s-transcript.pdf.

Brown, Claude. "The Language of Soul." *Esquire,* April 1968.

Brown, James. *James Brown: The Godfather of Soul.* New York: Macmillan, 1986.

Charles, Ray, with David Ritz. *Brother Ray: Ray Charles' Own Story.* New York: Da Capo, 1978.

Ellison, Mary. *The Black Experience.* New York: Harper, 1974.

"The Fire This Time: Cities." *Time,* August 4, 1967.

Garland, Phyl. "Eclipsed Singer Gains New Heights." *Ebony,* October 1967.

Gordon, Robert. *Respect Yourself: Stax Records and the Soul Explosion.* New York: Bloomsbury, 2013, p. 159.

Guralnick, Peter. *Sweet Soul Music.* New York: Harper & Row, 1986.

Hampton, Henry, and Steve Fayer. *Voices of Freedom: An Oral History of the Civil Rights Movement from the 1950s through the 1980s.* New York: Bantam, 1990.

Horowitz, David. *The Professors – The 101 Most Dangerous Academics in America.* New York: Regnery, 2006.

"Lady Soul: Singing Like It Is." *Time,* June 28, 1968.

Llorens, David. "Miracle in Milwaukee." *Ebony,* November 1967.

"Wilson Picket." *Ebony,* October 1968.

"The Magnificent Puts Soul Behind his Work." *Billboard,* May 23, 1964.

O'Neal, Jim, and Amy Van Singel, eds. *The Voice of the Blues.* New York: Rutledge, 2002.

Pearson, Hugh. *In the Shadow of the Panther: Huey Newton and the Price of Black Power in America.* New York: Perseus, 1994.

Rose, Cynthia. *Living in America: The Soul Saga of James Brown.* London: Serpent's Tail, 1990.

Salaam, Kaluma ya. "Historical Overviews of the Black Arts Movement." *Modern American Poetry.* Accessed May 5, 2018. http://www.english.illinois.edu/maps/blackarts/historical.htm.

Santoro, Gene. "James Brown." *Pulse,* October 1986.

Seale, Bobby. "Ten-Point Platform Program & the Formation of the Black Panther Party." February 23, 2015. https://www.linkedin.com/pulse/ten-point-platform-program-formation-black-panther-party-bobby-seale.

"Solomon Burke." *UPI News.* Accessed May 5, 2018. http://www.upi.com/topic/Solomon_Burke/news/2/

"Take Everything You Need, Baby." *Newsweek,* April 15, 1968.

Wilmer, Valerie. "Aretha … Lady Soul." *Downbeat,* August 8, 1968.

Chapter 12

Altman, Keith. "Just Call Me Helium." *Guitar World,* September 2001.

"At War With War." *Time,* May 18, 1970.

Ayers, Bill, Mark Rudd, Bernardine Dohrn, Jeff Jones, Terry Robbinson, Gerry Long, Steve Tappis et. al. "You Don't Need a Weatherman to Know Which Way the Wind Blows." *New Left Notes,* June 18, 1969. https://archive.org/details/YouDontNeedAWeathermanToKnowWhichWayTheWindBlows_925.

"Billy Cox." *Guitar Player,* May 1989.

Black, Johnny. *Jimi Hendrix: The Ultimate Experience.* New York: Thunder's Mouth, 1999.

Cady, Brian. "Roger Mayer: The Man Behind the Hendrix Sound." *Elmore,* March/April 2006.

Clapton, Eric. *Clapton: The Autobiography.* New York: Broadway, 2007.

Clark, Rick. "Wayne Kramer: Wayne's World: Wayne Kramer Talks About the MC5." *Goldmine,* April 17, 1992.

"Class of '69." *Newsweek,* June 23, 1969.

Considine, J. D. "Remember the Sabbath." *Guitar World,* June 1997), pp. 36–40.

Crowe, Cameron. "Jimmy Page and Robert Plant Talk." *Rolling Stone,* March 13, 1975.

Dannemann, Monika. *The Inner World of Jimi Hendrix,* New York: St. Martin's Press, 1995.

Di Perna, Alan. "Smoke Stack Lightning." *Guitar World,* September 2002.

"A Dignified Protest." *Time,* March 29, 1968.

Epstein, Dan. "Black Magic." *Guitar World,* July 2001.

Felder, Rob. "Black Sabbath." *Rolling Stone,* October 19, 1978.

Gabriel, Paul. "Sabbath, Bloody Sabbath: The Enduring Riff-Rock of Black Sabbath." *Discoveries* (June 1996), pp. 32–40.

Ghianni, Tim. "Interview with John Kay." John Kay & Steppenwolf. Accessed May 5, 2018. https://steppenwolf.com/p-4271-interview.html.

Gillies, Kevin. "The Last Radical." *Vancouver,* November 1998.

Gilmore, Mikal."The Allman Brothers." *Rolling Stone,* October 18, 1990.

Graham, Bill. *Bill Graham Presents: My Life Inside Rock and Out.* New York: Doubleday, 1992.

Henderson, David. *Jimi Hendrix: Voodoo Child of the Aquarian Age.* New York: Doubleday, 1978.

"History of Rock-and-Roll." ABC television series.

Isler, Scott. "I Had All These Ideas and Sounds in My Brain: Jimi Hendrix in His Own Words." *Musician,* November 1991.

"Jimi Hendrix in His Own Words." *Musician,* November 1991.

Kitts, Jeff. "To Hell and Back." *Guitar World,* August 1998.

Kubernik, Harvey. *Canyon of Dreams: The Music and Magic of Laurel Canyon.* New York: Sterling, 2009.

Lang, Michael. *The Road to Woodstock.* New York: HarperCollins, 2009.

LeMay, Gen. Curtis Emerson, with MacKinley Kantor, *Mission With LeMay: My Story.* New York: Doubleday, 1965.

"Lifting a Siege." *Time,* May 10, 1968.

McDermott, John. "Strange Brew." *Guitar World,* November 1997.

MC5. *Kick Out the Jams.* Elektra Records, 1969.

Mendelssohn, Jane. "Jimi Hendrix." *International Times,* February 18, 1969.

Milkowski, Bill. *Rockers, Jazzbos and Visionaries.* New York: Billboard, 1998.

"'My God! They're Killing Us.'" *Newsweek,* May 18, 1970.

Nixon, Richard. "Press Conference." *President's News Conference.* May 8, 1970. http://www.presidency.ucsb.edu/ws/?%20pid=2496.

Peck, Abe. *Uncovering the Sixties: The Life and Times of the Underground Press.* New York: Pantheon, 1985.

"The Rebellion of the Campus." *Newsweek,* May 18, 1970.

"Rebirth of the Blues." *Newsweek,* May 26, 1969.

Redding, Noel, and Carol Appleby. "Bad Trips: The End of the Jimi Hendrix Experience." *Musician,* September 1986.

Redding, Noel, and Carol Appleby. "Standing Next to A Mountain: Inside the Jimi Hendrix Experience." *Musician,* August 1986.

Reynolds, Simon. *Totally Wired: Postpunk Interviews and Overviews.* New York: Soft Skull, 2009.

"Report of the President's Commission on Campus Unrest." William W. Scranton, Chairman, Washington, D.C., U.S. Government Printing Office, 1970.

Robble, Andrew, and Debra Desalvo. "Talkin' Blues with the Midnight Rider: Gregg Allman." *Blues Revue,* April/May 1996.

"The Rock Family." *Life,* September 24, 1971.

Shaw, Arnold. *The Rock Revolution.* London: Collier, 1969.

Sinclair, John. *Guitar Army.* Detroit: Douglas, 1972.

Sylvan, Robin. *Traces of Spirit: The Religious Dimensions of Popular Music.* New York: NYU Press, 2002.

Thompson, Dave. "Jeff Beck." *Goldmine,* August 13, 1999.

Tolan, Tom. "40 Years Later, Woodstock Remains a Unique Journey." *Journal Sentinel,* August 8, 2009.

Tolinski, Brad. "Airwaves to Heaven." *Guitar World,* January 1998.

Varon, Jeremy. *Bringing the War Home: The Weather Underground, the Red Army Faction, and Revolutionary Violence in the Sixties and*

Seventies. Berkeley and Los Angeles: University of California Press, 2004.

Viorst, Milton. *Fire in the Streets: America in the 60s.* New York: Touchstone, 1979.

"Voice of Experience: Jimi Hendrix." *Newsweek,* October 9, 1967.

Walker, Daniel. *Rights in Conflict: The violent confrontation of demonstrators and police in the parks and streets of Chicago during the week of the Democratic National Convention of 1968. A report submitted by Daniel Walker, director of the Chicago Study Team, to the National Commission on the Causes and Prevention of Violence.* Accessed May 5, 2018. http://chicago68.com/ricsumm.html.

Webb, Martin. "Just Steal From Everybody: Ritchie Blackmore." *Guitar Player,* Nov. 1973.

Weidman, Rich. *The Doors FAQ: All That's Left to Know about the Kings of Acid Rock.* Milwaukee: Hal Leonard, 2011.

"Woodstock Remembered." *Rolling Stone,* August 24, 1989.

Chapter 13

"Battle of the Bands." Time, May 31, 1976, p. 44.

Doggett, Peter. *Are You Ready for the Country: Elvis, Dylan, Parsons and the Roots of Country Rock.* New York: Penguin, 2001.

"Down to Old Dixie and Back." Time, January 12, 1970.

Einarson, John. *Desperados: The Roots of Country Rock.* New York: Cooper Square, 2001.

"The Girls Letting Go." *Newsweek,* July 14, 1969.

Herbst, Peter. "Linda Ronstadt Interview." *Rolling Stone,* October 19, 1978.

Hilburn, Robert. "Carol King: Return to Simple Values." *Los Angeles Times,* December 3, 1971.

Hilburn, Robert. "Joni Mitchell: The Mojo Interview." *Mojo,* February 2008.

Kubernik, Harvey. *Canyon of Dreams: The Music and Magic of Laurel Canyon.* New York: Sterling, 2009.

Ruhlmann, William."Poco."*Goldmine,* August 20, 1993.

Smith, Joe. *Off the Record: An Oral History of Popular Music.* New York: Warner, 1988.

Soocher, Stan. "The Poco Reunion." *Musician,* February 1990.

"James Taylor: One Man's Family of Rock." *Time,* March 1, 1971.

White, Timothy. "Old Wounds, New Bandages: James Taylor on the Mend." *Musician,* April 1988.

Wild, David. "Joni Mitchell: A Conversation." *Rolling Stone,* May 30, 1991.

Zimmer, Dave. *Crosby, Stills and Nash: The Authorized Biography.* New York: St. Martin's, 1984.

Chapter 14

Bickhart, Jim. "Steely Dan: Mixing the Modes for the Masses." *Downbeat,* September 11, 1975.

"Birth of the First Rock Opera." *Sunday Telegraph,* May 18, 1969.

Carr, Roy. "The Who by Numbers." *New Musical Express,* July 17, 1976.

Coryell, Julie, and Laura Friedman. *Jazz-Rock Fusion: The People, The Music.* New York: Delta, 1978.

Davis, Miles with Quincy Troupe. *Miles: The Autobiography.* New York: Simon and Schuster, 1989.

Eder, Bruce. "The Moody Blues: Veteran Cosmic Rockers." *Goldmine,* October 28, 1994.

Fellezs, Kevin. "Emergency! Race and Genre in Tony Williams' Lifetime." *Jazz Perspectives* 2, no. 1 (May 2008): 1–27.

Fitch, Vernon. *Pink Floyd: The Press Reports.* Canada: Collector's Guide Press, n.d.

Flanagan, Bill. "Songwriter Heaven." *Musician,* November 1992.

Fox, Ted. *In the Groove: The People Behind the Music.* New York: St. Martin's, 1986.

Gaer, Eric. "Emerson, Lake and Palmer: A Musical Force." *Downbeat,* May 9, 1974.

Gallagher, Joe. "Carrying On with Blood, Sweat & Tears." *Downbeat,* July 24, 1969.

Hall, Russell. "Welcome to the Show! Emerson, Lake and Palmer." *Goldmine*, December 6, 1996.

"James Taylor: One Man's Family of Rock." *Time*, March 1, 1971.

Kiefer, Kit, ed. *They Called It Rock: The Goldmine Oral History of Rock 'N Roll, 1950–1970*. Iola: Krause, 1991.

Lyons, Len. *The Great Jazz Pianists*. New York: Da Capo, 1983.

McGrath, Rick, and Mike Quigley. "Chicago: Another Interview with Jimmy Pankow." April 12, 1970. https://www.rocksbackpages.com/Library/Article/chicago-another-interview-with-jimmy-pankow

Milkowski, Bill. *Rockers, Jazzbos and Visionaries*. New York: Billboard, 1998.

Milner, Ronald. "Rock and the Classics." *Guardian*, September 14, 1970.

Myers, Marc. *Why Jazz Happened*. Berkeley: University of California Press, 2013.

"Now, the Self-Centered Generation." *Time*, September 23, 1974.

"Peter Gabriel, Talks." *ZigZag*, May 1971.

"Return to Good-Times Rock." *Time*, June 2, 1975.

Roby, Steven, ed. *Hendrix on Hendrix: Interview and Encounters with Jimi Hendrix*. Chicago: Chicago Review Press, 2012, p. 230

"Rock Goes to College." *Time*, September 23, 1974.

Roeser, Steve. "Yes—Progressing Towards the New Millennium." *Goldmine*, March 13, 1998.

Ruhlmann, William. "Steely Dan: Ironic Distance and Tasty Licks." *Goldmine*, January 22, 1993.

Santana, Carlos. *The Universal Tone: Bringing My Story to Light*. New York: Little, Brown, 2014.

Smith, Arnold. "Billy Cobham: Percussive Ways, Commercial Means, Musician Ends." *Downbeat*, December 4, 1975.

Smith, Joe. *Off the Record: An Oral History of Popular Music*. New York: Warner, 1988.

Stamataky, Harry. "Larry Coryell: More to Come." *Downbeat*, November 9, 1972.

Woodard, Josef. "Career Swings: Stanley Clarke." *Downbeat*, November 1991.

Chapter 15

Bollenberg, John "Bobo." "Rodger Hodgson Interview." Progressive World.net. June 11, 2000. http://www.progressiveworld.net/html/modules.php?name=Interviews&rop=showcontent&id=156.

Brewster, Bill, and Frank Broughton. *Last Night a DJ Saved My Life: The History of the Disc Jockey*. New York: Grove, 1999.

Christopher, Rita. "Every Night Fever." *MacLean's*, May 15, 1977.

Considine, J. D. "Mean Business." *Guitar World*, December 2002.

Crowe, Cameron. "David Bowie Interview." *Playboy*, September 1976.

Di Perna, Alan. "Back from the Dawn of Funk: Billy Bass." *Musician*, December 1993.

Di Perna, Alan. "Larger than Life." *Guitar World*, October 1998.

Di Perna, Alan. "Mac in the Saddle." *Guitar World*, September 1997.

"Disco Takes Over." *Newsweek*, April 2, 1979.

"ELO: American Sees the Light." *Rolling Stone*, August 24, 1978.

"Elton John in His Own Words." Super Seventies Rock Site. Accessed May 5, 2018. http://www.superseventies.com/sseltonjohn.html.

"Elton John Interview." *Playboy*, January 1976.

"Freddie Mercury." *Goldmine*, December 27, 1991.

Fricke, David. "George Clinton." *Rolling Stone*, September 20, 1990.

"The Gorillas Are Coming." *Forbes*, July 10, 1978.

Greenberg, Peter S. "Rock and Big Bucks." *Playboy*, January 1981.

Gross, Jason. "David Johansen Interview." *Perfect Sound Forever*. Accessed May 5, 2018. http://www.furious.com/perfect/davidjohansen.html

"Growth Rocks the Record Industry." *Fortune*, April 23, 1979.

Guitar World Presents Legends of Lead Guitar. Milwaukee: Hal Leonard, 2001.

Halbersberg, Elaine. "Kiss: In Their Own Words." *Billboard*, January 21, 1989.

Heibutzki, Ralph. "Sly and the Family Stone." *Goldmine*, February 18, 1994.

"Hey, Mac." *Newsweek*, May 10, 1976.

Heylin, Clinton. *From the Velvets to the Voidoids: A Pre-Punk History for a Post-Punk World*. New York: Penguin, 1993.

"History of Rock-and-Roll." ABC television series.

"Hotspots of the Urban Night." *Time*, June 27, 1977.

Isler, Scott. "Gregg Geller." *Rolling Stone*, February 22, 1979.

"James Brown." *Musician*, February 1987.

Kiersh, Edward. *Where Are You Now, Bo Diddley?* New York: Dolphin, 1986.

Kohut, Joe, and John Kohut, ed. *Rock Talk*. Winchester, MA: Faber and Faber, 1994.

Leaf, David, and Ken Sharp. *KISS: Behind the Mask*. New York: Grand, 2003.

McCardell, Charles. "Kraftwerk." *Trouser Press*, November 1981.

Miller, Jim. "Britain Rocks America—Again." *Newsweek*, January 23, 1984.

"Now, the Self-Centered Generation." *Time*, September 23, 1974.

Pareles, John. "Kansas." *Rolling Stone*, August 23, 1979.

"Recycler." *Guitar World*, July 1997.

Ressner, Jeffrey. "Freddie Mercury: 1946–1991." *Rolling Stone*, January 9, 1992.

Robinson, Lisa. "Rock Talk." *Tucson Daily Citizen*, January 4, 1977.

"The Rockers Are Rolling in It." *Forbes*, April 15, 1973.

Sharp, Ken. "Roy Wood." *Goldmine*, September 30, 1994.

Smith, Joe. *Off the Record: An Oral History of Popular Music*. New York: Warner, 1988.

Smith, Michael. "Kansas: Songs for America." *Goldmine*, July 14, 2000.

"Style Counsel." *Magnet*, August/September 2002.

Swenson, John. "15 Years of Making Kisstory." *Billboard*, January 21, 1989.

Talese, Gay. *Thy Neighbor's Wife*. New York: Doubleday, 1980.

"Timothy Leary." *MacLean's*, November 15, 1976.

"Tyrannical King Coke." *Time*, April 16, 1973.

Werner, Craig. *A Change Is Gonna Come: Music, Race and the Soul of America*. Ann Arbor: University of Michigan, 2006.

"Where Have the Flowers Gone?" *Newsweek*, September 5, 1977.

White, Timothy. "Earthy Angels: The Bee Gees Talk Dirty and Influence People." *Rolling Stone*, May 17, 1979.

White, Timothy. "Last Tangos, New Beginnings: The Fleetwood Mac Nobody Knows." *Musician*, February 1989.

Wolfe, Tom. *Mauve Gloves and Madmen, Clutter and Vine*. New York: McGraw-Hill, 1976.

Chapter 16

"Anthems of the Blank Generation." *Time*, July 11, 1977.

Apter, Jeff. *Never Enough: The Story of The Cure*. New York: Omnibus Press, 2009.

Azerrad, Michael. "Searching for the Cure." *Rolling Stone*, September 7, 1989.

Blush, Steve, and George Petros, eds. *45 Dangerous Minds: The Most Intensive Interviews from Seconds Magazine*. New York: Creation, 2005.

Burgess, Anthony, and John Lombardi. "Plastic Punks." *Psychology Today*, November 1977.

Cioe, Crispin, and Rafi Zabor. "The New Reggae." *Musician*, November 1981.

Clapton, Eric. Speech. https://www.reddit.com/r/todayilearned/comments/2r3lg8/til_in_1976_eric_clapton_made_a_speech_at_a/.

Cocks, Jay. "The Ska Above, the Beat Below." *Time*, April 7, 1980.

Dancis, Bruce. "Artistic Control and Records Too." *In These Times*, June 4–17, 1980.

Dancis, Bruce. "It's Not Only Rock and Roll: Tom Robinson Talks to ITT." *In These Times*, July 16-22, 1979.

Dancis, Bruce. "Reggae Today: Losing Roots or Paving Way?" *In These Times*, October 25–31, 1978.

Darling, Cary. "An Interview with Joe Strummer." *The Rocket*, May 1984.

Davis, Jerome. *Talking Heads*. New York: Vintage, 1986.

Derienzo, Paul. "Punk Party Brings Back '70s Scenesters and Memories." *The Villager*, October 24, 2013.

Di Perna, Alan. "The Loud Prayer." *Guitar World*, February 1998.

Di Perna, Alan. "The Tall Cool One." *Guitar World*, October 1997.

Egan, Sean. "Nothing's Rotten with the Sex Pistols." *Goldmine*, March 24, 2000.

"Eyewitness." *Q Special Edition: Here's the True Story of Punk*. April 2002.

Flanagan, Bill. "Frontman: John Lydon." *Musician*, July 1994.

Fox, Ted. *In the Groove: The People Behind the Music*. New York: St. Martin's, 1986.

Gilmore, Mikal. "The Clash: Anger on the Left." *Rolling Stone*, March 8, 1979.

Gilmore, Mikal. "Psychodramas You Can Talk To." *Rolling Stone*, November 29, 1979.

Gimarc, George. *Punk Diary: 1970–1979*. New York: St. Martin's, 1994.

Goldberg, Michael. "T. Robinson's Straight Talk about Being Gay." *In These Times*, July 19–25, 1978.

Gross, Jason. "Rough Trade 2: Geoff Travis Interview." *Perfect Sound Forever*. November 1996. http://www.furious.com/perfect/rt.html.

Halasa, Malu. "The English Beat Can't Stop Dancing." *Rolling Stone*, November 13, 1980.

Harron, Mary. "Punk Is Just Another Word for Nothin' Left to Lose." *Village Voice*, March 28, 1977.

Henke, James. "The Clash: There'll Be Dancing in the Streets." *Rolling Stone*, April 17, 1980.

Heylin, Clinton. *Babylon's Burning: From Punk to Grunge*. New York: Canongate, 2007.

Heylin, Clinton. *From the Velvets to the Voidoids: A Pre-Punk History for a Post-Punk World*. New York: Penguin, 1993.

Hill, Michael. "Brat Pack." *Mojo*, February 2001.

Hunt, Chris. "The Damned." *Q Special Edition: Here's the True Story of Punk*. April 2002.

Isler, Scott. "Fear and Loathing on the West Coast." *Trouser Press*, June 1980.

Itzkoff, Dave. "A Word with John Lydon: Life as a 'Great Seething Ball' of Wisdom." *New York Times*, March 30, 2017.

"John Holmstrom: Floating in a Bottle of Formaldehyde." *MetroTimes*, February 4, 2004.

"Johnny Knows He's Not Mad. Can You Say That?" *Record Mirror*, December 11, 1976.

"Johnny's Top of the Pops with Me Says Mrs. Rotten." *Sounds*, June 4, 1977.

Kozak, Roman. *This Ain't No Disco: The Story of CBGB*. Boston: Faber & Faber, 1988.

Lydon, John. *Rotten: No Irish—No Blacks—No Dogs*. New York: St. Martin's, 1994.

McCormick, Moira. "Richard Hell." *Trouser Press*, November 1982.

McNeil, Legs. "The Devil Finds Work for Idol Hands to Do." *Spin*, September 1990.

McNeil, Legs, and Gillian McCain. *Please Kill Me: An Uncensored Oral History of Punk*. New York: Grove, 1996.

McNeil, Legs, and John Holmstrom. "We're a Happy Family." *Spin*, August 1986.

"Mick Jones." *Musician*, June 1995.

Miles. "The Clash: Eighteen Flight Rock." *New Musical Express*, December 11, 1976.

Noakes, Tim. "Genesis Breyer P-Orridge." *Medium*, October 19, 2016.

Palmer, Robert. "Joy Division." *Musician*, August 1988.

Peisch, Jeffrey, series producer. *History of Rock and Roll*. 10 episodes, film made for television. March 1995.

Perry, Mark. "We Love UHU." *Q Special Edition: Here's the True Story of Punk*. May 2002.

"Punk." *London Times*, November 28, 1976.

"Punk or Prep." *Mademoiselle*, June 1980.

Reynolds, Simon. *Totally Wired: Postpunk Interviews and Overviews*. New York: Soft Skull, 2009.

Rock Against Racism. Liner notes.

Savage, Jon. *England's Dreaming: Anarchy, Sex Pistols, Punk Rock and Beyond*. New York: St. Martin's, 2001.

Smith, Patti. *Just Kids*. New York: Harper Collins, 2010. P. 245.

Stokes, Paul. "The Art of Noise." *Q Special Edition: Here's the True Story of Punk*. May 2002.

"The Top 100." *Rolling Stone*, November 16, 1989.

Unterberger, Richie. *Unknown Legends of Rock 'n' Roll*. San Francisco: Miller Freeman, 1998.

Vermorel, Fred, and Judy Vermorel. *Sex Pistols: The Inside Story*. London: Omnibus, 1987.

Watrous, Peter. "Sting." *Musician*, December 1987.

"We Gotta Get Out of This Place." *Mojo*, October 2001.

Wild, David. "Elvis Costello Interview." *Rolling Stone*, June 1, 1989.

Wilkinson, Roy. "Buzzcocks." *Q Special Edition: Here's the True Story of Punk*. May 2002.

Wilson, Lois. "Gangsters." *Mojo*, May 2008.

Wilson, Lois. "Tatty Threads." *Q Special Edition: Here's the True Story of Punk*. May 2002.

"X-Ray Spex." *Mojo*, October 2001.

Young, Charles M. "Visions of Patti." *Rolling Stone*, July 27, 1978.

Zabor, Rafi. "John Lydon's PiL." *Musician*, November 1984.

Zuckerman, Ed. "The Rise of Rock Against Racism." *Rolling Stone*, December 14, 1978.

Chapter 17

Arnold, Gina. *Route 666: On the Road to Nirvana*. New York: St. Martin's, 1993.

Azerrad, Michael. *This Band Could Be Your Life*. New York: Little, Brown, 2001.

Blush, Steven. *American Hardcore: A Tribal History*. Los Angeles: Feral, 2001.

Donny the Punk. "The Dead Kennedys' State of Confusion." *Spin*, February 1986.

Emsminger, David. *Left of the Dial: Conversations with Punk Icons*. Oakland: PM Press, 2013.

Lee, Ranking Jeffrey (a.k.a. Jeffrey Lee Pierce). "Circle Jerks: A Hard Act to Swallow." *New York Rocker*, September 1981.

Goldberg, Michael. "Punk Lives." *Rolling Stone*, July 18–August 1, 1985.

Grad, David. "Fade to Black: The Rough and Ruly History of Hardcore Legends Black Flag." *Guitar World*, July 1997.

Looram, Ed. "Ian MacKaye." *Tokoin*, September 2003.

McDonnell, Evelyn. "X's New World Order." *Rolling Stone*, June 24, 1993.

Morris, Chris. "Bob Mould: Shaken, Stirred and Fueled." *Musician*, October 1994.

Pareles, Jon. "Henry Rollins: The Loner." *Musician*, April 1993.

Perry, Steve. "Achin' To Be Understood." *Musician*, February 1989.

Rhulmann, William. "X: They're Still Desperate, But They're Used to It." *Goldmine*, February 4, 1994.

Sinker, Daniel, ed. *We Owe You Nothing—Punk Planet: The Collected Interviews*. New York: Akashic, 2001.

Sommer, Tom. "Black Flag." *Trouser Press*, June 1983.

Spitz, Marc, and Brendan Mullen. *We Got the Neutron Bomb: The Untold Story of L.A. Punk*. New York: Three Rivers, 2001.

"Top 100." *Rolling Stone*, November 16, 1989.

Unterberger, Richie. "Chip Kinman Interview." Transcripts of *Unknown Legends of Rock 'n' Roll*. Accessed May 5, 2018. http://www.richieunterberger.com/kinman.html.

Chapter 18

Canemaker, John. "Over the Edge with MTV." *Print*, September/October 1992.

Cocks, Jay. "Why He's a Thriller." *Time*, March 19, 1984.

Connelly, Christopher. "Ratt: Lap Dogs of the Devil?" *Rolling Stone*, December 6, 1984.

Considine, John. "The Sons of Aerosmith." *Musician*, August 1988.

"The Copycats That Are Chasing Music Television." *Business Week*, September 3, 1984.

Dennison, Serge. *Tarnished Gold: The Record Industry Revisited*. New York: Transaction, 1986.

DiMartino, Dave. "Decalog." *Billboard*, December 23, 1989.

"Duran Duran." *Trouser Press*, October 1983.

"The Eurythmics." *Trouser Press*, October 1983.

Flanagan, Bill. "We Three Kings: The Top Managers." *Musician*, April 1991.

Fricke, David. "Dress Right!" *Rolling Stone*, July 23, 1981.

Green, Jim. "Culture Club Comes Clean." *Trouser Press*, June 1983.

"Human League." *Trouser Press*, August 1982.

"It Completely Cured Him." *Sun*, December 29, 2016.

Jaffee, Larry. "What Has Video Wrought: Part I." *Pulse!*, September 1986.

Jaffee, Larry. "What Has Video Wrought: Part II." *Pulse!*, October 1986.

"Joe Jackson." *Billboard*, December 23, 1989.

Kaplan, Peter. "MTV: 21st Century Box." *Esquire*, March 1983.

Lupo, Jane. "Spandau Ballet." *Trouser Press*, September 1981.

Mackay, Gillian. "The New Wizard of Pop." *MacLean's*, July 23, 1984.

"Midge Ure." *Blitz*, 1982.

Milano, Brett. "Def Leppard Roars Back." *Pulse*, September 1987.

Miller, Jim. "Britain Rocks America—Again." *Newsweek*, January 23, 1984.

Miller, Jim. "The Peter Pan of Pop." *Newsweek*, January 10, 1983.

"New York Meets Steve Strange." *Trouser Press*, 1982.

Perry, Steve. "Prince in the Purple Decade." *Musician*, November 1988.

Reynolds, Simon. *Totally Wired: Postpunk Interviews and Overviews*. New York: Soft Skull, 2009.

Rockmaker, Deirdre. "Def Leppard: The Heavy Metal Band You Can Bring Home to Your Mother." *Goldmine*, June 11, 1993.

Rosen, Steven. "On Fire." *Guitar World*, March 2003.

Rowland, Mark. "Dreaming: Def Leppard." *Musician*, April 1992.

Salewicz, Chris. "Kemp: A Revolt into Style." *The Face*, October 1982.

Scaggs, Austin. "Madonna Looks Back." *Rolling Stone*, October 29, 2009.

Schaffner, Nicholas. *The British Invasion*. New York: McGraw-Hill, 1983.

Silverman, Leigh. "Finding Fame without Fortune." *Rolling Stone*, September 21, 1989.

"Sing a Song of Seeing." *Time*, December 26, 1983.

"Spandau Ballet." *Trouser Press*, May 1982.

Swenson, John. "15 Years of Making Kisstory." *Billboard*, January 21, 1989.

Tannenbaum, Rob, and Craig Marks. *I Want My MTV: The Uncensored Story of the Music Video Revolution*. New York: Penguin, 2012.

"Top 100." *Rolling Stone*, November 16, 1989.

"Van Halen." *Musician*, August 1991.

"Van Halen." Warner Brother Press release for First Album. 1978.

"Visage." *Blitz*, 982, pp. 5–8.

Vozick-Levinson, Simon. "Quincy Jones on *Thriller*." *Entertainment*. February 7, 2008.

Young, Charles. "Def Leppard Pulls Out of the Fast Lane." *Musician*, December 1987.

Young, Jon. "Keys to the Future." *Trouser Press*, May 1982.

Zoglin, Richard. "MTV Faces a Mid Life Crisis." *Time*, June 29, 1987.

Chapter 19

"Amnesty's Human-Rights Trek Rocks the States." *Rolling Stone*, November 3, 1988.

"The Backstreet Phantom of Rock." *Time*, October 27, 1975.

Barol, Bill. "I Ain't Gonna Play Sun City." *Time*, October 28, 1985.

Cocks, Jay. "Band on the Run: U2 Soars." *Time*, April 27, 1987.

Cocks, Jay. "Roll Them Bones." *Time*, September 4, 1989.

DiMartino, Dave. "Decalog." *Billboard*, December 23, 1989.

DiMartino, Dave, and Ed Christman. "CD Edges Up on Cassette as Top Format." *Billboard*, June 23, 1990.

Flippo, Chet. "Bruce Springsteen." *Musician*, November 1984.

Forman, Bill. "R.E.M.: Diminished But Unafraid, R.E.M. Talks About Passion." *Pulse*, November 1998.

Garland, Susan. "Those Aging Boomers." *Business Week*, May 20, 1991.

Henke, James. "Springsteen." *Rolling Stone*, August 6, 1992.

Hilburn, Robert. "Q: What 'Star' to 5 Years to Shine? A: News 'Cover-boy' Bruce Springsteen." *Oregonian*, October 24, 1980.

Hutchinson, John. "Luminous Times: U2." *Musician*, October 1987.

Loder, Kurt. "Bruce Springsteen Interview." *Rolling Stone*, December 6, 1984.

Macdonald, Patrick. "Vinyl's Final Days." *Seattle Times*, January 21, 1990, p. L1-L2.

McBee, Susanna. "Are Today's Young a Disillusioned Generation?" *U.S. News and World Report*, January 23, 1984.

Nelson, Paul. "Springsteen Fever." *Rolling Stone*, July 13, 1978.

Olliffe, Michael. "R.E.M. in Perth." *On the Street*. January 17, 1995.

Orth, Maureen, Janet Huck, and Peter Greenberg. "Making of a Rock Star." *Newsweek*, October 27, 1975.

Peisch, Jeffrey, series producer. *History of Rock and Roll*. 10 episodes, film made for television. March 1995.

Ressner, Jeffrey. "Going, Going, Gone?" *Rolling Stone*, April 20, 1989.

"Story 1985-01-19." *BruceBase*. Accessed May 5, 2018. https://bruce-base.wikispaces.com/1985-01-19+-+GREENSBORO+COLISEUM%2C+GREENSBORO%2C+NC

Stout, Gene. "Rock Radio Drags On." *Seattle Post-Intelligencer*, July 17, 1988.

Tannenbaum, Rob, and Craig Marks. *I Want My MTV: The Uncensored Story of the Music Video Revolution*. New York: Penguin, 2012.

"Technology." *Time*, January 1, 1990.

"The Top 100." *Rolling Stone*, November 16, 1989.

Wenner, Jann. "Bono: The Rolling Stone Interview." *Rolling Stone*, November 5, 2005.

Chapter 20

Cocks, Jay. "Friends in Low Places." *Time*, March 30, 1992.

Cocks, J., and E. L. Bland. "Country Classicists." *Time*, September 24, 1990.

Decurtis, Anthony. "Ropin' the Whirlwind." *Rolling Stone*, April 1, 1993.

Doggett, Peter. *Are You Ready for the Country: Elvis, Dylan, Parsons and the Roots of Country Rock*. New York: Penguin, 2001.

Hirshberg, Charles. "He's Garth Brooks." *Life*, July 1992.

Light, Alan. "Forever Young." *Rolling Stone*, January 21, 1993.

Painton, Priscilla. "Country Rocks the Boomers." *Time*, March 30, 1992.

Pareles, Jon. "Garth Brooks: Genial Superstar." *New York Times*, September 7, 1992.

Pareles, Jon. "When Country Music Moves to the Suburbs." *New York Times*, November 25, 1990.

Pond, Steve. "The Playboy Interview: Garth Brooks." *Playboy*, June 1994.

Schoemer, Kaen. "On the Tube: Country Music Can't Go Down-Home Again." *New York Times*, February 9, 1992.

Chapter 21

Arnold, Gina. "Nirvana: Punk Philosophers." In *We Rock You So You Don't Have To: The Option Reader*, edited by Scott Becker. New York: Incommunicado, 1998.

Arnold, Gina. *Route 666: On the Road to Nirvana*. New York: St. Martin's, 1993.

Azerrad, Michael. *Come As You Are: The Story of Nirvana*. New York: Doubleday, 1993.

Azerrad, Michael. "Inside the Heart and Mind of Kurt Cobain." *Rolling Stone*, April 16, 1992.

Azerrad, Michael. *Our Band Could Be Your Life*. New York: Little Brown, 2001.

Azerrad, Michael. "When Things Get Heavy." *Rolling Stone*, November 3, 1988.

Bienstock, Richard. "Thrash of the Titans." *Guitar World*, August 2003.

Blush, Steve and George Petros, eds. *45 Dangerous Minds: The Most Intensive Interviews from Seconds Magazine*. New York: Creation, 2005.

Borzillo, Carrie. *Nirvana: The Day-by-Day Eyewitness Chronicle*. New York: Thunder Mouth, 2000.

Bosc, Michael. "Street Gangs No Longer Just a Big City Problem." *U.S. News and World Report*, July 16, 1984.

Browne, David. "Recordings View; Seattle Rock." *New York Times*, November 18, 1990.

Cameron, Keith. "Spirit of '88." *Mojo*, August 2008.

Coddington, Grace. "Grunge and Glory." *Vogue*, December 1992.

Darms, Lisa. *The Riot Grrrl Collection*. New York: Feminist Press, 2013.

DiMartino, Dave. "A Seattle Slew." *Rolling Stone*, September 20, 1990.

Di Perna, Alan. "The Defiant Ones." *Guitar World*, October 2003.

Di Perna, Alan. "Jackhammer of the Gods." In *Guitar World Presents Alternative Rock*, edited by Jeff Kitts, Brad Tolinski, and Harold Steinblatt. Milwaukee: Hal Leonard, 1999.

Di Perna, Alan. "Machine Head." *Guitar World*, April 1994.

Di Perna, Alan. "Never More: The Life and Death of Kurt Cobain." *Guitar World*, March 1999.

Drozdowski, Ted. "Full Metal Justice." *Musician*, January 1989.

Drozdowski, Ted. "Heavy Mettle." *Musician*, March 1997.

Dunn, Katherine. "Courtney Love." *Rolling Stone*, November 13, 1997.

Fricke, David. "Don't Tread on Me: Metallica's James Hetfield." *Rolling Stone*, April 15, 1993.

Fricke, David. "Heavy Metal Justice." *Rolling Stone*, January 12, 1989.

Fricke, David. "Life After Death: Courtney Love." *Rolling Stone*, December 15, 1994.

Fricke, David. "Our Man in Nirvana Rages on (and on) about Stardom, Fatherhood, His Feud with Pearl Jam." *Rolling Stone*, January 27, 1994.

Garbarini, Vic. "Architects of Grunge." *Guitar One*, May 2004.

Garcia, Guy. "Heavy Metal Goes Platinum." *Time*, October 14, 1991.

Gitter, Mike. "Somber No More?" *Pulse!*, September 1991.

Gold, Jonathan. "Trent Reznor of Nine Inch Nails." *Rolling Stone*, September 8, 1994.

Goldberg, Michael. "The Twisted Genius of Rock-and-Roll Poster Boy Frank Kozik." *Cover Story*, 1997. http://www.addict.com/1.01/Cover_Story/.

Grad, David. "Rock Steady: Rancid." *Guitar World*, August 1998.

Greene, Jo-Ann. "Welcome to Paradise: The Story of Green Day." *Goldmine*, September 15, 1995.

Halbersberg, Elianne. "The Majors." *Billboard*, May 6, 1989.

Henke, Ronald. "Kids Are Killing, Dying, Bleeding." *Fortune*, August 10, 1992.

Hochman, Steve. "Eddie's New Jam." *Los Angeles Times*, October 18 1992.

Holland, Dexter. "Opinion." *Musician*, June 1994.

Kelly, Christina. "Dad, I'm a Degenerate: D Generation." *Rolling Stone*, February 9, 1995.

Lanham, Tom. "Generation Why?" *Musician*, September 1994.

Macnie, Jim. "Soundgarden's Full Punk Power Slide." *Musician*, February 1990.

Moore, John. "Diamond Head: Living on Borrowed Time." *Goldmine*, June 11, 1993.

Mudrian, Albert. *Choosing Death: The Improbable History of Death Metal and Grindcore*. Los Angeles: Feral House, 2004.

Mundy, Chris. "Nirvana." *Rolling Stone*, January 23, 1992.

Neely, Kim. "Into the Unknown." *Rolling Stone*, June 16, 1994.

Pike, Jeff. "At Long Last, Seattle is Suddenly Hot." *Billboard*, August 18, 1990.

Podhoretz, John. "Metallic Rock That's Designed to Shock." *U.S. News and World Report*, September 7, 1987.

Postel, Eric. "Heavy Metal Thunder!" *Pulse*, September 1983.

Powers, Ann. "No Longer Rock's Playthings." *New York Times*, February 14, 1993.

Prato, Greg. *Grunge Is Dead: The Oral History of Seattle Rock Music*. New York: ECW, 2009.

Ramirez, Marc. "Bliss Out." *Pacific Magazine, Seattle Times/Seattle Post Intelligencer*, April 26, 1992.

Reid, Larry. "Smells Like Prozac." *The Rocket*, September 28/October 12, 1994.

Stout, Gene. "Rockin' and Rollin' the Boat." *Seattle Post-Intelligencer*, March 24, 1990.

Uchitelle, Louis. "America Isn't Creating Enough Jobs, and No One Seems to Know Why." *The New York Times*, September 6, 1992.

Unterberger, Richie. "Jack Endino Interview." Accessed May 6, 2018. http://www.richieunterberger.com/endino.html.

White, Richard. "Sub Pop: Indie Marketing Phenomenon." *Pulse!* (Independent Special), 1989.

Weidenbaum, Marc. "Re: Garage Days Revisited." *Pulse!*, September 1990.

Wiederhorn, Jon. "Bathed in Blood: The Incredible Oral History of the Florida Death-Metal Revolution." *Revolver*, January 2009.

Wiederhorn, Jon. "The Devil Inside." *Guitar World*, July 1998.

Yarm, Mark. *Everybody Loves Our Town: An Oral History of Grunge*. New York: Crown, 2011.

Chapter 22

Aledort, Andy. "Phish Scales." *Guitar World*, August 2000.

Aston, Martin. "2+2=5." *Mojo*, August 2006.

Bronson, Fred. "Remembering When the Spice Girls 'Wannabe' Hit Number 1." *Billboard*, February 22, 2017.

Considine, J. D. "Interview with Dave." *Guitar World Acoustic*.

Hall, Russell. "Widespread Panic." *Performing Songwriter*, June 2002.

Harris, John. *Britpop!: Cool Britannia and the Spectacular Demise of English Rock*. New York: Da Capo Press, 2004.

Harris, John. "The Britpop Years." *Independent*, May 6, 2003.

Harris, John. "A Shite Sports Car and a Punk Reincarnation." *New Musical Express*, April 10, 1993.

Kent, Nick. "Ghost in the Machine." *Mojo*, August 2006.

Kot, Greg. "Grateful Dead to Celebrate 50 Years at Soldier Field This Summer." *Chicago Tribune*, January 16, 2015.

Martell, Nevin. *Dave Matthews Band: Music for the People*. New York: Pocket Books, 2004.

McFarland, Melanie. "Don't Hate Me Because I'm Powerful." *Seattle Times*, August 2, 1998.

Perry, Andrew. "Last Orders." *Mojo*, April 2003.

Rowland, Mark. "Don't Sign Anyone Over 30." *Musician*, April 1998.

Sutcliff, Phil. "Top of the World, Man." *Q*, February 1996.

Chapter 23

Aaron, Charles. "What the White Boy Means When He Says Yo." *Spin*, November 1998.

Azerrad, Michael. "Public Enemy." *Rolling Stone*, September 22, 1988.

Batey, Angus. "Spin City." *Mojo*, August 2003.

Berman, Eric. "The Godfathers of Rap." *Rolling Stone*, December 23, 1993/January 6, 1994.

Bozza, Anthony. *Whatever You Say I Am: The Life and Times of Eminem*. New York: Crown, 2003.

Brewster, Bill, and Frank Broughton. *Record Players: DJ Revolutionaries*. New York: Black Cat, 2010.

Chang, Jeff. *Can't Stop Won't Stop: A History of the Hip-Hop Generation*. New York: St. Martin's, 2005.

Chuck D, with Yufuf Jah. *Fight the Power: Rap, Race and Reality*. New York: Delacorte, 1997.

Donloe, Darlene. "Mintin' Majors." *Billboard*, November 24, 1990.

Eliscu, Jenny. "50 Cent Goes Hollywood." *Rolling Stone*, November 25, 2004.

Ex, Kris. "Jay-Z." *Vibe*, December 2000.

Fernando, S. H. *The New Beats: Exploring the Music, Culture and Attitudes of Hip-Hop*. New York: Anchor, 1994.

Flanagan, Bill. "Black History: Speech Meets Curtis Mayfield." *Musician*, June 1993.

Forman, Murray, and Mark Anthony Neal, eds. *That's the Joint! The Hip-Hop Studies Reader*. New York: Routledge, 2004.

Gardner, Elysa. "Watching the Detectives." *Musician*, October 1994.

George, Nelson, Sally Barnes, Susan Flinker, and Patty Romanowski. *Fresh: Hip Hop Don't Stop*. New York: Random, 1985.

Gold, Jonathan. "The Day of the Dre." *Rolling Stone*, September 30, 1993.

"Greatest Albums of the Nineties." *Spin*, September 1999.

Heibutzki, Ralph. "The Hip Hop Revolution." *Goldmine*, May 24, 1996.

Henderson, Alex. "Artists on Image." *Billboard*, December 24, 1988.

Hirschberg, Lynn. "The Music Man: Can Rick Rubin Dave the Record Business?" *The New York Times Magazine*, September 2, 2007.

Hochman, Steve. "NWA: Keeping Attitude Alive." *Musician*, March 1991.

"Is Rock and Roll Dead?" *Rolling Stone*, December 13–27, 1990.

Light, Alan. "Boyz II Men." *Rolling Stone*, March 5, 1992.

Light, Alan. "Ice." *Rolling Stone*, August 20, 1992.

Light, Alan. "L.A. Rappers Speak Out." *Rolling Stone*, June 25, 1992.

Martinez, Gerald, Diana Martinez, and Andres Chavez. *What It Is … What It Was!: Black Film Explosion of the '70s in Words and Pictures*. New York: Hyperion, 1998.

McAdams, Janine. "A Message of Peace Outta Compton." *Billboard*, May 5, 1990.

Munoz, Lorenza. "Where Black and White Youth Meet." *Los Angeles Times*, October 9, 1999.

Nathan, David. "Jungle Brothers Bear Civilized Message." *Billboard*, March 3, 1990.

Nathan, David. "Lauryn Hill: Next Big Miss Thang." *Pulse!*, March 1999.

Nathan, David. "Major Labels Are Suddenly Singing a Different Tune." *Billboard*, December 24, 1988.

Nguyen, Hao. "Hip-Hop Gem: Ice-T's '6 in the Mornin'" Was Inspired by Schoolly D's "P. S. K. What Does It Mean?" Stop the Breaks. December 18, 2014. http://www.stopthebreaks.com/gems/ice-t-6-in-the-mornin-inspired-by-schoolly-d-psk.

O'Brien, Patti. "Rap It Up." *Rolling Stone*, July 12–26, 1990.

Pareles, Jon. "Run-D.M.C.: Making Rap Safe for Heavy Metal Fans." *Rolling Stone*, July 18/August 1, 1995.

Peisch, Jeffrey, series producer. *History of Rock and Roll*. 10 episodes, film made for television. March 1995.

Perkins, William Eric, ed. *Droppin' Science: Critical Essays on Rap Music and Hip Hop Culture*. Philadelphia: Temple University Press, 1996.

"Rapper Ice-T Defends Song Against Spreading Boycott." *New York Times*, June 19, 1992.

Rogers, Sheila. "New Edition's New Division." *Rolling Stone*, September 21, 1990.

Rowland, Mark. "Ice T: The Code of Many Colors." *Musician*, August 1991.

Rule, Sheila. "Rappers' Words Foretold Depth of Blacks' Anger." *The New York Times*, May 26, 1992.

Russell, Lisa. "M.C. Hammer." *People*, June 24, 1990.

Samuels, Allison. "From Raunch to Romance." *Newsweek*, April 6, 1998.

Samuels, Allison. "Straight Outta Cleveland." *Newsweek*, July 28, 1997.

Samuels, Allison, N'GaiCroal, and David Gates. "Battle for the Soul of Hip Hop." *Newsweek*, October 9, 2000.

Samuels, David. "Yo! MTV Unwrapped." *Spin*, September 1991.

Sanneh, Kelefa."Gettin' Paid: Jay-Z, Criminal Culture and the Rise of Corporate Rap." *New Yorker*, August 20 & 27, 2001.

Scaggs, Austin. "Jay-Z Interview." *Rolling Stone*, November 29, 2007.

Shaw, William. "A Bronx Tale." *Details*, November 1998.

Spady, James, Charles Lee, and Hesham Samy Alim. *Street Conscious Rap*. Philadelphia: Loh, 1999.

Stacey, Ringo. "Public Enemy – Chuck D Interview." *Quietus*, May 20, 2008.

Stout, Gene. "L.L. Proves Cool." *Seattle Post-Intelligencer*, May 17, 1991.

Toop, David. *Rap Attack 2: African Rap to Global Hip Hop*. New York: Serpent's Tail, 1991.

White, Armond. *Rebel for the Hell of It: The Life of Tupac Shakur*. New York: Thunder's Mouth, 1997.

"X-Men: Run-D.M.C. Look Back." *Pulse!*, July 1993.

Chapter 24

Baraka, Ras. "Return of the Hard." *The Source*, October 1991.

Brewster, Bill, and Frank Broughton. *Record Players: DJ Revolutionaries*. New York: Black Cat, 2010.

Considine, John. "2 Turntables and a Loud Guitar." *Guitar World*, November 1997.

Derogatis, Jim. "Deftones: Feed your Head." *Guitar World*, September 2003.

Di Perna, Alan. "Getting Better All the Time: Red Hot Chili Peppers." *Guitar World*, August 2002.

Di Perna, Alan. "Staind Class." *Guitar World*, September 2001.

Ehrlich, Dimitri. "Phat Cats and Punks." *Rolling Stone*, August 19, 1993.

"Faith No More." *Guitar World*, June 2003.

Flick, Larry. "Wind-Up's Creed Has 'Weathered' Success." *Billboard*, November 10, 2001.

Gill, Chris. "Got the Life." *Guitar World*, April 1999.

Gill, Chris. "Raising Hell." *Guitar World*, April 1999.

Graff, Gary. "Meet Kid Rock." *Guitar World*, February 2002.

Guitar One Presents Legends of the Lead Guitar: The Best of the Interviews 1995–2000. New York: Cherry Lane, 2001.

Gulla, Bob. "Forecast: Heavy Weathered." *Guitar One*, January 2002.

Heath, Chris. "Creed's Stairway to Heaven." *Rolling Stone*, February 28, 2002.

Levine, Daniel. "Black Sheep." In *Guitar World Presents Alternative Rock*, edited by Jeff Kitts, Brad Tolinski, and Harold Steinblatt. Milwaukee: Hal Leonard, 1999.

"Mike Bordin Interview." http://www.lunarpages.com/mrbungle/inter03.html.

"The New Power Generation." *Guitar World*, September 2001.

Nugent, Benjamin. "Rock at the Top." *Time*, December 17, 2001.

Paul, Alan. "Milk Money." *Guitar World*, May 2002.

Recording Industries Association of America Report 2000.

Ressner, Jeffrey. "Thrashers Pay Tribute to Rap." *Rolling Stone*, August 8, 1991.

Roeser, Steve. "Anthrax: Spreading the Metal." *Goldmine*, April 17, 1992.

Rowland, Mark. "Crap Killer." *Musician*, January 1993.

"World Overview." International Federation of the Phonographic Industry. 2000.

Chapter 25

Adegoke, Yinka. "Vivendi Chief Says Universal Will Keep Artists." *Reuters*, October 16, 2007.

Anderson, Chris. *The Long Tail: Why the Future of Business is Selling More of Less*. New York: Hyperion, 2006.

Brandle, Lars. "Radiohead in Direct-Licensing Deal." *Billboard*, October 9, 2007.

"Business: A Change of Tune; The Music Industry." *The Economist*, July 7, 2007.

Crosley, Hillary. "Ready for Duty." *Billboard*, September 22, 2007.

DeMain, Bill. "The Indie Power List." *Performing Songwriter*, December 2007.

Featherly, Kevin. "Long-Time File-Swappers Buy More Music, Not Less." *Newsbytes*, April 25, 2002.

"File Traders Could Do Hard Time." *Wired*, September 28, 2004.

Gabriella. "Interview with David Draiman." New York Rock. November 2000. http://76.12.46.30/interviews/2001/disturbed_int.asp.

Goodell, Jeff. "Steve Jobs Interview." *Rolling Stone*, December 25, 2003–January 8, 2004.

Grossman, Lev. "The Battle Over Music Piracy." *Time*, May 24, 2007.

Graham, Jefferson. "Does iTunes Finally Have a Rival?" *USA Today*, March 26, 2008.

Hirschberg, Lynn. "The Music Man." *The New York Times Magazine*, September 2007.

"iTunes Music Store Downloads Top One Billion Songs." *Apple Newsletter*, February 23, 2006.

International Federation of the Phonographic Industry. "Global Recorded Music Sales Down 5% in First Half of 2001." September 28, 2001, press release.

Kot, Greg. "A New Perspective from Radiohead's Thom Yorke." *San Diego Union-Tribune*, September 24, 2003.

Kot, Greg. *Ripped: How the Wired Generation Revolutionized Music*. New York: Scribner, 2009.

Langer, Andy. "The Insider: Scott Lapatine." *The Austin Chronicle*, March 16, 2007.

Leeds, Jeff. "This One's on Trent Reznor." *New York Times*, May 6, 2008.

Morrison, Allen. "Navigating the Digital Jungle." *Downbeat*, April 2015.

Reznor, Trent. Post on personal website. October 8, 2007.

Seabrook, John. "The Price of a Ticket." *The New Yorker*, August 10 & 17, 2009.

Seabrook, John. "Revenue Streams: Is Spotify the Music Industry's Friend or Foe." *The New Yorker*, November 24, 2014.

Smith, Ethan. "Sales of Music, Long in Decline, Plunge Sharply." *The Wall Street Journal*, March 21, 2007.

Thompson, Derek. "The Shazam Effect." *The Atlantic*, December 2014.

Westergren, Tim. "Music Genome Project Statement of Purpose." 2000.

"Woman Fined £100,000 for Illegal File Sharing." *Guardian Unlimited*, October 5, 2007.

Chapter 26

"About Music For America." Music for America Website. October 15, 2003. http://www.musicforamerica.org/about.

"About Punkvoter.com." Punkvoter Website. Accessed May 6, 2018. http://punkvoter.com/about/about.html.

"America … In God We Trust." Teen Ink. 2001.

Baker, James A., III, and Lee H. Hamilton. *The Iraq Study Group Report: The Way Forward - A New Approach*. New York: Vintage, 2006.

Ball, Jeffrey. "In Climate Controversy, Industry Cedes Ground." *Wall Street Journal*, January 23, 2007.

Bromley, Adrian. "Disturbing the Mainstream: CoC Talks to Dani Filth." Chronicles of Chaos. March 16, 2003. http://www.chroniclesofchaos.com/articles.aspx?id=1-579.

Davis, Kimberly. "The Many Faces of Kanye West." *Ebony*, June 2004.

DeMain, Bill. "Ben Harper: Stardust Melodies." *Performing Songwriter*, March/April, 2006.

Kalet, Hank. "The Music of Politics." *Progressive Populist*, April 16, 2004.

Malernee, Jamie. "Youth Vote Lost in Large Turnout in the 2004 Presidential Election." *South Florida Sun-Sentinel*, November 7, 2004.

Mayer, John. "Waiting on the World to Change – entry Number 1." Personal blog #329. http://www.johnmayer.com/blog#329.

McEvoy, Chris. "Political Rock 2004." *National Review,* August 9, 2004.

MTV/CBS. "News Poll: Environment." Conducted May 30 to June 9, 2006. Accessed May 6, 2018. https://www.rockthevote.com/wp-content/uploads/publications/research/mtv_cbs_environment_poll-2006.pdf

Neal, Chris. "Back from Bedlam." *Performing Songwriter*, November 2007.

"Our Mission." Hip-Hop Summit Action Network website.

Prozak, Spinoza Ray. "Interview: Quorthon." Anus. 2002. http://www.anus.com/metal/about/interviews/quorthon.

Riememschneider, Chris. "Younger Generation of Musicians Turns Political." *Star Tribune*, October 5, 2004.

Rock Against Bush, Vol. 1. Liner notes. Fat Wreck Chords, 2004.

"Satyr Interview." Metal-Experience.com. March 24, 2007. http://www.metal-experience.com/interviews/Interview%20Satyricon%20int.htm.

Schwarz, Paul. "An Extravagant Rebel Conquest: CoC Talks to Satyr of Satyricon." Chronicles of Chaos. April 3, 1999. http://www.chroniclesofchaos.com/articles.aspx?id=1-216.

Schwarz, Paul. "In Deep with the Deacons of the Dark Castle: CoC Chats with Shagrath and Silenoz from Dimmu Borgir." Chronicles of Chaos. April 29, 2004. http://www.chroniclesofchaos.com/articles.aspx?id=1-646.

Smit, Jackie. "Diabolical Masquerades: CoC Chats with Shagrath of Dimmu Borgir." Chronicles of Chaos. May 8, 2007. http://www.chroniclesofchaos.com/articles.aspx?id=1-996.

Smit, Jackie. "Lords of the Left Hand: CoC Chats with Nergal of Behemoth." Chronicles of Chaos. September 9, 2007. http://www.chroniclesofchaos.com/articles.aspx?id=1-1010.

Smith-Arcarese, August Mark. "Interview with Cradle of Filth." Nadamucho.com. December 8, 2003. http://www.nadamucho.com/cradle-of-filth.

Springsteen, Bruce. "Singing Out for Change." *Seattle Post-Intelligence*, August 12, 2004.

Tyrangiel, Josh. "Why You Can't Ignore Kanye." *Time*, August 29, 2005.

"Voices for Change." *Rolling Stone*, October 14, 2004.

"What Is MoveOn All About?" MoveOn Website. http://www.moveon.org/about.

Chapter 27

"Bloomberg: U.S. Consumers Most Negative on Economy Since Recession." *NewsMax Finance*, October 27, 2011.

Darden, Beville. "Blake Shelton." *The Boot.* September 6, 2011.

Doyle, Patrick. "Boozin' and Cruisin' with Country's Rowdiest Star." *Rolling Stone*, May 10, 2012.

Doyle, Patrick. "Eric Church on Scalpers, Bro-Country, and Blake Shelton Scandal." *Rolling Stone*, June 11, 2014.

"Singer's Rant on Obama Causes ESPN to Pull Intro." *Seattle Times*, October 4, 2011.

Sorkin, Andrew, Diana Henriques, Edmund Andrews, and Joe Nocera. "As Credit Crisis Spiraled, Alarm Led to Action." *New York Times*, October 1, 2008.

"Trace Adkins Talks Tea Parties, Sarah Palin on 'Anderson Cooper 360.'" *The Boot*, September 18, 2010.

Vallorani, Jared. "Aaron Lewis: The Tea Party's New Poster Child." *The Patriot Update.* April 19, 2011.

Webster, Tom. "The National Country P1 Study." Edison Media Research. Country Radio Seminar 38, Nashville. March 2007.

Chapter 28

Blake, Jimmy. "Has EDM Opened Doors or Slammed Them Shut in Dance Music?" *Newsbeat BBC*, July 20, 2016.

Brewster, Bill, and Frank Broughton. *Last Night a DJ Saved My Life: The History of the Disc Jockey*. New York: Grove, 1999.

Brewster, Bill, and Frank Broughton. *Record Players: DJ Revolutionaries*. New York: Black Cat, 2010.

Collin, Matthew. *Altered State: The Story of Ecstasy and Acid House*. London: Serpent's Tail, 1997.

Collin, Matthew. "Do You Think You Can Hide from Stardom?" *Mixmag*, August 1997.

Gabriella. "Interview of Liam Howlett and Keith Flint of Prodigy." New York Rock. November 1997. http://www.nyrock.com/features/prodigy_int.htm.

Hanson, Amy. "Massive Attack." *Goldmine*, August 14, 1998.

Horton, Sean. "An Interview with Daddy G." *aXis*, October, 1998.

Hoskyns, Barney. "Fatboy Slim Must Die." *Revolver*, Winter 2000.

Knopper, Steve. "Drugs, Death and Dance Music." *Rolling Stone*, September 26, 2013.

Ladouceur, Liisa. "The Revolution Will Not Be Colorized." *Pulse!*, November 1998.

Matos, Michaelangelo. *The Underground Is Massive*. New York: Harper Collins, 2015.

Reynolds, Simon. *Generation Ecstasy: Into the World of Techno and Rave Culture*. Boston: Little Brown, 1998.

Reynolds, Simon. "How Rave Music Conquered America." *The Guardian*, August 2, 2012.

Rubin, Mike. "Who Knew That Robots Were Funky?" *New York Times*, December 6, 2009.

Salamon, Jeff. "The Chemical Brothers." *Spin*, September 1999.

Sherburne, Philip. "Harder, Better, Faster, Stronger." *Spin*, October 2011.

Sisario, Ben. "Electronic Dance Concerts Turn Up Volume, Tempting Investors." *New York Times,* April 5, 2012.

Introduction

"Interview with Don Robey." *Billboard*, March 1957.

Index

Aarseth, Oystein, "Euronymous," 331–2
Abbruzzese, Dave, 279
Abrahams, Mick, 194
Abramson, Herb, 155
AC/DC, 270
Ace, Johnny, 20
Acheson, Dean, 77
Ackerman, Paul, 61
Adam Ant, 232
Adams, John, 2
Adamski, 342
Adkins, Trace, 337, 338
Adler, Bill, 298
Adler, Lou, 144, 145
Adolescents, 235, 236, 238
Aerosmith, 298
Agent Orange, 236
Agnew, Spiro, 139
Aguilar, Dave, 117
A Guy Called Gerald, 343
Ainsworth, Steve, 198
Alan Freed Show, 117
Albarn, Damon, 286, 287
Albin, Peter, 137, 138
Aldean, Jason, 336–8
Alice Cooper, 203–4, 212
Alice in Chains, 279, 327
Allen, Daevid, 141
Allen, Paul, 278
Allen, Richard, 3
Allender, Paul, 333
Allison, Jerry, 45
Allman, Duane, 165
Allman, Gregg, 165
Allman Brothers, 165
Almanac Singers, 76
Alpert, Herb, 212
Altamont Speedway festival, 174
Alter, Hobie, 69
alternative country, 266
Ament, Jeff, 279
American Bandstand, 117
American Federation of Musicians, 115
Anastasio, Trey, 288
Andersen, Eric, 88
Anderson, Brett, 285
Anderson, Ian, 194
Anderson, Jon, 196
Anderson, Katherine, 120
Anderson, Pink, 42
Andre 3000, 308
Andrew, Sam, 145
Angel Witch, 269, 270
Animal, Philthy, 270
The Animals, 116, 117, 141
Anthony, Michael, 249–50
Anthrax, 272, 309
Aphex Twin, 344
Appel, Mike, 257
Araya, Tom, 272
arenas, 205–6
Arm, Mark, 279
Armstrong, Billie Joe, 282
Arnold, Billy Boy, 13, 19, 115
Arnold, Eddy, 47
Aron, Evelyn, 16
Arrested Development, 301
Arvizu, Reginald, "Fieldy," 311
Asher, Peter, 180, 181
Asher, William, 71
Ashford, Rosalind, 120
Ashford, R. T., 9
Ashton, William, 102
Astaire, Fred, 245
Astronauts, 73
Atkins, Chet, 46
Atkins, Cholly, 123, 124, 126
Atkins, Juan, 341, 342

Aucoin, Bill, 202, 232
Austin, Lovie, 12
automobiles, 73–4
Avalon, Frankie, 59, 60, 70
Avicii, 349
Avory, Mick, 115
Axton, Mae, 39
Ayers, Kevin, 141
Ayler, Albert, 214
Azagthoth, Trey, 272, 273
Azoff, Irving, 319

Bachmann, Michele, 335
Bad Religion, 236
Baez, Joan, 85–9, 137, 259
Baker, Ginger, 168
Baker, James, 325
Baker, LaVern, 32
Baker, Roy Thomas, 206
Balin, Marty, 128, 136, 138, 140
Ballard, Florence, 123, 125
Ballard, Hank, 60
Balzary, Michael, "Flea," 310
Bambaataa, Afrika, 292, 294–7, 309
The Band, 178
Bangalter, Thomas, 347, 348
Banks, Bessie, 193
Baraka, Amiri, 150
Barber, Chris, 95, 107
Barbie dolls, 69
Barker, Danny, 12
Barnes, Chris, 273
Barnes, Ken, 261
Barnes, Richard, 114
Baron, Peter, 249
Barre, Martin, 194
Barrett, Richard, 64
Barrett, Syd, 141, 195
Barron, Jack, 345
Barron, Siobhan, 243
Barrow, Geoff, 345
Barrow, Tony, 97
Barry, Jeff, 65, 66, 115
Barth, Bill, 79
Barton, Geoff, 269
Basie, William "Count," 12, 30
Basquiat, Jean-Michel, 296
Bass, Ralph, 29
Bathory, 331
Bathory, Elizabeth, 331
Bauhaus, 229
Bay City Rollers, 218
Beach Boys, 69, 71–2, 73, 74, 144, 259
Beastie Boys, 298, 309, 327
Beatles, 90–105, 109, 111–13, 118, 124, 141
Beatniks, 89
Beats, 128–32, 136
Beattie, Jim, 343
Beaulieu, Priscilla, 56
Beccera, Jeff, 272
Beck, Jeff, 115, 168–9, 193
Becker, Walter, 191
Beckett, Steve, 344
Bee Gees, 210, 212
Behemoth, 324, 333
Bel-Airs, 70
Bell, Ricky, 303
Bell, Thom, 184, 185
Bell Biv DeVoe, 303
Belvederes, 64
Benjamin, Benny, 125
Bennett, Estelle, 66
Bennett, John, 61, 62
Bennett, Lerone, Jr., 151
Bennett, Ronnie, 65, 66
Bennett, Stanford, 4
Bennett, Veronica, 66
Bennington, Chester, 313

Benson, Renaldo, 126
Benton, Glen, 272, 274
Berle, Milton, 48
Berman, Jay, 321
Bernanke, Ben, 335
Berners-Lee, Tim, 315
Bernstein, Nils, 283
Berry, Bernard, 51
Berry, Bill, 260
Berry, Chuck, 15, 24–30, 55, 61, 72, 95, 106, 108, 109, 114, 117, 177
Berry, Jan, 72–3, 74
Besman, Bernie, 21
Best, Pete, 95, 96
Betrock, Alan, 218
Betts, Dickey, 165
Beuford, Carter, 289
B.G., 306
Biafra, Jello, 237, 238
Biden, Joseph, 338
Bienstock, Miriam, 155
big beat, 346–7
Big Bill Broonzy, 4, 5, 13, 14, 107, 151, 154
Big Bopper, 56
Big Brother and the Holding Company, 131, 135, 137, 138, 140, 144, 145
Big Daddy Kane, 301
Bigeou, Esther, 13
Big Four of Sun, 43
Big Walter Horton, 38
Bihari, Joe, 19, 20
Bihari, Saul, 19, 20
Bikini Kill, 282
Bill Haley and the Comets, 43, 108
Bingenheimer, Rodney, 236
Bird, Martina, 345
Black, Bill, 37, 38, 51
Black, Clint, 263, 264
Black, Pauline, 225
Black Arts Movement, 150
Black Dog, 344
Black Flag, 233–8, 271, 277, 309
black metal, 331–3
Blackmore, Ritchie, 172
Black Panther Party of Self-Defense, 149–50, 156–7, 174
black power, 149, 160
Black Rose, 227
Black Sabbath, 171–2, 259, 269, 309
Black Spades, 292
Blackwell, Chris, 25, 194, 224
Blackwood Brothers Quartet, 37
Blair, Tony, 285, 287
Blake, William, 130, 139
blaxploitation, 305
Bleyer, Archie, 46
Blige, Mary J., 304
Blind Lemon Jefferson, 5
Bloch, Ray, 101
Block, Herbert, 77
Blood, Sweat and Tears, 187, 191
Bloods, 292, 293
Blossoms, 65
Blow, Kurtis, 296, 297
Blower, Chuck, 31
Bluecaps, 46
Blue Notes, 184
Bluesbreakers, 107, 108
Blues Incorporated, 108
Blues Project, 187
Blues Traveler, 288, 289, 290
Blue Unicorn, 133
Blunt, James, 329
Blur, 285, 286, 287
Body Count, 299, 309
Boehner, John, 338
Bogart, Neil, 202, 209

Bolan, Marc, 200
Bolin, Tommy, 193
Bomb Squad, 300–1
Bonebrake, Don, 233
Bone Thugs-N-Harmony, 303
Bonham, John, 170–1
Bon Jovi, 251
Bon Jovi, Jon, 251
Bonniwell, Sean, 116
Bono, 253, 259–60
Bono, Sonny, 90
Booker T. Jones and the MGs, 156
Boomtown Rats, 258
Boon, D., 238
Boone, Pat, 31, 32
Bordin, Mike, "Puffy," 310
Borland, Wes, 311–12
Boston, 206
Bottum, Roddy, 310
Bowen, Jimmy, 45
Bowen, Michael, 132
Bowie, David, 199–201, 205, 243, 259
Boyce, Tommy, 105
Boyd, Eddie, 11
Boyd, Joe, 141
Boy George, 247
Boyz II Men, 303
Bracey, Ishmon, 4, 6
Bracken, James, 21
Bradford, Percy, 12
Bramah, Martin, 229
Brand, Stewart, 131
Brando, Marlon, 48, 50
Bratmobile, 282
B-Real, 292, 310
Brecker, Randy, 187, 191
Brenston, Jackie, 38, 44
Bridges, Jeff, 338
British Dixieland, 95
Britpop, 285–8
Brooker, Gary, 194
Brooks, Colleen Carroll, 264
Brooks, Garth, 264–6, 334, 337
Broonzy, Big Bill, 1, 4, 24, 108
Brown, Bobby, 303
Brown, Bruce, 70
Brown, Charles, 21
Brown, Claude, 146, 148
Brown, H. Rap, 149, 150
Brown, Ian, 345
Brown, James, 112, 117, 152, 154, 156, 157, 159, 207, 244, 294, 296
Brown, Jerry, 238
Brown, Jim, 4
Brown, Myra Gale, 56
Brown, Willie, 4
Browne, Jackson, 180, 259
Bruce, Jack, 168
Brunelle, Richard, 272, 273
Brusuelas, Joseph, 335
Bryan, Luke, 337
Bryant, Elbridge, 126
Buchla, Don, 190
Buck, Peter, 260
Buckingham, Lindsey, 207
Buckner, H. Taylor, 133
Buffalo Springfield, 179, 182, 183
Bunker, Clive, 194
Burckhard, Aaron, 277
Burdon, Eric, 116, 141
Burgess, Anthony, 214
Burgess, Sonny, 43
Burke, Solomon, 154, 155, 159
Burkett, Fat Mike, 326
Burlison, Paul, 34, 44
Burnette, Billy, 44
Burnette, Dorsey, 34, 44, 46
Burnette, Johnny, 34, 44–6